The Master Guide for Teams

edited by
Dana G. King, M.A.

CRC Press
Taylor & Francis Group
Boca Raton London New York

CRC Press is an imprint of the
Taylor & Francis Group, an **informa** business
A PRODUCTIVITY PRESS BOOK

Most Productivity Press books are available at quantity discounts when purchased in bulk. For more information, contact our Customer Service Department (800-394-6868). Address all other inquiries to:

Productivity Press
444 Park Avenue South, Suite 604
New York, NY 10016
United States of America
Telephone: 212-686-5900
Telefax: 212-686-5411
E-mail: info@productivityinc.com

Cover design by Carla Refojo
Cover illustration by Ana Capitaine
Text design by Janet Brandt and Jonathan Wills
Page composition by William H. Brunson, Typography Services
Art creation by Smith & Fredrick Graphics, Jonathan Wills, and Lorraine Millard
Printed by Malloy Lithographing in the United States of America

Library of Congress Cataloging-in-Publication Data

Michalski, Walter J.
      Six Sigma Tool navigator : the master guide for teams / Walter J. Michalski :
   edited by Dana G. King.
          p.   cm.
      Updated ed. of: Tool navigator. Portland Or. : Productivity Press, c1997
      ISBN 1-56327-295-4 (alk. paper)
      1. Total quality management.   2. Teams in the workplace.   3. Group problem solving.   4. Creative ability.   I. Michalski, Walter J. Tool navigator. II. Title.
      HD62.15.M29   2003
      658.4′036—dc21   2003006071
                                                                                                 CIP

This handbook is dedicated to my father Josef and to the memory of my mother Hildegard. Both instilled in me an attitude and work ethic of continuous education and process and quality improvement that has served me well both in my professional and personal life.

"If you want to teach people a new way of thinking, don't bother trying to teach them. Instead, give them tools, the use of which will lead to new ways of thinking."

—Buckminster Fuller

Publisher's Message   *xiii*

Preface   *xv*

Acknowledgments   *xix*

Introduction   *xxi*

Six Sigma Tool-Strings

Six Sigma Basics: Techniques and Considerations   6σ–1

Six Sigma Tools: Tool-Strings Examples   6σ–23

222 Tools in Flowchart Cross-Reference   6σ–26

65 Tool-Strings Flowchart Examples   6σ–33

Tool Navigator

  1 (IG)   5W2H Method   1

  2 (IG)   6-3-5 Method   3

  3 (AT)   Action and Effect Diagram (AED)   6

  4 (PP)   Action Plan   8

  5 (AT)   Activity Analysis   11

  6 (DC)   Activity Cost Matrix   14

  7 (PP)   Activity Network Diagram   17

  8 (IG)   Affinity Diagram   20

  9 (IG)   Analogy and Metaphor   23

10 (AT)   Analysis of Variance   26

11 (IG)   Attribute Listing   31

12 (PP)   Audience Analysis   33

13 (DM) Balance Sheet   35

14 (AT)   Bar Chart   37

15 (CI)   Barriers-and-Aids Analysis   39

16 (PP)   Basili Data Collection Method   41

17 (DC)   Benchmarking   44

18 (AT)   Block Diagram   47

19 (AT)   Box Plot   50

20 (IG)   Brainstorming   53

21 (IG)   Brainwriting Pool   55

22 (AT)   Breakdown Tree   58

23	(TB)	Buzz Group	61
24	(DC)	Case Study	63
25	(AT)	Cause and Effect Diagram (CED)	66
26	(AT)	Cause and Effect Diagram Adding Cards (CEDAC)	68
27	(IG)	Checkerboard Method	71
28	(IG)	Checklist	74
29	(DC)	Checksheet	76
30	(IG)	Circle of Opportunity	78
31	(DC)	Circle Response	81
32	(TB)	Circles of Influence	83
33	(DC)	Circles of Knowledge	86
34	(IG)	Circumrelation	89
35	(ES)	Cluster Analysis	92
36	(ES)	Comparison Matrix	95
37	(AT)	Competency Gap Assessment	98
38	(DC)	Conjoint Analysis	101
39	(DM)	Consensus Decision Making	103
40	(AT)	Control Chart - c (Attribute)	105
41	(AT)	Control Chart - p (Attribute)	109
42	(AT)	Control Chart - $\bar{X}$-R (Variable)	113
43	(DM)	Correlation Analysis	117
44	(AT)	Cost of Quality	121
45	(ES)	Cost-Benefit Analysis	124
46	(PP)	Countermeasures Matrix	126
47	(IG)	Crawford Slip Method	128
48	(ES)	Creativity Assessment	131
49	(ES)	Criteria Filtering	134
50	(IG)	Critical Dialogue	136
51	(DC)	Critical Incident	139
52	(AT)	Customer Acquisition-Defection Matrix	141
53	(DC)	Customer Needs Table	144
54	(AT)	Customer Satisfaction Analysis (CSA)	146
55	(DC)	Customer-First-Questions (CFQ)	149
56	(AT)	Cycle Time Flowchart	152
57	(DC)	Data Collection Strategy	156

58 (DM) Decision Process Flowchart 158

59 (DM) Decision Tree Diagram 160

60 (DC) Defect Map 164

61 (ES) Delphi Method 166

62 (CI) Deming PDSA Cycle 169

63 (AT) Demographic Analysis 171

64 (ES) Dendrogram 174

65 (PP) Deployment Chart (Down-Across) 176

66 (PP) Descriptive Statistics 179

67 (PP) Different Point of View 183

68 (PP) Dimensions Cube 186

69 (AT) Dot Diagram 189

70 (IG) Double Reversal 191

71 (CI) Events Log 194

72 (CI) Facility Layout Diagram 196

73 (ES) Factor Analysis 199

74 (CI) Failure Mode Effect Analysis (FMEA) 202

75 (AT) Fault Tree Analysis (FTA) 205

76 (TB) Fishbowls 208

77 (AT) Five Whys 211

78 (DC) Focus Group 213

79 (CI) Fog Index 216

80 (CI) Force Field Analysis (FFA) 218

81 (IG) Forced Association 221

82 (DM) Forced Choice 223

83 (AT) Frequency Distribution (FD) 225

84 (IG) Fresh Eye 228

85 (AT) Functional Map 230

86 (AT) Futures Wheel 233

87 (PP) Gantt Chart 236

88 (CI) Gap Analysis 239

89 (PP) Gozinto Chart 241

90 (AT) Histogram 243

91 (ES) House of Quality 246

92 (DM) Hypothesis Testing (Chi-Square) 250

93	(ES)	Idea Advocate	254
94	(IG)	Idea Borrowing	256
95	(IG)	Idea Grid	259
96	(DM)	Importance Weighting	262
97	(PP)	Influence Diagram	265
98	(DC)	Information Needs Analysis	267
99	(AT)	Interrelationship Digraph (I.D.)	270
100	(DC)	Interview Technique	273
101	(AT)	Line Chart	276
102	(ES)	Linking Diagram	278
103	(CI)	Major Program Status	280
104	(AT)	Markov Analysis	283
105	(ES)	Matrix Data Analysis	286
106	(PP)	Matrix Diagram	288
107	(ES)	Measurement Matrix	291
108	(IG)	Mental Imaging	294
109	(PP)	Milestones Chart	296
110	(IG)	Mind Flow	298
111	(CI)	Monthly Assessment Schedule	301
112	(IG)	Morphological Analysis	304
113	(DC)	Multiple Rating Matrix	307
114	(AT)	Multivariable Chart	309
115	(DM)	Multivoting	311
116	(AT)	Needs Analysis	314
117	(IG)	Nominal Group Technique (NGT)	316
118	(ES)	Nominal Prioritization	319
119	(AT)	Normal Probability Distribution	322
120	(ES)	Numerical Prioritization	326
121	(CI)	Objectives Matrix (OMAX)	329
122	(DC)	Observation	332
123	(ES)	Opportunity Analysis	335
124	(PP)	Organization Chart	337
125	(TB)	Organization Mapping	339
126	(CI)	Organization Readiness Chart	342
127	(TB)	Pair Matching Overlay	344

128	(ES)	Paired Comparison	347
129	(AT)	Panel Debate	350
130	(AT)	Pareto Chart	352
131	(IG)	Phillips 66	355
132	(PP)	Pictograph	357
133	(AT)	Pie Chart	359
134	(IG)	Pin Cards Technique	361
135	(DM)	Point-Scoring Evaluation	364
136	(AT)	Polygon	366
137	(AT)	Polygon Overlay	369
138	(CI)	Potential Problem Analysis (PPA)	372
139	(PP)	Presentation	375
140	(ES)	Prioritization Matrix—Analytical	377
141	(ES)	Prioritization Matrix—Combination	382
142	(ES)	Prioritization Matrix—Consensus	385
143	(AT)	Problem Analysis	388
144	(ES)	Problem Selection Matrix	391
145	(PP)	Problem Specification	393
146	(AT)	Process Analysis	396
147	(AT)	Process Capability Ratios	399
148	(PP)	Process Decision Program Chart (PDPC)	403
149	(AT)	Process Flowchart	406
150	(CI)	Process Mapping	410
151	(CI)	Process Selection Matrix	414
152	(PP)	Program Evaluation and Review Technique (PERT)	416
153	(PP)	Project Planning Log	419
154	(ES)	Project Prioritization Matrix	421
155	(CI)	Quality Chart	424
156	(DC)	Questionnaires	426
157	(AT)	Radar Chart	431
158	(DC)	Random Numbers Generator	433
159	(ES)	Ranking Matrix	436
160	(ES)	Rating Matrix	438
161	(TB)	Relationship Map	440

162	(PP)	Resource Histogram	443
163	(PP)	Resource Requirements Matrix	446
164	(DC)	Response Data Encoding Form	448
165	(DC)	Response Matrix Analysis	452
166	(CI)	Responsibility Matrix	455
167	(ES)	Reverse Brainstorming	457
168	(AT)	Risk Space Analysis	459
169	(CI)	Rotating Roles	462
170	(IG)	Round Robin Brainstorming	465
171	(AT)	Run Chart	468
172	(AT)	Run-It-By	471
173	(DC)	Sampling Method	474
174	(AT)	SCAMPER	477
175	(AT)	Scatter Diagram	479
176	(CI)	Scenario Writing	482
177	(ES)	Selection Matrix	484
178	(ES)	Selection Window	486
179	(IG)	Semantic Intuition	488
180	(CI)	Shewhart PDCA Cycle	490
181	(AT)	Snake Chart	492
182	(TB)	Sociogram	494
183	(ES)	Solution Matrix	497
184	(AT)	Standard Deviation	499
185	(DC)	Starbursting	502
186	(AT)	Stem-and-Leaf Display	505
187	(ES)	Sticking Dots	507
188	(IG)	Stimulus Analysis	509
189	(PP)	Storyboarding	512
190	(AT)	Stratification	516
191	(AT)	Stratum Chart	518
192	(DC)	Surveying	520
193	(PP)	SWOT Analysis	523
194	(AT)	Symbolic Flowchart	526
195	(AT)	Systems Analysis Diagram	529

196 (AT) Task Analysis   531

197 (TB) Team Meeting Evaluation   534

198 (TB) Team Mirror   537

199 (TB) Team Process Assessment   540

200 (AT) Thematic Content Analysis   542

201 (CI) Time Study Sheet   544

202 (AT) Timeline Chart   546

203 (PP) Top-Down Flowchart   548

204 (PP) Tree Diagram   551

205 (AT) Trend Analysis   554

206 (ES) Triple Ranking   557

207 (AT) Truth Table   560

208 (DC) Two-Dimensional Survey Grid   564

209 (AT) Two-Directional Bar Chart   567

210 (AT) Value Analysis   569

211 (AT) Value/Non-value-Added Cycle Time Chart   572

212 (AT) Variance Analysis   575

213 (ES) Venn Diagram   579

214 (DM) Weighted Voting   581

215 (AT) What-If Analysis   583

216 (PP) Why/How Charting   585

217 (IG) Wildest Idea Technique   588

218 (AT) Window Analysis   590

219 (AT) Wishful Thinking   593

220 (PP) Work Breakdown Structure (WBS)   595

221 (CI) Work Flow Analysis (WFA)   598

222 (AT) Yield Chart   601

Appendix—Statistical Tables   *605*

    Table A: Proportions of Area Under the Normal Curve   *605*

    Table B: Critical Values for the Distribution of t

       (Student's t)   *609*

    Table C: Critical Values for the Distribution of F *611*

    Table D: Critical Values for the Distribution

       of Chi-Square (x^2)   *619*

Table E: Critical Values for the Pearson's Product-
Moment Correlation Coefficient (r)   *621*

Abbreviated Bibliography   *623*

About the Author   *629*

Cross-Reference Index   *631*

Process Category Index   *635*

Six Sigma DFSS and PFSS Tools Listing   *638*

In our never ending quest for total quality and customer satisfacton, we have moved from Quality Circles to Team-based Organizations, from Total Quality Management to a work ethic of Six Sigma, and we have always been searching for the right tools to complete a complex project or finish a simple task. This revised edition of the *Six Sigma Tool Navigator*™, has the tools you need! Wouldn't it be powerful to have a resource that could provide you with the appropriate problem-solving tool every time you needed one? Like being able to access tools that are classified by process application—tools that focus on such things as idea generating, analyzing/trending, team building, or data collecting. Or having the ability to access the proper tools for a certain problem-solving phase you're in—like selecting and defining a problem or opportunity, identifying and analyzing causes or potential change, or developing and planning possible solutions or change. Or how about those times you wish you had an easy way to find a set of process tools that pertain to your area of interest, like research/statistics, engineering, manufacturing, marketing/sales, or customer/quality metrics? And how liberating would it be if you could refer to a *before-and-after* tool so you could determine your next step and achieve your final result—to implement continuous process improvement methods?

Six Sigma Tool Navigator™—*The Master Guide for Teams,* by Walter Michalski is a direct response to the many requests we've had from our customers to publish a compendium of tools for teams engaged in Six Sigma improvement activities. Here you will find 222 tools to implement major processes like Six Sigma, just-in-time, total productive maintenance, and quality assurance. This is not just a book of dry definitions. It is a true navigator that gives a classification of each tool by process application, description of various applications of the tool, possible links to before-and-after tools, and problem-solving phases most applicable for the tool. It also shows the ranking of category or work discipline in which the tool is most actively used or applied, helpful support information, a step-by-step procedure explaining how to use the tool, and an example of the display, output, or result of the tool's use. Finally, there are useful appendixes and statistical charts. And all of this is provided in an easy-to-use format (see the sample pages in the introduction).

Six Sigma Tool Navigator™ is the most comprehensive toolbox on the market—222 tools collected over 30 years. This book will enhance your team facilitation skills and assist you at every step in your diverse Six Sigma problem-solving or process-improvement efforts. We at Productivity Press are excited about this book because we know Walter Michalski has provided the definitive handbook for our customers. Never again will you complain, "If only I had the right tool!"

Many people contributed to the successful creation of this compendium, but particular gratitude must be given to Susan Swanson whose careful coordination of the myriad details related to art and text design and page composition turned this book of tools into a valuable tool itself. Our thanks go to all those who worked on this project: Mike Sinocchi, prepress editor and project manager; Emily Pillars, developmental editing; Janet Brandt and Jonathan Wills, text design; Lee Smith of Smith & Fredrick Graphics, art creation; Bill Brunson of Typography Services, text composition; Carla Refojo, cover design; and Ana Capitaine, cover illustration.

Maura May
Publisher

The *Six Sigma Tool Navigator*™ is a result of my constant search to discover additional, special, or more appropriate tools to enhance my team facilitation skills in diverse problem-solving or process-improvement efforts. The handbook itself presents 222 tools standardized in an easy-to-read format that includes a description of not only how to apply the tools but how to link them as well. It also provides a practical example with an illustration of how the tool is used in the team setting. In addition, the revised *Six Sigma Tool Navigator* now reflects a set of tool-strings or flowcharts of interconnected tools for Six Sigma teams. All 222 tools have been sorted and placed into flowcharts drawn for a specific purpose or outcome. This new element will be of great assistance to team-based organizations that desire to succeed with Six Sigma.

From my first involvement with quality circles in the 1960s to the present day of business process reengineering (BPR) and integrated product development (IPD) teams, I have collected books on tools and attended or presented workshops on tools either in the employee training environment or as adjunct faculty for the adult learner attending local universities. My first experience with Six Sigma came in 1995, when I was trained and certified as a Six Sigma instructor by Motorola, the originator of Six Sigma Quality. Since that time, I have trained and facilitated Six Sigma workshops for approximately 2,500 Engineers, managers, and company trainers. My ongoing review of literature and exchange of information with other Six Sigma and TQM practitioners resulted in many files and binders of collected tool information. While having so many tools available contributed to my flexibility as a facilitator, it became frustrating at times to search for half-remembered tools.

I have seen hardworking teams come to a screeching halt for the lack of "next-step" tools. I have seen bundles of rolled up flip charts in managers' offices, the output of many brainstorming sessions and other team activities, which had never moved beyond the idea generation phase because of the lack of appropriate tools. It has been said that if a hammer is your only tool, all problems begin to look like nails (source unknown). This handbook gives teams the tools to start and complete any task.

I have often been disappointed to find that seemingly "new" tools were the same or variations of tools that I knew by another name. TQM seminars, problem-solving workshops, books, and guides usually covered the basic seven management and seven statistical tools (see *Introduction*) and offered teams very few additional tools from which to select. During a recent review (2002) of available Six Sigma books, I have discovered with great feelings of pride that perhaps 90% of the tools listed in the *Six Sigma Tool Navigator*™ were recommended or discussed by various authors in their books. According to the experts, these tools are needed to be applied in the DFSS (Design for Six Sigma) and/or PFSS (Processing for Six Sigma) phases.

Clearly, a comprehensive handbook was needed. Based on my 30 years of collecting material and notes on tools and techniques, and a current extensive review of the literature, I set out to achieve the following objectives with this handbook:

1. Simplicity.

My first concern was that the handbook be written and formatted in very easy to understand language with clear illustrations. This concern came from my experience teaching research and statistics courses to undergraduate and graduate adult students and listening to their frequent complaints about being unable to read, let alone understand, the text. This simplification has been accomplished with step-by-step, detailed procedures, use of realistic data, and a final illustration that shows the outcome that teams would expect to see from the application of a particular tool.

2. Ready reference.

Second, I wanted this comprehensive handbook to be used by teams as a ready reference so they would no longer find it necessary to chase after other breakthrough tools. My intention was that this handbook could be used as a self-study text,

guide, or training material for continuous team reference or
for classroom instruction.

3. Thoroughness.

I set out to identify the most frequently used problem-solving
and process/quality improvement tools. This lengthy and thorough investigation resulted in the identification of 527 tool
names or titles. I was then able to effectively reduce those to
222 tools, since many tools were known by several names. My
final list accounted for 222 tools, covered by 396 commonly
referred to tool names.

4. Clear classification.

To assist in this classification effort, I sorted all tools into
major processes, including:

- TB–Team Building
- IG–Idea Generating
- DC–Data Collecting
- AT–Analyzing/Trending
- ES–Evaluating/Selecting
- DM–Decision Making
- PP–Planning/Presenting
- CI–Changing/Implementing

5. Appropriate tool selection.

My last challenge was to find a way to help the team select
the appropriate tool for any given situation or discipline and
identify when to use it within one of the six problem-solving
phases. This was accomplished through the design of a standard description process, which also provided the *before-and-
after* tools list. This standard format was used for all 222 tools
in the handbook.

My latest idea on tool selection was the development of Six Sigma
tool-strings—flowcharts showing in what sequence the tools have
to be completed in order to show a certain result, outcome, or

opportunity. This approach will provide instant tools linkage for Six Sigma teams.

I have made every effort to identify and credit the originators or sources of many of the tools presented in this handbook. I offer my sincere apology if I have overlooked anyone. I give special thanks to my contacts at the following organizations who granted permission to reprint certain information (see respective permission granted notices):

Conway Quality, Inc.

Juran Institute, Inc.

MIT, Center for Advanced Engineering Study and
   The W. Edwards Deming Institute

Phillip Crosby Associates, Inc.

Finally, I would also like to thank a very good friend and the statistics instructor who taught me much, John Timko. I am indebted to him for allowing me to reprint the statistical tables in the Appendix. His consulting firm, Statistics for Management, is located at 2112 Apricot Drive, Irvine, CA 92620, (949) 997-7535.

Please mail to me any tool or technique not described in this handbook for possible inclusion in a future edition. I thank you in advance for this information.

The *Six Sigma Tool Navigator*™ could not have materialized without the consistent support and timely advice of my own team, people whom I gratefully acknowledge for their ongoing encouragement to write this book.

First, I would like to give my special thanks to my wife Giovanna who, while waiting patiently for "my return," often gave a valuable, non-expert perspective during the drafting of the tools.

Many sincere thanks to my daughter, Dana Giovanna King, who, in spite of her busy schedule teaching and grading papers, spent many long hours editing and revising my drafts. Her constructive comments and rewriting suggestions helped immeasurably in producing the final draft. Her seven-year-old son, our Steven, really made my day whenever he kept me company in my workroom.

My sons, James Walter and Anthony Peter, also made their highly appreciated contributions. I thank Jim for his special counsel on all administrative matters and Tony for his much needed periodic typing assistance.

I am also indebted to my brother Peter Michalski for sharing his computer expertise, insights, and constructive evaluations.

Ms. Ana Castillo deserves many thanks and a "job well done" for her total typing effort, the monotonous retyping of revisions, and the final checking and formatting of the tools.

Finally, I want to thank the team at Productivity Press, who provided me with the much appreciated technical support.

Walter J. Michalski, Ed.D.

The Tools

Tools do not solve problems, people do. Just as a team facilitator makes it easier for a team of people to problem solve, so does the application of appropriate tools facilitate the process of problem solving.

This handbook represents the largest collection of tools to date; it is compiled and published as a master guide for team problem-solving and quality/process-improvement activities.

In order to make sense of this tool inventory and effectively use this extensive resource, the following features of this handbook should be considered:

- A classification of tools suggests the tool's particular process application.
- A category or work discipline in which the tool is most actively used or applied is given.
- Each tool is marked as applicable in one or more of six suggested problem-solving phases.
- Suggested links to before-and-after tools are given.
- All 222 tools are accounted for in a set of Six Sigma tool-strings that sequence and link the appropriate tools in order of completion for a particular team activity. Please refer to *Six Sigma Tool-Strings Examples.*
- A format has been used to describe and explain step-by-step how each tool is used by a team. Realistic source data or a problem/opportunity has been used to produce an expected output in a form of a matrix, sketch, flowchart, diagram, graph, table, map, list, or whatever a particular tool produces. The 11 components are as follows:

    1. tool number, name, and acronym
    2. tool *also-known-as* (aka)
    3. tool process category
    4. tool description
    5. typical application
    6. typically used by
    7. problem-solving phase

How to Use

This sample two-page spread details the components of each tool and its intended use.

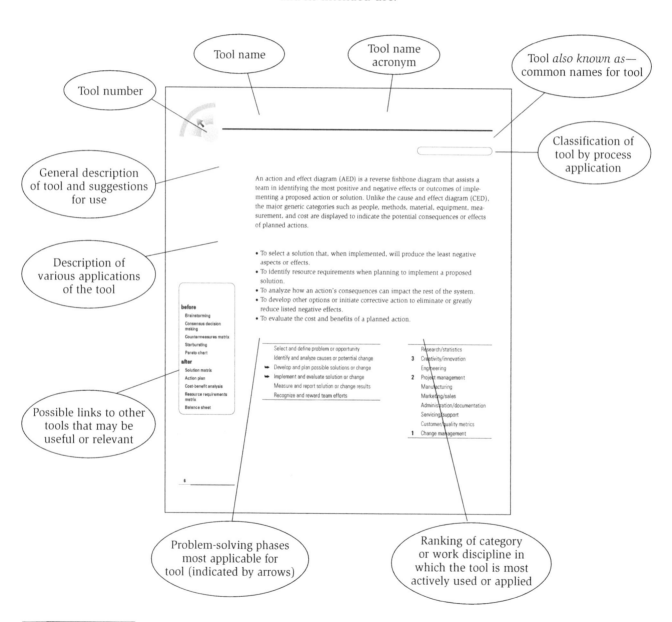

Tool name

Tool name acronym

Tool *also known as—* common names for tool

Tool number

Classification of tool by process application

General description of tool and suggestions for use

Description of various applications of the tool

Possible links to other tools that may be useful or relevant

Problem-solving phases most applicable for tool (indicated by arrows)

Ranking of category or work discipline in which the tool is most actively used or applied

Helpful and supporting information

Step-by-step procedure explaining how to use tool

Example of the display, output, or result of the tool's use

- Complete an action and effect diagram (AED) for all proposed solutions.
- Arrows are reversed in the action and effect diagram (AED).
- Positive and negative effects can be listed as pros and cons in order to compare them in several proposed solutions. Draw circles around strong negative effects indicated in the diagram(s).

Team reaches consensus on a proposed solution. See example *Provide "Tools for Teams" Training.*

Next, the team determines the major categories and places one in each category box.

Possible positive and negative consequences or effects are brainstormed and indicated with each category.

This process is continued until all ideas are recorded as shown in the example.

If more potential solutions are to be analyzed, an action and effect diagram (AED) for each possible solution is completed. The solution with the highest potential and the fewest negative aspects or effects is selected for implementation.

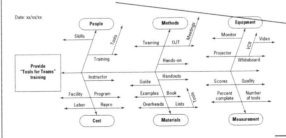

Date: xx/xx/xx

7

8. probable linkage with other tools (before and after)
9. notes and key points
10. step-by-step procedure
11. example of tool application (the output or result)

Appendix

The *Appendix* provides the necessary statistical tables used in inferential statistics or hypothesis testing.

Cross-Reference Index

The *Cross-Reference Index* allows a quick search for a particular tool if known by some other tool name. It is a cross-reference of 396 tool names listed in alphabetical order.

Process Category Index

The *Process Category Index* allows the classification of all 222 tools into eight specific groupings of tools to aid in the selection of an appropriate tool.

Six Sigma DFSS and PFSS Tools Listing

The *Six Sigma DFSS* and *PFSS Tools* Listing indicate which tools are most frequently used by Six Sigma teams in either or both phases of the Six Sigma process

In summary, this handbook is a powerful resource not only for teams, but also for managers, trainers, industrial engineers, and quality assurance people. It is for anyone who is interested in solving problems, developing new products, improving processes, and increasing customer satisfaction in a corporate culture committed to innovation, quality first, and continuous improvement.

What Is Six Sigma?

A review of the current literature on quality and process improvement frequently reflects a relatively new topic — Six Sigma. Created and pioneered in the 1980s by the Motorola organization, Six Sigma has, in recent years, spread to boardrooms, training departments, and cross-functional teams in major corporations. Although Motorola's original objective for Six Sigma was to focus on the reduction of defects in the manufacturing processes, it soon became clear that Six Sigma standards could also be applied to service organizations where the emphasis was placed on the reduction of errors made in administrative processes (document preparation), marketing and sales, distribution, and the various database and record-keeping functions.

The author was trained and certified by Motorola in 1995 as a Master Six Sigma trainer, and he has come to appreciate the systemic approach, the logic of required activities, and the use of bundled tools that can produce the measurable results organizations often failed to achieve under the umbrella of Total Quality Management (TQM).

What is Six Sigma? The current texts describe Six Sigma in many different ways — as an improved quality assurance program, an updated measurement/improvement process, a new methodology, a philosophy, a strategy, or a quality initiative. The author believes on a strictly stand-alone basis that not one of these terms will fully describe the true power of Six Sigma. A better definition would be that of a new work ethic, a top-to-bottom approach of how the organization performs to meet customer expectations. Two widely recognized gurus of Six Sigma, Mikel Harry and Richard Schroeder, authored an informative book on Six Sigma, *Six Sigma: The Breakthrough Management Strategy Revolutionizing the World's Corporations* (2000), in which they define Six Sigma. They see the strategy as "a business process that allows companies to drastically improve their bottom line by designing and monitoring everyday business activities in ways that minimize waste and resources while increasing customer satisfaction." In addition, Mikel Harry (2000, July) suggests three "primary vehicles for delivering breakthrough" drawn as a Venn Diagram showing three circles that overlap so that Six Sigma is centered and surrounded by MFSS (Managing for Six Sigma), DFSS (Designing for Six Sigma), and PFSS (Processing for

Six Sigma). For an example Venn Diagram and explanation, refer to tool # 213 in this book. According to Mikel Harry, Managing for Six Sigma (MFSS):

> is the underlying foundation of leadership for a Six Sigma initiative regardless of its nature. It is concerned with the creation, installation, initialization and utilization of the deployment plans, reporting systems and implementation processes that support PFSS and FDSS. The ultimate goal of MFSS is simple: to attain best in class business performance by improving the operational capability of an organization at an annualized rate of approximately 78% (Six Sigma learning curve) (p.75).

The author reviewed another definition for Six Sigma by Pande, Neuman, and Cavanagh (2000) and considers this an all-encompassing statement:

> [Six Sigma is] a comprehensive and flexible system for achieving, sustaining, and maximizing business success. Six Sigma is uniquely driven by close understanding of customer needs, disciplined use of facts, data, and statistical analysis, and diligent attention to managing, improving, and reinventing business processes (p.xi).

This truly new work ethic requires a cultural change of continuous commitment and training at all levels in the organization. This also means that resources are made available in an ongoing effort to reduce variation in every aspect of the business, e.g. product design, supplier-provided materials, internal processes, services, and administrative support. As Snee and Hoerl (2003) pointed out, "The essence of Six Sigma is about breakthrough business improvement, not incremental improvements. Six Sigma projects are defined to produce major improvement (30-60% or more) in process performance in less than 4-6 months with a significant [financial] impact. Such changes greatly change how business is conducted day-to-day."

On an operational level, Six Sigma can be linked directly to the measurement and statistical reporting of variation as measured under the Gaussian Curve. For a detailed explanation, refer to tool # 119, "Normal Probability Distribution," in this book. The curve shows ±4 Sigma. Sigma (σ) is a Greek alphabet letter that describes a measure of variability, or Standard Deviation (SD). Please refer to tool # 184 for description and examples of SD calculations. Motorola determined a long time ago that this measurement under the curve required a 1.5 Sigma process mean (nominal) shift, which would result in a shifted distribution to account for a long-term process drift, in either direction, under the curve and its stated specification limits. Out-of-specification results, with a mean process shift, therefore would indicate:

66,807	Defects for 3.0 Sigma (standard deviations)
6,210	Defects for 4.0 Sigma
233	Defects for 5.0 Sigma
and no more than	3.4 Defects for 6.0 Sigma [per million opportunities (DPMO) or parts per million (PPM)]

If the figure of 3.4 defects is converted to a percentage of yield, it would then show 99.99966%.

Percent yield indication with a 1.5 Sigma process shift is as follows:

At ±3 Sigma or 3 SD, a yield of 93.32% occurs.

At ±4 Sigma or 4 SD, a yield of 99.379% occurs

At ±5 Sigma or 5 SD, a yield of 99.9767% occurs

At ±6 Sigma or 6 SD, a yield of 99.99966% occurs

Six Sigma has come to represent a business culture with a strong focus on the reduction of variation in the design and process stages to minimize defects or errors. Since most organizations today are still operating at a 3 or 4 level Sigma, one can see from the figures above how many defects could reach the customer.

What is the difference between Six Sigma and TQM? Under TQM, teams attacked a specific problem or process to reduce defects or cycle time. The savings incurred were often small or could not be validated. Six Sigma tools and procedures, in comparison, are introduced early in the Design for Six Sigma (DFSS) phase and continue to be applied to Define, Measure, Analyze, Improve, and Control (DMAIC) in the processing phase. This difference results in much greater gains since virtually every department is involved. TQM programs and team problem-solving projects were linked to or managed by quality assurance professionals, whereas a Six Sigma work ethic ideally makes every employee a process improver, eventually reducing the number of "Quality Inspectors" throughout the organization.

Is Six Sigma a passing fad? A number of managers are very slow indeed in accepting or following the "new Six Sigma hype." They have seen many of the previous so-called quality initiatives come and fade away. From quality circles to cross-functional teams, from lean manufacturing to TQM, many of these organizational-change efforts did not show significant returns for the training, time, and resources required. Moreover, the tools themselves often prove to be recycled or outdated. Also, in today's world, the priority is still on productivity. Who has time to experiment with a new system, even when initial results show it to be superior?

Presently, Six Sigma work is performed in many organizations, regardless of size, products, or service offered. Corporate executives have read highly publicized reports on savings of billions of dollars realized in organizations such as Motorola, General Electric, Allied Signal, et al, companies that changed to a work ethic of Six Sigma. Now they are analyzing case studies for information on training and implementation requirements. One can gauge the interest in Six Sigma by the number of books, articles, and consulting agencies devoted to the subject that have appeared in recent years. It is true that most tools were used in many past efforts, but the clear difference now is how these tools are bundled/sequenced and rigorously applied by management and teams alike. This new edition of the *Six Sigma Tool Navigator*™ will be of great assistance for hardworking Six Sigma teams. The author came across some interesting information supplied by G. H. Watson (1998): "ASQ [American Society for Quality] has twice conducted a future study, once in 1996 and again in 1999. In both of the studies it was evident that the quality profession would shrink as the tools of quality are extended to the masses." *The Six Sigma Tool Navigator*™ will be the master guide to help accomplish this!

Rationale for Six Sigma

The establishment of a Six Sigma work ethic within your company will indeed become a strong driving force. It will significantly increase customer satisfaction and act as an enabler for an organization to reach world-class status among competitors. Furthermore, it will also:

- Promote a common language and understanding of teamwork in the quality arena within the organization.
- Tie directly into existing TQM, ISO-9000, or lean manufacturing activities.
- Assist in cost and cycle time reduction, defect rework, and waste elimination.
- Attack variation at the supplier, process, product, and service levels.
- Support the Malcolm Baldrige National Quality Award criteria.

An essential organizational benefit realized from the establishment and ongoing implementation challenges of Six Sigma quality is the strategic alignment and much-improved level of communications and teamwork among organizational units and the customer. Other more direct results are:

- Expanded market share;
- Higher returns on resource expenditures;
- Greatly enhanced engineering and manufacturing capability;
- On-time delivery through cycle time reductions;
- Cost reductions and improved financial results.

An important requirement is that all financial performance indicators must be validated by the organization's accounting unit. Six Sigma performance and consequent results are typically related to cost savings, time-to-market, customer satisfaction, and employee job satisfaction.

Neuscheier-Fritsch and Norris (2001, May) have the following comment:

> In conducting postmortems for clients, we have learned that one of the root causes for teams being perceived as less than successful is that the CFO [Chief Financial Officer]and his or her staff were not engaged in blessing the project's results. Without the organization's financial blessing, the improvements were discounted by the senior executives. "These improvements will not play on Wall Street" and "What do operating personnel know about translating results to the bottom line?" are a few comments senior executive made during debriefing (p.39).

Large corporations have reported some outstanding Six Sigma successes. Motorola, the originator of Six Sigma, reported $11 billion in savings over the last decade. The interesting story behind this success is that the company's drive to win the Malcolm Baldrige National Quality Award was actually responsible for developing the Six Sigma approach to quality. Motorola went on to win the award in 1988. Jack Welch, the former CEO [Chief Executive Officer] of General Electric (GE), claims that the Six Sigma initiative introduced and supported by his management team has resulted in more than $2 billion in cost savings. Allied Signal reduced their operations cost more than $2 billion. Allied Signal's management team (headed by Lawrence Bossidy) introduced Six Sigma to General Electric's CEO Jack Welch, who then immediately started his own push for Six Sigma at GE.

Regardless of organizational structure or function, deploying Six Sigma in an organization will improve:

- New business development (timely proposals);
- Supplier base (quality materials);
- Engineering (fewer design changes, document errors);

- Software programs/systems (reliability and compatibility);
- Manufacturing (reduced rework, scrap costs);
- All processes (less cycle time);
- Finance (open accounts and collections);
- Customer service (complaint handling);
- Human resources (staffing and turnover);
- Employees (improved job satisfaction and morale).

Six Sigma requires a great deal more attention to roles and responsibilities throughout the organization, including upper levels of management, Six Sigma champions, change agents, and a trained team of Master Black Belts, Black Belts, and Green Belts. In addition, Harry and Schroeder (2000) point out that Six Sigma stands for "a disciplined method of using extremely rigorous data-gathering and statistical analysis to pinpoint sources of errors and ways to eliminate them."

However, some concerns and precautionary measures must be taken to ensure that Six Sigma produces the success that corporate managers expect. Six Sigma is not a short-term program, but an ongoing and challenging approach to perfect quality based on a long-term performance plan. It must be interlocked with the organization's strategy and improvement goals at every level. It will require a significant amount of time and funding. A decision-making process must be in place to determine data collection and database administration costs, assess training needs from the Introduction to the DFSS phase, and define the priority criteria for important process selection. One important point to note: a small, incremental improvement from Six Sigma may not justify the costs involved in bring about process changes!

George Eckes, in his book *The Six Sigma Revolution* (2001), compiled a listing of Six Sigma concerns that included such issues as "failure to apply the concept of customer internally, recognizing management involvement, not just commitment, overemphasis on costs, and ignoring team dynamics as a root cause of project failures." Another major concern is overcoming Six Sigma resistance. Again, George Eckes discusses "four major types of resistance to Six Sigma" in his book *Making Six Sigma* last (2001). This is truly the first time that the author found a description of the types of resistance that not only makes sense but also reflects the author's experience gained from consulting work within organizations. The four major types of resistance are:

1. **Technical resistance** occurs when Six Sigma produces feelings of inadequacy or perceptions of stupidity in the stakeholder.

2. **Political resistance** occurs where the stakeholder sees Six Sigma as a personal loss. This loss could be real or perceived.
3. **Organizational resistance** occurs when the stakeholder experiences issues of control, pride, and a sense of loss of ownership because of Six Sigma.
4. **Individualized resistance** occurs when the stakeholder experiences fear and emotional paralysis because of high stress (pp. 61-62).

The literature reflects other concerns often expressed by people who resist and are still not convinced. It may be appropriate to mention these concerns here:

- Six Sigma implementation costs are too high for organizations that have fewer than 500 employees;
- Six Sigma is not for organizations with a tight budget or those that have difficulty providing the necessary resources;
- Six Sigma is *not* for managers who expect dramatic results within weeks or who set short-term goals;
- Six Sigma is just another quality program to try out;
- The perception of "Sick Sigma" in the organization by people in the organization (employees voice their resistance to implementing Six Sigma);
- Too much effort is required to convince the resisters of the value of Six Sigma;
- Six Sigma is attentive only to defects in manufacturing, a quantitative measurement, and is difficult to apply to service, since service often calls for a qualitative measurement;
- Six Sigma dismisses other proven quality tools;
- Six Sigma is simply a repackaging of old methods and tools;
- Six Sigma is primarily an evaluation toolkit, not a method to prevent poor quality;
- Data collected from inside or outside the organization may not be reliable or valid.

Six Sigma Training and Implementation

Company training is not often regarded as important when resources are required elsewhere to meet higher priorities. This changes with Six Sigma. Very structured and detailed training is necessary to provide the skills and knowledge that are needed to successfully implement the work ethic of Six Sigma. Without a focused and fully committed training effort, Six Sigma may fail in its early stages of development. So, who needs to be trained? According to Greg Bruce (2002), the "key players" in the total Six Sigma effort are:

- An executive leader — who is committed to Six Sigma and who promotes it.
- Champions — who remove barriers.
- Master Black Belts — who work as trainers, mentors, and guides.
- Black Belts — who work and manage the Six Sigma projects full-time.
- Green Belts — who assist Black Belts on a part-time basis (p.80).

An in-depth training program begins with a 2-3 day Six Sigma orientation session for executive management, and is typically followed with 5-8 days of Project Champion training. This consists of an overview of DFSS (DMADV) and PFSS (DMAIC), change management, Master Black Belt and Black Belt assistance, project management, resource allocation, process integration, and team dynamics.

Green Belts (GB) receive 10-15 days of training, mostly in the application of basic tools and techniques in the DMAIC stages. They receive a certificate for the successful completion of the formal training and assigned project tasks. They also assist Black Belts (BB) in the completion of Six Sigma projects. Black Belts' training often consists of 20-25 days that include all major components of Six Sigma work, an expanded mix of tools, inferential statistics, and the completion of two small Six Sigma projects within the learning cycle. The Black Belt will also receive a certificate of completion. The Master Black Belt (MBB) usually receives 2-3 weeks of additional training in financial results reporting, team conflict resolution, mentoring, and train-the-trainer information to train Black Belts and Green Belts. They also act as internal consultants for people assigned to Six Sigma projects.

The length of training programs varies from one practicing organization to another. This is also true for certification requirements. The tools and techniques presented in training programs for Green Belts, Black Belts, and Master Black Belts overlap greatly since they provide a common communication platform for Six Sigma teams.

The following is a selection of recurring training modules found in researched training programs that offer Green Belt and Black Belt certification:
- DFSS (DMADV) and PFSS (DMAIC) roadmaps.
- Sampling methods, instrument development.
- Data collection, and "Best Practices" benchmarking.
- Descriptive statistics (histograms, pie charts, scatter diagrams, etc.).
- Inferential statistics [hypothesis testing for t-distribution (student's "t"), analysis of variance (ANOVA), chi-square ("X^2"), correlation ("r"), etc.].
- Six Sigma process capability calculations.
- Variability-reduction techniques.

- Voice of the customer tools, quality function deployment.
- Design of experiment (DOE).
- Measurement systems analysis.
- Problem definition and selection.
- Problem-solving tools and techniques.
- Process analysis, cycle time reduction.
- Statistical process control (SPC) tools.
- Measurement and assessment tools.
- Project management and monitoring.
- Team dynamics and conflict resolution.
- Team building and facilitation skills.
- Team research and document preparation.
- Team project reporting and presentation.

A strong case is made for the inclusion of team-building/team dynamics training by George Eckes in *Six Sigma Team Dynamics* (2003). He points out that "many groups of individuals who call themselves a team end up failing miserably using either the DMAIC or the DMADV methodology — often, the reason behind their failure is poor team dynamics."

The implementation of Six Sigma across the organization requires careful planning, resource allocation, and funding for full-time employees trained and assigned to Six Sigma projects. Other costs will be incurred for consultants and trainers to train the initial core of selected Six Sigma people, and also to establish an administrative support and reward system. Forest Breyfogle (1999) believes that:

> Six Sigma can be the best thing that ever happened to a company. Alternatively, a company can find Six Sigma to be a dismal failure. It all depends on implementation. Organizations need to follow a road map that leads an organization away from a Six Sigma strategy built around "playing games with the numbers" to a strategy that yields long lasting process improvements with significant bottom-line results (p.111).

There are many opinions about how to successfully implement Six Sigma. General Electric relies on the strategy of implementation teams under the leadership of company executives, proven and accepted training programs, and a changing corporate culture that links a reward system to performance measurement. Some other considerations are:

- Creating a steering committee to develop an implementation plan.
- Developing measurable goals (ideally based on gap analyses such as benchmarking).
- Developing metrics to monitor Six Sigma project outcomes.
- Training top management levels, establishing a guidance committee.
- Communicating the Six Sigma quality strategy to all employees.
- Training Project Champions, Green Belts, and Black Belts.
- Defining customer requirements and processes.
- Performing benchmarking, identifying best suppliers.
- Identifying and selecting high-profile Six Sigma projects.
- Establishing Six Sigma teams to work on DFSS and PFSS projects.

In addition, Smith and Lee (2002) give good advice:

> to deploy strategic Six Sigma initiatives rapidly and with sufficient speed and scale to enforce optimal success that CEOs [among others] — ensure that the company is both passionate and consistent about how it stays in touch with customers [and] — recognize that success with strategic Six Sigma means making a full-time commitment and applying the manpower to ensure that Six Sigma projects succeed (pp.44-48).

Six Sigma requires a superior, criteria-based selection of projects that have a high probability of success. Please refer to tool # 154, *Project Prioritization Matrix*. The criteria for selection may be to increase customer satisfaction, at least 50% defect reduction, a process cycle time reduction of 50% or more, or an identifiable cost savings of $100,000 to $250,000 per project. Generally speaking, the number of Black Belts in some organizations represents roughly one percent of the workforce. The requirements for full-time Six Sigma employees will vary for the size and type of organization. At the start-up, one may consider a Project Champion, a Master Black Belt working with perhaps 15 Black Belts that lead 15 teams, and approximately 150 Green Belts to assist the Black Belts, a ratio of 1:15.

Black Belts working with teams are expected to complete 5-8 projects per year. For every 10-15 Black Belts, a Master Black Belt is devoted full time for support and training activities. Green Belts assist in research, form and facilitate teams, and under the leadership of Black Belts complete their own projects. Project Champions provide the resources and funding for the teams. They also remove any roadblocks that teams may encounter. In support of Six Sigma teams, Thomas Pyzdek, the author of *The Six*

Sigma Handbook (2001), cautions against four ineffective management support strategies:

- Command people to act as you wish,
- Change the rules by decree,
- Authorize circumventing of the rules,
- Redirect resources to the project.

Hopefully, organizations have gained the experience to avoid these dysfunctional activities in past TQM efforts.

Basic Six Sigma Metrics and Other Considerations

This section discusses some very important concepts, illustrates the power of these tools in the decision-making process, and explains some basic calculations relevant to Six Sigma design (DFSS) or process work (PFSS).

1. Change management

Frequently, executive management will only "react" when the dissatisfaction (customer complaints, amount of rework, increased costs, etc.) exceeds the costs (funding, resources) to fix the problem. This can be expressed as follows:

$$C = f(D + P + E) > \$$$

Where:

C = change — could be DFSS or PFSS
f = a function of
D = dissatisfaction — with the present state (problem)
P = process — that may be DMADV or DMAIC
E = expertise — trained Green Belts/Black Belts working with Six Sigma teams
> = greater than
$ = bottom-line costs to eliminate or reduce the problematic condition

2. A change in factorial experiments

The DFSS process includes many diverse tools, among them Design of Experiment (DOE) which attempts to identify, by checking the main effects and interactions, the optimum combination of factors (x) to meet a product design requirement (Y). D. H. Stamatis (2002) provides some advice:

The DMAIC model focuses on fixing problems, whereas DFSS [DMADV] focuses on prevention and robustness. Robustness is indeed the design's focal point if we are serious about improvement. The traditional model of Y = f(x) is no longer appropriate. We must focus on the Y = f(x, n). Therefore, the requirements at this stage are to optimize product and manufacturing/assembly process functions by testing in the presence of anticipated sources of variation [i.e. noise (n)] (p.48).

3. Defects/rework determine first-pass yield

The diagram below illustrates how defects during assembly can affect the total output or yield.

INPUT		STAGE 1		STAGE 2		STAGE 3		OUTPUT
Subassemblies		———		———		———		Result: 903 fully
and parts for	→	95%	→	96%	→	99%	→	assembled units
1,000 units		———		———		———		to the customer
		50 defects		38 defects		9 defects		
		950 units		912 units		903 units		

Yield = 1 — (97 defectives/1000 units) x 100 = 90.3%
Check: (.99 x .96 x .99) x 100 = 90.3%

4. SIPOC, a widely used tool in Six Sigma work

SIPOC is an acronym for Supplier-Input-Process-Output-Customer. It illustrates the process flow from supplier to customer. For a more detailed description, please refer to tool #195, *Systems Analysis Diagram*. Another SIPOC application example is shown below of an organization that is striving for Six Sigma quality. It assumes 1,000 video cassette recorders in production.

SUPPLIER		INPUT		PROCESS		OUTPUT		CUSTOMER
———		———		———		———		———
.985	→	.997	→	.994	→	.995	→	.998
———		———		———		———		———
Defective		Kitting,		Assembly		Tested out		Escaped
parts		document		defects		defects		defects
received		errors		(rework)		(QC)		(returns)
(15)		(3)		(6)		(5)		(2)

Therefore, product/process quality = $(.985 \times .997 \times .994 \times 995 \times .998) \times 100 = 96.9\%$

Also, cost of poor quality = defects per unit (DPU) x volume x mean cost/defect

Given that most organizations still work and produce at the 3-4 Sigma level of quality, this example does show that even small improvements at every stage will give a significant payback in total quality!

5. The concept of "defect budgeting"

This process is an objective approach to assign defect or error elimination activities to the organizational department identified as the source of the defects. For example, a Pareto chart (refer to tool #130 in this book) indicates:

    65% of the defects are caused during assembly

    15% of defects are due to faulty material from the supplier

    12% of defects are caused during painting

    8% of defects are traced to packaging and shipping

These results give first priority to assembly, and their given objective would point to a requirement of 65% reduction in defects in the overall assembly process. Next, the supplier would receive a reduction of faulty materials notice in order to close a 15% quality gap and so on, right across to all departments that have been identified as defects contributors.

6. A brainstorming tool that truly returns breakthrough ideas

Many times teams are disappointed with their own brainstorming results. They just do not come up with any fresh ideas that could make the difference! This book contains what this writer considers to be the best brainstorming tool — tool # 70, *Double Reversal*. This tool not only asks for the normal brainstorming input of ideas, it also asks the team for a second round of ideas to make this problem worse, as people always seem to be better at thinking of ways to destroy or make things worse. These ideas, once listed, are then negated and added to the original list of brainstormed ideas. It is truly amazing what ideas are produced, ideas that rarely would have been mentioned during normal, straightforward brainstorming.

7. Pugh-type decision-making methodology tools

Six Sigma books and articles frequently describe a scoring matrix called a Pugh Matrix used for comparing alternatives. It is popular because it is easy and fast to construct and allows many variations for scoring. The basic Pugh Matrix requires six basic steps, completed on a flipchart:

Step 1: Team brainstorms the criteria to be used for comparison.
Step 2: Team facilitator determines scoring — this could be a simple three-level score (+ , 0, –), or a five level score (+ 2, + 1, 0, -1, -2), or even finer.
Step 3: Team facilitator lists the alternatives to be compared.
Step 4: Team compares and assigns scores of + , 0, or – to alternatives.
Step 5: Team facilitator totals scores.
Step 6: Facilitator then ranks the top three choices (alternatives).

For a variation of this method, refer to tool #144, *Problem Selection Matrix.* Other matrix decision-making tools in this book are:
- Comparison Matrix, tool # 36.
- Paired Comparison, tool # 128.
- Selection Matrix, tool # 177.
- Solution Matrix, tool # 183.

8. Calculate and validate team results of quantitative and qualitative improvements

In team-based organizations, questions always come up regarding how one reports (converts) qualitative improvements into a dollar figure. Another concern is present whenever two or more teams are working in the same process area and report their results independently and at different times: how is the overall effect measured? It could indeed become very difficult to assess overall improvement cost savings. For example, suppose there are two teams working to reduce process cycle time, materials cost, or defects, and they have achieved the following improvements:

Presently, a work cell assembles **10 switches for $1,000** — this is the baseline measurement. $100 per switch before changes.

Team A has found a way to reduce material costs by **10%**	**10 switches for $900** — a quantitative result
Team B has conducted retraining and was able to reduce rework by **20%**	**12 switches for $1,000** — a qualitative result

Both teams report their success to the department manager. Team A reports a 10% cost savings, and Team B reports, two weeks later, a 20% cost savings. Is the manager correct in reporting an overall 30% reduction in costs? No! **The bottom line will only show an overall 25% saved, since $900 divided by 12 Units equals $75 per switch instead of the $100 before changes.**

The work cell now assembles   12 switches for $900 — Teams A and B
combined results $75 per switch **after changes**

The point is that whenever many teams work on several processes or known problem areas, careful accounting practices need to be in place to measure, with validity, a team's performance.

9. A powerful tool to measure progress of *all* Six Sigma implementation activities

Six Sigma Champions with overall reporting responsibility could use tool # 121, *Objectives Matrix* (OMAX), to verify the status of all Six Sigma implementation activities, or they could use it as an ongoing, monthly Six Sigma project progress reporting tool. This tool tracks work by percent completed on all stated objectives, shows what activities may fall behind schedule, and provides a composite index value that represents the combined progress of all activities.

10. Six Sigma (6σ) and the Shifted Probability Curve

The difference in quality levels can be explained by examining the figures below. With a *nonshifted* curve, only 2 defects per billion parts or opportunities would be expected. With a curve shifted $\pm 1.5\ \sigma$ from the center or the process nominal (can be controlled within the target area $\pm 1.5\ \sigma$), only 3.4 defects per million parts or opportunities would be expected. The table below can represent this relationship.

Shift	3σ	3.5σ	4σ	4.5σ	5σ	5.5σ	6σ
0	2700	465	63	6.8	0.57	0.034	0.002
$\pm 1.5\sigma$	66,803	22,800	6,200	1,350	233	32	3.4

Defects per Million Opportunities (DPMO) can be calculated as follows:
DPMO = DPU x 1,000000/parts count (for manufacturing) or
opportunities for errors (for service)
DPU = Defects per Unit
DPU = Number of defects found/number of units processed

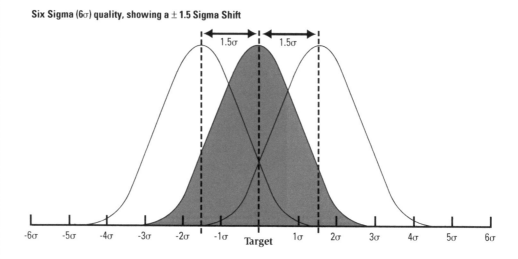

Six Sigma (6σ) quality, showing a ± 1.5 Sigma Shift

Why the ±1.5 Sigma shift? Mikel Harry, a recognized Six Sigma guru, has often claimed in his writings that there is a ±1.5σ shift in long-term, highly consistent processes. Sammy Shina (2002) explains this ±1.5σ shift, which has been widely adopted as a standard, as follows:

> The Six Sigma concept, as described by most companies, assumes that the average quality characteristic of parts being produced can vary as much as ±1.5σ Sigma from the specification nominal . . . This ±1.5 Sigma shift of the average was developed from history of process shifts from Motorola's own supply chain. This makes Six Sigma defect calculations inclusive of normal changes in the manufacturing process (p.41).

11. Understanding process capability

First, to aid in the understanding of some simple calculations, the reader should review some background information provided by tool # 119, *Normal Probability Distribution*, and tool # 184, *Standard Deviation*.

Sigma is a measure of variability. The smaller the computed value of Sigma (or standard deviation), the tighter the normal curve and, therefore, the more products or processes will appear near the nominal or target value.

Cp: Process capability is often defined as the range of natural process variation. It reflects the best ability to process or perform within established lower and upper specification limits (LSL — USL) and as measured to ± 3σ under the curve.

Cpk: Actual or located process capability is the measure of performance relative to the design target value under the curve.

At this point, the reader is asked to refer to tool # 147, *Process Capability Ratios,* for a detailed description and calculations of Cp and Cpk.

A Six Sigma (6σ) Distribution Curve

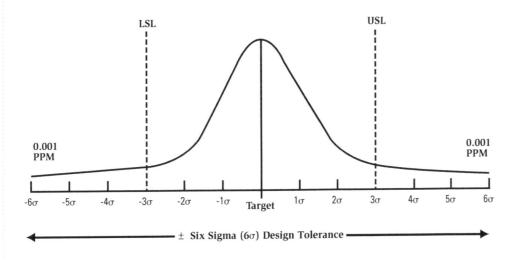

Example of design tolerance at $\pm 4\sigma$

USL = 14, LSL = 6, Nominal (target) = 10

Cp = design specification width / $\pm 3\sigma$ = 14 – 6/6 = 1.33
CPU (process capability upper) = 14 – 10 / 3 = 1.33
CPL (process capability lower) = 10 – 6 / 3 = 1.33

Cpk (actual Cp shifted 1.5σ = minimum of (CPU, CPL)
CPU = 4 + 1.5 / 3 = 1.833
CPL = 4 – 1.5 / 3 = .833
Therefore, Cpk = .833
Check two-sided: Cp = CPU + CPL / 2 = 1.833 + .833 / 2 = 1.33

Check: Cpk = Cp (1-k), k = Target – Actual / 1/2 (USL-LSL) = 10 -14/ $\frac{1}{2}$(14 – 6) = 1,
Cpk = 1.33 (1) = 1.33

Example of design tolerance at $\pm 6\sigma$

USL = 24, LSL = 12, Nominal (target) = 18
Cp = USL – LSL / ± 3 = 24-12 / 6 = 2
CPU = 24 – 18 / 3 = 2
Cpk = minimum (CPU, CPL) = CPU = 6 + 1.5 / 3 = 2.5
                                                          = CPL = 6 – 1.5 / 3 = 1.5
Check two-sided: Cp = CPU and CPL / 2 = 2.5 + 1.5 / 2 = 2

We can now construct a table of process capability (Cp):

Six Sigma	4.5 Sigma (1.5σ shifted)	Cpk
6	4.5	2.00
5	3.5	1.67
4	2.5	1.33
3	1.5	1.00

DFSS (Design for Six Sigma)

The DFSS process drastically changes the way organizations design their products, services, and processes. DFSS allows early prediction of overall design quality, including potential problems that may occur later. Subir Chowdhury (2000) claims that

> DFSS is the proper methodology because that is what DFSS is designed to attack — new products, services, or processes. Six Sigma's DMAIC, on the other hand, focuses on improvement . . . of existing products and services. This also reinforces my earlier point that Six Sigma does not have to be a prerequisite for DFSS (p.23).

The DFSS process also places an emphasis on total quality and customer satisfaction in the early design phases, to effectively and greatly reduce the need for product changes and process improvements. Snee, Heorl, and Hall (2003) stated that many organizations have now adopted the General Electric-developed **DMADV** roadmap of **D**efine, **M**easure, **A**nalyze, **D**esign, and **V**erify. This author also accepted this model and determines that this systemic approach uses the tools identified as DFSS tools in the *Six Sigma DFSS and PFSS Tools Listing* section at the end of this book (p.636). By including Six Sigma tools early into the design process, the probability of product or process failure is sharply reduced. It promotes creativity and innovation with a definite outcome of products and services of superior design.

A brief description of the DMADV roadmap stages will help to illustrate some examples of the tools used:

Define: Perhaps benchmarking will give some direction to what needs to be done. Also, Voice of the Customer tools such as House of Quality (Quality Function Deployment), Customer-First-Questions, Customer Needs Table. Others are Gap Analysis, Problem Specification, Process Mapping, Problem Analysis, Value Analysis, and the Five Whys.

Measure: Important tools are Data Collection Strategy, System Analysis (SIPOC), Measurement Matrix, Objectives Matrix (OMAX), Failure Mode and Effect Analysis (FMEA), Process Capability Ratios, Cost of Quality, Checksheet, Descriptive Statistics, Importance Weighting, Basili Data Collection Method, and Balance Sheet.

Analyze: Typically applied tools are Variance Analysis, Process Capability Ratios, Pareto Chart, Trend Line, Correlation/Regression, Process Analysis, Hypothesis Testing, most problem-solving tools such as the Five Whys, Problem Selection, Process Flowchart, Cause and Effect Diagram, and Work Flow Analysis.

Design: Tools that bring much to this stage are Design of Experiment (DOE) tools such as Analysis of Variance (ANOVA), Factor Analysis, Hypothesis Testing. Customer-First-Questions (Kano), Creativity Assessment, Forced Association, Semantic Intuition, Idea Borrowing, Phillips 66, Opportunity Analysis, Morphological Analysis, Checkerboard Method, Circumrelation.

Verify: Failure Mode and Effect Analysis (FMEA) results may provide a final check; Countermeasures Matrix, Yield Chart, Value Analysis, Point Scoring Evaluation, Customer Satisfaction Analysis, Measurement Matrix, Cost-Benefit Analysis.

Refer to *Six Sigma DFSS and PFSS Tools Listing* in this book for a complete listing of tools that could effectively be applied in the DFSS phase. Once the desired tools are identified, the reader should then find the flowchart containing the selected tools in the *Six Sigma Tools: Tool-Strings Examples* section, also in this book (p.6σ – 23).

PFSS (Process for Six Sigma)

Many would remember Shewhart's Plan-Do-Check-Act (PDCA) cycle as part of the toolbox for TQM. A more refined process is used within Six Sigma's **DMAIC** roadmap, which consists of the **D**efine, **M**easure, **A**nalyze, **I**mprove, and **C**ontrol stages. Simply put, Six Sigma teams use this roadmap to complete every quality or process improvement project. The team:

- Defines the customer's "wants" and/or satisfaction measures;
- Measures how existing processes perform;
- Analyzes data that points to root causes of problems;
- Improves processes by reducing variability and cycle time;
- Controls improved processes by anchoring them in place with new metrics or controls.

In order to research the appropriate tools, the *Six Sigma DFSS and PFSS Tools Listing* for the reader (p.636) identifies, via a simplified cross-reference, the tools deemed right for the **DMAIC** stages. It is of importance to note here that several tools will perform similarly; it may be necessary for the reader to consider several and then select one that fits best in the situation at hand. A brief description of the **DMAIC** roadmap stages will help to illustrate a few examples of tools used:

Define: Problem Specification, Process Mapping, Potential Problem Analysis, System Analysis (SIPOC), Voice of the Customer tools such as House of Quality (QFD), Customer-First-Questions, Customer Needs Table, the Five Whys, Information Needs Analysis, Objectives Matrix (OMAX), Problem Analysis, and Value Analysis.

Measure: Data Collection Strategy, Process Capability Ratios, Failure Mode and Effect Analysis (FMEA), Benchmarking, Cycle Time Flowchart, Basili Data Collection Method, Checksheet, Cost of Quality, Descriptive Statistics, Measurement Matrix, SWOT Analysis, Competency Gap Assessment, and Customer Satisfaction Analysis.

Analyze: Pareto Chart, Correlation/Regression, Variance Analysis, Activity Analysis, Hypothesis Testing, Conjoint Analysis, Cycle Time Flowchart, Force Field Analysis, Matrix Data Analysis, Multivariate Chart, Opportunity Analysis, Potential Problem Analysis, Stimulus Analysis, Importance Weighting, and Cause-and-Effect Diagram.

Improve: Factor Analysis, Checkerboard Method, Comparison Matrix, Criteria Filtering, Problem Selection Matrix, Problem Analysis, Process

Flowchart, Process Selection Matrix, SCAMPER, Solution Matrix, Value Analysis, What-If Analysis, Work Flow Analysis, Attribute Listing, Defect Map, and Why/How Charting.

Control: Control Charts, Cost-Benefit Analysis, Objectives Matrix (OMAX), Process Capability Ratios, Trend and Run Charts, Yield Chart, Stratum Chart, Quality Chart, Point-Scoring Evaluation, Monthly Assessment Schedule, Major Program Status, Basili Data Collection, Checklist, Checksheet, and Balance Sheet.

The *Six Sigma Tool Navigator*™, contains many additional tools for every stage of the **DMAIC** roadmap. Refer to the *Six Sigma DFSS and PFSS Tools Listing* and then find the selected tools in the *Six Sigma Tools: Tool-Strings Examples* section in this book.

Section References

Breyfogle, F. W. (1999, August). "Implementing Six Sigma." *The Management Forum* (111).

Bruce, G. (2000). *Six Sigma for Managers.* New York: McGraw-Hill, p. 80.

Chowdhury, S. (2000). *Design for Six Sigma.* Chicago: Dearborn Trade Publishing, p.23.

Eckes, G. (2001). *The Six Sigma Revolution.* New York: John Wiley & Sons, Inc., pp. 244-262.

Eckes, G. (2003). *Six Sigma Team Dynamics.* New York: John Wiley & Sons, Inc., p.3.

Eckes, G. (2001). *Making Six Sigma Last.* New York: John Wiley & Sons, Inc., pp. 61-62.

Harry, M. J. (2000, July). Abatement of Business Risk is Key to Six Sigma. *Quality Progress* (75).

Harry, M. and Schroeder, R. (2000). *Six Sigma: The Breakthrough Management Strategy Revolutionizing the World's Top Corporations.* New York: Currency Doubleday, p.9.

Neuscheier-Fritsch, D. and Norris, R. Capturing financial benefits from Six Sigma. *Quality Digest* (39).

Pande, P. S., Neuman, R. P., and Cavanagh, R. R. (2000). *The Six Sigma Way.* New York: McGraw-Hill, p. xi.

Pyzdeck, T. (2002). *The Six Sigma Handbook.* New York: McGraw-Hill, pp.234-235.

Shina, S. G. (2000). *Six Sigma for Electronics Design and Manufacturing.* New York: McGraw-Hill, p.41.

Smith, D., and Lee, J.B. (2002) *Strategic Six Sigma*. Hoboken, NJ: John Wiley & Sons, Inc., pp. 44-48.

Snee, R. D. and Heorl, R. W. (2003). *Leading Six Sigma*. Upper Saddle River, NJ: Prentice Hall, pp. 5, 232.

Stamatis, D. H. (2002, May). Guidelines for Six Sigma Design Review — Part Two. *Quality Digest* (48).

Watson, G. H. (1998, June). Bringing Quality to the Masses: The Miracle of Loaves and Fishes. *Quality Press* (16).

In an article authored by G.H. Watson[1], a point was made that in two separate ASQ studies (1996 & 1999) the evidence suggests that quality assurance professionals may slowly fade away if more tools were made available "to the masses." The Six Sigma Tool Navigator™ *can certainly train the masses!*

The new *Six Sigma Tool Navigator*™ reflects a great improvement since it now shows all 222 tools placed into easy-to-follow "Tool-Strings" flowcharts that sequence tools in the order of completion by a Six Sigma or any other team. This section was developed to fill a perceived need, which has been voiced frequently by the various teams utilizing the first edition Tool Navigator's 222 tools for problem solving, innovation and creativity, process/quality improvements, and other organizational change activities.

Although a "Links to Other Tools" feature accompanies every tool, teams with little experience in linking tools to achieve a particular outcome have had some difficulties in determining what tools are appropriate for a particular task. In addition, teams often did not know the sequence in which these tools should be used. In order to respond to this need, the author has developed a set of 65 "Tool-Strings" or flowcharts of interconnected tools for teams. All 222 tools have been accounted for and are included in the many different flowcharts designed to provide the desired outcome.

At times, the same tools are called by different names. The following are a few examples:

- SIPOC is shown as tool #195, *Systems Analysis Diagram*
- Quality Function Deployment is shown as tool #91, *House of Quality*
- Kano model is shown as tool #55, *Customer-First Question* (CFQ)
- Process Capability is shown as tool #147, *Process Capability Ratios*
- Voice of the Customer (VOC) is shown as tool #53, *Customer Needs Table*
- Simple Linear Regression is shown as tool # 43, *Correlation Analysis*

[1] Watson, G. H. "Bringing quality to the masses; the miracle of loaves and fish," Quality Progress, June 1998.

Since the above examples indicate the difficulty in selecting a tool by name or specific functionality, three reference aids are available in the *Six Sigma Tool Navigator*™ book:

1. A **Cross-Reference Index** that lists 396 tool names in an alphabetical order. Since many tools are known by different names, this cross-reference will direct the team to the appropriate tool.

2. A **Process Category Index** that classifies all tools into the following eight (8) categories:

TB — Team Building	ES — Evaluating/Selecting
IG — Idea Generating	DM — Decision Making
DC — Data Collecting	PP — Planning/Presenting
AT — Analyzing/Trending	CI — Changing/Implementing

3. A Six Sigma DFSS and PFSS Tools Listing that further suggests what tools are frequently worked through in these Six Sigma projects.

The "Tool-Strings" flowcharts are typically drawn as shown in the examples below. The team works through the linked tools, follows the arrows, and refers to the *Six Sigma Tool Navigator*™ for helpful information. Many flowcharts show the "OR" function, which allows the team to examine the tools and choose the correct tool to complete the process. Each flowchart box contains the following information:

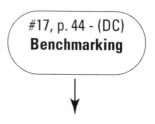

- #17 — The number of the tool (range 1-222)
- p.44 — The page number for this tool in the Tools section of the book
- DC — The tool's category, Data Collection (8 categories — see above listing)
- The tool's name as used in the Tools section book

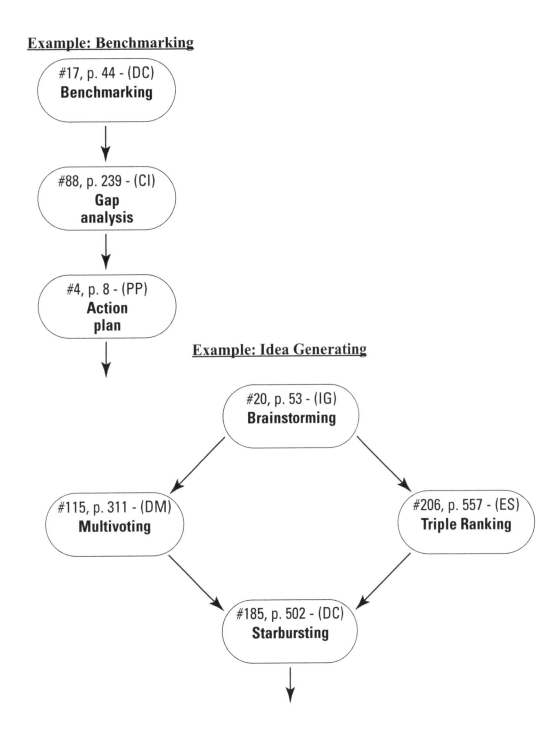

Example: Benchmarking

#17, p. 44 - (DC)
Benchmarking

#88, p. 239 - (CI)
**Gap
analysis**

#4, p. 8 - (PP)
**Action
plan**

Example: Idea Generating

#20, p. 53 - (IG)
Brainstorming

#115, p. 311 - (DM)
Multivoting

#206, p. 557 - (ES)
Triple Ranking

#185, p. 502 - (DC)
Starbursting

Note: Although many of these tools can be used in all Six Sigma work activities, the designations in the Six Sigma (6σ) column indicate frequent application in:

"D" — DFSS (Designing for Six Sigma)

"P" — PFSS (Processing for Six Sigma)

"B" — This tools is used in both DFSS and PFSS

"T" — Team-building and Socio-metric tools

6σ	Page Number	Tool Category	Title	Tool-Strings Flowchart number
B	#1	(IG)	5W2H Method	FC43
D	#2	(IG)	6-3-5 Method	FC61
P	#3	(AT)	Action and Effect Diagram (AED)	FC24
P	#4	(PP)	Action Plan	FC14, 28, 36, 47, 56, 60, 65
P	#5	(AT)	Activity Analysis	FC27
P	#6	(DC)	Activity Cost Matrix	FC33, 43
P	#7	(PP)	Activity Network Diagram	FC34
B	#8	(IG)	Affinity Diagram	FC12, 13, 17, 55
T	#9	(IG)	Analogy and Metaphor	FC20
D	#10	(AT)	Analysis of Variance	FC53
P	#11	(IG)	Attribute Listing	FC44
T	#12	(PP)	Audience Analysis	FC06
P	#13	(DM)	Balance Sheet	FC62
P	#14	(AT)	Barchart	FC30
P	#15	(CI)	Barriers-and-Aids Analysis	FC24
P	#16	(PP)	Basili Data Collection Method	FC47,
D	#17	(DC)	Benchmarking	FC41, 47, 56
P	#18	(AT)	Block Diagram	FC22
P	#19	(AT)	Box Plot	FC51
B	#20	(IG)	Brainstorming	FC01, 10, 12, 13, 19, 55
D	#21	(IG)	Brainwriting Pool	FC05, 58
P	#22	(AT)	Breakdown Tree	FC40
T	#23	(TB)	Buzz Group	FC06

6σ	Page Number	Tool Category	Title	Tool-Strings Flowchart number
P	#24	(DC)	Case Study	FC45
P	#25	(AT)	Cause and Effect Diagram (CED)	FC58
P	#26	(AT)	Cause and Effect Diagram Adding Cards (CEDAC)	FC58
D	#27	(IG)	Checkerboard Method	FC16
P	#28	(IG)	Checklist	FC01
P	#29	(DC)	Checksheet	FC30
D	#30	(IG)	Circle of Opportunity	FC44
B	#31	(DC)	Circle Response	FC46
T	#32	(TB)	Circles of Influence	FC04
B	#33	(DC)	Circles of Knowledge	FC06
D	#34	(IG)	Circumrelation	FC19
P	#35	(ES)	Cluster Analysis	FC10
P	#36	(ES)	Comparison Matrix	FC42
P	#37	(AT)	Competency Gap Assessment	FC57
D	#38	(DC)	Conjoint Analysis	FC37
B	#39	(DM)	Consensus Decision Making	FC11, 16, 27, 35, 42, 62
P	#40	(AT)	Control Chart — c (Attribute)	FC32
P	#41	(AT)	Control Chart — p (Attribute)	FC32
P	#42	(AT)	Control Chart — X-R (Variable)	FC32
D	#43	(DM)	Correlation Analysis	FC52
P	#44	(AT)	Cost of Quality	FC29, 30, 32
B	#45	(ES)	Cost-Benefit Analysis	FC07, 57
P	#46	(PP)	Countermeasures Matrix	FC21
D	#47	(IG)	Crawford Slip Method	FC38
B	#48	(ES)	Creativity Assessment	FC15, 16
P	#49	(ES)	Criteria Filtering	FC19, 55
T	#50	(IG)	Critical Dialogue	FC03, 64
P	#51	(DC)	Critical Incident	FC45, 64
B	#52	(AT)	Customer Acquisition-Defection Matrix	FC42
D	#53	(DC)	Customer Needs Table	FC39
B	#54	(AT)	Customer Satisfaction Analysis (CSA)	FC40
D	#55	(DC)	Customer-First-Questions (CFQ)	FC39
P	#56	(AT)	Cycle Time Flowchart	FC27
P	#57	(DC)	Data Collection Strategy	FC29, 31, 32, 39, 40, 42, 48, 49, 50, 52, 53, 54, 63, 65

6σ	Page Number	Tool Category	Title	Tool-Strings Flowchart number
P	#58	(DM)	Decision Process Flowchart	FC08
P	#59	(DM)	Decision Tree Diagram	FC08
P	#60	(DC)	Defect Map	FC31
B	#61	(ES)	Delphi Method	FC46
P	#62	(CI)	Deming PDSA Cycle	FC59
B	#63	(AT)	Demographic Analysis	FC40, 60
P	#64	(ES)	Dendrogram	FC37
P	#65	(PP)	Deployment Chart (Down-Across)	FC34
B	#66	(PP)	Descriptive Statistics	FC50
B	#67	(PP)	Different Point of View	FC05, 23, 40
T	#68	(PP)	Dimensions Cube	FC18
P	#69	(AT)	Dot Diagram	FC51
B	#70	(IG)	Double Reversal	FC09, 55
P	#71	(CI)	Events Log	FC14
P	#72	(CI)	Facility Layout Diagram	FC28
B	#73	(ES)	Factor Analysis	FC56, 62
P	#74	(CI)	Failure Mode Effect Analysis (FMEA)	FC23
P	#75	(AT)	Fault Tree Analysis (FTA)	FC21
T	#76	(TB)	Fishbowls	FC01
P	#77	(AT)	Five Whys	FC58
D	#78	(DC)	Focus Group	FC16, 46, 48, 60
T	#79	(CI)	Fog Index	FC06
P	#80	(CI)	Force Field Analysis (FFA)	FC56
D	#81	(IG)	Forced Association	FC19
B	#82	(DM)	Forced Choice	FC06
P	#83	(AT)	Frequency Distribution (FD)	FC50
B	#84	(IG)	Fresh Eye	FC25
P	#85	(AT)	Functional Map	FC62
P	#86	(AT	Futures Wheel	FC64
P	#87	(PP)	Gantt Chart	FC36
P	#88	(CI)	Gap Analysis	FC47, 56
P	#89	(PP)	Gozinto Chart	FC23
P	#90	(AT)	Histogram	FC50
D	#91	(ES)	House of Quality	FC37
D	#92	(DM)	Hypothesis Testing (Chi-Square)	FC54
B	#93	(ES)	Idea Advocate	FC06

6σ	Page Number	Tool Category	Title	Tool-Strings Flowchart number
B	#94	(IG)	Idea Borrowing	FC11
D	#95	(IG)	Idea Grid	FC42
B	#96	(DM)	Importance Weighting	FC07
P	#97	(PP)	Influence Diagram	FC65
B	#98	(DC)	Information Needs Analysis	FC08, 18, 45, 46, 47, 57, 59
T	#99	(AT)	Interrelationship Digraph (I.D.)	FC12
B	#100	(DC)	Interview Technique	FC48, 56
P	#101	(AT)	Linechart	FC30
B	#102	(ES)	Linking Diagram	FC24
B	#103	(CI)	Major Program Status	FC36
T	#104	(AT)	Markov Analysis	FC65
P	#105	(ES)	Matrix Data Analysis	FC37
P	#106	(PP)	Matrix Diagram	FC13, 33
B	#107	(ES)	Measurement Matrix	FC33
D	#108	(IG)	Mental Imaging	FC20
P	#109	(PP)	Milestones Chart	FC34
D	#110	(IG)	Mind Flow	FC15
P	#111	(CI)	Monthly Assessment Schedule	FC08, 14
D	#112	(IG)	Morphological Analysis	FC38
P	#113	(DC)	Multiple Rating Matrix	FC49
P	#114	(AT)	Multivariable Chart	FC32
B	#115	(DM)	Multivoting	FC26
B	#116	(AT)	Needs Analysis	FC57
B	#117	(IG)	Nominal Group Technique (NGT)	FC09, 19
P	#118	(ES)	Nominal Prioritization	FC06
D	#119	(AT	Normal Probability Distribution	FC50, 54
B	#120	(ES)	Numerical Prioritization	FC04
B	#121	(CI)	Objectives Matrix (OMAX)	FC61
P	#122	(DC)	Observation	FC31, 53
B	#123	(ES)	Opportunity Analysis	FC41, 43
T	#124	(PP)	Organization Chart	FC04, 28, 36
B	#125	(TB)	Organization Mapping	FC02, 04
B	#126	(CI)	Organization Readiness Chart	FC59
T	#127	(TB)	Pair Matching Overlay	FC03
B	#128	(ES)	Paired Comparison	FC07
T	#129	(AT)	Panel Debate	FC05

6σ	Page Number	Tool Category	Title	Tool-Strings Flowchart number
B	#130	(AT)	Pareto Chart	FC14
D	#131	(IG)	Phillips 66	FC06
P	#132	(PP)	Pictograph	FC51
P	#133	(AT)	Pie Chart	FC51
P	#134	(IG)	Pin Cards Technique	FC17
P	#135	(DM)	Point-Scoring Evaluation	FC17, 58
P	#136	(AT)	Polygon	FC50
P	#137	(AT)	Polygon Overlay	FC50
P	#138	(CI)	Potential Problem Analysis (PPA)	FC22, 44
T	#139	(PP)	Presentation	FC06, 09, 11, 21, 22, 25, 34, 39, 44, 63
P	#140	(ES)	Prioritization Matrix — Analytical	FC35
P	#141	(ES)	Prioritization Matrix — Combination	FC35
P	#142	(ES)	Prioritization Matrix — Consensus	FC35
P	#143	(AT)	Problem Analysis	FC12, 20, 21, 35, 57
P	#144	(ES)	Problem Selection Matrix	FC59
B	#145	(PP)	Problem Specification	FC17, 25, 31, 44
P	#146	(AT)	Process Analysis	FC26
D	#147	(AT)	Process Capability Ratios	FC32
B	#148	(PP)	Process Decision Program Chart (PDPC)	FC33
P	#149	(AT)	Process Flowchart	FC25
B	#150	(CI)	Process Mapping	FC25
P	#151	(CI)	Process Selection Matrix	FC27
P	#152	(PP)	Program Evaluation and Review Technique (PERT)	FC36
P	#153	(PP)	Project Planning Log	FC08, 20, 35
B	#154	(ES)	Project Prioritization Matrix	FC34
P	#155	(CI)	Quality Chart	FC31
B	#156	(DC)	Questionnaires	FC48, 53
P	#157	(AT)	Radar Chart	FC63
B	#158	(DC)	Random Numbers Generator	FC52
B	#159	(ES)	Ranking Matrix	FC09
B	#160	(ES)	Rating Matrix	FC09
P	#161	(TB)	Relationship Map	FC02
P	#162	(PP)	Resource Histogram	FC36
B	#163	(PP)	Resource Requirements Matrix	FC14, 35

6σ	Page Number	Tool Category	Title	Tool-Strings Flowchart number
D	#164	(DC)	Response Data Encoding Form	FC48, 53, 54
D	#165	(DC)	Response Matrix Analysis	FC41
B	#166	(CI)	Responsibility Matrix	FC36, 55
B	#167	(ES)	Reverse Brainstorming	FC10, 15
P	#168	(AT)	Risk Space Analysis	FC12, 17
P	#169	(CI)	Rotating Roles	FC02, 12
B	#170	(IG)	Round Robin Brainstorming	FC38
P	#171	(AT)	Run Chart	FC29
P	#172	(AT)	Run-It-By	FC05, 13, 18, 20
D	#173	(DC)	Sampling Method	FC29, 30, 32, 48, 49, 52, 53, 54
B	#174	(AT)	SCAMPER	FC26, 43
B	#175	(IG)	Scatter Diagram	FC52
P	#176	(CI)	Scenario Writing	FC64
P	#177	(ES)	Selection Matrix	FC45
P	#178	(ES)	Selection Window	FC11
D	#179	(IG)	Semantic Intuition	FC38
P	#180	(CI)	Shewhart PDCA Cycle	FC59
P	#181	(AT)	Snake Chart	FC41
T	#182	(TB)	Sociogram	FC03
B	#183	(ES)	Solution Matrix	FC28, 41, 43
B	#184	(AT)	Standard Deviation	FC50
D	#185	(DC)	Starbursting	FC10
P	#186	(AT)	Stem-and-Leaf Display	FC51
P	#187	(ES)	Sticking Dots	FC10
D	#188	(IG)	Stimulus Analysis	FC15
B	#189	(PP)	Storyboarding	FC55
P	#190	(AT)	Stratification	FC29
P	#191	(AT)	Stratum Chart	FC63
D	#192	(DC)	Surveying	FC48, 49, 54, 56
D	#193	(PP)	SWOT Analysis	FC62
P	#194	(AT)	Symbolic Flowchart	FC22
P	#195	(AT)	Systems Analysis Diagram	FC24
P	#196	(AT	Task Analysis	FC57
T	#197	(TB)	Team Meeting Evaluation	FC02, 03, 55
T	#198	(TB)	Team Mirror	FC01
T	#199	(TB)	Team Process Assessment	FC01

6σ	Page Number	Tool Category	Title	Tool-Strings Flowchart number
T	#200	(AT)	Thematic Content Analysis	FC49
P	#201	(CI)	Time Study Sheet	FC26
P	#202	(AT)	Timeline Chart	FC30
P	#203	(PP)	Top-Down Flowchart	FC23
P	#204	(PP)	Tree Diagram	FC13
P	#205	(AT)	Trend Analysis	FC65
B	#206	(ES)	Triple Ranking	FC55
P	#207	(AT)	Truth Table	FC21
B	#208	(DC)	Two-Dimensional Survey Grid	FC40, 60
P	#209	(AT)	Two-Directional Bar Chart	FC31
D	#210	(AT)	Value Analysis	FC37
P	#211	(AT)	Value/Non-Value-Added Cycle Time Chart	FC27
P	#212	(AT)	Variance Analysis	FC26
T	#213	(ES)	Venn Diagram	FC18
B	#214	(DM)	Weighted Voting	FC38
B	#215	(AT)	What-If Analysis	FC27, 33
B	#216	(PP)	Why/How Charting	FC61
B	#217	(IG)	Wildest Idea Technique	FC07
P	#218	(AT)	Window Analysis	FC11
B	#219	(AT)	Wishful Thinking	FC20
P	#220	(PP)	Work Breakdown Structure (WBS)	FC34, 36
P	#221	(CI)	Work Flow Analysis (WFA)	FC28
P	#222	(AT)	Yield Chart	FC29

1. Teaming   (FC01-FC14)

- FC01-Team Building: Team Dynamics Training 6σ-36
- FC02-Team Building: Identifying Organizational Interactions 6σ-37
- FC03-Team Building: Interpersonal Dynamics 6σ-38
- FC04-Team Communications: Organizational Relationships 6σ-39
- FC05-Team Communications: Collecting Information 6σ-40
- FC06-Team Communications: Information for Presentation 6σ-41
- FC07-Team Decision Making: Prioritizing Options 6σ-42
- FC08-Team Decision Making: Considering many Alternatives 6σ-43
- FC09-Team Decision Making: Applying Team Criteria 6σ-44
- FC10-Team Problem Solving: Identifying Problem Clusters 6σ-45
- FC11-Team Problem Solving: Window Analysis for Options 6σ-46
- FC12-Team Problem Solving: In-depth Analysis 6σ-47
- FC13-Team Problem Solving: Planning for Change 6σ-48
- FC14-Team Problem Solving: Continuous Improvement 6σ-49

2. Creativity (FC15-FC21)

- FC15-Creativity/Assessment: Non-linear Thinking Process 6σ-50
- FC16-Creativity/Assessment: Technical Improvements 6σ-51
- FC17-Creativity/Assessment: Grouping Generated Ideas 6σ-52
- FC18-Creativity/Assessment: Logical Thinking 6σ-53
- FC19-Creativity/Assessment: Relationships and Associations 6σ-54
- FC20-Creativity/Assessment: Non-logical Problem Solving 6σ-55
- FC21-Logical Thinking in Problem Solving 6σ-56

3. Process   (FC22-FC32)

- FC22-Process Improvement: Processing Operations 6σ-57
- FC23-Process Improvement: Technical Operations 6σ-58
- FC24-Process Improvement: Top-down Analysis for Change 6σ-59
- FC25-Process Improvement: Process Mapping and Analysis 6σ-60
- FC26-Process Improvement: Process Flow and Cycle Time 6σ-61
- FC27-Cycle Time Reduction: Work Flow Analysis 6σ-62
- FC28-Work Space Reduction: Work Flow Analysis 6σ-63

- FC29-Quality Reporting: Monitoring over Time   6σ-64
- FC30-Quality Reporting: Analysis of Trends   6σ-65
- FC31-Quality Reporting: Quality Charting   6σ-66
- FC32-Quality Reporting: Statistical Process Control Functions   6σ-67

4. Projects   (FC33-FC36)

- FC33-Project Management: Planning and Measurement   6σ-68
- FC34-Project Management: Prioritizing and Scheduling   6σ-69
- FC35-Project Management: Prioritization Analysis   6σ-70
- FC36-Project Management: Major Projects   6σ-71

5. Products/Services (FC37-FC44)

- FC37-Products/Services: Quality Function Deployment   6σ-72
- FC38-Products/Services: Generating Ideas   6σ-73
- FC39-Products/Services: Meeting Customer Expectations   6σ-74
- FC40-Products/Services: Customer Satisfaction Analysis   6σ-75
- FC41-Products/Services: Comparing Benchmark Data   6σ-76
- FC42-Products/Services: Repositioning of Products   6σ-77
- FC43-Products/Services: Checking for Improvements   6σ-78
- FC44-Products/Services: Finding Solutions to Problems   6σ-79

6. Research/Statistics   (FC45-FC54)

- FC45-Research Methods: Information Needs Analysis   6σ-80
- FC46-Research Methods: Collecting Specific Data   6σ-81
- FC47-Research Methods: Benchmarking   6σ-82
- FC48-Research Methods: Surveying   6σ-83
- FC49-Research Methods: Searching for Patterns   6σ-84
- FC50-Descriptive Statistics: Basic Data Analysis   6σ-85
- FC51-Descriptive Statistics: Data Displays   6σ-86
- FC52-Inferential Statistics: Hypothesis Testing — Correlation   6σ-87
- FC53-Inferential Statistics: Hypothesis Testing — ANOVA   6σ-88
- FC54-Inferential Statistics: Hypothesis Testing — Chi-Square   6σ-89

7. Organizational Change   (FC55-FC65)

- FC55-Organizational Change: Storyboarding Team Start-up   6σ-90
- FC56-Organizational Change: Benchmarking Activities   6σ-91

- FC57-Organizational Change: Needs Analysis   6σ-92
- FC58-Organizational Change: Root Cause Analysis   6σ-93
- FC59-Organizational Change: Continuous Improvement Cycle   6σ-94
- FC60-Organizational Measurement: Analyzing Survey Data   6σ-95
- FC61-Organizational Measurement: Developing Objectives   6σ-96
- FC62-Organizational Measurement: Strengths and Weaknesses   6σ-97
- FC63-Organizational Measurement: Change over Time   6σ-98
- FC64-Organizational Futuring: Discovering Outcomes   6σ-99
- FC65-Organizational Futuring: Responding to Predictions   6σ-100

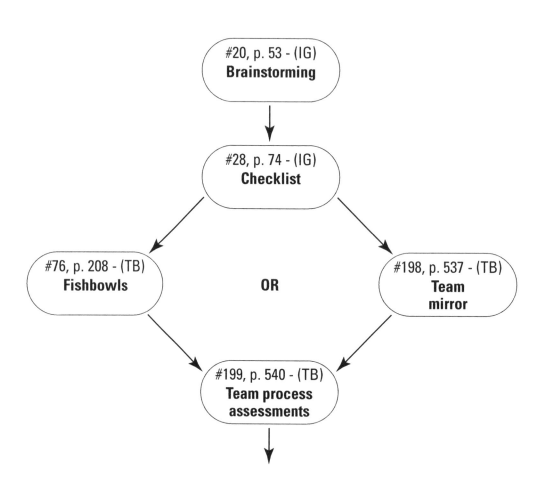

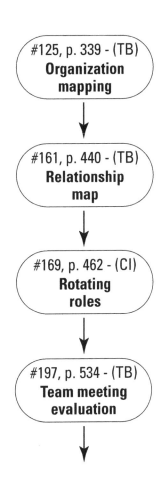

#125, p. 339 - (TB)
Organization mapping

#161, p. 440 - (TB)
Relationship map

#169, p. 462 - (CI)
Rotating roles

#197, p. 534 - (TB)
Team meeting evaluation

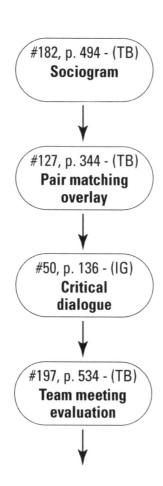

#182, p. 494 - (TB)
Sociogram

#127, p. 344 - (TB)
**Pair matching
overlay**

#50, p. 136 - (IG)
**Critical
dialogue**

#197, p. 534 - (TB)
**Team meeting
evaluation**

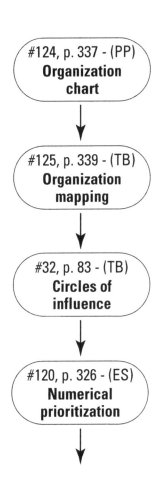

#124, p. 337 - (PP)
Organization chart

#125, p. 339 - (TB)
Organization mapping

#32, p. 83 - (TB)
Circles of influence

#120, p. 326 - (ES)
Numerical prioritization

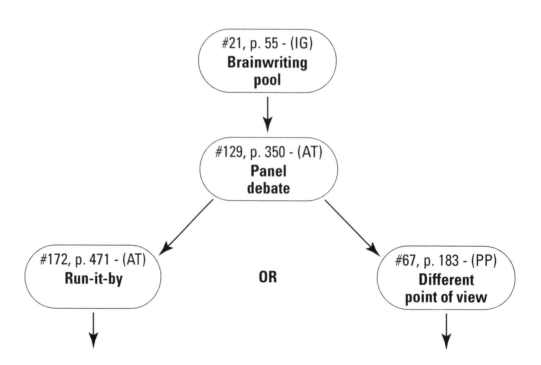

#21, p. 55 - (IG)
Brainwriting pool

#129, p. 350 - (AT)
Panel debate

#172, p. 471 - (AT)
Run-it-by

OR

#67, p. 183 - (PP)
Different point of view

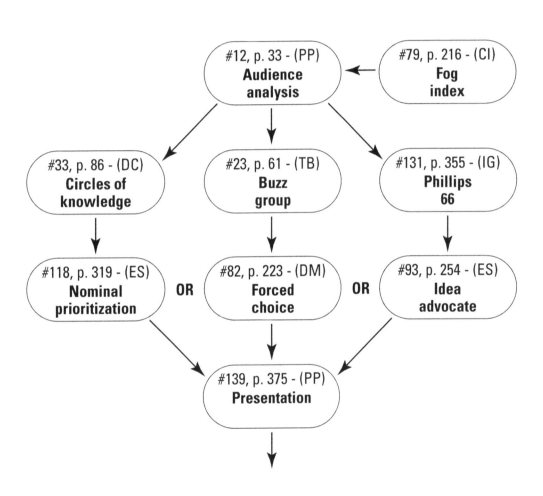

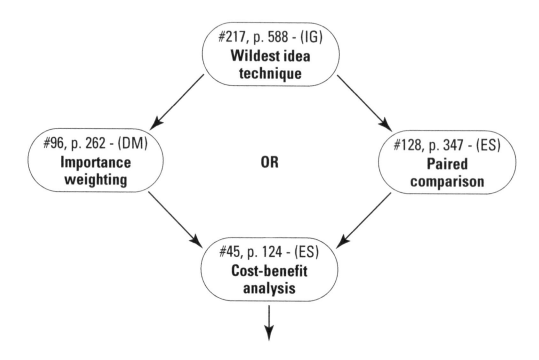

#217, p. 588 - (IG)
Wildest idea technique

#96, p. 262 - (DM)
Importance weighting

OR

#128, p. 347 - (ES)
Paired comparison

#45, p. 124 - (ES)
Cost-benefit analysis

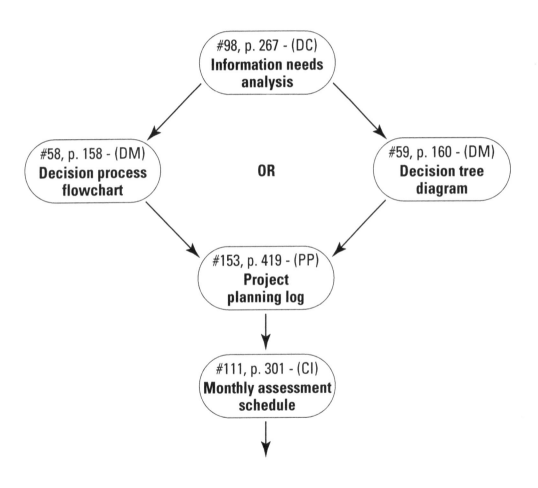

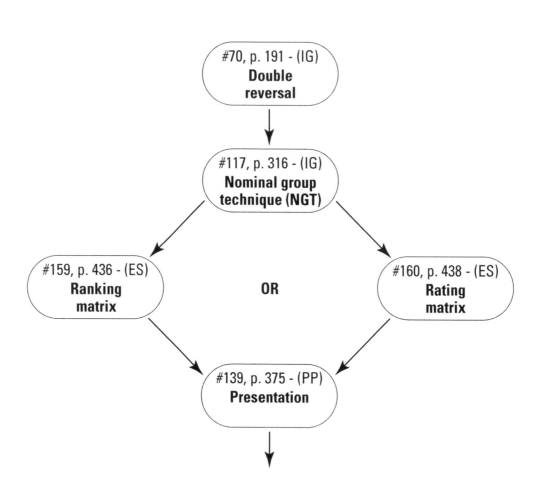

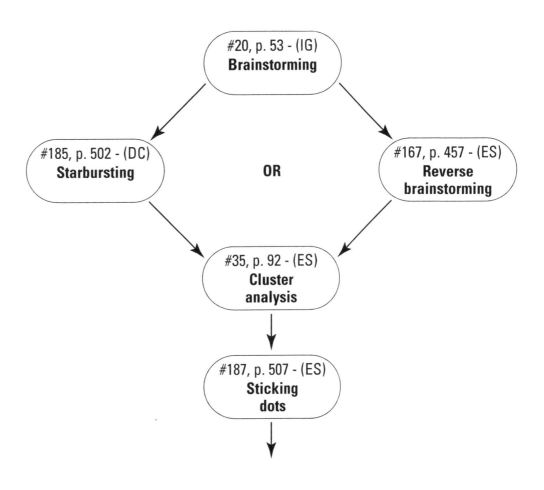

#20, p. 53 - (IG)
Brainstorming

#185, p. 502 - (DC)
Starbursting

OR

#167, p. 457 - (ES)
**Reverse
brainstorming**

#35, p. 92 - (ES)
**Cluster
analysis**

#187, p. 507 - (ES)
**Sticking
dots**

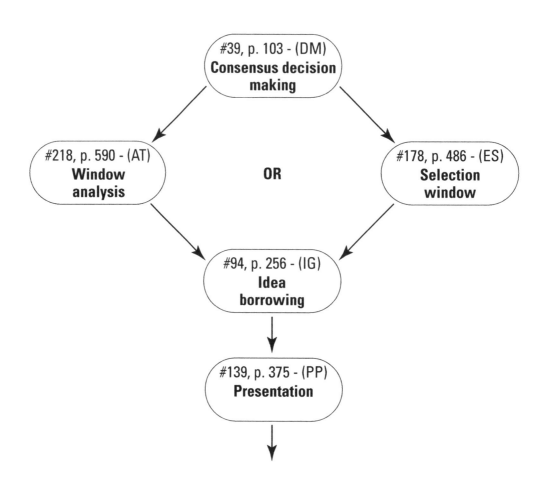

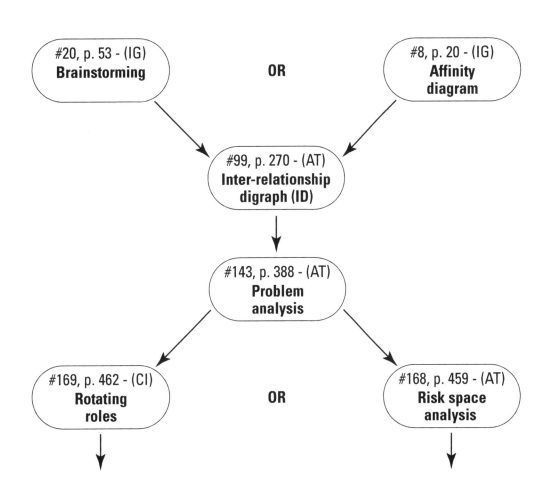

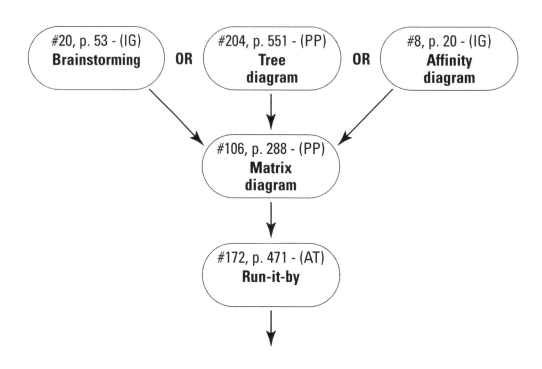

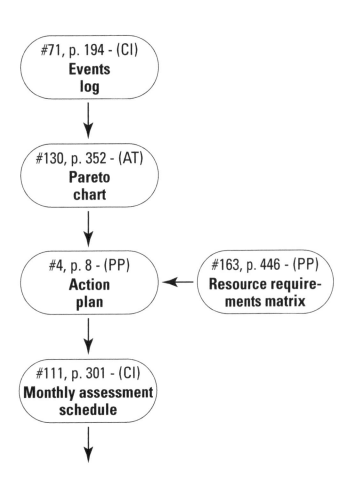

#71, p. 194 - (CI)
**Events
log**

#130, p. 352 - (AT)
**Pareto
chart**

#4, p. 8 - (PP)
**Action
plan**

#163, p. 446 - (PP)
**Resource require-
ments matrix**

#111, p. 301 - (CI)
**Monthly assessment
schedule**

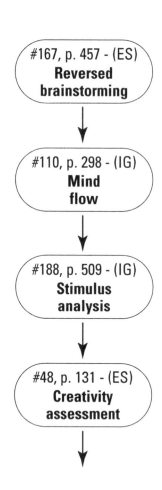

#167, p. 457 - (ES)
**Reversed
brainstorming**

#110, p. 298 - (IG)
**Mind
flow**

#188, p. 509 - (IG)
**Stimulus
analysis**

#48, p. 131 - (ES)
**Creativity
assessment**

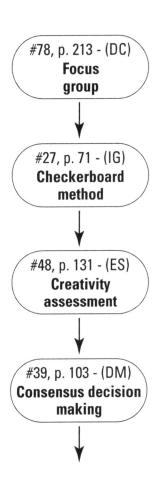

#78, p. 213 - (DC)
**Focus
group**

#27, p. 71 - (IG)
**Checkerboard
method**

#48, p. 131 - (ES)
**Creativity
assessment**

#39, p. 103 - (DM)
**Consensus decision
making**

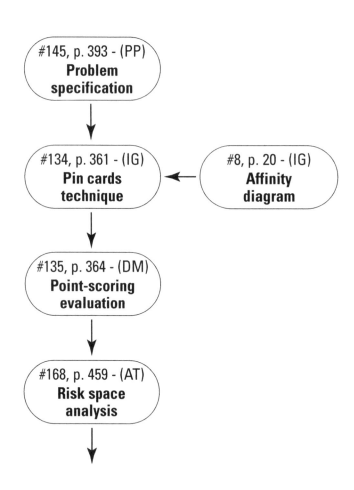

#145, p. 393 - (PP)
**Problem
specification**

#134, p. 361 - (IG)
**Pin cards
technique**

#8, p. 20 - (IG)
**Affinity
diagram**

#135, p. 364 - (DM)
**Point-scoring
evaluation**

#168, p. 459 - (AT)
**Risk space
analysis**

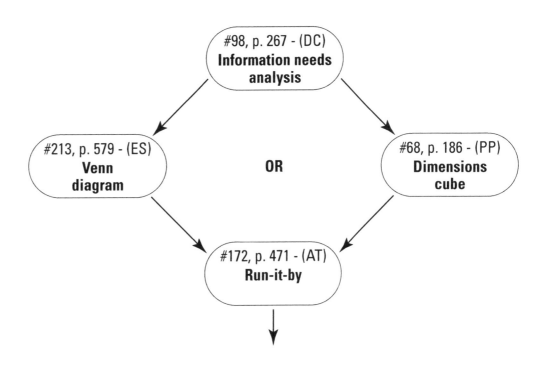

#98, p. 267 - (DC)
**Information needs
analysis**

#213, p. 579 - (ES)
**Venn
diagram**

OR

#68, p. 186 - (PP)
**Dimensions
cube**

#172, p. 471 - (AT)
Run-it-by

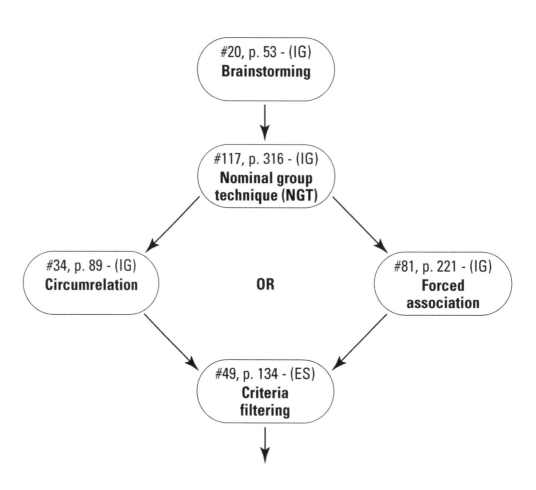

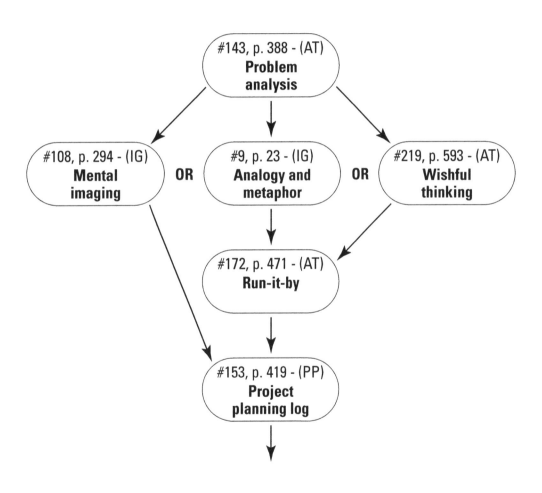

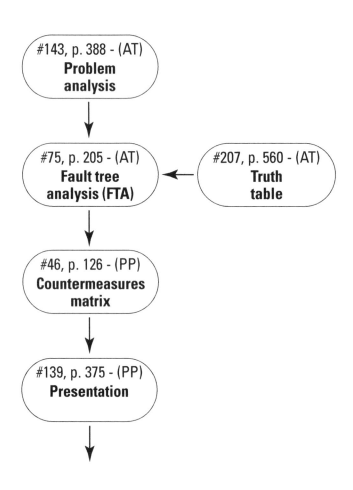

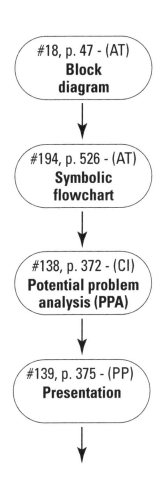

#18, p. 47 - (AT)
**Block
diagram**

#194, p. 526 - (AT)
**Symbolic
flowchart**

#138, p. 372 - (CI)
**Potential problem
analysis (PPA)**

#139, p. 375 - (PP)
Presentation

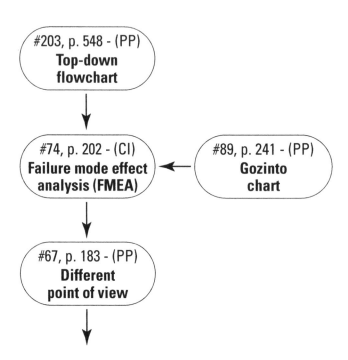

#203, p. 548 - (PP)
**Top-down
flowchart**

#74, p. 202 - (CI)
**Failure mode effect
analysis (FMEA)**

#89, p. 241 - (PP)
**Gozinto
chart**

#67, p. 183 - (PP)
**Different
point of view**

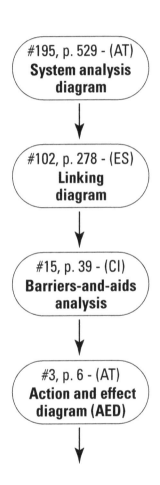

#195, p. 529 - (AT)
**System analysis
diagram**

#102, p. 278 - (ES)
**Linking
diagram**

#15, p. 39 - (CI)
**Barriers-and-aids
analysis**

#3, p. 6 - (AT)
**Action and effect
diagram (AED)**

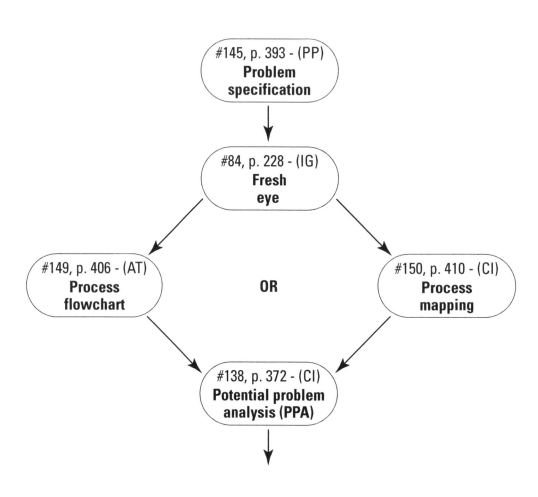

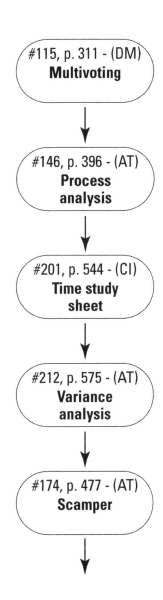

#115, p. 311 - (DM)
Multivoting

#146, p. 396 - (AT)
**Process
analysis**

#201, p. 544 - (CI)
**Time study
sheet**

#212, p. 575 - (AT)
**Variance
analysis**

#174, p. 477 - (AT)
Scamper

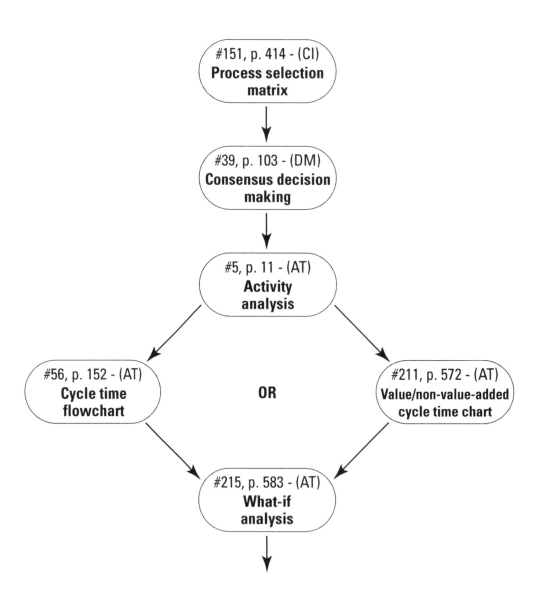

#151, p. 414 - (CI)
Process selection matrix

↓

#39, p. 103 - (DM)
Consensus decision making

↓

#5, p. 11 - (AT)
Activity analysis

#56, p. 152 - (AT)
Cycle time flowchart

OR

#211, p. 572 - (AT)
Value/non-value-added cycle time chart

#215, p. 583 - (AT)
What-if analysis

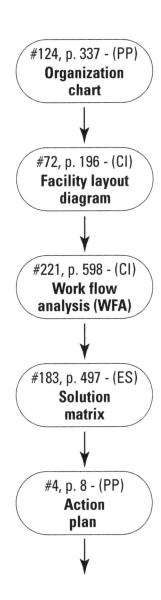

#124, p. 337 - (PP)
**Organization
chart**

↓

#72, p. 196 - (CI)
**Facility layout
diagram**

↓

#221, p. 598 - (CI)
**Work flow
analysis (WFA)**

↓

#183, p. 497 - (ES)
**Solution
matrix**

↓

#4, p. 8 - (PP)
**Action
plan**

↓

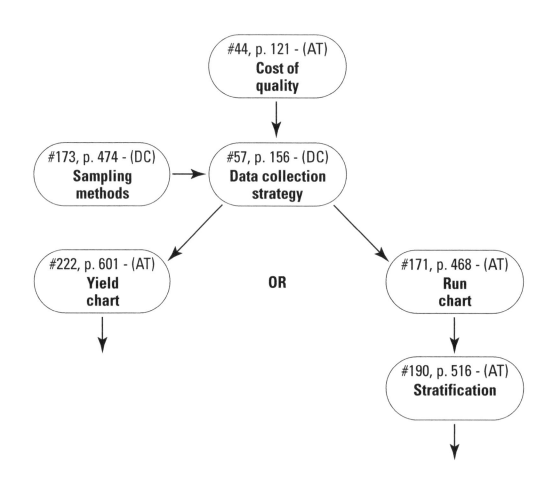

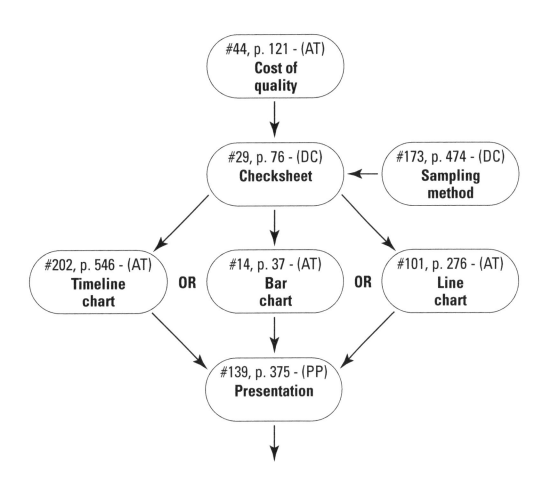

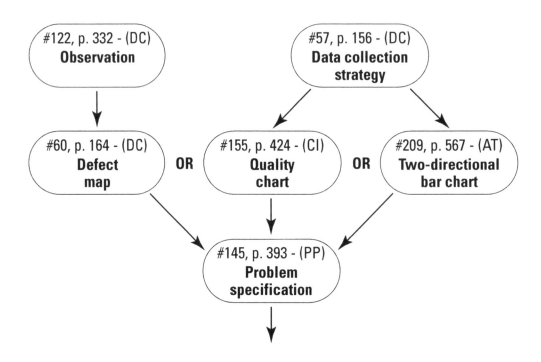

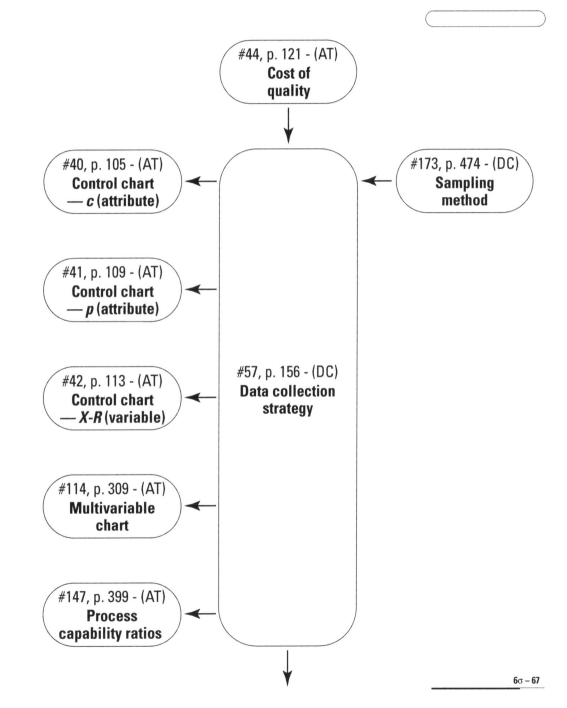

#44, p. 121 - (AT)
**Cost of
quality**

#40, p. 105 - (AT)
**Control chart
— *c* (attribute)**

#173, p. 474 - (DC)
**Sampling
method**

#41, p. 109 - (AT)
**Control chart
— *p* (attribute)**

#42, p. 113 - (AT)
**Control chart
— *X-R* (variable)**

#57, p. 156 - (DC)
**Data collection
strategy**

#114, p. 309 - (AT)
**Multivariable
chart**

#147, p. 399 - (AT)
**Process
capability ratios**

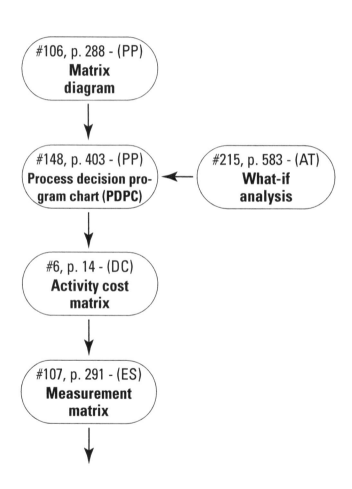

#106, p. 288 - (PP)
**Matrix
diagram**

#148, p. 403 - (PP)
**Process decision pro-
gram chart (PDPC)**

#215, p. 583 - (AT)
**What-if
analysis**

#6, p. 14 - (DC)
**Activity cost
matrix**

#107, p. 291 - (ES)
**Measurement
matrix**

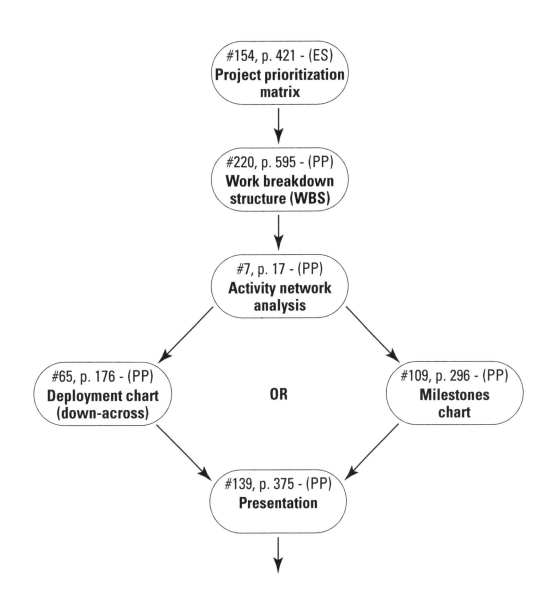

#154, p. 421 - (ES)
Project prioritization matrix

#220, p. 595 - (PP)
Work breakdown structure (WBS)

#7, p. 17 - (PP)
Activity network analysis

#65, p. 176 - (PP)
Deployment chart (down-across)

OR

#109, p. 296 - (PP)
Milestones chart

#139, p. 375 - (PP)
Presentation

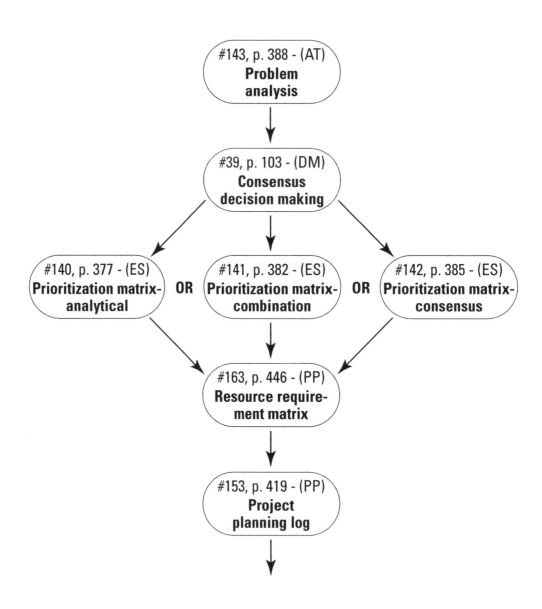

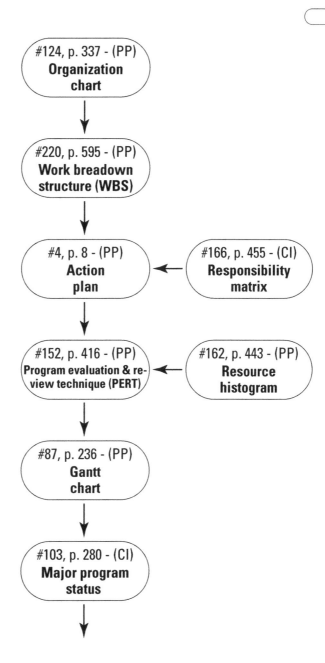

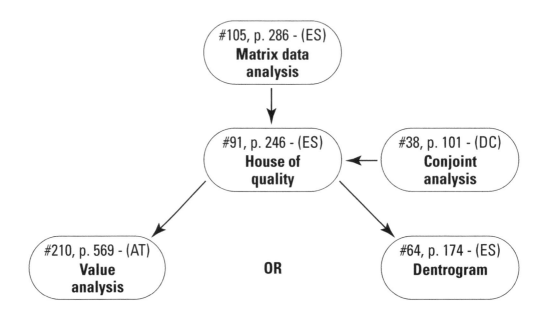

#105, p. 286 - (ES)
**Matrix data
analysis**

#91, p. 246 - (ES)
**House of
quality**

#38, p. 101 - (DC)
**Conjoint
analysis**

#210, p. 569 - (AT)
**Value
analysis**

OR

#64, p. 174 - (ES)
Dentrogram

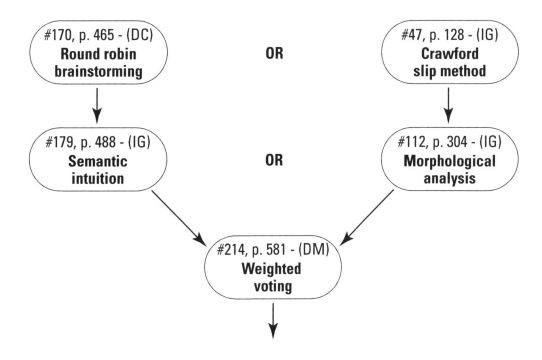

| #170, p. 465 - (DC) | | #47, p. 128 - (IG) |
| **Round robin brainstorming** | OR | **Crawford slip method** |

| #179, p. 488 - (IG) | | #112, p. 304 - (IG) |
| **Semantic intuition** | OR | **Morphological analysis** |

#214, p. 581 - (DM)
Weighted voting

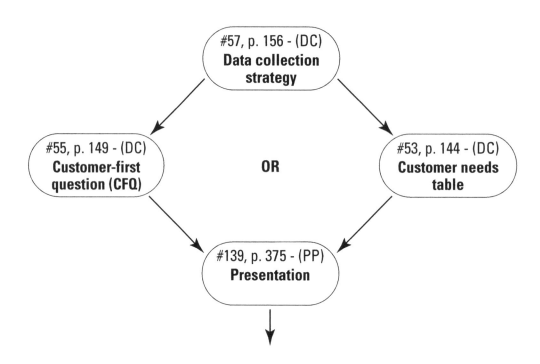

```
                    ┌──────────────────────┐
                    │  #57, p. 156 - (DC)  │
                    │   Data collection    │
                    │      strategy        │
                    └──────────────────────┘
                      ↙                  ↘
  ┌──────────────────────┐          ┌──────────────────────┐
  │  #55, p. 149 - (DC)  │          │  #53, p. 144 - (DC)  │
  │   Customer-first     │   OR     │   Customer needs     │
  │   question (CFQ)     │          │       table          │
  └──────────────────────┘          └──────────────────────┘
                      ↘                  ↙
                    ┌──────────────────────┐
                    │  #139, p. 375 - (PP) │
                    │    Presentation      │
                    └──────────────────────┘
                              ↓
```

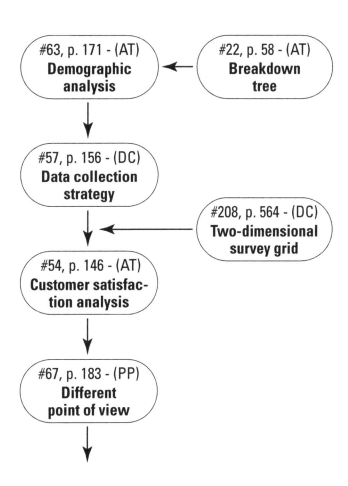

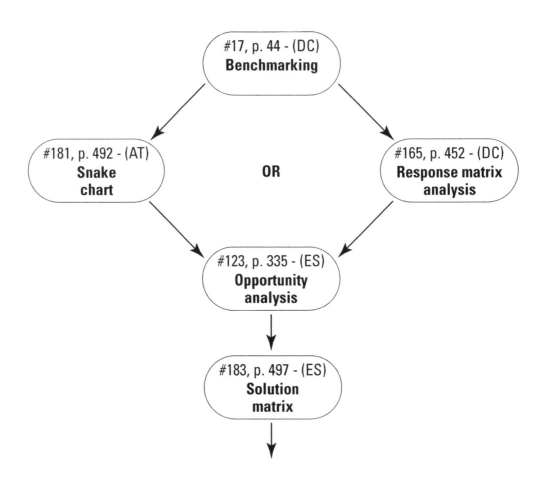

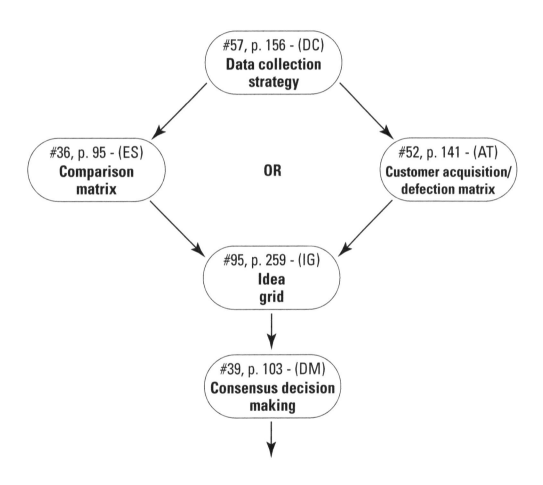

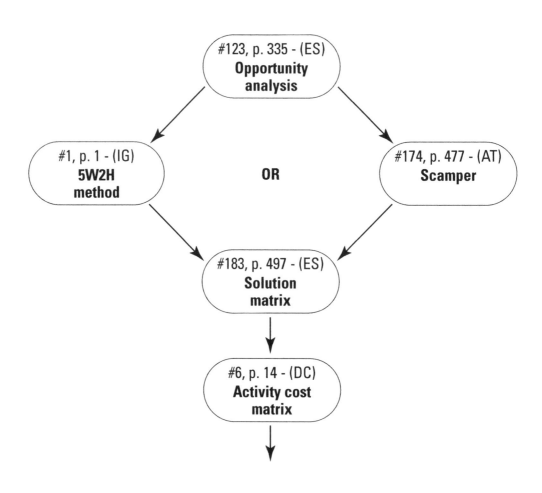

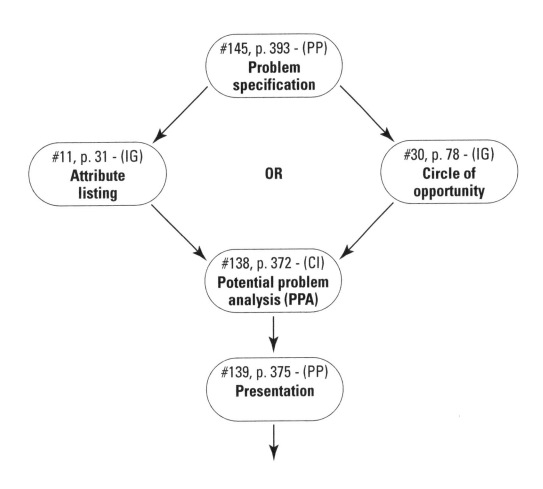

#145, p. 393 - (PP)
Problem specification

#11, p. 31 - (IG)
Attribute listing

OR

#30, p. 78 - (IG)
Circle of opportunity

#138, p. 372 - (CI)
Potential problem analysis (PPA)

#139, p. 375 - (PP)
Presentation

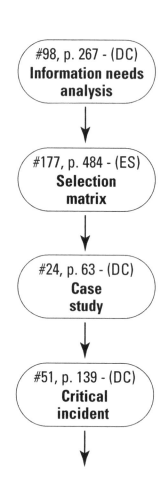

#98, p. 267 - (DC)
**Information needs
analysis**

#177, p. 484 - (ES)
**Selection
matrix**

#24, p. 63 - (DC)
**Case
study**

#51, p. 139 - (DC)
**Critical
incident**

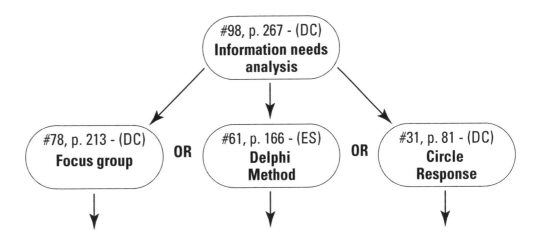

#98, p. 267 - (DC)
**Information needs
analysis**

#78, p. 213 - (DC)
Focus group

OR

#61, p. 166 - (ES)
**Delphi
Method**

OR

#31, p. 81 - (DC)
**Circle
Response**

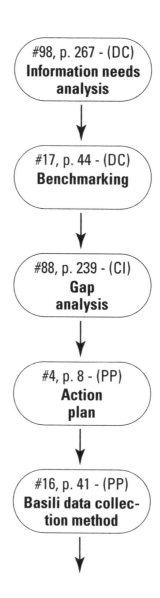

#98, p. 267 - (DC)
**Information needs
analysis**

↓

#17, p. 44 - (DC)
Benchmarking

↓

#88, p. 239 - (CI)
**Gap
analysis**

↓

#4, p. 8 - (PP)
**Action
plan**

↓

#16, p. 41 - (PP)
**Basili data collec-
tion method**

↓

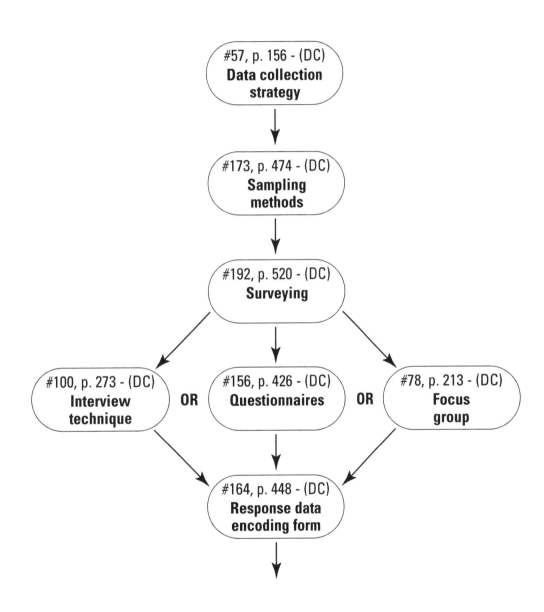

#57, p. 156 - (DC)
Data collection strategy

#173, p. 474 - (DC)
Sampling methods

#192, p. 520 - (DC)
Surveying

#100, p. 273 - (DC)
Interview technique

OR

#156, p. 426 - (DC)
Questionnaires

OR

#78, p. 213 - (DC)
Focus group

#164, p. 448 - (DC)
Response data encoding form

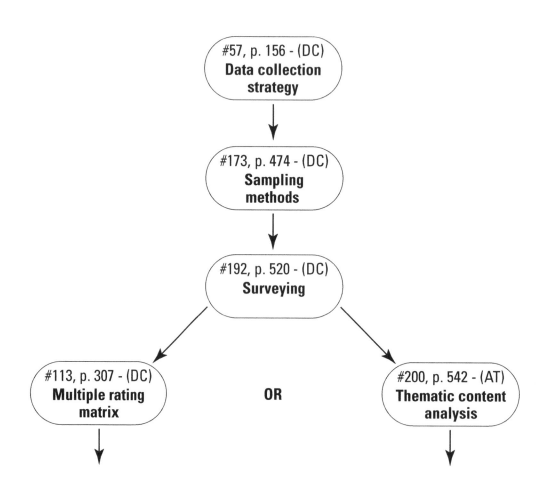

#57, p. 156 - (DC)
Data collection strategy

#173, p. 474 - (DC)
Sampling methods

#192, p. 520 - (DC)
Surveying

#113, p. 307 - (DC)
Multiple rating matrix

OR

#200, p. 542 - (AT)
Thematic content analysis

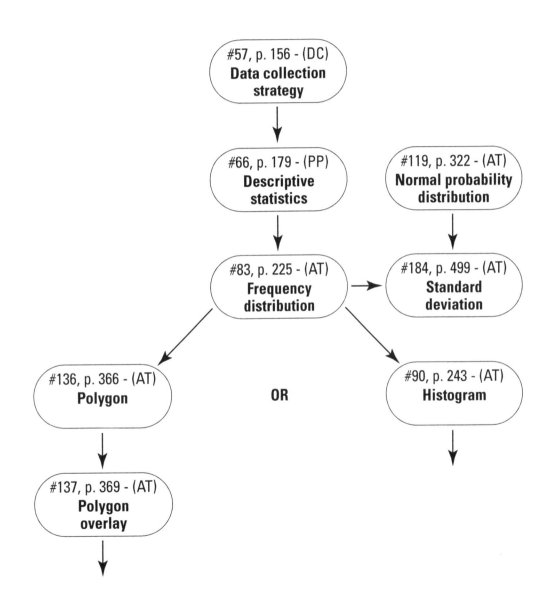

#57, p. 156 - (DC)
**Data collection
strategy**

#66, p. 179 - (PP)
**Descriptive
statistics**

#119, p. 322 - (AT)
**Normal probability
distribution**

#83, p. 225 - (AT)
**Frequency
distribution**

#184, p. 499 - (AT)
**Standard
deviation**

#136, p. 366 - (AT)
Polygon

OR

#90, p. 243 - (AT)
Histogram

#137, p. 369 - (AT)
**Polygon
overlay**

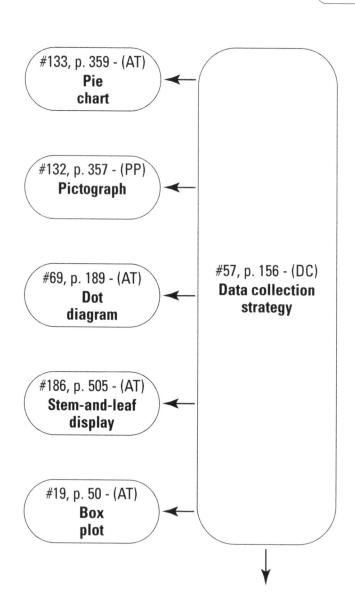

#133, p. 359 - (AT)
**Pie
chart**

#132, p. 357 - (PP)
Pictograph

#69, p. 189 - (AT)
**Dot
diagram**

#57, p. 156 - (DC)
**Data collection
strategy**

#186, p. 505 - (AT)
**Stem-and-leaf
display**

#19, p. 50 - (AT)
**Box
plot**

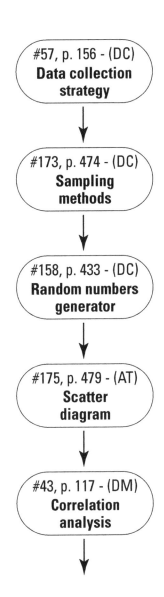

#57, p. 156 - (DC)
Data collection strategy

#173, p. 474 - (DC)
Sampling methods

#158, p. 433 - (DC)
Random numbers generator

#175, p. 479 - (AT)
Scatter diagram

#43, p. 117 - (DM)
Correlation analysis

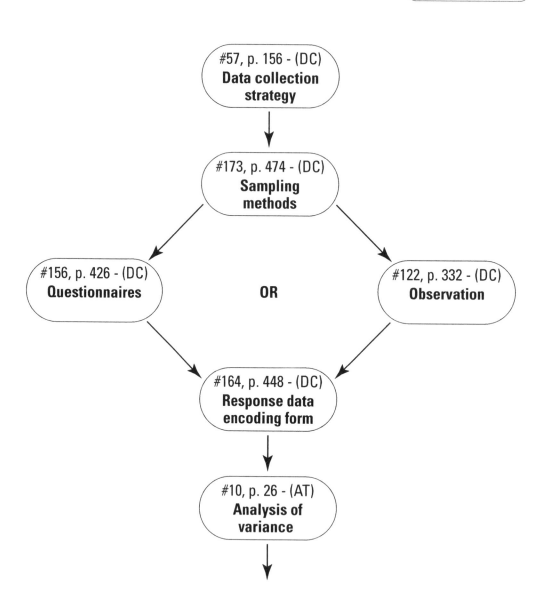

#57, p. 156 - (DC)
Data collection strategy

#173, p. 474 - (DC)
Sampling methods

#156, p. 426 - (DC)
Questionnaires

OR

#122, p. 332 - (DC)
Observation

#164, p. 448 - (DC)
Response data encoding form

#10, p. 26 - (AT)
Analysis of variance

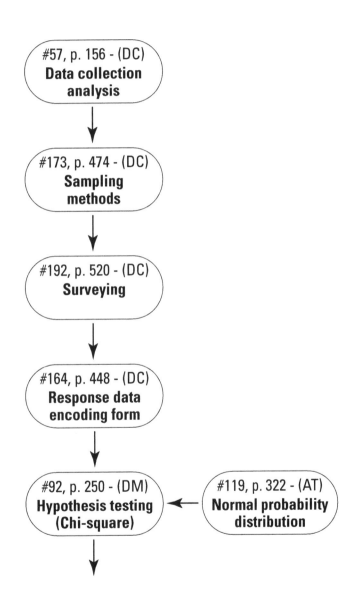

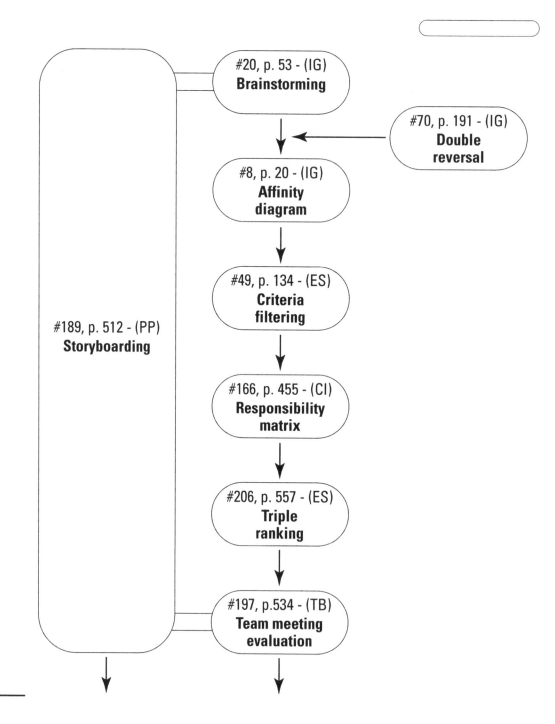

#20, p. 53 - (IG)
Brainstorming

#70, p. 191 - (IG)
**Double
reversal**

#8, p. 20 - (IG)
**Affinity
diagram**

#49, p. 134 - (ES)
**Criteria
filtering**

#189, p. 512 - (PP)
Storyboarding

#166, p. 455 - (CI)
**Responsibility
matrix**

#206, p. 557 - (ES)
**Triple
ranking**

#197, p.534 - (TB)
**Team meeting
evaluation**

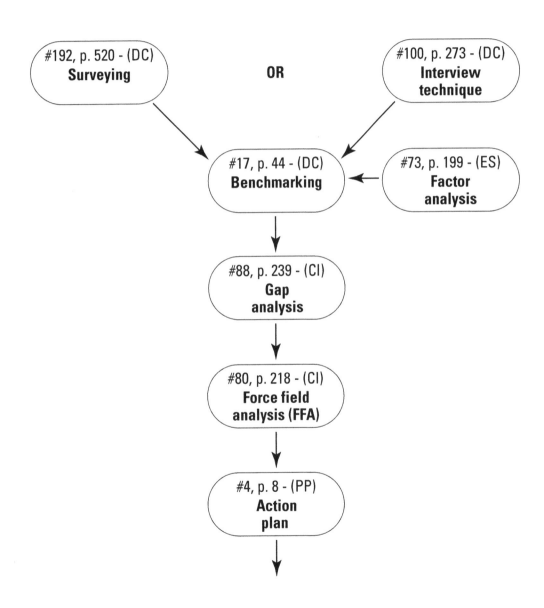

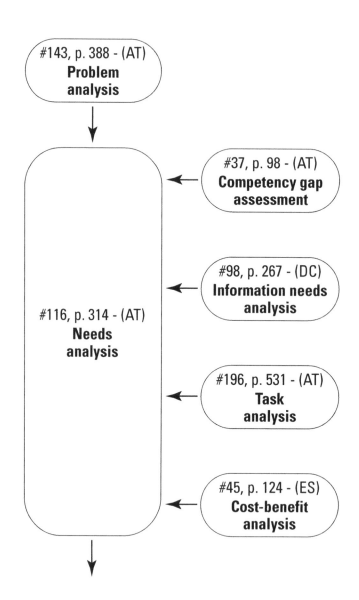

#143, p. 388 - (AT)
**Problem
analysis**

#37, p. 98 - (AT)
**Competency gap
assessment**

#98, p. 267 - (DC)
**Information needs
analysis**

#116, p. 314 - (AT)
**Needs
analysis**

#196, p. 531 - (AT)
**Task
analysis**

#45, p. 124 - (ES)
**Cost-benefit
analysis**

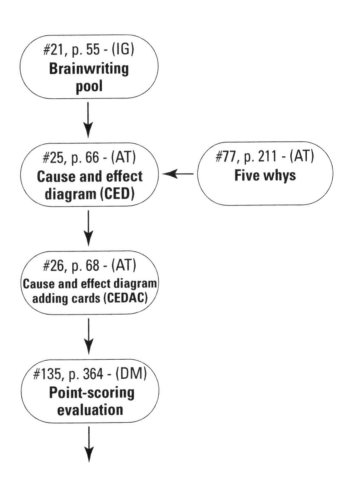

#21, p. 55 - (IG)
Brainwriting pool

#25, p. 66 - (AT)
Cause and effect diagram (CED)

#77, p. 211 - (AT)
Five whys

#26, p. 68 - (AT)
Cause and effect diagram adding cards (CEDAC)

#135, p. 364 - (DM)
Point-scoring evaluation

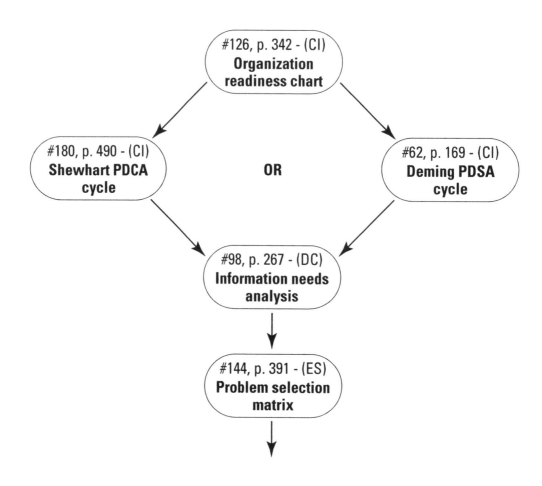

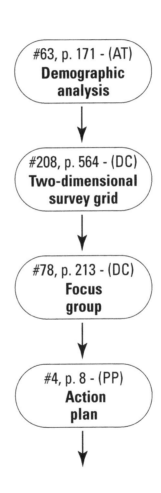

#63, p. 171 - (AT)
**Demographic
analysis**

#208, p. 564 - (DC)
**Two-dimensional
survey grid**

#78, p. 213 - (DC)
**Focus
group**

#4, p. 8 - (PP)
**Action
plan**

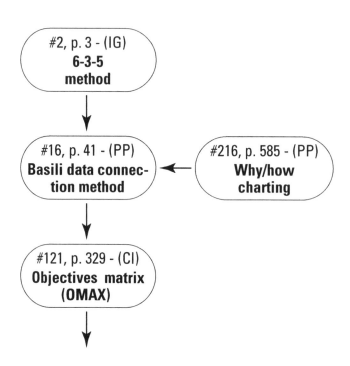

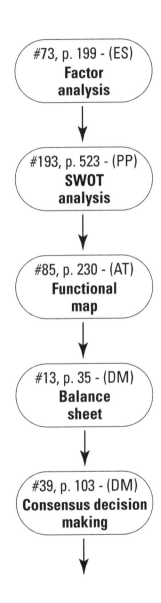

#73, p. 199 - (ES)
**Factor
analysis**

#193, p. 523 - (PP)
**SWOT
analysis**

#85, p. 230 - (AT)
**Functional
map**

#13, p. 35 - (DM)
**Balance
sheet**

#39, p. 103 - (DM)
**Consensus decision
making**

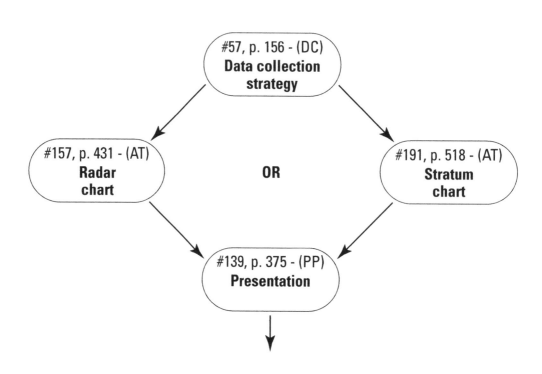

#57, p. 156 - (DC)
**Data collection
strategy**

#157, p. 431 - (AT)
**Radar
chart**

OR

#191, p. 518 - (AT)
**Stratum
chart**

#139, p. 375 - (PP)
Presentation

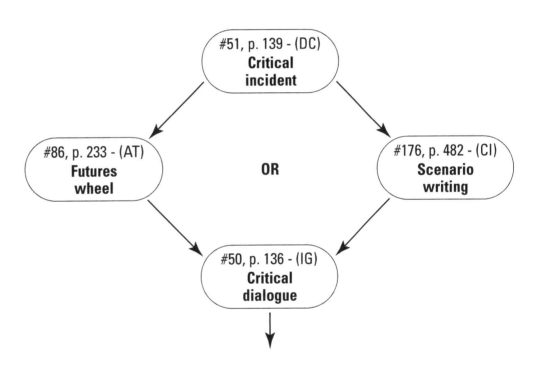

#51, p. 139 - (DC)
**Critical
incident**

#86, p. 233 - (AT)
**Futures
wheel**

OR

#176, p. 482 - (CI)
**Scenario
writing**

#50, p. 136 - (IG)
**Critical
dialogue**

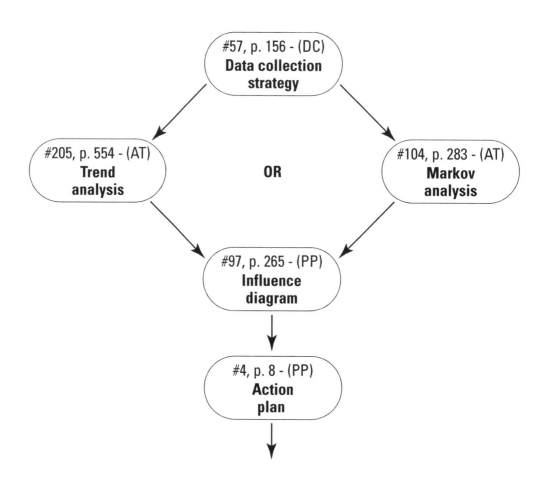

The 5W2H method is a very structured, idea-generating tool that asks a specific set of questions regarding a previously prepared problem or opportunity statement. This tool will force a team to consider and question every aspect of the problem or opportunity.

- To examine and question a process or product for the purpose of gaining improvement ideas.
- To identify potential problem or opportunity breakthroughs.
- To assist a team in generating new ideas.
- To discover overlooked issues or causes.

before

Events log
Checksheet
Brainstorming
Pareto chart
Problem specification

after

Starbursting
Problem analysis
Countermeasures matrix
Solution matrix
Work flow analysis (WFA)

➡ Select and define problem or opportunity
➡ Identify and analyze causes or potential change
➡ Develop and plan possible solutions or change
   Implement and evaluate solution or change
   Measure and report solution or change results
   Recognize and reward team efforts

Research/statistics
1 Creativity/innovation
Engineering
Project management
3 Manufacturing
Marketing/sales
Administration/documentation
Servicing/support
Customer/quality metrics
2 Change management

• Also refer to the SCAMPER tool for more options.

Display a prepared problem or opportunity statement to the team. See example *Reduce Hiring Cycle Time for Engineers*.

Describe the 5W2H chart and its headings of *Issue*, *5W2H*, *Question*, and *Consider*.

Participants respond with questions and countermeasures for completing the chart. Use additional flip-chart paper to record a large number of responses.

Review and date the completed chart.

Reduce Hiring Cycle Time for Engineers			Date: xx/xx/xx
Issue	5W2H Question		Consider
Purpose	Why	—do we need this process? —does it take so much time?	Outsource function
Activity	What	—are the activities involved? —are the essential activities?	Cycle time reduction
Place	Where	—is the process performed? —are the employment offices?	Centralization/ decentralization
Staff	Who	—is involved in this process? —needs to be involved?	Reduce approvals
Time	When	—is this process activated? —is this process completed?	Planning/ procedures
Method	How	—do we recruit? —is staffing practiced?	Re-engineering
Cost	How much	—does it cost for hiring? —can the cost be reduced?	Cost/ benefit analysis

The 6-3-5 method is a brainwriting technique that generates and develops ideas by asking six participants to write, within five minutes, three ideas on separate cards. These cards are then passed along to other participants for further refinement or additional ideas.

- To generate a large list of ideas for problem solving.
- To unlock the creativity in teams.
- To identify process or product-improvement opportunities.
- To refine or build on previously generated ideas.

before

Checklist

Checksheet

Observation

Interview technique

Problem specification

after

Criteria filtering

SCAMPER

Cluster analysis

Creativity assessment

Nominal group technique (NGT)

Select and define problem or opportunity

➡ Identify and analyze causes or potential change

➡ Develop and plan possible solutions or change

➡ Implement and evaluate solution or change

Measure and report solution or change results

Recognize and reward team efforts

Research/statistics

1 Creativity/innovation

Engineering

Project management

Manufacturing

Marketing/sales

Administration/documentation

Servicing/support

Customer/quality metrics

2 Change management

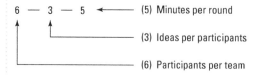

6 — 3 — 5 ← (5) Minutes per round

(3) Ideas per participants

(6) Participants per team

A problem statement is shared with a team of six participants. See example *Improve Customer Satisfaction*.

Several blank cards are handed out to each participant with the instruction to generate three ideas (one per card) within five minutes.

Each participant writes three ideas related to the problem statement.

After the five-minute first round, participants pass the cards with written ideas to the person on their left.

The participants read all ideas passed to them, further develop the ideas, or add additional ideas to the previously recorded idea.

After five minutes, the second round is started, using the process as outlined in steps 4–5 above.

This process continues until each participant receives back his or her own card written during round one.

Lastly, all ideas are clustered and recorded. The chart is dated and saved for the next action step.

Improve Customer Satisfaction	Date: xx/xx/xx
External	**Product**
Survey customers	No spare parts
Focus groups	Missing parts
Conduct interviews	Defective products
Random contact	Missing manual
Etc.	Etc.
Internal	**Service**
Complaint file	Make callbacks
Check "returns" records	Be on time
Warranty claims	Forms filled out completely
Ask customer reps	No appointment errors
Sort correspondence	60 day followup
Reorder process	"Know your product"
Ask quality assurance	Accurate information
Shipping problem log	Check Code of Conduct
Etc.	Etc.

An action and effect diagram (AED) is a reverse fishbone diagram that assists a team in identifying the most positive and negative effects or outcomes of implementing a proposed action or solution. Unlike the cause and effect diagram (CED), the major generic categories such as people, methods, material, equipment, measurement, and cost are displayed to indicate the potential consequences or effects of planned actions.

- To select a solution that, when implemented, will produce the least negative aspects or effects.
- To identify resource requirements when planning to implement a proposed solution.
- To analyze how an action's consequences can impact the rest of the system.
- To develop other options or initiate corrective action to eliminate or greatly reduce listed negative effects.
- To evaluate the cost and benefits of a planned action.

before

Brainstorming

Consensus decision making

Countermeasures matrix

Starbursting

Pareto chart

after

Solution matrix

Action plan

Cost-benefit analysis

Resource requirements matrix

Balance sheet

Select and define problem or opportunity
Identify and analyze causes or potential change
➡ Develop and plan possible solutions or change
➡ Implement and evaluate solution or change
Measure and report solution or change results
Recognize and reward team efforts

Research/statistics
3 Creativity/innovation
Engineering
2 Project management
Manufacturing
Marketing/sales
Administration/documentation
Servicing/support
Customer/quality metrics
1 Change management

6

- Complete an action and effect diagram (AED) for all proposed solutions.
- Arrows are reversed in the action and effect diagram (AED).
- Positive and negative effects can be listed as pros and cons in order to compare them in several proposed solutions. Draw circles around strong negative effects indicated in the diagram(s).

Team reaches consensus on a proposed solution. See example *Provide "Tools for Teams" Training.*

Next, the team determines the major categories and places one in each category box.

Possible positive and negative consequences or effects are brainstormed and indicated with each category.

This process is continued until all ideas are recorded as shown in the example.

If more potential solutions are to be analyzed, an action and effect diagram (AED) for each possible solution is completed. The solution with the highest potential and the fewest negative aspects or effects is selected for implementation.

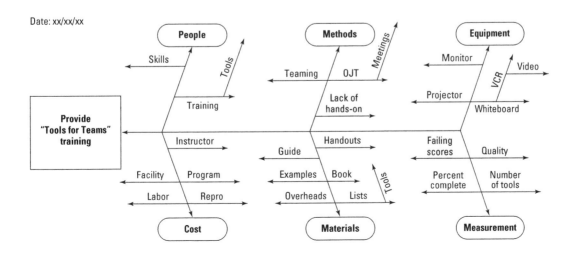

Date: xx/xx/xx

An action plan is a finalized document that displays action items, due dates, and other related information to successfully implement a solution or manage a project. The action plan breaks down an often complex project into smaller action items that are assigned to people who use stated resources to complete the tasks.

- To organize a team effort to implement a solution or process-improvement opportunity.
- To ascertain the progress of completion of listed action items and to verify overall schedule performance.
- To provide a project management tool for monitoring project status.

before

Project planning log

Project prioritization matrix

Work breakdown structure (WBS)

Resource requirements matrix

Milestones chart

after

Activity network diagram

Objectives matrix (OMAX)

Program evaluation and review technique (PERT)

Responsibility matrix

Resource histogram

	Select and define problem or opportunity
	Identify and analyze causes or potential change
➡	Develop and plan possible solutions or change
➡	Implement and evaluate solution or change
	Measure and report solution or change results
	Recognize and reward team efforts

	Research/statistics
	Creativity/innovation
	Engineering
1	Project management
	Manufacturing
	Marketing/sales
3	Administration/documentation
	Servicing/support
	Customer/quality metrics
2	Change management

- If the action plan's completion date is known, due dates for action items are developed moving backward in time.
- Openly display the action plan so that participants can verify status of completion.

The team brainstorms and identifies all required action items and their sequence of completion.

The facilitator draws an action plan on the whiteboard and lists all required action items and target dates. See example *Action Plan for Poster Development*.

Next, team participants or outside-the-team personnel are assigned the responsibility of completing the items.

All due dates are checked to ensure there are no conflicting time frames, and resource requirements (if known) are noted on the action plan.

The final plan is verified, signed off by the team, and dated as shown in the example.

After the action plan has been finalized, approved, and reproduced, a copy is posted on the bulletin board for future progress checks.

Action Plan for Poster Development

Action Plan Issue: 1	Team: Quality				Date: xx/xx/xx
Objective: Development of a TQM Poster					Approval: WJM
No.	Action items	Person responsible	Resources required	Target date	Actual date	Status disposition

No.	Action items	Person responsible	Resources required	Target date	Actual date	Status disposition
1	Prepare draft	J. Cowen	Review materials	2-1	2-6	Some definitions are missing
2	Typewritten info	S. Fagen	Word processing	4-1	3-15	Have J. C. check copy
3	Prepare artwork	J.L. (graphics)	Graphics request	5-1		
4	Check prepared draft	J. Cowen	——	7-1		
5	Revise draft and artwork	Team	——	8-1		
6	Cut printing plate	Bill S. (repro)	Print request	10-15		
7	Print color poster	"	Printshop materials	11-10		
8	Revise color shading	"	"	12-1		
9	Check poster quality	Team	Get feedback	12-5		
10	Request reproduction	WJM	Repro request	12-15		

An activity analysis is a very useful tool to account for the time spent in everyday work schedules, programs, or project activities. It allows an analyst to uncover unnecessary work activities, time taken to complete highly important to unimportant activities, and provides data helpful to make work more efficient and effective.

- To analyze and evaluate work and time requirements to complete the work.
- To identify ineffective work steps and procedures for the purpose of eliminating waste.
- To account for time used within an eight-hour day or other predetermined time period.

before

Time study sheet

Task analysis

Checksheet

Check list

Starbursting

after

Activity cost matrix

Value/nonvalue added cycle time chart

Process analysis

Breakdown tree

Cluster analysis

➥ Select and define problem or opportunity
➥ Identify and analyze causes or potential change
Develop and plan possible solutions or change
Implement and evaluate solution or change
Measure and report solution or change results
Recognize and reward team efforts

Research/statistics

Creativity/innovation

3 Engineering

Project management

2 Manufacturing

Marketing/sales

4 Administration/documentation

Servicing/support

Customer/quality metrics

1 Change management

• The following legend pertains to the example *Design Engineer—Two Work Days*.

Legend: ● = All value-added   Productive activity

　　　　 ◕ = Some value-added   Required activity

　　　　 ○ = Non-value-added   Nonproductive activity

An activity analysis form is prepared for the position, program, or project to be observed and analyzed. See example *Design Engineer—Two Work Days*.

Every activity that is considered important, time-consuming, or required work is timed and recorded on the form.

Other supporting activities are noted for the purpose of time accounting.

All activities are value-rated and coded as an *all, some, non*-value-added activity and recorded as such on the form, as shown in the example.

The totals column is summed to show time used in a specific period of time.

The form is completely filled out in order to provide background data for work simplification or process-improvement efforts.

Finally, the activity analysis form is reviewed and dated.

Design Engineer — Two Work Days

Name:		Date: 11/14/xx	VALUE	Evaluation			Analysis		
Team/Position: Design Engineer							Total		Contact Info.
Date	Time	Activity		Real Work	Routine Work	Busy Work	Hr	Min	
11/12	0745	Get coffee	○						
	0810	Check e-mail	◒		✓			50	
	0900	Return voice mail calls	◒		✓			45	
	0945	Break	○						
	1015	Call program office	●		✓			10	Pgm. J.L.
	1026	Revise drawing AX-221	●	✓			1	35	
	Noon	Lunch							
	1315	Revise drawing AX-255	●	✓			2	25	
	1540	Repro/graphics call	◒		✓			10	8-4445
	1600	Attend IPD meeting	○			✓		45	Weekly
	1650	Call repro	○		✓				8-4445
11/13	0810	Get coffee, talk to boss	○						
	0900	Talk to J.M. to coordinate	◒			✓		30	J.M.
	0930	Check e-mail	◒		✓			30	
	1000	Check voice mail, return calls	◒		✓			30	
	1030	Make calls on design changes	●	✓			1		Boston
	1130	Lunch meeting	○			✓			
	1315	Computer downtime	○						
	1330	Call software group	◒		✓			5	MIS-3
	1410	Supply parts data to G.K.	●	✓				20	G.K.
	1630	Leave for evening class	○						

Note: ● All value-added ◒ Some value-added ○ Non-value-added   Total | 9 | 35

The activity cost matrix is a useful cost data collection tool for the purpose of planning and budget preparation. In order to identify which personnel are involved in a major project, direct and supporting activities are listed and percent contribution estimated for each contributor.

- To determine departmental activities and associated cost data.
- To schedule personnel for completing specific project activities.
- To compare the ratio of contribution (effort) against the total project budget.

before

Information needs analysis

Data collection strategy

Interview technique

Audience analysis

Time study sheet

after

Deployment chart (down-across)

Action plan

Monthly assessment schedule

Gantt chart

Major program status

	Select and define problem or opportunity
➡	Identify and analyze causes or potential change
➡	Develop and plan possible solutions or change
➡	Implement and evaluate solution or change
	Measure and report solution or change results
	Recognize and reward team efforts

	Research/statistics
	Creativity/innovation
3	Engineering
1	Project management
4	Manufacturing
	Marketing/sales
2	Administration/documentation
	Servicing/support
	Customer/quality metrics
	Change management

- Use actual timekeeping data from previous project closing documentation to estimate percent cost of the various activities.
- To increase the validity of data to be stated in the activity cost matrix, department sources or subject matter experts (SME) should be contacted for specific information.

The first step requires a search for a previously completed project's historical data. Timekeeping (activity time) and cost data will greatly assist in the completing of an activity cost matrix. See example *Training Activities—Percent Cost*.

Interviews are conducted with department personnel or subject matter experts. Information on percent contribution to total project effort is collected.

Lastly, an activity cost matrix is completed and dated as shown in this example.

A copy is given to all involved parties for their review and feedback.

Training Activities — Percent Cost

Date: xx/xx/xx	Responsibility — % Contribution									
Analyst: A. Fisher										
Activity Costs for Training Workshop Development Activities	User	User — SME	Training analyst	Training developer	Training instructor	Training administrator	Graphic arts	Reproduction	Budgeting and finance	Facilities
1 Training course request	2	5	10							
3 User needs analysis	5	5	20							
4 Training proposal			20	5		2			90	5
5 User task analysis	15	5	20	10			4	5		
7 Workshop development		20		60						
7.3 Graphics and aids			2	3		2	96	5	5	
7.9 Formative evaluation		50	13	10						
8 Pilot workshop	5	5	5	5				4		
10 Workshop revision				2				3		
11 Train-the-trainer		5		5	20					5
12 Workshop participation	70	5			70					
13 Summitive evaluation			5		2	5				
15 Scheduling and administration	3				3	80		3	5	90
15.2 Material reproduction					2	5		80		
17 Master copy control			5		3	6				
Total contribution	100%	100%	100%	100%	100%	100%	100%	100%	100%	100%

Note: SME = Subject Matter Experts

The activity network diagram is a project planning and scheduling tool for product development or improvements. It graphically displays the sequential flow of activities, estimated time requirement and start/finish times, critical path, and interrelationship of activities.

- To map and schedule in a logical sequence all required activities in a project to be completed.
- To identify a critical path and resource allocations.
- To coordinate and control parallel activities, estimated completion times, and to meet critical data deadlines.

before

Work breakdown structure (WBS)

Top-down flowchart

Activity analysis

Project prioritization matrix

Process analysis

after

Responsibility matrix

Milestones chart

Gantt chart

Project planning log

Resource histogram

Select and define problem or opportunity

Identify and analyze causes or potential change

Develop and plan possible solutions or change

➥ Implement and evaluate solution or change

➥ Measure and report solution or change results

Recognize and reward team efforts

Research/statistics

Creativity/innovation

1 Engineering

3 Project management

2 Manufacturing

5 Marketing/sales

6 Administration/documentation

Servicing/support

Customer/quality metrics

4 Change management

Activity		
Task I.D.	ES	EF
Time	LS	LF

ES = Early Start
EF = Early Finish
LS = Late Start
EF = Late Finish

Bold Lines ➡ = Critical path = Represents
The longest completion time from starting
the first task to finishing the last task

Slack (Float):

1a − 1b − 1c = 24 days ∴ 0 days slack (critical path)
2a − 2b − 1c = 20 days ∴ 4 days slack
1a − 1b − 3b = 17 days ∴ 7 days slack
1a − 3a − 3b = 14 days ∴ 10 days slack

Complete a work breakdown structure (WBS) or similar data collection activity to identify and sequence project activities to be completed. See example *Development of a Statistical Process Control (SPC) Training Course*.

Sort and sequence all activities from left to right, determine parallel paths and interrelationship.

Complete, on post-its, all required information as shown in *notes and key points* and this example.

– Record name of activities, task identification, estimated completion time, and early/late start and finish times. For calculating the critical path, add all estimated times from start to finish of the project. This is also the longest completion time and the earliest time that the project can be completed. There is no slack (float) time.

– For calculating early start/finish times, add the estimated time for each task (left-to-right) to the cumulative duration of the preceding tasks.

– For calculating late start/finish times, subtract the estimated time for each task (right-to-left) from the late start (LS) time of the succeeding tasks.

– For calculating slack or float time, determine the differences (if any) between the early start (ES) and the late start (LS) for each task. Also, calculate slack in each path of the diagram as shown in the example.

Finalize the diagram by chaining all nodes and checking sequential and logical flow.

Check all information, title and date the chart.

Development of an SPC Training Course

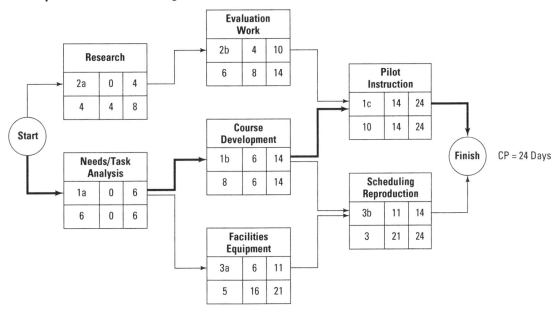

Note: ➤ Heavy line = critical path (CP)

First developed and used in the 1960s by Jiro Kawakita, the affinity diagram is the product of a team's brainstorming and consensus activities. This creative process gathers large amounts of data (ideas, issues, opinions, facts, etc.) and organizes them into logical groupings based on the natural relationships among items.

- Sort by affinity large volume of data.
- Identify key ideas for process improvement.
- Push for creativity and breakthroughs.
- Determine requirements for action plans.
- Point to potential solutions to problems.
- Identify patterns among seemingly unrelated factors.

before

Brainstorming

Brainwriting pool

Events log

Focus group

Consensus decision making

after

Interrelationship digraph (I.D)

Tree diagram

Action plan

Factor analysis

Potential problem analysis (PPA)

➡ Select and define problem or opportunity

➡ Identify and analyze causes or potential change

➡ Develop and plan possible solutions or change

   Implement and evaluate solution or change

   Measure and report solution or change results

   Recognize and reward team efforts

   Research/statistics

1 Creativity/innovation

   Engineering

   Project management

   Manufacturing

   Marketing/sales

   Administration/documentation

3 Servicing/support

   Customer/quality metrics

2 Change management

- Typical affinity: 6–8 participants, 6–10 groupings of ideas, 50–100 ideas. Connect interrelated groupings with ↔ and cause and effect with →.

Form a diverse team of 6–8 participants.

Write the issue or problem on a flip chart—no further explanation should be given. See example *Improvement of Employee Training*.

Participants generate and record ideas on 3 × 5 cards or post-its, one idea per card.

After approximately 15 minutes, cards are collected and randomly spread out on a large table or posted on a wall.

Participants sort cards in silence, placing related ideas into a grouping. Cards that do not fit are "loners" and kept outside the groups. Groups are reviewed and consensus is reached on ideas that are placed in a particular group.

A search takes place to select a card in each grouping that captures the meaning of that group. This card is considered to be the header and is placed on top of the group. If unable to do this step, a header card is created by the team.

Steps 3–6 are repeated to expand groupings, create others, and gain more ideas.

An affinity diagram is created by laying out groups. Place closely related groups together. Draw outlines for each group with the header card placed on top.

Team checks the final affinity diagram, makes modifications if needed, then titles and dates the diagram.

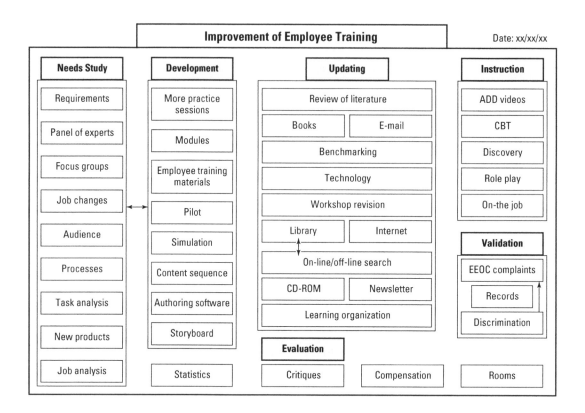

Improvement of Employee Training   Date: xx/xx/xx

Needs Study	Development	Updating	Instruction
Requirements	More practice sessions	Review of literature	ADD videos
Panel of experts	Modules	Books / E-mail	CBT
Focus groups	Employee training materials	Benchmarking	Discovery
Job changes	Pilot	Technology	Role play
Audience	Simulation	Workshop revision	On-the job
Processes	Content sequence	Library / Internet	
Task analysis	Authoring software	On-line/off-line search	
New products	Storyboard	CD-ROM / Newsletter	
Job analysis		Learning organization	

Validation

EEOC complaints

Records

Discrimination

Evaluation

| Statistics | Critiques | Compensation | Rooms |

To use an analogy or metaphor is to make an implied comparison between two things. Often creativity is stifled when we struggle with or resist addressing a perceived problem. In order to look at things differently, a team may create several analogies to clarify a problem or to place it into a different context. The ability to look at one thing (the current problem situation) and to see another (similar situation) can lead to the transfer of a potential solution to the real problem.

- To find transferable solutions to a problem by focusing attention away from the real problem.
- To engage in metaphorical thinking for the purpose of thinking creatively about some problem or opportunity.
- To compare and integrate different sets of concepts found in analogies and metaphors.

before

Forced choice

Forced association

Fresh eye

Brainstorming

Mental imaging

after

Semantic intuition

Checkerboard method

Creativity assessment

Run-it-by

Presentation

➥ Select and define problem or opportunity

➥ Identify and analyze causes or potential change

➥ Develop and plan possible solutions or change

Implement and evaluate solution or change

Measure and report solution or change results

Recognize and reward team efforts

Research/statistics

1 Creativity/innovation

Engineering

Project management

Manufacturing

Marketing/sales

Administration/documentation

Servicing/support

Customer/quality metrics

2 Change management

- Definitions (from *The Random House Dictionary*, 1978)

Analogy   1. "A partial similarity on which a comparison may be based."

             2. "A form of reasoning in which one thing is inferred to be similar to another thing in a certain respect on the basis of the known similarity in other respects."

Metaphor   "A figure of speech in which a term or phrase is applied to something to which it is not literally applicable in order to suggest a resemblance."

Simile   "A figure of speech in which two unlike things are explicitly compared."

A facilitator first displays a problem statement to the team.

The team thinks of analogies and attempts to solve every recorded analogy. The facilitator guides the discussions and records potential problem-solving ideas on flip charts.

Upon the conclusion of the discussion, the team translates or attempts to transfer ideas or problem solutions back to the original problem.

Finally, the team sorts and evaluates all information compiled. The best ideas for problem resolution are recorded for team action.

In the Workplace
Analogy:
• Excellent teamwork is a well-oiled machine.
• Fun at work is having a party.
• A coach is to a team as a facilitator is to a group.
Metaphor:
• Product life cycle — a blink in time
• Recognizing a problem — the tip of an iceberg
• Peak performance — a spark of energy
Simile:
• Getting cooperation is like pulling teeth.
• Finding a solution is like finding a needle in a haystack.
• The improved process runs like clockwork.

The analysis of variance is an inferential statistical technique designed to test for significance of the differences among two or more sample means. Some applications include the ability to make inferences about the population from which the samples were drawn, to identify differences or variations in statistical process control (SPC) analyses, and to provide for analysis and comparison of factorial designs in design of experiments (DOE).

- To identify differences or variance in productivity, quality, methods, factorial designs, performance, and many other applications.
- To check for variation among sample or group means.
- To perform hypothesis testing on interval (quantitative) data sets.

before

Variance analysis

Standard deviation

Process capability ratios

Normal probability distribution

Descriptive statistics

after

Problem specification

Work flow analysis (WFA)

Prioritization matrix

Process analysis

Problem analysis

➡ Select and define problem or opportunity
➡ Identify and analyze causes or potential change
   Develop and plan possible solutions or change
➡ Implement and evaluate solution or change
➡ Measure and report solution or change results
   Recognize and reward team efforts

1   Research/statistics
   Creativity/innovation
2   Engineering
   Project management
   Manufacturing
   Marketing/sales
   Administration/documentation
   Servicing/support
   Customer/quality metrics
3   Change management

- Definition: The analysis of variance (ANOVA) is a technique often applied in the field of inferential statistics to test whether the means of more than two quantative data sets of samples or populations differ.
- Variance analysis:

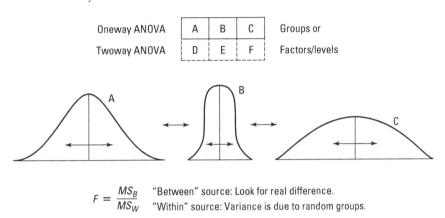

| Oneway ANOVA | A | B | C | Groups or |
| Twoway ANOVA | D | E | F | Factors/levels |

$$F = \frac{MS_B}{MS_W}$$ "Between" source: Look for real difference.
"Within" source: Variance is due to random groups.

- Refer to the *hypothesis testing* procedure (see tool 92). The analysis of variance test is frequently used in testing hypotheses.
- Partial analysis of variance (ANOVA) distribution table—critical values at the .05 level of significance. (Refer to the Appendix, Table C for complete ANOVA critical values table.)

F-Distribution: .05 One-Tail, .10 Two-Tail Test

$K-1 = 3-1 = 2$

$N - K = 15 - 3 = 12$

Degrees of freedom for denominator

Degrees of freedom for numerator

	1	2	3	4	5	6	7	8	9	10	12	15	20	24	30	40	60	120	∞
1	161	200	216	225	230	234	237	239	241	242	244	246	248	249	250	251	252	253	254
2	18.5	19.0	19.2	19.2	19.3	19.3	19.4	19.4	19.4	19.4	19.4	19.4	19.4	19.4	19.5	19.5	19.5	19.5	19.5
3	10.1	9.55	9.28	9.12	9.01	8.94	8.89	8.85	8.81	8.79	8.74	8.70	8.66	8.64	8.62	8.59	8.57	8.55	8.53
4	7.71	6.94	6.59	6.39	6.26	6.16	6.09	6.04	6.00	5.96	5.91	5.86	5.80	5.77	5.75	5.72	5.69	5.66	5.63
5	6.61	5.79	5.41	5.19	5.05	4.95	4.88	4.82	4.77	4.74	4.68	4.62	4.56	4.53	4.50	4.46	4.43	4.40	4.37
6	5.99	5.14	4.76	4.53	4.39	4.28	4.21	4.15	4.10	4.06	4.00	3.94	3.87	3.84	3.81	3.77	3.74	3.70	3.67
7	5.59	4.74	4.35	4.12	3.97	3.87	3.79	3.73	3.68	3.64	3.57	3.51	3.44	3.41	3.38	3.34	3.30	3.27	3.23
8	5.32	4.46	4.07	3.84	3.69	3.58	3.50	3.44	3.39	3.35	3.28	3.22	3.15	3.12	3.08	3.04	3.01	2.97	2.93
9	5.12	4.26	3.86	3.63	3.48	3.37	3.29	3.23	3.18	3.14	3.07	3.01	2.94	2.90	2.86	2.83	2.79	2.75	2.71
10	4.96	4.10	3.71	3.48	3.33	3.22	3.14	3.07	3.02	2.98	2.91	2.85	2.77	2.74	2.70	2.66	2.62	2.58	2.54
11	4.84	3.98	3.59	3.36	3.20	3.09	3.01	2.95	2.90	2.85	2.79	2.72	2.65	2.61	2.57	2.53	2.49	2.45	2.46
12	4.75	3.89	3.49	3.26	3.11	3.00	2.91	2.85	2.80	2.75	2.69	2.62	2.54	2.51	2.47	2.43	2.38	2.34	
13	4.67	3.81	3.41	3.18	3.03	2.92	2.83	2.77	2.71	2.67	2.60	2.53	2.46	2.42	2.38	2.34			
14	4.60	3.74	3.34	3.11															
15	4.54																		

First, daily product defect rates are collected on three different methods of production. See example *Three Production Methods and Their Daily Product Defect Rates*.

The Null Hypothesis (H_0) is stated: There is no statistically significant difference in the daily product defect rates and the production methods used measured at .05 alpha (level of significance) using a one-tailed F-test (ANOVA).

The eight-step hypothesis testing procedure is used to arrive at a decision (see Hypothesis Testing [CHI-square] for example).

The calculations are performed in this example.
Note: The analysis of variance calculations are time consuming and often difficult to calculate. Any basic software program on statistics will perform calculations and provide a printout similar to that shown in this example.

Finally, the test result is verified against the critical value located in the ANOVA distribution table (*notes and key points*). On the basis of the test result F-ratio $= 5.74$ and the critical value $= 3.89$ (which is lower), the Null Hypothesis (H_0) is rejected. There is a statistically significant difference in the three production methods and their daily product defect rates.

Three Production Methods and Their Daily Product Defect Rates

Step 1 Calculate method totals and means	Step 2 Calculate total sum of squared deviations from the grand mean $\overline{\overline{X}}$	Step 3 Calculate how much scores vary within group from $\overline{X}$ of group
Method A	$X - \overline{\overline{X}} = x \quad\quad x^2$	$X - \overline{X} = x \quad\quad x^2$
12	$12 - 7.7 = 4.3 = 18.5$	$12 - 10 = 2^2 = 4$
11	$11 - 7.7 = 3.3 = 10.9$	$11 - 10 = 1^2 = 1$
11	$11 - 7.7 = 3.3 = 10.9$	$11 - 10 = 1^2 = 1$
9	$9 - 7.7 = 1.3 = 1.7$	$9 - 10 = 1^2 = 1$
7	$7 - 7.7 = 0.7 = 0.5$	$7 - 10 = 3^2 = 9$
$\Sigma\ 50$	42.5	16
$\overline{X} = 10$		
Method B		
10	$10 - 7.7 = 2.3 = 5.3$	$10 - 7 = 3^2 = 9$
4	$4 - 7.7 = 3.7 = 13.7$	$4 - 7 = 3^2 = 9$
6	$6 - 7.7 = 1.7 = 2.9$	$6 - 7 = 1^2 = 1$
8	$8 - 7.7 = 0.3 = 0.1$	$8 - 7 = 1^2 = 1$
7	$7 - 7.7 = 0.7 = 0.5$	$7 - 7 = 0^2 = 0$
$\Sigma\ 35$	22.5	20
$\overline{X} = 7$		
Method C		
4	$4 - 7.7 = 3.7 = 13.7$	$4 - 6 = 2^2 = 4$
5	$5 - 7.7 = 2.7 = 7.3$	$5 - 6 = 1^2 = 1$
7	$7 - 7.7 = 0.7 = 0.5$	$7 - 6 = 1^2 = 1$
6	$6 - 7.7 = 1.7 = 2.9$	$6 - 6 = 0^2 = 0$
8	$8 - 7.7 = 0.3 = 0.1$	$8 - 6 = 2^2 = 4$
$\Sigma\ 30$	24.5	10
$\overline{X} = 6$	$SS_t = 89.5$	$SS_w = 46$
Grand total Σ 115 **Grand mean** $\overline{\overline{X}} = 7.7$	SS_t = the sum of all squared deviations of the individual scores from the grand mean of all scores	SS_w = the sum of squared deviations of all the scores in each group from the mean of that group

Three Production Methods and Their Daily Product Defect Rates (continued)

Step 4

Calculate the sum of all squared deviations of the group means from the grand mean times the number of scores per group (between)!

Method	$\bar{X} - \bar{\bar{X}} = x$	$x^2 \times n$
A	$10 - 7.7 = 2.3$	$5.3 \times 5 = 26.5$
B	$7 - 7.7 = 0.7$	$0.5 \times 5 = 2.5$
C	$6 - 7.7 = 1.7$	$2.9 \times 5 = \underline{14.5}$
		$SS_B = 43.5$

Step 5

Calculate degrees of freedom (df):

df for $SS_t = N - 1$	$15 - 1 = 14$	
df for $SS_B = K - 1$	$3 - 1 = 2$	⟵ Numerator
df for $SS_w = N - K$	$15 - 3 = 12$	⟵ Denominator
$SS_t = SS_B + SS_w$	$89.5 = 43.5 + 46$	

Step 6

Calculate the means squares:

$$MS_B = \frac{SS_B}{K\text{-}1} = \frac{43.5}{2} = 21.8$$

$$MS_w = \frac{SS_w}{N\text{-}K} = \frac{46}{12} = 3.8$$

Step 7

Calculate the F-ratio:

$$F = \frac{MS_B}{MS_w} = \frac{21.8}{3.8} = 5.74$$

Step 8

Determine if statistically significant:

F-ratio table at 2 df ⟶ and 12 df ↓ at $\alpha = .05$ (one-tailed test) = 3.89, ∴ we reject H_0

Step 9

A typical printout table:

Source of variation	Sum of Squares	df	Mean squares	F-ratio	F-probability $\alpha = .05$
Between-groups	43.5	2	21.8	5.74	3.89
Within-groups	46.0	12	3.8		
Total	89.5	14			

Developed by Robert Crawford during the 1930s, the attribute listing technique is an idea-generating tool for identifying process, product, and service improvement opportunities. Attributes of a product, service, or process are systematically changed or substituted to search for problem solutions or improvement ideas.

- To modify product, process, or service characteristics in order to bring problem-solving or improvement ideas to the surface.
- To examine essential problem-related attributes to possibly change or modify them in order to eliminate or reduce the problem.

before

Brainstorming
Defect map
Stimulus analysis
Fresh eye
Circles of knowledge

after

Circle of opportunity
Information needs analysis
Opportunity analysis
Creativity assessment
Presentation

	Select and define problem or opportunity
➡	Identify and analyze causes or potential change
➡	Develop and plan possible solutions or change
	Implement and evaluate solution or change
	Measure and report solution or change results
	Recognize and reward team efforts

- To keep a session focused, limit the use of attributes to seven per session.

	Research/statistics
1	Creativity/innovation
	Engineering
	Project management
	Manufacturing
	Marketing/sales
	Administration/documentation
	Servicing/support
2	Customer/quality metrics
3	Change management

First, the problem statement is discussed. See example *Copier Copy Tray Pins Break Frequently*.

All characteristics or attributes of the product, process, or service are listed.

Next, the problem-related, essential characteristics are identified and recorded.

Lastly, the modification or substitution of all characteristics is systematically discussed by team participants. This often results in finding a solution to the problem or an improvement opportunity as shown in the example.

The recorded information is dated.

Problem: Copier Copy Tray Pins Break Frequently   Date: xx/xx/xx

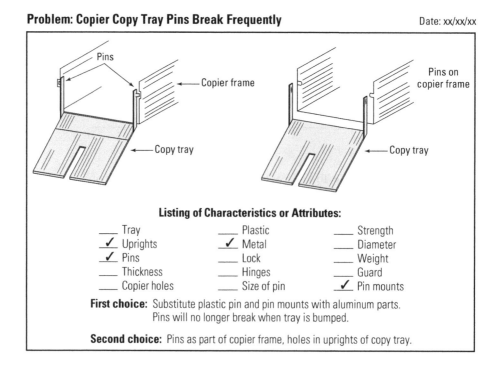

Listing of Characteristics or Attributes:

___ Tray	___ Plastic	___ Strength
✓ Uprights	✓ Metal	___ Diameter
✓ Pins	___ Lock	___ Weight
___ Thickness	___ Hinges	___ Guard
___ Copier holes	___ Size of pin	✓ Pin mounts

First choice: Substitute plastic pin and pin mounts with aluminum parts. Pins will no longer break when tray is bumped.

Second choice: Pins as part of copier frame, holes in uprights of copy tray.

An audience analysis assists in the developing of an effective strategy for giving a presentation or conducting a workshop. Data collected and analyzed will point to appropriate material content and a more focused preparation for the presenter or facilitator.

- To prepare for a presentation or facilitation of a workshop.
- To uncover the needs and expectations of an audience.
- To gather data for planning and developing a quality presentation.

before

Demographic analysis
Survey profile
Surveying
Circle response
Interview technique

after

Presentation
Consensus decision making
Team meeting evaluation
Value analysis
Different point of view

➡ Select and define problem or opportunity
➡ Identify and analyze causes or potential change
➡ Develop and plan possible solutions or change
Implement and evaluate solution or change
Measure and report solution or change results
Recognize and reward team efforts

Research/statistics
Creativity/innovation
Engineering
Project management
Manufacturing
2 Marketing/sales
Administration/documentation
1 Servicing/support
3 Customer/quality metrics
Change management

- Audience research, data collection, and analysis will depend greatly on purpose and situation. Focus or areas of concern would determine instrumentation and methods applied.

In order to collect data necessary to perform an audience analysis, a set of questions needs to be developed for a particular audience to ensure that appropriate response data is available.

Data collection methods include surveys, interviews, focus groups, meetings with supervisory personnel, historical data, job descriptions, plans, records, and technical documentation.

The data is analyzed and brief comments and notes recorded on a summary form as shown in the example.

This data is considered and used to develop a presentation or to customize an existing workshop.

Presentation for Design Engineers

Audience Analysis — Date xx/xx/xx	Research Notes
1. Audience's Identity/Membership? – Design engineering group – Satellite division	– Check terminology
2. Audience's Purpose/Objectives? – Learn design to cost – Cones of tolerance applications	– Review DTC – Review equations
3. Audience's Needs/Expectations? – Case studies, current info – Benchmarking info	– Update current files
4. Audience's Knowledge/Experience? –Modular to Systems' Level – 6–10 years of experience	✓ – Mostly specialized
5. Audience's Constraints/Concerns? – Division politics, work ethic –Job security	– Just went through reengineering
6. Audience's Willingness/Involvement? – Will participate in exercises – Willing to share lessons	✓ Jones' feedback indicates strong participation
7. Audience's Values/Attitudes? – Learning organization concept – Positive, low risk takers	– Great – Why?
8. Audience's Composition/Profile? – Senior engineers, college – Ph.D. – Cutting-edge technology, high specialization	– Revise handouts

Note: Attach Audience Analysis Worksheet to preserve detail.

A balance sheet is used to identify and review the pros and cons of several listed alternatives and to facilitate discussion for the purpose of guiding a team closer to consensus. The information provided from using this tool can also serve as a rationale for or against implementing a proposed change in activity or a solution to a problem.

- To determine a course of action on the basis of assessing the pros and cons.
- To supply the information necessary for a team to make a decision.
- To provide a quick approach for reaching team consensus.

before

Consensus decision making

Brainstorming

Crawford slip method

Circle response

Buzz group

after

Starbursting

Multivoting

Team meeting evaluation

Team process assessment

Consensus decision making

Select and define problem or opportunity

Identify and analyze causes or potential change

➡ Develop and plan possible solutions or change

➡ Implement and evaluate solution or change

Measure and report solution or change results

➡ Recognize and reward team efforts

Research/statistics

Creativity/innovation

Engineering

3 Project management

Manufacturing

Marketing/sales

Administration/documentation

Servicing/support

2 Customer/quality metrics

1 Change management

- Balance sheets have two columns labeled *Pros* (+) and *Cons* (−).

A facilitated team identifies and selects two or more alternatives to solve a problem, implement an improvement program, or initiate an organizational change effort.

A whiteboard is used to record the alternatives. A balance sheet is drawn showing alternatives and two columns, *Pros* and *Cons*. See example *Twenty-four Hours of TQM Training within One Year for Every Employee in the Organization?*

Participants systematically discuss the pros and cons of each alternative and generate short statements to be placed in the pros and cons columns.

When all alternatives have been discussed and pros and cons recorded, the facilitator guides team participants toward a decision by consensus. The decision could be for or against the activity, or simply point to a compromise.

Twenty-four Hours of TQM Training within One Year for Every Employee in the Organization?

Cascading 24 Hours of TQM Training	Date: xx/xx/xx
Pros	Cons
• Every employee will be TQM trained	• Most employees will not use the training
• Spreads employee involvement	• Many employees will not have time
• More problem-solving teams	• Would drain too many resources
• Will increase job satisfaction	• Will not affect most job classifications
• A good investment of time and money	• To train all is too costly and time consuming
• Promotes teamwork and communications	• Hard to involve everyone — too busy now

Train Every Employee within One Year	
• Will have all employees trained by ____	• Cannot release all employees to training
• Resources can be made available	• Will be a hardship to prioritize resources
• Become competitive and world class	• Haste makes waste, hard to control
• Develop a strong commitment	• Difficult to get support at all levels
• Learn from other companies	• Could learn from internal experts

A simple bar chart is useful to present information for a quick problem or opportunity analysis. It provides a comparison of quantities of items or frequencies of events within a particular time period.

- To display a "snapshot" comparison of categories.
- To depict the relationship between variations over time.
- To illustrate process variability or trends.
- To indicate a potential problem area (high or low frequencies).

before

Data collection strategy

Frequency distribution (FD)

Checksheets

Events log

Observation

after

Pie chart

Stratification

Variance analysis

Pareto chart

Presentation

⮕ Select and define problem or opportunity
⮕ Identify and analyze causes or potential change
  Develop and plan possible solutions or change
  Implement and evaluate solution or change
  Measure and report solution or change results
⮕ Recognize and reward team efforts

Research/statistics
Creativity/innovation
Engineering
1 Project management
Manufacturing
3 Marketing/sales
Administration/documentation
2 Servicing/support
Customer/quality metrics
Change management

- Care should be taken not to insert more than five bars or cover more than five time periods. This would make the Bar Chart cluttered and difficult to interpret.
- f = frequency

Collect data from sources such as a checksheet. See example *Customer Complaints*.

Construct a bar chart. Apply the 3:4 ratio rule. The height of the *Y* axis must be 75 percent of the length (100 percent) of the *X* axis.

Label the axes and insert the bars as shown in the example.

Check all information and date the bar chart.

Date: xx/xx/xx

Type	Week 1					Week 2					Week 3					Week 4					Total
	M	T	W	T	F	M	T	W	T	F	M	T	W	T	F	M	T	W	T	F	
Ordering	‖	‖	⦀⦀	‖	⦀	‖	‖‖	‖‖	‖‖	⦀⦀	⦀	⦀⦀	‖	⦀⦀‖		⦀⦀	‖‖	‖	⦀⦀	‖‖	66
Shipping	‖	‖		‖	‖	‖		⦀			‖	‖		‖	‖	‖	‖		‖		20
Billing	‖	‖		‖		‖		‖		⦀	‖	‖			⦀	‖	‖	‖		‖	20
Defect	‖	‖	⦀⦀	⦀⦀	‖	‖	‖	‖‖	‖	‖	‖		‖	⦀⦀		‖	‖	‖	‖	⦀	41
Service	⦀⦀	‖	‖‖	⦀	⦀⦀	‖	‖	⦀⦀	‖	⦀⦀	⦀⦀	⦀⦀	‖	⦀⦀	‖	⦀⦀‖	‖	⦀⦀	‖	⦀⦀	69
Total	11	6	14	12	11	7	7	18	6	14	13	12	5	18	5	15	9	11	9	13	216

Customer Complaints

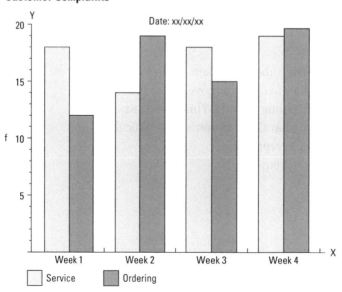

Date: xx/xx/xx

The barriers-and-aids analysis tool can be used to perform a preliminary check on what needs to be accomplished to successfully implement change. Elements pushing for change (aids) and against change (barriers) are identified and recorded. Barriers that must be overcome are noted and countermeasures to eliminate or greatly reduce them are developed.

- To identify elements that resist the implementation of solutions or improvements.
- To anticipate and verify potential problems that must be resolved.
- To allow a clearer understanding of the process.

before

Gap analysis

Interview technique

Focus group

Problem analysis

Process analysis

after

Consensus decision making

Action plan

Resource requirements matrix

Action and effect diagram (AED)

Potential problem analysis (PPA)

➥ Select and define problem or opportunity

➥ Identify and analyze causes or potential change

➥ Develop and plan possible solutions or change

Implement and evaluate solution or change

Measure and report solution or change results

Recognize and reward team efforts

Research/statistics

2 Creativity/innovation

Engineering

Project management

Manufacturing

Marketing/sales

Administration/documentation

3 Servicing/support

Customer/quality metrics

1 Change management

Definitions:
- Barriers are hindering, restraining elements.
- Aids are driving, helping elements.
- Countermeasures are potential solutions.

The team facilitator reviews the barriers-and-aids tool with the team. Participants take some time to discuss the process involved.

The performance objective is displayed on a whiteboard. See example *Establishment of a Project Management System for Site Engineers*.

Next, a list of barriers is brainstormed and recorded as vertical columns on the whiteboard. Barriers are elements that will resist and hinder the change process.

Participants now identify aids and record them next to the barriers. Aids are elements that will assist and support the change process.

This process continues until all barriers and aids have been identified and recorded. The two columns are checked for redundancy and revised, if needed.

Lastly, the heading *Countermeasures* is placed on the whiteboard and participants are asked to generate ideas that could eliminate or greatly reduce the barriers as shown in the example.

As the last step, the completed matrix is checked, dated, and saved for the planning of countermeasures activities.

Establishment of a Project Management System for Site Engineers	Date: xx/xx/xx
Aids	Barriers
• Will allow performance contracts	• Threat to engineer's autonomy
• Establishes accountability	• Produces competitive work ethic
• Sets time frames and due dates	• Resistance to change
• Improves intergroup communications	• Under observation
• Receive fair performance appraisal	• Invalid assumptions
• Use standard forms and procedures	• Requires re-setup of project files
	• Will force more workload and stress
	Countermeasures
	• Provide training on the new PMS to engineers
	• Explain interactive features and reports generation
	• Provide on-site assistance

Note: Each site engineer previously managed his/her own work projects and schedule.

The Basili data collection method is a process of establishing a performance measurement system that can be applied throughout the organization. First introduced by V. R. Basili (1984), this eight-step model interlocks goals with performance questions and with metrics that respond to the questions stated.

- To create specialized metrics that will measure goal attainment.
- To design a data collection methodology that is supportive of performance measurement requirements.

before

Process analysis

Information needs analysis

Major program status

Delphi method

Questionnaires

after

Objectives matrix (OMAX)

Run-it-by

Data collection strategy

Action plan

Surveying

	Select and define problem or opportunity
	Identify and analyze causes or potential change
	Develop and plan possible solutions or change
➥	Implement and evaluate solution or change
➥	Measure and report solution or change results
	Recognize and reward team efforts

	Research/statistics
	Creativity/innovation
4	Engineering
3	Project management
	Manufacturing
	Marketing/sales
	Administration/documentation
	Servicing/support
1	Customer/quality metrics
2	Change management

Hierarchy of Goal — Questions — Metrics

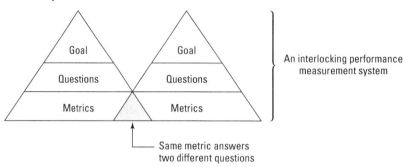

An interlocking performance measurement system

Same metric answers two different questions

A team is assembled for the purpose of determining data collection goals. See example *Data Collection for Integrated Product Development (IPD)*.

Answers to a list of questions are brainstormed. These questions point to specific data requirements necessary to measure goal attainment aspects.

To provide specific performance data, metrics are developed and documented.

An easy-to-use data collection form is designed.

The data collection and validation process is started.

Collected data are analyzed for anomalies.

Results are communicated to process owners and other involved groups.

The team determines how the results of performance measurement can be utilized to improve processes.

Data Collection for Integrated Product Development (IPD)

Goal 1: Compile benchmarking data

Question 1: What is average cycle time for process "A"?

    Metric 1: Reduce process "A" cycle time by 35% by xx/xx/xx

    Metric 2: Map key processes by xx/xx/xx

Goal 2: Acquire IPD customer input data

Question 2: How many QFD matrices are required?

    Metric 3: House of Quality matrix completed by xx/xx/xx

    Metric 4: Determine internal capability by xx/xx/xx

Question 3: How can suppliers meet requirements?

    Metric 5: Determine supplier capability by xx/xx/xx

    Metric 6: Verify supplier parts Cp data for $X-Y-Z$

Notes: Partial data collection plan.

Same metric answers two different questions.

Benchmarking, made popular by Robert C. Camp, is a data collection method that identifies and measures similar processes, products, and services against those of organizations considered best-in-class. All benchmarking projects, inside or outside the organization, generally collect and compare strategic, performance, or process benchmarks for the purpose of identifying gaps in performance and establishing gap-closing action plans.

- To identify areas that require process improvement.
- To verify and measure an organization's performance against that of the competition.
- To research trends and performance data of similar organizations for the purpose of developing strategic action plans.

before

Data collection strategy

Idea grid

Interview technique

Surveying

Customer needs table

after

Action plan

Activity cost matrix

Information needs analysis

Force field analysis (FFA)

Competency gap

➡ Select and define problem or opportunity	**1** Research/statistics
➡ Identify and analyze causes or potential change	Creativity/innovation
Develop and plan possible solutions or change	Engineering
Implement and evaluate solution or change	Project management
➡ Measure and report solution or change results	Manufacturing
Recognize and reward team efforts	**4** Marketing/sales
	Administration/documentation
	Servicing/support
	2 Customer/quality metrics
	3 Change management

- Quantitative and qualitative data is collected in a benchmarking project as shown in the example. A different version of the benchmarking process can be illustrated.

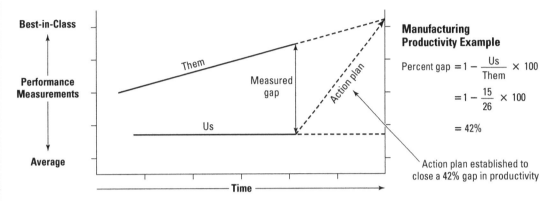

$$\text{Percent gap} = 1 - \frac{\text{Us}}{\text{Them}} \times 100$$

$$= 1 - \frac{15}{26} \times 100$$

$$= 42\%$$

Action plan established to close a 42% gap in productivity

Recommendation: An action plan for closing any existing gap should also consider the competitor's trendline in order to reach at least parity at some future date (goal).

First, the benchmarking team identifies processes to benchmark that are of great importance to the customer and the organization. See example *Training and Development Services*.

Similar organizations are targeted and selected on the basis of their excellence in certain fields.

Partnerships are formed with selected organizations. A set of common operational definitions is developed for processes, key characteristics, and metrics.

Desired benchmark data is collected (exchanged), using various data collection methods such as interviews, surveys, historical files, and other methods.

Collected benchmarks are analyzed and best-in-class performance data identified.

A gap analysis is performed and priorities established for certain identified areas in need of improvement.

Finally, an action plan is developed to close the performance gaps.

Training and Development Services Date: xx/xx/xx

Quantitative (Numeric)	Year xxxx	This Co.	Co. A	Co. B	Co. C	Co. D
1. Total no. of employees / Total no. of T&D trainers	Efficiency ratio	2367:1	1230:1	80:1	488:1	667:1
2. Total T&D budget (actual) / Total student hrs	$/Student hr.	$12.50	$36.23	$13.60	$45.16	$22.17
3. Total hrs of trainer platform time / Total trainer hrs available	% Platform time	54%	NA	20%	NA	40%
4. Total student hrs / Total T&D students	Hrs/student	28	40	208	51	8
Qualitative (Processes)						
A. Training of employees inside vs. outside (cost)	Effectiveness ratio	1:1.59	NA	1:2	NA	1.10:1
B.[1] Utilizing inside trainers vs. outside trainers	Expertise %	100%	95%	73%	98%	100%
C.[1] Develop courses inside vs. purchase from outside	Expertise %	90%	95%	80%	95%	20%
D. Cross-training activity — percent backup for courses	Flexibility %	100%	100%	100%	100%	67%

Notes: [1]Benchmarks B–C (self-sufficiency)
NA = No benchmark data available

The block diagram illustrates, at an overview level, how a process flows from function to function or from unit to unit within an organization. The diagram uses blocks to reflect the most important activities and links them together by connecting lines that represent material or communication flows.

- To provide a high-level view of a process.
- To promote an understanding of process function and sequence.
- To identify cross-functional unit interfacing.

before

Process analysis

Work flow analysis (WFA)

Problem analysis

Work breakdown structure (WBS)

Systems analysis diagram

after

Organization chart

Process mapping

Potential problem analysis (PPA)

Functional map

Activity analysis

	Select and define problem or opportunity
➡	Identify and analyze causes or potential change
➡	Develop and plan possible solutions or change
➡	Implement and evaluate solution or change
	Measure and report solution or change results
	Recognize and reward team efforts

	Research/statistics
	Creativity/innovation
5	Engineering
1	Project management
	Manufacturing
4	Marketing/sales
3	Administration/documentation
	Servicing/support
2	Customer/quality metrics
	Change management

The team identifies all functions or activities within a process and checks where the start and stop functions are, as determined by team consensus. See example *Development of an Employee Training Program*.

The functions are sequenced and drawn on a whiteboard or flip charts in a block diagram format.

The team verifies that all blocks (functions) are accounted for and drawn in the proper sequence to accurately reflect the current process.

Finally, additional supporting information is added and the diagram is dated, as shown in the example.

Development of an Employee Training Program

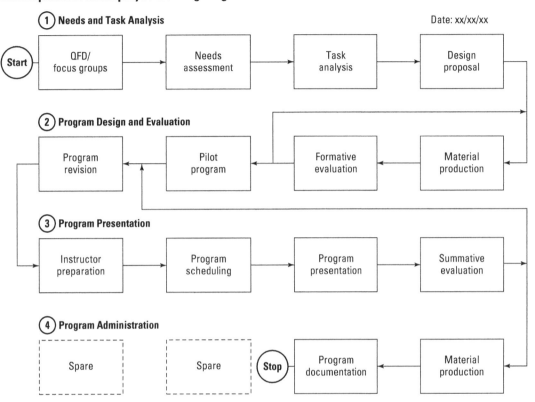

① Needs and Task Analysis   Date: xx/xx/xx

Start → QFD/ focus groups → Needs assessment → Task analysis → Design proposal

② Program Design and Evaluation

Program revision ← Pilot program ← Formative evaluation ← Material production

③ Program Presentation

Instructor preparation → Program scheduling → Program presentation → Summative evaluation

④ Program Administration

Spare   Spare   **Stop**   Program documentation ← Material production

The box plot illustrates a distribution of data showing location and spread of values, skewness, and possible outliers (extremely high or low scores). Although a box plot is less detailed than a histogram, it is quite useful in that it will display extreme variations in the data plotted.

- To identify outliers in a data set.
- To compare groups of data for significant differences in patterns.
- To check for improvement in data after a process change has been made.

before

Data collection strategy

Stem and leaf display

Observation

Dot diagram

Sampling methods

after

Variance analysis

Problem analysis

Process analysis

Potential problem
analysis (PPA)

What-if analysis

Select and define problem or opportunity

➡ Identify and analyze causes or potential change

Develop and plan possible solutions or change

Implement and evaluate solution or change

➡ Measure and report solution or change results

Recognize and reward team efforts

1 Research/statistics

Creativity/innovation

3 Engineering

Project management

2 Manufacturing

Marketing/sales

Administration/documentation

Servicing/support

Customer/quality metrics

Change management

Use the following equation to calculate ranks for quartiles:

For this example:

– Median rank $= \dfrac{1 + n}{2} = \dfrac{1 + 24}{2} = 12.5$

Median rank $= 12$

– Rank of lower quartile (L.Q.) $= \dfrac{1 + \text{int}\,[(1 + n)/2]}{2} = \dfrac{1 + 12}{2} = 6.5$

int $=$ integer only, discard decimal

– Rank of upper quartile (U.Q.) $= (n + 1) - \text{L.Q.} = (24 + 1) - 6.5 = 18.5$

To identify outliers use the following:
– Check for larger data values:

U.Q. $+ 1.5 \times$ (U.Q. $-$ L.Q.) $= 35 + 1.5 \times (35 - 18) = 60.5$

– Therefore defect scores 61 and 65 are outliers at the high end of the distribution.
– Check for smaller data values:

L.Q. $- 1.5 \times$ (U.Q. $-$ L.Q.) $= 18 - 1.5 \times (35 - 18) = -7.5$

– The lowest data value $= 5$; therefore there is no outlier at the low end of the distribution.

Data is collected and identified by recording the collection period, data source, and exact description of what is supposed to be measured. See example *Operator Defects Covering Four 6-Day Weeks*.

A table of rank-ordered data is constructed and median, lower and upper quartiles calculated. See *notes and key points* for the calculations used in this example.

A box plot is constructed as shown. Ensure that outliers are identified and marked.

Check all data values, box plot dimensions and outlier values, date the plot, and make final notes on the pattern or variation of the data.

Operator Defects Covering Four 6-Day Weeks

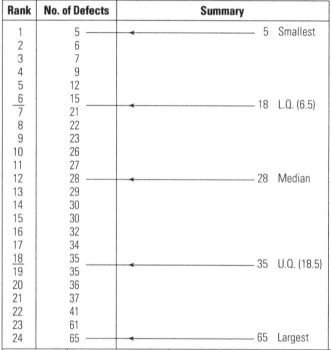

Rank	No. of Defects	Summary
1	5	5 Smallest
2	6	
3	7	
4	9	
5	12	
6	15	18 L.Q. (6.5)
7	21	
8	22	
9	23	
10	26	
11	27	
12	28	28 Median
13	29	
14	30	
15	30	
16	32	
17	34	
18	35	35 U.Q. (18.5)
19	35	
20	36	
21	37	
22	41	
23	61	
24	65	65 Largest

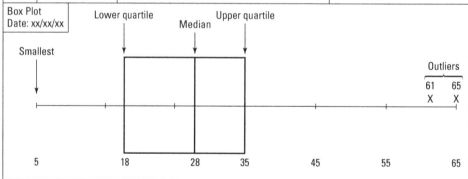

Box Plot
Date: xx/xx/xx

Lower quartile   Median   Upper quartile

Smallest

Outliers
61 65
X   X

5   18   28   35   45   55   65

Brainstorming is an idea-generating tool widely used by teams for identifying problems, alternative solutions to problems, or opportunities for improvement. This tool originated in 1941 by Alex F. Osborne, when his search for creative ideas resulted in an unstructured group process of interactive "brain-storming" that generated more and better ideas than individuals could produce working independently.

- To unlock the creativity in teams.
- To generate a large list of ideas for problem solving or a list of problem areas for decision making or planning.
- To develop creative alternative solutions.
- To identify improvement opportunities.
- To start innovation in processes, products, and services through team participation.

before

Data collection strategy

Checksheet

Team mirror

Surveying

Interview technique

after

Triple ranking

Multivoting

Nominal group technique (NGT)

SCAMPER

Cluster analysis

➡ Select and define problem or opportunity
➡ Identify and analyze causes or potential change
Develop and plan possible solutions or change
Implement and evaluate solution or change
Measure and report solution or change results
Recognize and reward team efforts

Research/statistics
1 Creativity/innovation
Engineering
Project management
Manufacturing
Marketing/sales
Administration/documentation
3 Servicing/support
Customer/quality metrics
2 Change management

- Accept one idea at a time; team members can "pass."
- Encourage members to think of the wildest ideas; they often trigger others!
- Accept expanding, improving, and combining ideas of others (piggy-backing).
- Do not allow instant evaluation of ideas, criticism, or remarks.
- Avoid wandering or side discussions.

Form a team of approximately 6–10 people.

Communicate brainstorming guidelines and set time limit (approximately 15–20 minutes).

State purpose for session; discuss specific problem or topic. See example *Improve Quality*.

Establish a positive, nonthreatening setting and encourage all members to participate in a free-wheeling expression of ideas.

Record, on flip charts, all ideas generated; the emphasis is on quantity, not quality.

When the team has run out of ideas, review and clarify each idea (no discussion).

Allow some time for ideas to incubate.

Identify or prioritize useful ideas.

Improve Quality

Flip chart 1

Session 8/19/xx
Topic: Improve Quality
– More training
– Short due dates
– Inexperience
– No communication
– Missing information
– What is a defect?
– Constant changes
– No inspections
– Too much work
– Many interruptions
– Group conflict
– Incorrect testing

Flip chart 2

Session 8/19/xx
– Lack of proper tools
– Low job satisfaction
– Specifications unclear
– Lack of instructions
– Low morale, motivation
– Lack of metrics
– Involve customers
– Stressful work
– Equipment problems
– Lack of data
– Need problem-solving teams
– No procedures
End of Ideas

Developed by the Battelle Institute of Frankfurt, Germany, the brainwriting pool is an idea-generating tool that uses a nonverbal approach to record ideas from each team participant. Similar to brainstorming, participants think of ideas to solve a problem or improve a process. Cards or sheets of paper are used to record the ideas; they then are pooled in order to be exchanged and examined by others. This results in additional related or "build-on" ideas.

- To collect more focused, developed ideas.
- To allow participants to build on each other's ideas.
- To allow idea generation regarding a controversial topic and maintain the contributor's anonymity.
- To avoid interpersonal conflict or intimidation by dominant participants.

before

Checklist
6-3-5 method
Sticking dots
Interview technique
Buzz group

after

Consensus decision making
Criteria filtering
Weighted voting
Multivoting
Numerical prioritization

➡ Select and define problem or opportunity
Identify and analyze causes or potential change
➡ Develop and plan possible solutions or change
Implement and evaluate solution or change
Measure and report solution or change results
Recognize and reward team efforts

	Research/statistics
1	Creativity/innovation
	Engineering
3	Project management
	Manufacturing
4	Marketing/sales
	Administration/documentation
	Servicing/support
	Customer/quality metrics
2	Change management

- A variation is the gallery method. Several flip chart sheets are posted around the room and participants circulate and record their ideas. As participants move around the room and read the ideas of others, they often get other, related ideas that they add to the list.

Six to eight team participants are seated around a table.

A topic or problem is displayed on a flip chart. See example *Operator Work Scheduling*.

Each team participant silently writes four ideas or responses on a card or sheet of paper.

Each participant places his or her sheet in the center of the table (the pool), exchanging it for another sheet placed there by another participant.

Ideas on the sheet are examined, other related ideas are added, or listed ideas are used to build on or think of new ideas. The sheet is then returned to the pool and exchanged for another sheet.

This process continues for approximately 30 minutes. At the end of this time, all ideas are posted on flip charts for later evaluation.

Operator Work Scheduling

Sheet #1 Ideas:
- Schedule by seniority
- Verify voluntary requests
- Etc.

Sheet #2 Ideas:
- Assign on a rotational basis
- Open schedule
- Etc.

Sheet #(*n*) Ideas:
- Operators input their preference
- Allow trade-offs

Final List of Ideas   Date: xx/xx/xx
- Operators reach consensus on scheduling method to be used
- Start scheduling with voluntary requests first
- Strictly follow established scheduling procedures
- Etc.

A breakdown tree is used in statistical analysis when population or sample variables need to be displayed and analyzed. Using the breakdown tree format, variables and their respective frequencies, subgroups, and category headings can be easily illustrated.

- To break down population or sample variables into more defined subgroups.
- To format data for the purpose of profiling or describing relationships.
- To display data in the descriptive analysis section of statistical reports.

before

Demographic analysis

Audience analysis

Sampling methods

Tree diagram

Data collection strategy

after

Pie chart

Polygon overlay

Pictograph

Snake chart

Bar chart

Select and define problem or opportunity

➥ Identify and analyze causes or potential change

Develop and plan possible solutions or change

Implement and evaluate solution or change

➥ Measure and report solution or change results

Recognize and reward team efforts

1 Research/statistics

Creativity/innovation

Engineering

Project management

Manufacturing

2 Marketing/sales

3 Administration/documentation

Servicing/support

Customer/quality metrics

Change management

- Do not break down data to fewer than five respondents or units of analysis.
- Report frequencies (in parentheses) rather than percentages. Optional: A frequency distribution table can be constructed showing relative frequency (percent) for listed variables.

The researcher organizes and summarizes demographic response data by category and/or variables. See example *Demographic Analysis of Design Engineers*.

A tree diagram is drawn with branches representing categories and variables.

Frequencies (in parentheses) are inserted at respective branches of the breakdown tree.

All data entries are checked for accuracy by totaling all columns. In this example, they should add up to 122.

The chart is dated and used in various reports.

Demographic Analysis of Design Engineers

Gender	Age	Experience (Years)	Education (Ph.D.)	
		0-7 (45)	Yes (31)	
			No (14)	
	20-40 (80)	8-15 (26)	Yes (20)	
			No (6)	
		15+ (9)	Yes (2)	
			No (7)	
Male (101)		0-7 (6)	Yes (3)	
			No (3)	
	41-70 (21)	8-15 (3)	Yes (1)	
			No (2)	
		15+ (12)	Yes (1)	
			No (11)	
(N = 122)		0-7 (11)	Yes (6)	
			No (5)	
	20-40 (16)	8-15 (5)	Yes (4)	
			No (1)	
		15+ (0)	Yes (0)	
			No (0)	
Female (21)		0-7 (2)	Yes (1)	
			No (1)	
	41-70 (5)	8-15 (2)	Yes (2)	
			No (0)	
		15+ (1)	Yes (1)	
			No (0)	

Note: N = 122, Number of design engineers = 122

The buzz group technique is of great assistance to team facilitators or presenters when there is a lack of participation or intra-group communication and more involvement is desired. It can be used to initiate discussion on perceived problems, to share experiences and lessons learned, or to achieve team consensus.

- To explore in detail, and with full participation, process improvement opportunities or ideas for problem resolution.
- To receive each participant's feedback on some issue or experience.
- To involve all persons in the learning process.

before

Circle response

Circles of knowledge

Round robin brainstorming

Interview technique

Surveying

after

Consensus decision making

Phillips 66

Critical dialogue

Wildest idea technique

Presentation

➡ Select and define problem or opportunity
➡ Identify and analyze causes or potential change
➡ Develop and plan possible solutions or change
   Implement and evaluate solution or change
   Measure and report solution or change results
➡ Recognize and reward team efforts

- Buzz group size: 4–6 participants.
- Position chairs in a circle so that participants face each other.

	Research/statistics
1	Creativity/innovation
	Engineering
3	Project management
	Manufacturing
	Marketing/sales
	Administration/documentation
	Servicing/support
	Customer/quality metrics
2	Change management

The team facilitator, instructor, or presenter states the purpose for buzzing, asks participants to face one another, and informs all buzz groups that they have approximately eight minutes to "buzz" their topic. Each buzz group selects a spokesperson.

A problem, issue, or idea is displayed to all buzz groups. Groups begin to sort, discuss, or summarize information. See example *Identify Cycle Time Reduction Tools*.

After the allowed time limit, buzz groups are asked to report their findings or ideas.

The facilitator, instructor, or presenter records findings or ideas on flip charts for everyone to see.

Information generated is dated and used on the spot or saved for later reference.

Identify Cycle Time Reduction Tools

Date: xx/xx/xx

The case study method is a systematic approach used to describe, analyze, and bring to the surface potential solutions to a problem situation or business issue of fair complexity. A case study stimulates critical thinking and requires researchers to apply their problem-solving and decision-making skills to develop recommendations in a case report.

- To improve a researcher's critical evaluation, problem-solving and decision-making skills.
- To obtain lessons learned from analyzing the significant factors in an actual situation.
- To explore the issues of a problem or situation brought to the surface during a case analysis.

before

Information needs analysis

Data collection strategy

Benchmarking

Cluster analysis

Thematic content analysis

after

Scenario writing

Factor analysis

Value analysis

Consensus decision making

Different point of view

Select and define problem or opportunity

➡ Identify and analyze causes or potential change

➡ Develop and plan possible solutions or change

Implement and evaluate solution or change

Measure and report solution or change results

Recognize and reward team efforts

1 Research/statistics

Creativity/innovation

Engineering

Project management

Manufacturing

3 Marketing/sales

Administration/documentation

Servicing/support

Customer/quality metrics

2 Change management

- When drafting the case report:
  - Background information should be brief.
  - All relevant data must be included.
  - Supporting documents must be attached.
- Basic format of case report:
  - Main problem statement
  - Significant and relevant factors
  - Potential solutions/action and analysis of solutions/action
  - Conclusions and recommendations

The researcher carefully reads and analyzes the case information.

The main problem area is isolated and all significant and relevant factors are considered. A specific problem statement is developed.

Next, potential solutions are evaluated and a recommended course of action is prepared. The evaluation or solutions is based on a thorough discussion of the advantages and disadvantages of each.

Conclusions are briefly listed. A more detailed explanation follows all stated recommendations as to what precisely needs to be accomplished to solve the problem or issue.

A final case report is prepared.

The Study of Motorola's Six Sigma Work Ethic

Research Material on the Concept of Six Sigma Quality

. . . Motorola, a recipient of the Malcolm Baldrige National Quality Award, established goals . . . to improve products and services . . . to achieve Six Sigma capability . . . a culture of continual improvements . . . total customer satisfaction . . .

Part of Researcher's Case Report

Conclusions

The establishment of Six Sigma quality would indeed become a strong driving force to significantly increase customer satisfaction and act as an enabler to reach world class status among competitors. Furthermore:

- it would promote a common language and understanding of quality within the organization

- it directly ties into a work ethic of TQM, ISO-9000, and Integrated Product Development Teams (IPDT)

- as a powerful tool, it assists in cost and cycle time reduction, waste elimination, and attacks variation at the supplier, process, product, and service level

- it supports the Malcolm Baldrige National Quality Award criteria

Recommendations

The implementation of Six Sigma across the organization requires careful planning, effective training, and resource allocation for pilot studies, development of metrics, data collection/bases, and administrative procedures that include an organizational performance appraisal and reward system. The following reflect the basic considerations:

- Communicate the Six Sigma Quality strategy and roll-out plan. Start training core personnel.

- Define the organization's products and services.

- Identify suppliers and determine needs to be met.

- Determine desired customer characteristics and needs.

- Baseline processes for creating products and services. Establish metrics and procedures.

- Reduce variation, costs, cycle time, waste, and defects from the process.

- Measure results for continuous improvement.

The cause and effect diagram is a fishbone diagram that typically displays major, generic categories such as people, methods, materials, equipment, measurement, and environment that cause an effect, often perceived as a problem. First applied by Kaoru Ishikawa in 1950, this diagram is used to systematically analyze cause and effect relationships and to identify potential root causes of a problem.

- To assist a team to reach a common understanding of a complex problem.
- To expand the team's thinking and consider all potential causes.
- To define the major categories or sources of root causes.
- To organize and analyze relationships and interactive factors.
- To identify factors that could improve a process.

before

Brainstorming
Five whys
Brainwriting pool
5W2H method
6-3-5 method

after

Problem specification
Work flow analysis (WFA)
Pareto chart
Countermeasures matrix
Problem analysis

➥ Select and define problem or opportunity
➥ Identify and analyze causes or potential change
Develop and plan possible solutions or change
Implement and evaluate solution or change
Measure and report solution or change results
Recognize and reward team efforts

	Research/statistics
	Creativity/innovation
	Engineering
	Project management
3	Manufacturing
	Marketing/sales
	Administration/documentation
2	Servicing/support
4	Customer/quality metrics
1	Change management

- Generic category designation may be substituted. Example: "procedures" for "methods," or "facilities" for "equipment," etc.
- Do not overload categories. Establish another category if more detail is desired.

Reach consensus on a problem to be analyzed. See example *Missed Reproduction Schedules*.

Determine the major categories and place one in each category box.

Brainstorm possible causes for each category and enter them in a fishbone fashion by drawing arrows to the main arrow (category) as shown in the example.

Continue to ask questions using the Five Whys tool to search for root causes. Insert and connect potential causes to the various other contributing factors.

When ideas or causes can no longer be identified, further analyze the diagram to identify additional data collection requirements for problem solving.

Missed Reproduction Schedules

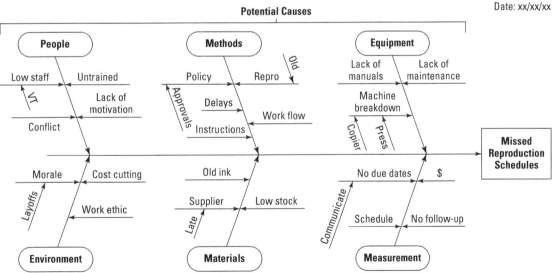

Developed and first introduced in 1978 by Sumitomo Electric Industries of Japan, the cause and effect diagram adding cards (CEDAC) is a fishbone diagram that typically displays major, generic categories such as people, methods, materials, equipment, measurement, and environment that cause an effect, often perceived as a problem. This diagram is used to systematically analyze cause and effect relationships and to identify potential root causes of a problem. An additional feature of adding cards by those outside the team allows the capture of more ideas from others in an expanded involvement in the problem-solving process. Once the basic diagram is completed and posted, cards or notes indicating more causes or ideas are attached.

- To assist a team in reaching a common understanding of a complex problem and to share this information with others for more input.
- To expand the team's thinking and to consider all potential causes.
- To post and share a completed cause and effect diagram (CED) for the purpose of allowing others to add potential causes or ideas.
- To define the major categories or sources of root causes.
- To organize and analyze relationships and interactive factors.
- To identify factors that could improve a process.

before

Cause and effect diagram (CED)

Brainstorming

Brainwriting pool

6-3-5 method

Five ways

after

Problem specification

Work flow analysis (WFA)

Process analysis

Countermeasures matrix

Pareto chart

➡ Select and define problem or opportunity
➡ Identify and analyze causes or potential change
  Develop and plan possible solutions or change
  Implement and evaluate solution or change
  Measure and report solution or change results
  Recognize and reward team efforts

  Research/statistics
  Creativity/innovation
  Engineering
  Project management
3 Manufacturing
  Marketing/sales
  Administration/documentation
2 Servicing/support
4 Customer/quality metrics
1 Change management

- This tool is an expansion of the cause and effect diagram (CED).
- Generic category designations may be substituted. Example: *Procedures* for *methods*, or *facilities* for *requirement*, etc.
- Do not overload categories. Establish another category if more detail is desired.

Reach consensus on a problem to be analyzed. See example *Missed Reproduction Schedules*.

Determine the major categories and place one in each category box.

Brainstorm possible causes for each category and enter in a fishbone fashion by drawing arrows to the main arrow (category), as shown in the example.

Continue to ask questions using the Five Whys tool to search for root causes. Insert and connect potential causes to the various other contributing factors.

When the team feels that the diagram is complete, a final and much larger diagram is drawn.

The diagram is posted in a hallway or on bulletin boards with an invitation for others to examine and possibly add their causes or ideas on available cards or Post-its to the respective categories on the diagram.

After a specified period of time, the diagram is removed and revised to include the additional information. A completed, smaller diagram is reposted with a thank you note.

The team now advances to the next step of further analysis, additional data collection, and problem solving.

Missed Reproduction Schedules

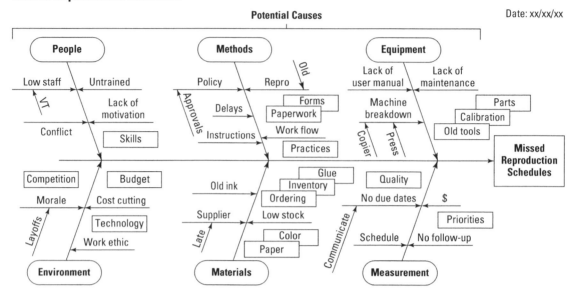

The checkerboard method uses an interrelational matrix to plot interrelationships or the effects of various factors on one another. By combining possible concepts, features, and capabilities, powerful combinations of (or ideas for) feasible new products and services are produced.

- To generate ideas for new products and services.
- To increase team creativity and innovation.
- To discover process improvement opportunities.
- To identify interrelationships or linkages.

before

Brainstorming

Data collection strategy

Observation

Focus group

Checklist

after

Creativity assessment

Run-it-by

Presentation

Consensus decision making

Different point of view

➥ Select and define problem or opportunity
➥ Identify and analyze causes or potential change
Develop and plan possible solutions or change
Implement and evaluate solution or change
Measure and report solution or change results
Recognize and reward team efforts

Research/statistics
1 Creativity/innovation
4 Engineering
Project management
Manufacturing
3 Marketing/sales
Administration/documentation
Servicing/support
Customer/quality metrics
2 Change management

- Do not create matrices greater than vertical (20) × horizontal (25).
- Legend: ○ High Potential
  △ Low Potential
  □ (Blank) No Potential

Construct a matrix and determine if available factors are of sufficient detail to insert into the matrix. See example *Telephone Communication Equipment*.

Complete the vertical and horizontal columns as shown in the example.

Match all factors in the vertical columns with the factors in the horizontal column. Not every pairing will be applicable.

As this process of matching continues, rate potential application of feasibility by indicating ○ for high and △ for low potential.

Finally, date the completed matrix and reach consensus on the next steps.

Telephone Communications Equipment (New Features and Capabilities)

Date: xx/xx/xx

Applications

○ = High Potential △ = Low Potential

Equipment	Activity sensor	Smoke alarm	Security loop	Auto dial	Wake up	Door check	All locked	Pet check	Pet exit	Remote check	Room monitor	TV interface	Remote switch	Remote scanner	Gas on/off	Ring neighbor	Time lights	Message transfer	Search file	Inventory DB	Leave message
Phone		△		△				△	○				○	○	○	○	○	○	○	○	○
Video phone	△		○		○	△	○												△	△	△
Speaker phone				○		○			○												△
Fax machine			△										△	○					○	○	△
Answering machine										○				○			○		○		○
Alarm phone	○		○	○	△						△		△	○	△						
Intercom		○				△		△	○		○										○
Recorder	○		△				△			○	○			○				△	○	○	○
Call Distrib														△	○	△	○				△
Timer	△		△	○	○	○	○	△	△	△			△	○		○					○
Transfer		○											△	△	△	△	○			○	△
Scanner										○	○		△	△		△	△	○	○		
Call waiting										○							○				△
Call forward		○											△		○		○				△
Call block										△		△	△			△				△	
Call priority		○	○	△	△					△					○		○			○	

○ = High Potential △ = Low Potential

A checklist is a useful tool for guiding a team's activities and progress, providing important steps and information in a procedure, collecting and organizing data, and helping in the idea generation process for product development and problem solving. Checklists can also be useful as work instructions and safety checks.

- To prevent the omission of critical steps in a process or procedure.
- To question if certain items or ideas have been completed or considered.
- To collect and organize data for problem analysis.

before

Data collection strategy

Observation

Questionnaires

Critical incident

Thematic content analysis

after

SCAMPER

What-if analysis

SWOT analysis

Stimulus analysis

Problem specifications

	Select and define problem or opportunity
➡	Identify and analyze causes or potential change
	Develop and plan possible solutions or change
➡	Implement and evaluate solution or change
	Measure and report solution or change results
	Recognize and reward team efforts

	Research/statistics
4	Creativity/innovation
	Engineering
	Project management
2	Manufacturing
	Marketing/sales
5	Administration/documentation
3	Servicing/support
	Customer/quality metrics
1	Change management

- Some of the most common checklists cover the following areas:
  - New product development
  - Problem prevention
  - Idea generation for solutions
  - Start-up and progress
  - Selection or prioritization
  - Work instructions
  - Data collection and recording

As a first step, the purpose and intended use of the checklist is determined.

Research is then performed to ensure that the developed checklist covers all requirements, provides all options, or asks for specific data to be recorded. See example *Checklists for Teaming*.

When constructing the checklist, provide space for checking off completed steps, ideas, or data items, as shown in the example.

Ask subject matter experts to review the final draft of a checklist to ensure that nothing of importance has been overlooked or omitted.

Perform final revisions and pilot the checklist.

Checklists for Teaming   Date: xx/xx/xx

✓	Team Start-Up Sequence
	Organizational readiness?
	Top management support?
	A champion coordinating?
	Volunteers for teams?
	Schedule and facility ready?
	Team training available?
	Team role assignments made?
	Team norms established?
	Mission and goals developed?
	Problem specification stated?
	Team meetings scheduled?

✓	Team Norms
	Start and end on time
	No off-side conversations
	Participate—active contribution
	Assists keeping team focused
	Avoid interrupting others
	Equal status for all
	No evaluation of team members
	Allow process flexibility
	Be open to new ideas
	Help facilitate
	Complete assigned action item

✓	Generate Ideas for Solutions
	Change materials
	Change work instructions
	Change color or symbols
	Change shape or format
	Change size or amount
	Change design or style
	Change person or place
	Rearrange sequence
	Rearrange parts

A checksheet is a simple form designed to record and quantify facts and data over a period of time. The construction of the checksheet should be tailored to collect data on specific categories and location of defects, frequency of events, or possible causes.

- To observe an operation and record specific data over a period of time.
- To acquire a short-term observation of process variability on the current situation.
- To identify what potential problem should be addressed first.
- To confirm the effects of problems.

before

Data collection strategy

Observation

Surveying

Interview technique

Focus group

after

Stratum chart

Histogram

Frequency distribution (FD)

Box plot

Pareto chart

➡ Select and define problem or opportunity
➡ Identify and analyze causes or potential change
   Develop and plan possible solutions or change
➡ Implement and evaluate solution or change
   Measure and report solution or change results
   Recognize and reward team efforts

3	Research/statistics
	Creativity/innovation
	Engineering
	Project management
2	Manufacturing
	Marketing/sales
4	Administration/documentation
	Servicing/support
1	Customer/quality metrics
	Change management

Types of frequently used Checksheets:
- To count occurrences (Tally 卌).
- To measure activities (amounts, time, etc.)
- To locate problems or defects (Defect Map)

Identify data to be collected. See example *Customer Complaints*.

Design checksheet for easy data capture.

Collect data for the stated time period. Example: 20 days.

After a specified period, total the check marks and input this data into the problem-solving process. Date the checksheet.

Note: For another type of checksheet, see the defect map approach.

Customer Complaints

Date: xx/xx/xx

Type	Week 1					Week 2					Week 3					Week 4					Total
	M	T	W	T	F	M	T	W	T	F	M	T	W	T	F	M	T	W	T	F	
Ordering	II	I	卌	I	III	II	IIII	IIII	IIII	卌	III	卌	I	卌I		卌	IIII	II	卌	IIII	66
Shipping	I	II		II	I	I		III			II	I		II	I	I	I		II		20
Billing	I	I		I		I		II		III	I	I			III	II	I	II		I	20
Defect	II	I	卌	卌	II	I	II	IIII	I	I	II		II	卌		I	I	II	I	III	41
Service	卌	I	IIII	III	卌	II	I	卌	I	卌	卌	卌	II	卌	I	卌I	II	卌	I	卌	69
Total	11	6	14	12	11	7	7	18	6	14	13	12	5	18	5	15	9	11	9	13	216

The circle of opportunity technique is a process of randomly selecting problem-related characteristics or attributes and, by free association, arriving at original and new ideas or possible solutions. As associations are formed or links completed, new relationships, insights, or possibilities produce additional novel ideas for consideration and study by a team.

- To discover new meanings, relationships, or word associations and, by concentrated study, to produce new thoughts on solving problems or improving products and services.
- To free-associate attributes for the purpose of surfacing original ideas for problem solving or process improvement.
- To selectively study randomly linked word combinations in search of ideas or solutions.

before

Attribute listing
Fresh eye
Mental imaging
Forced choice
Circumrelation

after

Stimulus analysis
Idea advocate
Opportunity analysis
Information needs analysis
Value analysis

Select and define problem or opportunity
➡ Identify and analyze causes or potential change
➡ Develop and plan possible solutions or change
Implement and evaluate solution or change
Measure and report solution or change results
Recognize and reward team efforts

Research/statistics
1 Creativity/innovation
Engineering
Project management
Manufacturing
Marketing/sales
Administration/documentation
Servicing/support
3 Customer/quality metrics
2 Change management

- To ensure randomness, a pair of dice is needed to select characteristics or attributes listed around a closed circle (circle of opportunity).

The team facilitator displays a problem statement to the team participants. See example *Problem: Frequent Machine Downtime.*

A circle of opportunity is constructed as shown in the example.

Problem-related characteristics are identified by the team. The facilitator records these around the twelve circle of opportunity segments.

The facilitator throws one die to determine the first characteristic, then throws both dice to determine the second characteristic.

The team collectively free-associates using individual and combined word characteristics. The facilitator records on flip charts any associations and resulting ideas or insights as they are produced by the participants.

Connections or links to the problem are surfaced and analyzed. Any thoughts that may help to finalize a solution to the problem are also recorded.

Collectively, the participants produce a potential solution statement as seen in the example.

The circle of opportunity is dated and shown to the process owner.

Problem: Frequent Machine Downtime   Date: xx/xx/xx

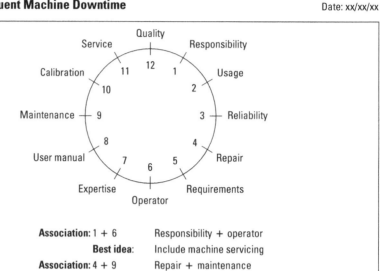

Association: 1 + 6   Responsibility + operator
Best idea: Include machine servicing
Association: 4 + 9   Repair + maintenance
Best idea: Train operators in maintenance/repair

Potential Solution: Rewrite the machine operator job description to include the servicing and maintenance of the equipment. This will prevent excessive work delays due to machine downtime.

The circle response technique is ideal for quickly collecting data from participants without forming a team or setting up a session for this purpose. A facilitator or trainer uses this impromptu method to get a response from each participant on a stated question or issue.

- To acquire on-the-spot responses or ideas from a group of participants.
- To promote involvement of all participants in a learning process.
- To check what, individually, participants can contribute.

before

Audience analysis

Buzz group

Different point of view

Run-it-by

Surveying

after

Consensus decision making

Circles of knowledge

Thematic content analysis

What-if analysis

Idea advocate

➥ Select and define problem or opportunity
➥ Identify and analyze causes or potential change
➥ Develop and plan possible solutions or change
    Implement and evaluate solution or change
    Measure and report solution or change results
➥ Recognize and reward team efforts

	Research/statistics
	Research/statistics
1	Creativity/innovation
4	Engineering
	Project management
5	Manufacturing
3	Marketing/sales
	Administration/documentation
6	Servicing/support
	Customer/quality metrics
2	Change management

- If there are more than 20 participants, have some participants work together in pairs and input a joint idea or response.
- Establish a time limit of 30 seconds per person to generate an idea or response.

The facilitator or trainer asks participants to form a circle so that everyone can see and hear each other.

On a flip chart, a question or issue is displayed to participants. Everyone is asked to respond with an answer or idea to recommend. See example *Recommendations to Review the Literature*.

The facilitator explains the procedure, mentions that they have only about a minute to respond, and explains that no evaluation or interruptions will be allowed.

Starting with one participant and moving around the circle, everyone gives his or her input, which is recorded on a flip chart.

Once every participant has responded, the facilitator summarizes the data and ends the session by thanking each participant and suggesting that this process may be repeated.

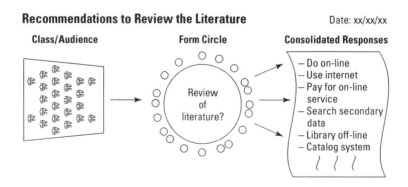

Recommendations to Review the Literature   Date: xx/xx/xx

Class/Audience   Form Circle   Consolidated Responses

Review of literature?

- Do on-line
- Use internet
- Pay for on-line service
- Search secondary data
- Library off-line
- Catalog system

The circles of influence tool allows a team to verify the extent of its self-management, decision-making authority, and problem-solving capability. Circles are used to display forces or problems that are within the team's influence or that are outside the team's influence.

- To evaluate problems and forces influencing a team's performance.
- To identify a team's areas of responsibility and influence.
- To verify team management and authority.
- To empower a team by increasing its influence and defining accountability.

before

Brainstorming

Consensus decision making

Team process assessment

Buzz group

Team mirror

after

Relationship map

Sociogram

Delphi method

Critical dialogue

Multivoting

Select and define problem or opportunity

➟ Identify and analyze causes or potential change

➟ Develop and plan possible solutions or change

Implement and evaluate solution or change

➟ Measure and report solution or change results

Recognize and reward team efforts

	Research/statistics
2	Creativity/innovation
	Engineering
	Project management
	Manufacturing
	Marketing/sales
4	Administration/documentation
	Servicing/support
3	Customer/quality metrics
1	Change management

- Each participant takes no more than 10 minutes to list problems for consideration.
- Use coding such as A-1, B-1, C-1, etc., to designate problems placed into circles of influence A-B-C.

The team's facilitator draws three circles of influence on a flip chart and explains the purpose and application of this tool. A team discussion follows.

The facilitator starts the team by providing an example problem for each circle of influence. Further clarification takes place to ensure that each participant understands the process.

Participants are asked to develop a list of existing and perceived problems that affect the team's present performance.

Once participants have completed their lists, the facilitator collects these lists for encoding and charting problems. See example *A Team's Problem-Solving Ability*.

All listed problems are discussed and consensus is reached on where problems should be charted: circle A, B, or C. The first problem determined to be in circle A should be encoded as A-1.

All charted problems are recorded on flip charts titled *Circle A*, *Circle B*, and *Circle C*, as shown in the example. A discussion follows on the team's ability to control or influence problems.

Finally, the team explores ways to increase the team's influence, expand on its area of responsibility, and, therefore, improve team performance.

A Team's Problem-Solving Ability

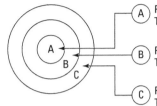

A — Problems can be solved by the team.
The team is in control.

B — Problems can be influenced by the team.
The team is not in control.

C — Problems encountered by the team.
The team has no control or influence.

Date: xx/xx/xx

Circle A	Circle B	Circle C
A-1 Membership	B-1 Inter-group participation	C-1 Customer contacts
A-2 Work assignments	B-2 Rules	C-2 Work ethic
A-3 Safety	B-3 Schedule	C-3 Policy
A-4 Performance	B-4 Reports	C-4 Regulatory
A-5 Communications	B-5 Resources	C-5 Compensation
A-6 Cooperation	B-6 Turnover	C-6 Contracts
A-7 Relationships		

The circles of knowledge tool is a technique that can be used during a team session, staff meeting, or in the classroom to involve every participant in considering and providing feedback on a problem, issue, or a stated question. This technique can be repeated, impromptu, several times to collect information on the topic being discussed or presented.

- To involve each participant in the meeting or learning process in order to verify understanding or review previously covered material.
- To focus participants on some issue or question that requires instant response.
- To further explore a problem, issue, or question and to collect participants' responses.

before

Buzz group

Audience analysis

Circle response

Different point of view

Surveying

after

Consensus decision making

Presentation

Idea advocate

Thematic content analysis

What-if analysis

➥ Select and define problem or opportunity
➥ Identify and analyze causes or potential change
➥ Develop and plan possible solutions or change
  Implement and evaluate solution or change
  Measure and report solution or change results
➥ Recognize and reward team efforts

	Research/statistics
1	Creativity/innovation
	Engineering
2	Project management
	Manufacturing
	Marketing/sales
3	Administration/documentation
	Servicing/support
	Customer/quality metrics
4	Change management

- Can best be used if an audience numbers 12–25 participants.
- Complete session should take no longer than 30 minutes.

A facilitator or trainer breaks up the audience into circles of 5–6 participants. Circles move away from each other so that the simultaneous discussions will not cause noise interference. Someone in each circle takes on the role of the recorder.

The facilitator or trainer displays on a flip chart a question, problem, or issue to participants. Everyone is asked to respond with an answer, idea, or recommendation. See example *Development of a Marketing Proposal.*

The facilitator next explains the rules of this activity. Simply, no participant may "pass," evaluate, or criticize other participants' input, or interrupt the process in any way.

The recorder records all responses as they come from each participant around the circle.

At the end of approximately 20 minutes, all circles rejoin and the recorded information is displayed for all to see.

The facilitator restates the question, problem, or issue and asks each recorder to present the recorded information while the other recorders check their own flip charts for redundent information.

This process continues until all information is presented. The facilitator rewrites or consolidates the information on a flip chart to save for later reference as shown in the example.

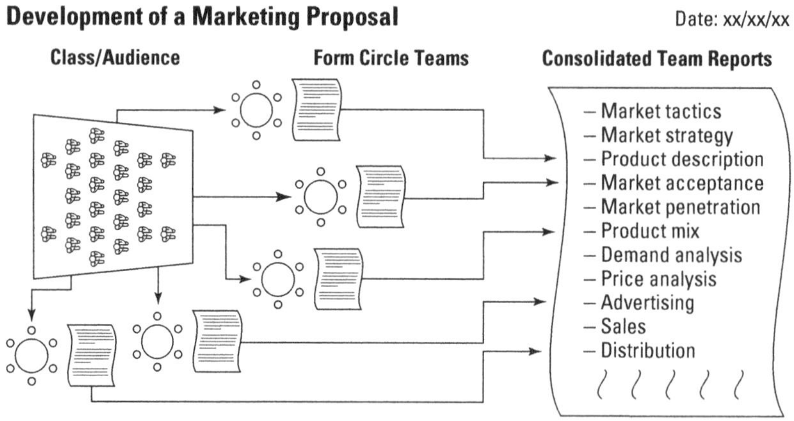

Development of a Marketing Proposal

Date: xx/xx/xx

Class/Audience   **Form Circle Teams**   **Consolidated Team Reports**

- Market tactics
- Market strategy
- Product description
- Market acceptance
- Market penetration
- Product mix
- Demand analysis
- Price analysis
- Advertising
- Sales
- Distribution

The circumrelation method is an idea generation tool developed by Frank Laverty. Using three freely spinning disks, each with factors recorded in respective sections, forced relationships are possible by rotating the disks so that different factors, one from each disk, are lined up to form a combination of factors. Combinations are evaluated for useful ideas or potential solutions.

- To examine related problem factors by combining three different factors at a time in an attempt to produce some ideas for problem resolution.
- To discover novel ideas for process improvement.
- To utilize a systemic approach to problem solving.

before

Problem specification

Brainstorming

Phillips 66

Brainwriting pool

Focus group

after

Criteria filtering

Run-it-by

Different point of view

Consensus decision making

Wildest idea technique

➥ Select and define problem or opportunity
➥ Identify and analyze causes or potential change
Develop and plan possible solutions or change
Implement and evaluate solution or change
Measure and report solution or change results
Recognize and reward team efforts

Research/statistics
1 Creativity/innovation
Engineering
Project management
Manufacturing
3 Marketing/sales
Administration/documentation
Servicing/support
Customer/quality metrics
2 Change management

Circumrelator Assembly

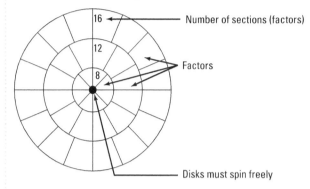

Number of sections (factors)

Factors

Disks must spin freely

- For individual or team idea generation.
- A basic circumrelator has three disks measuring 3, 5, and 7 inches in diameter. A fourth disk is optional.
- Disks are divided into 8, 12, and 16 sections. Multiplying 8 × 12 × 16 = 1536 factor combinations or forced relationships.

The team (or individual) reviews the previously specified problem.

Three major areas related to the problem are identified. See example *Circumrelation: Reduce Defect Level*. People issues, equipment maintenance, and defect types are all related to a reduce defect level.

The team brainstorms factors for each major area. This process is continued until the team stops generating factors.

Using the nominal group technique (NGT), the team reduces the number of generated factors in each major area to 8-12-16.

Factors are now recorded in the sections of the three major areas on the three disks.

The search for idea-producing combinations calls for the rotation of one disk at a time, lining up different combinations (forced relationships).

The team assesses all combinations and records any ideas that warrant further consideration in order to solve the problem. See idea in example shown.

Reduce Defect Level

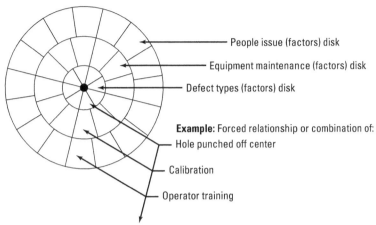

People issue (factors) disk

Equipment maintenance (factors) disk

Defect types (factors) disk

Example: Forced relationship or combination of:
Hole punched off center

Calibration

Operator training

Idea for reducing defect level: Train operators to be able to calibrate equipment

The cluster analysis tool is best utilized after a brainstorming session to organize data by subdividing different ideas, items, or characteristics into relatively similar groups, each under a topical heading. Mainly a discovery tool, it often surfaces perceived problem areas, concerns, or items that naturally belong together.

- To classify data into natural groupings on the basis of similar or related characteristics.
- To identify most important characteristics to be considered in developing a problem specification.
- To develop a more homogeneous group of items from a large list of dissimilar items.
- To identify differences among customer, employee, or supplier groups in regard to quality perception and performance issues.

before

Brainstorming

Brainwriting pool

6-3-5 method

Double reversal

Starbursting

after

Problem specification

Pareto chart

Opportunity analysis

Force field analysis (FFA)

Nominal group technique (NGT)

➥ Select and define problem or opportunity	
➥ Identify and analyze causes or potential change	
Develop and plan possible solutions or change	
Implement and evaluate solution or change	
Measure and report solution or change results	
Recognize and reward team efforts	

	Research/statistics
1	Creativity/innovation
	Engineering
3	Project management
	Manufacturing
5	Marketing/sales
	Administration/documentation
	Servicing/support
4	Customer/quality metrics
2	Change management

- Cluster analysis is simply a classification process that combines similar objects, items, ideas, variables, or issues into categories or groups.

The team facilitator displays the flip charts of previously brainstormed data to the team. See example *Clustering Brainstormed Data: Improve Quality.*

The team looks at all items and suggests general or topical headings for similar items. They become the cluster names.

The facilitator records all suggested cluster names and asks participants to sort or organize items to be placed under each cluster name. As participants call out items, the facilitator designates the items on the flip charts with the first letter of the cluster name as shown in the example.

Once all items have been designated, a final chart of formed clusters (groups) is drawn.

The resulting cluster chart is dated and saved for future reference.

Clustering Brainstormed Data: Improve Quality

Cluster Names
P = People
I = Information
T = Technical
C = Causes
S = Solutions

Flip chart 1

Session 8/19/xx

Topic: Improve Quality

S – More training
C – Short due dates
P – Inexperience
I – No communication
I – Missing info
T – What is a defect?
T – Constant changes
C – No inspections
C – Too much work
C – Many interruptions
P – Group conflict
C – Incorrect testing

Flip chart 2

Session 8/19/xx

C – Lack of proper tools
P – Low job satisfaction
I – Specifications unclear
I – Lack of instructions
P – Low morale
T – Lack of metrics
S – Involve customers
C – Stressful work
C – Equipment problems
T – Lack of data
S – Need problem-solving teams
I – No procedures
    End of ideas

Resulting Clusters				Date: xx/xx/xx
People	**Information**	**Technical**	**Causes**	**Solutions**
– Group conflict	– No communications	– Constant changes	– Equipment problems	– More training
– Low job satisfaction	– Missing info	– Lack of metrics	– Lack of proper tools	– Involve customers
– Low morale	– Specifications unclear	– Lack of data	– Short due dates	– Need problem-solving teams
– Inexperience	– Lack of instructions	– What is a defect?	– Many interruptions	
	– No procedures		– Incorrect testing	
			– Lack of instruction	
			– Stressful work	
			– No inspections	
			– Too much work	

A comparison matrix assists with the analysis process to identify existing gaps between an organization and its competitors, to determine the profitability potential of a product or service, or to discover other problems that may require immediate attention. When gaps, problems and profitability potential are known, a company can more effectively position its future products and services.

- To identify problem areas and areas where resources should best be allocated.
- To compare organizational capability with that of competitors.
- To perform market demand futuring for products and services.

before

Data collections strategy

Benchmarking

Conjoint analysis

Information needs analysis

Customer-first-questions (CFQ)

after

Resource requirements matrix

Opportunity analysis

Gap analysis

Starbursting

Action plan

➡ Select and define problem or opportunity

  Identify and analyze causes or potential change

➡ Develop and plan possible solutions or change

  Implement and evaluate solution or change

➡ Measure and report solution or change results

  Recognize and reward team efforts

	Research/statistics
	Creativity/innovation
	Engineering
	Project management
	Manufacturing
1	Marketing/sales
	Administration/documentation
2	Servicing/support
3	Customer/quality metrics
4	Change management

- A rating system of non-numeric symbols can be used in place of numeric values or non-numeric ratings. Optional: ● = 5 (strong); ○ = 3 (moderate); □ = 1 (weak).

A facilitated cross-functional team decides upon a data-collection strategy to gather historical and forecasted information about the products/services.

The team identifies core productions/services and lists them in order of importance or value to the organization. See example *Softhelp Software Company*.

Appropriate markets or market segments are agreed upon.

The team selects a rating system.
Note: Non-numeric figures can be used in place of numeric values or non-numeric ratings.

Data is collected and discussed, and findings are plotted on the comparison matrix as shown in the example.

The team reviews the completed matrix and writes a short rationale for each product/service rating.

A final report, which describes potential, leverage points, future requirements, etc., is written and attached to the comparison matrix and submitted to management.

Softhelp Software Company   Date: xx/xx/xx

Product or Service \ Market or Market Segment	Domestic		International		Supplier	Specific industry
Software package A (product)	F	◯	F	●		
	P	☐	P	☐		
Software package B (product)	F	●	F	◯		
	P	☐	P	☐		
Technical support (service)	F	●	F	●		
	P	☐	P	☐		
System maintenance (service)	F	●	F	●		
	P	☐	P	◯		

● = 5 (strong)   ◯ = 3 (moderate)   ☐ = 1 (weak)

Notes: Market demand/strength:
(P) Present = current product/service performance
(F) Future = future potential of product/service

The competency gap assessment tool can be applied to measure organizational competencies or individual abilities to perform relative to the perceived importance of activities to be completed. Analysis of response data will directly point to individual or organizational performance gaps.

- To collect customer feedback data on the perceived importance of tasks versus displayed competency in the performance of tasks.
- To check for any performance gaps between provided service and expected service.
- To verify a possible education and training need for employees.

before

Surveying

Interview technique

Questionnaires

Observation

Task analysis

after

Needs analysis

Different point of view

Gap analysis

Force field analysis (FFA)

SWOT analysis

➡ Select and define problem or opportunity

➡ Identify and analyze causes or potential change

Develop and plan possible solutions or change

Implement and evaluate solution or change

➡ Measure and report solution or change results

Recognize and reward team efforts

1	Research/statistics
	Creativity/innovation
	Engineering
	Project management
	Manufacturing
	Marketing/sales
	Administration/documentation
4	Servicing/support
2	Customer/quality metrics
3	Change management

Competency Gap Assessment

This instrument can also be used to measure customer satisfaction simply by changing the questions and rating headings: Example:

Servicing of Generators—Various Field Sites
Please evaluate the quality of service and importance of such service to you for each category. Circle the selected number.

Service	*Importance*
0 = Poor	0 = To no extent
1 = Fair	1 = To some extent
2 = Good	2 = To a great extent
3 = Very Good	3 = To a very great extent

Category	*Service*	*Importance*	*D-Score*
1. Staff's professionalism during site visit	0 1 2 3	0 1 2 3	—
2. Equipment ready and calibrated	0 1 2 3	0 1 2 3	—

———————————————————— etc. ————————————————————

All respondents' negative difference scores should be added to arrive at a total of negative D-Scores. The top five, ranking from highest to lowest total score, will indicate the most severe performance gaps and exactly what subject or skill dimension they represent.

The first step requires the identification of an important area to be measured. Candidates could be identified at the individual, group, or organizational level. See example *Professional Roles and Competencies.*

A set of items or dimensions that cover the critical area to be measured must be identified.

The survey rating form is developed and field tested.

After the final revisions have been made, the survey rating form is administered to targeted employees or customers.

Survey responses are "difference scored," and all negative difference scores totaled by item or dimension.

Finally, the D-Score totals are ranked from high to low, as shown in the example. These performance gaps provide the input data for an action plan to close these gaps.

Professional Roles and Competencies

Listed below are managerial knowledge and skill requirements (dimensions) supportive of contemporary aspects in management. Please respond by circling one of the
numbers for each category. Also, the ratings are as follows: The number "3" = High,
"2" = Medium, "1" = Low, and "0" = No "Ability" or "Importance."

	What is your ability to perform in this dimension?	How important is this dimension in your position?	
Planning Dimensions	Ability	Importance	D-Score
1. Use futuring tools	3 2 1 0	3 2 1 0	___
2. Communicate vision/strategy	3 2 1 0	3 2 1 0	___
3. Develop business plans	3 2 1 0	3 2 1 0	___
④ Prepare proposals/reports	3 2 1 0	3 2 1 0	___
5. Construct "what if" scenarios	3 2 1 0	3 2 1 0	___
6. Perform hoshin planning	3 2 1 0	3 2 1 0	___

Example Question No. 4

Dimension	Ability	Importance	
④ Prepare proposals/reports	3 2 ① 0	③ 2 1 0	-2

In this example the respondent circled a "1" (Low) for "Ability" and a "3" (High) for
"Importance." Subtracting the "Importance" rating from the "Ability" rating will give
us a powerful "Difference Score" of –2. Any negative "Difference Score" would indicate a competency gap, a need for further development. Also, the higher the negative
score, the greater the existing discrepancy.

Conjoint analysis is a marketing research tool used by many companies to verify the customers' perception of value for most product or service features. It provides integrated product development teams (IPDT) with detailed information on the features customers want and expect in new products or services.

Every product is considered a package of features. To assess the contribution a feature will make to the overall value of the product, a rating schema is used. The sum of all customer-supplied ratings for all identified features will yield the perceived value to the customer.

- To determine which combination of product or service features are valued highest by customers in a target market.
- To provide preference data as input in the product innovation and development process.
- To verify the value a customer places on each of a product's features.
- To compare overall customer value of a product or service to that of a competitor's product or service.

before

Data collection strategy

Customer-first-questions (CFQ)

House of quality

Focus group

Customer needs table

after

Interview technique

Surveying

Competency gap assessment

Customer satisfaction analysis (CSA)

Consensus decision making

➥ Select and define problem or opportunity

➥ Identify and analyze causes or potential change

➥ Develop and plan possible solutions or change

   Implement and evaluate solution or change

➥ Measure and report solution or change results

   Recognize and reward team efforts

4	Research/statistics
3	Creativity/innovation
	Engineering
	Project management
	Manufacturing
2	Marketing/sales
	Administration/documentation
	Servicing/support
1	Customer/quality metrics
	Change management

- Product or service features are rated on a scale of 1 to 10. See example Value of Safety (Valsafe) = 10, where 1 is lowest, 5 is average, and 10 is of highest value.

Identify features most valued by the customer. See example *Conjoint Analysis of an Electric Can Opener.*

Profile the product's typical customer.

Select a sample of potential customers (the target matrix) to participate in the data collection process.

Develop a product-features rating form. List your product and competing products.

Interview prospective customers and have them rate product features on a scale from 1–10.

Total the values for each product. (The assumption is made that the product with the highest total value or utility to customers would capture the greatest market share.) Besides showing how product stacks up to the competition, a conjoint analysis identifies the features customers want the most. This information allows the design team to alter the product to suit customer demand prior to product release.

Electric Can Opener

Conjoint Analysis Table		Date: xx/xx/xx
Feature	**Rating** (1 - 10)	**Value**
Price	4	Valpric = 4
Performance	9	Valperf = 9
Flexibility	6	Valflex = 6
Size	3	Valsize = 3
Attractiveness	3	Valattr = 3
Ease of operation	7	Valoper = 7
Safety	2	Valsafe = 2
Maintenance/service	4	Valserv = 4
		Total product rating = 38

The consensus decision making tool is an interactive process in which all team participants openly communicate their ideas and reserve feedback and other points of view. The process continues until all team participants are able to accept and support a team decision even though some may not completely agree with it. Reaching consensus often requires greater individual participation, clear communication, and some compromise on well-considered decisions.

- To reach agreement on a proposed action or next step in a problem-solving effort.
- To gain general agreement and support on a particular idea or issue.
- To allow team participants the opportunity to express and defend their point of view.
- To avoid conflict or rush to a decision.

before

Brainstorming

Brainwriting pool

Futures wheel

Affinity diagram

Window analysis

after

Team process assessment

Resource requirements matrix

Objectives matrix (OMAX)

Responsibility matrix

Action plan

➥ Select and define problem or opportunity

➥ Identify and analyze causes or potential change

➥ Develop and plan possible solutions or change

 Implement and evaluate solution or change

 Measure and report solution or change results

➥ Recognize and reward team efforts

	Research/statistics
3	Creativity/innovation
	Engineering
2	Project management
	Manufacturing
	Marketing/sales
	Administration/documentation
4	Servicing/support
	Customer/quality metrics
1	Change management

- Consensus is reached when:
  - All participants have presented their views.
  - Participants fully understand, accept, and will support the team decision.
  - Even if some participants are not fully satisfied or cannot completely agree with the decision, they do feel that they "can live with it" and will not oppose it.

The team displays a final list of ideas, a proposed problem solution, or process improvement activity. See example *Increase Customer Contact Time for Complaint Handling*.

Team participants clarify all issues, share views, and listen to other ideas or concerns. Ensure that all actively participate in this discussion.

After all information has been shared and alternatives considered, the team develops general agreement with care being taken to avoid conflict, participants taking sides, or outright blocking of compromise.

Lastly, the team creates a final decision statement and verifies that all participants understand and are willing to support their decision.

Increase Customer Contact Time for Complaint Handling   Date: xx/xx/xx

Team Aims for Consensus

Team Reached Consensus

A control chart is a graph that plots randomly selected data over time in order to determine if a process is performing to requirements or is, therefore, under statistical control. The chart displays whether a problem is caused by an unusual or special cause (correctable error) or is due to chance causes (natural variation) alone.

- To determine if a process is performing to upper and lower control-limit requirements (process is kept in control).
- To monitor process variations over time, with regard to both special or chance causes.
- To identify opportunities for improving quality and to measure process improvement.
- To serve as a quality measurement technique.

before

Standard deviation
Sampling methods
Observation
Checksheet
Events log

after

Process capability ratios
Variance analysis
Descriptive statistics
Process analysis
Work flow analysis (WFA)

➡ Select and define problem or opportunity	
➡ Identify and analyze causes or potential change	
Develop and plan possible solutions or change	
➡ Implement and evaluate solution or change	
➡ Measure and report solution or change results	
Recognize and reward team efforts	

2	Research/statistics
	Creativity/innovation
4	Engineering
	Project management
1	Manufacturing
	Marketing/sales
	Administration/documentation
	Servicing/support
3	Customer/quality metrics
	Change management

Types of Control Charts	
Data Required	**For Specific Chart**
Quantitative Variable Data Continuous or measurements *Example:* size, downtime, dimensions, activities per day, etc.	• $\bar{X} - R$ chart[†] (average $\bar{X}$ and range "R" of samples) • $\bar{X} - S$ chart (average $\bar{X}$ and standard deviations "S" of samples)
Qualitative Attribute Data Discrete or counts *Example:* Complaints, rework, missed due dates, delays, rejects, etc.	• c chart[‡] (number of defects in a subgroup) • np chart (number of defective units in a subgroup) • p chart[††] (percentage defective) • μ chart (defects per unit)

Most commonly used charts:

    [†]For variable data: $\bar{X}$-R Chart

    [‡]For attribute data: c Chart

    [†‡]For attribute data: p Chart

Note: For a description of other charts refer to a reference on statistical process control (SPC).

- c Chart (attribute data)
- Sample data: Minumum (25) samples, subgroups must be of equal size (sample size is constant).
- Calculations: See c Chart example.

$$\bar{c} \text{ (Avg.)} = \frac{\text{Total number of defects}}{\text{Number of samples}}, \bar{c} = \frac{350}{25}, \bar{c} = 14$$

Upper Control Limit:

$$\text{UCL} = \bar{c} + 3\sqrt{\bar{c}}, \text{UCL} = 14 + 3\sqrt{14}, \text{UCL} = 25.22$$

Lower Control Limit:

$$\text{LCL} = \bar{c} - 3\sqrt{\bar{c}}, \text{LCL} = 14 - 3\sqrt{14}, \text{LCL} = 2.78$$

Determine the type of attribute control chart to be used. See example *Typing: Errors per Page* (attribute control chart—Type *c*).

Collect at least 25 samples of data; subgroups must be of equal size.

Prepare a type *c* chart and continue to record collected data as shown. See example chart.

After all 25 subgroups (samples) have been recorded, perform all required calculations. See *notes and key points* above for example.

Plot and connect plotted points to form a trendline. Verify that the trendline points reflect recorded averages ($\bar{c}$).

Analyze plotted data for significant variance or patterns. Date the chart.

Typing Errors per Page

Source: Admin. **Process:** Typing **Characteristic:** Errors per page **Frequency:** Daily

$\bar{c} = 14.0$ $UCL = 25.22$ $LCL = 2.78$ **Prepared by:** W.J.M **Calculation date:** xx/xx/xx

Date	10/1	2	3	4	5	10/6	7	8	9	10	10/11	12	13	14	15	10/16	17	18	19	20	10/21	22	23	24	10/25
Time	5 PM				5 PM	1 PM				1 PM	5 PM				5 PM	1 PM				1 PM	5 PM				5 PM

Subgroups	1	2	3	4	5	6	7	8	9	10	11	12	13	14	15	16	17	18	19	20	21	22	23	24	25
Sample size (n)	20	20	20	20	20	20	20	20	20	20	20	20	20	20	20	20	20	20	20	20	20	20	20	20	20
Number (c)	12	18	13	10	19	24	8	16	14	8	16	16	14	19	27	7	9	12	15	10	12	13	13	14	18

Notes: 1. Samples taken at 5 PM for five day periods frequently have a higher error average

A control chart is a graph that plots randomly selected data over time in order to determine if a process is performing to requirements and is, therefore, under statistical control. The chart displays whether a problem is caused by an unusual or special cause (correctable error) or is due to chance causes (natural variation) alone.

- To determine if a process is performing to upper and lower control-limit requirements (process is kept in control).
- To monitor process variations over time, with regard to both special or chance causes.
- To identify opportunities for improving quality and to measure process improvement.
- To serve as a quality measurement technique.

before

Variance analysis
Sampling methods
Observation
Checksheet
Events log

after

Process capability ratios
Standard deviation
Descriptive statistics
Process analysis
Work flow analysis (WFA)

➡ Select and define problem or opportunity	
➡ Identify and analyze causes or potential change	
Develop and plan possible solutions or change	
➡ Implement and evaluate solution or change	
➡ Measure and report solution or change results	
Recognize and reward team efforts	

2	Research/statistics
	Creativity/innovation
4	Engineering
	Project management
1	Manufacturing
	Marketing/sales
	Administration/documentation
	Servicing/support
3	Customer/quality metrics
	Change management

Types of Control Charts	
Data Required	**For Specific Chart**
Quantitative Variable Data Continuous or measurements *Example:* size, downtime, dimensions, activities per day, etc.	• $\bar{X} - R$ chart[†] (average $\bar{X}$ and range "R" of samples) • $\bar{X} - S$ chart (average $\bar{X}$ and standard deviations "S" of samples)
Qualitative Attribute Data Discrete or counts *Example:* Complaints, rework, missed due dates, delays, rejects, etc.	• c chart[‡] (number of defects in a subgroup) • np chart (number of defective units in a subgroup) • p chart[††‡] (percentage defective) • μ chart (defects per unit)

Most commonly used charts:

†For variable data: $\bar{X}$-R Chart

‡For attribute data: c Chart

†‡For attribute data: p Chart

Note: For a description of other charts refer to a reference on statistical process control (SPC).

– p Chart (attribute data)

– Sample data: Minimum (25) samples, subgroups size may vary (sample size varies). Subgroup size is typically 50 or greater to show defectives per subgroup of 4 or greater.

Note: Subgroup size (n) should be within + or − 20% of the average size or control limits need to be recalculated.

Calculations: See p Chart example.

$$\bar{p} \text{ (Avg.)} = \frac{\text{Total number of defectives}}{\text{Total number of units}} = \frac{183}{1526} = .12 \text{ or } 12\%$$

$$\bar{n} \text{ (Avg.)} = \frac{\text{Total number of units}}{\text{Total number of samples}} = \frac{1526}{25} = 61$$

Upper Control Limit:

$$\text{UCLp} = \bar{p} + 3\sqrt{\frac{(\bar{p} \times (100\% - \bar{p})}{n}}$$

$$= 12 + 3\sqrt{\frac{12 \times (100 - 12)}{61}} = 12 + 3\sqrt{\frac{1056}{61}}$$

$$= 12 + 3\sqrt{17.31} = 12 + 12.48$$

$$= 24.48$$

Lower Control Limit:

$$\text{LcLp} = \bar{p} - 3\sqrt{\frac{(\bar{p} \times (100\% - \bar{p})}{n}}$$

$$= 12 - 12.48 \text{ (from above)}$$

$$= -.48$$

Note: Often the answer is negative. Therefore the lower control limit is at zero!

Determine the type of attribute control chart to be used. See example *Paint Rejects per Hour* (attribute control chart—type *p*).

Collect at least 25 samples of data; subgroups can vary but must have at least 50 units to show defectives per subgroup of 4 or greater.

Prepare a type *p* chart and continue to record collected data as shown. See example chart.

After all 25 subgroups (samples) have been recorded, perform all required calculations. See *notes and key points* above for example.

Plot and connect plotted points to form a trendline. Verify that the trend-line points reflect percentage of defectives.

Finalize and date the chart.

Paint Rejects per Hour

Source: Mfg. **Process:** Painting **Characteristic:** Paint rejects/hour **Frequency:** Once/day

Prepared by: W.J.M **Calculation date:** xx/xx/xx

$\bar{p} = 12$ UCL = 24.5 LCL = 0

$UCL_p = 24.5$ $\bar{p} = 12$ $LCL_p = 0$

% Defective axis: 27, 24, 21, 18, 15, 12, 9, 6, 3, 0

Subgroups	1	2	3	4	5	6	7	8	9	10	11	12	13	14	15	16	17	18	19	20	21	22	23	24	25
Date	10/1					10/6					10/11					10/16					10/21				10/25
Time	5 PM				5 PM	1 PM				1 PM	5 PM				5 PM	1 PM				1 PM	5 PM				5 PM
Sample size (n)	60	55	65	62	61	60	60	59	60	59	60	62	63	65	66	56	60	61	62	67	59	60	61	64	59
Number (np)	5	8	7	9	10	6	7	7	8	9	9	7	11	9	8	7	6	5	6	7	9	6	5	6	6
Defective (%)	8	15	11	15	16	10	12	12	13	15	15	11	17	14	12	13	10	8	10	10	15	10	8	9	10

Notes: 1. Number of defectives per subgroup = np

2. Sample size must be greater than 50 to show 4 or more defects per subgroup

3. Average sample size ($\bar{n}$) = 61 (1526 ÷ 25 = 61)

A control chart is a graph that plots randomly selected data over time in order to determine if a process is performing to requirements or is, therefore, under statistical control. The chart displays whether a problem is caused by an unusual or special cause (correctable error) or is due to chance causes (natural variation) alone.

- To determine if a process is performing to upper and lower control-limit requirements (process is kept in control).
- To monitor process variations over time, with regard to both special or chance causes.
- To identify opportunities for improving quality and to measure process improvement.
- To serve as a quality measurement technique.

before

Variance analysis
Sampling methods
Observation
Checksheet
Events log

after

Process capability ratios
Standard deviation
Descriptive statistics
Process analysis
Work flow analysis (WFA)

➥ Select and define problem or opportunity
➥ Identify and analyze causes or potential change
   Develop and plan possible solutions or change
➥ Implement and evaluate solution or change
➥ Measure and report solution or change results
   Recognize and reward team efforts

2 Research/statistics
   Creativity/innovation
4 Engineering
   Project management
1 Manufacturing
   Marketing/sales
   Administration/documentation
   Servicing/support
3 Customer/quality metrics
   Change management

Types of Control Charts	
Data Required	**For Specific Chart**
Quantitative Variable Data Continuous or measurements *Example:* size, downtime, dimensions, activities per day, etc.	• $\bar{X} - R$ chart† (average $\bar{X}$ and range "R" of samples) • $\bar{X} - S$ chart (average $\bar{X}$ and standard deviations "S" of samples)
Qualitative Attribute Data Discrete or counts *Example:* Complaints, rework, missed due dates, delays, rejects, etc.	• c chart‡ (number of defects in a subgroup) • np chart (number of defective units in a subgroup) • p chart†‡ (percentage defective) • μ chart (defects per unit)

Most commonly used charts:

  †For variable data: $\bar{X}$-R Chart
  ‡For attribute data: c Chart
  †‡For attribute data: p Chart

Note: For a description of other charts refer to a reference on statistical process control (SPC).

– $\bar{X}$-R Chart (variable data)
– Sample data: Random sampling, minimum (20) samples, minimum (5) data points in each subgroup.
– Calculations: See $\bar{X}$-R Chart example

Table of Factors for $\bar{X}$ & R Charts			
Data Points in Subgroup (*n*)	**Factors for $\bar{X}$ Chart**	**Factors for R Chart**	
	A2	**Upper–D3**	**Lower–D4**
2	1.880	0	3.268
3	1.023	0	2.574
4	.729	0	2.282
5	.577	0	2.114
6	.483	0	2.004
7	.419	.076	1.924
8	.373	.136	1.864
9	.337	.184	1.816
10	.308	.223	1.777

$$\bar{X} = \frac{\Sigma \times}{n}, \bar{X} = \frac{\text{Sum of measurements}}{\text{Number of samples}}$$

$$\bar{R} = H{-}L, R = \text{Highest} - \text{Lowest measurements}$$

$$\bar{\bar{X}} = \frac{\Sigma \bar{x}}{k}, \bar{\bar{X}} = \frac{\text{Sum of averages } (\bar{X})}{\text{Number of subgroups}}, \bar{\bar{X}} = \frac{99.94}{20}, \bar{\bar{X}} = 5.00$$

$$\bar{R} = \frac{\Sigma R}{k}, \bar{R} = \frac{\text{Sum of ranges } (R)}{\text{Number of subgroups}}, \bar{R} = \frac{4.78}{20}, \bar{R} = .24$$

$$\text{UCL}_{\bar{x}} = \bar{\bar{X}} + A_2\bar{R}, \text{UCL}_{\bar{x}} = 5.00 + (.577 \times .24), \text{UCL}_{\bar{x}} = 5.14$$

$$\text{LCL}_{\bar{x}} = X - A_2\bar{R}, \text{LCL}_{\bar{x}} = 5.00 - (.577 \times .24), \text{LCL}_{\bar{x}} = 4.86$$

$$\text{UCL}_R = D_4\bar{R}, \text{UCL}_R = 2.114 \times .24, \text{UCL}_R = .51$$

$$\text{LCL}_R = D_3\bar{R}, \text{Factor} = 0, \text{therefore LCL}_R = 0$$

Determine the type of variance control chart to be used. See example *Connector Wire* (variables control chart—type $\bar{X}$-R).

Collect at least 20 samples of data, 5 measurements per sample. Sampling should be random and according to a set frequency over a period of time.

Prepare a type $\bar{X}$-R Chart and record collected data as shown. See example chart.

After all 20 subgroups (samples) have been recorded, perform all required calculations. See *notes and key points* above for example.

Plot and connect plotted points to draw trendlines. Verify that trendline points reflect recorded averages ($\bar{X}$) and ranges (R).

Analyze plotted data for significant variance or patterns.

Connector Wire

Date: xx/xx/xx
Source: E-5

Process: Connector wire

Characteristic: Length: 15 cm

Frequency: Daily

$\bar{\bar{X}} = 5.00$ UCL = 5.14   LCL = 4.86 $\bar{R} = .24$ UCL = .51   LCL = 0   USL = 4.8   LSL = 5.2

Time	09:00	10:00	11:00	12:00	14:00	15:00	16:30	17:00	17:30	18:00	18:30	19:00	20:00	21:00	22:30	23:00	23:30	24:00	01:00	02:00
1	4.81	5.05	5.15	4.95	4.94	4.90	4.91	4.90	5.11	4.99	5.00	4.88	4.99	5.25	4.99	5.01	4.70	5.20	5.04	4.84
2	4.80	5.10	4.83	5.14	5.12	5.13	5.11	5.09	5.12	5.08	5.06	5.14	4.90	5.27	4.95	5.09	4.69	5.18	5.06	4.95
3	4.90	4.99	4.95	5.06	5.04	4.92	5.10	4.82	4.93	4.83	4.90	5.07	4.98	5.18	4.90	4.91	4.70	5.25	5.00	5.11
4	5.11	5.21	4.99	5.01	4.81	5.02	5.17	5.03	5.18	5.04	5.05	5.07	4.98	5.25	5.26	5.00	4.85	5.26	4.97	5.04
5	5.19	4.81	5.08	5.02	4.95	5.03	5.00	5.01	5.02	5.02	4.96	4.84	4.92	5.20	4.70	4.95	4.70	5.30	4.98	4.98
6																				
7																				
Total	24.81	25.16	25.00	25.18	24.86	25.00	24.85	24.85	25.36	24.96	24.97	25.00	24.77	26.16	24.08	24.96	23.64	26.19	25.05	24.92
Avg. ($\bar{X}$)	4.96	5.03	5.00	5.04	4.97	5.00	4.97	4.97	5.07	4.99	4.99	5.00	4.95	5.23	4.82	4.99	4.73	5.24	5.01	4.98
Range (R)	.39	.40	.32	.19	.31	.23	.26	.27	.25	.25	.16	.30	.09	.09	.56	.18	.16	.12	.09	.16

Sample measurements

$\bar{X}$ chart: 5.20, UCL 5.14, 5.10, $\bar{\bar{X}}$ 5.00, 4.90, LCL 4.86, 4.80

R chart: 56, UCL 51, 49, 42, 35, 28, $\bar{R}$ 24, 21, 14, 7, 0

The correlation analysis (hypothesis testing) procedure is utilized to measure the strength of the relationship or correlation (if any) between two variables or data sets of interest. A scatter diagram is usually completed to show, visually, the approximate correlation before the correlation coefficient is calculated.

- To measure the strength of a relationship (correlation) between two variables of interest.
- To calculate the correlation coefficient in order to accept or reject the stated null hypothesis (H_0), or, in other words, to test whether or not a statistically significant relationship exists between two variables.

before

Data collection strategy
Sampling method
Descriptive statistics
Scatter diagram
Standard deviation

after

Information needs analysis
Trend analysis
Response matrix analysis
SWOT analysis
Presentation

Select and define problem or opportunity
➥ Identify and analyze causes or potential change
Develop and plan possible solutions or change
Implement and evaluate solution or change
➥ Measure and report solution or change results
Recognize and reward team efforts

1 Research/statistics
   Creativity/innovation
2 Engineering
   Project management
   Manufacturing
   Marketing/sales
   Administration/documentation
   Servicing/support
3 Customer/quality metrics
   Change management

Sufficient supporting information is presented here to provide a good overview of the hypothesis testing procedure using a correlation test to illustrate the sequential steps involved to arrive at a decision. It is suggested, however, that the reader refer to a text on statistics for additional information and examples.

This is the recommended eight-step procedure for testing a null hypothesis (H_0) *(Note: Pearson's* r, *the product-moment correlation coefficient, is used for this example).*

1. Data Source: Errors made in document processing
   Variable X = number of documents processed per day
   Variable Y = number of errors per day

2. Research and null hypothesis (H_1 - H_0)
   H_1: There is a statistically significant relationship (correlation) in an increase of documents processed with an increase in errors per day.
   H_0: There is no statistically significant relationship (correlation) in an increase of documents processed with an increase of errors per day measured at .05 level of significance using a Pearson's product-moment correlation test.

3. Test used: Simple PPM two-tailed correlation test.

4. Level of significance used: .05

5. Degrees of freedom: 10 ($n - 2$), 12 pairs in our example.

6. Test result : r = .853

7. Critical value: .576 (See Pearson's Table in the Appendix, Table E.)

8. Decision: *Reject the H_0!* (If the test result is higher than the critical value, the H_0 is rejected. The test result is in the rejection region under the curve.)
   – Pearson's product-moment equations:

   $$r = \frac{\Sigma XY}{(n)(Sx)(Sy)} \qquad \text{Degrees of freedom: } df = n - 2$$

   $$S = \sqrt{\frac{\Sigma(X - \bar{x})^2}{n - 1}} \qquad \text{(Refer to standard deviation in this book.)}$$

Critical Values Table for Correlation Coefficient

No. of Pairs	(df) Degrees of Freedom	Level of Significance				
		.20	.10	.05	.01	.001
3	1	0.951	.988	.997	1.000	1.000
4	2	0.800	.900	.950	.990	.999
5	3	0.687	.805	.878	.959	.991
6	4	0.608	.729	.811	.917	.974
7	5	0.551	.669	.755	.875	.951
8	6	0.507	.621	.707	.834	.925
9	7	0.472	.582	.666	.798	.898
10	8	0.443	.549	.632	.765	.872
11	9	0.419	.521	.602	.735	.847
12	10	0.398	.497	.576	.708	.823
13	11	0.380	.476	.553	.684	.801
14	12	0.365	.457	.532	.661	.780
15	13	0.351	.441	.514	.641	.760
16	14	0.338	.426	.497	.623	.742
17		0.327	.412	.482	.606	.725

Data has been collected in order to check if there is any correlation in documents processed and errors found in processing. See example *Errors Made in Document Processing—Is There a Statistically Significant Correlation?*

A scatter diagram is prepared as shown in this example.
Note: Refer to scatter diagram in this book for additional information.

Prepare a table for calculating the correlation coefficient r. Insert the data (docs and errors) into columns X and Y as shown.

– Calculate the average $\bar{X}$ of column X, and $\bar{Y}$ of column Y.

– Subtract $\bar{X}$ from X scores and get small x, the deviation score.

– Subtract $\bar{Y}$ from Y scores and get small y, the deviation score.

– Square small x to get x^2.

– Square small y to get y^2.

- Multiply small x times small y to get xy.

– Total column xy and insert into r equation.
  Note: Refer to standard deviation in this handbook to calculate the standard deviation S_x and S_y.

Complete the calculations to get r, the correlation coefficient. Refer to the hypothesis testing steps as outlined in *notes and key points* on the previous page.

**Errors Made in Document Processing—
Is There a Statistically Significant Correlation?**

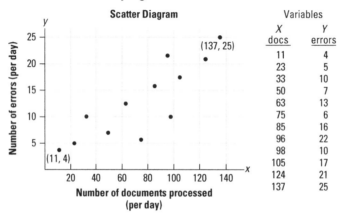

Scatter Diagram

(137, 25)

(11, 4)

Number of errors (per day)

Number of documents processed
(per day)

Variables	
X	Y
docs	errors
11	4
23	5
33	10
50	7
63	13
75	6
85	16
96	22
98	10
105	17
124	21
137	25

Calculations

$\bar{X} = 75$ $\bar{Y} = 13$ $S_x = \sqrt{\dfrac{\Sigma x^2}{n}}$, $S_x = 38.2$ $S_y = \sqrt{\dfrac{\Sigma y^2}{n}}$, $S_y = 6.84$

Days	Docs X	Errors Y	x	y	x^2	y^2	xy
4	11	4	−64	−9	4096	81	576
2	23	5	−52	−8	2704	64	416
9	33	10	−42	−3	1764	9	126
8	50	7	−25	−6	625	36	150
3	63	13	−12	0	144	0	0
6	75	6	0	−7	0	49	0
7	85	16	10	3	100	9	30
12	96	22	21	9	441	81	189
1	98	10	23	−3	529	9	−69
10	105	17	30	4	900	16	120
5	124	21	49	8	2401	64	392
11	137	25	62	12	3844	144	744
$n = 12$	$\Sigma X = 900$	$\Sigma Y = 156$	$\Sigma x = 0$	$\Sigma y = 0$	$\Sigma x^2 = 17{,}548$	$\Sigma y^2 = 562$	$\Sigma xy = 2674$

$r = \dfrac{\Sigma xy}{(n)(S_x)(S_y)}$

$r = \dfrac{2674}{(12)(38.2)(6.84)}$

$r = .853$

Critical value (see table) = .576
Therefore we reject the Null Hypotheses (H_0).

The cost of quality technique can be used as a powerful tool to identify and break down the readily apparent and the more hidden costs of quality activities. Costs are associated with conformance (prevention and assessment activities) and nonconformance (internal and external failures) factors.

- To identify total quality costs of operations.
- To analyze quality costs for the purpose of discovering cost savings and process improvement opportunities.
- To educate the work force on the cost of quality or lack of quality.

before

Data collection strategy

Activity cost matrix

Interview technique

Focus group

Starbursting

after

Cost-benefit analysis

Balance sheet

Presentation

Process analysis

Run-it-by

Select and define problem or opportunity

➡ Identify and analyze causes or potential change

➡ Develop and plan possible solutions or change

Implement and evaluate solution or change

Measure and report solution or change results

Recognize and reward team efforts

Research/statistics

Creativity/innovation

1 Engineering

Project management

2 Manufacturing

Marketing/sales

Administration/documentation

Servicing/support

3 Customer/quality metrics

4 Change management

Estimating Cost of Quality (COQ):

$$COQ = \frac{\text{Total time spent on COQ elements}}{\text{Total project time}} \times \frac{\text{Total cost of}}{\text{project time}}$$

A facilitator team brainstorms and lists all quality factors for the purpose of estimating total operational cost.

Team participants receive assignments to collect actual cost data wherever possible. Other costs for quality-related activities need to be estimated by the process owners or department managers.

The facilitator sorts costs into conformance and nonconformance. See example *Cost of Quality (COQ) Measurement*.

The team searches the cost data for the major cost items and discusses alternatives to lower these costs.

A list of potential cost-saving action items is drawn up. This could also be a list of potential process improvements to greatly reduce or eliminate quality-related costs.

Participants use the checklist in this example to generate other ideas for further consideration and analysis.

Cost of Quality (COQ) Measurement

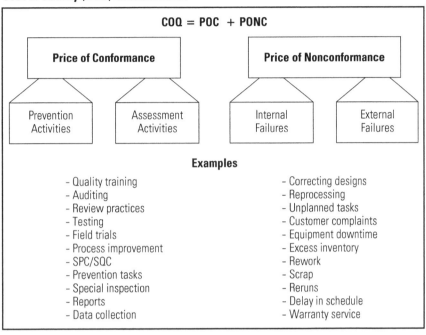

COQ = POC + PONC

Price of Conformance	Price of Nonconformance

Prevention Activities	Assessment Activities	Internal Failures	External Failures

Examples

- Quality training
- Auditing
- Review practices
- Testing
- Field trials
- Process improvement
- SPC/SQC
- Prevention tasks
- Special inspection
- Reports
- Data collection

- Correcting designs
- Reprocessing
- Unplanned tasks
- Customer complaints
- Equipment downtime
- Excess inventory
- Rework
- Scrap
- Reruns
- Delay in schedule
- Warranty service

The cost-benefit analysis provides the team with the ability to estimate the costs associated with potential benefits of implementing a proposed solution or process-improvement opportunity. This analysis is especially useful when several options need to be evaluated for financial impact; the final selection should return the greatest overall benefit for incurred cost.

- To compare among several options and select the option that offers the greatest return for the cost of implementation.
- To prepare a financial cost-benefit analysis for decision makers.
- To provide a cost-data rationale for proposing the implementation of a solution.
- To verify the cost effectiveness of a solution.

before

Information needs analysis

Data collection strategy

Activity cost matrix

Consensus decision making

Resource requirements matrix

after

Cost of quality

Starbursting

What-if analysis

Different point of view

Presentation

➥ Select and define problem or opportunity

 Identify and analyze causes or potential change

➥ Develop and plan possible solutions or change

➥ Implement and evaluate solution or change

 Measure and report solution or change results

 Recognize and reward team efforts

Research/statistics

Creativity/innovation

Engineering

Project management

Manufacturing

2 Marketing/sales

3 Administration/documentation

 Servicing/support

 Customer/quality metrics

1 Change management

- When calculating costs, use actual labor and material rates. Remember, your conclusions are only as good as the data they are based on!
- Costs-benefit ratio = Benefits ÷ Costs

The team first identifies the various costs involved for the activities to be completed within the options to be evaluated.

Costing data are collected from some qualified source. These data cover labor rates, material costs, transportation, expenses, fees, and other charges. See example *Provide Statistical Process Control (SPC) Training*.

The team next discusses the various options, selects those that show the greatest potential, and performs the calculations of total costs.

Options are costed out and compared using a benefits/cost ratio as shown in the example.

A final decision is made and the cost-benefit analysis data are saved for the development of a proposal or action plan.

Provide Statistical Process Control (SPC) Training

Date: xx/xx/xx

Option A: Engage external trainer to conduct (6) 2-day SPC workshops for 100 employees		Option B: Prepare internal trainer to conduct the 2-day SPC workshops for 100 employees	
$ 2,250	Airfare (3 roundtrips, conduct 2 classes per trip)	$ 750	Airfare for company trainer to be cross-trained
1,560	Expenses (12 days × $130 per day)	700	Expenses (5 days workshop and research)
2,500	Materials ($25 per student)	3,000	Train-the-trainer charge
9,500	Tuition ($95 per student)	10,000	Master copy and repro rights
350	Shipping materials	1,080	Internal trainers' prep time ($45 per hr × 24 hrs)
120	Local reproduction	4,320	conduct (6) 2-day classes (labor $360 per day)
$16,280		1,200	repro of 100 training binders
		$21,050	

Benefit Estimate: Reduction of an estimated 25 hours of rework per week. Savings ($) = 25 hrs × 50 wks × $30/hr = $37,500 per year	
Notes: Tuition discounted to $95 per employee *Benefits/Cost ratio = 2.30* *Based on the higher benefit/cost ratio, this is the better option.*	*Notes: Labor rates fully loaded* *Benefits/Cost ratio = 1.78*

A countermeasures matrix documents a problem and identifies causes, solutions (countermeasures), and implementation priorities. Priority is established by team rating based on the importance or feasibility of recommended action items. This matrix provides input data for developing an action plan.

- To identify next steps in the problem-solving process.
- To document the team's findings and recommended actions.
- To prioritize required resources for process improvement implementation activities.

before

Idea grid

Cause and effect diagram (CED)

Problem analysis

Process analysis

Solution matrix

after

Cost-benefit analysis

What-if analysis

Resource requirements matrix

Project planning log

Action plan

	Select and define problem or opportunity
➥	Identify and analyze causes or potential change
➥	Develop and plan possible solutions or change
	Implement and evaluate solution or change
	Measure and report solution or change results
	Recognize and reward team efforts

- *Importance* rating scale: 1–5, 5 being the most important. This attribute can be substituted for feasibility, etc.
- Action priority: Highest team total is number 1 priority for implementation.

	Research/statistics
	Creativity/innovation
	Engineering
2	Project management
4	Manufacturing
	Marketing/sales
	Administration/documentation
3	Servicing/support
5	Customer/quality metrics
1	Change management

The team facilitator prepares, on a whiteboard or flip charts, a counter-measures matrix and reviews the requirements for completing the matrix. See example *Team Attrition Countermeasures*.

The participants engage in discussion to identify countermeasures and required action items to resolve the problem.

Next, the team rates the action items on the basis of importance or feasibility of implementation. A scale of 1–5 is used, 5 being the most important or feasible.

The facilitator tabulates the ratings and indicates action priorities on the matrix.

The matrix is dated and submitted for action planning.

Team Attrition Countermeasures

Problem: Teams Experience Increased Member Attrition					Date xx/xx/xx
Identified Causes	Proposed Countermeasures	Recommended Action Items	Participant Importance Rating[†]	Team Total	Action Priority
1. Lack of leadership	Rotate team leadership	Draw up schedule	3, 4, 1, 5, 4, 2, 4, 3	26	2
2. Lack of commitment	Check rewards and recognition	Revise policy	3, 5, 2, 1, 1, 4, 3, 4	23	3
3. Lack of participation	Obtain commitment	Participant selection	4, 3, 2, 2, 2, 1, 5, 2	21	4
4. Participant's workload	Balance schedule	Schedule by consensus	4, 5, 5, 3, 4, 3, 3, 5	32	1[‡]
5. Lack of progress	Provide training	Attend team training	2, 3, 1, 1, 2, 3, 4, 1	17	5

Notes: [†]*Importance scale 1–5, 5 being most important*
    [‡]*Highest priority for taking action*

Pioneered by C. C. Crawford, the Crawford Slip method is a structured approach used to collect a large number of ideas from a group. A facilitator first displays a problem statement or issue, then participants generate ideas and write them on a provided slip of paper or 3 × 5 index card. Since this is an anonymous process, more candid and creative ideas result.

- To generate anonymously ideas on how to deal with a sensitive issue or topic.
- To identify real and perceived problem areas in the organization.
- To collect ideas for process, product, or service improvement.
- To produce potential problem-solving solutions.

before

Buzz group

Weighted voting

Sticking dots

Checklist

Interview technique

after

Value analysis

Criteria filtering

Mutivoting

Consensus decision making

Nominal group technique (NGT)

➠ Select and define problem or opportunity	Research/statistics
➠ Identify and analyze causes or potential change	**1** Creativity/innovation
➠ Develop and plan possible solutions or change	Engineering
Implement and evaluate solution or change	**4** Project management
Measure and report solution or change results	Manufacturing
Recognize and reward team efforts	**2** Marketing/sales
	Administration/documentation
	Servicing/support
	Customer/quality metrics
	3 Change management

- The Crawford Slip method of brainstorming:

Advantages

- Any size group (small to large).
- Any seating arrangement.
- Broader participation (includes less expressive participants).
- Large quantity of ideas.
- Good for sensitive topics since participants' input is anonymous, without team interaction.
- Easier process of sorting ideas.

Disadvantages

- Overall slow process.
- Cannot build on other ideas (piggybacking).
- Written ideas may not be legible or clear.
- Written ideas may be stated as a word when they require a lengthy paragraph.

A facilitator explains the procedure to the team (or large group) and hands out slips of paper or 3 × 5 index cards to each participant.

A flip chart with a written problem statement or an issue to be brainstormed is displayed to the team.

Participants respond by writing their ideas on the provided papers, one idea per paper or card, and then pass them to the facilitator. See example *Perceived Organizational Problems*.

This process continues for approximately 25 minutes, and the rest of the additional ideas are handed to the facilitator.

If this process was completed with a relatively small team of 6–12 participants, ideas can now be sorted by frequency and category. Ideas from a large group would require sorting and analysis at a later date.

Perceived Organizational Problems

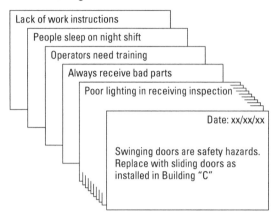

Lack of work instructions
People sleep on night shift
Operators need training
Always receive bad parts
Poor lighting in receiving inspection

Date: xx/xx/xx

Swinging doors are safety hazards.
Replace with sliding doors as
installed in Building "C"

Developed by Leo Moore, the creativity assessment technique is applied as a sorting and rating process to a long list of brainstormed ideas. It should help teams with evaluation and categorization by selecting ideas on the basis of predetermined criteria.

- To categorize a list of generated ideas using team-established criteria.
- To evaluate and sort ideas into groups.
- To screen ideas or solutions considered for implementation.

before

Brainstorming

Round robin brainstorming

Brainwriting pool

Pin cards technique

Criteria filtering

after

Consensus decision making

Cluster analysis

Solution matrix

Selection matrix

Presentation

➡ Select and define problem or opportunity

➡ Identify and analyze causes or potential change

➡ Develop and plan possible solutions or change

Implement and evaluate solution or change

Measure and report solution or change results

Recognize and reward team efforts

Research/statistics

1 Creativity/innovation

2 Engineering

Project management

Manufacturing

Marketing/sales

Administration/documentation

3 Servicing/support

Customer/quality metrics

4 Change management

- The categorization scheme is often dependent on the type of data and the situation encountered.
  - Ideas can be categorized into levels of difficulty using Roman numerals for designating levels, such as:

    I = easy to do; II = hard to do; III = most difficult to do
  - Other criteria can be used to determine value, importance, cost, and resources required:

    I = few resources required; II = considerable resources required;

    III = a great many resources required.

The team's facilitator displays flip charts of previously brainstormed ideas. See example *Improve Quality*.

The participants establish the criteria for assessment. In this example, the criteria are easy to do, hard to do, and most difficult to do.

The facilitator writes the respective category headings on three flip charts, and participants evaluate and organize ideas into the three categories as shown in this example.

After all ideas have been categorized, the three resulting categories I–III are reviewed and dated.

Lastly, the team presents the three idea categories to upper management for further evaluation and action.

Improve Quality

Flip chart 1

Session 8/19/xx

Topic: Improve Quality

- More training
- Short due dates
- Inexperience
- No communication
- Missing info
- What is a defect?
- Constant changes
- No inspections
- Too much work
- Many interruptions
- Group conflict
- Incorrect testing

Flip chart 2

Session 8/19/xx

- Lack of proper tools
- Low job satisfaction
- Specifications unclear
- Lack of instructions
- Low morale, motivation
- Lack of metrics
- Involve customers
- Stressful work
- Equipment problems
- Lack of data
- Need problem-solving teams
- No procedures

End of Ideas

I – Easy to Do

- Missing info
- No inspections
- Too much work
- Many interruptions
- Incorrect testing
- Lack of proper tools
- Specifications unclear
- Equipment problems

II – Hard to Do

- More training
- Inexperience
- No communications
- What is a defect?
- Constant changes
- Lack of instructions
- Lack of metrics
- Stressful work
- Lack of data
- Need PS teams
- No procedures

III – Most Difficult to Do

- Short due dates
- Group conflict
- Low job satisfaction
- Low morale, motivation
- Involve customers

The criteria filtering technique is a screening methodology that uses certain criteria to sort identified problem areas into two categories, one of *easy-to-do* "low hanging fruit activities" requiring relatively few resources, and the other of *hard-to-do* activities that require a more extensive problem-solving approach and, therefore, more resources to solve a problem.

- To prioritize team activities on the basis of high impact—low resource requirements.
- To identify quick fix opportunities.
- To brainstorm selection criteria to be used as a filter to screen out *easy-to-do* problem-solving activities.

before

Criteria rating form

Consensus decision making

Activity analysis

Countermeasures matrix

Project prioritization matrix

after

Run-it-by

What-if analysis

Five whys

Value analysis

Cycle time flowchart

➡ Select and define problem or opportunity

➡ Identify and analyze causes or potential change

➡ Develop and plan possible solutions or change

➡ Implement and evaluate solution or change

   Measure and report solution or change results

   Recognize and reward team efforts

- The selection criteria should be determined by team consensus and should cover resource requirements such as time, cost, expertise, quantity, quality, legal, safety, and approval authorization levels.

   Research/statistics

   Creativity/innovation

   Engineering

2 Project management

4 Manufacturing

   Marketing/sales

   Administration/documentation

3 Servicing/support

   Customer/quality metrics

1 Change management

As a first step, the team brainstorms appropriate criteria that will screen and sort potential problem-solving or improvement opportunities into two categories, *easy-to-do* and *hard-to-do*.

The established criteria is displayed on a flip chart alongside a recommended list of problem-solving or process-improvement opportunities.

Using the criteria as a filter, the team screens every item on the list by answering the questions (criteria) as seen in the example.

Lastly, a new list of easy-to-do items is compiled, dated, and assigned for action.

Training Improvement Opportunities
(Activity #6 – Revise Training Registration Form)

Criteria (Filter)		Date: xx/xx/xx
Estimated hours ($\leq$ 160)	Yes ✓	No ___
Cost to implement ($\leq$ $500)	Yes ✓	No ___
Adverse impact?	Yes ___	No ✓
Legal involved?	Yes ___	No ✓
Safety involved?	Yes ___	No ✓
Support organizational goals?	Yes ✓	No ___
Outside expertise required?	Yes ___	No ✓
Estimated schedule ($\leq$ 3 months)	Yes ✓	No ___

Note: This activity is categorized as "easy to do."

Team participants use critical dialogue to engage in an open and meaningful flow of thought, exploring and giving serious attention to surfaced ideas. It also provides for common understanding and agreement on solutions to problems or opportunities for improvement. Additionally, critical dialogue gives an opportunity for involving all team participants in the sharing of information and the receiving of valuable feedback.

- To openly explore the issues and receive constructive feedback during a deep and meaningful sharing of thoughts or ideas on an issue.
- To involve all team participants in a natural flow of conversation leading to a common understanding of the issue or problem at hand.
- To consider ideas or a variety of possible decisions.

before

Circles of knowledge

Buzz group

Run-it-by

Different point of view

Fishbowls

after

Consensus decision making

Starbursting

What-if analysis

Barriers-and-aids analysis

Force field analysis (FFA)

➡ Select and define problem or opportunity

➡ Identify and analyze causes or potential change

➡ Develop and plan possible solutions or change

Implement and evaluate solution or change

Measure and report solution or change results

Recognize and reward team efforts

Research/statistics

1   Creativity/innovation

Engineering

2   Project management

Manufacturing

Marketing/sales

Administration/documentation

Servicing/support

4   Customer/quality metrics

3   Change management

- Team facilitators must be careful whenever controversial issues are addressed. Conducting a dialogue about certain issues may result in debating the issues!

The practice of critical dialogue requires an experienced facilitator. The team or group of people seeks out someone who has experience in group dynamics and conflict resolution.

The facilitator arranges a table and chairs to form a circle to establish a sense of equality among participants and to ensure that everyone can see and hear one another.

Next, the facilitator introduces the general concept of critical dialogue, sets a time limit for the session, and asks participants to recall a good, in-depth conversation between equals.

Participants are asked to share their experience and state what characteristics of that conversation made it a good, effective exchange of thoughts.

The facilitator records these characteristics on the flip chart and asks all participants to reflect on the them.

Skillfully, the facilitator introduces a topic to the participants and allows participants to engage in critical dialogue. See example *Team Recognition and Reward*.

From time to time, the facilitator may find it necessary to intervene in order to clarify process steps or assist in reducing confusion or frustration.

Lastly, the facilitator closes the session by asking participants for their ideas or supporting comments and summarizes these on a flip chart for later reference.

Team Recognition and Reward

Date: xx/xx/xx

The critical incident process is recommended when some issue or aspect of a case under study needs to emphasized or deserves special attention. The critical incident is discussed and on-the-spot comparisons to other real life situations are made.

- To relate critical incidents or lessons learned to one's own experience.
- To learn what has worked for others.
- To analyze cases for the purpose of discovering approaches that will prevent future problems.

before

Data collection strategy

Information needs analysis

Interview technique

Buzz group

Case study

after

Critical dialogue

Starbursting

Different point of view

Circles of knowledge

Panel debate

➥ Select and define problem or opportunity

➥ Identify and analyze causes or potential change

➥ Develop and plan possible solutions or change

   Implement and evaluate solution or change

   Measure and report solution or change results

   Recognize and reward team efforts

- The Critical Incident method can be used to focus on some critical aspect of a case when performing a case study.

1	Research/statistics
	Creativity/innovation
	Engineering
	Project management
	Manufacturing
2	Marketing/sales
	Administration/documentation
	Servicing/support
	Customer/quality metrics
3	Change management

The team receives a handout to be read that describes a success story, a missed opportunity, or a changed project outcome. See example *Studying the Importance of Customer Satisfaction*.

After all participants have familiarized themselves with the case, an outline of the most important points made is drawn on a whiteboard or flip charts. Limit the list to four or five items for discussion.

The critical incident is identified and analyzed by the participants.

Last, participants discuss lessons learned and how this analysis can best benefit them.

Studying the Importance of Customer Satisfaction

"Moments of Truth"
The only thing that counts is a satisfied customer.   —Jan Carlzon, SAS Jan Carlzon, president of Scandinavian Airlines System (SAS), feels that employees have 50 million chances every year, the *Moments of Truth,* to demonstrate to the traveling customer a personal commitment to achieve complete customer satisfaction through their interaction with the customer every time. **Question:** What are your moments of truth?

The customer acquisition-defection matrix is a very useful tool to gauge customer brand loyalty, to track competitors' market share, and to identify trends in customer needs, expectations, or behavior.

- To identify customer product purchase flows among different product brand names in comparison to the company's existing market share.
- To plot market share data of previous product purchase percentage to new product purchase percentage.
- To measure percent change in product demand; to track customer defection rates.
- To develop a benchmarking plan for targeting the strongest competitors.

before

Data collection strategy

Measurement matrix

Interview technique

Surveying

Questionnaires

after

Customer satisfaction analysis (CSA)

Customer-first-questions (CFQ)

Benchmarking

Failure mode effect analysis

Countermeasures matrix

➡ Select and define problem or opportunity

➡ Identify and analyze causes or potential change

   Develop and plan possible solutions or change

➡ Implement and evaluate solution or change

➡ Measure and report solution or change results

   Recognize and reward team efforts

4 Research/statistics
   Creativity/innovation
5 Engineering
   Project management
   Manufacturing
3 Marketing/sales
   Administration/documentation
   Servicing/support
1 Customer/quality metrics
2 Change management

- The data collection process should include the search and verification of secondary data, such as market share studies, company annual reports, trendlines, or any other summarized customer behavior information.

The first step requires an extensive and highly focused data collection on the product under analysis. Market share data, customer buying behavior, and market/technology trends need to be examined.

Product-specific data such as previous ownership percentage, repurchase percentage, and competitors' gain/loss percentages are collected.

A customer acquisition-defection matrix is constructed and percentages listed in the appropriate squares associated with particular brand names. See example *Purchase of Home Water Heaters*.

– Brand A is this company's location on the matrix. It shows that 42 percent of Brand A customers purchased another Brand A home water heater from this company, 10 percent purchased Brand B, 7 percent purchased Brand C, etc.

– Referring to Brand B on the matrix, 45 percent of all Brand B heater customers repurchased a Brand B heater, 9 percent purchased a Brand A heater, 8 percent purchased a Brand F heater, and so on.

Next, total all row percentages for each brand and indicate this total in the percentage column.

Lastly, check all plotted data and calculations, and date the matrix.

Purchase of Home Water Heaters

Date: xx/xx/xx		Brand A	Brand B	Brand C	Brand D	Brand E	Brand F	Brand G	Brand H	%	
Customer Aquisition/Defection											
Old heater unit %	Brand A	42	10	–	3	1	12	4	7	79	All brands total %
	Brand B	9	45	1	3	–	8	2	6	74	
	Brand C	4	4	16	4	–	5	1	6	40	
	Brand D	3	2	–	28	1	5	2	4	45	
	Brand E	6	8	1	1	13	6	–	2	37	
	Brand F	7	6	–	3	–	61	4	7	88	
	Brand G	3	5	1	–	–	6	26	2	43	
	Brand H	2	3	–	–	–	4	3	35	47	
New heater unit %										*	

* Total percentages will not equal 100% due to missing data for other brands

The customer needs table helps integrated product development teams (IPDT) translate customer needs and wants into required designs that may meet customer expectations prior to the potential development of new products or service development.

- To identify customer needs and wants in a new product or service.
- To translate voice of the customer information into design requirements.
- To reduce the amount of potential engineering change orders (ECO).

before

Surveying

Interview technique

Focus group

Demographic analysis

Buzz group

after

Customer-first-questions (CFQ)

Value analysis

Factor analysis

Conjoint analysis

Customer satisfaction analysis (CSA)

➡ Select and define problem or opportunity

➡ Identify and analyze causes or potential change

➡ Develop and plan possible solutions or change

  Implement and evaluate solution or change

  Measure and report solution or change results

  Recognize and reward team efforts

	Research/statistics
	Creativity/innovation
4	Engineering
	Project management
	Manufacturing
1	Marketing/sales
	Administration/documentation
2	Servicing/support
3	Customer/quality metrics
	Change management

- Data collection methods: Customer surveys, interviews, focus groups, benchmarks, similar product data, summarized studies, product demos, and others.
- This is a powerful resource tool, ideally used with quality function deployment (QFD).

An integrated product development team (IDPT) selects a methodology of collecting information of a proposed product or service. See example *Development of a Portable Coffee Maker.*

Potential customers are randomly selected and questioned on the various listed characteristics and factors shown in the customer needs table.

All customer response data is organized and placed into the customer needs table as shown in this example.

The table is reviewed by the team, dated, and presented to a QFD team or given directly to the process owners throughout the organization.

Development of a Portable Coffeemaker

#	Customer Demographics	Customer Needs/Wants	Product / Service Usage					Date xx/xx/xx
			Who	What	When	Where	How
1	F, 25, secretary	Coffee anytime	Evening student	Make coffee	Evening classes	Classrooms	One cup at a time
2	M, 45, construction worker	Coffee at construction site	Construction worker	Coffee or hot water	All day	Construction sites	General breaks
3							
4							
5							

#	Expected Quality	Reworded Needs/Wants	Reliability	Function/ Ease of Use	Safety	Cost	Special Requests
1	*Hot* coffee	Instant operation	Works every time	Plug in or battery-operated	No burns	Below $80	Ready timer
2	Does not leak	Placed anywhere	Long battery operation	Easy to clean	No electrical shorts	Range $30 to $50	No rust
3							
4							
5							

A customer satisfaction analysis (CSA) is a highly structured survey approach to determine and measure customer satisfaction levels in terms of experienced quality, perceived value, and the importance placed on characteristics of provided products and services.

- To compare customer satisfaction ratings for the organization's products or services to the competitor's products or services.
- To measure customer satisfaction levels for products and services.
- To gather customer information for the purpose of improving products or services.
- To identify problem areas in product or service quality.

before

House of quality

Customer-first-questions (CFQ)

Interview technique

Weighted voting

Nominal group technique (NGT)

after

Consensus decision making

Starbursting

Different point of view

Run-it-by

Multiple rating matrix

➥ Select and define problem or opportunity

➥ Identify and analyze causes or potential change

➥ Develop and plan possible solutions or change

Implement and evaluate solution or change

Measure and report solution or change results

Recognize and reward team efforts

	Research/statistics
	Creativity/innovation
	Engineering
	Project management
	Manufacturing
3	Marketing/sales
	Administration/documentation
4	Servicing/support
1	Customer/quality metrics
2	Change management

- Relative weight points must total 20 and be distributed across listed customer satisfaction product/service characteristics.
- Perceived value/quality ratings are assigned a value from 1 to 5. A rating of 1 = poor; 2 = fair; 3 = good; 4 = very good; and 5 = excellent.
- The lowest rating total is 20 (all 20 relative weight points × value/quality ratings of 1); the highest rating total is 100 (all 20 relative weight points × value/quality ratings of 5).

Customer feedback data is examined to identify problem areas for certain products or services.

The team develops a customer profile for the product or service under analysis.

Next, customer satisfaction characteristics of the product or service are identified and placed on flip chart.

The team facilitator draws a customer satisfaction matrix on a flip chart and inserts all characteristics. See example *Lawnmower Repair Service*.

The team then discusses the importance of each characteristic and assigns a relative weight to it.

Next, consensus is reached on a value/quality rating for each characteristic.

Finally, the facilitator calculates weighted ratings for each characteristic and arrives at a rating total.

The team checks all calculations; the customer satisfaction matrix is dated and given to the process owners for consideration and action.

Lawnmower Repair Service

Date xx/xx/xx

	Customer Satisfaction Characteristics	Relative Weight	×	Value / Quality Rating	=	Weighted Rating
1	Phone service	1	×	1	=	1
2	Parts in stock	1	×	2	=	2
3	Wait time	2	×	3	=	6
4	Cost	4	×	5	=	20
5	Staff expertise	2	×	4	=	8
6	Warranty	3	×	2	=	6
7	Repair quality	7	×	5	=	35
8			×		=	
9			×		=	
10			×		=	
					Rating total:	**78**

Notes: Distribute 20 relative weight points across listed customer satisfaction characteristics
Assign value / quality rating of 1–5
Minimum rating total = 20, maximum rating total = 100

First introduced by Hewlett-Packard, the customer-first questions tool is used by integrated product development teams (IPDT) to predict a customer's reaction to a new product or service. Early data collection in the customer-research process is quite difficult because customers often cannot state their needs; they may not know enough about the product/service to assist, or they simply do not recognize existing gaps or problems. Data collection methodology is helpful as a first step in reducing the risk involved in anticipating customer needs and wants.

- To identify customer needs and wants and input this data into the product innovation process.
- To respond to CFQ with additional data, product features that, from the customers point of view, are, as categorized in the matrix, presumed, expected, or delighted.
- To reduce the risk of predicting what exactly the customers expectations are.
- To reduce the number of product design changes during the development process.

before

Data collection strategy

Benchmarking

Thematic content analysis

Customer needs table

Morphological analysis

after

Conjoint analysis

House of quality

Focus group

Surveying

Customer satisfaction analysis (CSA)

Select and define problem or opportunity	**1** Research/statistics
➥ Identify and analyze causes or potential change	**4** Creativity/innovation
➥ Develop and plan possible solutions or change	Engineering
Implement and evaluate solution or change	Project management
Measure and report solution or change results	Manufacturing
Recognize and reward team efforts	**3** Marketing/sales
	Administration/documentation
	Servicing/support
	2 Customer/quality metrics
	Change management

- A response to CFQ can come from two approaches:
  1. Broad customer research utilizing various data collection tools for customer input.
  2. Less customer research, but an increased emphasis on a more flexible, robust design, with possible misuse of product considerations designed into the product to lessen the potential for ongoing engineering changes.
- The CFQ methodology described has been adapted, modified, and used by many companies. The process has been, in this example, expanded to include the Kano model (see Step 5) as well.

The first step requires an integrated product development team to brainstorm possible data-collection methodologies and to develop instrumentation to answer these questions:

- What customer problems does our product/service solve that our competitors do not?

- What benefits does our product/service offer that our competitors do not?

- What motivates the customer to purchase our product/service over that of our competitors?

Next, a CFQ matrix is created with the above questions placed in the top half of the matrix. See example *CFQ Matrix for a Bicycle*.

Data is collected utilizing methodologies such as benchmarking, survey, focus group, quality function deployment (QFD), or customer satisfaction analysis (CSA).

A careful check of data is completed and responses to CFQ questions are formulated. The responses are then recorded in the bottom half of the matrix.

Now apply the Kano model. To do this, the team assumes the role of the customer and categorizes the product's/service's features as belonging to any of the categories listed below. (For our purposes, the "model" is not a graph or other visual; it is merely a way to categorize and label information for easy reference.) After the features have been identified this way, label them on the matrix by placing a (P), (E), or (D) in the columns to the right of the features.

(P) Presumed—Features customers assume the product/service will have.

(E) Expected—Features customers expect such a new product/service to have.

(D) Delighted—Features customers do not expect. These are what really "sell" the customer.

A program check is necessary at this stage. If a lack of data is obvious, more research needs to be done.

Note: The integrated product development team may choose to make design changes to the product or service after completing this exercise. Remember that such changes will be small in comparison to the benefits derived from increased customer satisfaction.

CFQ Matrix for a Bicycle

Date: xx/xx/xx

CFQ #1 **Problems**	CFQ #2 **Benefits**	CFQ #3 **Motivational Factors**
What customer problems does our product/service solve that our competitors don't?	What benefits does our product/service offer that our competitors don't?	What motivates the customer to purchase our product/ service over our competition?
IPD Team Responses to the CFQ		

• Comfortable seat (E)*
• Tires don't go flat (D)
• Chain doesn't (P)
  disengage
• Less maintenance (E)
 	
↓
	• Variety of colors (P)
	• Converts to stationary (D)
	  bike
	• Travel air pump (E)
	• Multiple gears (P)
	
	↓
		• Low cost (E)
		• Built-in radio (D)
		• Increased safety (E)
		• Better warranty (P)
		
		↓

* Applied Kano identification = (P), (E), or (D)

A cycle time flowchart accounts for all activities and time required from the start point to the stop point of a process. The intent of using this tool is to identify non-value-adding activities, bottlenecks, excessive loops, approvals, and delays. The flowchart is constructed by a team that owns the process. Participants have a good understanding of the activities and therefore are best suited to collectively produce the cycle time of the overall process.

- To identify non-value-adding activities and excessive delay time in a process.
- To capture the "as is" process flow in order to have better team understanding of the process for further problem-solving efforts.
- To draw a detailed flowchart for the purpose of completing redesign, problem resolution, and cycle time reduction activities.

before

Process mapping

Problem specification

Pareto chart

Potential problem analysis (PPA)

Systems analysis diagram

after

Process analysis

Problem analysis

Activity analysis

What-if analysis

Force field analysis (FFA)

➡ Select and define problem or opportunity
➡ Identify and analyze causes or potential change
  Develop and plan possible solutions or change
  Implement and evaluate solution or change
  Measure and report solution or change results
  Recognize and reward team efforts

  Research/statistics
  Creativity/innovation
  Engineering
2 Project management
3 Manufacturing
  Marketing/sales
  Administration/documentation
4 Servicing/support
  Customer/quality metrics
1 Change management

Symbols and scale:

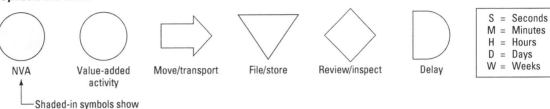

						S	=	Seconds
NVA	Value-added activity	Move/transport	File/store	Review/inspect	Delay	M	=	Minutes
						H	=	Hours
						D	=	Days
						W	=	Weeks

└─ Shaded-in symbols show non-value-added activities

Connectors example:

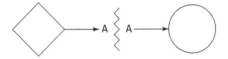

When stating an activity's cycle time, indicate (A) for *actual time*, (E) for *estimated time*.

The team facilitator assembles a team that consists of representatives (process owners) of the process to be the subject of the cycle time flowchart. A whiteboard is prepared to draft out the flowchart.

The team determines the start and stop points of the process. The appropriate scale of time to be used is also determined.

Using team-provided input, the team facilitator, using flowchart symbols, sequentially connects all activities in the process, showing sequence number, what is being done, who does it, and how much time is used to complete each activity. Time is stated as actual (A) or estimated (E). See example *Department Budgeting Process*.

Next, the team checks the charts for completeness, correct task sequence, and task-identifying information.

Finally, the completed cycle time flowchart on the whiteboard is copied onto the flowchart template and the information is summarized. The chart is dated and kept for cycle time reduction work.

Department Budgeting Process

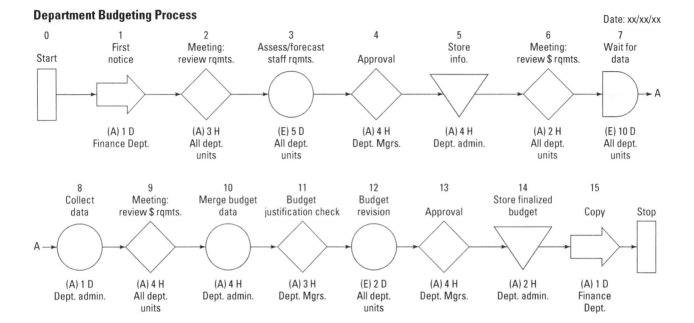

0	1	2	3	4	5	6	7
Start	First notice	Meeting: review rqmts.	Assess/forecast staff rqmts.	Approval	Store info.	Meeting: review $ rqmts.	Wait for data
	(A) 1 D Finance Dept.	(A) 3 H All dept. units	(E) 5 D All dept. units	(A) 4 H Dept. Mgrs.	(A) 4 H Dept. admin.	(A) 2 H All dept. units	(E) 10 D All dept. units

8	9	10	11	12	13	14	15
Collect data	Meeting: review $ rqmts.	Merge budget data	Budget justification check	Budget revision	Approval	Store finalized budget	Copy / Stop
(A) 1 D Dept. admin.	(A) 4 H All dept. units	(A) 4 H Dept. admin.	(A) 3 H Dept. Mgrs.	(E) 2 D All dept. units	(A) 4 H Dept. Mgrs.	(A) 2 H Dept. admin.	(A) 1 D Finance Dept.

Cycle Time Flowchart for Department Budgeting Process

Seq. no.	Cycle time Est.	Cycle time Act.	Symbol	Activity description
1		8	◯ ◇ ⇨ D ▽	First notice
2		3	◯ ◇ ⇨ D ▽	Meeting: review rqmts.
3	40		◯ ◇ ⇨ D ▽	Assess/forecast staff rqmts.
4		4	◯ ◇ ⇨ D ▽	Approval
5		4	◯ ◇ ⇨ D ▽	Store info
6		2	◯ ◇ ⇨ D ▽	Meeting: review dollar rqmts.
7	80		◯ ◇ ⇨ D ▽	Wait for data
8		8	◯ ◇ ⇨ D ▽	Collect data
9		4	◯ ◇ ⇨ D ▽	Meeting: review dollar rqmts.
10		4	◯ ◇ ⇨ D ▽	Merge budget data
11		3	◯ ◇ ⇨ D ▽	Budget justification check
12	16		◯ ◇ ⇨ D ▽	Budget revision
13		4	◯ ◇ ⇨ D ▽	Approval
14		2	◯ ◇ ⇨ D ▽	Store finalized budget
15		8	◯ ◇ ⇨ D ▽	Copy
16	–	–	◯ ◇ ⇨ D ▽	Stop
17			◯ ◇ ⇨ D ▽	
18			◯ ◇ ⇨ D ▽	
19			◯ ◇ ⇨ D ▽	
20			◯ ◇ ⇨ D ▽	
21			◯ ◇ ⇨ D ▽	
22			◯ ◇ ⇨ D ▽	
23			◯ ◇ ⇨ D ▽	
24			◯ ◇ ⇨ D ▽	
25			◯ ◇ ⇨ D ▽	
26			◯ ◇ ⇨ D ▽	
27			◯ ◇ ⇨ D ▽	
28			◯ ◇ ⇨ D ▽	
29			◯ ◇ ⇨ D ▽	
30			◯ ◇ ⇨ D ▽	

	Est.	Act.	Symbol	
Value added / Non-value added	56	12	◯ Activity	Time scale: ☐ Seconds
		20	◇ Review/inspect	☐ Minutes
		16	⇨ Move/transport	[X] Hours
	80		D Delay	☐ Days
		6	▽ File/store	☐ Weeks
◯◯	136	54	Total time: 190 hours	Date: xx/xx/xx

The data collection strategy tool provides an approach for collecting data on any process prior to, during, or after an intervention has taken place. It considers data type requirements and sampling and evaluation methods, and it organizes and describes data in statistical terms.

- To decide on a course of action on the basis of data collected.
- To prioritize problems to be worked on.
- To verify process capability.
- To monitor process improvement.

before

Brainstorming

Consensus decision making

Questionnaires

Gap analysis

Checklist

after

Stratification

Control chart

Polygon overlay

Multivarible chart

Pareto chart

➡ Select and define problem or opportunity
➡ Identify and analyze causes or potential change
   Develop and plan possible solutions or change
   Implement and evaluate solution or change
➡ Measure and report solution or change results
   Recognize and reward team efforts

1	Research/statistics
	Creativity/innovation
	Engineering
5	Project management
6	Manufacturing
4	Marketing/sales
	Administration/documentation
7	Servicing/support
2	Customer/quality metrics
3	Change management

- A data collection strategy form can be developed to meet any data collection need. Refer to statistics information sources for sample size determination, sampling methods, and descriptive and inferential test calculations.

The team determines what data needs to be collected to assist in problem specification, confirm defect rates, or measure specific performance expectations. See example *Operator Training Results at Facility X*.

The team decides on the method and location of the data to be collected. The data collection strategy form is completed as shown in the example.

A data collection assignment is given to a team participant or someone familiar with the process.

After the data have been collected, they are organized and summarized. Basic groups will display certain data and statistical treatment will provide additional information for consideration by the team.

Operator Training at Facility X

Data Collection Stategy			
Measurement *Operator training results at facility X*			
Supports a unit performance objective		Yes _✓_	No ____
Data collection method	*Survey—Primary data questionnaire, operator files, HR records*		
Data source(s)	*Population: all operators—A, B, and C shift*		
Sampling method	*Stratified (ensures representativeness)*		
Data types/scales	*Interval and nominal (demographics)*		
Data display methods	*Histogram, pie chart, FD tables and respondent profile*		
Statistical test(s)	*Mean, medium, range, variance, standard deviation*		
Measuring method	*10/1/96 and 10/1/97—verify operator records*		
Secondary data	*World class organizations' training efforts*		
Other	*Trg. hrs., cost/operator, OJT vs. formal hours, % of productive time*		
Requirements	**Who will**	**Initials**	**Date**
✓ Demographics	Measure (1)	*WJM*	*xx/xx/xx*
✓ Frequency	Collect data (2)	*WJM*	*xx/xx/xx*
✓ Time periods	Analyze data (3)	*WJM*	*xx/xx/xx*
✓ Percentage	Write report (4)	*SJJ*	*xx/xx/xx*
✓ Amount	Follow-up (5)	*WJM*	*xx/xx/xx*
Rate			
✓ Duration			
Other *Benchmarking data*			

The decision process flowchart is a decision-making tool that greatly assists managers and teams in arriving at better decisions. Additionally, possible alternatives are branched in a logical path that helps to consider the potential outcomes of decisions made.

- To use a logical approach in the search for a best course or action.
- To improve the decision-making process.
- To identify critical path or high priority.

before

Influence diagram

Decision tree diagram

Information needs analysis

Process mapping

Consensus decision making

after

Activity analysis

Action plan

Cost of quality

Cost-benefit analysis

Potential problem analysis (PPA)

➥ Select and define problem or opportunity

➥ Identify and analyze causes or potential change

➥ Develop and plan possible solutions or change

　Implement and evaluate solution or change

　Measure and report solution or change results

　Recognize and reward team efforts

- Construct the flowchart so that each decision fork presents a Yes/No (mutually exclusive) option.
- Decision outcomes may reflect personal or team bias.
- Recommendation to avoid complexity: No more than five decision points.

1	Research/statistics
	Creativity/innovation
2	Engineering
3	Project management
	Manufacturing
	Marketing/sales
	Administration/documentation
	Servicing/support
	Customer/quality metrics
4	Change management

First, the team participants discuss the application of this tool to ensure that everyone understands the process involved.

The team decides on the issue, topic, or problem to be flowcharted. See example *Should Engineering Assistants Attend Marketing Workshops?*

Next, a list of questions is developed to serve as headings for the decision points of the various "logical flow" branches.

A whiteboard is used to flowchart. At this point some revisions of the questions may be necessary.

Upon completion of the flowchart, possible decisions are surfaced by the team through the analysis of every path using the flowchart, as shown in the example.

Finally, the completed decision process flowchart is reviewed and dated.

Should Engineering Assistants Attend Marketing Workshops?

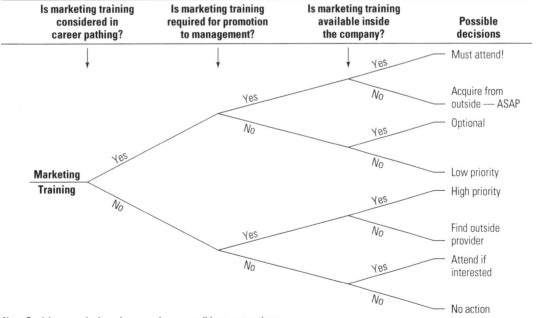

Note: Decisions may be based on experience, conditions, perceptions.

A decision tree diagram displays the outcomes or expected values of several possible alternatives and the likelihood, expressed as percent probability, of their happening. Restated, the diagram allows a manager or team to rationally analyze alternative branches and select the best possible choice of action or outcome (utility).

- To analyze all possible alternatives in a decision situation.
- To assist the decision-making process.
- To decide on a course of action by considering outcomes and probabilities in the analysis.

<table>
<tr><td>➥ Select and define problem or opportunity</td><td></td><td>Research/statistics</td></tr>
<tr><td>➥ Identify and analyze causes or potential change</td><td></td><td>Creativity/innovation</td></tr>
<tr><td>➥ Develop and plan possible solutions or change</td><td>4</td><td>Engineering</td></tr>
<tr><td>Implement and evaluate solution or change</td><td>1</td><td>Project management</td></tr>
<tr><td>Measure and report solution or change results</td><td></td><td>Manufacturing</td></tr>
<tr><td>Recognize and reward team efforts</td><td></td><td>Marketing/sales</td></tr>
<tr><td></td><td></td><td>Administration/documentation</td></tr>
<tr><td></td><td></td><td>Servicing/support</td></tr>
<tr><td></td><td>3</td><td>Customer/quality metrics</td></tr>
<tr><td></td><td>2</td><td>Change management</td></tr>
</table>

before

Tree diagram

Consensus decision making

Influence diagram

Relationship map

Activity analysis

after

Action plan

Opportunity analysis

Potential problem analysis (PPA)

What-if analysis

Risk space analysis

Decision Tree Diagram Definitions and Symbols:

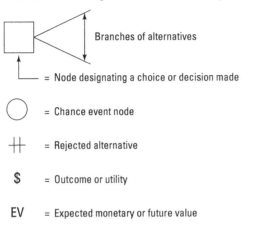

= Node designating a choice or decision made

◯ = Chance event node

╫ = Rejected alternative

$ = Outcome or utility

EV = Expected monetary or future value

P = Probability: A decimal number between .00 – 1.00

– Backward induction: The backward calculating of expected values (EV) needed to make a decision.
– Probability values (.00 - 1.00) are usually based on prior experience or historical data.
– It is recommended that the reader refer to any text on statistics for additional background information on probability and decision trees.

As a first step, the following information must be collected by the researcher in order to formulate a decision strategy for a particular concern, issue, or problem:

– A clearly defined concern, issue, or problem statement.
– The number and description of possible alternatives.
– The percent chance (probability) for each particular event (branch).
– The projected outcome (utility) for each possible branch. This is often based on historical data or experience.

See example *Should Human Resources Provide Statistical Process Control (SPC) Training?*

Once all data has been collected, a decision tree diagram is drawn, showing all alternatives and chance event branches.

Next, outcomes and probabilities values are placed next to each branch. In this example, dollar *outcomes* were forecasted revenues from operation supervisors to pay for their employees' training charges. *Probabilities* were based on the results of a student survey to check their interest in attending SPC training (F = for, A = against attending). The alternatives for supervisors (yes, no, or uncertain) were the normal choices supervisors had in managing their training budget.

The backward induction process calculations are estimated monetary values (EV) for nodes numbers 1–3. Calculations in this example are shown in the table associated with the decision tree.

On the basis of the calculations, node number 1, the alternative that reflects supervisory support for the SPC training, is considered the first choice. It also allows the HR training department to recapture training expenses for developing and conducting this training for employees.

Alternatives number 2 and number 3 are marked ╫ to designate the risky and, therefore, rejected alternatives.

Should HR Provide Statistical Process Control (SPC) Training?   Date: xx/xx/xx

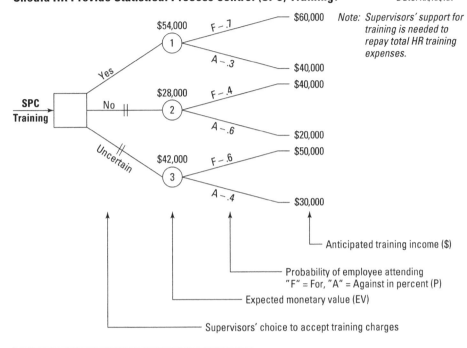

Note: Supervisors' support for training is needed to repay total HR training expenses.

— Anticipated training income ($)

— Probability of employee attending
  "F" = For, "A" = Against in percent (P)

— Expected monetary value (EV)

— Supervisors' choice to accept training charges

Node	P	$	P	$	EV
1	(.7)	(60,000)	+ (.3)	(40,000)	= $54,000
2	(.4)	(40,000)	+ (.6)	(20,000)	= $28,000
3	(.6)	(50,000)	+ (.4)	(30,000)	= $42,000

Note: The HR training department needs to receive a minimum of $40,000 to recapture development of training costs.

A defect map displays the location of defects and simplifies the process of data collection and repair. Problem locations are marked so that repair staff know where to look.

- To point to the location of defects or problems on rejected products.
- To mark or check off the locations of defects on an assembly diagram for the purpose of collecting frequency data of the various defects observed.

before

Data collection strategy

Checksheet

Checklist

Observation

Quality chart

after

Pareto chart

Problem specification

Failure mode effect analysis

Potential problem analysis (PPA)

Countermeasures matrix

➡ Select and define problem or opportunity
➡ Identify and analyze causes or potential change
    Develop and plan possible solutions or change
    Implement and evaluate solution or change
    Measure and report solution or change results
    Recognize and reward team efforts

- Use checksheets to record and summarize various defect map data.

	Research/statistics
	Creativity/innovation
4	Engineering
	Project management
1	Manufacturing
	Marketing/sales
3	Administration/documentation
	Servicing/support
2	Customer/quality metrics
	Change management

A defect map can be drawn for specific parts, assemblies, or complete units of product. Assembly drawings can also be used as defect maps. See example *Sub-Assembly No. 314—Location of Defects*.

During inspection of parts, assemblies, or units, the observed location of defects is marked on defect maps.

Defect types, locations, and frequencies are summarized on a checksheet as shown in the example.

Use this type of historical defect data to prepare a problem specification statement.

Provide notes on drawings, and date all documentation.

Sub-Assembly No. 314 – Location of Defects

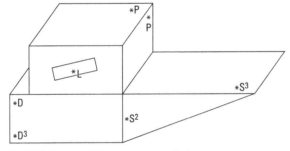

SA – 314	Date: xx/xx/xx
Defects	**Total**
D = Dent	4
S = Scratch	5
P = Paint	2
L = Label	1
Total	12

Note: D^3 stands for three dents in specified area.

The Delphi method is a very structured approach used to acquire written opinion or to receive feedback about a problem on detailed questionnaires sent to experts. Used by the Rand Corporation during the 1950s, the use of questionnaires prevents interpersonal interaction that can often stifle individual contribution whenever some participants dominate the discussion. Participants' anonymous responses are shared, and each participant can revise his or her response on the basis of reading other opinions. After repeating this process several times, the convergence of opinion will lead to team consensus.

- To solicit opinions or ideas from a jury of experts, anonymously circulate questionnaires repeatedly for revisions and consolidation in order to arrive at a final forecast, choice, or action plan.
- To generate ideas by a group of experts, allow them to revise their own ideas after having read all other ideas, and finally have a summarized statement that reflects group consensus.
- To forecast trends in economic and technological forces that may affect the organization.

before

Questionnaires

Circles of influence

Buzz group

Critical incident

Different point of view

after

Presentation

Run-it-by

Action and effect
diagram (AED)

What-if analysis

Barriers-and-aids
analysis

➡ Select and define problem or opportunity

➡ Identify and analyze causes or potential change

➡ Develop and plan possible solutions or change

➡ Implement and evaluate solution or change

➡ Measure and report solution or change results

  Recognize and reward team efforts

  Research/statistics

1 Creativity/innovation

  Engineering

  Project management

  Manufacturing

3 Marketing/sales

  Administration/documentation

  Servicing/support

  Customer/quality metrics

2 Change management

- No direct contact, debate, or exchange of information is allowed among the participants.
- Participants must be given enough time to prevent hasty responses or opinions.

The first activity is to identify and select a team of participants. A trained facilitator coordinates this process and thoroughly explains the Delphi method's objectives and processes to the participants.

Participants, isolated from each other, are sent detailed questionnaires, problem statements, or preliminary forecasts for their response or opinion. See example *Forecast the Consequences Resulting from the Establishment of Integrated Product Development Teams (IPDT)*.

The completed questionnaires, problem statements, or forecasts are summarized by the facilitator and anonymously redistributed to the participants.

Participants read all of the responses. Participants may or may not choose to revise their own response(s).

Steps 3 and 4 are repeated until participants stop revising their own responses. At this point, team consensus is reached.

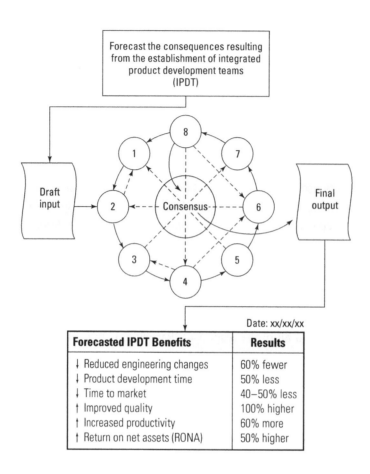

Forecast the consequences resulting from the establishment of integrated product development teams (IPDT)

Draft input

Consensus

Final output

Date: xx/xx/xx

Forecasted IPDT Benefits	Results
↓ Reduced engineering changes	60% fewer
↓ Product development time	50% less
↓ Time to market	40–50% less
↑ Improved quality	100% higher
↑ Increased productivity	60% more
↑ Return on net assets (RONA)	50% higher

The Deming PDSA cycle is a method of continually improving products, services, and processes. A small scale, low risk plan-do-study-act activity is often used to verify the feasibility of proposed ideas or change. Great for organizational learning, the PDSA cycle allows experimentation and study prior to full-scale implementation.

- To provide a structured problem-solving and process-improvement methodology.
- To assess proposed problem solutions or recommended process-improvement ideas.
- To improve the quality of work through constant change.
- To identify and measure the effects and outcomes of initial, trial efforts.

before

Critical dialogue

Gap analysis

Systems analysis diagram

Process mapping

Force field analysis (FFA)

after

Basili data collection method

Run-it-by

Different point of view

Presentation

Action plan

Select and define problem or opportunity

Identify and analyze causes or potential change

➡ Develop and plan possible solutions or change

➡ Implement and evaluate solution or change

➡ Measure and report solution or change results

Recognize and reward team efforts

Research/statistics

Creativity/innovation

Engineering

2 Project management

Manufacturing

Marketing/sales

Administration/documentation

3 Servicing/support

Customer/quality metrics

1 Change management

- In 1990, Deming changed plan-do-check-act (PDCA) to plan-do-study-act (PDSA). He believed that if one simply "checks" something, one does not perform an in-depth study, and important data may be missed.
- Cross-reference to the Shewhart PDCA cycle for a variation of this process.

Plan (P) an organizational change. See example *Improve Statistical Process Control (SPC) Training*.

Do (D) perform the change activities.

Study (S) the quantitative and qualitative data collected on the effects of change.

Act (A) on lessons learned and implement the change throughout the organization.

Repeat this PDSA cycle for further improvements.

Improve Statistical Process Control (SPC) Training   Date: xx/xx/xx

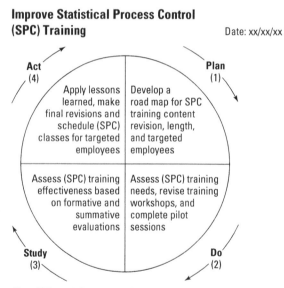

Act (4)
Apply lessons learned, make final revisions and schedule (SPC) classes for targeted employees

Plan (1)
Develop a road map for SPC training content revision, length, and targeted employees

Study (3)
Assess (SPC) training effectiveness based on formative and summative evaluations

Do (2)
Assess (SPC) training needs, revise training workshops, and complete pilot sessions

Note: This cycle is repeated for further improvement.

The demographic analysis tool is of great value when objective data is needed to describe and profile an audience or potential customer group. Data collection is accomplished through the use of various methods, such as surveys, interviews, or other summarized data sources. Demographic data analysis provides the researcher with an understanding of what is needed or expected by a customer and what decisions must be made to ensure that the information, products, or services meet these needs.

- To develop a demographic profile of the audience or customer to assist in the decision-making process.
- To collect data for the purpose of product or service targeting.

before

Surveying

Interview technique

Questionnaires

Starbursting

Circle response

after

Customer needs table

Presentation

Hypothesis testing
(chi-square)

Task analysis

Descriptive statistics

➡ Select and define problem or opportunity
➡ Identify and analyze causes or potential change
   Develop and plan possible solutions or change
   Implement and evaluate solution or change
   Measure and report solution or change results
➡ Recognize and reward team efforts

1 Research/statistics
   Creativity/innovation
   Engineering
   Project management
   Manufacturing
2 Marketing/sales
3 Administration/documentation
   Servicing/support
   Customer/quality metrics
   Change management

- Partial listing of demographic data items:

Group A
- Gender
- Age
- Religion
- Race
- Marital status
- Household composition

Group B
- Home ownership
- Time at location
- Zip code
- Location

Group C
- Education
- Hobbies
- Languages spoken
- Affiliations
- Certifications
- Travel

Group D
- Employment
- Income
- Occupational group
- Group membership

A demographic analysis requires the development of a demographic data collection instrument. Questions or demographic items need to be identified by the research team. Refer to data groups A–D above, item sources for most frequently asked questions.

Data are typically collected using survey, interview, focus group, product demos, or secondary data collection methods.

Data are sorted, organized, and summarized for analysis. A demographic profile can now be developed for specific purposes. See example *Marketing Research Data*.

The profile is used in marketing research reports or descriptive statistics data.

Marketing Research Data	Date: xx/xx/xx
Product Targeting Information / Customer Profile	

More often than not the potential buyer
- is married
- is 36–50 years of age
- has 14 or more years of education
- has worked 10 or more years for the company
- holds a supervisory position in the company
- owns a home
- resided at least 10 years at present location
- frequently travels overseas
- has an income level of $80,000+

Note additional data requirements:
- Product preference: Competition A __ B __ C __
- Household composition
- Zip code

The dendrogram displays, in a tree-type classification format, clusters of characteristics or ideas to be analyzed for potential breakthroughs in product design and development. It can also be used to detail possible solutions to problems or examine process improvement opportunities.

- To search for potential product innovations.
- To break down and classify large data sets.
- To review and question ideas for problem resolution or process improvement.

before
Cluster analysis
Brainwriting pool
Crawford slip method
Delphi method
Focus group

after
House of quality
Activity analysis
Factor analysis
Opportunity analysis
Creativity assessment

➥ Select and define problem or opportunity
➥ Identify and analyze causes or potential change
➥ Develop and plan possible solutions or change
    Implement and evaluate solution or change
    Measure and report solution or change results
    Recognize and reward team efforts

- Dendrograms are often used to display the outcomes or results of cluster analyses.

    Research/statistics
3   Creativity/innovation
1   Engineering
    Project management
    Manufacturing
    Marketing/sales
    Administration/documentation
    Servicing/support
    Customer/quality metrics
2   Change management

The team facilitator describes the use of a dendrogram and asks the team to brainstorm items within an area of interest. See example *Development of a Better Classroom Pointer*.

The facilitator draws the dendrogram on a whiteboard as the participants further break down a selected characteristic or idea.

The participants discuss preferred ideas and select one for product innovation or problem analysis, as shown in this example.

The participants review the flowdown of characteristics or ideas and date the dendrogram.

Development of a Better Classroom Pointer

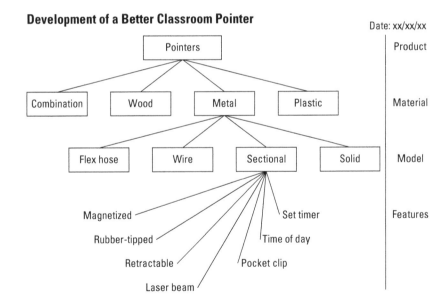

Date: xx/xx/xx

A deployment chart reflects the sequence of required activities and the persons or teams responsible for completing them. The chart's down-across construction also indicates approximately when, by due dates, these activities are scheduled to be completed.

- To provide a process or project overview of activities, people involved, activity sequence, and completion dates.
- To illustrate a process flow for teams to refer to during problem-solving or process-improvement efforts.

before

Demographic analysis

Consensus decision making

Circle response

Checklist

Problem analysis

after

Action plan

Resource histogram

Project planning log

Events log

Major program status

| Select and define problem or opportunity |
| Identify and analyze causes or potential change |
| ➡ Develop and plan possible solutions or change |
| ➡ Implement and evaluate solution or change |
| Measure and report solution or change results |
| Recognize and reward team efforts |

	Research/statistics
	Creativity/innovation
	Engineering
1	Project management
	Manufacturing
	Marketing/sales
3	Administration/documentation
	Servicing/support
	Customer/quality metrics
2	Change management

- Deployment chart activities start at top-left of chart and move down-across. Due date (end of activity) is lined-up laterally with the bottom line of the activity box.
- Optional: A due date column is not necessary if due dates are placed on top of respective activity box.

The facilitator draws an outline of a deployment chart (down-across) on a whiteboard. The process or project to be charted is reviewed and clarified.

Team participants brainstorm required activities. See example *Poster Development Process*.

With the assistance from the participants, activity blocks are drawn into the columns that reflect who or what group is performing this activity.

Activities are inserted from the top down and across to show directionality and elapsed time. Lines are drawn to sequentially link all activity blocks in a downward flow.

A column with due dates of respective activities is constructed as the last activity to complete the chart as shown.

The team reflects the process flow of the chart, makes any revisions, and dates the chart.

Poster Development Process

Date: xx/xx/xx

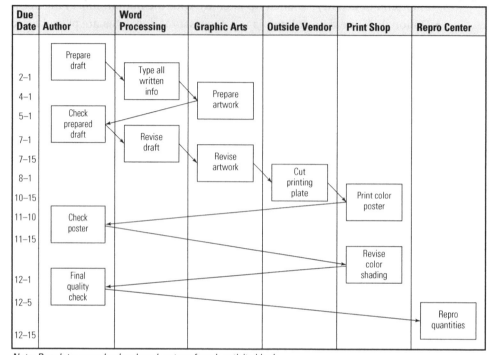

Due Date	Author	Word Processing	Graphic Arts	Outside Vendor	Print Shop	Repro Center
	Prepare draft					
2–1		Type all written info				
4–1			Prepare artwork			
5–1	Check prepared draft					
7–1		Revise draft				
7–15			Revise artwork			
8–1				Cut printing plate		
10–15					Print color poster	
11–10	Check poster					
11–15						
					Revise color shading	
12–1	Final quality check					
12–5						
						Repro quantities
12–15						

Note: Due dates can also be placed on top of each activity block.

Descriptive statistics are the procedures used to organize, summarize, and describe data that were collected over time or as a result of a data collection process during a research project. The statistical calculations provide measures of central tendency and measures of dispersion, which are often used as supporting information in the decision-making process.

- To summarize research data into meaningful forms using standard statistical techniques.
- To describe, in statistical terms, collected data for reporting purposes.
- To use statistical data to improve the decision-making process.

before

Data collection strategy

Sampling method

Random numbers generator

Standard deviation

Frequency distribution (FD)

after

Process capability ratios

Control chart

Correlation analysis

Analysis of variance

Hypothesis testing (Chi-square)

Select and define problem or opportunity

Identify and analyze causes or potential change

Develop and plan possible solutions or change

➥ Implement and evaluate solution or change

➥ Measure and report solution or change results

Recognize and reward team efforts

1 Research/statistics

Creativity/innovation

2 Engineering

3 Project management

4 Manufacturing

Marketing/sales

Administration/documentation

Servicing/support

Customer/quality metrics

Change management

The normal probability distribution is a symmetrical, bell-shaped distribution frequently used in statistical analyses. The arithmetic mean ($\bar{X}$), median ($\tilde{X}$), and mode ($\hat{X}$) are of equal value and are located at the center and peak of the curve. These measures are averages and therefore considered measures of central tendency. Measures of dispersion are measures under the curve, moving horizontally left or right to identify area or probability. Among others, standard deviations (S), z-values (z), and percentiles (%) are most often used in descriptive and inferential statistics.

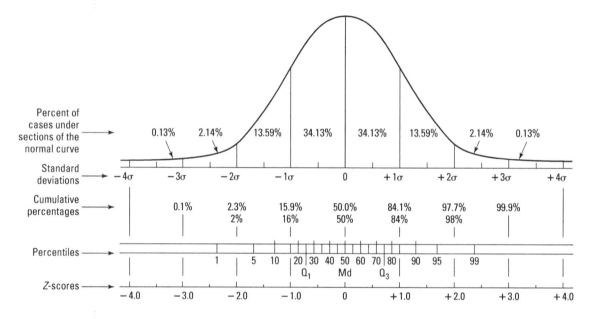

Symbols and Definitions:

Population   *Sample*

N = Population size n = Sample size

μ = Population mean $\bar{X}$ = Sample mean

σ^2 = Population variance S^2 = Sample variance

σ = Population standard deviation S = Sample standard deviation

Variance: σ^2 (sigma squared) is the average of the squared deviation scores (x) of the observations from the mean ($\bar{X}$).

Standard deviation: σ (Sigma) is the square root of the average of the squared deviation scores (x) of the observations from the mean ($\bar{X}$).

Deviation scores: (x) Found by subtracting the mean ($\bar{X}$) from each observation or data value.

X, Y = Any observation, measurement, data value, or score (X for the first data set, Y for the second data set.)

x, y = Deviation score found by: $x = X - \bar{X}$

$\bar{X}, \bar{Y}$ = The Mean: The arithmetic average.

$\tilde{X}, \tilde{Y}$ = The Median: The midpoint observation or value of observations that have been ordered from low to high. Half of the observations are above and half of the observation are below the median, or middle observation.

$\overset{\Delta}{X}, \overset{\Delta}{Y}$ = The Mode: The values of the observation that appear most frequently in a data set.

R = The Range: Highest value-lowest value of observations in a data set.

z = The z-score: The distance between a specific value of an observation (X) and the mean ($\bar{X}$) divided by the standard deviation (S). The z value is used to access the "Proportions of Area Under the Normal Curve" table to determine the area or probability. (See Appendix, Table A.)

Σ = The sum of (the summation sign).

SK = Skewness: to check if distribution has positive or negative skewness.

Equations:

$$R = (H{-}L) + 1 \qquad \bar{X} = \frac{\Sigma X}{n} \qquad S^2 = \frac{\Sigma (X - \bar{X})^2}{n - 1}$$

$$S = \sqrt{\frac{\Sigma (X - \bar{X})^2}{n - 1}} \qquad SK = \frac{3\,(\bar{X} - \tilde{X})}{S} \qquad Z = \frac{X - \bar{X}}{S}$$

Note: n–1 is used when total observations = ≤30.

The raw data are organized by sorting, sequencing, grouping, or placing them into matrices or tables.

Basic measures of central tendency, measures of dispersion, and z-scores to percentiles under the normal probability curve can now be calculated. See example *Document Wire Extension Measurement*.

All calculations are checked and used in reports or presentations as supporting information.

Document Wire Extension Measurements

Refer to #8 (*notes and key points*) for the equations used below.

X	$-$	$\bar{X} = x$	x^2			Date: xx/xx/xx
19.2	$-$	$20 = -.8$	.64			Note: All measurements in centimeters (cm).
19.5	$-$	$20 = -.5$	.25	$S^2 = \dfrac{\Sigma\, x^2}{n-1}$		
19.6	$-$	$20 = -.4$	.16			
19.8	$-$	$20 = -.2$	.04	$S^2 = \dfrac{2.28}{10}$		
19.9	$-$	$20 = -.1$	.01			
20.0	$-$	$20 = 0$	0	$S^2 = .228$		
20.1	$-$	$20 = +.1$	.01			
20.2	$-$	$20 = +.2$	.04	$S = \sqrt{.228}$		
20.4	$-$	$20 = +.4$	.16			
20.4	$-$	$20 = +.4$	.16	$S = .477$		
20.9	$-$	$20 = +.9$	.81			
$\Sigma = 220.0$		0	$\Sigma\, x^2 = 2.28$			

$\bar{X} = \dfrac{220}{11}$ | $R = 20.9 - 19.2$ | $\tilde{X} = 20$

$\bar{X} = 20$ | $R = 1.7$ | $\overset{\Delta}{X} = 20.4$

Z - Score for 19.2:

$$Z = \frac{19.9 - 20}{.477}$$

$$Z = -1.68$$

Z - Score for 20.9:

$$Z = \frac{20.9 - 20}{.477}$$

$$Z = 1.89$$

% Area under the curve:

$-1.68 \longrightarrow 4.65\%\,*$

% Area under the curve:

$1.89 \longrightarrow 97.06\%\,*$

Refer to "Percentage of Area Under the Normal Curve" in Table A of the Appendix to check percentage (%); also described in "Normal Probability Distribution" in this book.

The different point of view tool is ideal for a team to use to acquire a second opinion or an outsider's view to verify that a potential solution to a problem has been well thought out. Another application of this tool is to predict how other people may react to a team's proposal or what may be asked during a team's presentation.

- To allow further clarification of the problem.
- To solicit more information to gain further insight into issues, concerns, or consequences.
- To determine if important issues have been overlooked.
- To consider the view or input of people outside the team.

before

Double reversal

Reverse brainstorming

Delphi method

Focus group

Presentation

after

Thematic content analysis

Gap analysis

Team rating

Solution matrix

Response matrix analysis

	Select and define problem or opportunity
	Identify and analyze causes or potential change
➥	Develop and plan possible solutions or change
	Implement and evaluate solution or change
	Measure and report solution or change results
➥	Recognize and reward team efforts

	Research/statistics
2	Creativity/innovation
	Engineering
3	Project management
	Manufacturing
4	Marketing/sales
5	Administration/documentation
	Servicing/support
	Customer/quality metrics
1	Change management

• Suggested groups to provide different points of view are users, customers, process owners, subject matter experts, people affected by a change, and people who are responsible for the work unit or implementation activities.

The team has developed a proposed solution to a problem, an action plan, or a process improvement opportunity. See example *Changing the Parts Data Base Update Procedure*.

The team determines the people whose points of view may differ on the basis of position, work duties, interests, etc. A copy of the proposal is distributed to selected people or groups as shown in the example.

Different points of view are collected from the selected people and groups.

The next activity requires the team to complete a thematic content analysis to identify common strands of thought, clusters of similar ideas, recommendations for revisions, or agreement on possible action items.

Having identified essential revisions based on the different points of view, the team completes the revised work and presents a finalized proposal or action plan for implementation.

Changing the Parts Database
Update Procedure

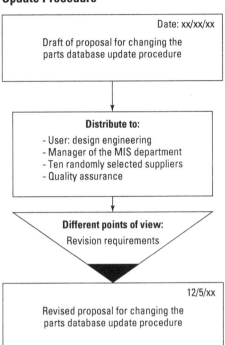

Date: xx/xx/xx

Draft of proposal for changing the
parts database update procedure

Distribute to:

- User: design engineering
- Manager of the MIS department
- Ten randomly selected suppliers
- Quality assurance

Different points of view:

Revision requirements

12/5/xx

Revised proposal for changing the
parts database update procedure

A dimension cube enables researchers to identify general dimensions of a structure, model, program, or process. It provides a means to study relationships, to estimate resource requirements, and to consider alternative action plans.

- To show the dimensions of something.
- To prevent the omission of some important element from planning or investigation work.
- To present a model of a process or concept.

before

Data collection strategy

Process analysis

Needs analysis

Consensus decision making

Influence diagram

after

Presentation

Benchmarking

Resource requirements matrix

Cluster analysis

Process selection matrix

Select and define problem or opportunity
Identify and analyze causes or potential change
➡ Develop and plan possible solutions or change
➡ Implement and evaluate solution or change
Measure and report solution or change results
Recognize and reward team efforts

1	Research/statistics
	Creativity/innovation
	Engineering
	Project management
	Manufacturing
2	Marketing/sales
	Administration/documentation
	Servicing/support
3	Customer/quality metrics
	Change management

- Typical applications for a dimension cube:
  - Total quality concepts
  - Human resource elements
  - Basic dimensions of education
  - Human behavior modeling
  - Technology roadmaps
  - Strategic planning dimensions
  - Performance/process models

The researcher reviews the information on the topic or concept to be modeled. See example *Basic Dimensions of Total Quality Management/ Continuous Improvement*.

Dimension headings are identified and relevant items clustered under each heading.

A dimensions cube is drawn and the items are recorded with each heading on one side of the cube as shown in the example.

The dimension cube is shown to others for additional input or revision recommendations.

The finalized dimension cube is attached to a paper or proposal as a supporting document.

Basic Dimensions of Total Quality
Managment/Continuous Improvement

The TQM/CI cube

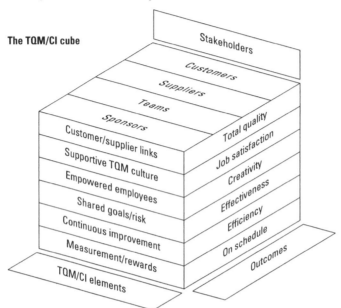

A dot diagram tool allows data to be displayed for quick analysis. Observations of some sets of numbers are dotted along a scale to indicate a natural tendency to form a normal (bell-shaped) distribution, or to show clustering around a central value. It can also be used to check for patterns in recorded data.

- To display the relationship or distance between the numbers (observations) in a small sample or population of numbers (≤30).
- To provide quick measurements of range and average, and to show the dispersion of data.

before

Data collection strategy

Sampling methods

Observation

Checksheet

Surveying

after

Stem-and-leaf display

Problem analysis

Monthly assessment schedule

Descriptive statistics

Demographic analysis

➥ Select and define problem or opportunity

➥ Identify and analyze causes or potential change

Develop and plan possible solutions or change

Implement and evaluate solution or change

Measure and report solution or change results

Recognize and reward team efforts

1 Research/statistics

Creativity/innovation

Engineering

Project management

Manufacturing

Marketing/sales

Administration/documentation

Servicing/support

2 Customer/quality metrics

Change management

- A dot diagram should not be used for more than 30 observations.
- Numbers that are off the scale should be reported as outliers.

Collect and record data. Sort values (numbers) from low to high. See example *Recorded Lost Calls*.

Draw a horizontal line and mark or scale units of measurement, as shown in the example.

Place a dot for each value (number) and continue until all numbers have been dotted. When finished dotting, the dot diagram displays all values and how often they occurred.

If desired, basic statistical analysis can be completed as shown.

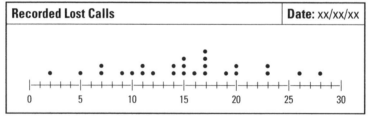

| Recorded Lost Calls | Date: xx/xx/xx |

Note: Range = (H − L), R = (28 − 2) + 1, R = 27
Mean (average) = 390 : 26 = 15
Mediam (value of middle number) = 15
Mode (most frequently occurring number) = 17

The double reversal is a reversed thinking process that allows teams to continue with idea generating after they have run out of ideas or simply have found no novel way of looking at the problem. This tool requires an issue, idea, or goal to be reversed or stated in a negative form in order to gain more ideas of what could cause the problem. Reversing again each reversed idea should produce potential action steps to consider in the problem solution phase.

- To identify the less obvious ideas for problem resolution.
- To expand the list of ideas developed during a classical brainstorming session.
- To search for additional process or quality improvement opportunities.
- To recover from an unproductive brainstorming effort.
- To further clarify a problem to gain more solution ideas.

before

Brainstorming

Round robin brainstorming

Focus group

Crawford slip method

Brainwriting

after

Sticking dots

Opportunity analysis

Consensus decision making

Multivoting

Process selection matrix

➥ Select and define problem or opportunity
➥ Identify and analyze causes or potential change
➥ Develop and plan possible solutions or change
   Implement and evaluate solution or change
   Measure and report solution or change results
   Recognize and reward team efforts

   Research/statistics
1 Creativity/innovation
   Engineering
   Project management
   Manufacturing
   Marketing/sales
   Administration/documentation
   Servicing/support
3 Customer/quality metrics
2 Change management

- Reversed also means, for this tool application, the negated or negative form of the idea presented.

The team reviews the session objective or desired improvement goal. See example *Reduce the Percentage of "No Shows" in Scheduled Training Workshops*.

A list of ideas, previously brainstormed, is displayed and discussed.

The next action taken is to reverse the objective. See example *Increase the percentage of "No Shows" in Scheduled Training Workshops*.

The team now brainstorms how to make the condition or problem worse—the reversed or negative form of the objective.

Once the reversed ideas have been recorded, the team reverses again all ideas—the double reversal process.

The final step is to add all newly developed ideas to the previous list. The team now has some fresh, different potential solutions to the problem.

Reduce the Percentage of "No-Shows"   Date: xx/xx/xx
in Scheduled Training Workshops

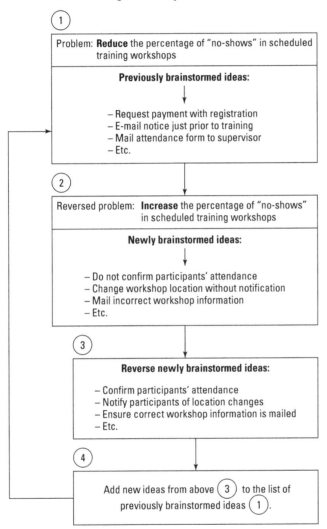

① **Problem: Reduce** the percentage of "no-shows" in scheduled training workshops

Previously brainstormed ideas:

– Request payment with registration
– E-mail notice just prior to training
– Mail attendance form to supervisor
– Etc.

② **Reversed problem: Increase** the percentage of "no-shows" in scheduled training workshops

Newly brainstormed ideas:

– Do not confirm participants' attendance
– Change workshop location without notification
– Mail incorrect workshop information
– Etc.

③ **Reverse newly brainstormed ideas:**

– Confirm participants' attendance
– Notify participants of location changes
– Ensure correct workshop information is mailed
– Etc.

④ Add new ideas from above ③ to the list of previously brainstormed ideas ①.

*Note: The result is a **longer** list of brainstormed ideas.*

An events log is a historical data trace for critical operations. It provides background information on process variation, changes in operations, supplier problems, and other information useful to problem-solving teams. Entries are made by anyone directly involved in the process and are checked frequently by the process owner.

- To detect any early trends that may result in a loss of quality or productivity.
- To collect data for the purpose of monitoring operations.
- To maintain a problem prevention procedure.

before

Observation

Data collection strategy

Checklist

Process analysis

Problem analysis

after

Defect map

Countermeasures matrix

Quality chart

Monthly assessment schedule

Action plan

➥ Select and define problem or opportunity
➥ Identify and analyze causes or potential change
➥ Develop and plan possible solutions or change
  Implement and evaluate solution or change
  Measure and report solution or change results
  Recognize and reward team efforts

Research/statistics
Creativity/innovation
Engineering
Project management
1 Manufacturing
Marketing/sales
2 Administration/documentation
Servicing/support
Customer/quality metrics
3 Change management

- Events are considered to be changes in people, equipment, tools, methods, forms, measurements, materials, suppliers, or environment. Frequently occurring problems must be included in the events log for possible future problem-solving activities.

An events log is started the first day of every month by the unit manager.

Entries are made for every event and each entry is coded for a specific meaning. See example *Work Cell #5—Daily Operations*.

The unit manager checks the events log on a daily basis for variations, patterns, trends, problem areas, etc.

Events logs are used in staff meetings and filed for future reference if needed.

Work Cell #5 — Daily Operations

WC #5 — Product Line: Scope Assembly				Period: 2/1/xx — 3/1/xx
Date	Time	Code	Comments	By
2/1/xx	08:00	2	Absent	J.H.
2/2/xx	09:00	12	Scrap — "D" lens — scratch	A.L.
"	15:30	12	Scrap — "D" lens — 12 lenses scratched	A.L.
2/3/xx	11:30	1	Jay off sick	S.P.
2/4/xx	10:15	14	Inspector found more defective "D" lenses	A.L.
"	13:20	14	Supplier notified by receiving inspection	A.L.
2/5/xx	07:45	11	Delay, parts shortage	A.L.
2/6/xx	15:50	10	Work reassignments (to loan)	J.H.
			includes documents	
2/27/xx	09:30	9	Form 96	R.I.
2/28/xx	14:20	4	Calibration schedule — 2 hrs.	D.O.

Codes – changes		Codes – problems
1 - Operator	7 - Set-up	11 - Material shortage
2 - Expeditor	8 - Process	12 - Scrap
3 - Inspector	9 - Form/drwg.	13 - Rework
4 - Equipment	10 - Other	14 - Defective part
5 - Tooling		15 - Downtime
6 - Material		16 - Control charts

A facility layout diagram displays floor layouts, manufacturing or service process flows, employee movement, possible bottlenecks, excessive cycle time, and other possible inefficiencies in the present layout. This tool prepares a layout of equipment, work areas, and storage areas useful in work flow analysis (WFA) and improvement efforts.

- To create a floor plan of the facility for tracing employee movement.
- To identify possible co-location of activities and shorter distances of required movement.
- To map process flows and loopbacks.

before

Process flowchart

Cycle time flowchart

Opportunity analysis

Mental imaging

Interview technique

after

Work flow analysis (WFA)

Activity analysis

Variance analysis

Potential problem analysis

What-if analysis

➡ Select and define problem or opportunity

➡ Identify and analyze causes or potential change

➡ Develop and plan possible solutions or change

Implement and evaluate solution or change

Measure and report solution or change results

Recognize and reward team efforts

	Research/statistics
	Creativity/innovation
2	Engineering
	Project management
3	Manufacturing
	Marketing/sales
4	Administration/documentation
	Servicing/support
	Customer/quality metrics
1	Change management

For easy reference to any work area, use grid labeling of facility layout. Example:

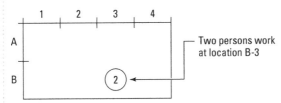

First, identify and observe the facility or work area for the normal work flow, equipment location, and the number of employees normally assigned to workstations. See example *Reproduction Facility Layout*.

Using drafting paper, prepare a facility layout diagram showing all major items or equipment, furniture, and other objects or areas of interest.

Name all drawn items, complete grid reference labeling, and identify the number of people working at certain locations.

Finally, check for accuracy and date the diagram.

Reproduction Facility Layout

Date: xx/xx/xx

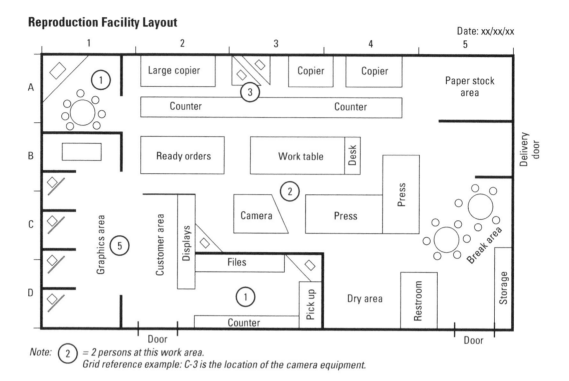

Note: ② = 2 persons at this work area.
Grid reference example: C-3 is the location of the camera equipment.

A factor analysis is an assessment technique that surfaces product, process, or service factors that may require immediate attention or further analysis. Similar to benchmarking, product and/or service factor ratings are compared to best in class or to one's own organization to determine competitive strengths and weaknesses.

- To assess best in class processes.
- To compare product and service ratings with those of the competition.
- To identify problem areas for the assignment to problem-solving teams.

<table>
<tr><td>➡</td><td>Select and define problem or opportunity</td></tr>
<tr><td>➡</td><td>Identify and analyze causes or potential change</td></tr>
<tr><td></td><td>Develop and plan possible solutions or change</td></tr>
<tr><td>➡</td><td>Implement and evaluate solution or change</td></tr>
<tr><td></td><td>Measure and report solution or change results</td></tr>
<tr><td></td><td>Recognize and reward team efforts</td></tr>
</table>

	Research/statistics
2	Creativity/innovation
1	Engineering
	Project management
	Manufacturing
3	Marketing/sales
	Administration/documentation
	Servicing/support
	Customer/quality metrics
4	Change management

before

Benchmarking

Matrix data analysis

Linking diagram

Customer needs table

Organization readiness chart

after

SWOT analysis

Gap analysis

Radar chart

SCAMPER

Value analysis

- Factorial ratings can reflect customer satisfaction, best practices, overall quality, design, or process categories.
- Optional ratings: 4 = very high; 3 = high; 2 = medium; 1 = low. Other rating scales can be used.
- The overall or category of factors rating is an average of all factor ratings within a particular category.

An integrated product development team (IDPT) selects the most important product or service factors to be analyzed. See example *TV/Cable Providers—Service Factors Analysis*.

Next, competitors are identified for data collection on the selected factors. Sources of data are customer satisfaction surveys, benchmarking partnerships, secondary data, interviews, documentation, and others.

Data from competitors and one's own organization are verified, rated, and organized into category of factors groupings.

A factor analysis table is constructed and ratings recorded for each listed factor. Also, a category of factors average is calculated and recorded.

Finally, the factor analysis table is checked for completeness, dated, and presented to the respective process owners.

TV/Cable Providers — Service Factors Analysis

Date: xx/xx/xx

Service Factors	A 4	A 3	A 2	A 1	B 4	B 3	B 2	B 1	C 4	C 3	C 2	C 1	Our 4	Our 3	Our 2	Our 1
Ordering/scheduling	(1.75)				(2.75)				(3.50)				(2.50)			
– Customer service			■			■			■					■		
– Product availability			■		■					■				■		
– Wait period				■				■	■						■	
– Flexibility			■			■				■					■	
Pricing/billing	(2.00)				(3.25)				(2.50)				(3.00)			
– Rate structure			■			■				■				■		
– Bundling			■			■					■			■		
– Info detail		■			■						■			■		
– Billing errors				■		■			■						■	
Installation/support	(1.50)				(3.50)				(3.25)				(2.25)			
– On-site visit			■		■					■				■		
– Ease of use				■		■					■					■
– Complaint handling			■		■				■						■	
– Repair service			■			■				■				■		

Notes: Service quality ratings: 4 = very high, 3 = high, 2 = medium, 1 = low
(1.75) = average category of factors rating (2 + 2 + 2 + 1 divided by 4, 7 ÷ 4 = 1.75).

A failure mode effect analysis (FMEA) is a technique that allows a cross-functional team to identify potential failure modes or causes of failures that may occur as a result of design or process deficiencies. This analysis, furthermore, produces estimates of the effects and level of severity of failures, and it provides recommendations for corrective design or process changes.

- To consider potential failure modes, causes, effects, and corrective action to be taken.
- To predict the reliability of complex products and processes.
- To assess the impact of failures on internal and external customers.
- To identify ways for a product or subsystem to fail meeting specifications.

before

Fault tree analysis (FTA)
Process flowchart
Process analysis
Activity analysis
Variance analysis

after

Countermeasures matrix
Defect map
Dendrogram
Pareto chart
Events log

➡ Select and define problem or opportunity
➡ Identify and analyze causes or potential change
➡ Develop and plan possible solutions or change
   Implement and evaluate solution or change
   Measure and report solution or change results
   Recognize and reward team efforts

   Research/statistics
   Creativity/innovation
1 Engineering
   Project management
2 Manufacturing
   Marketing/sales
4 Administration/documentation
3 Servicing/support
   Customer/quality metrics
   Change management

Failure mode effect analysis (FMEA) applications:
- *Design FMEA:* Covers all new designs and major design changes to existing products or systems. Considerations: Process capability, assembling space/access for tooling, performance (test) design deviations.
- *Process FMEA:* Covers all planned manufacturing of assembly processes. Considerations: Manufacturing/fabrication, assembly, receiving/inspection, testing/inspection.

Optional scales for FMEA applications:
- Probability of failure *occurrence* (1–10): 1 = remote chance of failing, 10 = very high chance of failing.
- Degree of failure *severity* (1–10): 1 = not noticeable to the customer, 10- critical failure, probable loss of customer.
- Probability of failure *detection* (1–10): 1 = extremely low chance of escaping defects; 10 = very high chance of escaping defects.
- *Risk Assessment:* The higher the risk priority number (RPN), the more important is the task to eliminate the cause of failure.

RPN = *occurrence* rating × *severity* rating × *detection* rating.

A cross-functional team determines the potential failure modes of a design or process. See example *Power Relay Switch Design and Assembly.*

FMEA forms are distributed to the team's participants and all items on the form are explained and discussed.

Scales and ratings for failure occurrence, severity, and detection are agreed upon and respective rating values assigned for each failure mode, as shown in the example.

The FMEA matrix is completed and checked for accuracy. Finally, recommended action items are assigned.

The finalized FMEA matrix is dated and presented to the process owner.

Power Relay Switch Design and Assembly

Design/Process: Power Relay Assembly									Date: xx/xx/xx Issue No. 1	
Component and No.: Relay Coil									Team: Power Operators	
Department: Manufacturing									Process Owner: J.K. Nelson	
Potential mode of failure	Potential cause of failure	Potential effect of failure	Design/ process controls	Probablitity of failure occurance	Degree of failure severity	Probablitity of failure detection	Risk priority number	Recommended preventive action	Results or comments
Open winding	Boken coil wire	Relay does not operate	Cp, SPC	2	10	1	20	Pretest	Approved
Intermittent shorting	Lack of insulation	Burn out relay	Visual inspection	3	6	4	72	Change insulation	Assigned to J.P.

Note: Scales are 1–10 for occurence, severity, and detection ratings.
See description of rating scales for additional information.

The fault tree analysis (FTA) was first introduced by Bell Laboratories. It is a logical tool that assists in the uncovering of potential root causes of defects or equipment failures. It can, however, be applied to administrative areas as well. Similar to a tree diagram, the output is the result of various levels of contributing factors or potential causes for failure.

The logic behind this diagram uses *and* and *or* function gates to illustrate symptoms of failure down to real root causes. As shown in the fault tree analysis, an *or* (+) function gate will, for example, have an output of *few inquiries* as a result of input *low interest*, *lack of info*, or both. On the other hand, an *and* (•) function gate will show a true output of *unprepared instructor* only if all *and* inputs are true. This type of analysis, therefore, provides great insight into the interrelationships among the various cause and effect conditions.

- To allow a backward approach to systematically identify potential causes of failures.
- To provide an overview of interrelationships between causes and failures.
- To break down failure indications into more detailed input branches.

before

Problem specification

Checklist

Failure mode effect analysis

Dendrogram

Events log

after

Countermeasures matrix

Potential problem analysis (PPA)

What-if analysis

Process analysis

Problem analysis

➡	Select and define problem or opportunity		Research/statistics
➡	Identify and analyze causes or potential change		Creativity/innovation
➡	Develop and plan possible solutions or change	**4**	Engineering
	Implement and evaluate solution or change		Project management
	Measure and report solution or change results	**2**	Manufacturing
	Recognize and reward team efforts		Marketing/sales
			Administration/documentation
		3	Servicing/support
			Customer/quality metrics
		1	Change management

The fault tree is drawn using two logic gates interconnected in various functions.

Three input *and* gate, which requires all three inputs present to have an output.

Two input *or* gate, which requires at least one input to be present to have an output.

Note: This tool works well with other major tools, such as quality function deployment, metrics, and management by policy.

The first step for a team is to write down the failure as an output for the top *or* gate (Level 1). See example *Problem! An Ineffective Training Program for Integrated Product Development Teams (IPDT)*.

Determine what input (symptoms) could be considered a contributing element (Level 2).

Continue breaking down the failure with additional gate levels (Levels 3, 4 or more).

Always ask yourself: Can this gate output be true with any input (*or* function), or does all input need to be present for a true gate output (*and* function)?

Lastly, finalize and date the diagram.

Problem: An Ineffective Training Program for Integrated Product Development Teams (IPDT)

Date: xx/xx/xx

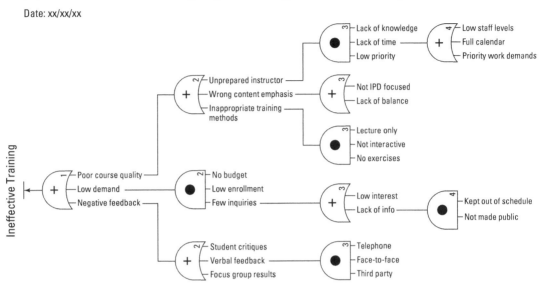

Fishbowls are very structured and facilitated discussions on some problem or issue by half of the team's participants while the other half of the team observes the process. After a predetermined time period, both halves switch roles. Fishbowls are ideal for team dynamics to serve as team training, as well as to explore in-depth an issue or problem.

- To train teams to communicate effectively, have discussions among equals, and promote an open sharing of ideas.
- To keep participants focused on an issue or problem.
- To start a problem-solving effort.
- To observe and analyze team dynamics.

before

Sociogram

Buzz group

Observation

Circle response

Circles of influence

after

Rotating roles

Different point of view

Consensus decision making

Critical dialogue

Presentation

➥ Select and define problem or opportunity

➥ Identify and analyze causes or potential change

➥ Develop and plan possible solutions or change

Implement and evaluate solution or change

Measure and report solution or change results

Recognize and reward team efforts

Research/statistics

1 Creativity/innovation

Engineering

Project management

Manufacturing

Marketing/sales

Administration/documentation

Servicing/support

Customer/quality metrics

2 Change management

- Ensure that participants switch roles only as directed.
- Each participant's input is limited to 1 minute per input.
- Total time for the fishbowl activity is 60 minutes.

The facilitator provides an overview of the fishbowl process. Participants draw numbers and are divided into odd and even numbers. At the beginning, the odd-numbered participants are seated in the inner circle, the fishbowl. Even-numbered participants take a seat in the outer circle.

Next, the facilitator displays the issue to be discussed, informs the inner ring when the discussion starts and that they have 30 minutes to discuss the issue. A moderator is selected and receives a prepared set of questions to keep the discussion stimulating and challenging. Participants are asked to keep their input to 1 minute per issue. The moderator takes notes on the discussion for team sharing. See example *How Do We Change the Culture in an Organization?*

The participants of the outer ring are assigned roles as observers. Their silent note taking will capture data on conflict, interruptions, drifting to other issues, dominant or less expressive participants, and other situations.

The facilitator starts the clock and the discussion and observations take place. After 30 minutes, the fishbowl is stopped and the observers provide feedback on their observations.

Roles are switched and the outer ring participants (even numbers) move to the inner ring. Steps 2 through 4 above are repeated to complete the fishbowl.

Both moderators share their discussion notes and a joint discussion may now take place on the issue, as shown in the example.

How Do We Change the Culture in an Organization?

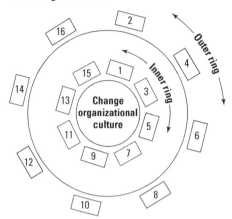

Fishbowl Observations	Date: xx/xx/xx

Team Dynamics
 – Some dominant individuals

 – Some participants struggled

 – Timing was frustrating to some

Discussion items
 – Involve people in any change

 – Teach learning organization concepts

 – How do we build trust?

The five whys uses a systematic questionnaire technique to search for root causes of a problem. The technique requires participants to ask "why?" at least five times, or work through five levels of detail. Once it becomes difficult to respond to "why?," the probable cause may have been identified.

- To identify the reason(s) for an abnormal condition or situation.
- To identify the root causes(s) of a problem.
- To start a data collection process.

before
Tree diagram
Checksheet
Cause and effect diagram (CED)
Defect map
Problem specification

after
Countermeasures matrix
Shewhart PDCA cycle
Force field analysis (FFA)
Gap analysis
Action plan

➥ Select and define problem or opportunity
➥ Identify and analyze causes or potential change
Develop and plan possible solutions or change
Implement and evaluate solution or change
Measure and report solution or change results
Recognize and reward team efforts

	Research/statistics
3	Creativity/innovation
	Engineering
4	Project management
	Manufacturing
	Marketing/sales
	Administration/documentation
	Servicing/support
2	Customer/quality metrics
1	Change management

- While asking "five whys," do not switch to asking "who." The focus is on the process of the problem, not the person involved.
- Continue to ask "why" beyond the arbitrary five times if necessary to get to the root cause of a problem.

Complete a problem statement by describing a perceived problem in specific terms. See example *The Night Shift Productivity Output Is Often Lower than That of the Day Shift.*

Ask the first "why" question. Why does this problem exist?

Continue to ask "why" questions until the root causes are identified. This process may take more than "five whys"!

Write a next step statement for solving the problem.

State a (perceived) problem: Date: xx/xx/xx

The night shift productivity output is often lower than that of the day shift.

Ask "Why" 1 *Why is productivity lower on the night shift?*

Response: *Punch presses model X are frequently switched off by quality inspectors.*

Ask "Why" 2 *Why are these particular presses switched off?*

Response: *Nightshift operator cannot calibrate model X presses.*

Ask "Why" 3 *Why cannot operators maintain and calibrate this model?*

Response: *The operators have not been trained on this model.*

Ask "Why" 4 *Why were operators not trained on this model?*

Response *Some presses of this model were recently placed into service. Factory training was provided to day shift operators.*

Ask "Why" 5 *Why did night shift operators not receive this training?*

Response: *The training department does not have update training in the punch press workshop.*

Root cause(s) of the perceived problem identified?

Yes. Punch press model X is presently not covered in the company's training program for operators. All PP model X operators need update training.

The focus group method is a relatively flexible process to collect the insights, opinions, ideas, and recommendations of targeted participants. Information collected in a focus group session can be clarified, explored, and expanded on immediately. Data can be preliminary or follow-up to support or confirm an intervention. The use of focus groups should be considered when it is important to involve groups that will be affected by an organizational change, when there is a clear need for subject matter expertise, or when proposed activities need to be "run by" representatives of the user organization.

- To gain insights into general problem areas or customer satisfaction concerns.
- To verify a users' group's perception of product or service quality.
- To collect technical data from experts in the field.
- To obtain in-depth, qualitative feedback on proposed organizational change.

before

Data collection strategy
Audience analysis
Run-it-by
Buzz group
Circle response

after

Questionnaires
Surveying
Interview technique
Competency gap assessment
Consensus decision making

➡ Select and define problem or opportunity
➡ Identify and analyze causes or potential change
➡ Develop and plan possible solutions or change
Implement and evaluate solution or change
Measure and report solution or change results
Recognize and reward team efforts

Research/statistics
3 Creativity/innovation
Engineering
Project management
Manufacturing
2 Marketing/sales
Administration/documentation
Servicing/support
1 Customer/quality metrics
4 Change management

- A focus group should consist of 8–12 participants.
- Participants are selected on the basis of their insight and potential contribution to achieve the session's objectives.
- The focus group session should be facilitated by a moderator and take no longer than 3 hours.
- A neutral facility, away from the work location, is of great benefit.

The Focus Group process owner and the moderator jointly develop a clear goal statement to determine (1) who the representatives are, (2) how many participants should be involved, and (3) what the composition (level and/or functions) of the focus group should be. See example *Identification of Sequence Steps for Research and Statistical Analysis.*

The moderator develops an outline and main topic description for the session.

Participants are identified and contacted by mail at least three weeks before the actual session. A follow-up call is required to confirm attendance.

The session is started by introducing the moderator and recorder, reviewing of the focus group objectives, and displaying the topic statement, or if appropriate, prepared questionnaires.

During the session, prepared questions are asked and responses are recorded on flip charts by the recorder(s). If needed, questions are clarified for the participants. The focus group process should allow everyone the opportunity to respond to every question asked.
Note: It is important that the moderator keep his or her comments neutral.

Finally, a final check is made to ensure that all participants responded to all questions (there may have been a "pass" on some questions). Ask participants if everything was covered. Display all the flip charts for verification of responses collected. Record any changes or rewrites.

Identification of Sequence Steps for Research and Statistical Analysis
1. Idea (Area of Interest)
2. Topic Selection (Focus)
3. Review of Literature (on-line/ off-line)
4. Research Questions Formulation
5. H_1 and H_0 Hypotheses Formulation
6. Research Design / Methodology Determination
7. Proposal–Objectives of Research
8. Population Definition
9. Sample Size Determination
10. Sampling Method Identification
11. Development of Instrumentation
12. Field Testing of Instruments
13. Instruments Revisions
14. Data Collection and Follow-up
15. Encoding Data and Profiling of Data
16. Data Input and SPSS (Stats Software)
17. Descriptive and Inferential (H_0) Testing
18. 8-Step H_0 Testing Procedure
19. Findings vs. Secondary Data Evaluation
20. Conclusions (Inferences)
21. Research Outcome Evaluation (Panel of Experts)
22. Final Report

Developed by Robert Gunning, the fog index stands for the reading level required to understand written information. Computing the fog index allows a writer to assess at what reading level he or she is currently writing and what adjustments, if any, are needed to write for a particular audience.

- To determine a reading level requirement for one's writing.
- To estimate an educational level needed to understand written information.

before

Audience analysis

Surveying

Questionnaires

Cluster analysis

Starbursting

after

Thematic content
analysis

Case study

Critical incident

Presentation

Storyboarding

➡ Select and define problem or opportunity
➡ Identify and analyze causes or potential change
   Develop and plan possible solutions or change
   Implement and evaluate solution or change
➡ Measure and report solution or change results
   Recognize and reward team efforts

Research/statistics
Creativity/innovation
Engineering
Project management
Manufacturing
1 Marketing/sales
2 Administration/documentation
Servicing/support
Customer/quality metrics
Change management

- Calculating Robert Gunning's Fog Index:

$$F.I. = 0.4 (A + B)$$

Where: $.4$ = A constant

A = Average number of words
per sentence

B = Number of words with
three or more syllables

Take a random sample of 100 to 200 words of written material.

Count the number of sentences found in the sample.
Note: Independent clauses are counted as sentences.

Divide the total number of words in the sample by the number of sentences. This will result in the average number of words per sentence. See example *Using these Written Process Steps*.

Identify and count the number of words having three or more syllables. *Note: Exclude words that may qualify because of -es, -ed, -ing, or words that are capitalized or compounded.*

Add the totals of Step 3 and Step 4 above and multiply the total by 0.4 to get the fog index. This result identifies the level of reading ability one should have to understand these written process steps.

Using These Written Process Steps

Sample: This tool's process steps numbers 1–5

Total number of words = 127

Total number of sentences = 10
 —Average number of words per sentence = 12.7

Total number of words having three or more syllables = 13

F.I. = 0.4 (12.7 + 13)

F.I. = 10.3

The force field analysis (FFA) is a widely recognized and effective tool for organizational change. According to Kurt Lewin (1951), who developed FFA, a successful change requires the elimination of *restraining forces* that hinder the move toward desired change by *driving forces*. Additionally, if opposing forces in a force field are equal, no change will result. A team uses FFA in a problem-solving effort to identify all forces that prevent the *as is state* (the problem) from changing to a *desired state* (solution). Ideally, change occurs when the as is state is *unfrozen*, moved to a desired state and *refrozen* to institutionalize the change.

- To analyze a problem situation and identify the contributing forces or root causes of the problem.
- To consider change factors that may suggest a solution to a problem or an opportunity for improvement.
- To isolate and prioritize key elements for analysis and action.
- To organize and process information required in an organizational change project.

before

Round robin brainstorming

Interview technique

Cause and effect diagram (CED)

Gap analysis

Focus group

after

Idea borrowing

Why/how charting

Barriers-and-aids analysis

Action plan

Consensus decision making

➡ Select and define problem or opportunity	
➡ Identify and analyze causes or potential change	
➡ Develop and plan possible solutions or change	
Implement and evaluate solution or change	
Measure and report solution or change results	
Recognize and reward team efforts	

	Research/statistics
	Creativity/innovation
	Engineering
2	Project management
	Manufacturing
	Marketing/sales
5	Administration/documentation
3	Servicing/support
4	Customer/quality metrics
1	Change management

Drawing of arrows may differ in two ways:

– The *length* of arrow ⟶ is equal to the amount of force, or,

– The *heavier* the arrow ➤, the stronger the force.

Directionality of forces:

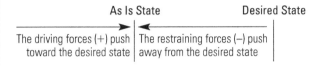

As Is State	Desired State
The driving forces (+) push toward the desired state	The restraining forces (–) push away from the desired state

The team facilitator first draws a basic FFA chart on a whiteboard.

The team's goal is inserted in the chart, and participants discuss the process. See example *Goal: "Tools for Teams" Training for Engineers.*

The team brainstorms and lists on the whiteboard driving forces for the desired state and restraining forces that may hinder or block outright the change.

Next, the team determines the strength of the forces and indicates that strength—with the length of the arrow associated with each force. The longer the arrow, the stronger the force (see *notes and key points*).

Strategies are discussed among team members to *eliminate* or *greatly reduce the restraining forces* and to *add to or strengthen the driving forces* to achieve the goal.

Finally, the team develops an action plan that reflects all activities required to implement the change.

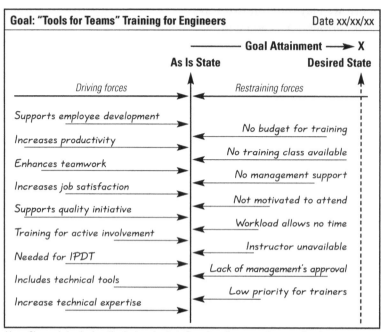

Goal: "Tools for Teams" Training for Engineers Date xx/xx/xx

Goal Attainment ⟶ X

As Is State   Desired State

Driving forces   *Restraining forces*

Supports employee development

Increases productivity

Enhances teamwork

Increases job satisfaction

Supports quality initiative

Training for active involvement

Needed for IPDT

Includes technical tools

Increase technical expertise

No budget for training

No training class available

No management support

Not motivated to attend

Workload allows no time

Instructor unavailable

Lack of management's approval

Low priority for trainers

*Note: Change is institutionalized when the As Is State is unfrozen, performance level
is moved to Goal Attainment, and the Desired State is then refrozen.*

The forced association technique is an idea generation tool that allows a team to associate or connect pairs of unrelated concepts, ideas, or terms to search for potential solutions, improved processes, or new products and services.

- To generate ideas for new products and services.
- To provide an opportunity for team creativity and innovation.
- To allow an individual or team to think in many different ways.

before

Brainstorming

Brainwriting pool

Phillips 66

Reverse brainstorming

Focus group

after

Criteria filtering

Run-it-by

Different point of view

Consensus decision making

Team process assessment

	Select and define problem or opportunity
➥	Identify and analyze causes or potential change
➥	Develop and plan possible solutions or change
	Implement and evaluate solution or change
	Measure and report solution or change results
	Recognize and reward team efforts

	Research/statistics
1	Creativity/innovation
4	Engineering
	Project management
	Manufacturing
3	Marketing/sales
	Administration/documentation
	Servicing/support
	Customer/quality metrics
2	Change management

- Brainstorm several lists of 10 concepts, ideas, and terms. This enables a team to significantly increase the number of possible connections.

The team brainstorms four or five lists of 10 unrelated concepts, ideas, or terms.

The team then mixes all items of randomly selected items and assigns them to two columns. See example *Sports with Marketing Research*.

The team systematically scans each pair and checks for emerging ideas.

This process continues and potential ideas are recorded.

Lastly, the team performs criteria filtering to produce a list of high potential or great ideas.

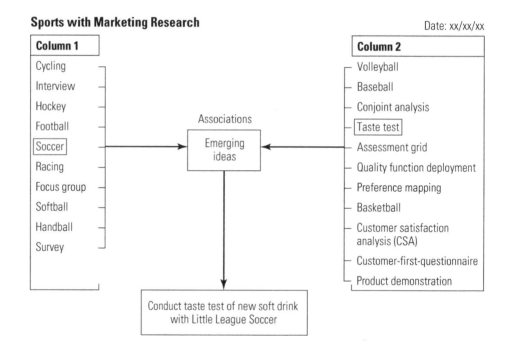

Sports with Marketing Research

Date: xx/xx/xx

The forced choice technique is a team decision making process in which previously identified options are compared against team-established criteria. Criteria may include implementation time, cost of change, feasibility, effectiveness, and so on. Options are systematically compared with all other options, and a tally mark is assigned to the option considered best. Total marks for each option determine ranking.

- To identify a preferred alternative or choice on the basis of rating and ranking criteria.
- To search for quick results and choices.
- To arrive at a team decision from a list of options.

before

Brainstorming

Consensus decision making

Starbursting

Problem selection matrix

Solution matrix

after

Numerical prioritization

Cost-benefit analysis

Resource requirement matrix

Factor analysis

What-if analysis

Select and define problem or opportunity

➡ Identify and analyze causes or potential change

➡ Develop and plan possible solutions or change

Implement and evaluate solution or change

Measure and report solution or change results

Recognize and reward team efforts

Research/statistics

Creativity/innovation

Engineering

3 Project management

Manufacturing

Marketing/sales

2 Administration/documentation

Servicing/support

Customer/quality metrics

1 Change management

- If two options receive the same number of evaluation marks (see this example, options number 3-4), then rank this tie as 5.5 for both to account for rank positions 5-6.
- Lowest rank is considered best option.

The facilitator displays a list of previously recorded options for solutions or improvements. See example *Reduce Defects per Unit (DPU) Levels*.

Next, the facilitator asks participants if any of the options shown need clarification.

The criteria or standard for evaluation of options against each other is discussed and finalized.

The team starts to compare each option against all other options in descending order, for example, option 1 and option 2 as compared to stated criteria. Best option receives a tally mark. Continue with options 1 and 3, etc.

When all options have been compared with option 1, then option 2 is compared with all subsequent options and best options receive a mark. This process continues until all comparisons have been made.

The number of marks are totaled and the highest total is assigned rank 1. Rank 1 is the best option for lowering the DPU level quickly, as shown in this example.

Reduce Defects per Unit (DPU) Levels   Date: xx/xx/xx

Criteria: Length of Time to Show Results	Evaluation	Rank
1. Establish robust design procedures	IIII	9.5
2. Increase test equipment efficiency	IIII I	4
3. Suppliers provide parts process capability data	IIII	5.5
4. Retrain assembly line employees	IIII	5.5
5. Establish process/quality improvement teams	IIII III	2
6. Improve quality assurance measures	IIII II	3
7. Reduce process cycle time	II	8
8. Improve equipment calibration/maintenance	IIII IIII	1
9. Perform research and benchmarking	III	7
10. Implement a just-in-time system	I	9.5

Note: Option #8 (rank 1) would be the quickest to show DPU level reduction results.

A frequency distribution can display in table format quantitative (class intervals) as well as qualitative (categories) data organized in a meaningful order. The FD is often used to group data for histogram, pie chart, or other tools.

- To determine how data is distributed over an acceptable range of upper and lower limits.
- To sort and group raw data.
- To show distribution ratios (percent).

<table>
<tr><td>→</td><td>Select and define problem or opportunity</td><td>1</td><td>Research/statistics</td></tr>
<tr><td>→</td><td>Identify and analyze causes or potential change</td><td></td><td>Creativity/innovation</td></tr>
<tr><td></td><td>Develop and plan possible solutions or change</td><td>4</td><td>Engineering</td></tr>
<tr><td></td><td>Implement and evaluate solution or change</td><td></td><td>Project management</td></tr>
<tr><td></td><td>Measure and report solution or change results</td><td>2</td><td>Manufacturing</td></tr>
<tr><td></td><td>Recognize and reward team efforts</td><td>6</td><td>Marketing/sales</td></tr>
<tr><td></td><td></td><td>7</td><td>Administration/documentation</td></tr>
<tr><td></td><td></td><td>3</td><td>Servicing/support</td></tr>
<tr><td></td><td></td><td>5</td><td>Customer/quality metrics</td></tr>
<tr><td></td><td></td><td></td><td>Change management</td></tr>
</table>

before

Checksheet
Observation
Data collection strategy
Surveying
Interview technique

after

Histogram
Linechart
Pie chart
Two-directional bar chart
Trend analysis

Preparation for Grouping of Data

- Determine the range(s) of the distribution
  $R = (H - L) + 1$
- For smaller data sets, $N = \, <100$: number of class intervals (C.I.) between 5–10
  For larger data sets, $N = \, >100$: number of class intervals (C.I.) between 10–20.
- Width of the class interval to be 2, 3, 5, 10, 20 for smaller numbers. (Add zeros for larger data sets.)
- Select number of class intervals:

  number of C.I. $= \dfrac{R \longleftarrow \text{Range}}{2, 3, 5, 10, 20 \longleftarrow \text{C.I. Width}}$

- Check if the lowest data point in the data set is divisible an equal number of times as those by the C.I. width. If not, select the next lower data point that is.

Count the number (N) of data points or observations (customer complaints per day):

16 11 15 22 31	Count = 30	⑩ 15 17 21 25	
19 10 24 14 26		11 15 18 22 26	
17 22 16 12 27		12 16 19 22 27	
14 13 16 24 28		13 16 19 22 28	
19 29 21 22 19		14 16 19 24 29	High = 31
18 15 17 19 25		14 17 19 24 ㉛	Low = 10

Identify highest and lowest data point.

Calculate range (R): $R = (H - L) + 1$
$$= (31 - 10) + 1 = 22$$

Determine the number of class intervals (C.I.) and width:

number of C.I. $= \dfrac{22}{2, ③, 5, 10, 20} = 7.33 \text{ or } 8$

width = 3   Must be between 5–10

Construct frequency distribution table to display columns for: class interval, class frequency (f), and relative frequency (rf), which is expressed in percent of total (N).

Note: 9 is used as the lowest score since 10 was not divisible by the C.I. of 3 without a remainder.

Insert prepared data into the FD table. See example *Customer Complaints per Day* (quantitative data). Date the table.

Note: For categorical data, construct a FD table as shown in example for customer response data.

Customer Complaints per Day

A. Customer Complaints/Day		Period = 30 days
Class Interval	Class *f*	Class *rf* (%)
9–11	2	6.67
12–14	4	13.33
15–17	7	23.33
18–20	5	16.67
21–23	4	13.33
24–26	4	13.33
27–29	3	10.00
30–32	1	3.33
Date xx/xx/xx	30	100.00

B. Customer Response Data	Total Respondents = 26	
Category	(*N*)	%
Strongly agree	6	23.08
Agree	7	26.92
Neither	3	11.54
Disagree	5	19.23
Strongly disagree	3	11.54
Missing response	2	7.69
Date xx/xx/xx	26	100.00

The fresh eye technique searches for new or unique ideas to a previously analyzed problem. Process owners often have difficulties looking at a problem from an unbiased view. The fresh eye technique allows other, uninvolved people to generate and pass on some innovative ideas on how to solve the problem.

- To stimulate a fresh look at the problem.
- To search for unique or more promising ideas to solve a problem or improve a process.
- To involve outside-the-process people in the idea generation.

before

Reverse brainstorming

Double reversal

Pin cards technique

Activity analysis

Brainstorming

after

Consensus decision making

Different point of view

Action plan

Run-it-by

Presentation

➡ Select and define problem or opportunity
➡ Identify and analyze causes or potential change
➡ Develop and plan possible solutions or change
    Implement and evaluate solution or change
    Measure and report solution or change results
    Recognize and reward team efforts

Research/statistics
1 Creativity/innovation
  Engineering
  Project management
  Manufacturing
2 Marketing/sales
  Administration/documentation
3 Servicing/support
  Customer/quality metrics
  Change management

- There are two variations of the fresh eye technique:
  - Individual or team search for other problem-solving ideas.
  - Asking people outside the team or process to think of problem-solving ideas.

The team decides to use the fresh eye technique to improve the chances of discovering additional, unique, or innovative ideas.

The previously developed problem statement is rechecked for content and clarity. The team may decide to restate the problem in different, yet clear and concise terms. See example *Improve the Effectiveness of Team Training*.

The problem statement is typed and distributed to some people who are interested in assisting but who are outside the problem or have little experience with the undesirable situation.

After approximately one week, all ideas from outsiders are collected and their potential evaluated by the team.

Finally, the team may find that this process may give them some other fresh ideas or build on their previous list of ideas.

Improve the Effectivness of Team Training

List of previously generated ideas

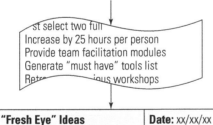

st select two full
Increase by 25 hours per person
Provide team facilitation modules
Generate "must have" tools list
Retr━━━━ious workshops

"Fresh Eye" Ideas	Date: xx/xx/xx
Perform "just-in-time" training	
Allow team participants to input into the training process	
Convert structured modules into team exercises	
Use case studies of successful teams as background for training module development	
Place training into an employee's personal development plan	

A functional map is a multipurpose tool that can illustrate many organizational issues such as capability, performance, competitive behavior, costs and profits, market share, and others. It is often used to display important relationships, time trends, interactions, and SWOT analysis factors: strengths, weaknesses, opportunities, and threats.

- To determine what actions need to be taken.
- To communicate important issues and factors to management.
- To plot performance variables.

before

Data collection strategy

Benchmarking

Matrix data analysis

Comparison matrix

Matrix diagram

after

Cost-benefit analysis

Balance sheet

Action plan

Basili data collection method

Measurement matrix

➡ Select and define problem or opportunity

➡ Identify and analyze causes or potential change

➡ Develop and plan possible solutions or change

Implement and evaluate solution or change

Measure and report solution or change results

Recognize and reward team efforts

Research/statistics

Creativity/innovation

2 Engineering

1 Project management

Manufacturing

3 Marketing/sales

Administration/documentation

4 Servicing/support

Customer/quality metrics

Change management

- Applications for functional maps:
  - Product development
  - Market share
  - Competition/gap analysis
  - Technology/innovation
  - Research and development
  - Products and service
  - Performance characteristics
  - Customer behavior

The first action item for team participants is to collect background data relevant to the topic to be displayed on a functional map. Benchmarking, case analyses, trade journals, and other sources should be reviewed for this purpose.

Once the appropriate data has been collected, the team decides on the forms of functional maps to be used. See *notes and key points* for some considerations.

Two or three sets of variables are used to develop the maps. See example *Product Price/Performance Comparison*.

Completed maps are verified by the team and appropriate experts in the field. Revisions are made and all maps are dated.

Product Price/Performance Comparison

Team: <u>Marketing</u>   Date: xx/xx/xx

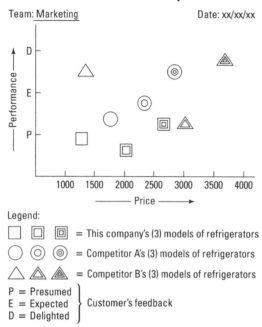

Legend:

▢ ▣ ▩ = This company's (3) models of refrigerators

◯ ◎ ⊚ = Competitor A's (3) models of refrigerators

△ △ ▲ = Competitor B's (3) models of refrigerators

P = Presumed
E = Expected   } Customer's feedback
D = Delighted

The futures wheel is a tool used to forecast or predict trends in possible reactions to or associated consequences for an initial event, idea, or action taken. The consideration here is that every initial event may have several first-order consequences, they in turn may have second-order consequences, and so continue until a very detailed level of breakdown is achieved.

- To identify possible reactions or consequences for proposed problem-solving or process-improvement ideas.
- To assess possible future impact on people or processes.
- To check that every issue has been considered prior to implementing an action plan.
- To avoid unpleasant surprises before future actions are taken.

before

Reverse brainstorming

Brainstorming

Double reversal

Organization readiness chart

Trend analysis

after

Action plan

Mind flow

Rating matrix

Force field analysis (FFA)

Process analysis

	Select and define problem or opportunity
➡	Identify and analyze causes or potential change
➡	Develop and plan possible solutions or change
➡	Implement and evaluate solution or change
	Measure and report solution or change results
	Recognize and reward team efforts

	Research/statistics
1	Creativity/innovation
	Engineering
4	Project management
	Manufacturing
3	Marketing/sales
5	Administration/documentation
	Servicing/support
	Customer/quality metrics
2	Change management

Futures wheel symbolics:

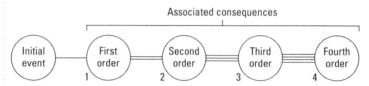

The team assembles around a whiteboard or two, side-by-side standing easels with flip charts.

An event, idea, trend, or action is recorded inside a large circle, which is the initial event or step. See example *Support a Work Ethic of TQM*.

The team now brainstorms possible first-order (1) consequences to the inital events. Circles are drawn and connected to the center circle.

Next, circles are drawn for the second-order (2) consequences, connected with parallel lines to signify second order as seen in the example.

The team completes this futures wheel and records all consequences.

Finally, the team discusses the completed futures wheel and identifies all precautionary or preliminary action items that need attention before implementation to reduce the risk of unpleasant surprises.

The futures wheel is checked and dated.

Support a Work Ethic of TQM

Date: xx/xx/xx

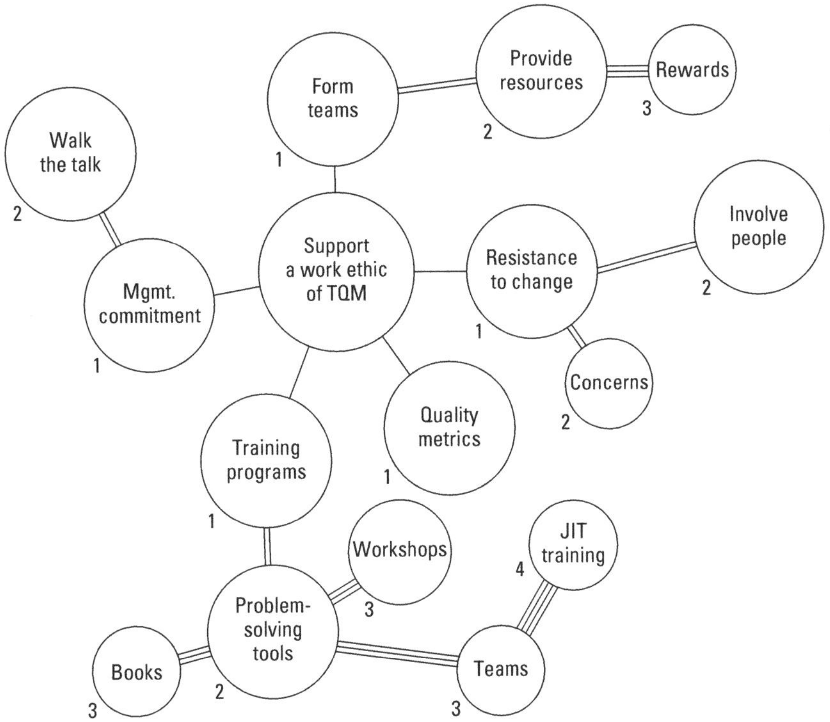

A Gantt chart effectively documents the schedule of planned activities, milestone dates, and the assigned responsibility for completing the activities. Used as a project management tool, it tracks and monitors completion of goals, possible delays, and time left to target achievement. Critical milestone dates are placed on horizontal activity bars to enable the comparison of planned to actual performance. It is used as supporting data in a project status report.

- To schedule and monitor sequenced project activities.
- To determine resource requirements, task responsibility, and time duration of the overall schedule of the project.
- To manage the completion of a project.

before

Resource histogram

Responsibility matrix

Monthly assessment schedule

Work breakdown structure (WBS)

Program evaluation and review technique (PERT)

after

Basili data collection method

Objectives matrix (OMAX)

Action plan

Major program status

Events log

Select and define problem or opportunity
Identify and analyze causes or potential change
➡ Develop and plan possible solutions or change
Implement and evaluate solution or change
➡ Measure and report solution or change results
Recognize and reward team efforts

Research/statistics
Creativity/innovation
Engineering
1 Project management
Manufacturing
Marketing/sales
Administration/documentation
Servicing/support
3 Customer/quality metrics
2 Change management

- Legend: Various symbols are used. For this example:

☐ Scheduled ■ Completed • Critical milestone date

- Optional: To identify activity completed

The team facilitator records all necessary activities of a project on a flip chart. Activities were identified by team participants who represent or have knowledge of the work that needs to be completed.

A basic Gantt chart is drawn on a whiteboard with a list of activities ordered by sequence of completion. See example *Typical Research Project Activities and Time Frames*.

The team estimates the time required for each activity. On that basis, an activity completion date (due date) is associated with every listed activity and recorded. Horizontal bars are drawn to represent time duration and the begin/end dates for each activity, as shown in the example.

Lastly, ownership (responsibility) is determined or assigned for the completion of each activity.

The team checks activities, sequence and duration, makes final revisions, and dates the chart. Once the chart is finalized, it is given to the project manager.

Typical Research Project Activities and Time Frames

Employee Acceptance of the Establishment of Flextime																			Date: xx/xx/xx
Task no.	Task	Due date	J	F	M	A	M	J	J	A	S	O	N	D					Owner
1	Topic selection	2–1	▮																HR director
2	Objectives-proposal	3–1	▮•																HR/labor
3	Research questions and hypothesis	3–1	▮																Researcher
4	Research design	3–1	▮																Researcher
5	Review of literature	5–15	▬▬▬▬•▬																Library staff
6	Population definition	6–1				▮													Researcher
7	Sampling	6–15				▮													"
8	Instrument development	6–20				▬▬													"
9	Field testing	7–15						▬▬											Training staff
10	Data collection	9–1						▬□•											Administration
11	Follow-up	9–20						□											"
12	Data-entry-SPSS	9–30							□										Quality staff
13	Descriptive statistics	10–10							□										"
14	Inferential statistics	10–10							□										"
15	Findings/results	10–20							□•										Researcher
16	Report evaluation by panel of experts	11–1							□										Company reps
17	Revisions	11–15							□										Researcher
18	Final report	12–1							□•										"
Notes: □ Scheduled ▬ Completed • Milestone																			

The gap analysis tool is an ideal method to determine resources and action plans required to close a performance gap. This gap is identified as an outcome of comparing current performance or status to desired performance or future status by means of benchmarking, market research, or other results data comparisons.

- To analyze benchmarking gaps (differences).
- To provide input data for organizational change.
- To expedite data collection for the planning process.
- To identify requirements for reaching future goals.

before

Benchmarking

Checklist

Comparison matrix

Radar chart

Deming PDSA cycle

after

Action plan

Force field analysis (FFA)

Barriers-and-aids analysis

Milestones chart

Numerical prioritization

Select and define problem or opportunity

Identify and analyze causes or potential change

➡ Develop and plan possible solutions or change

Implement and evaluate solution or change

➡ Measure and report solution or change results

Recognize and reward team efforts

- All differences should be evaluated and prioritized for the development of an action plan.

Research/statistics

3 Creativity/innovation

Engineering

2 Project management

Manufacturing

Marketing/sales

Administration/documentation

Servicing/support

Customer/quality metrics

1 Change management

Prepare a gap analysis worksheet as shown in the example *Employee Training*.

Fill in column (1), reflecting the Present State of some actual performance state.

Indicate the desired performance, the Future State in column (2).

List all necessary Requirements in column (3) in order to move from column (1) to column (2).

Under each listed requirement, identify all resources needed to effect the change.

Employee Training

Human Resources—Training and Development Section		Date : xx/xx/xx
Present State (1)	**Requirements (3)**	**Future State (2)**
1. Lack of diversity training for the workforce.	1. Develop a diversity training program • Conduct train-the-trainer sessions • Pilot the program • Verify resources required, budget staff, schedule, etc.	1. Conduct diversity training for all employees.
2. Average training per employee is 12 hours/year.	2. Perform training needs analysis • Identify training program and materials • Budget training • Establish a balanced training schedule	2. Increase average training per employee to 24 hours/year.
3. Insufficient training staff — four trainers.	3. Hire three more trainers • Place an ad for open positions • Set up and perform interviews • Make offer	3. Augment training staff to seven trainers.

The Gozinto chart is a vertical tree diagram that displays hierarchical levels of detail of a complete product assembly to ship process. Developed by A. Vazsonyi, this project planning tool is of great value for kitting, bill of materials (BOM) auditing, parts/number identification, and operator training.

- To breakdown a product into its parts.
- To flow out the assembly process.
- To cross-reference parts data with the hierarchical levels of assembly.

➡ Select and define problem or opportunity
➡ Identify and analyze causes or potential change
Develop and plan possible solutions or change
Implement and evaluate solution or change
Measure and report solution or change results
Recognize and reward team efforts

Research/statistics
Creativity/innovation
Engineering
1 Project management
3 Manufacturing
Marketing/sales
4 Administration/documentation
Servicing/support
Customer/quality metrics
2 Change management

- Gozinto chart numbering is by levels and BOM or part identification number. Example: 3015: 3 for level 3, 015 for bill of material or part ID number.
- This is a similar approach to the work breakdown structure (WBS) chart.

before

Tree diagram

Work breakdown structure (WBS)

Information needs analysis

Process analysis

Work flow analysis (WFA)

after

Failure mode and effect analysis

Task analysis

Potential problem analysis

Dendrogram

Activity analysis

List all parts required to completely assemble the product.

Draw a hierarchy of assembly, showing levels of detail from the top down to the basic level of parts.

Provide identification of parts; name and number each part charted.

Check completeness of chart and date.

Mousetrap — Assembly to Ship

Date: xx/xx/xx

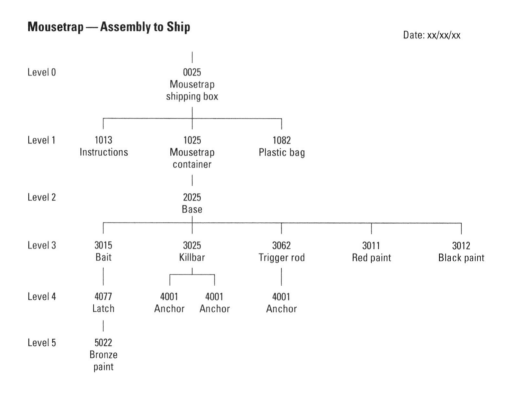

A histogram is a column graph that displays the central tendency, process variability and relative frequency of collected data. Typically taken from a frequency distribution, a histogram is very effective in providing a visual presentation of how actual measurements of characteristics vary around a target or specification value.

- To show problematic process variations from a desired result or value.
- To determine if the process variability within a data distribution is within specification limits.
- To identify shifts in process capability.
- To verify changes in the process after improvements have been made.

before
Checksheet
Frequency
distribution (FD)
Events log
Observation
Box plot
after
Pareto chart
Multivariable chart
Presentation
Pie chart
Stratification

➥ Select and define problem or opportunity
➥ Identify and analyze causes or potential change
   Develop and plan possible solutions or change
➥ Implement and evaluate solution or change
➥ Measure and report solution or change results
   Recognize and reward team efforts

1   Research/statistics
    Creativity/innovation
    Engineering
2   Project management
4   Manufacturing
5   Marketing/sales
    Administration/documentation
    Servicing/support
3   Customer/quality metrics
    Change management

- Preparation for grouping:
- Determine the range (R) of the distribution

$$R = (H - L) + 1$$

- For small data sets ($N < 100$): Number the class intervals (C.I.) between 5–10, if ($N > 100$): Number the class intervals (C.I.) between 10–20.
- Width of C.I. to be 2, 3, 5, 10, 20 for smaller samples, add zeros for larger data sets.
- Select number of class intervals by calculating:

$$\text{number of C.I.} = \frac{R \longleftarrow \text{Range}}{2, 3, 5, 10, 20 \longleftarrow \text{C.I. width}}$$

- Check to determine if lowest data point in the data set is divisible an equal number of times by the C.I. width. If not, select the next lowest data point that is equally divisible.

Count the number (N) of data points or observations (daily rework hours):

16	11	15	22	31	Count = 30	⑩	15	17	21	25
19	10	24	14	26		11	15	18	22	26
17	22	16	12	27		12	16	19	22	27
14	13	16	24	28		13	16	19	22	28
19	29	21	22	19		14	16	19	24	29
18	15	17	19	25		14	17	19	24	㉛

High = 31

Low = 10

Identify highest and lowest data point.

Calculate range (R): $R = (H - L) + 1$
$$= (31 - 10) + 1 = 22$$

Determine the number of class intervals (C.I.) and width:

$$\text{number of C.I.} = \frac{22}{2, ③, 5, 10, 20} = 7.33 \text{ or } 8$$

width = 3

Must be between 8–10

List resulting Class Intervals (C.I.) and frequency (*f*):

C.I.	*f*
9–11	2
12–14	4
15–17	7
18–20	5
21–23	4
24–26	4
27–29	3
30–32	1

Construct a histogram. Apply the 3:4 ratio rule: The height of the *Y* axis must be 75 percent of the length (100 percent) of the *X* axis.

Complete the histogram to display the number of rework hours completed during the last 30 days. Date the histogram.

Histogram — Completed Rework Hours

Date: xx/xx/xx

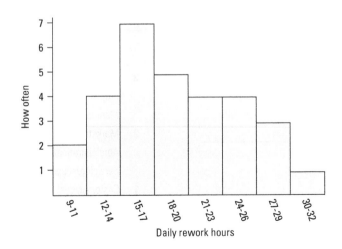

The house of quality matrix is an important tool for translating customer requirements and expectations into appropriate design and product characteristics. Starting with marketing and engineering, a house of quality matrix will ensure that characteristics are considered and acted on at every stage of product development. It is considered a must for integrated product development teams (IPDT) in that it forces cross-functional communications and teamwork in the planning, engineering, and manufacturing activities and aligns them to achieve quality and customer satisfaction.

- To provide an interlocking matrix that reflects customer needs and wants and necessary design features to be included in a product in order to gain maximum product acceptance.
- To translate customer requirements and expectations into quantitative, technical language.
- To minimize potential problems and engineering change orders by carefully mapping out functional requirements as they relate to the voice of the customer.

before

Benchmarking

Interview technique

Circles of knowledge

Audience analysis

Information needs analysis

after

Comparison matrix

Problem specification

Consensus decision making

Weighted voting

Force field analysis (FFA)

➡ Select and define problem or opportunity

Identify and analyze causes or potential change

➡ Develop and plan possible solutions or change

Implement and evaluate solution or change

Measure and report solution or change results

Recognize and reward team efforts

	Research/statistics
	Creativity/innovation
3	Engineering
	Project management
	Manufacturing
2	Marketing/sales
	Administration/documentation
	Servicing/support
1	Customer/quality metrics
4	Change management

The house of quality matrix is the first of many matrices linked together to carry the customer requirements through to manufacturing. The process known as quality function deployment (QFD) translates customer requirements (the *whats*) into technical requirements (the *hows*). The *hows* in turn become the *whats* for linking matrices to capture requirements in greater and greater detail.

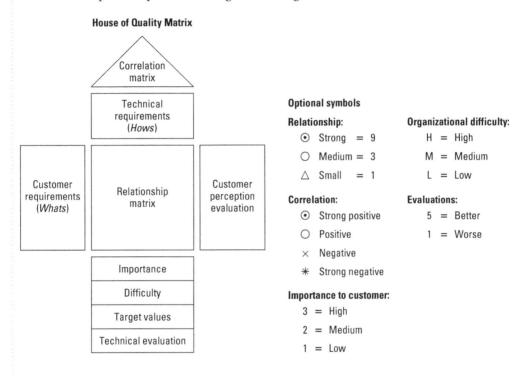

House of Quality Matrix

Optional symbols

Relationship:
⊙   Strong   = 9
○   Medium = 3
△   Small   = 1

Organizational difficulty:
H = High
M = Medium
L = Low

Correlation:
⊙   Strong positive
○   Positive
×   Negative
✳   Strong negative

Evaluations:
5 = Better
1 = Worse

Importance to customer:
3 = High
2 = Medium
1 = Low

Example of Importance Weighting:

Importance to customer	Materials: low cost	
3	○	3 x 3 = 9
3		
1	○	1 x 3 = 3
2		
2		
2	△	2 x 1 = 2
1	○	1 x 3 = 3
3	⊙	3 x 9 =27
2		
3	○	3 x 3 = 9

53

To develop a house of quality for a particular product, great care must be taken to assemble a cross-functional team that reflects representation from each required discipline of the organization.

The first action of the team requires a data collection process that acquires customer requirements and expectations and benchmark data for a competitive analysis. See example *Multi-Purpose Personal Copier*.

The team facilitator draws the basic house of quality on flip charts. Since the development of the house will take several team sessions, work needs to be completed in a structured, systematic way.

All customer requirements (whats) and their associated importance to the customer ratings are listed in the matrix.

Next, the team determines the technical requirements (hows) and the target values. The matrix is being completed as decisions are made.

The benchmark data, customer perception of competitors (A + B) and this organization, are analyzed and recorded in the matrix.

Technical evaluation data from competitors (A + B) and this organization's capability are analyzed, evaluated, and recorded in the matrix.

The team is now ready to perform the following tasks as shown in the example:

– Correlate the technical requirements.
– Verify relationships between customer requirements and technical requirements pairs.
– Calculate importance weighting. See example in *notes and key points*.
– Rate, by team consensus, organizational difficulty.

Finally, the team facilitator, after having drafted the complete house of quality matrix, asks the team to check information and calculations.

The house of quality matrix is finalized and distributed to all representatives. This matrix will also provide the input data for the next matrix to be developed.

Multi-Purpose Personal Copier

Date: xx/xx/xx

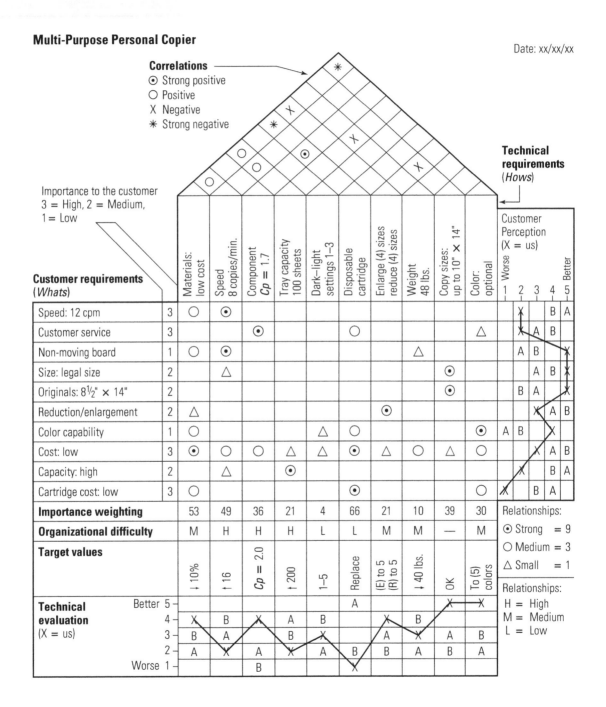

Hypothesis testing is a decision-making procedure that requires a random sample to be taken from a defined population and, through statistical testing, the difference or relationship of the hypothesized population mean and the actual sample mean is determined. Since the null hypothesis (H_0) assumes no statistical significant difference or relationship, a test result is measured against critical value (level of significance) to decide if the null hypothesis is a reasonable statement and should not be rejected, or if the observed difference or relationship is statistically significant and therefore should be rejected.

- To reject or not reject a stated null hypothesis (H_0).
- To perform inferential statistics—that is, to make inferences to a defined population on the basis of test results from a sample of that population.
- To use a systematic process or decision rule to make a decision.

before

Data collection strategy

Demographic analysis

Sampling methods

Surveying

Descriptive statistics

after

Response data encoding form

Two-dimensional survey grid

Response matrix analysis

Information needs analysis

SWOT analysis

➡ Select and define problem or opportunity
➡ Identify and analyze causes or potential change
  Develop and plan possible solutions or change
➡ Implement and evaluate solution or change
➡ Measure and report solution or change results
  Recognize and reward team efforts

1 Research/statistics
   Creativity/innovation
2 Engineering
   Project management
   Manufacturing
   Marketing/sales
   Administration/documentation
   Servicing/support
4 Customer/quality metrics
3 Change management

Note: Sufficient supporting information is presented here to provide a good overview of the hypothesis-testing procedure using the chi-square test to illustrate the sequential steps involved to arrive at a decision. It is suggested, however, that the reader refer to a text on statistics for additional information and examples.

Recommended procedure for testing a null hypothesis

(Note: A chi-square (χ^2) test is used for this example):

1. *Data Source:* Customer satisfaction visits by executives
   - Business unit visited: ☐ X   ☐ Y
   - Corrective action required: ☐ Yes   ☐ No

2. *Research and Null Hypotheses (H_1 – H_0)*
   H_1: There is a statistically significant relationship in the number of action items required to be done as a result of customer visits by executives to business units X and Y.
   H_0: There is no statistically significant relationship in the number of action items required to be done as a result of customer visits by executives to business units (X) and (Y) measured at .05 level of significance using a χ^2 test of independence.

3. *Test used:* Chi-square (χ^2) test of independence

4. *Level of significance used:* .05

5. *Degrees of freedom:* 1   df = $(c - 1)(r - 1)$

6. *Test result:* $\chi^2 = 3.63$

7. *Critical value:* 3.841 (See *Chi-Square Distribution Table*)

8. Decision: Accept H_0! (If the test result is lower than the critical value, the H_0 is accepted. The test result is in the acceptance region under the curve.)

   Chi-square analysis: A contingency matrix table constructed to cross-classify at least two characteristics and to test whether they are related. These tables can be configured to have 2 × 2, 2 × 3, 2 × 4, 2 × 5, 3 × 5, 4 × 5, or 5 × 5 cells.

Example: A 2 × 5 matrix

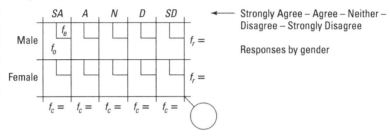

Strongly Agree – Agree – Neither –
Disagree – Strongly Disagree

Responses by gender

Nominal data (data by name) is used:

Example: — Technical$_1$ — Hourly$_2$ — Management$_3$
— SA_1 — A_2 — N_3 — D_4 — SD_5
— True — False — Uncertain
— Male — Female

Symbolics:

x^2 = Chi – square statistics
f_o = Frequency observed
f_e = Frequency expected
f_c = Frequency column
f_r = Frequency row
df = Degrees of freedom
Alpha .05 = Level of significance (95% confidence)
N = Total number of responses (data points)
r = Row
c = Column

Equations:

$$\chi^2 = \sum \frac{(f_o - f_e)^2}{f_e}$$

$$f_e = \frac{f_r \times f_c}{N}$$

$$df = (c - 1)(r - 1)$$

Partial Chi-Square Distribution Table

(Refer to Table D in the Appendix for a complete table of critical values for x^2.)

Degrees of Freedom n	0.10	0.05	0.02	0.01 ← Level of Significance
1	2.706	3.841	5.412	6.635
2	4.605	5.991	7.824	9.210
3	6.251	7.815	9.837	11.341
4	7.779	9.488	11.668	13.277
5	9.236	11.070	13.388	15.086
6	10.645	12.592	15.033	16.812
7	12.017	14.067	16.622	18.475
8	13.362	15.507	18.168	20.090

Critical Value

Note: This example points to a critical value of 3.841 using df = 1 with .05 level of significance.

Data has been collected as a result of customer satisfaction visits by executives. As a result of these visits, the following data were tabulated:

	Corrective Action
Business Unit X	Yes = 22, No = 6
Business Unit Y	Yes = 14, No = 12

Since the data shown are nominal (qualitative) data, a chi-square test is used to perform a hypothesis testing procedure (see *notes and key points*).

Steps 1 through 8 of the hypothesis testing procedure are completed. The calculations are found in the example shown.

The decision rule reflected that the null hypothesis (H_0) has been accepted. There is no statistical significant relationship in business units with corrective action items required.

Customer Satisfaction Visits by Executives

Data source:

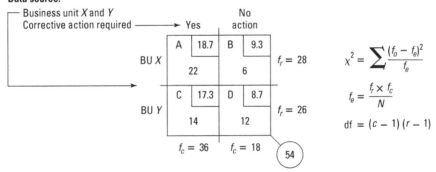

To calculate f_e:

(A) $\dfrac{28 \times 36}{54} = 18.7$ $\chi^2 = \dfrac{(22 - 18.7)^2}{18.7} + \dfrac{(6 - 9.3)^2}{9.3} + \dfrac{(14 - 17.3)^2}{17.3} + \dfrac{(12 - 8.7)^2}{8.7}$

(B) $\dfrac{28 \times 18}{54} = 9.3$ $\chi^2 = \quad .58 \quad + \quad 1.17 \quad + \quad .63 \quad + \quad 1.25$

(C) $\dfrac{26 \times 36}{54} = 17.3$ $\chi^2 = \quad 3.63 \quad$ | Table at .05 = **3.841** $\therefore$ Accept H_0

There is no statistically significant relationship.

(D) $\dfrac{26 \times 18}{54} = 8.7$ If cell C = 12 *yes* votes, then χ^2 for cells A–D would be .74 + 1.41 + .87 + 1.65 respectively for a total X of 4.67, and therefore would reject H_0 at alpha .05!

First used by the Battelle Institute of Frankfurt, Germany, the idea advocate is an excellent idea-evaluation tool. The team assigns the role of idea advocate to a participant who promotes a particular idea as the most valuable from a list of previously generated ideas. The more an idea advocate promotes different ideas, the more powerful the selection process, since every idea is fully examined by the evaluating team.

- To ensure fair examination of all ideas.
- To give every presented idea equal chance of being selected.
- To uncover the positive aspects of every idea presented.

before

Phillips 66

Presentation

Basili data collection method

Rating matrix

Buzz group

after

Problem selection matrix

Different point of view

Barriers-and-aids analysis

Run-it-by

Needs analysis

➡ Select and define problem or opportunity
  Identify and analyze causes or potential change
➡ Develop and plan possible solutions or change
  Implement and evaluate solution or change
  Measure and report solution or change results
  Recognize and reward team efforts

- Consideration should be given to also assigning a devil's advocate for a more balanced assessment of certain proposed ideas.

	Research/statistics
1	Creativity/innovation
	Engineering
3	Project management
	Manufacturing
4	Marketing/sales
	Administration/documentation
	Servicing/support
	Customer/quality metrics
2	Change management

The team reviews a list of previously generated ideas.

The next task is to assign idea advocate roles to: (a) the person who proposed the idea, (b) the person who will implement the idea, and (c) the person who strongly argues in support of selecting the idea.

The team examines each idea as it is presented by an idea advocate who explains why selecting the idea makes sense and why the idea would indeed be the best among all others.

After all idea advocates have presented their ideas, the team reaches consensus on which idea has the highest potential to solve a problem or improve a process.

Select Best Training Method

Date: xx/xx/xx

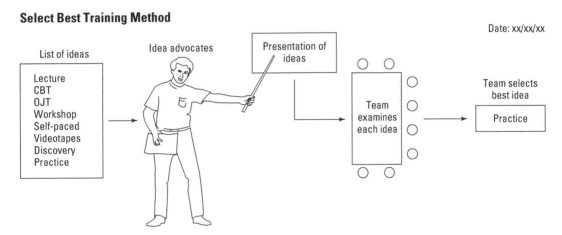

Note: CBT = computer-based-training
       OJT = on-the-job training

The idea borrowing technique allows team participants to bring to the surface ideas from inside and outside the organization or through their own creativity. Team-established criteria is used to rate and select the top-rated ideas considered for implementing.

- To surface best practices, technological innovations, and perceived good ideas.
- To supplement brainstorming and benchmarking activities.
- To stimulate the creativity of employees.

before

Information needs analysis

Benchmarking

Fresh eye

Wildest idea technique

Mental imaging

after

Idea advocate

Run-it-by

Creativity assessment

Why/how charting

Presentation

➡ Select and define problem or opportunity

    Identify and analyze causes or potential change

➡ Develop and plan possible solutions or change

    Implement and evaluate solution or change

    Measure and report solution or change results

➡ Recognize and reward team efforts

	Research/statistics
1	Creativity/innovation
2	Engineering
	Project management
	Manufacturing
4	Marketing/sales
	Administration/documentation
	Servicing/support
	Customer/quality metrics
3	Change management

- Suggested idea selection criteria and scales:

Source of Idea	Potential Use	Estimated Implementation Costs
3 = Self (original)	5 = High	3 = Acceptable
2 = Internal	3 = Medium	2 = Marginal
1 = External	1 = Low	1 = Unacceptable

- To select the best idea, multiply columns Source × Potential × Costs. Rank ideas: highest total = best idea.

The team facilitator reviews the idea borrowing technique with the team and answers any questions participants may have at this point.

Participants silently list their ideas on provided paper. Ideas may be best practices, innovations, untried employee suggestions, benchmarking discoveries, and so forth.

After some predetermined idea-generation time, the facilitator asks participants to share their ideas. All ideas are listed on a whiteboard or flip charts.

The team discusses all ideas and, through consensus, identifies the top 15–20 ideas. The facilitator prepares a matrix containing this final list of ideas. See example *List of Ideas to Upgrade Employee Training*.

Next, the team decides on a set of criteria and associated scales to be used to rate all ideas.

All ideas are rated and ranked in accordance with the established criteria, as shown in this example.

Finally, the team prepares a presentation for presenting the ideas to upper management.

List of Ideas to Upgrade Employee Training

Description of Ideas	Source of Idea	Potential Use of Idea	Estimated Implementation Costs	Idea Selection	
				Total	Rank
Exchange and/or share trainers with other organizations	3	1	2	6	3
Ask employees to review the literature and present on contemporary topics	2	3	3	(18)	1
Make available internet access for technology update	1	5	1	5	4
Contract university faculty for special topic sessions	1	3	1	3	6
Engage recognized company subject matter experts to present on specific skill areas	1	5	3	15	2
Ask employees to team-develop their own training modules	2	1	2	4	5

Note: (1) **Source** **Potential** **Cost**
      3 = *self*   5 = *high*   3 = *acceptable*
      2 = *internal*   3 = *medium* 2 = *marginal*
      1 = *external* 1 = *low*   1 = *unacceptable*

(2) *Multiply columns: Source × Potential × Costs*

(3) (18) *highest total is best idea.*

First developed by Richard Vaughn (1978), the idea grid is considered an effective idea-generating tool because it provides an instant visualization of a potential market niche or an opportunity for marketing a new product. Ideas are generated when each grid quadrant is analyzed for product positioning options in comparison to the competitors' researched product positions on the idea grid.

- To identify a marketing opportunity and develop the appropriate strategy.
- To properly position one's product in the market.
- To reposition existing products and services.

before

Information needs analysis

Case study

Interview technique

Comparison matrix

Different point of view

after

Benchmarking

Gap analysis

Idea borrowing

Consensus decision making

Presentation

➥ Select and define problem or opportunity

➥ Identify and analyze causes or potential change

➥ Develop and plan possible solutions or change

Implement and evaluate solution or change

Measure and report solution or change results

Recognize and reward team efforts

Research/statistics

Creativity/innovation

Engineering

Project management

Manufacturing

1 Marketing/sales

Administration/documentation

3 Servicing/support

2 Customer/quality metrics

Change management

- Explanation of idea grid quadrant designations:
  - High involvement—Data and perceptions of high cost products. Example: Cars, trucks, appliances.
  - Low Involvement—Data and perception of low cost products. Example: Household items, books, supplies.
  - Think—Customer collects hard facts, specifications, consumer report-type data to decide on product.
  - Feel—Customers are emotionally involved; feelings play a large role in the decision to purchase.

The marketing team first completes the usual data collection process to acquire competitors' product information, marketing data, and product quality and performance data in order to position competitors on the idea grid.

The team next studies the idea grid and considers the four alternatives for the positioning of the product. See example *"Easystats" Primer for Statistics Courses*.

Background information: Required statistics courses in university degree programs are perceived as difficult by math haters. The team has reviewed five different textbooks on statistics and found all five to be difficult reading. Therefore, a need exists to provide an "Easystats" primer to assist students in the learning process.

Idea grid quadrant analysis:

- Alternative 1: *High involvement* with *Think*
  Convert the idea of an "Easystats" primer into a computer-based training program for students to pace themselves through statistics. Disadvantage: High program cost, requires computer equipment.

- Alternative 2: *High involvement* with *Feel*
  Create an interactive, study-group workshop using "Easystats" primer materials. This option requires group meetings. Benefits are instant communication and clarification.

- Alternative 3: *Low involvement* with *think*
  Market the "Easystats" primer as a supplement to various textbooks on statistics. Disadvantage is that student may think this supplement to be optional.
- Alternative 4: *Low involvement* with *feel*
  Market the "Easystats" primer as a stand-alone text with an easy to understand step-by-step set of instructions and examples. The "Easystats" primer drives out anxiety and allows students to enjoy the course.

Finally, the team reaches consensus on the positioning of the "Easystats" primer as shown in this example.

"Easystats" Primer for Statistics Courses   Date: xx/xx/xx

	Think	**Feel**
High involvement		
Low involvement	A • B • D • C • E •	• "Easystats" Primer

Note: A–E are various textbooks on statistics by various authors.

An importance weighting matrix is useful in a decision-making process where a particular product must be chosen on the basis of importance to the problem-solving or improvement-opportunity effort. A relative weight (percentage) is assigned to each characteristic as a multiplier to a product rating. The product with the highest weighted total is chosen as rank (1) importance.

- To compare and select a product or service on the basis of importance weighting considerations.
- To apply importance weighting in the decision-making process.
- To identify the best choice.

before

Multivoting

Starbursting

Matrix diagram

Information needs analysis

Opportunity analysis

after

Prioritization matrix

Consensus decision making

Matrix data analysis

Nominal group technique (NGT)

Cost-benefit analysis

➥ Select and define problem or opportunity
　Identify and analyze causes or potential change
➥ Develop and plan possible solutions or change
➥ Implement and evaluate solution or change
　Measure and report solution or change results
　Recognize and reward team efforts

1　Research/statistics
　Creativity/innovation
　Engineering
4　Project management
　Manufacturing
　Marketing/sales
　Administration/documentation
　Servicing/support
2　Customer/quality metrics
3　Change management

- Sum of all distributed factor weights must equal 1.00 (100%)
- Rating scales: 1 to 5, 5 being most supportive.
    - 1 to 10, 10 being most supportive.
    - Also, 1 to 10 provides greater precision.
- Ranking: Lowest rank (1) is of highest importance

The team facilitator lists all products or services to be considered in the decision-making process.

Next, the technique of importance weighting is reviewed with the participants and key product or service-related characteristics identified. See example *Videotape Purchase Decision*.

Participants reach consensus on the distribution of importance weight factor for all characteristics.
Note: Sum of weight factors must equal 1 (100 percent).

The participants rate all products (or services) using a scale of 1 to 5, 5 being most supportive.

Each product (or service) rating is multiplied by the weight factor and recorded as shown. This process continues until all products have been "weight" calculated as shown in the example.

Finally, the calculated products are summed and ranked. Rank (1) is the selection made.

The matrix is dated and given to the process owner.

Videotape Purchase Decision Date: xx/xx/xx

Key Support Area / Videotape Choices	Customer satisfaction	Communications	Productivity	Resources	Teaming	Quality	Weight Factor	
	.25	.10	.15	.10	.20	.20		
Managing change	4	3	4	4	4	5	4.10	(1)
	1.00	.30	.60	.40	.80	1.00		
Managing stress	2	5	3	2	4	2	2.85	3
	.50	.50	.45	.20	.80	.40		
Managing conflict	5	5	2	1	4	1	3.15	2
	1.25	.50	.30	.10	.80	.20		
Managing time	3	1	5	4	3	1	2.80	4
	.75	.10	.75	.40	.60	.20		
Managing projects	1	3	5	4	2	2	2.50	5
	.25	.30	.75	.40	.40	.40		

Note: Rating Scale: 1–5, 5 is high

Weighted totals ⟶
Weighted rankings ⟶

Note: (1) Rank 1 is the best selection.

The influence diagram is used to plan or forecast the flow of processes and possible outcomes. Since it illustrates a pathway to achieving a desired goal and identifies potential blockages or pitfalls, it therefore has a direct influence on the decision-making process.

- To identify factors that can affect the action steps required to reach a goal.
- To plan major events.
- To envision possible consequences and cause and effect relationships; to plan to avoid potential problem areas.

before

Interview technique

Relationship map

Circles of influence

Dimensions cube

Value analysis

after

Decision process flowchart

Futures wheel

Opportunity analysis

Why/how charting

Action plan

Select and define problem or opportunity

➡ Identify and analyze causes or potential change

➡ Develop and plan possible solutions or change

Implement and evaluate solution or change

Measure and report solution or change results

Recognize and reward team efforts

Research/statistics

Creativity/innovation

Engineering

2 Project management

Manufacturing

1 Marketing/sales

Administration/documentation

Servicing/support

Customer/quality metrics

3 Change management

- Draw an influence diagram from left (sources, ideas) to right (decision, outcome). The flow is similar to that of a reversed tree diagram.

Participants of a futuring team select a goal to be diagrammed. See example *Update Training Methods*.

Participants next identify required action steps, potential problem areas, and interrelationships of actions.

The facilitator records all input on flip charts. The team attempts to sort all recorded items into some logical sequence of action.

Next, the facilitator draws an influence diagram on a whiteboard using the somewhat sequenced information from the flip charts.

Participants assist the facilitator in the diagramming process by discussing the flow, branches, and the soundness of recorded information.

Lastly, the diagram is checked a final time, dated, and saved for further action.

Upgrade Training Methods

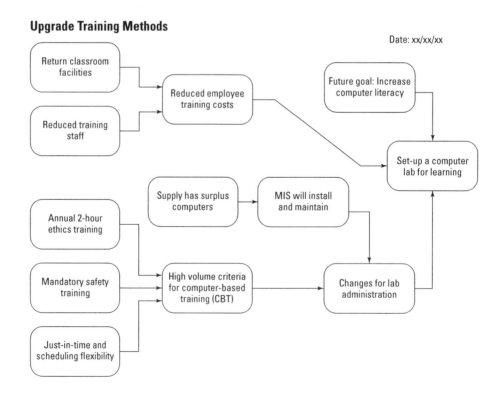

An information needs analysis allows the researcher to quickly check to see what information is available and what information needs to be researched. A systematic flow directs the researcher to consider various information sources and the data collection methods to be used.

- To identify information needs for implementing a particular project.
- To acquire knowledge through applied research methods.
- To determine what information is needed to begin a problem-solving effort.

before

Data collection strategy

Surveying

Questionnaires

Sampling methods

Thematic content analysis

after

Project planning log

Interview technique

Customer needs table

Process analysis

Problem analysis

➡ Select and define problem or opportunity

➡ Identify and analyze causes or potential change

➡ Develop and plan possible solutions or change

Implement and evaluate solution or change

Measure and report solution or change results

Recognize and reward team efforts

2 Research/statistics

Creativity/innovation

Engineering

Project management

Manufacturing

Marketing/sales

Administration/documentation

Servicing/support

Customer/quality metrics

1 Change management

- Recommendation: All libraries have an information handout for completing a review of literature using local equipment and catalog-access information. Ask for this information and save time.

The first step requires the development of a problem statement to direct the information needs analysis to a specific area or category. See example *Establishment of Self-Directed Work Teams (SDWT)*.

From the problem statements, two or three research questions are stated to further focus on information needs.

Using the information needs analysis flow diagram, the following information sources are considered, as shown in the example:

- Information sources
- Data requirements
- Review of literature
- Related information

Next, specific research and data collection assignments are allocated to all team participants.

Finally, all information is sorted and reviewed.

Establishment of Self-Directed Work Teams (SDWT)

Problem statement	*The company has no experience in organizing and supporting SDWTs.*

Research questions(s)	*Will SDWTs improve the quality of products/services?* *Will SDWTs improve employee morale?*

Information sources

People	*Outside consultants experienced in teaming*
Documents	*Quality manual, books on teams*
Benchmarks	*World-class organization examples*
Tools/tapes	*Videotapes on teaming, tools, communications*
Training	*Workshops on SDWTs, team facilitation*

Data requirements

Primary data	*Conduct surveys, focus groups, meetings*
Secondary data	*Acquire case studies, typical team reports*

Review of literature

On-line	*Search databases – Key descriptor = teaming*
Off-line	*Books, magazines, interviews*

Category background   *Teaming in organizations*

Topic specific   *Self-directed, self-managed work teams*

Detail   *Implementation, management, rewards*

Related information	*Empowerment, motivation, group decisions*

An interrelationship digraph displays causal relationships in a complex network of contributing factors. This digraph maps out a problem issue by establishing links among related ideas or issues.

- To understand and clarify interrelationships between ideas or issues in a complex problem.
- To identify root causes of a potential problem.
- To discover key cause and effect relationships.
- To find connections that influence other factors within a process.

before

Affinity diagram

Brainstorming

Focus group

Cause and effect diagram (CED)

Problem specification

after

Tree diagram

Linking diagram

Potential problem analysis (PPA)

Opportunity analysis

Criteria rating form

➡ Select and define problem or opportunity

➡ Identify and analyze causes or potential change

Develop and plan possible solutions or change

Implement and evaluate solution or change

Measure and report solution or change results

Recognize and reward team efforts

	Research/statistics
1	Creativity/innovation
	Engineering
	Project management
	Manufacturing
	Marketing/sales
	Administration/documentation
3	Servicing/support
	Customer/quality metrics
2	Change management

Legend:

In **2** | Out **2**

Related idea

In **1** | Out **5**

Major cause

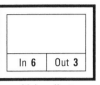

In **6** | Out **3**

Major effect

- Use 6–8 participants
- Collect or generate 10–30 ideas

Acquire collected data from an affinity diagram or brainstorming session.

Reach consensus on some problem or key issue to be considered. See example *What Causes Teams to Succeed?*

Use an idea-generation tool such as brainstorming or affinity diagram to produce ideas.

Collect all ideas on cards or post-it notes as they are produced; place these around the card that has the problem or key issue statement.

After the flow of ideas has slowed, look for relationships between each and every idea. Draw arrows pointing to either the causes or effects. Continue until all placed ideas have been verified.

Finalize an I.D. using encoding information as shown in *notes and key points*. Count the number of arrows coming into each idea (in) and the number of lines leaving the same idea (out).

Identify ideas or issues that are major causes (MC) or effects (ME). Use double boxes or bold boxes respectively. Date the interrelationship digraph.

What Causes Teams to Succeed?

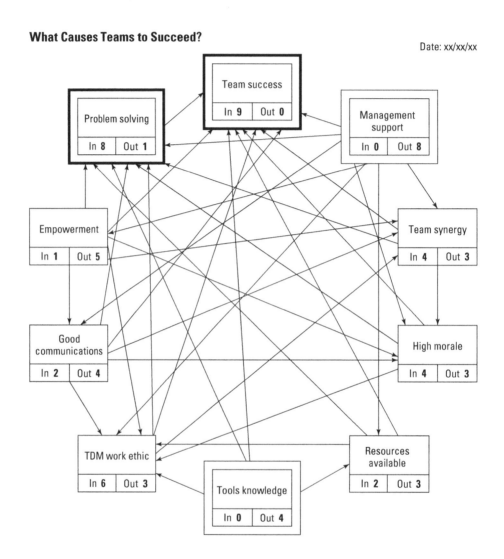

The interviewing technique is a highly structured, survey data-collection methodology to gather technical, experiential, or specialized information from individuals or groups. Face-to-face interviewers directly question respondents on location, whereas telephone interviewing, although very efficient, has been overused lately and no longer provides a good response rate. Interviews provide quality data on the basis that the interviewer can, on the spot, clarify questions or ask follow-up questions to further probe for meaningful data.

- To gather data from a small sample of some identified population to discover additional or specific information on problem situations or improvement opportunities.
- To measure employee perceptions, attitudes and reactions to problem areas, organizational change, or the company's leadership.
- To supplement or validate data collected previously by other survey methods for the purpose of defining customer expectations.
- To receive feedback on specific experiences or from certain targeted respondents.

before

Data collection strategy

Sampling methods

Audience analysis

Observation

Circle response

after

Critical dialogue

Response data encoding form

Consensus decision making

Run-it-by

What-if analysis

Select and define problem or opportunity	
➡ Identify and analyze causes or potential change	
Develop and plan possible solutions or change	
Implement and evaluate solution or change	
➡ Measure and report solution or change results	
➡ Recognize and reward team efforts	

3	Research/statistics
	Creativity/innovation
	Engineering
	Project management
	Manufacturing
1	Marketing/sales
	Administration/documentation
4	Servicing/support
2	Customer/quality metrics
5	Change management

- To reduce interviewer bias, an interviewer must use neutral language, open-ended questions, follow the question sequence and wording as outlined on the schedule (questionnaire), and record responses exactly as given by the respondent.

Advantages	Disadvantages
– Two-way communications	– Lack of anonymity
– No misunderstood questions	– Possible interviewer bias
– Flexible, quickly organized	– Often time-consuming
– Complete answers	– Scheduling difficulties
– Higher response rate	– Small sample data

A decision is made to perform face-to-face interviews for gathering specific information.

Identify information needed. See example *Interview Schedules for Manufacturing/Service Operations*.

Develop a set of specific interview questions.

Prepare interview schedule (questionnaire).

Select random sample of targeted population.

Contact selected respondents, state purpose, and schedule.

Meet respondent for face-to-face interview (restate purpose of interview).

Ask questions exactly as stated and sequenced from the prepared interview schedule.

Record responses as given (ensure understanding).

After completing the questionnaire, ask respondent for additional input or comments.

Thank the respondent for the information.

Interview Schedules for Manufacturing/ Service Operations

Organization/Location/Participants: ABC Manufacturing–Inspectors	Date: xx/xx/xx	Time: 10:30 AM
Purpose of interview: Quality assurance procedures	Interviewer: W.J.M.	

Manufacturing

   1. How many types of spring assemblies are there?

   2. What sampling method is used: _____table _____random

   3. Frequency rate: _____1/wk _____1/m _____4/yr

   4. How are inspection results recorded?

   5. Who gets the information?

   6. Is statistical process control used? _____Yes _____No

   Etc.

Service/administration

   1. What is the current customer complaint rate?

      _____5–10 _____11–20 _____21–40

   2. How are complaints compiled and recorded?

   3. Who acts on this data: _____QA _____Supv. _____Other

   4. What happens to the customer?

   5. What is being done to correct the problems?

   6. How are problem-solving efforts prioritized?

   Etc.

A simple line chart is an ideal method for showing trends in quality, quantity, cost, customer satisfaction, and so on. It is often a first indication that some problem exists during the monitoring and tracking of quality performance data.

- To monitor and track data over a period of time.
- To show a trendline analysis.
- To display change in quality performance.
- To identify shifts from predetermined averages.

➡ Select and define problem or opportunity
➡ Identify and analyze causes or potential change
  Develop and plan possible solutions or change
➡ Implement and evaluate solution or change
➡ Measure and report solution or change results
  Recognize and reward team efforts

Research/statistics
Creativity/innovation
Engineering
1 Project management
2 Manufacturing
3 Marketing/sales
   Administration/documentation
   Servicing/support
4 Customer/quality metrics
   Change management

- To enhance the interpretation of a line chart, a "goal for improvement" or a "standard" line should be drawn to verify actual performance to the desired goal or standard.

before
Frequency distribution (FD)
Checksheet
Observation
Focus group
Surveying

after
Stratification
Multivariable chart
Trend analysis
Pie chart
Pareto chart

Collect data from some source, such as a checksheet. See example *Customer Complaints*.

Type	Week 1					Week 2					Week 3					Week 4					Total
	M	T	W	T	F	M	T	W	T	F	M	T	W	T	F	M	T	W	T	F	
Ordering	‖	‖	卌	‖	‖‖	‖	‖‖‖	‖‖‖	‖‖‖	卌	‖‖	卌	‖	卌‖		卌	‖‖‖	‖	卌	‖‖‖	66
Shipping	‖	‖		‖	‖	‖		‖‖			‖	‖		‖	‖	‖	‖		‖		20
Billing	‖	‖		‖		‖		‖		‖‖	‖	‖			‖‖	‖	‖	‖		‖	20
Defect	‖	‖	卌	卌	‖	‖	‖	‖‖‖	‖	‖	‖		‖	卌		‖	‖	‖	‖	‖‖	41
Service	卌	‖	‖‖‖	‖‖	卌	‖	‖	卌	‖	卌	卌	卌	‖	卌	‖	卌‖	‖	卌	‖	卌	69
Total	11	6	14	12	11	7	7	18	6	14	13	12	5	18	5	15	9	11	9	13	216

Construct a line chart and apply the 3:4 ratio rule: The height of the *Y* axis must be 75 percent of the length of the *X* axis.

Label the axes, plot and connect the data points, and draw the line as encoded in the legend. Date the line chart.

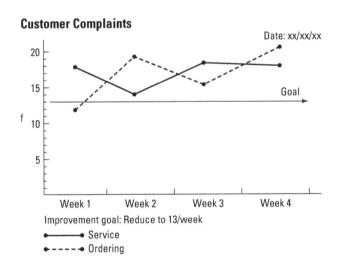

Customer Complaints

Date: xx/xx/xx

Goal

f

Week 1   Week 2   Week 3   Week 4

Improvement goal: Reduce to 13/week

•———• Service
•----• Ordering

A linking diagram helps a team to narrow down an important issue, problem, or situation by listing all the factors that need to be considered and linked to a particular department or business unit for corrective or process improvement action. Importance weighting is often used to prioritize listed factors.

- To narrow down complex issues into related and contributing factors for analysis.
- To link potential action to organizational units responsible for completing the action.
- To group business units that control a particular process.

before

Brainstorming

Surveying

Attribute listing

Interview technique

Benchmarking

after

SWOT analysis

Gap analysis

Force field analysis

Barriers-and-aids analysis

Cost-benefit analysis

➡ Select and define problem or opportunity
➡ Identify and analyze causes or potential change
   Develop and plan possible solutions or change
   Implement and evaluate solution or change
   Measure and report solution or change results
   Recognize and reward team efforts

- To indicate importance, value, or any other factor, a weight can be assigned to each element. Typically, scale of weight is 1–5 or 1–10, 10 being the highest rating.

	Research/statistics
	Creativity/innovation
1	Engineering
	Project management
2	Manufacturing
3	Marketing/sales
	Administration/documentation
4	Servicing/support
5	Customer/quality metrics
	Change management

A problem, issue, or condition is written on a whiteboard or flip chart.

The team narrows down the problem, issue, or condition by identifying potential action items or solutions. See example *Goal—Increase Market Share by 25 Percent*.

Next, participants rate the items (objectives) by their importance. The scale for weighting is usually 1–10, 10 being most important.

Once all of the factors have been listed, organizational units are identified that are directly involved in the completion or supporting of an action item.

Finally, a line is drawn to link involved organizational units to specific factors (items). This will provide some idea of complexity and resource requirement.

The completed linking diagram is checked for completeness and accuracy and then dated.

Goal: Increase Market Share by 25 Percent

Objectives	Weight	Department
Accelerate new product development, reduce time to market	10	Design Engineering
		Customer Service
Develop a SPC training program	5	Procurements
		Human Resources
Reduce latent defects by 50%	7	Manufacturing
		Mgmt. Info. Systems
Establish integrated product development teams (IPDT)	8	Quality
		Finance
Benchmark competitors products and services	7	Supply and Transport.
		Marketing/Sales
Perform customer satisfaction surveys	8	Legal/Regulatory
Reduce material and inventory costs	6	Product Planning

Note: Scale of weight: 1 = *lowest,* 10 = *highest importance*

A major program status matrix is used to display and report the status of a major program or project by using a color rating system. It indicates where progress is being made and if a project is on schedule, or where corrective action is required to improve quality or prevent further delays. This status chart is an ideal instrument for updating process owners during a staff meeting or as an attachment to a status report.

- To report the status of a major program or project.
- To assist a program manager with the overall management of resources.
- To surface potential problem areas in work-completion schedules or resource allocation management.

before

Data collection strategy

Objectives matrix (OMAX)

Basili data collection method

Gantt chart

Program evaluation and review technique (PERT)

after

Countermeasures matrix

Presentation

Project planning log

Barriers-and-aids analysis

Force field analysis (FFA)

Select and define problem or opportunity	Research/statistics
Identify and analyze causes or potential change	Creativity/innovation
Develop and plan possible solutions or change	Engineering
➡ Implement and evaluate solution or change	2 Project management
➡ Measure and report solution or change results	Manufacturing
Recognize and reward team efforts	Marketing/sales
	3 Administration/documentation
	Servicing/support
	1 Customer/quality metrics
	Change management

- Color coding to reflect major program status is optional. Numeric or symbolic ratings can be substituted for color ratings.

Color coding (rating) example:

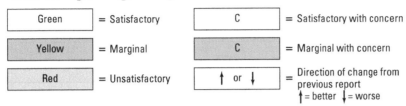

Green	= Satisfactory		C	= Satisfactory with concern
Yellow	= Marginal		C	= Marginal with concern
Red	= Unsatisfactory		↑ or ↓	= Direction of change from previous report ↑ = better ↓ = worse

First, the team establishes a focal point to receive the status of the various programs.

Representatives from each program team report their program's status to the focal point, often the data analyst who prepares the major program status report.

The team discusses the overall impact of each report and reaches consensus on the rating to be assigned. See example *Military Contract USA-XXXX-X Radar-Mobile*.

The major program status matrix is finalized (or updated), checked for accuracy, approved by the team, and dated.

Finally, the major program status matrix is presented to the respective process owners or attached to a status report mailed to the process owners or customer.

Military Contract USA-XXXX-X Radar-Mobile

Org. Unit	Team	Program	Budget Costs	Master Schedule	Contract Admin.	Technical Progress	Quality Status	General Trends
Division A	Radar	RUM						
Division B	Optics	RUM-O	C↑			C		
Division F	Electronics	RUM-E					↓	↓
Contracts	—	USA-XXXX						
Supplier	—	USA-XXXX-1		C			C	
MIS–L	Docs	DB-Radar					C	
Canada Ofc.	—	Research			C			
Human Resources	R. Support	USA-XXXX-HR						

Notes: Green = Satisfactory   Yellow = Marginal   Red = Unsatisfactory

C = With Concern   ↑↓ = Direction of change from previous report

A Markov analysis is used to identify employee movement through the various positions within an organizational unit. A matrix displays the percentage of employees who stayed in their position, who were promoted or demoted, or who left the department or company. The analysis results provide valuable information for the forecasting and budgeting of personnel.

- To forecast staffing and training requirements.
- To track the movement of personnel through the organization.
- To identify patterns of job changes.

before

Information needs analysis

Data collection strategy

Demographic analysis

Task analysis

Cluster analysis

after

Problem specification

Presentation

Cost-benefit analysis

Resource requirements matrix

Action plan

➡ Select and define problem or opportunity
➡ Identify and analyze causes or potential change
   Develop and plan possible solutions or change
   Implement and evaluate solution or change
➡ Measure and report solution or change results
   Recognize and reward team efforts

   Research/statistics
   Creativity/innovation
   Engineering
1 Project management
   Manufacturing
   Marketing/sales
2 Administration/documentation
   Servicing/support
   Customer/quality metrics
3 Change management

• Typical employee movement

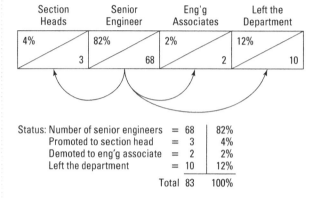

Section Heads	Senior Engineer	Eng'g Associates	Left the Department
4%	82%	2%	12%
3	68	2	10

Status: Number of senior engineers = 68 82%
Promoted to section head = 3 4%
Demoted to eng'g associate = 2 2%
Left the department = 10 12%
Total 83 100%

All personnel movement throughout the department or company is monitored and recorded for specific period of time. See example *1996 Employee Movement—Engineering*.

A Markov analysis matrix is developed for a particular organizational unit, and the previously collected staff-change data is inserted into the matrix cells.

Percentages are computed, row totals are verified for accuracy, and original budget totals added.

The finalized matrix is dated and presented to organization's management.

199x Employee Movement — Engineering

Year 199x	Department Managers	Section Heads	Senior Engineers	Engineering Associates	Left the Department
Department managers	83% 5				17% 1
Section heads	9% 1	64% 7	9% 1		18% 2
Senior engineers		4% 3	82% 68	2% 2	12% 10
Engineering associates			13% 12	78% 72	9% 8
Budgeted	6	11	82	80	21

Note: See notes and key points for matrix description.

The matrix data analysis tool is essentially a display of data characteristics used by integrated product development teams (IPDT) to perform market research and describe products and services. Matrix data is arranged for easy visualization and comparisons. Relationships between data variables shown on both axes are identified using symbols for importance or numerical values for evaluations.

- To determine the representative characteristics of customer or products.
- To perform market research.
- To verify the strength of relationships among variables.

before

Demographic analysis
House of quality
Benchmarking
Surveying
Starbursting

after

Risk space analysis
Opportunity analysis
Fresh eye
Window analysis
Idea grid

Select and define problem or opportunity
➡ Identify and analyze causes or potential change
➡ Develop and plan possible solutions or change
Implement and evaluate solution or change
➡ Measure and report solution or change results
Recognize and reward team efforts

1 Research/statistics
2 Creativity/innovation
Engineering
Project management
Manufacturing
3 Marketing/sales
Administration/documentation
Servicing/support
Customer/quality metrics
4 Change management

- Recommendation: Use symbols that stand out and are easily differentiated if the location of data on the matrix is not identified by name. See example ■, ●, ▲, +, etc. All circled symbols reflect this organization's data or quadrant location.

The team first determines what characteristics need to be analyzed. This process may be influenced by some product or service concern, loss of market share, or unfavorable benchmarking results. See example *Comparison of Nontraditional Degree Programs.*

A research and data collection process is performed to acquire the data to be charted on the matrix data analysis chart. Data may come from surveys, interviews, focus groups, historical records, benchmarks, or published sources. Ensure that appropriate scales are used to position or calculate data.

Next, team consensus is required to plot the comparison data on the chart. Care must be taken to ensure the unbiased positioning of the organization's data, as shown in this example.

The completed chart is discussed, all relationships are reviewed, and a summary statement is prepared. Finally, the chart is dated and presented to the process owners.

Comparison of Nontraditional Degree Programs

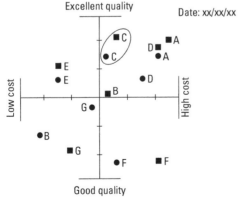

Notes: – Graduate degree programs = ●
– Undergraduate degree programs = ■
– University/college designation = A – G
– ◯ = This organization's data or quadrant location.

A matrix diagram is a planning tool that displays two or more sets of characteristics, functions, ideas, or issues. The scanning and comparing of items results in relationship "connections" or cause and effect interactions that can be useful in problem, opportunity, or task requirement analysis.

- To assign responsibility for action ideas.
- To identify opportunities for improvement.
- To search for possible problem causes.
- To compare the respective strengths of alternative choices.
- To match functions with resource needs.

before

Affinity diagram

Tree diagram

Interrelationship digraph (I.D.)

Work Breakdown Structure (WBS)

Process flowchart

after

Matrix data analysis

Activity network diagram

Process decision program chart

Attribute listing

Customer acquisition-defection matrix

Select and define problem or opportunity	
➡ Identify and analyze causes or potential change	
Develop and plan possible solutions or change	
➡ Implement and evaluate solution or change	
Measure and report solution or change results	
Recognize and reward team efforts	

6	Research/statistics
	Creativity/innovation
1	Engineering
	Project management
2	Manufacturing
	Marketing/sales
5	Administration/documentation
4	Servicing/support
3	Customer/quality metrics
	Change management

"L" shaped	"T" shaped	"Y" shaped	"X" shaped	"C" shaped
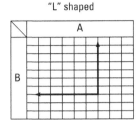	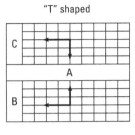	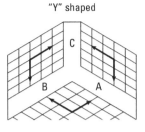	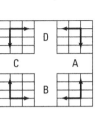	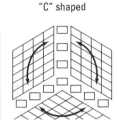

Matrix format	Sets of items	Application/notes	Sets
"L"	2	Check for related items Most frequently used matrix	A → B
"T"	3	Check for related items Two combined "L" matrices	A < B / C
"Y"	3	Check for interactions among (3) sets of items	A → B \ C
"X"	4	Check for interactions among (4) sets of items	A → B ↑ ↓ D ← C
"C" (cube)	3	Check for linkage between A-B-C	A → B ↓ C

Optional symbols — some examples

| ⊙ = High = 9 |
| ○ = Medium = 3 |
| △ = Low = 1 |

| ⊙ = Primary responsibility |
| ○ = Secondary responsibility |
| △ = Information only |

| ● = Strong relationship |
| ○ = Medium relationship |
| X = Weak relationship |

Collect two or more sets of items from a brainstorming list, tree diagram, affinity diagram, or other source.

Select a particular matrix format. See example *Improvement Tools Application by Function.*

Construct a matrix diagram and insert sets or items.

Select a set of symbols to show relationship or connection.

Identify relationships, agree on the strength (use the appropriate symbol) of the relationship, and place the symbol at the intersecting points on the matrix.

Verify that all items have been changed and date the matrix diagram.

Improvement Tools Application by Function

Date: xx/xx/xx / Tools / Function	QFD	SPC	JIT	CTM	BPR	CSA	Survey	Benchmarking	DOE	IPD	Metrics
Research	○	○				○	⊙	⊙	⊙	△	
Planning	⊙			○	⊙			⊙		⊙	△
Finance											⊙
Project mgmt.		△	△	⊙			△	○		⊙	⊙
Administration				⊙							⊙
Engineering	○	○	△	△	⊙			○	⊙	○	○
Manufacturing		⊙	⊙	⊙	△			△	○	△	○
Quality	⊙	⊙	○	△		⊙	△	○	△	△	⊙
Marketing	○		△			⊙	⊙	○		△	○
Sales/service	○	△	△	△		⊙	⊙	△		△	○

⊙ = High   ○ = Medium   △ = Low

Note: QFD = Quality function deployment
          SPC = Statistical process control
          JIT   = Just-in-time
          CTM = Cycle time management
          CSA = Customer service analysis
          DOE = Design of experiments
          IPD   = Integrated product development

The measurement matrix tool provides a powerful progress report in that it calculates and summarizes overall goal achievement performance in an organization. Goals are stated in measurable format and are based on agreed-upon standards. Periodic measurement tracks and records performance.

- To track organizational goal achievement and report results.
- To provide a performance measurement matrix for the organization.

before

Action plan

Benchmarking

Information needs analysis

Organization readiness chart

Needs analysis

after

Major program status

Objectives matrix (OMAX)

Presentation

Hypothesis testing

Monthly assessment schedule

Select and define problem or opportunity

➡ Identify and analyze causes or potential change

Develop and plan possible solutions or change

➡ Implement and evaluate solution or change

Measure and report solution or change results

Recognize and reward team efforts

Research/statistics

Creativity/innovation

Engineering

2   Project management

Manufacturing

Marketing/sales

3   Administration/documentation

Servicing/support

1   Customer/quality metrics

Change management

- Relative weight is distributed across objectives in accordance with the importance of each objective. The sum of relative weights equals 100.
- Use benchmarks or an industry standard for establishing goals.
- To measure progress, multiply improvement rating times relative weight for each circled performance indicator value. The sum of all calculations for all circled values gives the current total.

A team identifies requirements and objectives. Performance benchmark data or industry standards are used to determine measurable goals.

A measurement matrix template is used to record objectives, performance metrics, and goals. In addition, the team reaches consensus on the relative weight distribution across all stated objectives. See example *Performance Measurement Matrix*.

All intermediate levels of performance between 0 and 10 in the improvement ratings are filled in as shown in the example.

Later, to track performance, periodically measure progress and circle level of goal achievement. Multiply the improvement rating times the relative weight assigned for each goal and sum the total to obtain overall current performance.

Performance Measurement Matrix

Date: xx/xx/xx

	Quality Initiatives					
Objectives requirements	Integrated product development	Employee retraining	ISO-9000	Quality	Customer satisfaction	Competitive analysis
Preformance metrics	Number of IPD teams started	Percent of employees retrained	Percent of orientation meetings	Percent defects reduction	Percent complaints reduction	Completed studies
Relative weight	20	20	10	25	20	5
Benchmarks	20	50%	100%	20%	10%	3

sum = 100

Improvement rating

Circle current actual performance

							Possible totals
Goal → 10	18	40%	100%	20%	10	2	1000 Goal met
8	15	35	(80)	17	(8)	1	200 No gain
6	12	(30)	60	(14)	6	0	0 Worse
4	(9)	25	40	11	4	0	
Baseline → 2	6	20	20	8	2	(0)	**Previous total**
0	3	15	0	5	1	0	480

Current total

Improvement rating × weight	80	120	80	150	160	10	600

The mental imaging technique suggests using imagination or visualization to identify key relationships in problem areas, solutions to problems, or ways to process improvement. Any creative ideas are switched or associated with a different condition, process, product, or service to search for a breakthrough idea.

- To create experiences or images of potential solutions to problems.
- To visualize the ideal outcome or situation.
- To identify barriers to solutions or improved performance.

before

Fresh eye

Wishful thinking

Morphological analysis

Stimulus analysis

Mind flow

after

Creativity assessment

Wildest idea technique

What-if analysis

Checkerboard diagram

Different point of view

Select and define problem or opportunity

➡ Identify and analyze causes or potential change

➡ Develop and plan possible solutions or change

Implement and evaluate solution or change

Measure and report solution or change results

Recognize and reward team efforts

Research/statistics

1 Creativity/innovation

2 Engineering

Project management

Manufacturing

Marketing/sales

Administration/documentation

Servicing/support

Customer/quality metrics

Change management

- Select a quiet and comfortable workplace or location.
- Ensure that there is no chance of interruptions during the mental imaging session.

The first task for this process is to locate a quiet place that will not be subjected to frequent interruptions.

Mental imaging works best if a person or a team first performs some relaxation techniques.

Next, imagination or visualization of the solved problem, ideal conditions, or drastic improvements take place. Ideas are generated and are recorded on slips of paper. See example *Tool Navigator Marketing*.

After approximately 30–45 minutes, all generated images are discussed. From this exercise, some general idea or trend will emerge as the ideal or most effective solution or improvement.

The team continues to identify the gaps between the existing to ideal situation and starts a discussion on how to reach the ideal situation.

A preliminary action plan is developed that describes the best idea(s) and how they could be implemented, as shown in the example.

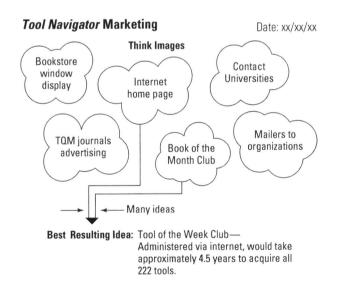

Tool Navigator **Marketing**   Date: xx/xx/xx

Think Images

Bookstore window display

Internet home page

Contact Universities

TQM journals advertising

Book of the Month Club

Mailers to organizations

Many ideas

Best Resulting Idea: Tool of the Week Club—Administered via internet, would take approximately 4.5 years to acquire all 222 tools.

A milestones chart displays all activities (milestones) and their corresponding start and completion dates. It is used to manage and monitor a project and can serve as a supporting document when attached to a project status report.

- To plan and schedule project activities.
- To track and monitor the progress of a project.
- To aid project status reporting.

before

Deployment chart
(Down-across)

Action plan

Countermeasures matrix

Project planning log

Activity analysis

after

Major program status

Monthly assessment
schedule

Objectives matrix (OMAX)

What-if analysis

Presentation

Select and define problem or opportunity

Identify and analyze causes or potential change

➥ Develop and plan possible solutions or change

➥ Implement and evaluate solution or change

Measure and report solution or change results

Recognize and reward team efforts

- Legend: ▆▆▆▆ complete
  ⬚ incomplete
- Optional: Include a column to provide space for listing who or which team has responsibility for completing each activity.

Research/statistics

Creativity/innovation

Engineering

1 Project management

Manufacturing

Marketing/sales

3 Administration/documentation

Servicing/support

Customer/quality metrics

2 Change management

The team first identifies all major activities of the project to be scheduled.

The team constructs a milestones chart and lists all identified activities in the order of completion. See example *Poster Development Process*.

The team estimates the time required to complete each activity and assigns a completion date to each.

Next, the team draws a horizontal bar for each activity, placing the bar in accordance with start and completion dates in sequential order along the milestones chart, as shown in the example.

The team then checks all information and dates the chart.

Poster Development Process

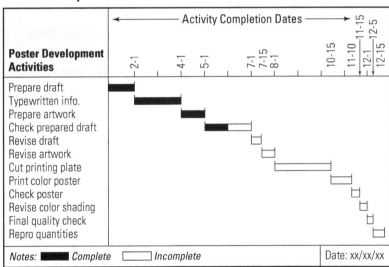

The mind flow technique produces a simple diagram of a team member's interconnecting brain activities, thereby enhancing the team's creativity and quality of thought when the resulting information is compared and added to from other diagrams. The result is a nonlinear approach to thinking—a mind flow diagram that reflects the creative generation of ideas, opens up new insights into problematic conditions or maps new possibilities for improving existing processes.

Note: More advanced Mind Mapping™ techniques were first introduced by Tony Buzan (1974). Buzan advocates Mind Mapping™ for note taking, creative writing, and problem-solving.

- To map complex situations by acquiring, collating, and connecting thoughts and data to a central topic on problem statement.
- To creatively identify requirements and connect details to main issues.
- To stimulate a team to surface new ideas in a problem-solving effort.
- To clarify links between ideas and processes and reflect relevant elements of major activities.

before

Brainstorming

Idea borrowing

Audience analysis

Fresh eye

Circles of knowledge

after

Futures wheel

Starbursting

Cluster analysis

Problem analysis

Cause and effect diagram (CED)

➡ Select and define problem or opportunity	
➡ Identify and analyze causes or potential change	
Develop and plan possible solutions or change	
Implement and evaluate solution or change	
Measure and report solution or change results	
Recognize and reward team efforts	

	Research/statistics
1	Creativity/innovation
3	Engineering
	Project management
	Manufacturing
	Marketing/sales
	Administration/documentation
	Servicing/support
	Customer/quality metrics
2	Change management

• Use symbols or images when appropriate. See example: $ ⊗ ☺ ☎ ▤ ◷

The team seeks an experienced facilitator for the mind flow process. Then the facilitator assists in setting up the mind flow exercise for the team.

A conference room with a whiteboard must be scheduled. A whiteboard works better than flip charts because it is easier to revise information during the session. Also, a set of color markers should be obtained.

At the beginning of the session, the facilitator explains the basic mind flow process. Drawing brief sketches on the whiteboard will assist in the understanding of connecting, clustering, coding, and mapping the information.

One team participant should volunteer to copy the mind flow diagram from the whiteboard as the team develops and records the information.

The team brainstorms or refers to an idea or problem to be used in the mind flow process. See example *Training Consultant's Work*.

A circle is drawn on the whiteboard and initial responses (key branches) are connected to the center.

The team continues to add information to the key branches in greater detail, creating more branches with yet greater detail as shown in the example.

Once the mind flow diagram is completed, a final check is performed and the diagram is dated.

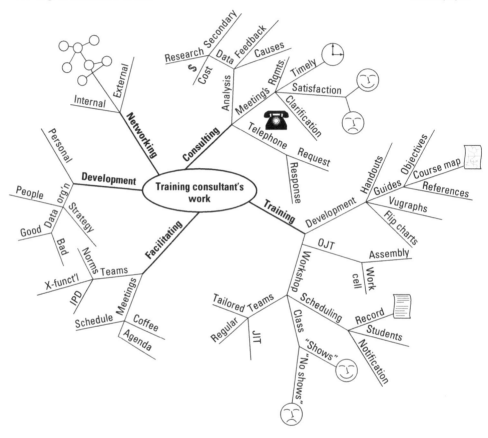

A monthly assessment schedule displays all sequential activities of a project, program, or some scheduled event. It reflects the milestone start and completion dates, the length of scheduled activities, and early completion or slipped dates. It serves as a valuable attachment for any status report.

- To assess monthly the status of scheduled activities for the purpose of overall project management.
- To plan and schedule a project, program or major event.
- To monitor the progress of a project.

before

Gap analysis

Force field analysis (FFA)

Barriers-and-aids analysis

Activity analysis

Checklist

after

Action plan

Consensus decision making

Measurement matrix

Countermeasures matrix

Presentation

	Select and define problem or opportunity
➡	Identify and analyze causes or potential change
➡	Develop and plan possible solutions or change
➡	Implement and evaluate solution or change
➡	Measure and report solution or change results
	Recognize and reward team efforts

	Research/statistics
	Creativity/innovation
1	Engineering
2	Project management
3	Manufacturing
	Marketing/sales
7	Administration/documentation
4	Servicing/support
5	Customer/quality metrics
6	Change management

Schedule milestone dates description:

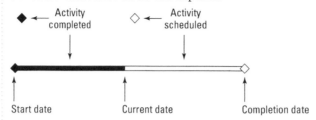

A team assembles for the purpose of identifying and placing into sequential order all of the activities to complete a project, program, or major event. See example *Annual Corporate-wide TQM Symposium Plan*.

A monthly assessment schedule form is used to list all activities.

Next, the team reaches consensus on the length of the listed activities and the start and completion dates of each activity.

The draft of the schedule is completed by inserting all milestone dates and connecting lines under the schedule covering a specific time period, as shown in this example.

The team verifies all information, dates the chart, and attaches the chart to an action plan.

Annual Corporate-Wide TQM Symposium Plan

Date: xx/xx/xx

Symposium Day: June 19, 199x

TQM Symposium Team Schedule / Scheduler: J.K. Smith	Jan					Feb				Mar				Apr			
	3	10	17	24	31	7	14	21	28	7	14	21	28	4	11	18	25
1. Select site location	◆	▬	▬	▬	▬	▬											
2. Negotiate arrangements						◆	▬	▬	▬								
3. Announce symposium										◆▬							
4. Identify dept. reps.			◆														
5. Call for papers						◆											
6. Establish guidelines				◆	▬												
7. Collect papers										◆							
8. Evaluate papers										◆▬		◇					
9. Select papers												◇					
10. Notify selectees													◇				
11. Finalize papers															◇		
12. Establish agenda					◆	▬	▬	▬	▬	▬					◇		
13. Format symposium										◆▬							◇
14. Select speakers											◇	▬	◇				
15. Concurrent sessions											◇			◇			
16. Develop rqmts. list											◇	◇					
17. Appoint coordinator												◇					
18. Develop hosting plan														◇			
19. Check budget/admin.					◆				◆			◇					◇
20. Awards and recognition														◇		◇	
21. Design proceedings									◆▬	▬					◇		
22. — Complete graphics																◇	◇
23. — Finalize master																	◇
24. — Repro copies																	
25. Speaker dry runs																	◇
26. Final status check																	
27. Symposium set-up																	
28. Symposium day																	

Note: For activities #18 → 32 completion dates, see page 2 of this schedule.   ↑ Current date

Morphological analysis is a tool used to surface new or improved products or services. Usually three or more dimensions are identified for a particular subject or problem, and variations for each dimension are brainstormed to develop lists of attributes. By scanning the attributes in each dimension, useful or interesting combinations are discovered that may form a new or improved product or service, or may be the solution to a problem.

- To discover new or improved products or services.
- To combine various attributes in search for a solution to a problem.
- To surface useful ideas by combining different variations of identified dimensions of a product or service.

before

Attribute listing

Forced choice

Circumrelation

Circle of opportunity

Forced association

after

Creativity assessment

Mental imaging

Checkerboard method

Idea advocate

Presentation

➥ Select and define problem or opportunity
➥ Identify and analyze causes or potential change
➥ Develop and plan possible solutions or change
   Implement and evaluate solution or change
   Measure and report solution or change results
   Recognize and reward team efforts

   Research/statistics
1 Creativity/innovation
4 Engineering
   Project management
   Manufacturing
3 Marketing/sales
   Administration/documentation
   Servicing/support
   Customer/quality metrics
2 Change management

- Three- or four-dimensional morphological analyses are the most common approaches. A dimension is further defined as a characteristic, variation, factor, or aspect.

Applications	Material	Features
1 _____	1 _____	1 _____
2 _____	2 _____	2 _____
3 _____	3 _____	3 _____
4 _____	4 _____	4 _____
5 _____	5 _____	5 _____

These *dimensions* are also referred to as *parameters* or *attribute listings*

Note: This example has three dimensions with five variations in each: $5 \times 5 \times 5 = 125$ *possible combinations.*

The team selects a problem, product, or service to be analyzed. See example *Additional Uses for Picture Frames.*

Dimensions are identified and recorded as headings on flip charts.

Next, the team brainstorms attributes (variations) of each dimension. The facilitator clarifies each response, if needed, and records responses on the flip chart. This process continues until the team stops generating attributes.

The other dimensions are brainstormed and attributes listed on respective flip charts.

The facilitator moves all flip charts close together and participants combine the possibilities by linking the various useful attributes listed on each flip chart (one per flip chart or column).

Useful, potential, or interesting combinations are marked using different colors of flip chart markers.

Date all flip charts.

**Additional Uses for
Picture Frames**   Date: xx/xx/xx

Applications	Material	Features
(Calendar)	Wood	Attachable
Picture	Plastic	(Adjustable)
Bulletin	(Brass)	Expandable
Sign	Styrofoam	Reshapeable
Poster	Cardboard	Interlocking
Flag	Sheet metal	Hang
		Stand
Shelf	Glass	
Clock	Plywood	(Mountable)

Note: Many interesting combinations are possible.

The multiple rating matrix scaling technique is used when response choices to survey questions fit a multiple set of items on the same topic. Circled or connected response choices then form a profile that often displays a trend, a state, a lack of something, or condition being measured.

- To identify a respondent's perception or position on some topic.
- To measure the strength of related item ratings.
- To collect survey data in a very efficient and practical way.

before

Data collection strategy

Information needs analysis

Stratification

Starbursting

Sampling methods

after

Questionnaires

Surveying

Cluster analysis

Interview technique

Organization readiness chart

Select and define problem or opportunity
➡ Identify and analyze causes or potential change
Develop and plan possible solutions or change
Implement and evaluate solution or change
➡ Measure and report solution or change results
Recognize and reward team efforts

- Recommendation: Do not exceed a 7-point numerical scale. Respondents normally classify things into a range from 2 to 7; above 7, some precision is lost.

1   Research/statistics
    Creativity/innovation
2   Engineering
    Project management
    Manufacturing
3   Marketing/sales
    Administration/documentation
    Servicing/support
4   Customer/quality metrics
    Change management

First, the research analyst determines the topic and items to be rated. See example *Employee Job Satisfaction Ratings*.

A draft of a multiple rating matrix is constructed and shown to a cross-section of potential respondents for their feedback on format, content, and clarity.

On the basis of the input received, matrix revisions may be necessary.

Next, the multiple rating matrix is mailed and response data collected.

Responses for each item are averaged and plotted on the multiple rating matrix as a profile composite, as shown in the example.

Date the completed profile composite.

Employee Job Satisfaction Ratings   Date: xx/xx/xx

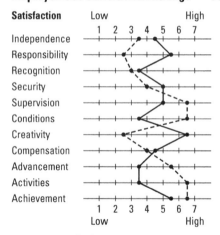

———— = Engineers
- - - - - - - - = Human Resource Specialists

Note: Profiles are composites of responses.

A multivariable chart is used to measure time-series data of multiple variables reflecting process capability variance. This chart provides process variable correlation and interaction information that is not usually found when examining traditional control charts one at a time.

- To construct an overlay of certain process variables normally recorded on control charts.
- To allow time-series analysis of process variables.
- To identify possible problem causes.
- To contribute to design of experiments (DOE) and statistical process control (SPC) activities.

before

Control chart
Data collection strategy
Checksheet
Checklist
Standard deviation

after

Variance analysis
Process capability ratios
Analysis of variance
Potential problem analysis (PPA)
Trend analysis

➥ Select and define problem or opportunity
➥ Identify and analyze causes or potential change
   Develop and plan possible solutions or change
   Implement and evaluate solution or change
   Measure and report solution or change results
   Recognize and reward team efforts

1	Research/statistics
	Creativity/innovation
3	Engineering
	Project management
2	Manufacturing
	Marketing/sales
	Administration/documentation
	Servicing/support
4	Customer/quality metrics
	Change management

- Note that it is difficult plotting process variables along matching time spans. Also, scaling of upper and lower specification limits (USL-LSL) for process variables may be limited to the base variable with the greatest upper and lower deviation from the specification target value.

First, acquire the target and upper and lower specification values from design engineering, manufacturing, or the quality department.

Identify two to four related process variables. See example *Painting Quality*.

Draw a chart, with the center line labeled *spec* (target) value and upper and lower horizontal lines designated *USL* and *LSL* respectively.

Designate the *x*-axis with the proper time scale. The *x*-axis represents an amount of time for the variable with the longest time span.

Identify process variables and encode for plotting and analysis purposes.

Take measurements and plot by connecting data points.

Date the chart and keep for later reference.

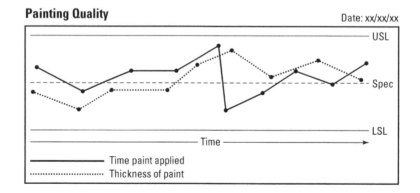

Painting Quality   Date: xx/xx/xx

The multivoting tool is used by teams to reduce a long list of items to a few items perceived as most important. Multivoting is a preferred list reduction method in that the final selection of top items is supported by all participants, since their votes directly contributed to the final items list.

- To perform a democratic, quick item selection process to arrive at a decision based on votes given for a particular item by each participant of the team.
- To apply a series of votes to reduce a long list of items to a few most important or popular items.
- To identify and prioritize problems or activities from a large, previously brainstormed list.

before

Brainstorming

Selection window

Phillips 66

Round robin brainstorming

Affinity diagram

after

Team process assessment

Project planning log

Activity analysis

Action and effect diagram (AED)

Action plan

➡ Select and define problem or opportunity
➡ Identify and analyze causes or potential change
➡ Develop and plan possible solutions or change
   Implement and evaluate solution or change
   Measure and report solution or change results
   Recognize and reward team efforts

   Research/statistics
   Creativity/innovation
   Engineering
2 Project management
   Manufacturing
4 Marketing/sales
   Administration/documentation
   Servicing/support
3 Customer/quality metrics
1 Change management

- Ideal for large groups and long lists. Never multivote down to one item only!
- Multivoting on a list of 30–50 items can reduce the list to 4–6 items.
- Voting round rules
  - Only one vote per item.
  - *First Round:* Vote for one half (one-third for long list) of listed items.
  - *Second Round*: Vote for one-half of remaining items.
  - *Next Rounds:* Repeat step two until the list is reduced to 4–6 items.

The team facilitator displays a list of items on a flip chart or whiteboard and explains the multivoting process to the team.

All participants vote for one-half of all items (the first round) and record their choices. See example *List of 33 Customer Complaints*.

The facilitator collects all votes and identifies items selected. Items with the fewest votes are eliminated and the remaining 17 votes are circles on the flip charts for all participants to see.

All participants vote again (second round) for one-half of the reduced list of items and record their choices. Reminder, one vote per item!

The facilitator collects all votes and repeats the process as in step 3.

A third round reduces the list to 5 choices, as seen in the example.

The last step calls for the drawing up of a final, prioritized list of 5 items. This list determines what next steps in the problem-solving process need to be taken by the team. Finally, date the prioritized list.

List of 33 Customer Complaints

Date: xx/xx/xx

List	1st Round	2nd Round	3rd Round	Final List
1. Missing manual	2			
	3			
	4			
	5			
	6	4		
10. Repair service	10	6		
	12	12	4	4 – Insulators
	13	17	12	12 – Scratches
	17	18	17	17 – No instructions
	18	21	21	21 – Defective lock
20. Billing error	21	23	23	23 – Shipping damage
	23	29		
	25	30		
	29			
	30			
	31			
33. Late delivery	32			

Note: List reduction from 33 to 17 to 9 to 5 items.

The primary goal of a needs analysis is to determine what needs to be accomplished to close an existing gap between actual and desired performance. To adequately assess requirements, a systematic study of organizational processes, job performance tasks, and employee needs is performed to identify potential solutions and process improvements to close performance gaps.

- To assess and develop solutions to close identified performance gaps or discrepancies.
- To analyze the needs of the organization.
- To study the organization and its processes to determine what employees need to perform their jobs.

before

Data collection strategy

Information needs analysis

Audience analysis

Interview technique

Surveying

after

Task analysis

Cost-benefit analysis

Activity analysis

Circles of knowledge

Action and effect diagram (AED)

Select and define problem or opportunity
➡ Identify and analyze causes or potential change
➡ Develop and plan possible solutions or change
Implement and evaluate solution or change
Measure and report solution or change results
Recognize and reward team efforts

1 Research/statistics
Creativity/innovation
Engineering
2 Project management
Manufacturing
Marketing/sales
3 Administration/documentation
Servicing/support
Customer/quality metrics
Change management

- Needs analyses are based on data collection. The basic procedure requires, as a minimum, information and statistical data on the following: people, processes, documentation, reporting relationships, organizational resources, performance goals and measurements, and performance plans and results.

The team establishes the goals for the needs analysis to be performed.

A plan is developed to acquire the data required to determine performance gaps and potential solutions. See example *Employee Performance Improvement*.

Team participants research, collect, and analyze the data. Alternative solutions and process improvements are finalized.

A list of resource requirements is compiled for the recommended gap-closing and process-improvement activities.

A proposal and action plan is developed and submitted to management.

Employee Performance Improvement

Problem Description	• Identify symptoms and evidence • Clarify conditions and results • State employees involved or affected
Problem Quantification	• Measure number of employees (job titles) • Show impact on operations, locations • Quantify productive time, defects, costs
Problem Definition	• Identify performance gaps • Define actual performance • Define desired performance
Problem Classification	• Categorize learning/skills deficiencies • Determine job/organization conditions • Classify behavior, motivation causes
Potential Solutions	• Determine training needs • Simplify job, improve processes • Enrich job, check rewards and recognition
Cost of Solutions	• Estimate the cost of employee training • Determine work simplification costs • Calculate costs of rewards and recognition
Benefit of Solutions	• Describe training benefits • Estimate process improvement benefits • List the benefits of increased job satisfaction
Solution Implementation	• Evaluate and select the best solution • Identify resource requirements • Develop an action plan and schedule

The nominal group technique (NGT) is used primarily to generate ideas, prioritize, and reach team consensus in a very structured, facilitated session. Originally developed by A. Delbecq and A. Van de Ven (1968), NGT has become increasingly popular as a means for participants to have an equal voice in the item or problem selection and decision-making process.

- To identify and reach consensus on the most important ideas, items, or problems so the team can advance to the next step in a problem-solving effort.
- To prioritize from a list of generated ideas or items with balanced team participation and without conflict.
- To gain participants' commitment by allowing each to fully participate in an idea-generation and -selection process.

before

Audience analysis

Circles of knowledge

Brainwriting pool

Phillips 66

Consensus decision making

after

Project planning log

Action and effect diagram (AED)

Force field analysis (FFA)

Action plan

Responsibility matrix

➥ Select and define problem or opportunity	
➥ Identify and analyze causes or potential change	
➥ Develop and plan possible solutions or change	
Implement and evaluate solution or change	
Measure and report solution or change results	
Recognize and reward team efforts	

	Research/statistics
2	Creativity/innovation
	Engineering
3	Project management
	Manufacturing
5	Marketing/sales
	Administration/documentation
	Servicing/support
4	Customer/quality metrics
1	Change management

- Although many variations exist, NGT works best if:
  - It is a facilitated session with 8–10 participants.
  - Individual, silent idea generation is used for about 10–15 minutes.
  - Each participant ranks the top five items using a priority/importance/value point scale of 5 for most preferred (highest rank) to 1 for least preferred (lowest rank) items.

The team facilitator displays, on a flip chart, a problem statement or open-ended question. See example *Ideas for Improving Teaming*.

Participants silently generate ideas on provided 3×5 cards.

When participants have finished, or after 15 minutes, the facilitator collects and records ideas in a round robin fashion by asking each participant to read his or her written ideas. No evaluation or criticism of ideas is allowed.

Step 3 above is repeated until all ideas have been recorded. Participants may "pass" at any time during this process.

Once the facilitator has recorded all ideas on the flip chart or whiteboard, participants may ask to have some ideas clarified. Ideas may also be modified or combined to promote understanding.

Next, the facilitator asks each participant to list five ideas from the recorded list of ideas that they prefer, writing down only one idea per 3×5 card. Individuals rank each idea according to a priority/importance/value point scale, 5 points being the highest and 1 point being the lowest.

The facilitator tabulates the votes and, using the point totals, lists the team's top five ideas and dates the chart as shown in the example.

The team discusses the results and establishes the next steps.

Ideas for Improving Teaming (Team of 10 Participants)

Date xx/xx/xx

Generated List of Ideas	Ranking (1–5)	Top 5
A Job rotation	A–3	3
B Team training	B–5, 4, 3, 5, 5	(22)
C Rewards / recognition	C–5, 2, 4	(11)
D Team facilitation	D–4, 4, 5, 2	(15)
E Open communication	E–3, 3, 3, 1	10
F Involved management	F–3, 1, 2	6
G Job sharing	G–1, 2	3
H Tools training	H–2, 4, 5, 2, 3	(16)
I Cross-functional teams	I–2, 3	5
J Learning communities	J–1, 3	4
K Teaming guidelines	K–1, 4	5
L Time allocation	L–2, 5, 5, 2, 4	(18)
M Self-directed work teams	M–1, 5	6
N Team sharing rally	N–1	1
O IPD teams	O–4, 1	5
P Team newsletters	P–2	2
Q Budget more money for teams	Q–3, 5	8
R Improve evaluation process	R–4, 4, 1, 1	10

Note: Ideas B, L, H, D, and C are the top 5 ideas.

The nominal prioritization tool is an easy and quick method for a team to team-prioritize from a list of items, proposed actions, or various options. It can also be used to team-select a particular problem or opportunity from a previously brainstormed list.

- To prioritize from a list of brainstormed items or options.
- To involve all team participants in the selection process of the preferred choices.
- To determine a "next-step" approach in a team problem-solving effort.

before
Brainstorming
Brainwriting pool
Crawford slip method
Double reversal
Importance weighting

after
Consensus decision making
Starbursting
Different point of view
Run-it-by
Criteria filtering

➥ Select and define problem or opportunity
Identify and analyze causes or potential change
➥ Develop and plan possible solutions or change
Implement and evaluate solution or change
Measure and report solution or change results
➥ Recognize and reward team efforts

Research/statistics
Creativity/innovation
Engineering
Project management
4 Manufacturing
Marketing/sales
3 Administration/documentation
2 Servicing/support
Customer/quality metrics
1 Change management

• Optional approach: A team facilitator may provide participants the opportunity to present and explain why they considered certain items as their second and third selections.

The team facilitator displays a flip chart with a list of items or options. See example *Prioritizing a Data Collection Method*.

Team participants are asked to review the entire list and select the top three choices.

Every participant moves to the flip chart and marks the top or most important choice by writing a 3, marks the second choice a 2, and the third choice a 1. All marked choices also require the participants' initials for possible future reference. This concludes the preliminary selection process.

The team facilitator totals up the scores of all selected items and ranks the top three choices. The highest scored item is, therefore, also what the team considers the most important item.

In the next step, participants give a rationale for selecting their most important choice. This discussion should be limited to 2–3 minutes per participant.

Once all participants have a chance to explain why a particular change was made, participants are now given the opportunity to change their selections.

Lastly, the facilitator retotals, if needed, all selections, and lists the final top three choices on a flip chart and dates the chart.

Prioritizing a Data Collection Method

Date: xx/xx/xx

Data Collection Methods	Preliminary Totals ⟶	Σ	Post-discussion Totals ⟶	Σ
Focus group	③JC, ①AS, ③SD, ①JS	8	⊗JS → ③JS ③MB	13
Interviewing	②GB, ②SD, ②JS	6		6
Survey research	③GB, ②AS, ①SD, ③JS	9	⊗JS → ①JS	7
Panel session	①GB, ②MB	3		3
Case analysis	③AS, ①MB	4		4
Literature review	②JC	2		2
Consultants	②FO, ③MB	5	⊗MB	2
Observations	①JC	1		1
Secondary data		0		0
Forum discussion	③FO	3		3
Historical files	①FO	1		1

Team results: Focus group (13)   — First choice
              Survey research (7) — Second choice
              Interviewing (6)   — Third choice

The normal probability distribution is used extensively in statistical process control (SPC) applications, the profiling and describing of various data distributions, and in the hypothesis testing procedures (inferential statistics) found in scientific research. The concepts of normally distributed sample data provide the basis for inferences made about a population based on samples taken from the source population.

- To illustrate variability of data.
- To apply the "normal" pattern concepts to statistical process control activities.
- To demonstrate data significance, allow transformations, and display measurement scales and their relationship under the curve.

before

Data collection strategy

Surveying

Frequency distribution (FD)

Standard deviation

Cluster analysis

after

Descriptive statistics

Process capability ratios

Analysis of variance

Control chart

Response matrix analysis

Select and define problem or opportunity
➡ Identify and analyze causes or potential change
Develop and plan possible solutions or change
Implement and evaluate solution or change
➡ Measure and report solution or change results
Recognize and reward team efforts

1 Research/statistics
Creativity/innovation
2 Engineering
Project management
Manufacturing
Marketing/sales
Administration/documentation
Servicing/support
3 Customer/quality metrics
Change management

- The normal probability distribution is a symmetrical, bell-shaped distribution frequently used in statistical analyses. The arithmetic mean, ($\bar{x}$) median ($\tilde{x}$) and mode ($\hat{x}$) are of equal value and are located at the center and peak of the curve. These measures are averages and therefore considered measures of central tendency. Measures of dispersion are measures under the curve, moving horizontally left or right to identify areas or probability, among others, standard deviations (S), z-values (z), and percentiles (%) are most often used in descriptive and inferential statistics.

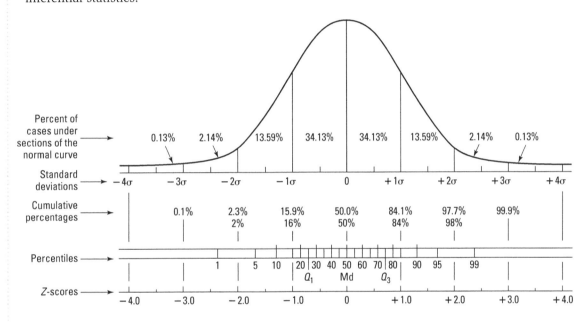

- Please refer to Appendix, Table A, "Proportions of Area Under the Normal Curve," for a detailed table.

Percentage of Area Under the Normal Curve

Example: To find the area under the curve for z-score = 1.89, move down the "Z" column to 1.8 and across to .09 column and locate .9706. This would be the 97.06% as shown.

97.06% of area

Z → Z = 1.89

Z	0.00	0.01	0.02	0.03	0.04	0.05	0.06	0.07	0.08	0.09
0	.5000	.5040	.5080	.5120	.5160	.5199	.5239	.5279	.5319	.5359
0.1	.5398	.5438	.5437	.5517	.5557	.5596	.5636	.5675	.5714	.5753
0.2	.5793	.5832	.5871	.5910	.5948	.5987	.6026	.6064	.6103	.6141
0.3	.6179	.6217	.6255	.6293	.6331	.6368	.6406	.6443	.6480	.6517
0.4	.6554	.6591	.6628	.6664	.6700	.6736	.6772	.6808	.6844	.6879
0.5	.6915	.6950	.6985	.7019	.7054	.7088	.7123	.7157	.7190	.7224
0.6	.7257	.7291	.7324	.7357	.7389	.7422	.7454	.7486	.7517	.7549
0.7	.7580	.7611	.7642	.7673	.7704	.7734	.7764	.7794	.7823	.7852
0.8	.7881	.7910	.7939	.7967	.7995	.8023	.8051	.8079	.8106	.8133
0.9	.8159	.8186	.8212	.8238	.8264	.8289	.8315	.8340	.8365	.8389
1.0	.8413	.8438	.8461	.8485	.8508	.8531	.8554	.8577	.8599	.8621
1.1	.8643	.8665	.8686	.8708	.8729	.8749	.8770	.8790	.8810	.8830
1.2	.8849	.8869	.8888	.8907	.8925	.8944	.8962	.8980	.8997	.9015
1.3	.9032	.9049	.9066	.9082	.9099	.9115	.9131	.9147	.9162	.9177
1.4	.9192	.9207	.9222	.9236	.9251	.9265	.9276	.9292	.9306	.9319
1.5	.9332	.9345	.9357	.9370	.9382	.9394	.9406	.9418	.9429	.9441
1.6	.9452	.9463	.9474	.9484	.9495	.9505	.9515	.9525	.9535	.9545
1.7	.9554	.9564	.9573	.9582	.9591	.9599	.9608	.9616	.9625	.9633
1.8	.9641	.9649	.9658	.9664	.9671	.9678	.9686	.9693	.9699	.9706
1.9	.9713	.9719	.9726	.9732	.9738	.9744	.9750	.9756	.9761	.9767
2.0	.9773	.9778	.9783	.9788	.9793	.9798	.9803	.9808	.9812	.9817
2.1	.9821	.9826	.9830	.9834	.9838	.9842	.9846	.9850	.9854	.9857
2.2	.9861	.9864	.9868	.9871	.9875	.9878	.9881	.9884	.9887	.9890
2.3	.9893	.9896	.9898	.9901	.9904	.9906	.9909	.9911	.9913	.9916
2.4	.9918	.9920	.9922	.9925	.9927	.9929	.9931	.9932	.9934	.9936
2.5	.9938	.9940	.9941	.9943	.9945	.9946	.9948	.9949	.9951	.9952
2.6	.9953	.9955	.9956	.9957	.9959	.9960	.9961	.9962	.9963	.9964
2.7	.9965	.9966	.9967	.9968	.9969	.9970	.9971	.9972	.9973	.9974
2.8	.9974	.9975	.9976	.9977	.9977	.9978	.9979	.9979	.9980	.9981
2.9	.9981	.9982	.9983	.9983	.9983	.9984	.9985	.9985	.9986	.9986
3.0	.99865	.99869	.99874	.99878	.99882	.99886	.99889	.99893	.99896	.99900
3.1	.99903	.99906	.99910	.99913	.99915	.99918	.99921	.99924	.99926	.99929
3.2	.99931	.99934	.99936	.99938	.99940	.99942	.99944	.99946	.99948	.99950
3.3	.99952	.99953	.99955	.99957	.99958	.99960	.99961	.99962	.99964	.99965
3.4	.99966	.99967	.99969	.99970	.99971	.99972	.99973	.99974	.99975	.99976
3.5	.99977	.99978	.99978	.99979	.99980	.99981	.99981	.99982	.99983	.99983

Z	0.00	0.01	0.02	0.03	0.04	0.05	0.06	0.07	0.08	0.09
-3.5	.00023	.00022	.00022	.00021	.00020	.00019	.00019	.00018	.00017	.00017
-3.4	.00034	.00033	.00031	.00030	.00029	.00028	.00027	.00026	.00025	.00024
-3.3	.00048	.00047	.00045	.00043	.00042	.00040	.00039	.00038	.00036	.00035
-3.2	.00069	.00066	.00064	.00062	.00060	.00058	.00056	.00054	.00052	.00050
-3.1	.00097	.00094	.00090	.00087	.00085	.00082	.00079	.00076	.00074	.00071
-3.0	.00135	.00131	.00126	.00122	.00118	.00114	.00111	.00107	.00104	.00010
-2.9	.0019	.0018	.0017	.0017	.0016	.0016	.0015	.0015	.0014	.0014
-2.8	.0026	.0025	.0024	.0023	.0023	.0022	.0021	.0021	.0020	.0019
-2.7	.0035	.0034	.0033	.0032	.0031	.0030	.0029	.0028	.0027	.0026
-2.6	.0047	.0045	.0044	.0043	.0041	.0040	.0039	.0038	.0037	.0036
-2.5	.0062	.0060	.0059	.0057	.0055	.0054	.0052	.0051	.0049	.0048
-2.4	.0082	.0080	.0078	.0075	.0073	.0071	.0069	.0068	.0066	.0064
-2.3	.0107	.0104	.0102	.0099	.0096	.0094	.0091	.0089	.0087	.0084
-2.2	.0139	.0136	.0132	.0129	.0125	.0122	.0119	.0116	.0113	.0110
-2.1	.0179	.0174	.0170	.0166	.0162	.0158	.0154	.0150	.0146	.0143
-2.0	.0228	.0222	.0217	.0212	.0207	.0202	.0197	.0192	.0188	.0183
-1.9	.0287	.0281	.0274	.0268	.0262	.0256	.0250	.0244	.0239	.0233
-1.8	.0359	.0351	.0344	.0336	.0329	.0322	.0314	.0307	.0301	.0294
-1.7	.0446	.0436	.0427	.0418	.0409	.0401	.0392	.0384	.0375	.0367
-1.6	.0548	.0537	.0526	.0516	.0505	.0495	.0485	.0475	.0465	.0455
-1.5	.0668	.0655	.0643	.0630	.0618	.0606	.0594	.0582	.0571	.0559
-1.4	.0808	.0793	.0778	.0764	.0749	.0735	.0721	.0708	.0694	.0681
-1.3	.0968	.0951	.0934	.0918	.0901	.0885	.0869	.0853	.0838	.0823
-1.2	.1151	.1131	.1112	.1093	.1075	.1057	.1038	.1020	.1003	.0985
-1.1	.1357	.1335	.1314	.1292	.1271	.1251	.1230	.1210	.1190	.1170
-1.0	.1587	.1562	.1539	.1515	.1492	.1469	.1446	.1423	.1401	.1379
-0.9	.1841	.1814	.1788	.1762	.1736	.1711	.1685	.1660	.1635	.1611
-0.8	.2119	.2090	.2061	.2033	.2005	.1977	.1949	.1922	.1894	.1867
-0.7	.2420	.2389	.2358	.2327	.2297	.2266	.2236	.2207	.2177	.2148
-0.6	.2743	.2709	.2676	.2643	.2611	.2578	.2546	.2514	.2483	.2451
-0.5	.3085	.3050	.3015	.2981	.2946	.2912	.2877	.2843	.2810	.2776
-0.4	.3446	.3409	.3372	.3336	.3300	.3264	.3228	.3192	.3156	.3121
-0.3	.3821	.3783	.3745	.3707	.3669	.3632	.3594	.3557	.3520	.3483
-0.2	.4207	.4168	.4129	.4090	.4052	.4013	.3974	.3936	.3897	.3859
-0.1	.4602	.4562	.4522	.4483	.4443	.4404	.4364	.4325	.4286	.4247
-0	.5000	.4960	.4920	.4880	.4840	.4801	.4761	.4721	.4681	.4641

Collect a sample of data for the purpose of checking quality goals, process capability, or probability of defects (excessive variability). See example *Normalizing Sample Data for SPC Applications*.

Calculate the population mean (μ) and standard deviation (σ).

Transform any measurement, using the *z*-score equation as shown in this example.

Refer to the *Proportions of Area Under the Normal Curve* table to locate the percentage of probability of area under the curve (See Appendix, Table A.)

Normalizing Sample Data for SPC Applications

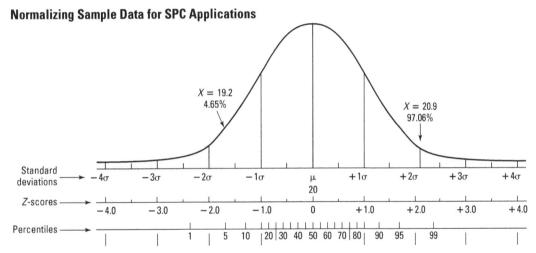

Wire extension measurements — sample data in cm
X = 19.2, 19.5, 19.6, 19.8, 19.9, 20.0, 20.1, 20.2, 20.4, 20.4, 20.9
μ = 20
σ = .477

To normalize (transform): $z = \dfrac{x - \mu}{\sigma}$

For lowest measurement

$z = \dfrac{19.2 - 20}{.477}$

$z = -1.68$

.0465 ← NPD table value

% = 4.65

For highest measurement

$z = \dfrac{20.9 - 20}{.477}$

$z = 1.89$

.9706 → NPD table value

% = 97.06 (47.06 + 50%)

Note: Establishing maximum/minimum values of length for wire extensions would allow the prediction of % "defects" area under the normal probability curve. Also see standard deviation (tool 184) and process capability ratios (tool 147) in this handbook for further information.

Introduced by Richard Bolles, the numerical prioritization tool is reflective of a systematic process of ranking items by preference or user's choice. Similar to paired comparisons, this choosing between paired items will result in a ranking frame of all listed items. This process simply guides the user (or team) through the item prioritization process without undue user bias.

- To prioritize a list of action items, problems, or choices.
- To allow a team decision to be made on the basis of comparing all options on a list.
- To combine the individual rankings of team participants to arrive at an unbiased collective team ranking of items.
- To reach team consensus without lengthy discussion.

before

Consensus decision making

Importance weighting

Criteria filtering

Phillips 66

Countermeasures matrix

after

Action plan

Project planning log

Cost-benefit analysis

Basili data collection method

Action and effect diagram (AED)

➥ Select and define problem or opportunity
➥ Identify and analyze causes or potential change
Develop and plan possible solutions or change
Implement and evaluate solution or change
Measure and report solution or change results
Recognize and reward team efforts

Research/statistics
Creativity/innovation
Engineering
Project management
Manufacturing
3 Marketing/sales
4 Administration/documentation
Servicing/support
1 Customer/quality metrics
2 Change management

- If any item numbers are circled the same number of times, the tie can be broken by checking which number was circled when the selection was made between the pair of item numbers which are tied.

The team develops or introduces a list of 10 items to be numerically prioritized. See example *Prioritization of Customer Satisfaction Tools*.

A nine column (A–I) matrix is constructed on a flip chart (see example). The list of 10 items is placed alongside the matrix; in easy view of all team participants.

Participants start their individual ranking by comparing item 1 with item 2 of column *A* and circling their choice. Moving down the column, this ranking is continued for each pair of items and in all remaining columns until the last choice has been circled in column *I*. If there are fewer than 10 items on your list, stop when the last choice in the column has been circled.

The next step is to total the number of times a particular item was chosen. Place the totals in the item chart.

The 10 items are ranked from highest number of circles (choices) to the lowest number of circles. The resulting rank-ordered list reflects an individuals numerical prioritization.

When individual scoring has been completed, tallies are added to get a team total.

Rank again the total scores of items to get the team's decision.

Lastly, date the final list.

Prioritization of Customer Satisfaction Tools

A	B	C	D	E	F	G	H	I
1 (2)								
1 (3)	2 (3)							
1 (4)	(2) 4	3 (4)						
(1) 5	(2) 5	(3) 5	(4) 5					
(1) 6	(2) 6	(3) 6	(4) 6	(5) 6				
1 (7)	2 (7)	3 (7)	4 (7)	5 (7)	6 (7)			
1 (8)	2 (8)	3 (8)	4 (8)	5 (8)	6 (8)	7 (8)		
1 (9)	2 (9)	3 (9)	4 (9)	5 (9)	6 (9)	7 (9)	8 (9)	
(1) 10	(2) 10	(3) 10	(4) 10	(5) 10	(6) 10	(7) 10	(8) 10	(9) 10

Total Scores	Individual Ranking	Team Total Scores	Team Ranking		Customer Satisfaction Tools	Date: xx/xx/xx
3	7			1.	Focus group	
5	5			2.	Conjoint analysis	
5	5			3.	Customer-first-questions (CFQ)	
5	5			4.	Customer feedback worksheet	
2	8			5.	Two-dimensional survey grid	
1	9			6.	Selection window	
7	3			7.	Voice of the customer table (VOCT)	
8	2			8.	House of quality	
9	1			9.	Customer satisfaction analysis (CSA)	
0	10			10.	Interview technique	

Note: #1 rank is the highest individual ranking (priority) for the tool Customer Satisfaction Analysis (CSA).

The objectives matrix (OMAX) is a powerful reporting form that allows the monitoring of the completion rate for all stated objectives within the area of project management. Originally recommended by Felix and Riggs (1983), and presented by S. L. Dockstader (1987), this tool can serve as a principle document to report on status and provide a scoring mechanism that measures, at any time, overall performance.

- To track organizational performance against a set of change objectives.
- To measure progress made and provide a composite index of goal attainment.
- To provide a detailed status report of progress made to upper management.

before

Basili data collection method

Milestones chart

Timeline chart

Monthly assessment schedule

Action plan

after

Run-it by

What-if analysis

Presentation

Problem analysis

Major program status

Select and define problem or opportunity	
Identify and analyze causes or potential change	
Develop and plan possible solutions or change	
➡ Implement and evaluate solution or change	
➡ Measure and report solution or change results	
Recognize and reward team efforts	

4	Research/statistics
	Creativity/innovation
	Engineering
2	Project management
	Manufacturing
	Marketing/sales
	Administration/documentation
	Servicing/support
1	Customer/quality metrics
3	Change management

- Scores 0–10 reflect the progress of completing the objectives. In the example shown, objective 2, *Conduct 100 orientation sessions* is 45 percent complete (see *Current performance*). This equates to a score of 4.5 (see score in column two), which is then multiplied by weight of 5 to arrive at value of 22.5.
- Frequency of measurement is determined by the process owners or upper management.

The first step calls for the development of measurable objectives to be inserted in the OMAX form. See example *General Goal—Establish IPD Teams*. (Refer to the example in the objective matrix table—calculations and steps.)

The team develops the countables for each objective column. The example *Establish 20 IPD Teams* will have 0 to 20 associated with score 0 to 10.

The team considers the weight or importance of each objective and reaches consensus on the weight multipliers to be assigned to all objectives as shown in the example (see *Weight*). Note that the *Weight* row total must equal 100.

Whenever a performance measurement is needed, the *Current performance (completed)* row is filled in with actual data.

The respective scores are identified and inserted in the score row. Example: The score 2 is associated with 4 in column one, which reflects also *Current performance (completed)* of 4 IPD teams established.

General Goal: Establish 20 Integrated Product Development (IPD) Teams

Objective No.	1	2	3	4	5	6	7	
Objectives/measures (Due 1/2/xx)	Establish 20 IPD teams	Conduct 100 orientation sessions	Train 20 team facilitators	Sign-up 200+ volunteers	Identify "Tools for Teams" training	Budget status: $200,000	Data collection and team reporting systems in place	Date
Current performance (completed)	4	45	6	90	5	40	10	xx/xx/xx

Score								
10 —	20	100	20	200	100%	200K	100%	
9 —	18	90	18	180	90	180	90	
8 —	16	80	16	160	80	160	80	
7 —	14	70	14	140	70	140	70	
6 —	12	60	12	120	60	120	60	
5 —	10	50	10	100	50	100	50	
4 —	8	40	8	80	40	80	40	
3 —	6	30	(6)	60	30	60	30	
2 —	(4)	20	4	40	20	(40)	20	
1 —	2	10	2	20	10	20	(10)	
0 —	0	0	0	0	0%	0	0%	

Score	2	4.5	3	4.5	.5	2	1	
Weight	25	5	20	25	5	10	10	Index
Value	50	22.5	60	112.5	2.5	20	10	277.5

Notes: 1. Reference attached cell objectives and rating information sheets.

2. (4) Reflects completion.

The observation technique is a direct and real-time method to determine and collect facts and data currently existing in a given workplace or situation. Observations and interview responses are systematically recorded on a worksheet or form specifically developed for documenting the information. No assumptions or speculations are made by the observer during data collection. Observations often serve as background data for problem-solving or process-improvement efforts.

- To obtain current data to verify existing problems or performance discrepancies.
- To collect performance data needed by a team to continue the problem-solving process.
- To study actual operations on location in order to fully document the process.
- To validate historical data used in recent research activities.

before

Data collection strategy

Sampling methods

Audience analysis

Checklist

Time study sheet

after

Frequency distribution (FD)

Checksheet

Activity analysis

Opportunity analysis

Problem specification

➥ Select and define problem or opportunity
➥ Identify and analyze causes or potential change
    Develop and plan possible solutions or change
➥ Implement and evaluate solution or change
    Measure and report solution or change results
    Recognize and reward team efforts

2 Research/statistics
    Creativity/innovation
    Engineering
    Project management
    Manufacturing
    Marketing/sales
    Administration/documentation
    Servicing/support
1 Customer/quality metrics
3 Change management

- A multipurpose observation form or worksheet should be used to record observed technical data, work activities, process interactions, or interview responses.
- An ideal data collection technique if information filtering needs to be avoided.

First, review practices and procedures, job descriptions and work instructions, or product/service information relevant to the workplace or situation to be observed.

Discuss observation schedule, time and place, who and what will be observed with the appropriate managers or process owners.

Using a prepared observation worksheet or form, record observations. See example *Types of Observations—Worksheets*.

Lastly, examine recorded information, circle key data or events, and write a final report, using the observation worksheet as an attachment.

Date all observation worksheets.

Types of Observations — Worksheets

(1)

Organization:	Unit:	Location:	Function:	Date:
ABC MFG.	#2	Workcell #5	Final assembly	xx/xx/xx

Purpose of observation: Cycle time reduction	Sample/selection process: Random sampling	Observer: W.J.M.

Observations at their work location:
1. Workstation 4 & 5: Combine tasks?
2. Operators at workstation #4 wait for work

(2)

Observations at customer site:
1. Product "A" – insufficient stock
2. Sales people point to sharp edges – product "D" packaging

(3)

Observations at test site:
1. Unit's power supply gets extremely hot
2. Frequent circuit breaker tripping

(4)

Observations by "mystery shopper:"
1. Waited (20) minutes at "appliances" – Station "B"
2. Station "F" rep. very helpful in locating item "X"

(5)

Monitoring of telephone calls

1. Complaint handling

Call duration
#5 – 1.5 Minutes
#11 – 2.5 Minutes
#16 – 1.0 Minute

2. Recording complaints

Complaint type	
A – Service	ⵜⵜⵜ I
B – Exchange	II
C – Payment	III

The opportunity analysis is an effective tool for a team to evaluate and select the most preferred opportunity among many. Similar to criteria filtering, identified improvement opportunities are rated against criteria such as organizational importance, feasibility of completion, and potential benefit against resources needed to implement the top-rated choice.

- To identify and plan for implementing the most preferred improvement opportunity.
- To provide a structured approach for teams to select high potential change.
- To determine and use criteria for profitable resource allocation.

before

Cluster analysis

Consensus decision making

Idea advocate

Buzz group

Checkerboard method

after

Risk space analysis

What-if analysis

Cost-benefit analysis

Sticking dots

Run-it by

➡ Select and define problem or opportunity

➡ Identify and analyze causes or potential change

➡ Develop and plan possible solutions or change

➡ Implement and evaluate solution or change

　 Measure and report solution or change results

　 Recognize and reward team efforts

Research/statistics

2 Creativity/innovation

　 Engineering

3 Project management

　 Manufacturing

　 Marketing/sales

　 Administration/documentation

　 Servicing/support

　 Customer/quality metrics

1 Change management

- Legend: (H) = High, 3 points; (M) = Medium, 2 points; (L) = Low, 1 point.
- Overall highest-rated improvement opportunity should be the top candidate for completion.

As a first step, the team facilitator introduces the opportunity analysis process. Rating criteria and final ranking is also discussed.

A prepared flip chart listing all of the opportunities is shown for the team to review and discuss.

Next, all criteria is clarified in order to have full understanding for the rating of listed improvement opportunities. See example *Reduction of Defects per Unit (DPU) Level*.

The team evaluates (rates) each opportunity, reaching consensus in the process.

A final ranking occurs and the top-rated improvement opportunity is identified.

The final chart is dated and next steps are briefly discussed.

Reduction of Defects Per Unit (DPU) Level

Date: 11/15/xx Improvement Opportunities	Organizational Importance			Feasibility of Completion			Potential Benefit			Rank
	H	M	L	H	M	L	H	M	L	
1. Select best suppliers		M			M			M		5
2. Involve the customer	H				M		H			2.5
3. Increase testing efficiency		M				L			L	7
4. Use parts of known process capability	H				M		H			2.5
⑤. Apply robust design principles	H			H			H			①
6. Reduce process variation	H				M			M		4
7. Provide SPC training			L	H					L	6

Note: Opportunity number 5 is highest ranked.
    Three Hs = 9 points = rank ①.

An organization chart typically shows the hierarchy and reporting relationships of functional units and their lines of communication and coordination. An organization chart is developed to provide employees with a common understanding of intergroup activities, communication channels, and levels of authority within the organization.

- To describe the formal organization.
- To show an organization's divisions and subdivisions, functional relationships, and links of communication and responsibility.

before

Block diagram

Process analysis

Tree diagram

Work breakdown structure (WBS)

Work flow analysis

after

Organizational mapping

Process mapping

Markov analysis

Task analysis

Systems analysis diagram

Select and define problem or opportunity

➡ Identify and analyze causes or potential change

Develop and plan possible solutions or change

Implement and evaluate solution or change

Measure and report solution or change results

➡ Recognize and reward team efforts

Research/statistics

Creativity/innovation

Engineering

1 Project management

Manufacturing

Marketing/sales

2 Administration/documentation

Servicing/support

Customer/quality metrics

Change management

- An organization chart is drawn from top to bottom, left to right. Organizations frequently show a hierarchical structure, with the highest level of authority at the top of the chart.
- Solid lines indicate the direct or controlling relationships, dashed lines indicate indirect or coordinating relationships.

The team determines the organization to be charted and lists all divisions and subdivisions, direct and indirect relationships, lines of communications and responsibility.

A traditional organization is drawn on a whiteboard or flip chart. See example *Employee Training and Development Organization*.

The finalized chart is checked for accuracy and dated.

Employee Training and Development Organization

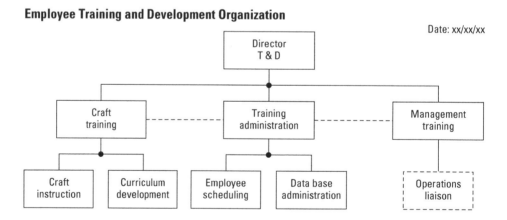

The organization mapping technique examines the team's relationships with other teams or business units within the organization. A map illustrates communication links and the frequency and importance of interactions. Recorded notes suggest improvement areas.

- To illustrate and define a team's relationships within an organization.
- To map ongoing interactions and to search for ways to improve those interactions.

before

Circle response

Sociogram

Buzz group

Observation

Consensus decision making

after

Relationship map

Deployment chart (down-across)

Run-it-by

Team mirror

Presentation

➥ Select and define problem or opportunity
➥ Identify and analyze causes or potential change
 Develop and plan possible solutions or change
 Implement and evaluate solution or change
 Measure and report solution or change results
 Recognize and reward team efforts

Research/statistics

Creativity/innovation

Engineering

Project management

Manufacturing

Marketing/sales

Administration/documentation

1 Servicing/support

2 Customer/quality metrics

3 Change management

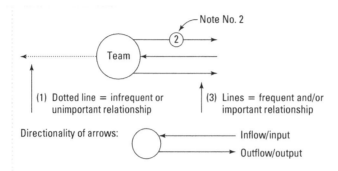

The team facilitator explains the purpose and application of this tool. A circle is drawn in the center of a whiteboard to start the organization mapping process.

Participants identify linkages and relationships with other teams or business units and establish the frequency and importance of these relationships. See example *Reproduction Team Services*.

Systematically, a map is drawn that displays links, partnerships, frequency and importance of relationships, and contact identification.

The participants engage in a discussion that explores improvements in the current network and problems that need to be resolved.

Notes are added to the organization map, a final check is performed so that the map reflects the current status, and finally, the map is dated.

Reproduction Team Services

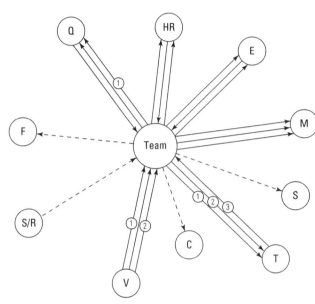

Interactions	
HR	– Human Resources
E	– Engineering
M	– Manufacturing
S	– Sales
T	– Training
C	– Consultants
V	– Vendors
S/R	– Shipping/receiving
F	– Finance
Q	– Quality

Notes: Q–1: Let's invite quality section to assist us in our
              quality improvement efforts
       V–1: Negotiate faster turnaround times
       V–2: Return damaged stock
       T–1: Need longer time frames to print
       T–2: Updating of course masters required
       T–3: We need to be more responsive to customers

The organization readiness chart is used by planning committees or research teams to verify that the organization is ready and capable of implementing a major change effort. The chart requires open communication and analysis in order to be an effective planning tool.

- To verify an organization's readiness and capability for planned change.
- To identify preliminary tasks that need to be accomplished to ensure success.

before

Data collection strategy

Venn diagram

Organization mapping

Two-dimensional survey grid

Markov analysis

after

SWOT analysis

Action plan

Resource requirements matrix

Barriers-and-aids analysis

Problem specification

➥ Select and define problem or opportunity

Identify and analyze causes or potential change

➥ Develop and plan possible solutions or change

Implement and evaluate solution or change

➥ Measure and report solution or change results

Recognize and reward team efforts

- The readiness scale is a recommendation only. Teams should adjust thresholds as desired.

Research/statistics

Creativity/innovation

Engineering

2 Project management

Manufacturing

Marketing/sales

3 Administration/documentation

Servicing/support

Customer/quality metrics

1 Change management

The planning committee or research team openly discusses the readiness of the organization. See example *Ready for Self-Directed Work Teams?*

All meeting participants fill in the chart, calculate a total score, and return the chart to the team facilitator.

A flip chart is used to record all total scores and "high concern" scores that may indicate problem areas or opportunities for improvement.

Following the display of scores, additional discussion takes place for the purpose of formulating required action.

Charts are dated and saved for future reference.

Ready for Self-Directed Work Teams?   Date: xx/xx/xx

Mark "0" for No Concern   "2" for Some Concern   "4" for High Concern

1. _____ A supportive climate in the organization

2. _____ Ongoing commitment to total quality management

3. _____ Active employee involvement is evident

4. _____ Employee share in the decision-making process

5. _____ Management's guidance and expectation for teams (at start-up)

6. _____ Supervisory staff's attitude toward teaming

7. _____ Rewards and recognition for teams

8. _____ Resource commitment (financial, facilities, equipment)

9. _____ Organizational constraints (personnel, budget, priorities)

10. _____ Consultation and evaluation support is available

11. _____ Communication channels (interfacing, reporting, feedback)

12. _____ Training of team members (team dynamics, problem-solving tools)

13. _____ Commitment to team meeting schedules and action items

14. _____ Availability of administrative forms and procedures (for teams)

15. _____ Other_____

_____ Total Score

Readiness Scale: 0–15 = ready to start; 16–30 = more preparation required; 31+ = lack of readiness

The pair matching overlay technique searches for an ideal mentor-protégé match or partnership. This match-up results when both mentors and protégés indicate their first and second choices (of partners) among the listed names on a matrix. This matrix is eventually overlaid with all choices to display the matching sets of names.

- To effectively match mentors and protégés to the satisfaction of both.
- To provide a quality personal development alternative that assists highly ranked potential candidates to prepare for higher job responsibilities.
- To find mentor-protégé partnerships that are mutually selected by both parties.

before

Circle of opportunity

Demographic analysis

Circles of influence

Surveying

Starbursting

after

Critical dialogue

Interview technique

Different point of view

Run-it-by

Consensus decision making

➥ Select and define problem or opportunity

  Identify and analyze causes or potential change

➥ Develop and plan possible solutions or change

  Implement and evaluate solution or change

  Measure and report solution or change results

➥ Recognize and reward team efforts

Research/statistics

Creativity/innovation

Engineering

Project management

Manufacturing

Marketing/sales

2 Administration/documentation

1 Servicing/support

  Customer/quality metrics

3 Change management

- Returned matrices are overlaid to check for mutual choices of partners: 1 = first choice, 2 = second choice.

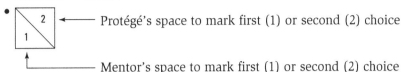 Protégé's space to mark first (1) or second (2) choice

Mentor's space to mark first (1) or second (2) choice

- Do not exceed a 15 × 15 matrix configuration of names.
- For best results: Reproduce 40 copies of the mentor-protégé matrix and provide each participant with a copy to record their preferences, if any.

Two lists of names are drawn-up: One is a list of available mentors and the other is a list of high potential candidates, or protégés.

A pair matching overlay matrix is used to display the names of identified mentors and protégés. Their organizational unit or department affiliation is also shown. See example *Searching for Mutually Agreeable Partnerships*.

Once the matrix is finalized, copies are made and mailed to all listed mentors and protégés to allow them to indicate their first and second choices.

Upon return of the completed matrices, mentor-protégé matches are identified by overlaying the choices of mentor and protégé matrices.

A final pair matching overlay matrix can be completed with all matches or partnerships identified as shown in the example of a partially completed matrix.

Date the final matrix.

Searching for Mutually Agreeable Partnerships

Date: xx/xx/xx

Org. Unit/Dept. → Mentor ↓ / Protégé →	HR 1 Name	BM 2 Name	F 3 Name	S 4 Name	CO 5 Name	M 6 Name	CO 7 Name	Div. A 8 Name	Div. B 9 Name	Div. C 10 Name	L 11 Name	HR 12 Name	BM 13 Name	Div. L 14 Name	PO 15 Name
Div. L — Name 1															2
Div. C — Name 2															
S — Name 3				1 / 1											
CO — Name 4															
F — Name 5	2					2 / 1							2		
L — Name 6															
M — Name 7													1		
DI — Name 8								2							
CO — Name 9	1 / 1									1					
PO — Name 10															
HR — Name 11															1
Div. A — Name 12				2 / 1											
Div. B — Name 13										2 / 2					
BM — Name 14															
HR — Name 15															

Notes:

⬜ 2 / 1 ← Protégé's first (1) or second (2) choice

↑ Mentor's first (1) or second (2) choice

The paired comparison tool requires all team participants to make choices on several pairs of items (options) such as problems, potential solutions, or activities, in order to arrive at a team decision. In other words, team participants can vote their individual preference, which, when totaled with the other participants' votes, will produce a team ranking of listed items.

- To quantify team participants' preferred items (choices) for the purpose of arriving at team consensus.
- To force a team to consider the advantages and disadvantages of all listed options, to make comparisons, and to determine the most preferred choice among all options.
- To prioritize a list of problems, potential solutions, or action items.

before

Weighted voting

Consensus decision making

Phillips 66

Criteria filtering

Countermeasures matrix

after

Project planning log

Action and effect diagram (AED)

What-if analysis

Cost-benefit analysis

Action plan

➥ Select and define problem or opportunity

Identify and analyze causes or potential change

➥ Develop and plan possible solutions or change

Implement and evaluate solution or change

Measure and report solution or change results

Recognize and reward team efforts

Research/statistics

Creativity/innovation

Engineering

2 Project management

Manufacturing

Marketing/sales

Administration/documentation

Servicing/support

3 Customer/quality metrics

1 Change management

- Compare six or fewer items (options) since the number of comparisons increase significantly with the increase of items.
This can be calculated by: comparisons $= \dfrac{N\,(N-1)}{2}$

# of items	# of comparisons
2	1
3	3
4	6
5	10
6	15
7	21
8	28
9	36
10	45

The team decides to attend a workshop of some quality-related topic. The team's eight participants have choices of Hoshin planning, benchmarking, cycle time management (CTM), and design of experiments (DOE). See example *Workshop Attendance Options*.

A paired comparison grid is drawn on a flip chart. The four training choices are listed in column *Choice* as in the example shown.

Each participant considers every pair of choices and decides which is the preferred choice. One participant tracks the votes as all choices are voted on by all participants. The total votes for each comparison must equal eight, since every participant receives only one vote and *no* participant is allowed to pass!

Upon completion of voting on choices, and once all votes are recorded, the numbers in the pair columns are totaled. The highest number (total) in the totals column reflect the team's preferred choice of training. *Note: The team's decision (total score = 17) calls for cycle time management (CTM) workshop attendance.*

Date the final chart.

Workshop Attendance Options

Date: xx/xx/xx

Choice	A or B	A or C	A or D	B or C	B or D	C or D	Totals
A	3	2	5				10
B	5			3	6		14
C		6		5		6	(17)
D			3		2	2	7

Choices

A – *Hoshin planning*
B – *Benchmarking*
C – *Cycle time management (CTM)*
D – *Design of experiments (DOE)*

Note: Cycle time management is preferred choice.

A panel debate technique allows a team of panelists with diverse knowledge, experience, or opinions to debate and share their insights on a topic, problem situation, or improvement opportunity. All participants, by questioning, gain valuable and current information to promote a more in-depth understanding of a specific study topic or problem issue.

- To provide access to current information and expertise from internal or external experts.
- To allow participants to interact with a panel of experts for the purpose of collecting specific information.
- To consult with people who have been recognized as experts in their field.

before

Brainstorming

Buzz group

Fishbowls

Rotating roles

Consensus decision making

after

Different point of view

Run-it-by

Fresh eye

Critical dialogue

Presentation

➡ Select and define problem or opportunity

Identify and analyze causes or potential change

➡ Develop and plan possible solutions or change

Implement and evaluate solution or change

➡ Measure and report solution or change results

Recognize and reward team efforts

	Research/statistics
3	Creativity/innovation
4	Engineering
	Project management
5	Manufacturing
1	Marketing/sales
	Administration/documentation
6	Servicing/support
2	Customer/quality metrics
	Change management

- Limit the size of a panel to 4 to 5 people.
- Assign a panel moderator to keep the debate moving along.
- Allow enough time so that key points and all questions (or prepared questions) can be discussed.

The team leader or facilitator contacts and schedules the members of the panel, experts in the field who can greatly contribute to the problem situation the team is presently researching.

Participants brainstorm the information that is needed and formulate questions prior to the actual panel debate.

The team facilitator, in the role of the moderator, facilitates the introductions and starts the debate/discussion. See example *Panel Debate on ISO-9000 Training Issues*.

A designated recorder records responses and key information during this interaction and date the document.

After completion of the panel debate, the team summarizes keypoints, identifies questions left unanswered, and discusses the next steps.

Panel Debate on ISO-9000 Training Issues

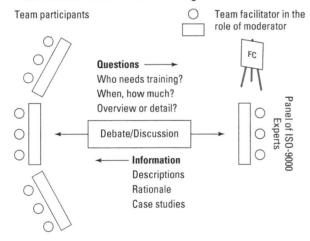

The Pareto chart is a bar chart arranged in a descending order of size or importance from left to right to separate and display the critical few from the trivial many causes of a problem. It is named after Vilfredo Pareto who, in the late 1800s, postulated the 80/20 role, which states that 80 percent of the trouble is due to 20 percent of the causes. The Pareto chart will also show the cumulative percentage for each cause on the chart.

- To prioritize potential causes of a problem.
- To establish and verify cause and effect.
- To reach consensus on what needs to be addressed first.
- To identify improvement opportunities.
- To measure success of corrective action.

before

Checksheet
Data collection strategy
Sampling methods
Frequency distribution
Yield chart

after

Problem specification
Process analysis
Problem analysis
Process mapping
Action plan

➥ Select and define problem or opportunity	
➥ Identify and analyze causes or potential change	
Develop and plan possible solutions or change	
➥ Implement and evaluate solution or change	
➥ Measure and report solution or change results	
Recognize and reward team efforts	

	Research/statistics
	Creativity/innovation
	Engineering
	Project management
2	Manufacturing
5	Marketing/sales
	Administration/documentation
3	Servicing/support
4	Customer/quality metrics
1	Change management

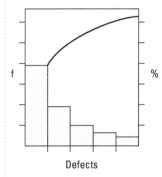

Left vertical scale = frequency of defects
Right vertical scale = percentage of defects
Horizontal scale = types of defects
Trendline = cumulative percentage of defect

Identify the data source. See example *Tape Unit Assembly Defects*.

Calculate percentages for totals of each type of defect.

Draw a Pareto chart as shown in the *notes and key points* above.

Designate left and right vertical scales.

Draw the bars in accordance with total defects per type.

Construct the cumulative line (left to right) by adding the respective percentage for each defect type and connect plots with straight lines, as shown in the example.

Title the Pareto chart; include time period covered and source of data.

Tape Unit Assembly Defects

Tape Unit Assembly Defects (April)	Quantity	%*
A – Unit surface (scars/scratches)	70	47
B – Sub-assembly (defective)	12	8
C – Mounting parts (incorrect/missing)	8	5
D – Insulators (cracked/missing)	23	15
E – Wire (incorrect length)	10	7
F – Assembling (incorrect)	7	5
G – Soldering (% fill rejects)	15	10
H – Labeling (missing/incorrect)	5	3
	150	100

* Rounded

Date: xx/xx/xx

Source: Final assembly 3-A

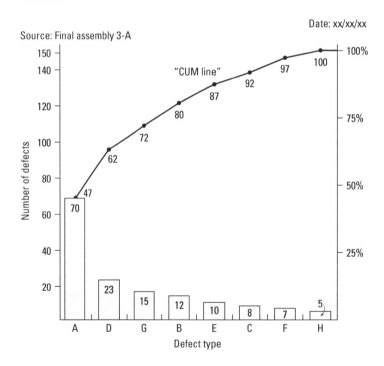

354

The Phillips 66 method was originated by Donald Phillips of Hillsdale College for the purpose of getting more involvement—questions, ideas, or opinions—from a large conference group. In order to effectively do this, the audience (large group) is divided into small groups of six people each and after some discussion, these groups present their results to the conference panel or leader.

- To start a problem-solving effort by involving a great number of people to discuss the issues involved and present potential solutions.
- To generate a large number of ideas from a large group or audience.
- To collect and evaluate several sets of ideas generated by a few loosely assembled small groups.

before

Data collection strategy

Audience analysis

Interview technique

Presentation

Nominal group technique (NGT)

after

Consensus decision making

Idea advocate

Creativity assessment

Gap analysis

Importance weighting

➡ Select and define problem or opportunity

➡ Identify and analyze causes or potential change

➡ Develop and plan possible solutions or change

Implement and evaluate solution or change

Measure and report solution or change results

Recognize and reward team efforts

	Research/statistics
1	Creativity/innovation
4	Engineering
	Project management
	Manufacturing
3	Marketing/sales
	Administration/documentation
	Servicing/support
	Customer/quality metrics
2	Change management

- The original Phillips 66 process called for the dividing of a large group into smaller groups of 6 people each and to allow 6 minutes per small group for discussing a problem or generating ideas.
- The small group size (5–10) should be adjusted in accordance with the size (25–100) of the large groups. Also, small group discussion time may need to be increased up to 30 minutes.

A large group of 25–100 people is subdivided into small teams of 5–10 people each. If possible, teams move to a different location so that they will not be overheard by other teams.

The team selects a spokesperson who will record and present the team's ideas.

Next, a well-defined problem or an issue is presented for discussion. After a 6–30 minute discussion, ideas are recorded. See example *Generate Ideas for New Product Development*.

Each team evaluates their ideas, reduces the many to a few promising ideas, and presents them to the conference facilitator or panel.

All teams return to their seats and the facilitator or panel receives the recorded ideas from each team.

The entire set of ideas is either saved for later evaluation or is displayed to the audience and discussed on the spot.

Generate Ideas for New Product Development

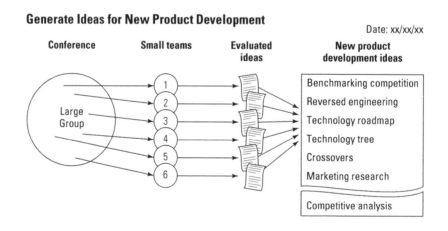

A pictograph is a visual representation of recorded data. A picture, diagram or symbol is used to indicate a specific quantity of the product or item being recorded on the graph for easy interpretation.

- To plot collected data using pictures or symbols for visual impact.
- To show quantities of items in a report or other publication.

➡	Select and define problem or opportunity
➡	Identify and analyze causes or potential change
	Develop and plan possible solutions or change
	Implement and evaluate solution or change
	Measure and report solution or change results
	Recognize and reward team efforts

	Research/statistics
	Creativity/innovation
	Engineering
	Project management
1	Manufacturing
	Marketing/sales
2	Administration/documentation
3	Servicing/support
4	Customer/quality metrics
	Change management

- When drawing a pictograph, care must be taken not to distort the relationships between scales and quantities.

before

Data collection strategy

Checksheet

Observation

Frequency distribution (FD)

Variance analysis

after

Pareto chart

Problem specification

Quality chart

Potential problem analysis (PPA)

Countermeasures matrix

The team collects and summarizes the data to be plotted.

The team constructs a pictograph and scales it on the basis of data totals. See example *TQM Teams—Total Meeting Hours*.

The team plots the data using a picture symbol to visually represent the quantity of items.

The team checks the totals and dates the graph.

TQM Teams — Total Meeting Hours

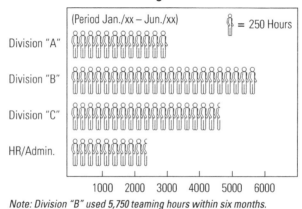

Note: Division "B" used 5,750 teaming hours within six months.

A pie chart presents data very efficiently and is useful for general comparison of parts or ratios. The circular graph illustrates the relationship of the various parts, each part representing a percentage of the whole.

- To display the relative contributions of different subcategories of data.
- To identify ratios or proportions.
- To establish priorities for action.
- To focus on problems or causes.

before

Frequency distribution (FD)

Checksheet

Observation

Surveying

Focus group

after

Two-directional bar chart

Demographic analysis

Cost-benefit analysis

Pareto chart

Presentation

➟ Select and define problem or opportunity
➟ Identify and analyze causes or potential change
  Develop and plan possible solutions or change
➟ Implement and evaluate solution or change
➟ Measure and report solution or change results
  Recognize and reward team efforts

- The parts of a pie chart must total 100 percent. Group small percentage items and label them "other." Draw no more than 10 parts, using alternate fill patterns or colors.

1   Research/statistics
    Creativity/innovation
    Engineering
2   Project management
    Manufacturing
3   Marketing/sales
    Administration/documentation
4   Servicing/support
5   Customer/quality metrics
    Change management

Collect the data and verify accuracy. See example *Cost of Quality Budget*.

Identify data categories and determine percentage for each.

Draw circle for the pie chart; include a small circle in the center to represent the whole.

Label each part (category) and indicate its percentage.

Use different shading, fill patterns, or color for parts. Date the pie chart.

"Cost of Quality" Budget   Date: xx/xx/xx

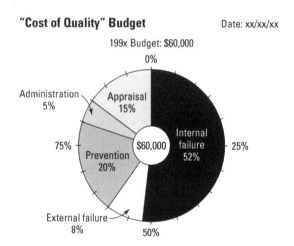

Developed by Wolfgang Schnelle, the pin cards technique is a brainwriting process to generate ideas on colored cards that are categorized and displayed to all participants for further sorting and clarification. This process includes an effective idea stimulation feature that assists participants to think of more ideas during the writing process.

- To generate ideas to solve a problem or improve a process.
- To allow equal participation in a team brainwriting process.
- To produce many ideas quickly and without filtering from other participants.

<table>
<tr><td>

before

Brainwriting pool

Mental imaging

Fresh eye

Stimulus analysis

Circle response

after

Morphological analysis

Sticking dots

Creativity assessment

Cluster analysis

Criteria filtering

</td><td>

➡ Select and define problem or opportunity

➡ Identify and analyze causes or potential change

➡ Develop and plan possible solutions or change

Implement and evaluate solution or change

Measure and report solution or change results

Recognize and reward team efforts

</td><td>

Research/statistics

1 Creativity/innovation

Engineering

Project management

Manufacturing

Marketing/sales

Administration/documentation

Servicing/support

Customer/quality metrics

2 Change management

</td></tr>
</table>

- Pin cards technique advantages:
  - It allows equal participation by all participants.
  - It produces more ideas than basic brainstorming.
  - Color-coded cards identify originator of idea (for later clarification, if needed).
  - Displayed ideas can easily be examined by all participants for combining ideas, modifying or building on each other's ideas.
- Pin cards technique disadvantages:
  - Participants not passing cards quickly may cause bottlenecks in the process.
  - Participants may perceive a time pressure to generate ideas.
  - Quick passing of idea cards leave little time for idea incubation.
  - Some participants may not wish to have their ideas openly displayed.

The team facilitator displays a flip chart with the problem statement and explains how the pin cards technique is performed. See example *Ideas for Improving Inter-team Communications*.

Every participant receives approximately 10 cards of the same color; each participant receives different-colored cards.

Participants recheck the problem statement, ask for clarification if needed, and begin writing ideas on their cards, one idea per card. Completed cards are passed to the person on their immediate right.

Participants have the option to pick up any cards from the person on their left and read it. This may stimulate participants to think of additional ideas.

After 30–45 minutes of brainwriting, the facilitator asks all participants to collect their cards and pin them on a wall or tape them to flip charts or a whiteboard. Cards are assembled by category or common group.

Participants read all cards, move some to a matching group or category, ask for clarification on others, and continue this process until completed.

Ideas for Improving Inter-Team Communications

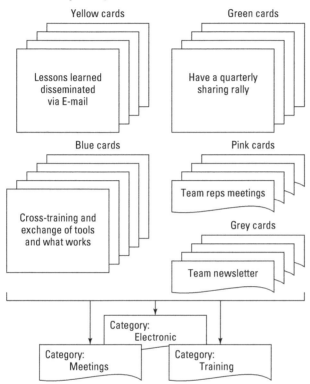

A point-scoring evaluation rates the importance, value, or preference of listed solutions, factors, or issues by the assignment of points to every alternative, not to exceed a team-set maximum of 100 or 1000 points of all listed alternatives. This rating system effectively supports a team's consensus decision-making effort.

- To review and rate all listed alternatives.
- To select, by numerical rating, a team's preferred solution, factor, or issue.
- To team-rate the importance, value, or best option of a matrix of factors.

before

Selection matrix
Rating matrix
Ranking matrix
Weighted voting
Solution matrix

after

Problem selection matrix
Project prioritization matrix
Starbursting
Run-it-by
Different point of view

	Select and define problem or opportunity
➡	Identify and analyze causes or potential change
➡	Develop and plan possible solutions or change
	Implement and evaluate solution or change
➡	Measure and report solution or change results
	Recognize and reward team efforts

- When point-scoring, use a total of 100 or 1000 points for the distribution across problems, elements, conditions, factors, issues, or ideas.

1	Research/statistics
	Creativity/innovation
2	Engineering
	Project management
	Manufacturing
3	Marketing/sales
	Administration/documentation
	Servicing/support
4	Customer/quality metrics
	Change management

The team facilitator reviews the process of point-scoring with the team.

A point-scoring matrix is drawn on a flip chart or whiteboard. All factors are discussed and recorded in the matrix. See example *Company TQM and Employee Involvement Events*.

Next, the team decides on the maximum number of points to be distributed: 100 or 1000 points. In this example 100 points were distributed.

The facilitator now guides the participants through the evaluation of each listed alternative and arrives at a team rating of points to be assigned to reach the preferred alternative.

The point-scoring matrix is filled and all columns are added to show the highest total. This is the preferred alternative. In this example, 95 points reflect the team's choice.

The matrix is checked for accuracy and dated.

Company TQM and Employee Involvement Events

Date: xx/xx/xx / Value to the Company	Type of Event — IPD Day lessons learned	Company sharing rally	Company TQM symposium	Learning organization conference	Max. points
Quality improvement	15	20	20	20	25
Shared learning	20	10	15	20	20
Training support	15	10	15	15	15
Teaming communications	15	15	15	15	15
Supports org. objectives	20	10	20	25	25
Totals	85	65	85	(95)	100

Note: IPD = Integrated product development
TQM = Total quality management

A polygon is a line graph that displays the central tendency, process variability, and relative frequency of collected data. Typically taken from a frequency distribution, a polygon is very effective in providing a visual representation of how actual measurements of a characteristic vary around a target or specification value.

- To determine if the process variability within a data distribution is within specification limits.
- To show problematic process variations from a desired result or value.
- To reflect shifts in process capability.
- To verify changes in the process after improvements have been made.

before

Checksheets

Frequency distribution (FD)

Events log

Observation

Dot diagram

after

Pareto chart

Multivariable chart

Presentation

Pie chart

Stratification

➡ Select and define problem or opportunity
➡ Identify and analyze causes or potential change
   Develop and plan possible solutions or change
➡ Implement and evaluate solution or change
➡ Measure and report solution or change results
   Recognize and reward team efforts

1	Research/statistics
	Creativity/innovation
	Engineering
4	Project management
3	Manufacturing
5	Marketing/sales
	Administration/documentation
	Servicing/support
2	Customer/quality metrics
	Change management

Preparation for Grouping of Data

- Determine the range(s) of the distribution
  $R = (H - L) + 1$
- For smaller data sets, $N = \; < 100$: number of class intervals (C.I.) between 5–10
  For larger data sets, $N = \; > 100$: number of class intervals (C.I.) between 10–20.
- Width of the class interval to be 2, 3, 5, 10, 20, for smaller numbers. (Add zeros for larger data sets.)
- Select numbers of class intervals:

  number of C.I. $= \dfrac{R}{2,\ 3,\ 5,\ 10,\ 20}$ $\longleftarrow$ Range

  $\longleftarrow$ C.I. width

- Check to see if the lowest data point in the data set is divisible an equal number of times by the C.I. width. If not, select the next lower data point that is.

Count the number (N) of data points or observations (see example *Completed Rework Hours*) and sequence them from low to high.

16 11 15 22 31	Count = 30	⑩ 15 17 21 25	
19 10 24 14 26		11 15 18 22 26	
17 22 16 12 27		12 16 19 22 27	
14 13 16 24 28		13 16 19 22 28	
19 29 21 22 19		14 16 19 24 29	High = 31
18 15 17 19 25		14 17 19 24 ㉛	Low = 10

Identify highest and lowest data point.

Calculate range (R): $R = (H - L) + 1$
$= (31 - 10) + 1 = 22$

Determine the number of class intervals (C.I.) and width:

number of C.I. $= \dfrac{22}{2,\ ③\ 5,\ 10,\ 20} = 7.33$ or 8

Width = 3   Must be between 5–10

List resulting class intervals (C.I.):

C.I.	f
9–11	2
12–14	4
15–17	7
18–20	5
21–23	4
24–26	4
27–29	3
30–32	1

Note: 9 was used as the lowest score since 10 was not divisible by the C.I. of 3 without a remainder.

Construct a polygon. Apply the 3:4 ratio rule: The height of the vertical axis (Y) must be 75 percent of the length of the horizontal axis (X). Complete the polygon by plotting dots at the height (frequency) and the midpoint of each Class Interval. Connect all dots with straight lines.

Label both axes and date the polygon.

Completed Rework Hours

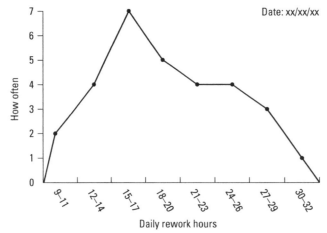

A polygon overlay is a graphical representation of many data variables, encoded for quick comparisons. It is a statistical tool that shows trendlines and correlations found in historical data.

- To plot data for forecasting purposes.
- To allow results comparisons.
- To verify status of progress.
- To provide supporting data in a problem-solving effort.

before

Data collection strategy

Observation

Events log

Surveying

Frequency distribution (FD)

after

Trend analysis

Process analysis

Pie chart

Stratification

Presentation

➡ Select and define problem or opportunity

➡ Identify and analyze causes or potential change

Develop and plan possible solutions or change

➡ Implement and evaluate solution or change

Measure and report solution or change results

Recognize and reward team efforts

1	Research/statistics
	Creativity/innovation
4	Engineering
3	Project management
	Manufacturing
6	Marketing/sales
	Administration/documentation
	Servicing/support
5	Customer/quality metrics
2	Change management

- Do not exceed five data variables on one chart; it may become difficult to scale every variable if vertical scales cannot be used for more than one variable. If there is a great numerical difference that requires separate vertical scale designations (upper/lower limits), a common denominator must be used to align scales from the zero point on the overlay graph.

Draw the vertical axis to be 75 percent of the horizontal axis. This 3:4 ratio rule is used to ensure unbiased graph construction. See example *Company Reengineering and Retraining Results*.

Identify the number of scales and their upper and lower limits required to include all data points.

Encode and name different data sets.

Graph data, anchoring it to its specific scale.

Verify that all raw data have been accounted for and properly converted to corresponding frequencies and positions on the graph.

Ensure that the title of the graph and all designations provide accurate descriptions of the data. Use notes if necessary to guarantee clarity.

If desired, continue to plot data for ongoing trendline analyses.

**Company Reengineering and Retraining Results
(Employee Training and Development)**

Date: xx/xx/xx

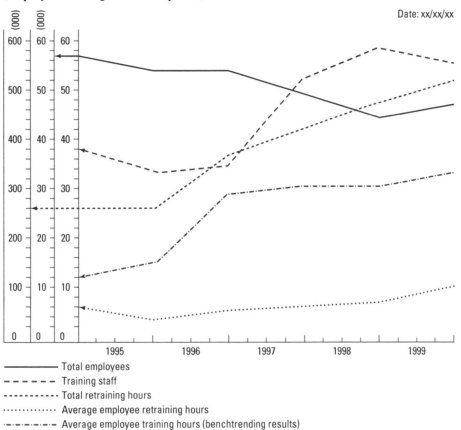

—————— Total employees
– – – – – Training staff
- - - - - - - - Total retraining hours
· · · · · · · · · · · · Average employee retraining hours
·–·–·–·– Average employee training hours (benchtrending results)

The potential problem analysis (PPA) is a tool used for minimizing the probability of solution implementation failure by identifying potential problems and possible countermeasures.

- To anticipate and analyze potential problems.
- To identify potential problems that could cause delays, difficulties, or outright failure in the implementation of a solution.
- To estimate the risk of project failure and the cost of prevention.

➡	Select and define problem or opportunity
➡	Identify and analyze causes or potential change
➡	Develop and plan possible solutions or change
	Implement and evaluate solution or change
	Measure and report solution or change results
	Recognize and reward team efforts

	Research/statistics
4	Creativity/innovation
2	Engineering
	Project management
3	Manufacturing
	Marketing/sales
	Administration/documentation
	Servicing/support
	Customer/quality metrics
1	Change management

before

Problem analysis

Activity analysis

Barriers-and-aids analysis

Reverse brainstorming

Action and effect diagram (AED)

after

Action plan

Resource requirements matrix

Consensus decision making

Countermeasures matrix

Facility layout diagram

- The team may identify potential problems as seen from this example.

  What? Parts not available when needed

  Where? At "parts assembly" workstations

  When? First 10 days of each month

  Who? Required by operators of all shifts

  Extend? Could shut down the assembly process

- Suggested definitions and scales.

  R – Risk in implementation (1–10): The amount of risk a potential problem may bring to the implementation of a solution. A rating of 1 stands for very little risk, a rating of 10 may prevent implementation altogether.

  P – Probability of occurrence (1–10): An estimate of probability for a potential problem to materialize. A rating of 1 is very low, 10 is extremely high.

  RP – Residual probability (1–10): A reestimated probability for a potential problem to occur after appropriate countermeasures may prevent a potential problem from appearing. A rating of 1 is very low, 10 is extremely high.

  C – The estimated cost of countermeasures or contingency plans. L = low cost, M = medium cost, H = high cost.

First, a facilitated team determines a set of solution implementation goals and all activities required to successfully reach these goals.

Using the reverse brainstorming method, a list of potential problems is developed and recorded on a whiteboard.

The list of potential problems is used to draw a table of potential problem analysis. See example *Implementation of a Just-in-Time (JIT) Manufacturing System*.

The facilitator asks participants to analyze each potential problem by asking: what? where? when? who? and to what extent? This will provide more detailed information for risk estimation.

Next, the team discusses the amount of risk each potential problem brings to the implementation effort. After reaching consensus on the risk estimates, the probability of problem occurrence is estimated. Ratings are placed with the potential problems in the table, as shown in this example.

Team discussion follows on the possible prevention of potential problems. Countermeasures are identified, and the residual probability of occurrence estimated. The residual probability is estimated on the basis of a greatly reduced probability of problem occurrence after countermeasures have been placed into effect.

Lastly, contingency plans are agreed upon just in case the countermeasures will not significantly affect the most serious problems.

To complete the potential problem analysis table, costs are estimated for countermeasures and contingency plans.

The team reviews the table, makes final revisions, dates the table, and presents this analysis to the process owners.

Implementation of a Just-in-Time (JIT) Manufacturing System

Date: xx/xx/xx

ID	Possible Causes of Potential Problems	R	P	Countermeasures to Prevent Problems	RP	C	Contingency Plans for High-Risk Problems	C
A	Suppliers cannot meet delivery schedule	8	5	Select and certify more suppliers	2	M	Acquire (purchase) supplier company	H
B	Parts not available when needed	10	7	Rearrange work, balance supply	4	M	Stock critical parts	M
C	Managers show resistance to change	5	4	Get managers involved early	2	L	Rotate, transfer decision-making	L
D	No direct operator involvement	5	9	Establish self-directed work teams	4	M	— — —	
E	Bottlenecks exist; no workflow balance	6	7	Perform process and cycle time analyses	3	H	— — —	
F	Lack of operator JIT training	4	8	Schedule operator JIT training	0	M	Engage outside training firm	M
G	No self-inspection methods in place	3	8	Develop practices and procedures	0	L	— — —	

Notes: R = Risk, P = Probablility, RP = Residual Probablity
Scale 1–10, 1 = Low
C = Cost: L = Low, M = Medium, H = High

A presentation is an activity from which both team participants and process owners receive benefits. Presentations show a team's progress, achievement, or a proposal for action. Another purpose for a presentation is to obtain approvals and commitments from the organization's decision makers.

- To report on a team's progress.
- To communicate essential information.
- To update management on projects, changes, or potential problem areas.

before

Audience analysis

Information needs analysis

Case study

Critical incident

Brainstorming

after

Different point of view

Run-it-by

Starbursting

Interview technique

Resource requirement matrix

Select and define problem or opportunity

Identify and analyze causes or potential change

Develop and plan possible solutions or change

Implement and evaluate solution or change

➥ Measure and report solution or change results

➥ Recognize and reward team efforts

Research/statistics

Creativity/innovation

Engineering

1 Project management

Manufacturing

3 Marketing/sales

Administration/documentation

4 Servicing/support

Customer/quality metrics

2 Change management

- When preparing and making a presentation avoid the following:
  - Unnecessary information
  - Unfamiliar jargon or acronyms
  - Putting others on the spot
  - Blaming people or departments
  - Bypassing levels of responsibility
  - Visuals with information overload

Periodically a team decides to present the status of its problem-solving efforts. A presentation can also be arranged by any group that wishes to communicate important information to a particular audience.

The team selects a participant to take overall responsibility to coordinate the activities required to develop and conduct the presentation.

The presentation is developed using a checklist. See example *Preparing a Presentation*.

The rest of the team assists in the completing of the action items as shown in the checklist.

The presenter rehearses the presentation with the team. This provides the opportunity for team members to critique the presentation and then rehearse and fine tune it for maximum effectiveness.

Preparing a Presentation

Checklist for Effective Presentations
☐ Identify the objective of the presentation
☐ Analyze the audience
☐ Estimate time requirements
☐ Construct the presentation
– Introduction — state importance
– Body — focus on main points
– Conclusion — summarize essentials
☐ Assemble supporting information
☐ Create visuals
☐ Develop handouts
☐ Invite process owners, key decision makers
☐ Check out facilities (adequate chairs and tables)
☐ Check out A/V equipment (good working order)
☐ Anticipate and prepare for questions
☐ Start and stop on time!

First introduced by T. L. Saaty (1988), prioritization matrices are used to prioritize a particular project, issue, or option on the basis of team-established, weighted criteria. Three variations of matrix construction are used: (A) full analytical criteria method, (B) consensus criteria method, and (C) the combination interrelationship digraph/matrix method. Variation (A), the analytical method, is the most frequently used method.

- To apply team consensus criteria to select and decide on further action.
- To prioritize among activities, issues, or options based on weighted criteria.
- To select and prioritize recommended change options.
- To allocate limited resources to the most important option.

before

Tree diagram

Consensus decision making

Task analysis

Information needs analysis

Nominal group technique (NGT)

after

Action plan

Objectives matrix (OMAX)

Responsibility matrix

Process mapping

Resource requirements matrix

➥ Select and define problem or opportunity
Identify and analyze causes or potential change
Develop and plan possible solutions or change
➥ Implement and evaluate solution or change
Measure and report solution or change results
Recognize and reward team efforts

Research/statistics
Creativity/innovation
5 Engineering
1 Project management
3 Manufacturing
Marketing/sales
Administration/documentation
4 Servicing/support
Customer/quality metrics
2 Change management

- The full analytical criteria method is very complex and time consuming; it is used when the decision outcome is of utmost importance to the team or organization.
- Refer to Thomas L. Saaty's book *Decision Making for Leaders*, University of Pittsburgh (1988) for additional information on prioritization processes.

The team decides what project, issue, or option needs to be prioritized.

The team selects a particular prioritization matrix method to be constructed. The full analytical criteria method is used.

The team agrees to prioritize, for example, data collection methods and establish a list of criteria (see first matrix). This matrix serves to rank the established criteria using the "importance" scale, as shown.

Construct matrices (second to fourth) to rank data collection methods such as survey, interview, focus group, benchmarking, and quality function deployment (QFD). Apply the same rating scale for *cost*, *time/effort*, and *amount of data*. See matrix 2-4.

Construct a (fifth) matrix that rates (prioritizes) the overall best data collection method on the basis of the previously developed weighted criteria and data collection method ranks. In the example shown, *survey* is overall best data collection method.

Check all calculations and date all charts.

Full Analytical Criteria Method
Example: Prioritization of Data Collection Methods

(First Matrix)   Date: xx/xx/xx

Criteria Ranking	Cost	Speed	Time/effort	Amount of data	Row totals	%
Cost		$\overset{*}{5}$	$\overset{1*}{\frac{1}{5}}$	$\frac{1}{10}$	5.3	12.4
Speed	$\frac{1}{5}$		1	$\frac{1}{10}$	$\overset{**}{1.3}$	$\overset{***}{3.0}$
Time/effort	5	1		$\frac{1}{10}$	6.1	14.3
Amount of data	10	10	10		30.0	70.3
Column totals	15.2	16	11.2	.3	42.7	100

Legend:

1 = Equal importance
5 = Great importance
10 = Greatest importance
$\frac{1}{5}$ = Less importance
$\frac{1}{10}$ = Least importance

(continued)

Notes:

	Cost	Speed
Cost		5
Speed	$\frac{1}{5}$	

* *Read across the rows and when recording a weight such as 1, 5, 10 into a row cell (Example: cost is of "great importance" (5) as compared to **speed**), its reciprocal 1, $\frac{1}{5}$, $\frac{1}{10}$ must be recorded into the corresponding column cell (speed = $\frac{1}{5}$) since **cost** and **speed** was already rated.*

** *Convert fraction to decimals ($\frac{1}{5}$ = .20) to make calculations*

*** ***Speed*** *rated significantly lower and therefore will not be considered in further analysis.*

(Second Matrix)

Date: xx/xx/xx

Cost

Cost	Survey	Interview	Focus group	Benchmarking	QFD	Row totals	%
Survey		$\frac{1}{10}$	$\frac{1}{10}$	$\frac{1}{10}$	$\frac{1}{10}$	.4	.6
Interview	10		5	$\frac{1}{5}$	5	20.2	29.5
Focus group	10	$\frac{1}{5}$		$\frac{1}{5}$	1	11.4	16.7
Benchmarking	10	5	5		5	25.0	36.5
QFD	10	$\frac{1}{5}$	1	$\frac{1}{5}$		11.4	16.7
Column totals	40	5.5	11.1	.7	11.1	68.4	100

Legend:

- 1 = Equal cost
- 5 = Great cost
- 10 = Greatest cost
- $\frac{1}{5}$ = Less cost
- $\frac{1}{10}$ = Least cost

(Third Matrix)

Date: xx/xx/xx

Time/Effort	Survey	Interview	Focus group	Benchmarking	QFD	Row totals	%
Survey		$\frac{1}{10}$	$\frac{1}{10}$	$\frac{1}{10}$	$\frac{1}{10}$	.4	.5
Interview	10		5	1	5	21.0	28.0
Focus group	10	$\frac{1}{5}$		$\frac{1}{10}$	1	11.3	15.1
Benchmarking	10	1	10		10	31.0	41.3
QFD	10	$\frac{1}{5}$	1	$\frac{1}{10}$		11.3	15.1
Column totals	40	1.5	16.1	1.3	16.1	75.0	100

Legend:

1 = Equal time/effort
5 = Great time/effort
10 = Greatest time/effort
$\frac{1}{5}$ = Less time/effort
$\frac{1}{10}$ = Least time/effort

(Fourth Matrix)

Date: xx/xx/xx

Amount of Data	Survey	Interview	Focus group	Benchmarking	QFD	Row totals	%
Survey		10	10	5	10	35	58.0
Interview	$\frac{1}{10}$		5	1	5	11.1	18.4
Focus group	$\frac{1}{10}$	$\frac{1}{5}$		$\frac{1}{5}$	1	1.5	2.5
Benchmarking	$\frac{1}{5}$	1	5		5	11.2	18.6
QFD	$\frac{1}{10}$	$\frac{1}{5}$	1	$\frac{1}{5}$		1.5	2.5
Column totals	.5	11.4	21	6.4	21	60.3	100

Legend:

1 = Equal amount of data
5 = Great amount of data
10 = Greatest amount of data
$\frac{1}{5}$ = Less amount of data
$\frac{1}{10}$ = Least amount of data

(Fifth Matrix)   Date: xx/xx/xx

Prioritization	Cost (.124)*	Time/Effort (.143)	Amount of Data (.703)	Row totals	%
Survey	.006** / .001***	.005 / .001	.580 / .408	.410	(42.1)
Interview	.295 / .037	.280 / .040	.184 / .129	.206	21.2
Focus group	.167 / .021	.151 / .022	.025 / .018	.061	6.3
Benchmarking	.365 / .045	.413 / .059	.186 / .131	.235	24.2
QFD	.167 / .021	.151 / .022	.025 / .018	.061	6.3
Column totals	.125	.144	.704	.973	100

Notes:
*   *(.124) Taken from first matrix (criteria) – see % Column:* 12.4%
**   *(.006) Taken from second matrix (cost) – see % Column: .6%, continue for third and fourth matrix (time/effort, amount of data).*
***   *(.001) – Multiply .006 × .124 = .001*

(42.1) Survey is overall best data collection method.

First introduced by T. L. Saaty (1988), prioritization matrices are used to prioritize among projects, issues, or options on the basis of team-established, weighted criteria. Three variations of matrix construction are used: (A) the full analytical criteria method, (B) the consensus criteria method, and (C) the combination interrelationship digraph/matrix method. Variation (C), the combination method, is used when strongly related options must be reduced to one or two.

- To apply team consensus criteria to select and decide on further action.
- To prioritize among activities, issues, or options based on weighted criteria.
- To select and prioritize recommended change options.
- To allocate limited resources to the most important option.

before

Tree diagram

Consensus decision making

Task analysis

Information needs analysis

Nominal group technique (NGT)

after

Action plan

Objectives matrix (OMAX)

Responsibility matrix

Process mapping

Resource requirements matrix

➡ Select and define problem or opportunity
  Identify and analyze causes or potential change
  Develop and plan possible solutions or change
➡ Implement and evaluate solution or change
  Measure and report solution or change results
  Recognize and reward team efforts

  Research/statistics
  Creativity/innovation
5 Engineering
1 Project management
3 Manufacturing
  Marketing/sales
  Administration/documentation
4 Servicing/support
  Customer/quality metrics
2 Change management

- *The combination I.D./data matrix method*
  This method is easy to complete; however, great care must be given when relationship or cause and effect ratings are determined. It may be necessary to recheck the entire final matrix in order to verify consistency of ratings.
- Refer to Thomas L. Saaty's book *Decision Making for Leaders*, University of Pittsburgh (1988) for additional information on prioritization processes.

The team decides what project, issue, or option needs to be prioritized.

Select a particular prioritization matrix method to be constructed. There are three alternatives:

- Full analytical criteria method
- Consensus criteria method
- Combination ID/matrix method

The team agrees to prioritize the best data collection approach. See example *Combination ID/Matrix Method Matrix*.

Next, the team determines the strength of the relationship, if any, by comparing each element with all other elements, as shown in the example matrix.

Complete the *Total in*, *Total out*, and *Strength* columns. This will complete the matrix.

Recheck all symbols and calculations and date the matrix.

Combination ID/Matrix Method

Example: Most Value-Added Data Collection Activity

Date: xx/xx/xx		1	2	3	4	5	6	7	8	Total in	Total out	Strength
1	Instrument construction		↑△	↑⊙		↑△	↑△	↑⊙	↑⊙	0	6	30
2	Reliability test	←△		⊙	↑○	↑○			↑△	2	3	17
3	Field testing	←⊙	↑⊙			↑⊙	↑△	↑△	↑△	1	5	30
4	Collection method		←○				△	↑⊙	○	3	1	16
5	Validity test	←△	←○	←⊙					↑△	3	1	14
6	Data encoding	←△		←△	↑△			←○	←⊙	4	1	15
7	Number of questions	←⊙		←△	←⊙		↑○		↑○	3	2	25
8	Scaling	←⊙	←△	←△	↑○	△	↑⊙	←○		5	2	27

Legend:

⊙ =	9	=	Strong relationship
○ =	3	=	Medium relationship
△ =	1	=	Weak relationship
← =	in	=	Cause or influence
↑ =	out	=	Effect or influenced

Notes: – *There is a strong relationship ⊙ between instrument construction (1) which **causes** the need for field testing (3).*

– *Also, the quality of instrument construction (1) **influences** (↑ out) field testing (3) results.*

First introduced by T. L. Saaty (1988), prioritization matrices are used to prioritize among particular projects, issues, or options on the basis of team-established, weighted criteria. Three variations of matrix construction are used: (A) the full analytical criteria method, (B) the consensus criteria method, and (C) the combination interrelationship digraph/matrix method. The *consensus* criteria method is used when a team experiences difficulty in arriving at a decision.

- To apply team consensus criteria to select and decide on further action.
- To prioritize among activities, issues, or options based on weighted criteria.
- To select and prioritize recommended change options.
- To allocate limited resources to the most important option.

before

Tree diagram

Consensus decision making

Task analysis

Information needs analysis

Nominal group technique (NGT)

after

Action plan

Objectives matrix (OMAX)

Responsibility matrix

Process mapping

Resource requirements matrix

➥ Select and define problem or opportunity

Identify and analyze causes or potential change

Develop and plan possible solutions or change

➥ Implement and evaluate solution or change

Measure and report solution or change results

Recognize and reward team efforts

	Research/statistics
	Creativity/innovation
5	Engineering
1	Project management
3	Manufacturing
	Marketing/sales
	Administration/documentation
4	Servicing/support
	Customer/quality metrics
2	Change management

- *The consensus criteria method*
  This method is less difficult and more flexible for a team to use when prioritizing. Simple consensus for criteria weighting and ranking techniques can be used.
- Refer to Thomas L. Saaty's book *Decision Making for Leaders*, University of Pittsburgh (1988) for additional information on prioritization processes.

The team decides what project, issue, or option needs to be prioritized.

Select a particular prioritization matrix method to be constructed. There are three alternatives:

- Full analytical criteria method
- Consensus criteria method
- Combination ID/matrix method

The team agrees to prioritize data collection methods and establishes a list of criteria. See example *Consensus Criteria Method*.

Next, the team ranks data collection methods as shown in the matrix.

All matrix cells are calculated and row totals indicated as shown in the matrix.

Check calculations and date the matrix.

Consensus Criteria Method

Example: Prioritization of data collection methods

Date: xx/xx/xx	Collection cost	Response time	Collector's time/effort	Data quantity	Anonimity	Total
Method (Criteria)	.65	1.04	1.35	1.66*	.30	
Survey	7** / 4.55 ***	2 / 2.08	7 / 9.45	7 / 11.62	6 / 1.80	29.50 ****
Interview	2 / 1.30	4 / 4.16	2 / 2.70	5 / 8.30	1 / .30	16.76
Observation	5 / 3.25	3 / 3.12	6 / 8.10	1 / 1.66	5 / 1.50	17.63
Focus group	4 / 2.60	6 / 6.24	5 / 6.75	3 / 4.98	2 / .60	21.17
Quality function deployment	3 / 1.95	5 / 5.20	4 / 5.40	2 / 3.32	3 / .90	16.77
Literature review	6 / 3.90	7 / 7.28	3 / 4.05	4 / 6.64	7 / 2.10	23.97
Benchmarking	1 / .65	1 / 1.04	1 / 1.35	6 / 9.96	4 / 1.20	14.20

Notes:

*   Team members' consensus to weight the criteria:
  Team members distribute the value of 1.0 *across the (5) criteria.*
  Example: *For data quantity, the five team members' combined*
  weightings = 1.66 *(calculated by adding .40 + .33 + .25 + .33 + .35).*

**   Team members' ranking of data collection methods:
  7 = highest rank – most favorable, 1 = *lowest rank – least favorable*
  Example: *The survey method is lowest in data collection costs.*

***   Multiply in each cell, rank x criteria value.
  Example: 7 x .65 = 4.55

**** Total across each row to identify (prioritize) best overall method
  Example: 4.55 + 2.08 + 9.45 + 11.62 + 1.80 = 29.50

The problem analysis tool is often the first attempt by a problem-solving team to document what is known and, on the basis of this preliminary data, what other or additional information needs to be collected to assist in the problem-solving process. A completed problem analysis document also aids in the understanding of the problem by team participants and process owners.

- To document initial problem information and observations for a problem-solving team.
- To capture all relevant data for input into the problem-solving process.
- To promote a common understanding of the problems' significance.

before

Data collection strategy

Process selection matrix

Problem specification

Checksheet

5W2H method

after

Information needs analysis

Pareto chart

Cause and effect diagram

Potential problem analysis (PPA)

Variance analysis

➥ Select and define problem or opportunity

➥ Identify and analyze causes or potential change

➥ Develop and plan possible solutions or change

    Implement and evaluate solution or change

    Measure and report solution or change results

    Recognize and reward team efforts

    Research/statistics

    Creativity/innovation

    Engineering

2 Project management

    Manufacturing

    Marketing/sales

3 Administration/documentation

    Servicing/support

    Customer/quality metrics

1 Change management

- The suggested problem analysis form can be modified to more closely reflect a certain type of organization or the intended use by problem-solving or process improvement teams.

The facilitator explains the problem analysis process and asks participants to examine a provided problem analysis form.

Using a whiteboard or flip charts, the facilitator records information provided on the problem issue. Information may also have come from documents introduced into the meeting.

Next, the recorded information is selectively used to complete the problem analysis form. See example *Employee Opinion Survey: Dissatisfaction with Work Schedules*.

Team consensus provides the basis for agreement on the final wording to be entered on the problem analysis form, tasks 1-8. Some information may need to be verified or collected in order to fully complete the form as shown in the example.

The form is dated, next steps are discussed, and, as an outcome of this discussion, action items are assigned to all team participants to continue the problem-solving process.

Employee Opinion Survey: Dissatisfaction with Work Schedules

Problem Analysis Form

Team: *DollarSavers*   Date: *xx/xx/xx*   Contact: *J.M. Walters*   Dept: *HR*

1. Prepare a concise problem statement
   The 1997 EOS results reflect a 32% increase in employee dissatisfaction with existing work schedules. Work schedules were changed to increase production.

2. Describe the primary purpose of the solution
   - *To improve employee job satisfaction and morale*
   - *To prevent a downturn of productivity, attendance*
   - *To maintain a high standard of quality*

3. Determine the problem's significance in terms of customers and impact
   Customers will experience delivery delays, slipped schedules. Dissatisfied employees often experience more defects, have decreased output rates, and overall lower performance. The company will experience delays, less revenues, increased costs in overtime.

4. State symptoms, effects, conditions, and other relevant information
   - *Manufacturing department reports decreased productivity and missed due dates*
   - *Quality department reports an increase in defects, rework, and scrap metrics*
   - *Human resources department reports increased turnover and absenteeism*

5. Identify probable causes, contributing factors, key variances
   The work schedules were changed to allow a third shift to meet increased demand. Shifts are 6-3, 3-10, and 10-6 around the clock. Departments report increased tardiness.

6. Name customers, employees, process owners, decision makers
   - *Customers: hardware stores (machine tools)*
   - *Employees: assembly line operators, inspectors*
   - *Process owners: manufacturing, engineering, quality departments*

7. List information needs and due dates
   - *Collect productivity and quality results data (8/15)*
   - *Collect from HR: demographics, turnover, attendance, overtime (8/31)*
   - *Survey all manufacturing and quality assurance employees (10/10)*

8. Propose potential solutions
   - *Expand facilities, purchase additional equipment to open an additional assembly line*
   - *Establish flextime in the organization*
   - *Outsource subassembly type work*

Note: Attach additional pages, or relevant supporting data.

A problem selection matrix allows the team to choose a particular problem on the basis of discussion and team rating against listed criteria. A major consideration in the selection process is the impact that identified problems currently have on customer satisfaction, defect per unit level, and process cycle time.

- To select a problem for a team.
- To differentiate among several problem conditions in order to determine which problem must be worked on first.
- To rank order identified problems by team-established importance criteria.

➡ Select and define problem or opportunity
➡ Identify and analyze causes or potential change
   Develop and plan possible solutions or change
   Implement and evaluate solution or change
   Measure and report solution or change results
   Recognize and reward team efforts

Research/statistics
Creativity/innovation
Engineering
3 Project management
Manufacturing
Marketing/sales
Administration/documentation
Servicing/support
2 Customer/quality metrics
1 Change management

before
Variance analysis
Cause and effect diagram (CED)
Five whys
Process analysis
Benchmarking
after
Problem specification
Information needs analysis
Action plan
Decision process flowchart
Problem analysis

- Teams should consider only problems that generally fall into the team's area of responsibility.
- A basic scale of $(+)$ = *yes*, (0) = *uncertain*, $(-)$ = *no* may be used in the selection process.
- Optional: Values can be assigned to symbols: $(+)$ = 5, (0) = 3, $(-)$ = 1.

The team facilitator prepares a problem selection matrix and records previously noted problem areas.

Team participants brainstorm rating criteria and reach consensus on 4-5 important categories. See example *Assembly Section "C"—Production Problems*.

Participants rate all problem areas against stated criteria and rank problem areas accordingly, as shown in the example.

The team facilitator completes the problem selection matrix, circles problem area selected, and dates the matrix.

Assembly Section "C"— Production Problems

Date: xx/xx/xx

	Problems Areas	Team Has Control	Short Time	Resources Available	Affects Customer	Team Ranking
1	Lack of work instructions	+	+	O	+	①
2	Lack of operator training	+	+	−	O	2
3	Higher parts reject rate	−	+	O	O	4
4	Increase in rework hours	O	−	O	+	3

Notes: – The rating symbols are: (+) = yes, (–) = no, (O) = uncertain.
– The team selects problem area No. 1, rank ① to be worked on first.

The problem specification tool provides team members with a shared understanding of a problem. Moreover it points to an orderly first step of collecting specific, appropriate data for the purpose of writing a problem statement that clearly defines the unacceptable "as is" situation, any process variance, or its potential causes. The problem specification should also describe the "should be" state of the situation or process to be improved.

- To establish a problem-solving goal or improvement target.
- To clarify a vague condition perceived as a problem.
- To collect data relevant to the problem and possibly indicative of the root causes.
- To satisfy the need for more data.

before

Data collection strategy

Interview technique

Multivariable chart

Cause and effect diagram (CED)

Pareto chart

after

What-if analysis

Process mapping

Work flow analysis (WFA)

Process analysis

Systems analysis diagram

➥ Select and define problem or opportunity
➥ Identify and analyze causes or potential change
   Develop and plan possible solutions or change
   Implement and evaluate solution or change
   Measure and report solution or change results
   Recognize and reward team efforts

	Research/statistics
	Creativity/innovation
6	Engineering
4	Project management
2	Manufacturing
	Marketing/sales
	Administration/documentation
3	Servicing/support
5	Customer/quality metrics
1	Change management

- A superior problem specification reflects measurable data: Quantitatively expressed data are numbers, percentages, frequencies, time periods, amounts, rate durations, etc. Qualitatively expressed data are perceptions, demographics, or any nominal data scales.

The team starts the problem specifiction process by discussing the current situation; this situation is called the *as is* on the problem specification form. Expand the information to include all recorded data and verbal input. See example *Problem Specification—Quality of Service*.

Next, the preferred situation, called *should be* on the form, is discussed. This ideal state reflects a perceived gap in process performance from the *as is* state.

Close the performance gap between the two states by filling in the information as illustrated by numbers 1 and 2 on the example problem specification form.

Using the information compiled in 1 and 2 on the example, complete the form by providing the appropriate information for the two columns: *problem occurs* 3 and *problem is resolved* 4 .

In the final step, develop a final problem statement that encompasses the critical elements of the problem as developed on the form.

The team finalizes the problem statement shown as 5 on the form; team consensus is reached, and the entire team signs off on it.

Quality of Service

Problem Specification—Quality of Service Date xx/xx/xx

❶ As is situation/condition

  Service cycle time is 12 days, the customer
  satisfaction index rating is low, and recalls
  average 7 per month.

❷ Should be target/goal

  Cycle time = 8.5 days, CSI rating = high,
  and recalls average 3 per month
  (per benchmark data)

When

❸ Problem occurs

  – At the end of the month (last six months)
  – Missed service calls

❹ Problem is resolved

  – Balanced scheduling
  – More training
  – Concerns for quality

Where

  – All service areas
  – Business districts

  – Timely service regardless of service area

Impact

  – 15% increase in customer complaints

  – Less than 2% recalls on service calls

People/Groups

  – Service department technicians

  – Service department technicians
    provide better quality service

Related Information

  – Pareto analysis and customer satisfaction survey results are available

❺ Final problem statement

  The previous six months' service calls schedule produced a 15% increase of customer complaints.
  Causes appear to be lengthy cycle time (delays) and quality of service (recalls).

The process analysis technique helps to trace the source of variation and is, therefore, a useful method to identify root causes of a problem. Process analysis is typically performed using an activity-level process flowchart and by asking a series of questions to explore or justify excessive cycle time, approvals, improper sequence, delays, and other process deficiencies.

- To review, analyze, and improve an existing process.
- To identify process improvement opportunities.
- To fine-tune processes in an organizational change project.

before

Symbolic flowchart
Organization chart
Process mapping
Process flowchart
Cycle time flowchart

after

Activity analysis
Variance analysis
Work flow analysis (WFA)
Facility layout diagram
Decision process
flowchart

➡ Select and define problem or opportunity
➡ Identify and analyze causes or potential change
➡ Develop and plan possible solutions or change
 Implement and evaluate solution or change
 Measure and report solution or change results
 Recognize and reward team efforts

 Research/statistics
 Creativity/innovation
 Engineering
 Project management
2 Manufacturing
 Marketing/sales
4 Administration/documentation
3 Servicing/support
 Customer/quality metrics
1 Change management

- To construct a process flow, several tools are available:
  - process flowchart
  - symbolic flowchart
  - process mapping
  - cycle time flowchart
  - activity analysis

  Using any one of these will allow a process improvement team to achieve established team goals.
- The given list of 10 process analysis questions is optional. The number and content of questions may change in accordance with the complexity of any given process.

As a prerequisite activity, a facilitated team develops a process flowchart at the activity-level for the process selected.

A set of standard process analysis questions is displayed by the facilitator. The team reviews the questions, adds, deletes, or revises questions to fully cover the process to be analyzed.

Using the finalized list of questions, the team discusses all activities in the process and provides responses to the questions.

Finally, the facilitator asks participants to recheck all responses, makes final revisions, and dates the list.

The information serves as an input to a variance analysis process, a logical next step for the team.

Symbolic Flowchart for the Facilitation of Process Mapping

Date: xx/xx/xx

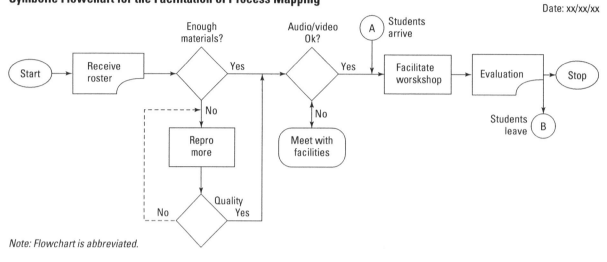

Note: Flowchart is abbreviated.

Typical Process Analysis Questions	Date: xx/xx/xx

1. Are the connected tasks performed in a logical sequence?
   No, materials check should have been done earlier

2. Does the defined process show more than two loopbacks?
   Yes

3. Do individual tasks have relatively long cycle times?
   No

4. Does every task add value to the process?
   No, audio-visual check does not add value to this process.

5. Are there redundant tasks?
   No

6. Does the process reflect excessive delays?
   No

7. Does the process contain sources of key variance?
   No

8. Are there more than two approval requirements?
   No

9. Can the process flow be changed to reduce tasks?
   Yes, remove materials and A/V checks

10. Does this process have a high level of consistency?
    Yes

Process capability ratios are calculated to determine the process variation that comes from natural or special causes. These ratios, also called C_p and C_{pk} Indices, relate the process variability to the design specification (tolerance) that reflects the customer's expectation or requirements. C_p is listed to characterize the capability, and C_{pk} is used to measure actual process performance.

- To estimate how well the process meets customer requirements.
- To monitor and measure product quality.
- To verify process variability to design specifications.
- To promote communications among design engineering, suppliers, and manufacturing.

before

Standard deviation

Sampling methods

Descriptive statistics

Normal probability distribution

Control chart

after

Variance analysis

process flowchart

Process analysis

Activity analysis

Basili data collection method

➡ Select and define problem or opportunity
➡ Identify and analyze causes or potential change
   Develop and plan possible solutions or change
   Implement and evaluate solution or change
➡ Measure and report solution or change results
   Recognize and reward team efforts

Research/statistics
Creativity/innovation
1 Engineering
Project management
2 Manufacturing
Marketing/sales
Administration/documentation
Servicing/support
3 Customer/quality metrics
4 Change management

- Definitions of process capability ratios:
  - C_p: A measure of ideal or potential process capability. The C_p index reflects the best ability of a process to perform within lower and upper design specification limits (LSL $\leftrightarrow$ USL).
  - C_{pk}: A measure of actual or located process performance. The C_{pk} index reflects the actual, located process mean relative to the design target value.
  - CPU: Upper process capability
  - CPL: Lower process capability
  - μ or $\bar{\bar{X}}$: Process average

- Equations for calculating C_p and C_{pk}:

(A) $\quad C_p = \dfrac{\text{Design tolerance}}{\text{Process variation}}, C_p = \dfrac{USL - LSL}{\pm 3\sigma}, C_p = \dfrac{USL - LSL}{6\sigma}$

or

(B) $\quad CPU = \dfrac{USL - \mu}{3\sigma}, CPL = \dfrac{\mu - LSL}{3\sigma}$

(A) $\quad C_{pk} = C_p\,(1 - k) \quad$ Where $k = \dfrac{\left|\begin{matrix}\text{Target} & & \text{Actual} \\ \text{mean point} & - & \text{mean point}\end{matrix}\right|}{1/2\ (USL - LSL)}$

or

(B) $\quad C_{pk} = \text{Minimum of (CPU, CPL)}$

- Process capability:

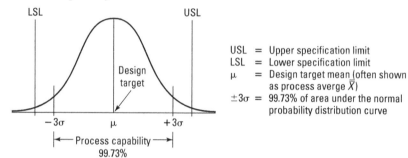

USL = Upper specification limit
LSL = Lower specification limit
μ = Design target mean (often shown as process averge $\bar{X}$)
$\pm 3\sigma$ = 99.73% of area under the normal probability distribution curve

Note: Refer to "Proportions of Area Under the Normal Curve" table in the Appendix, Table A, for additional information.

A team is formed with the goal of reduced process variability.

Through the data collection process, process data such as specific product specifications tolerances, control charts, samples of measurements, and historical data calculations, are acquired. See example *Fax Paper Extension Wire Measurements*.

Sample data are organized and summarized using descriptive statistics. A recommendation is made to read some background tools contained in this book:

- Descriptive statistics (tool 66)
- Normal probability distribution (tool 119)
- Standard deviation (tool 184)

Using process means and standard deviations, the C_p capability ratios can be calculated and compared.

Note: Measurement in this example is centimeters (cm).

An action plan is developed on the basis of the actual process performance results calculated. Required activities usually require reduction of process variations or recentering of the process within the specifications.

Fax Paper Extension Wire Measurements

C_p — Process capability and variability

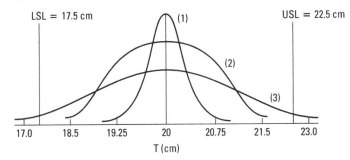

– Distribution #1: This is an *ideal* or *best* process.

$\sigma = .25, \pm 3\sigma = 1.5$

$$C_p = \frac{22.5 - 17.5}{1.5}$$

$$C_p = 3.33$$

– Distribution #2: This is a *capable* process.

$\sigma = .50, \pm 3\sigma = 3$

$$C_p = \frac{22.5 - 17.5}{3}$$

$$C_p = 1.67$$

– Distribution #3: This is an *uncapable* process.

$\sigma = 1, \pm 3\sigma = 6$

$$C_p = \frac{22.5 - 17.5}{6}$$

$$C_p = .83$$

Note: Shaded areas outside the specification limits display nonconformance to design specs.

C_pk — Actual or Located Process Performance

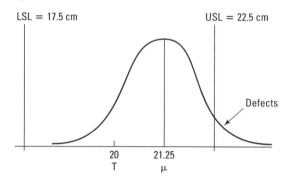

LSL = 17.5 cm   USL = 22.5 cm

Defects

20   21.25
T   μ

$$C_{pk} = C_p (1 - K) \qquad K = \frac{|\quad 20 - 21.25 \quad|}{1/2 \; (22.5 - 17.5)}$$

$$C_{pk} = 1.67 \; (1 - .5) \qquad K = \frac{-1.25}{2.50}$$

$$C_{pk} = .83 \qquad\qquad K = .5$$

Alternate method of calculating C_p, C_pk:

– Distribution #2: *Capable* process.

$$\text{CPU} = \frac{22.5 - 20}{1.5} \qquad \text{CPL} = \frac{20 - 17.5}{1.5}$$

$$\text{CPU} = 1.67 \qquad\qquad \text{CPL} = 1.67$$

– Distribution #3: *Uncapable* process.

$$\text{CPU} = \frac{22.5 - 21.25}{1.5} \qquad \text{CPL} = \frac{21.25 - 17.5}{1.5}$$

$$\text{CPU} = .83 \qquad\qquad\quad \text{CPL} = 2.5$$

– Check: $\dfrac{.83 + 2.5}{2} = 1.67$

C_{pk} = Minimum of (83, 2.5)
C_{pk} = .83 as calculated above.

The process decision program chart (PDPC) is a contingency planning tool used to assist in establishing an implementation action plan for a complex project that has a high degree of uncertainty for successful and timely completion. This tool, which uses a very structured approach, identifies plan activities, asks what-if questions to uncover potential problem areas, and develops countermeasures for any problems that might occur.

- To perform contingency planning prior to implementing a complex activity problem or solution with high uncertainty.
- To determine possible countermeasures in order to minimize any problems that may surface when an unfamiliar activity is performed.
- To anticipate problems and consider consequences due to errors or gaps in planning.

before

Tree diagram
Problem specification
Matrix diagram
Weighted voting
Process analysis

after

Countermeasures matrix
Starbursting
Solution matrix
Action plan
Variance analysis

Select and define problem or opportunity
➡ Identify and analyze causes or potential change
➡ Develop and plan possible solutions or change
Implement and evaluate solution or change
Measure and report solution or change results
Recognize and reward team efforts

Research/statistics
3 Creativity/innovation
Engineering
2 Project management
Manufacturing
Marketing/sales
Administration/documentation
4 Servicing/support
Customer/quality metrics
1 Change management

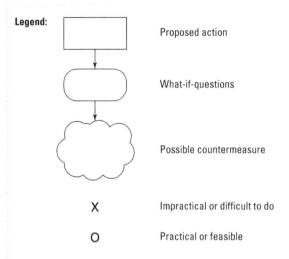

Legend:

Proposed action

What-if-questions

Possible countermeasure

X   Impractical or difficult to do

O   Practical or feasible

The team refers to a previously completed data collection and analysis. This data source can be a tree diagram, matrix diagram, a problem specification, or some other tool reference.

The next step is to construct a PDPC chart as outlined in the example *Conversion of an Assembly Line to Work Cells*.

First, list the project goal, followed by a lower level of primary activities detailed further into required tasks. Ensure that all activities have been considered from the data source.

For each task or requirement, ask what-ifs. See example What if there is an interruption in production output? What if there is equipment downtime?

For every what-if, consider what countermeasures can be taken. Connect what-ifs and countermeasures to the tasks to complete the chart. Designate countermeasures as practical and feasible = 0, or impractical and difficult = X.

Review the chart, make revisions if needed, and provide date of issue.

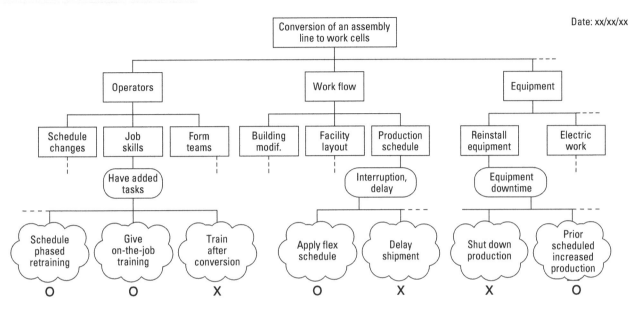

Date: xx/xx/xx

Conversion of an assembly line to work cells		

Operators
- Schedule changes
- Job skills
  - Have added tasks
    - Schedule phased retraining — O
    - Give on-the-job training — O
    - Train after conversion — X
- Form teams

Work flow
- Building modif.
- Facility layout
- Production schedule
  - Interruption, delay
    - Apply flex schedule — O
    - Delay shipment — X

Equipment
- Reinstall equipment
  - Equipment downtime
    - Shut down production — X
    - Prior scheduled increased production — O
- Electric work

A process flowchart illustrates the major activities, sequence, and flow connections of a work process or project. The flowchart helps a team gain a common understanding of the overall process and its interrelationships. The flowchart can be used to identify problem areas, document a process, or serve as a planning tool for process improvement.

- To illustrate the flow or process steps in manufacturing a product, providing a service, or managing a project.
- To provide a common understanding of a complex process.
- To recommend an improved process to the process owner.

before

Information needs analysis

Systems analysis diagram

Variance analysis

Problem analysis

Pareto chart

after

Process mapping

Problem specification

Opportunity analysis

Work flow analysis (WFA)

Action plan

➡ Select and define problem or opportunity	
➡ Identify and analyze causes or potential change	
➡ Develop and plan possible solutions or change	
Implement and evaluate solution or change	
Measure and report solution or change results	
Recognize and reward team efforts	

	Research/statistics
	Creativity/innovation
2	Engineering
5	Project management
3	Manufacturing
	Marketing/sales
	Administration/documentation
4	Servicing/support
	Customer/quality metrics
1	Change management

- Legend for process flow chart symbols:

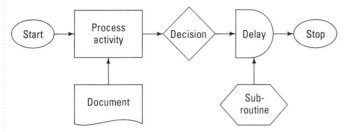

Note: Ensure that participants represent and cover all process areas to be flowcharted.

As a first step, the team facilitator assembles a team whose participants thoroughly understand all aspects of the process. See example *Reengineering Human Resources*.

The overall scope of the process flowchart is determined. A starting and stopping point is identified.

Next, participants identify all major process steps and the sequence of completion. Reviews, delays, documents, reports, and other important activities are recorded on another flipchart.

The facilitator uses a whiteboard to start drawing the process flowchart. The participants assist the facilitator in drawing and connecting all process steps in the correct sequence.

Depending on the level of detail agreed upon, additional information can be noted along with the process steps, as shown in the example.

Finally, the process flowchart is verified for accuracy and dated.

Reengineering Human Resources

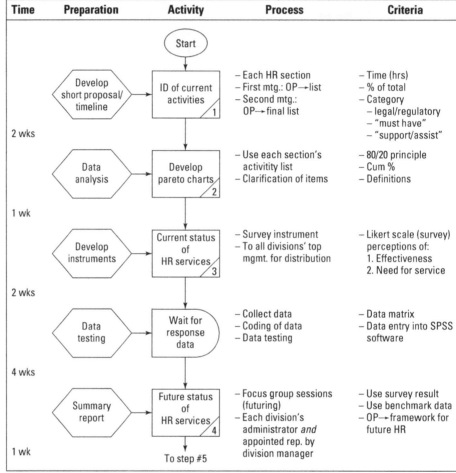

Time	Preparation	Activity	Process	Criteria
		Start		
2 wks	Develop short proposal/ timeline	ID of current activities 1	– Each HR section – First mtg.: OP→list – Second mtg.: OP→final list	– Time (hrs) – % of total – Category – legal/regulatory – "must have" – "support/assist"
1 wk	Data analysis	Develop pareto charts 2	– Use each section's activitity list – Clarification of items	– 80/20 principle – Cum % – Definitions
2 wks	Develop instruments	Current status of HR services 3	– Survey instrument – To all divisions' top mgmt. for distribution	– Likert scale (survey) perceptions of: 1. Effectiveness 2. Need for service
4 wks	Data testing	Wait for response data	– Collect data – Coding of data – Data testing	– Data matrix – Data entry into SPSS software
1 wk	Summary report	Future status of HR services 4	– Focus group sessions (futuring) – Each division's administrator *and* appointed rep. by division manager	– Use survey result – Use benchmark data – OP→framework for future HR
		To step #5		

Notes: OP = Output   *(continued)*
      SPSS = Statistical Package for Social Sciences (a software program for statistical analysis)

Reengineering Human Resources, *continued*

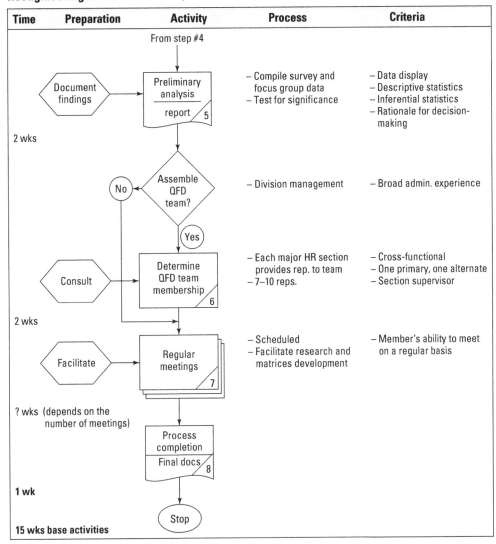

Time	Preparation	Activity	Process	Criteria
		From step #4		
	Document findings	Preliminary analysis / report 5	– Compile survey and focus group data – Test for significance	– Data display – Descriptive statistics – Inferential statistics – Rationale for decision-making
2 wks		Assemble QFD team? No / Yes	– Division management	– Broad admin. experience
	Consult	Determine QFD team membership 6	– Each major HR section provides rep. to team – 7–10 reps.	– Cross-functional – One primary, one alternate – Section supervisor
2 wks				
	Facilitate	Regular meetings 7	– Scheduled – Facilitate research and matrices development	– Member's ability to meet on a regular basis
? wks (depends on the number of meetings)		Process completion / Final docs 8		
1 wk		Stop		
15 wks base activities				

The process mapping tool is of great value for teams in documenting the existing process. It identifies and maps all cross-functional processes, process owners (organizations), metrics, and estimated processing time or mapped activities. A finalized process map ensures a thorough understanding of the "as is" process and provides baseline input data for a process improvement team.

- To mark a visual map of the process in order to perform the analysis necessary for identifying problematic conditions.
- To identify, map, analyze, and prepare *as is* and *should be* process maps.
- To draw a map for process understanding and to discover potential areas for improvement.
- To reduce cycle time of mapped activities.

before

Affinity diagram

Systems analysis diagram

Pareto chart

Potential problem analysis (PPA)

Needs analysis

after

Cycle time flowchart

Gap analysis

Force field analysis (FFA)

Barriers-and-aids analysis

Activity analysis

➡ Select and define problem or opportunity

➡ Identify and analyze causes or potential change

Develop and plan possible solutions or change

Implement and evaluate solution or change

Measure and report solution or change results

Recognize and reward team efforts

Research/statistics

Creativity/innovation

4 Engineering

2 Project management

3 Manufacturing

Marketing/sales

Administration/documentation

Servicing/support

Customer/quality metrics

1 Change management

- Symbols and scale:

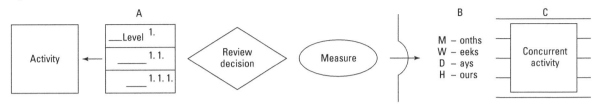

A – Optional level of detail for activities
B – Time scale: Months (M), Weeks (W), Days (D), Hours (H).
C – Four organizations performing activity concurrently

- "Connectors" example:

- A process map can be developed at the macro, mini, or micro level of an organizational process.

A team facilitator assembles a team of cross-functional representatives to assist the development of the process map.

The team decides on the level of detail to be mapped—that is macro (overview), mini (most activities), and micro (very detailed, specific tasks).

Next, the process start and stop points are determined.

As a prerequisite activity, four flip charts are prepared to serve as input data to the process-mapping procedure:

- A listing of all organizations or work groups. Sequence list in order of occurrence.

- A listing of all major functions or activities. Sequence list in order of occurrence.

- A listing of all reviews, audits, approvals, or other decision-making activities. Sequence list in order of occurrence.

– A listing of all measurements (metrics) in the following categories: process, results, resources, and customer satisfaction. Sequence list in order of occurrence.

The team facilitator, on a whiteboard, draws the process map as directed and checked by the team. The listings of process sequences "organizations," "major functions," "decision-making," and "metrics" are referenced, in order of occurrence, to map out the complete process. See example *Process: Prepare Draft of Action Plans*.

Finally, the team checks the completed map, final revisions are made, and the map is titled and dated. The facilitator redraws the process map on flip charts for future reference.

Process: Prepare draft of action plans
Goal: New process—Improve project management documentation

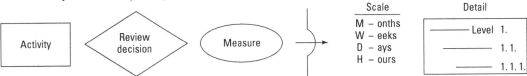

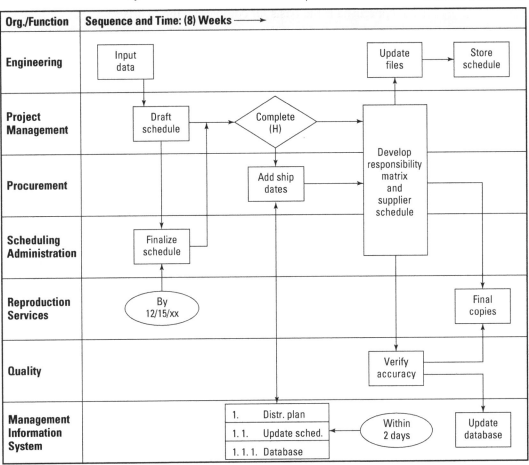

A process selection matrix uses a set of criteria for prioritization to determine a team's first choice. Typically, the team establishes the criteria and rating method. Team consensus is the basis for completing the matrix.

- To prioritize processes, projects, or systems to be used in a problem-solving or major organizational change effort.
- To identify a process or tool that promises the greatest return on total investment.
- To determine ways to improve the organization.

Select and define problem or opportunity

Identify and analyze causes or potential change

➡ Develop and plan possible solutions or change

➡ Implement and evaluate solution or change

Measure and report solution or change results

Recognize and reward team efforts

	Research/statistics
	Creativity/innovation
3	Engineering
2	Project management
4	Manufacturing
	Marketing/sales
	Administration/documentation
	Servicing/support
	Customer/quality metrics
1	Change management

- If two total scores are tied, add both ranks and divide to assign median to both rank positions. Example: Two scores = 19 for rank position (2) and (3), therefore 2 + 3 = 5/2 = 2.5. Rank 2.5 is assigned to both positions, as shown in the example.

before

Cost-benefit analysis

Benchmarking

Consensus decision making

Process analysis

Potential problem analysis (PPA)

after

Activity cost matrix

Action plan

Information needs analysis

Decision process flowchart

Basili data collection method

The team facilitator prepares a selection matrix and lists all previously determined processes. See example *Organizational Change—Process Selection*.

Participants brainstorm a set of criteria to be used in the rating process.

Next, participants rate each process on a scale of *high, medium, low* using the consensus decision-making technique.

The facilitator records each rating and totals all rows.

Finally, the process selection matrix is dated and Rank 1 (best choice) is circled.

Organizational Change—Process Selection

Date: xx/xx/xx Process Selection	Customer Impact	Implementation Feasibility	Employee Motivation	Organization's Competitiveness	Return on Investment	Total	Rank
Just-in-time (JIT) manufacturing	H	L	M	M	H	17	4.5
Integrated product development	H	H	H	H	M	23	①
Self-managed work teams	M	H	H	M	M	19	2.5
Hoshin planning system	L	M	L	L	L	7	6
ISO-9000 quality system	H	M	M	H	M	19	2.5
Business process reengineering	M	L	H	H	M	17	4.5

Notes: *High = 5, medium = 3, low = 1*
  Ranking: Highest total is best choice, rank ①

Developed in the 1950s by the U.S. Navy, the PERT network is of extreme importance in project management. It is designed to assist in the planning and controlling of projects and new product development efforts. Drawn as a network with various paths, it displays Critical Path sequence, expected activity time and variance, and overall time to completion.

- To plan, schedule, and control a new program or product development effort.
- To document and track a complex project.
- To designate critical path and show other interrelationships.
- To ensure time and resource management, and to reduce project costs through coordination and communication.

before

Work breakdown structure (WBS)

Project planning log

Process analysis

Milestones chart

Activity analysis

after

Responsibility matrix

Gantt chart

Resource histogram

Selection matrix

Resource requirements matrix

Select and define problem or opportunity	
Identify and analyze causes or potential change	
Develop and plan possible solutions or change	
➥ Implement and evaluate solution or change	
➥ Measure and report solution or change results	
Recognize and reward team efforts	

	Research/statistics
	Creativity/innovation
2	Engineering
1	Project management
4	Manufacturing
	Marketing/sales
5	Administration/documentation
	Servicing/support
	Customer/quality metrics
3	Change management

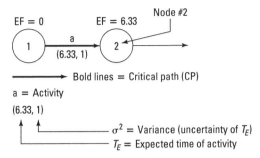

EF = 0   EF = 6.33   Node #2

1 —a→ 2
(6.33, 1)

———→ Bold lines = Critical path (CP)

a = Activity

(6.33, 1)

σ^2 = Variance (uncertainty of T_E)
T_E = Expected time of activity

Calculations:

$$T_E = \frac{(a + 4m + b)}{6} \qquad \sigma^2 = \left[\frac{(b - a)}{6}\right]^2$$

a = Optimistic time estimate
b = Pessimistic time estimate
m = Most likely time estimate

Activity	a	m	b	T_E	σ^2
a	4	6	10	6.33	1
b	3	5	10	5.5	1.36
c	2	2	2	2	0
d	6	7	7	6.83	.03
e	4	8	12	8	1.77
f	6	9	16	9.66	2.78
g	5	7	11	7.33	1
h	4	4	10	5	1
i	2	10	12	9	2.78
j	4	4	4	4	0

Collect data on project activities. See example *Update a Customer Database System*.

Construct a preliminary network, account for all required activities, and calculate expected time (T_E) and variance (σ^2) for each.

Determine and highlight critical path (CP), and calculate early finish (EF) for each node.

Check all network linkages and calculations and date the finalized PERT network.

Program Evaluation Review Technique—Update a Customer Database System

Date: xx/xx/xx

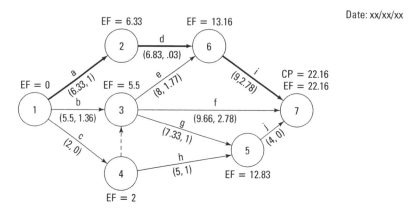

The project planning log documents all planned activities to resolve a problem or implement a process improvement opportunity. The log organizes and sequences action items and completion dates; it indicates individual or team responsibility and the review and follow-up requirements.

- To plan and schedule a problem-solving or organizational change project.
- To assign and monitor change activities.
- To propose and map out an implementation effort.

before

Action plan

Resource requirements matrix

Force field analysis (FFA)

Gap analysis

Project prioritization matrix

after

Information needs analysis

Monthly assessment schedule

Influence diagram

Measurement matrix

Presentation

Select and define problem or opportunity

Identify and analyze causes or potential change

➡ Develop and plan possible solutions or change

➡ Implement and evaluate solution or change

➡ Measure and report solution or change results

Recognize and reward team efforts

Research/statistics

Creativity/innovation

Engineering

1   Project management

Manufacturing

Marketing/sales

3   Administration/documentation

Servicing/support

Customer/quality metrics

2   Change management

- A project planning log can serve as an input or source document for developing a more detailed action plan.

A listing of all major activities required to complete the project is developed and recorded on a project planning log. See example *Retrain Human Resource Specialists*.

Information is added as to how these activities are to be performed and in what sequence.

Identification of individuals or teams responsible for completing these activities and associated due dates is completed.

Follow-up activities and review procedures are added to activities on an as required basis.

The draft project planning log is reviewed by all team participants and revisions are suggested and completed.

The project planning log is dated and distributed to all involved parties.

Retrain Human Resource Specialists

Date: xx/xx/xx

Team: Eagles	**Solution:** Revise/Update HR Training			
Major Tasks	Process/Methods	Due	Name	Follow-Up
1. Identify needs	Perform needs study	4/1/xx	J.P.	Review docs
2. Review of current HR practices	Review of HR literature	6/1/xx	Team	Sort/file by 6/15/xx
3. Acquire case studies	Consolidate secondary data	7/10/xx	K.L.	—
4. Engage subject matter experts	Identify/contact (3) SMEs	7/30/xx	K.L.	Interviews
5. Identify tasks	Perform task analysis	9/1/xx	J.P.	Contact HR personnel
6. Job descriptions	Update	10/1/xx	K.L.	—
7. Develop training	Build HR modules	12/20/xx	T & D	Interface with T & D
8. Train-the-trainer	Match experience with HR modules for trainer I.D.	1/15/xx	HR staff	Check schedules

Note: SME = subject matter experts

The project prioritization matrix is a valuable tool used to allocate resources where they are needed most. The need to prioritize projects by some established criteria is not a new issue for project teams. A project prioritization matrix will allow a systematic approach to identifying project importance.

- To prioritize projects by an established set or criteria.
- To ensure correct and timely resource allocation.
- To document a decision-making process that establishes a rule indicating when a project should be activated.

before

Milestones chart

Gap analysis

Force field analysis (FFA)

Fault tree analysis (FTA)

Brainstorming

after

Work breakdown structure (WBS)

Resource requirements matrix

Project planning log

Timeline chart

Gantt chart

	Select and define problem or opportunity
	Identify and analyze causes or potential change
➡	Develop and plan possible solutions or change
➡	Implement and evaluate solution or change
	Measure and report solution or change results
	Recognize and reward team efforts

	Research/statistics
	Creativity/innovation
3	Engineering
1	Project management
	Manufacturing
	Marketing/sales
	Administration/documentation
	Servicing/support
	Customer/quality metrics
2	Change management

- The threshold value is set either by the team or some outside source.
- Relative weights must add up to a total of 100.
- Do not exceed 15 items to be rated.
- Multiplier values are 0–5.

The team develops a list of brainstormed criteria for the project, program or activity. See example *Form and Train an Integrated Project Development Team* (IPDT). See items 1–11, the established criteria for this example.

The second step is to distribute the relative weight assignments for a total of 100 points across all criteria.

A baseline is set for the total number of points that will designate the value of the priority (this value will serve as the threshold). Compute the possible number of total points as follows: relative weight (100) $\times$ highest multiplier for perceived value (5) = 500.

The team rates each item on the chart for its perceived value on a scale of one to five, five being highest.

The next calculation is to multiply weight $\times$ rating for each item and insert the total into the bottom row of boxes.

The team sums up the points for the total point score and verifies the total against the threshold determined in Step 3 above. Since the overall rating of 401 points exceeds the threshold value of 350, this project should be completed.

Form and Train an Integrated Product Development Team (IPDT)

1	2	3	4	5	6	7	8	9	10	11	12	13	14	15	Item No.
Support master schedule	External customer	Internal customer	Resources available	Approvals expected	Aligned to goals	Came recommended	Company policy	Best value option	Learning opportunity	Capable of doing					Project/program/activity *Form and train an integrated product development team (IPDT)* Date: *xx/xx/xx*
10	10	2	8	10	10	13	8	15	6	8					Relative weight ⟨ 100

Perceived value rating																Multiplier
X	X							X							5	High
		X		X	X	X									4	
			X						X						3	
			X												2	
								X							2	
															1	Low
															0	None

50	50	4	32	30	40	52	32	75	12	24					Weight × rating
															⟨ Points *401*

Notes: Threshold value = 350. Exceeding this value will designate priority.

A quality chart is used to monitor quality metrics within any operation of an organization. The chart is a simple data collection form that reflects actual data and the results of continuous improvement efforts toward an established performance goal.

- To publicly display the results of problem-solving teams on particular quality concerns.
- To monitor and track quality metrics within the organization.
- To identify quality of performance discrepancies.

➡ Select and define problem or opportunity
➡ Identify and analyze causes or potential change
  Develop and plan possible solutions or change
➡ Implement and evaluate solution or change
  Measure and report solution or change results
  Recognize and reward team efforts

	Research/statistics
	Creativity/innovation
	Engineering
	Project management
3	Manufacturing
	Marketing/sales
2	Administration/documentation
	Servicing/support
	Customer/quality metrics
1	Change management

- Quality charts can be used for any function within the organization. Ideally, they display historical data, recent data trends, and established goals for quality improvement.

before

Information needs analysis

Data collection strategy

Sampling methods

Checksheet

Observation

after

Problem analysis

Potential problem analysis (PPA)

Cost of quality

Process analysis

Countermeasures matrix

A preprinted quality chart is publicly displayed in a hallway or other open space.

A problem-solving team decides on the type of data and over what period of time the data is to be collected.

The quality chart is prepared to reflect the quality concerns, type of data, quarters, weekly dates, and the established goal(s). See example *Missed "24-Hour Turnaround" Customer Complaint Handling*.

Data is collected and posted on an ongoing basis, as shown in this example.

The team continues to work on the identified problem areas and measures its improvement programs.

Missed "24-Hour Turnaround" Customer Complaint Handling

Questionnaires are useful in a data collection process that requires a large amount of data on a specific topic or problem area. The use of questionnaires is cost-effective, administratively less time consuming, and flexible for different mailing modes such as direct mail, electronic mail, or fax. Questionnaires must be carefully designed to provide valid, reliable, and unbiased response data. In order to increase the usually low response rate for mailed questionnaires, a follow-up telephone call or remailing is helpful.

- To complete an organizational research project that uses a self-administered questionnaire for data collection.
- To collect specific data from a large group in a relatively short time at reasonable cost.

before

Data collection strategy

Sampling methods

Demographic analysis

Starbursting

Information needs analysis

after

Response data encoding form

Surveying

Interview technique

Checksheet

Fog index

➡ Select and define problem or opportunity
➡ Identify and analyze causes or potential change
   Develop and plan possible solutions or change
   Implement and evaluate solution or change
   Measure and report solution or change results
➡ Recognize and reward team efforts

1	Research/statistics
	Creativity/innovation
	Engineering
	Project management
	Manufacturing
3	Marketing/sales
	Administration/documentation
4	Servicing/support
2	Customer/quality metrics
5	Change management

- Keep the questionnaire as short as possible. Only ask questions necessary for this data collection requirement.
- Avoid open-ended responses. They are difficult to tabulate and analyze.
- Group together questions of a particular format for easier completion and analysis.
- Use multiple choice matrix questions for large data volume.
- Prevent researcher bias when phrasing questions.
- Use a panel of experts to review the draft questionnaire to check for clarity, understanding, and completeness.
- Field-test completed questionnaires to reduce ambiguity. Use a similar group of respondents for this task.

As a first step, a team decides on the specific data requirements. A list of preliminary questions is developed.

The questionnaire is developed using appropriate questionnaire construction guidelines. A research text reference can be very helpful in this task. See example *Various Question Formats and Example Questions*.

The draft questionnaire is verified by all team participants so that the required data will be collected using the number and type of questions listed.

A small sample of the identified population of respondents is asked to assist in the field testing of the questionnaire. Final revisions are made.

On the basis of the size of the predetermined population, a sample is taken and questionnaires are mailed.

As the questionnaires are returned, the team checks the questionnaires (see response data encoding form), calculates a response rate, and decides if a follow-up mailing is needed.

Various Question Formats and Example Questions

Section I—Demographic data examples

Please respond to the following questions. Enter the numbers of your choices in the appropriate boxes on the right.

xx **Your team membership** ☐
  1 = Engineering
  2 = Manufacturing
  3 = Quality
  4 = Human Resources

xx **Employment status** ☐
  1 = Full-time (32 hours or more per week)
  2 = Part-time (31 hours or less per week)

xx **Gender** ☐
  1 = Female
  2 = Male

xx **Years in present position** ☐
  1 = Less than 2 years
  2 = 2–4 years
  3 = Over 4 years

xx **Trained in team dynamics, problem solving** ☐
  1 = Overview only
  2 = Classroom—internal
  3 = On-the-job training
  4 = Workshop—external
  5 = Two or more

Section II—Matrix, probing, contingency, and branching question examples

xx **What training workshop is of particular interest to you?**

	Degree of interest		
	Great interest	Some interest	No interest
Design of experiments (DOE)	( )$_1$	( )$_2$	( )$_3$	☐
Cycle time management (CTM)	( )$_1$	( )$_2$	( )$_3$	☐
Management by policy (MBP)	( )$_1$	( )$_2$	( )$_3$	☐

xx **Primary method of acquiring customer data?** ☐
  1 = Quality function deployment
  2 = Customer satisfaction survey
  3 = Focus group
  4 = Other (please specify) _____

xx **How often do you use customer interviews?** ☐
  ( )$_1$ Once per year   ( )$_2$ Occasionally   ( )$_3$ Never

xx **If your answer above was "Never," we would appreciate a brief explanation.**

xx **Were the instructions in the user manual clear?**
  1 = Yes (Please skip to question #xx) ☐
  2 = No (Please skip to question #xx) ☐

(continued)

Various Question Formats and Example Questions, *continued*

Section III—Likert scales examples

	Very satisfied	Satisfied	Neither satisfied nor dissatisfied	Dissatisfied	Very dissatisfied	
Perceived *satisfaction* ratings						
xx Information is available when needed.	5	4	3	2	1	☐
xx The team organization meets our needs.	5	4	3	2	1	☐
Perceived *agreement* ratings						
xx There is open communication throughout the department.	5	4	3	2	1	☐
xx There is management commitment at the team level.	5	4	3	2	1	☐
Perceived *attainment* ratings						
xx I feel empowered in my team.	5	4	3	2	1	☐
xx I truly feel part of a team.	5	4	3	2	1	☐

Section IV—Various scales examples

Horizontal numerical scales: Example—Importance of issue

xx   **Question: User manuals must be updated**

Extremely important   1   ②   3   4   5   *Extremely unimportant*

Semantic differential scales: Example—Opinion check

xx   **Question:** Place a ✓ in the space on each line below to indicate your opinion of proposed changes in customer support.

xx   Will work   ___ ✓ ___ ___ ___ ___ ___   Will not work
                 1   2   3   4   5   6   7

xx   Effective   ___ ___ ✓ ___ ___ ___ ___   Not effective
                 1   2   3   4   5   6   7

Multiple rating matrix: Example—Perception ratings

Questions:

	Extremely safe				Extremely risky		
xx Changing existing service procedures	1	2	③	4	5	6	7
xx Decision making to the lowest levels	1	2	3	4	⑤	6	7

Multiple rating grid: Example—Customer satisfaction evaluation

Excellent 1 2 3 4 5 Poor

CSA Teams ⟶	Action	Guidance	Cross-functional	Process
xx Attendance	1	3	3	2
xx Tools usage	2	4	4	1
xx Progress	2	2	3	1

Note: CSA = customer satisfaction analysis   *(continued)*

Various Question Formats and Example Questions, *continued*

Ad hoc scales: Example—Comparison of general characteristics for a profile construction

xx **CSA Teams** ⟶

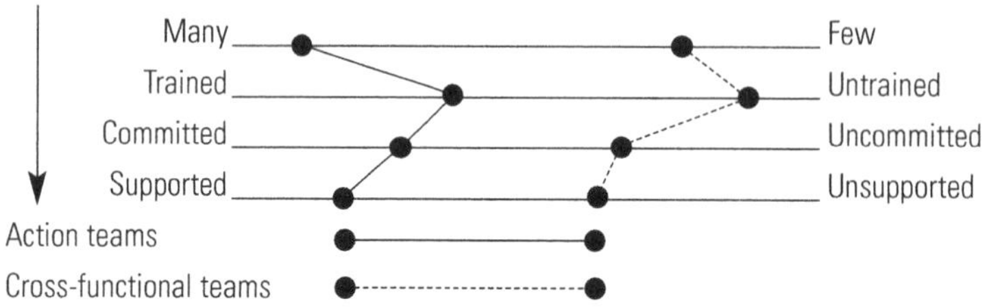

Many _____●───────────●_____ Few
Trained _____●_____ Untrained
Committed _____●_____ Uncommitted
Supported _____●_____ Unsupported

Action teams ●───────●

Cross-functional teams ●- - - - - - - ●

Section V—Open-ended questions/examples

xx **Did this questionnaire cover all issues?**

1 = Yes ☐

2 = No (If "No," what was left out? ☐

_____

xx **Anything you wish to comment on?**

_____
_____
_____

A radar chart is a very useful indicator of the status quo in relation to an ideal state or a vision. It can be used to verify gaps in operational performance, benchmark one unit against the other, show current trends, display percent completion, or reflect on overall organization's strengths and weaknesses.

- To visually display existing gaps in both current and planned organizational performance.
- To show shifts in the organization's strengths and weaknesses.
- To perform a reality check against an ideal state or vision.
- To report trends in resource allocations or progress made.

before

Affinity diagram

Brainstorming

Data collection strategy

Benchmarking

Organization readiness chart

after

Gap analysis

Storyboarding

Project prioritization matrix

Consensus decision making

Force field analysis (FFA)

➡ Select and define problem or opportunity
➡ Identify and analyze causes or potential change
  Develop and plan possible solutions or change
  Implement and evaluate solution or change
➡ Measure and report solution or change results
  Recognize and reward team efforts

1 Research/statistics
  Creativity/innovation
  Engineering
  Project management
  Manufacturing
4 Marketing/sales
  Administration/documentation
  Servicing/support
3 Customer/quality metrics
2 Change management

- The scale of assessment for a radar chart is measured from the center of the chart as follows:
  – 0 to 50 percent (identifies gaps, completion percent)
  – SD - D - A - SA [checks for team agreement—ratings are strongly disagree (SD), disagree (D), agree (A), strongly agree (SA)].

Reach consensus on the themes or elements to be measured with the radar chart.

Collect or verify the data to be plotted. See example *Shift in Company Trainer's Activities (1980 vs. 1996)*.

Prepare a flip chart displaying the radar chart with appropriate scaling along the spokes.

Plot the 1980 data as shown; then plot the 1996 data using encoded lines connecting every marked location on each spoke.

Check that all data has been plotted as scaled on each spoke.

Provide legend, indicate other supporting information, and date the radar chart.

Shift in Company Trainer's Activities (1980 vs. 1996)

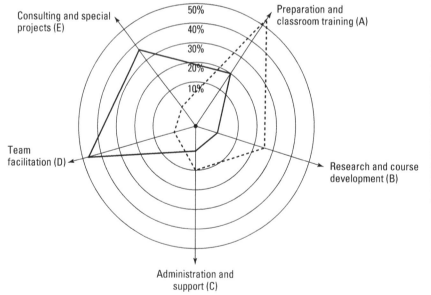

Date: xx/xx/xx

Overlay legend:
- - - - - = 1980
——— = 1996

Shifts:

	From 1980 →	to 1996
(A)	55%	20%
(B)	25%	5%
(C)	10%	5%
(D)	5%	45%
(E)	5%	35%
	100%	100%

The random numbers generator is a research and statistics tool that conveniently allows a simple random sampling process to be completed in a completely unbiased fashion within a relatively short time. A simple random sampling method allows each member of a population an equal probability to be included in a sample drawn from the same population.

- To generate a valid sample from an identified population using a simple random sampling method.
- To provide a convenient method of selecting an unbiased sample of predetermined size from a target population.

<table>
<tbody>
<tr><td>before</td></tr>
<tr><td>Data collection strategy</td></tr>
<tr><td>Sampling methods</td></tr>
<tr><td>Demographic analysis</td></tr>
<tr><td>Audience analysis</td></tr>
<tr><td>Consensus decision making</td></tr>
</tbody>
</table>

before

Data collection strategy

Sampling methods

Demographic analysis

Audience analysis

Consensus decision making

after

Normal probability distribution

Surveying

Interview technique

Observation

Analysis of variance

Select and define problem or opportunity

➡ Identify and analyze causes or potential change

Develop and plan possible solutions or change

Implement and evaluate solution or change

➡ Measure and report solution or change results

Recognize and reward team efforts

1 Research/statistics

Creativity/innovation

Engineering

Project management

Manufacturing

4 Marketing/sales

Administration/documentation

Servicing/support

2 Customer/quality metrics

3 Change management

- During the extracting of the numbers for the random sample from the random numbers generator, skip the numbers that: 1) are repeated, and 2) are higher than the highest number in the population range. Example: If population size is 100, skip number 101 if it should come up in the table.

Determine or estimate the size of the target population that will be used as the source for a random sample.

On the basis of the population size, look up the required size of the sample by referring to a sample size determination table found in most statistics textbooks.

The next step considers the size of the sample to be taken. The identified number of employees = 100. At first, a list of employee names or identification numbers is prepared to reflect 00–99. Referring to a sample size determination table (at the 95 percent confidence level), the sample size for N = 100 was found to be 80. See example *A Random Sampling of 80 from 100 Employees*.

Using a random numbers generator table (RNGT), select a random sample. First, an unbiased starting point needs to be identified. The selecting of a starting point can be accomplished in three ways: 1) Ask a person to point to any number on the RNGT; 2) face away from the tale and using a pencil behind your back, mark a number of the RNGT for a starting point, or 3) use a watch or calendar to retrieve the numbers (any digits are fine) to be used as a starting point on the RNGT. Suppose that the unbiased starting point selected was 591, this would give you 59 as the first number since the population range is only 00–99 (counting down vertically the first, then the second column to the tenth 5 × 5 matrix, two spaces to the right is 591). The next five numbers are 18, 68, 31, 67, and 00. This process of selecting numbers continues until all 80 numbers have been drawn for the sample.

Note: Skip any repeated number that comes up and any number that is greater than 79! (Remember, 00–79 = 80 numbers.)

Cross-reference the selected numbers to the employees. This is your random sample.

Random Sampling of 80 from 100 Employees

```
114 384 154 666 772   061 895 087 971 800   390 089 597 357 754   824 812 826 765 791   927 969 090 264 194
541 583 495 653 782   317 825 477 409 843   878 103 587 802 467   061 719 963 602 431   392 696 126 417 578
839 068 452 733 209   410 906 416 988 729   255 598 866 464 985   230 753 722 917 504   610 727 641 022 602
674 541 265 731 866   735 920 983 783 674   087 653 490 588 723   603 178 589 675 899   275 786 972 607 817
753 015 626 574 733   035 166 735 829 372   816 781 986 503 711   748 622 286 833 779   385 578 034 676 019

942 761 642 692 697   301 591 182 683 316   098 595 537 432 631   160 536 459 046 053   735 607 753 739 749
234 099 944 513 874   670 007 011 647 536   809 695 481 080 065   883 779 194 724 702   656 462 633 744 842
999 538 554 716 800   411 713 530 575 586   515 791 970 262 653   632 296 600 774 805   636 340 898 032 432
466 849 276 886 746   778 913 286 765 059   319 061 309 794 713   219 732 425 538 145   157 862 805 726 606
948 950 792 739 629   727 148 724 654 876   385 624 443 051 959   811 022 309 347 647   707 830 793 974 608

115 747 904 883 055   788 165 912 025 696   603 915 021 892 521   631 875 915 872 160   668 698 700 953 639
920 709 749 489 777   774 784 739 534 713   822 910 397 685 608   888 949 829 193 882   614 745 440 045 804
773 978 580 665 733   828 559 872 004 005   794 820 452 803 580   130 993 944 777 644   667 748 318 638 828
460 253 604 651 728   074 802 928 946 817   782 503 571 902 768   722 088 884 188 393   427 749 799 487 548
744 837 021 454 586   865 674 011 740 314   787 848 513 072 720   478 921 621 969 793   035 890 929 613 786

759 758 000 364 378   175 356 797 088 300   888 683 055 644 686   623 076 880 061 656   504 911 910 084 708
938 850 580 573 941   823 779 134 587 563   790 782 829 670 822   917 971 990 742 407   895 895 644 199 653
030 669 827 306 768   194 768 781 561 827   956 019 668 600 691   682 406 676 134 600   905 246 926 492 900
865 644 339 556 659   918 928 382 874 437   549 763 722 640 641   708 433 776 956 876   096 529 599 908 236
727 826 675 502 464   513 819 827 922 894   707 747 574 546 806   717 998 554 889 011   097 634 613 303 458

436 569 795 937 828   528 782 753 057 993   428 597 766 162 952   091 830 970 569 691   819 507 722 242 510
062 912 669 084 708   312 284 638 325 790   909 881 959 831 446   468 843 749 546 688   884 447 631 236 122
135 970 900 547 954   483 382 945 226 592   854 313 905 951 760   448 790 381 958 077   754 074 752 045 791
811 188 230 795 228   563 801 319 089 201   514 497 440 903 744   706 391 434 951 897   442 867 527 186 701
591 834 823 978 321   888 932 658 108 551   843 866 977 308 083   710 045 651 060 819   614 021 903 837 712

804 728 550 913 392   017 697 941 450 577   990 471 522 667 669   112 188 839 773 431   065 502 676 911 584
431 864 794 120 596   563 128 410 020 123   708 981 564 474 549   021 377 983 709 476   738 580 173 669 761
486 328 136 782 658   669 457 521 637 998   516 043 259 715 529   819 852 035 695 815   165 912 625 996 159
979 724 668 766 886   176 346 933 742 522   726 865 859 608 702   867 624 055 826 670   035 858 831 965 663
045 713 942 565 229   426 976 608 736 937   941 032 664 643 944   760 758 644 873 777   707 950 503 679 892

758 183 787 738 059   749 936 647 733 131   896 524 304 636 542   653 585 034 713 777   636 606 269 548 450
852 962 830 979 392   312 936 791 986 201   803 074 728 738 373   024 863 973 087 836   974 138 948 693 042
207 775 495 717 177   497 437 072 775 785   051 697 823 678 567   883 508 801 724 951   738 999 422 928 315
827 749 437 509 639   585 413 403 725 552   854 684 065 747 859   716 544 642 643 034   536 615 719 590 773
011 716 617 785 976   445 481 695 729 079   865 613 900 948 660   560 779 801 681 557   357 017 586 857 662

666 508 532 746 153   684 460 095 982 832   488 861 681 791 461   893 599 711 604 061   993 471 261 968 494
708 635 756 008 060   729 373 954 877 962   971 729 792 538 253   638 755 859 055 054   932 788 665 097 080
555 612 512 792 281   159 607 960 879 536   527 495 445 789 509   317 754 067 737 204   892 605 824 162 015
700 791 919 989 736   076 635 859 937 879   880 586 830 905 914   732 064 535 928 561   595 381 790 568 931
814 906 004 406 919   029 754 796 796 616   333 956 146 607 580   669 857 726 887 977   539 551 403 559 895
```

Table developed by Walter J. Michalski, Ed.D. (1997)

The ranking matrix tool is applied when rank ordering several options on the basis of a set of team-established criteria or guidelines. Comparing options against each other, ranks are assigned to each option to determine the "best" or "worst" standing of all listed and ranked options on the matrix.

- To determine a preferred or perceived best problem solution or process-improvement opportunity.
- To assist a team in reaching consensus.
- To cross-validate any other assessment technique, such as a rating matrix.
- To simply rank order all available options on the basis of comparing all options against established criteria.

before

Data collection strategy
Brainstorming
Brainwriting pool
Affinity diagram
Focus group

after

Run-it-by
Different point of view
Problem specification
Action plan
Point-scoring evaluation

➥ Select and define problem or opportunity
   Identify and analyze causes or potential change
➥ Develop and plan possible solutions or change
➥ Implement and evaluate solution or change
➥ Measure and report solution or change results
➥ Recognize and reward team efforts

- Assign rank 1–5 in accordance with how well each training method meets the criteria. Rank 1 (low) is the preferred method; lowest total score is overall best training method.

5	Research/statistics
	Creativity/innovation
	Engineering
4	Project management
	Manufacturing
3	Marketing/sales
	Administration/documentation
	Servicing/support
2	Customer/quality metrics
1	Change management

The team determines the criteria for ranking the options. See example *Overall Best Training Method*.

A ranking matrix is constructed and all criteria is listed across the top with a respective scale and translation, as seen in the example.

All options to be ranked are listed in the vertical matrix column.

Each option is ranked in comparison to all other options.

All ranks are added across to arrive at a total value. The lowest total ranks as the best option.

Overall Best Training Method

Date: xx/xx/xx **Ranking of Training Methodologies**	Training Cost	Instructor Time	Participant Demand	Equipment Needs	Test Administration	
	Rank 1–5 (1 is best)					**Total**
Lecture/ presentation	1	5	5	1	3	15
Computer-based	5	4	2	5	2	18
Case study	2	2	4	2	4	14
Research/ discovery	3	1	3	3	5	15
Hands-on practice	4	3	1	4	1	*13

Notes: * Lowest score is overall ranked **best** training method.

The rating matrix tool is used to rate a list of options against a team-established set of necessary criteria or guidelines in order to identify the perceived "best" option. Greater weight can be assigned to a more important criterion using a multiplier factor. The lowest total score on the rating matrix suggests the best option.

- To evaluate and rate a number of options available to the team.
- To determine a preferred or perceived best problem solution or process-improvement opportunity.
- To assist a team in reaching consensus.
- To decide on what action the team should take as the next step.

before

6-3-5 method

Brainwriting pool

Brainstorming

Data collection strategy

Focus group

after

Action plan

Run-it-by

Potential problem analysis (PPA)

Project planning log

Different point of view

➡ Select and define problem or opportunity
   Identify and analyze causes or potential change
➡ Develop and plan possible solutions or change
➡ Implement and evaluate solution or change
➡ Measure and report solution or change results
➡ Recognize and reward team efforts

5 Research/statistics
   Creativity/innovation
   Engineering
4 Project management
   Manufacturing
3 Marketing/sales
   Administration/documentation
   Servicing/support
2 Customer/quality metrics
1 Change management

- Assign ratings of 1–5 in accordance with how well each training method meets the criteria. A rating of 1 (low) is the preferred method; the lowest total score is the overall best training method.
- If a particular criterion is perceived to be of higher importance, a multiplier factor can be applied as shown in the example. The rating is multiplied by the multiplier factor to give the criterion greater weight, or in other words, a higher rating score.

The team determines the criteria and scales to be used for rating all options. See example *Overall Best Training Method*.

A rating matrix is constructed with the rating criteria and scales shown on top. Ensure that all numerical scales and translations do not conflict with "lower rating is better" approach.

The team rates how well each option meets the established criteria. If a particular criterion is suggested to be more important, a multiplier value can be assigned for greater weight as seen in the example.

After all options have been rated, the scores are added across the matrix to arrive at total scores. The lowest total score is rated as the best option.

Date the matrix and provide the information to the process owner.

Overall Best Training Method

Date: xx/xx/xx **Rating of Training Methodologies**	*Training Cost* 1 - Low 5 - High	*Instructor Time* 1 - Short 5 - Long	*Participant Demand* 1 - High 5 - Low	*Equipment Needs* 1 - Low 5 - High	*Test Administration* 1 - Easy 5 - Hard	**Total**
Lecture/ presentation	2 × 3 = 6	5	5	1 × 2 = 6	3	21
Computer-based	3 × 3 = 9	1	3	5 × 2 = 10	2	25
Case study	2 × 3 = 6	3	3	1 × 2 = 2	5	19
Research/ discovery	2 × 3 = 6	2	4	2 × 2 = 4	5	21
Hands-on practice	2 × 3 = 6	2	1	3 × 2 = 6	2	*17

Notes: Training Cost importance weight multiplier (×3)
        Equipment Needs importance weight multiplier (×2)
    * Lowest score is overall rated **best** training method.

The relationship map directs the emphasis on people and their interactions among teams from different functional units. It helps a team visualize the process steps and brainstorm some process-improvement ideas. The map also fosters a common understanding of the overall process.

- To show relationship and interactions of teams working together to reach a common goal.
- To map out process steps for the purpose of surfacing process-improvement opportunities.

before

Organization mapping

Sociogram

Circle response

Observation

Circles of influence

after

Process mapping

Deployment chart (down-across)

Process analysis

Different point of view

Potential problem analysis (PPA)

➥ Select and define problem or opportunity

➥ Identify and analyze causes or potential change

➥ Develop and plan possible solutions or change

Implement and evaluate solution or change

Measure and report solution or change results

Recognize and reward team efforts

Research/statistics

Creativity/innovation

Engineering

Project management

Manufacturing

Marketing/sales

Administration/documentation

1 Servicing/support

Customer/quality metrics

2 Change management

Similar to a process map, a relationship map uses some basic symbols:

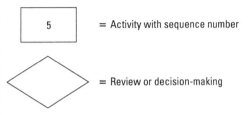

5	= Activity with sequence number

= Review or decision-making

The team facilitator reviews, with the participants, the steps for constructing a relationship map.

Next, all teams or functional units that are involved in the process are listed on a whiteboard. See example *Preliminary Analysis: ISO-9000 Implementation*.

Process steps are identified and sequenced in order of completion.

The relationship map is completed by fully connecting all process activities following the sequence steps as shown in the example.

Notes are added to fully explain what the relationships are and what is being accomplished.

Finally, the map is dated and distributed to all interested parties.

Preliminary Analysis: ISO-9000 Implementation

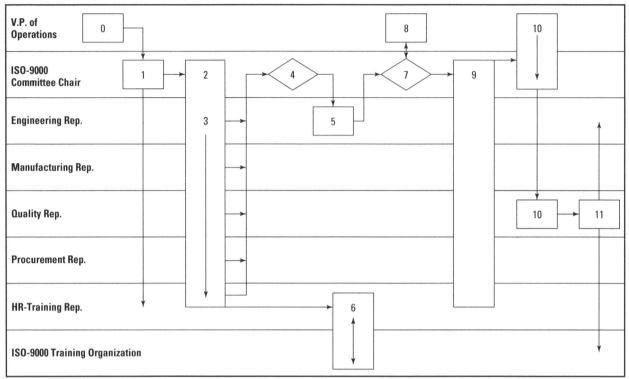

Process Sequence Steps:

0. V.P. of Operations appoints ISO-9000 chair.
1. Company ISO-9000 review committee established.
2. Company representatives attend orientation meeting.
3. Research tasks assigned
   - Engineering — Proposal development
   - Manufacturing — Data collection requirements
   - Quality — Quality manual development
   - Procurement — Supplier involvement
   - HR (training) — Training requirements
4. Researched information reviewed.
5. Engineering compiles proposal information.
6. Training contacts outside ISO-9000 source.
7. Proposal draft reviewed and forwarded to operations.
8. Next step authorization received.
9. Representatives prepare budgets for their respective units.
10. Quality department appointed leadership role.
11. First ISO-9000 implementation committee meeting scheduled.

A resource histogram provides the means of evaluating a project's resource requirements and resource availability. It enables a project manager to determine where resources need to be reallocated and load leveled over the duration of the project. Without resource leveling, the project's requirements (loading) tend to fluctuate. The resource histogram, therefore, reflects the work packages and schedules where load leveling may be possible.

- To indicate potential resource problems and the need to perform load leveling to balance requirements.
- To provide a general understanding of the needed resources for a project over a specific period of time.
- To optimize resource allocation and prevent extreme fluctuations in the availability of resources.

before

Work breakdown structure (WBS)

Program evaluation and review technique (PERT)

Project prioritization matrix

Resource requirements matrix

Force field analysis (FFA)

after

Responsibility matrix

Action plan

Gantt chart

Objectives matrix (OMAX)

Presentation

Select and define problem or opportunity	
Identify and analyze causes or potential change	
➡ Develop and plan possible solutions or change	
➡ Implement and evaluate solution or change	
Measure and report solution or change results	
Recognize and reward team efforts	

	Research/statistics
	Creativity/innovation
2	Engineering
1	Project management
3	Manufacturing
	Marketing/sales
4	Administration/documentation
	Servicing/support
	Customer/quality metrics
	Change management

- A resource histogram should be drawn after a requirements (load) leveling activity has been completed.
- Load leveling results in fewer scheduling problems.
- If resources are leveled, associated costs are also leveled.
- Methods of leveling resource utilization:
  - Delay activities that have no impact on other activity start times.
  - Eliminate certain work segments or activities.
  - Substitute less resource-consuming activities.
  - Change to different resources.

The project manager and his team discuss the project schedule and work packages that need to be completed during a specific time period.

A work breakdown structure (WBS) is checked to determine the resource requirements (loading) needed to complete all listed work packages. A schedule showing when the resources are required is drawn-up. See example *Skilled Labor Requirements After Leveling*.

The work packages' start and finish dates are checked to ensure that any resource leveling using some of the work packages will not adversely affect the project schedule.

All work packages are calculated for monthly resource requirements and balanced across the schedule to prevent any extreme fluctuations in the requirements.

A resource histogram is built by overlaying the monthly resource requirements across the schedule as shown in the example.

Finally, the histogram is checked for accuracy and dated.

Skilled Labor Requirements after Leveling

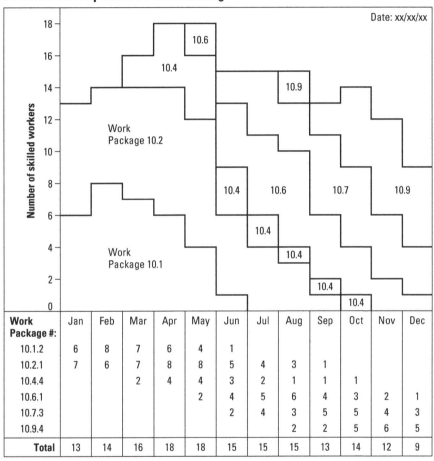

Date: xx/xx/xx

Work Package #:	Jan	Feb	Mar	Apr	May	Jun	Jul	Aug	Sep	Oct	Nov	Dec
10.1.2	6	8	7	6	4	1						
10.2.1	7	6	7	8	8	5	4	3	1			
10.4.4			2	4	4	3	2	1	1	1		
10.6.1					2	4	5	6	4	3	2	1
10.7.3						2	4	3	5	5	4	3
10.9.4								2	2	5	6	5
Total	13	14	16	18	18	15	15	15	13	14	12	9

The resource requirements matrix reflects an estimated total cost for implementing an activity or major project. Required resource categories are identified and associated costs calculated. Costs are summed by resource categories and activities to provide a common understanding for planning and budgeting purposes.

- To plan and budget for implementation activities or process changes.
- To estimate total project costs.
- To provide supporting data for decision making.

before

Information needs analysis

Consensus decision making

Case study

Checklist

Dimensions cube

after

Activity cost matrix

Cost-benefit analysis

Balance sheet

Comparison matrix

Matrix data analysis

	Select and define problem or opportunity
	Identify and analyze causes or potential change
➦	Develop and plan possible solutions or change
➦	Implement and evaluate solution or change
	Measure and report solution or change results
	Recognize and reward team efforts

	Research/statistics
	Creativity/innovation
2	Engineering
1	Project management
3	Manufacturing
	Marketing/sales
5	Administration/documentation
4	Servicing/support
	Customer/quality metrics
	Change management

- Identification of probable resource categories and required activities within these categories is part of the preliminary data collection.
- Calculate averages of actual incomes, times, costs, etc., to increase degree of accuracy in calculated total resource costs.

A planning team systematically identifies required activities, personnel, facilities equipment, material, services, and other resources needed to implement or complete an activity or project.

The team recorder uses a whiteboard to draw a resource requirements matrix and inserts all identified data into the matrix. See example *An Active Cross-Functional Team Cost Estimate*.

Cost averages are calculated or estimated and recorded into the appropriate cells of the matrix, as shown in this example.

Finally, all rows and columns are summed, calculations are checked, and the matrix is dated.

An Active Cross-Functional Team Cost Estimate   Date: xx/xx/xx

Estimated Annual Team Maintenance Costs	Team Participants	Facilities/ Utilities	Equipment Media/Computer	Materials/ Supplies	$ Totals
Orientation/ forming	2,000	100	—	200	2,300
Team training	8,000	300	800	900	10,000
Ongoing meetings	29,000	5,000	—	1,000	35,000
Action items	26,000	—	5,000	300	31,300
Administration support	8,000	400	1,000	300	9,700
$ Totals	73,000	5,800	6,800	2,700	$88,300

Notes: Team description: eight participants, (50) two-hour meetings per year, average income: $60,000 per year.

The response data encoding form can be viewed as a data matrix that contains transcribed response choices from data collection instruments. It serves as a data entry form, data source for a respondent's profile, and data consolidation sheet.

- To serve as a recording sheet to hold survey data summarized for data entry into the statistical testing process.
- To sort and record survey data on a data matrix that displays respondents' identification numbers (rows) by response choice variables (columns).

before

Data collection strategy
Questionnaires
Surveying
Interview technique
Observation

after

Demographic analysis
Survey profile
Audience analysis
Presentation
Polygon overlay

Select and define problem or opportunity	
➥ Identify and analyze causes or potential change	
Develop and plan possible solutions or change	
Implement and evaluate solution or change	
➥ Measure and report solution or change results	
Recognize and reward team efforts	

1	Research/statistics
	Creativity/innovation
6	Engineering
	Project management
	Manufacturing
4	Marketing/sales
2	Administration/documentation
5	Servicing/support
3	Customer/quality metrics
	Change management

- Each form can accommodate 50 respondents' data for a maximum of 30 questions.
- Enter the digit 9 for any missing response.

Sort all returned data collection instruments by identification number, or write identification number on instruments. See example *Sample Survey Questionnaire (partial), ID #12*.

Starting with respondent 1 of questionnaire 1, transfer all recorded response choices to the appropriate row and columns on the response data encoding form. In this example, respondent 12 data is recorded as shown. The row shows partial data—see questionnaire items.

Verify that all data has been accurately transcribed. Record a 9 for any missing response choices.

Date the response data encoding form

Sample Survey Questionnaire (partial)

Section I—Demographic Data

Please respond to the following questions. Enter the numbers of your choices in the appropriate boxes on the right.

1. Year of graduation (completion)
   1 = 1981 2 = 1982 3 = 1983 4 = 1984

   $\boxed{2}$

2. Sex
   1 = Male 2 = Female

   $\boxed{2}$

5. Number of dependents during the greater part (over half) of your program attendance.
   1 = 1 (only yourself); 2 = 2 or 3; 3 = 4 or more

   $\boxed{}$

Section II—Personal Achievement Aspects of Graduates

9. Age at program completion
   1 = 25 years or less
   2 = 26–30
   3 = 31–35
   4 = 36–40
   5 = 41–45
   6 = 46–50
   7 = 51 or more

   $\boxed{2}$

Section III—Perceived Extent of Goal Attainment

Please enter in the boxes the numbers that reflect your judgments about the personal results of completing the program. Use the scale in the box at right.

14. Satisfaction in having a degree $\boxed{3}$

15. Personal growth/development $\boxed{4}$

16. Increased independence/confidence $\boxed{5}$

17. Preparation for career change $\boxed{3}$

18. Promotion $\boxed{4}$

19. Job change $\boxed{4}$

> 5 = To a very great extent
> 4 = To a great extent
> 3 = To a moderate extent
> 2 = To a small extent
> 1 = To no extent

Section IV—Perceived Satisfaction Ratings of Program Aspects

Please enter in the boxes the numbers that reflect your ratings of personal satisfaction for the program. Use the scale in the box at right.

24. Overall program content (curriculum) $\boxed{4}$

25. Management theory $\boxed{4}$

26. Personal and professional assessment (portfolio) $\boxed{3}$

> 5 = Very satisfied
> 4 = Satisfied
> 3 = Neither satisfied nor dissatisfied
> 2 = Dissatisfied
> 1 = Very dissatisfied

Response Data Encoding Form

Date: xx/xx/xx

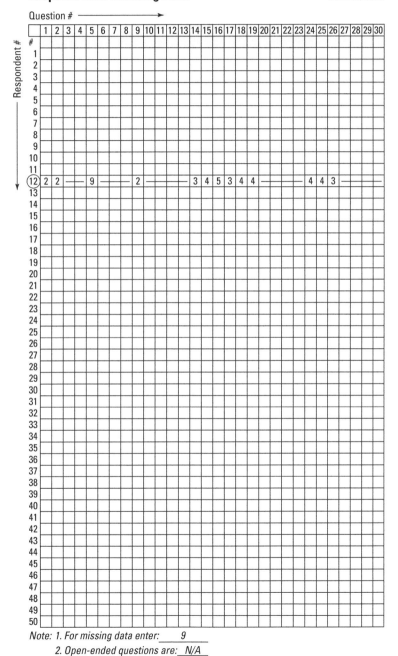

Note: 1. For missing data enter:___9___

      2. Open-ended questions are:_ N/A _

      3. Page 1 of___1___

The response matrix analysis is often used to summarize rating responses from customers or team members on product characteristics and service quality, or to select a particular alternative from among several. Profiling rating averages to compare against benchmark or other standards will show perception differences or performance gaps.

- To summarize and profile raters' responses.
- To choose among many complex alternatives.
- To verify customer satisfaction for products or services.
- To identify gaps in perception or performance when comparing one set of ratings against another.

before

Questionnaires

Surveying

Interview technique

Demographic analysis

Focus group

after

Hypothesis testing
(chi-square)

Solution matrix

Different point of view

Run-it-by

Descriptive statistics

➥ Select and define problem or opportunity

➥ Identify and analyze causes or potential change

➥ Develop and plan possible solutions or change

Implement and evaluate solution or change

Measure and report solution or change results

Recognize and reward team efforts

1 Research/statistics

Creativity/innovation

Engineering

Project management

Manufacturing

2 Marketing/sales

Administration/documentation

Servicing/support

3 Customer/quality metrics

Change management

- Profiling of data is frequently used to compare against an industry average, benchmark data, customer satisfaction, or established organizational goal metrics.
- Optional four- or five-point rating scales are used to rate factors:

4 = Excellent	5 = Excellent
3 = Good	4 = Very good
2 = Fair	3 = Good
1 = Poor	2 = Fair
	1 = Poor

The team develops a listing of product or service factors to be rated and profiled (compared) against customer benchmark data.

The team facilitator explains the rating scale to be used and asks participants to rate each factor. See example *Team Response Analysis— Fax Machine.*

All ratings are recorded on a whiteboard and summarized. Averages are calculated for each factor.

Customer benchmark averages are added, and both sets of rating averages are profiled as shown in the example.

The matrix is verified for accuracy and dated.

Team Response Analysis—Fax Machine

Factors	Team Ratings**					Sum	Avg.	BM*	Profiling
									1　2　3　4　5
Price	2	4	3	4	5	18	3.6	2.2	
Performance	3	5	4	2	5	19	3.8	1.8	
Programming	2	4	5	5	5	21	4.2	2.0	
Flexibility	2	3	1	3	2	11	2.2	2.4	
Attractiveness	1	2	2	5	5	15	3.0	1.6	
Ease of operation	2	4	4	4	5	19	3.8	2.0	
Memory capacity	3	4	2	3	3	15	3.0	1.8	
Set-up/controls	3	2	1	4	2	12	2.4	1.0	
Print quality	2	3	1	2	5	13	2.6	2.0	
Maintenance/service	4	5	4	4	4	21	4.2	2.0	
Total	24	36	27	36	41				
Date: xx/xx/xx									

Notes: *BM = Customer benchmark data used for comparison.
　　　　** Team ratings: 1 = Poor, 2 = Fair, 3 = Good, 4 = Very good, 5 = Excellent

A responsibility matrix is used to identify decisions to be made, major activities to be completed, and persons or groups involved in a change project. Project management requires constant tracking of activities and schedule; a responsibility matrix provides the assignments and understanding of employees' roles and resources required to complete a project.

- To display decision requirements, activities to be completed, and key personnel involved in a project management setting.
- To provide a common understanding of a project's people and resource requirements and allocation.

before

Problem analysis

Checklist

Demographic analysis

Circle response

Consensus decision making

after

Resource histogram

Action plan

Basili data collection method

Project planning log

Milestones chart

	Select and define problem or opportunity
	Identify and analyze causes or potential change
➡	Develop and plan possible solutions or change
➡	Implement and evaluate solution or change
	Measure and report solution or change results
	Recognize and reward team efforts

	Research/statistics
	Creativity/innovation
	Engineering
1	Project management
	Manufacturing
	Marketing/sales
3	Administration/documentation
	Servicing/support
	Customer/quality metrics
2	Change management

- No cell may contain more than one role.
- Avoid splitting primary responsibility (R) for action.
- Avoid assigning too many approvals (A) to any one item.
- Coding: Typical codes have been assigned in this example. Additional designations may be needed.

A facilitated planning team or committee identifies major project activities and responsibilities.

The facilitator creates a responsibility matrix on a whiteboard and requests participants' assistance in completing the matrix. Activities and actors are listed. See example *Establishment of Continuous Improvement Teams*.

Next, participants determine personnel assignments and respective roles in the completion of project activities. A coding scheme is used as shown in this example.

Finally, the completed responsibility matrix is checked, revised, and dated.

Establishment of Continuous Improvement Teams

Date xx/xx/xx

Decisions or Activities	Person or Team									
	HR Director	OPS Manager	Team Leader	Team Facilitator	Team Members	Budget Admin.	Shift A Supervisor	Shift B Supervisor	Quality Director	VP of OPS
Member recruitment	S	A	R	—	I	S	I	I	I	C
Schedule/facilities	I	A	R	S	I	S	C	C	I	—
Administrative support	S	S	R	—	I	A	I	I	C	—
Role assignments	—	A	R	C	I	—	—	—	—	—
Team guidelines	R	S	S	C	I	—	I	I	A	—
Team training	R	A	—	S	I	S	I	I	C	—
Recognition rewards	R	S	I	I	I	S	I	I	C	A

Codes: A = Approval role   R = Responsibility for action   S = Support role;
          C = Consultation role   I = Information/notification role   — = Irrelevant

Reverse brainstorming can be used as a final evaluation technique through the critical questioning of the value or applicability of previously team-generated ideas. In addition, this process attempts to uncover potential problems or other serious consequences when an idea or proposed solution is implemented.

- To minimize the risk prior to the implementation of an idea or proposed solution.
- To reverse brainstorm ideas for weaknesses or serious consequences.
- To criticize ideas for the purpose of reducing many to a few overall "best" ideas.

before

Data collection strategy

Surveying

Interview technique

Observation

Checklist

after

Action and effect diagram (AED)

Sticking dots

Multivoting

Weighted voting

Nominal group technique (NGT)

➥ Select and define problem or opportunity
➥ Identify and analyze causes or potential change
➥ Develop and plan possible solutions or change
   Implement and evaluate solution or change
   Measure and report solution or change results
   Recognize and reward team efforts

Research/statistics
1 Creativity/innovation
Engineering
Project management
Manufacturing
Marketing/sales
Administration/documentation
3 Servicing/support
Customer/quality metrics
2 Change management

- Team size should be limited to the 8–12 participants who previously generated the list of ideas.
- Reverse brainstorming may not be appropriate to use for more than 10 ideas.
- Since this tool promotes criticisms or the severe questioning of previously generated ideas, care must be taken not to "tear down" every good idea!

The team displays a final list of previously brainstormed ideas that passed preliminary evaluation—a reduced list at this point. See example *Increase Operator Job Satisfaction*.

One by one, all ideas are questioned or criticized for possible shortcomings, problems, weaknesses, or serious consequences if implemented.

After all ideas have been evaluated and the potential solutions to problem areas of each idea considered and analyzed, the team selects one (or more) "best" idea that would hold a minimum amount of risk when implemented.

Increase Operator Job Satisfaction

Final List of Previously Brainstormed Ideas that Passed Preliminary Evaluation	Date: xx/xx/xx
1. Establish flextime for operators	
2. Change to self-management	
③ More on-the-job training	
4. They perform equipment maintenance	
5. They do their own job scheduling	
6. Change assembly line to work cells.	
7. Provide optional 4/40 work week.	
⑧ Rotate job assignments	
9. Enrich the present job	
⑩ Form teams for process improvement	

Final Doable List of Ideas After Exhaustive Critical Questioning and Analysis
③ More on-the-job training
8. Rotate job assignments
⑩ Form teams for process improvement

Consensus Reached on "Best" Idea for Immediate Implementation
8. Rotate job assignments

The risk space analysis tool is used by teams to ensure early detection of potential problems in any proposed change activities or to assist in the understanding of plan/action outcome uncertainty. In the area of risk management, a risk space analysis plot allows the identification of risk factors, determines if certain risks need to be controlled, and suggests what evaluation and decision making is required to proceed with a particular strategy or action plan.

- To identify controllable and uncontrollable risk factors.
- To assess risk based on data collected from similar past events.
- To provide an understanding of uncertainty inherent in a change plan.
- To manage risk or uncertainty by systematically addressing the decisions that need to be made about the risk.

before

Data collection strategy

Thematic content analysis

SWOT analysis

Systems analysis diagram

Information needs analysis

after

Variance analysis

Run-it-by

What-if analysis

Organization readiness chart

Project planning log

➟ Select and define problem or opportunity
➟ Identify and analyze causes or potential change
Develop and plan possible solutions or change
➟ Implement and evaluate solution or change
Measure and report solution or change results
Recognize and reward team efforts

1	Research/statistics
	Creativity/innovation
	Engineering
3	Project management
	Manufacturing
5	Marketing/sales
	Administration/documentation
4	Servicing/support
	Customer/quality metrics
2	Change management

- Optional: A severity rating of 1–5 could be assigned to plotted risk factors.
- *Primary data* are data/information collected first-hand by the researcher: surveys, interviews, observations, focus groups, etc.
- *Secondary data* are summarized data/information collected by the researcher during a review of the literature: case studies, statistics, research findings, historical data, etc.

Collect primary data from data sources such as interviews, surveys, quality function deployment (QFD), focus groups, and brainstorming sessions.

Collect secondary data. Review relevant on-line and off-line literature, "best practices," benchmarking data, research reports, case studies, etc.

Select the appropriate data for the process change under consideration. See example *Identification of Risk Factors in Business Process Reengineering (BPR) Work.*

Using flip charts, create several categories of concern, issues, or related process activities. Consider the following headings: *process*, *people*, *requirements*, *schedule*, *cost*, *environment*, and others. Beneath the category headings list potential risks that pertain to those areas.

Draw a risk space analysis plot as shown in the example. Now, ask yourself if the risks you identified are (1) controllable or not controllable, or (2) observable or not observable. Your answers will tell you where to record the items on the plot. After completing this step, date the plot.

For future reference, draft a list of the reasons why you placed the risk factors where you did.

Identification of Risk Factors in Business Process Reengineering (BPR) Work

Date: xx/xx/xx

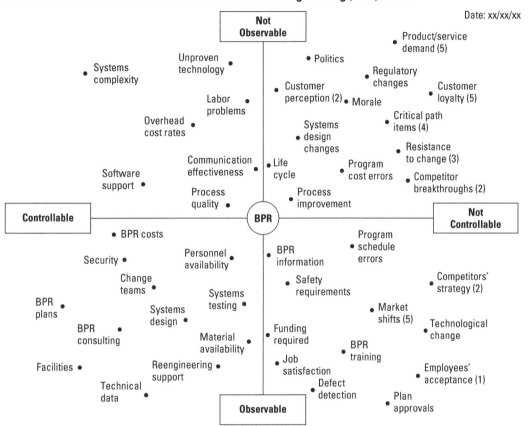

Note: Severity Rating: 1 = Low, 5 = High

The rotating roles activity is a very effective tool for expanding a team's perspectives on the possible consequences or problems resulting from organizational change or from implementation efforts for process, product, or service improvements. Rotating between roles allows participants to bring forward different views in that role or position as a process owner or stakeholder, views that often do not surface unless you "act out" a particular role.

- To collect more perspectives or views on the problem at hand.
- To identify the concerns, issues, or opportunities for a team's consideration before taking action.
- To see different possibilities by "acting out" a particular process owner's role or position in the organization.

before

Different point of view

Circles of influence

Fishbowls

Customer acquisition/defection matrix

Interview technique

after

Presentation

Critical dialogue

Team meeting evaluation

Starbursting

What-if-analysis

Select and define problem or opportunity	
➡ Identify and analyze causes or potential change	
➡ Develop and plan possible solutions or change	
Implement and evaluate solution or change	
Measure and report solution or change results	
Recognize and reward team efforts	

	Research/statistics
2	Creativity/innovation
	Engineering
3	Project management
	Manufacturing
	Marketing/sales
4	Administration/documentation
	Servicing/support
	Customer/quality metrics
1	Change management

- Works best with 5–8 participants.
- Have one prepared flip chart for each role.
- Rotate one space at a time until all participants have had each role.
- No "pass" is permitted!

The facilitator prepares a wheel with participants' names and writes the problem in the center of the wheel. Role cards and a flip chart for each role must also be prepared. See example *Potential Problems with the Establishment of Flextime*.

Participants are seated around the table and the facilitator explains the purpose and rules of the activity.

Every participant views the problem from his/her present role and records concerns, insights, ideas, or recommendations on the appropriate flip chart prepared for this role. After everyone has finished, the wheel is rotated one position or, as an option, participants move to the next chair.

This process of rotation continues, and ideas are recorded on the flip charts, until all participants have rotated through all roles. No "pass" is allowed.

The facilitator ends the session and compiles flip chart information for the team's next step in the problem solving or quality improvement effort as shown in the example.

Potential Problems with the
Establishment of Flextime

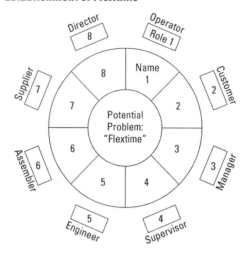

Points of view	Date: xx/xx/xx
– Difficult timekeeping procedures	
– Less absenteeism (single parents)	
– Quality of work life	
– Customer cannot reach employee	
– Effective communications during core hours	

– Scheduling problems (staff meetings, etc.)
– Performance observation/appraisal

The round robin brainstorming tool is a variation of the classical brainstorming in that the team facilitator calls in turn on participants (round robin style) to give their ideas, which are then recorded on a flip chart. This technique is ideal in providing every participant, including those less expressive, an equal chance to contribute, and it greatly slows down the more dominant individuals.

- To gather ideas quickly and without filtering from participants.
- To generate ideas, possible root causes, or potential solutions.
- To ensure that every participant of a team receives equal recognition to voice their ideas.

before

Demographic analysis

Sticking dots

Buzz group

Interview technique

Checklist

after

Wildest idea technique

Starbursting

Consensus decision making

Criteria filtering

Multivoting

➡ Select and define problem or opportunity

➡ Identify and analyze causes or potential change

➡ Develop and plan possible solutions or change

   Implement and evaluate solution or change

   Measure and report solution or change results

   Recognize and reward team efforts

   Research/statistics

1 Creativity/innovation

   Engineering

   Project management

   Manufacturing

   Marketing/sales

   Administration/documentation

   Servicing/support

3 Customer/quality metrics

2 Change management

- The round robin brainstorming tool:

Advantages
- An egalitarian status among participants.
- No individual domination of the process.
- Broader participation (including less expressive participants).
- More focused ideas.
- Hitchhiking or "piggy-backing" on ideas of others.

Disadvantages
- Difficulty for participants to wait their turn.
- Perception of wasting time when waiting one's turn.
- Stifled spontaneity.
- Perceived pressure on participants to respond when their turn comes up.

The team acquires an "outside-the-group" facilitator.

The facilitator explains the round robin brainstorming process and displays a flip chart with the following rules: one idea at time, take turns, no idea evaluation, "pass" is allowed, wild ideas accepted, piggy-back of ideas.

A problem statement or topic is displayed to all participants. See example *Reduce the Student "No Show" Rate in Scheduled Training*.

Participants call out, round robin, their ideas. The facilitator records all ideas on a flip chart. Often, when participants see the ideas of others, they build on these or think of other related ideas.

This process continues, and ideas are recorded until all participants have passed during a round.

The facilitator dates the flip charts, thanks the participants, and closes the session.

Reduce the Student "No Show" Rate in Scheduled Training	Date xx/xx/xx
– Confirm seats	– Mail advanced sign-up form
– Mail reminder notices	– Call students just before class
– Check registration	– E-mail students
– Early registration	– Mail roster to department head
– Distribute schedule	– Check administrative process
– Notify supervisor	– Prove training report monthly
– Inform students of changes	– Ask students how to improve
– Bill the department	– Call other training units
– Notify supervisor on "no shows"	– Benchmark the process
– Record all "no shows"	– Overbook
– Verify classroom schedule	– Charge fee regardless
– Ensure no scheduling conflict	

A run chart is a simple monitoring tool that indicates a trend of change or process over a specified time. Observed data is plotted in sequence and connected by a line to show runs. Run charts can be used for monitoring any variation from an average, the increasing/decreasing trends in performance or defects, or any other change in normal data patterns.

- To observe process variation over time.
- To plot data for the purpose of identifying any changes or trends in the average.
- To receive an early warning of a potential problem due to an observed pattern of plotted data that shows an undesirable trend or variation.

before

Checksheet
Observation
Data collection strategy
Polygon
Surveying

after

Problem specification
Process analysis
Problem analysis
Potential problem analysis (PPA)
Monthly assessment schedule

➡ Select and define problem or opportunity
➡ Identify and analyze causes or potential change
   Develop and plan possible solutions or change
   Implement and evaluate solution or change
➡ Measure and report solution or change results
   Recognize and reward team efforts

1 Research/statistics
   Creativity/innovation
   Engineering
3 Project management
4 Manufacturing
   Marketing/sales
   Administration/documentation
   Servicing/support
   Customer/quality metrics
2 Change management

- A run chart is simply a chart showing runs and trends. It is not as powerful as a control chart that determines if a process is in or out of control on the basis of calculated upper and lower control limits.
- A rough indication of a potential problem may be the consecutive increase or decrease of six or more points in row (a run).
- Another indication of a process change may be the consecutive run of nine or more points on one side of a plotted average ($\bar{x}$) center line of the run chart.
- Plot at least twelve data points to increase the probability of observing a meaningful pattern.

If possible, collect historical data of the process to be observed. This will provide a baseline, or an average, for the run chart to be constructed. See example *"Tools for Teams" Training Participant Attendance*.

Develop a run chart showing time horizontally and a discrete or continuous interval scale vertically.

Plot the observations (measurements) in sequential order as they are collected. Connect data points with straight lines.

As the run chart is developed, check for trends, variations, or indications of potential problems.

Date and save run charts for formulating a problem specification.

"Tools for Teams" Training Participant Attendance

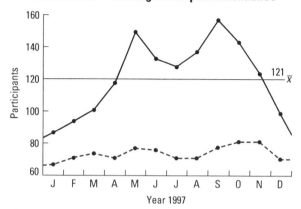

Notes: - - - - - *1996 participant attendance*
Average ($\overline{x}$) = 121 *participants/month*

The run-it-by tool is used by a team to present ideas or proposals to process owners, experts, or other interested groups for the purpose of obtaining additional data, recommendations, or just second opinions. Selected individuals and groups are encoded on a diagram for expected positive, negative, or neutral feedback that will provide the team with new insights and concerns. Additionally, this tool can assist a team to establish interest and gain support from those who are instrumental in the decision-making process.

- To run-it-by critical individuals to obtain first reactions, second opinions, or positions on the proposed idea or action plan.
- To involve affected parties early to minimize resistance to change.
- To uncover potential pitfalls or weaknesses in proposed ideas or action plans.
- To obtain agreement and support from affected individuals or groups.

before

Presentation
Delphi method
Gap analysis
Force field analysis (FFA)
House of quality

after

Thematic content analysis
Action plan
Solution matrix
Process analysis
Process mapping

Select and define problem or opportunity
Identify and analyze causes or potential change
➡ Develop and plan possible solutions or change
Implement and evaluate solution or change
Measure and report solution or change results
➡ Recognize and reward team efforts

	Research/statistics
1	Creativity/innovation
	Engineering
3	Project management
	Manufacturing
	Marketing/sales
4	Administration/documentation
	Servicing/support
	Customer/quality metrics
2	Change management

• Drawn circles are encoded to record who:

$+$ = is supportive, in agreement with prepared action

$-$ = is opposed, resistant to proposed action

N = is neutral to proposed action

The team writes a proposed idea or action into a large circle. See example *Convert Assembly Line "C" to Work Cells*.

The team brainstorms affected process owners, users, supporting groups, and other interested parties. Circles are drawn around the center circle and identified parties recorded inside the circles.

Consensus is reached on who may be supportive $(+)$, opposed $(-)$, or neutral (N) to the proposed idea or action. Symbols are placed near the circles as shown in the example.

The team develops a plan and rationale for contacts to be made.

The team contacts individuals and groups to present the team's position on the proposed idea or action.

Feedback is recorded for additional consideration and action.

Convert Assembly Line "C" to Work Cells

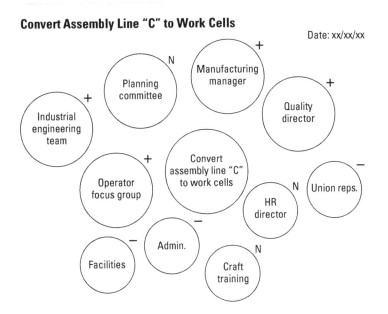

The sampling methods provide teams with the ability to identify and collect sufficient data from targeted populations or processes in order to determine the state of quality, customer perception, or opinion on some issue with reasonable confidence in the results measured. Other considerations for sampling rather than taking the whole population are the savings in cost and time, the impossibility of reaching or checking every member of a population, and the proven adequacy of the different sampling methods for most research applications.

- To collect sample data that is considered representative of the population under observation.
- To estimate the number and distribution of failures, defects, or complaints over a specified period of time.
- To uncover problems or customer dissatisfaction through the application or appropriate sampling methods.
- To obtain answers to research questions or to validate prior research findings.

before

Data collection strategy

Audience analysis

Demographic analysis

Consensus decision making

Multivoting

after

Interview technique

Surveying

Random numbers generator

Observation

Questionnaires

Select and define problem or opportunity	
➡ Identify and analyze causes or potential change	
Develop and plan possible solutions or change	
➡ Implement and evaluate solution or change	
➡ Measure and report solution or change results	
Recognize and reward team efforts	

1	Research/statistics
	Creativity/innovation
	Engineering
3	Project management
	Manufacturing
5	Marketing/sales
	Administration/documentation
	Servicing/support
2	Customer/quality metrics
4	Change management

- Also refer to tool 158, random numbers generator, in this handbook.
- Refer to textbooks on statistics for additional and more detailed information on the various sampling methods.

Define the population to be sampled. Determine the size, strata or make-up, location, and general characteristics. This step is important in that it will suggest a particular sampling method to be used by the researcher. See example *Illustration of the Most Frequently Used Sampling Methods*.

Determine the sample size. Reference should be made to a sample size determination table found in most textbooks on statistics. The proper sample size assists in ensuring a high degree of validity in the research process.

Select a representative sample from the targeted population. The most common sampling methods are:

Simple Random Sampling   Every member of the population has an equal chance to be included in the sample. A popular method is the use of a random numbers generator, a convenient process to draw a considered valid sample.

Systematic Sampling   A variation of random sampling in which members of a population are selected at a predetermined interval (sampling frame) from a listing, time period, or space. Once a random starting point has been established, even every n^{th} number of a sampling frame (population) is selected for the sample.

Stratified Sampling   A sampling method that addresses the differences of subgroups, called strata, and ensures that a representative percentage is drawn from each stratum to form the sample.

Cluster Sampling   This sampling method is often used to save time and cost when a population is widely dispersed. Dividing a geographic area (or facility) into clusters is a first step. Following this step, clusters are then sampled.

Once the sampling is complete, a data collection plan and the appropriate data collection instruments are used to carefully collect required data.

Notes are kept on the sampling method and process used for later reference in a summary report.

Illustration of the Most Frequently Used Sampling Methods

| Population ↓ | Sample ↓ |

Simple random sampling

Systematic sampling

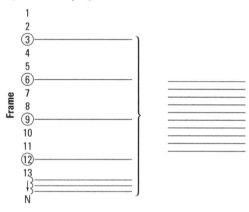

Stratified sampling

Cluster sampling

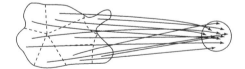

The SCAMPER tool is an outcome of the creative facilitation work performed by Alex F. Osborne in the 1950s. Consisting of a checklist of simple questions, this tool can be used by a team to explore the issues and question everything to formulate new, fresh ideas. Problem-solving teams often produce many solution ideas when responding to the SCAMPER questions asked.

- To question and identify improvement opportunities for processes, products, and services.
- To formulate alternative ideas for problem solving or process change.
- To produce a large number of solution ideas.

before

Brainstorming
Checksheet
Defect map
Pareto chart
Events log

after

Starbursting
Countermeasures matrix
Problem analysis
Process analysis
Solution matrix

➡ Select and define problem or opportunity
➡ Identify and analyze causes or potential change
➡ Develop and plan possible solutions or change
　 Implement and evaluate solution or change
　 Measure and report solution or change results
　 Recognize and reward team efforts

　 Research/statistics
1 Creativity/innovation
　 Engineering
3 Project management
　 Manufacturing
　 Marketing/sales
　 Administration/documentation
　 Servicing/support
　 Customer/quality metrics
2 Change management

- The mnemonic SCAMPER (developed by Bob Eberle) stands for:

  S - Substitute?
  C - Combine?
  A - Adapt?
  M - Modify? Magnify?
  P - Put to other uses?
  E - Eliminate? Minimize?
  R - Reverse? Rearrange?

Assemble a representative team with knowledge of the topic, issue, or problem to be analyzed. See example *Defective Flashlight Switch*.

One by one, the idea-spurring SCAMPER questions are presented to the team.

Participants discuss the questions and formulate ideas. Responses are recorded as the SCAMPER checklist or questions are completed.

Defective Flashlight Switch

SCAMPER Questions—Defective Switch	Date xx/xx/xx
S – Can we *substitute* a more reliable switch?	
C – *Combine* slide switch assembly with the signaling button?	
A – What ideas or concepts can be *adapted* from other similar switches?	
M – *Modify* the switch to have fewer parts?	
P – Can the switch be *put* to other uses?	
E – Can the switch be *eliminated* or exchanged?	
R – How can we *rearrange* the components of the switch to a more robust design?	

The scatter diagram is an analysis tool that plots related pairs of variables (factors) to display a pattern of relationship or correlation. This tool is extremely useful in detecting possible causes of a problem, the strength of the relationship, and how the change of one variable can affect the other.

- To determine if a relationship exists between two sets of data.
- To demonstrate that a change in one activity or condition will affect the other.
- To verify a possible cause to an observed effect.
- To illustrate process improvement.

before

Checksheet

Data collection strategy

Events log

Defect map

Cause and effect diagram (CED)

after

Presentation

Information needs analysis

Trend analysis

Potential problem analysis (PPA)

Cost of quality

	Select and define problem or opportunity
➡	Identify and analyze causes or potential change
	Develop and plan possible solutions or change
➡	Implement and evaluate solution or change
➡	Measure and report solution or change results
	Recognize and reward team efforts

1	Research/statistics
	Creativity/innovation
	Engineering
	Project management
3	Manufacturing
5	Marketing/sales
	Administration/documentation
4	Servicing/support
2	Customer/quality metrics
6	Change management

• Scatter patterns of correlation:

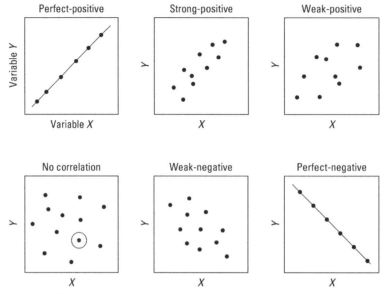

Notes: – ⊙ Identical paired-data points
– To calculate a correlation coefficient, regression statistical techniques
need to be used. Refer to tool 43, correlation analysis, in this handbook.

Select two sets of data (variables) for plotting. See example *Errors Made in Document Processing*.

Sort or rank the data pairs from low to high for both data sets.

Construct a diagram and scale both axes in accordance with observed data pairs, from low numbers to high numbers of occurrence. For example, the X axis reflects a scale from 0 to 140 documents processed per day, the Y axis shows a scale from 0 to 25 errors made per day.

Plot related data pairs on the grid—the diagram. Be careful in measuring the exact location of the intersecting point.

Label and date the scatter diagram.

Errors Made in Document Processing

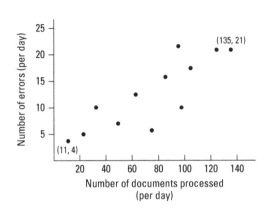

Date: xx/xx/xx

Variables

X docs	Y errors
11	4
23	5
33	10
50	7
63	13
75	6
85	16
96	22
98	10
105	17
124	21
135	21

The scenario writing technique is a process of forecasting some future state by examining the details and interactions of different events of change. As in gap analysis, the process starts with the status quo and moves to a desirable end state, identifying the required actions to get there.

- To forecast and write a description of a future state.
- To hypothesize how continuous change will affect future events.
- To imagine the actual conditions that will exist at some future date.

before
Gap analysis
Case study
Force field analysis
Mental imaging
Trend analysis

after
Opportunity analysis
Cost-benefit analysis
Consensus decision making
Countermeasures matrix
Variance analysis

Select and define problem or opportunity
➡ Identify and analyze causes or potential change
➡ Develop and plan possible solutions or change
Implement and evaluate solution or change
Measure and report solution or change results
Recognize and reward team efforts

	Research/statistics
1	Creativity/innovation
	Engineering
	Project management
	Manufacturing
2	Marketing/sales
	Administration/documentation
	Servicing/support
	Customer/quality metrics
3	Change management

- Scenario writing is similar to futuring, a visualization of some future, ideal state.
- A constructed scenario should be clear, concise, and incorporate as much detail as possible.

A team decides to construct a scenario for the present organization, such as a description of the organization in the year 2002. See example *Futuring the Learning Organization.*

Participants discuss probable events and changes leading up to the future state of the organization.

To more accurately forecast a realistic picture of the future organization, a list of specific considerations is developed, as shown in this example.

Lastly, the desired end state is summarized. This written scenario of the future organization could be very useful in the visioning and planning process.

Futuring the Learning Organization

Trust
Dialogue
Study Teams
Practice Fields
Learning Community
Learning Laboratory

**The Ideal
End State**

Building a Learning Organization
(Some considerations)

- Learn about concepts, strategies, and tools for building a learning organization
- Start sharing information throughout the organization—include customers and suppliers
- Establish study teams and learning forums
- Create a vision of becoming a learning organization—communicate to all employees
- Establish structures and procedures that support openness and collaboration
- Communicate learning organization goals on the basis of honest assessment and trust

A selection matrix helps a researcher to identify the appropriate tool, method, or procedure for a specific task. Once a team has developed the criteria to be used for deciding on a selection, the matrix is examined and the item that best fits the criteria is chosen.

- To select an appropriate tool, methodology, or procedure needed to perform a task.
- To facilitate the decision process by matching established criteria to choices under consideration.
- To compare all available alternatives.

before

Data selection strategy

Sampling methods

Random numbers generator

Information needs analysis

Demographic analysis

after

Response data encoding form

Decision tree diagram

Process analysis

Cluster analysis

Case study

Select and define problem or opportunity
➥ Identify and analyze causes or potential change
Develop and plan possible solutions or change
Implement and evaluate solution or change
➥ Measure and report solution or change results
Recognize and reward team efforts

1 Research/statistics
Creativity/innovation
Engineering
3 Project management
Manufacturing
4 Marketing/sales
Administration/documentation
Servicing/support
Customer/quality metrics
2 Change management

- The *high, medium, low* rating assigned in the example may vary with different processes used to collect the data needed.

The team facilitator leads a discussion on the process for establishing a set of criteria to be used for deciding on a tool, method, or procedure.

A previously recorded list of items is copied onto a selection matrix form. See example *Choosing a Data Collection Method*.

Participants rate all items using the established criteria. The items that best match the requirements are selected as shown in the example. In our example, process flexibility and data accessibility were the primary considerations.

The facilitator dates the matrix and assigns necessary next step action items.

Choosing a Data Collection Method

Date: xx/xx/xx

Data Collection Methods	Collection Time			Collection Cost			Process Flexibility			Data Reliability			Data Accessibility			Selection
	H	M	L	H	M	L	H	M	L	H	M	L	H	M	L	
Survey research		X			X		X				X		X			
Questionnaires		X				X		X			X				X	
Interviews	X			X			X				X		X			✓
Observations	X			X					X	X			X			
Secondary data	X				X				X	X					X	
Focus group			X		X		X				X		X			✓
Panel of experts			X		X		X			X			X			✓
Panels		X			X				X		X			X		
Forum		X			X				X		X			X		
Case study	X				X		X			X					X	
Critical incident	X				X				X		X				X	
Work records	X				X				X		X			X		
Best practices		X				X			X		X				X	
Simulations		X		X			X			X			X			

Note: H = high, M = medium, L = low

The selection window is a great tool for the initial identification and analysis of problematic conditions, improvement opportunities, and action alternatives. It organizes a team's ideas to establish a focus and criteria to select a potential "best" alternative.

- To prioritize an action to be taken on the basis of established criteria.
- To maintain focus and promote understanding of a business issue deemed important.
- To select an alternative that can be successfully pursued with presently available resources.
- To reach team consensus on a plan of action.

before

Consensus decision making

Paired comparison

Critical dialogue

Different point of view

Run-it-by

after

Basili data collection method

Opportunity analysis

Activity analysis

Project planning log

Action plan

	Select and define problem or opportunity
➡	Identify and analyze causes or potential change
➡	Develop and plan possible solutions or change
	Implement and evaluate solution or change
	Measure and report solution or change results
	Recognize and reward team efforts

- The use of this tool is greatly enhanced when team consensus is reached on the determination of scales and the wording of alternatives in each window quadrant.

	Research/statistics
	Creativity/innovation
	Engineering
1	Project management
	Manufacturing
4	Marketing/sales
	Administration/documentation
5	Servicing/support
2	Customer/quality metrics
3	Change management

The team discusses the issues involved and reaches consensus on which alternative actions are to be considered.

Each alternative is considered on the basis of how it would best support the primary purpose of this analysis. See example *Increase Customer Satisfaction*.

The team facilitator draws a selection window on a flip chart. Scales are determined by team consensus.

Each alternative is reexamined as to *Importance* and *Customer Satisfaction* and written into the respective quadrant of the window, as shown in the example.

Increase Customer Satisfaction

Think Service

		Low	High
Importance	High	Action required	Strengths
	Low	No action	Overkill
		Performance	

Think Satisfaction

		Low	High
Importance	High	Defective units	On-time delivery
	Low	Billing errors	Low-cost service calls
		Customer satisfaction	

Semantic intuition is an idea-generating tool used by teams to create a product or process invention by combining words from two or three previously brainstormed lists all related to a problem area. Developed by the Battelle Institute (Frankfurt), the idea is to back into an invention by first naming it, then checking to see if it is feasible to implement. This is the reverse of the usual process of inventing first and then implementing.

- To discover an invention by word association.
- To search for creative solutions to a problem.
- To identify word combinations that may result in a new product, process, or service.

before

Brainstorming

Forced association

Forced choice

Idea borrowing

Round robin brainstorming

after

Analogy and metaphor

Checkerboard method

Creativity assessment

Run-it-by

Presentation

➡ Select and define problem or opportunity
➡ Identify and analyze causes or potential change
　 Develop and plan possible solutions or change
　 Implement and evaluate solution or change
　 Measure and report solution or change results
　 Recognize and reward team efforts

　 Research/statistics
1 Creativity/innovation
　 Engineering
　 Project management
　 Manufacturing
3 Marketing/sales
　 Administration/documentation
　 Servicing/support
　 Customer/quality metrics
2 Change management

- Two- and three-word combinations may increase the probability of finding inventions.
- For use by individuals or teams of 6–8 participants.

The first step requires the team to define a problem area. See example *Lack of Funds to Purchase Training Equipment for Each Classroom*; Solution: Portable Flip Chart Easel.

The team brainstorms two or three wordlists that are linked or related to the problem. Wordlists are displayed side-by-side for the team to view during this process.

Next, words are combined or associated to form new names or potential ideas. The team systematically scans all wordlists in order to surface many combinations.

Discussions take place on word combinations that need further exploration. An attempt is made to visualize a new product, process, or service.

Potential inventions are listed by circling the words and connecting the words with lines (links) drawn from one wordlist to the other(s), as shown in the example.

Lack of Funds to Purchase Training Equipment for Each Classroom
Solution: Portable Flip Chart Easel

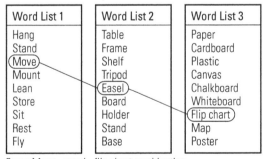

Word List 1	Word List 2	Word List 3
Hang	Table	Paper
Stand	Frame	Cardboard
Move	Shelf	Plastic
Mount	Tripod	Canvas
Lean	Easel	Chalkboard
Store	Board	Whiteboard
Sit	Holder	Flip chart
Rest	Stand	Map
Fly	Base	Poster

From: Move—easel—flip chart combination
To: Portable—easel—flip chart invention

The Shewhart PDCA cycle is a structured cyclical approach for the continuous improvement of processes, products, or services. The plan-do-check-act cycle is usually tried first on a limited basis to test and validate the benefits of change prior to a full-scale implementation effort.

- To provide a set of guidelines for a systemic application of problem solving steps, for validation of quality improvement opportunities, or for the verification of design criteria in new product development.
- To test an improvement idea for possible large-scale implementation.
- To continuously improve the quality of processes, products, and services.
- To transition from an idea exploration stage to a trial pilot project.

before

Variance analysis

Systems analysis diagram

Gap analysis

Force field analysis (FFA)

Process mapping

after

Project planning log

Objectives matrix (OMAX)

Work flow analysis (WFA)

Barriers-and-aids analysis

Action plan

Select and define problem or opportunity

Identify and analyze causes or potential change

➡ Develop and plan possible solutions or change

➡ Implement and evaluate solution or change

➡ Measure and report solution or change results

Recognize and reward team efforts

- Cross-reference to the Deming PDSA cycle (tool 62) for a variation of this process.

Research/statistics

Creativity/innovation

Engineering

2 Project management

4 Manufacturing

Marketing/sales

Administration/documentation

3 Servicing/support

Customer/quality metrics

1 Change management

Plan (P) a product, service, problem solution, or process improvement. See example *From Product Development to Customer Satisfaction*.

Do (D) the activity planned, conduct an experiment, or pilot the change.

Check (C) the results or effects of change. Analyze the collected data.

Act (A) on lessons learned. Mark decision on large-scale production or implementation, abandonment, or activity, or the repeating of cycle steps 1–4 for continued improvement.

From Product Development to Customer Satisfaction

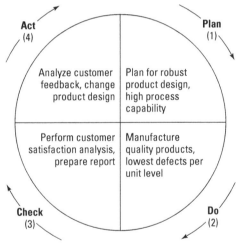

Note: This cycle is repeated for further improvement

The snake chart provides a quick comparison of products and services across attributes or product/service characteristics previously determined to be important to the customer on the basis of customer ratings. These results identify gaps in performance and therefore point to attributes that require improvement action.

- To compare customer-provided attribute ratings for products/services.
- To conduct a quick performance gap analysis by analyzing competitor's data.

before

Data collection strategy

Benchmarking

Nominal prioritization

Attribute listing

Cluster analysis

after

Customer satisfaction analysis (CSA)

Customer-first-questions (CFQ)

Information needs analysis

Problem selection matrix

Action plan

➡ Select and define problem or opportunity

➡ Identify and analyze causes or potential change

➡ Develop and plan possible solutions or change

   Implement and evaluate solution or change

➡ Measure and report solution or change results

   Recognize and reward team efforts

- Customer rating scale should be 1–10, 10 being most important.
- Do not rate more than 10 attributes of product or service at a time.

2 Research/statistics

   Creativity/innovation

   Engineering

   Project management

   Manufacturing

3 Marketing/sales

   Administration/documentation

   Servicing/support

1 Customer/quality metrics

   Change management

Collect benchmark data on competitor's product or service to be compared and analyzed. See example *Electronic Typewriter—Comparison Based on Customer Ratings*.

Develop a snake chart frame and scale according to rating scale.

Draw horizontal bars to represent competitor's and your organization's customer ratings for the selected product or service attributes.

Check all plotted information and date the chart.

Electronic Typewriter—Comparison Based on Customer Ratings

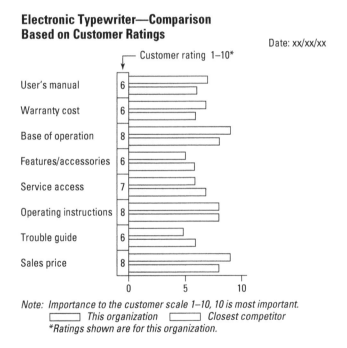

Note: Importance to the customer scale 1–10, 10 is most important.
☐ This organization   ☐ Closest competitor
*Ratings shown are for this organization.

The sociogram is an interaction diagram that illustrates intrateam communication patterns, interpersonal dynamics, and compatibility among team participants. Introduced by J. L. Moreno in 1934, the sociogram is helpful in promoting partnerships, team cohesiveness, and mutual acceptance; it therefore allows more participation and openness in teams.

- To diagram a team's interpersonal relationships and cooperation.
- To obtain an understanding of intrateam interactions and acceptance of team participants.

before

Demographic analysis

Circles of influence

Audience analysis

Organization mapping

Observation

after

Critical dialogue

Relationship map

Rotating roles

Pair matching overlay

Resource histogram

Select and define problem or opportunity

➡ Identify and analyze causes or potential change

➡ Develop and plan possible solutions or change

Implement and evaluate solution or change

Measure and report solution or change results

Recognize and reward team efforts

Research/statistics

Creativity/innovation

Engineering

Project management

Manufacturing

Marketing/sales

Administration/documentation

3 Servicing/support

2 Customer/quality metrics

1 Change management

- Sociogram legend:

Selector ————→ Selected
Rejecter ——//—→ Rejected
Mutual ←————→ Choice (or acceptance)

- A variation of showing interactions is to draw the number of choices (mentions) given or received:

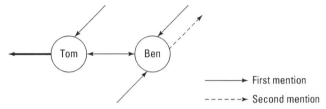

————→ First mention
----→ Second mention

- Limit to 10 the number of people in a sociogram.

Periodically, the team facilitator, coach, or a designated team participant performs observations of team behavior and interpersonal communications.

Notes on communication patterns, acceptance, and rejection, "who interacts with whom" (Moreno), and amount of participation are collected.

Next, a sociogram is drawn and shared with the team. An open discussion follows on ways to improve the team's performance.

A list of possible improvements is developed.

Team Interpersonal Dynamics

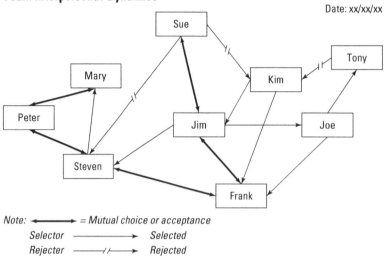

Date: xx/xx/xx

Note: ◄───► = Mutual choice or acceptance

Selector ────► Selected

Rejecter ──//──► Rejected

The solution matrix is a method to document the various possible solutions for a particular problem. Solutions are rated and ranked to determine the best choice that has the highest chance of success. Criteria for rating is often feasibility, customer value, and change effectiveness.

- To rate and rank all solutions and identify a workable, best choice.
- To analyze proposed solutions on the basis of significant factors affecting the solution.
- To avoid guessing at the best solution.

before

Countermeasures matrix

Decision tree diagram

Consensus decision making

Factor analysis

Different point of view

After

Activity cost matrix

Action plan

Cost-benefit analysis

Balance sheet

Basili data collection method

Select and define problem or opportunity

Identify and analyze causes or potential change

➡ Develop and plan possible solutions or change

Implement and evaluate solution or change

➡ Measure and report solution or change results

➡ Recognize and reward team efforts

Research/statistics

Creativity/innovation

Engineering

Project management

Manufacturing

Marketing/sales

Administration/documentation

Servicing/support

2 Customer/quality metrics

1 Change management

- Rating criteria is optional. Care must be taken that rating designations of *high*, *medium*, or *low* will not conflict with other criteria. For example, if solution *implementation time* is *low,* this is a highly (*high*!) desirable characteristic.

The team facilitator displays all proposed solutions on a whiteboard or flip chart. A matrix format is used. See example *Reduce the Current Defects per Unit (DPU) Level*.

Participants brainstorm a set of criteria that is recorded into the solution matrix as shown in this example. Consensus is reached on a rating scale.

Each proposed solution is rated against the listed criteria. This process continues until all proposed solutions have been rated.

Next, all rows are totaled by the facilitator and ranked from highest total (rank 1) to lowest total, as shown in this example. The proposed solution ranked 1 is considered the best or preferred solution.

Finally, the completed solution matrix is dated and presented to the process owner.

Reduce the Current Defects Per Unit (DPU) Level

Date xx/xx/xx

Solutions	Change Effectiveness	Implementation Feasibility	Customer Impact	Total	Rank
Train suppliers, ask for C_p data	M	L	H	9	2.5
Implement statistical process control (SPC)	L	H	M	9	2.5
Reduce process cycle time	M	M	L	7	4
Perform C_p studies, benchmark	L	L	L	3	5
Apply robust design principles	H	M	H	13	①

Notes: *high* = 5, *medium* = 3, *low* = 1
  Ranking: Highest total is best choice, rank ①

The standard deviation is a powerful building block to perform descriptive and inferential statistics in research, project management, quality assurance, education and training, and many other disciplines. Used in many statistical formulae, it assists in the understanding of variability in data distributions. Considered a unit of measurement, a smaller standard deviation simply states that the data distribution is more homogeneous or has less variance.

- To identify the extent of variability in a data set.
- To assist in statistical analyses such as process capability, analysis of variance (anova), design of experiments, and others.
- To compare two or more data distributions.

before

Data collection strategy

Observation

Questionnaires

Surveying

Frequency distribution (FD)

after

Process capability ratios

Correlation analysis

Normal probability distribution

Control chart

Analysis of variance

Select and define problem or opportunity

➥ Identify and analyze causes or potential change

Develop and plan possible solutions or change

Implement and evaluate solution or change

➥ Measure and report solution or change results

Recognize and reward team efforts

1 Research/statistics
   Creativity/innovation
2 Engineering
   Project management
3 Manufacturing
4 Marketing/sales
   Administration/documentation
   Servicing/support
   Customer/quality metrics
5 Change management

- Definition: The standard deviation is a measure of variability within a population or a sample of data. A more technical definition describes the standard deviation as the square root of the average of the squared deviations of the observations from the mean ($\bar{X}$).

  - Standard deviation of the population: σ (sigma):

$$\sigma = \sqrt{\frac{\Sigma(X - \mu)^2}{N}}$$

  Where: Σ = Sum of
  X = Observations
  μ = Population avg.
  N = Population size

  - Standard deviation of the sample: S:

$$s = \sqrt{\frac{\Sigma(X - \bar{X})^2}{n - 1^*}}$$

  Where: Σ = Sum of
  X = Observations
  $\bar{X}$ = Sample mean (average)
  n = Sample size

  Note: n – 1 *is used when the sample size is ≤30.*

- Normal probability distribution

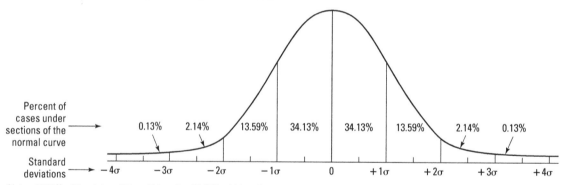

Percent of cases under sections of the normal curve

0.13%   2.14%   13.59%   34.13%   34.13%   13.59%   2.14%   0.13%

Standard deviations → −4σ   −3σ   −2σ   −1σ   0   +1σ   +2σ   +3σ   +4σ

Note: *68.26% of the data will be within ± 1σ, 95.45% within ± 2σ, and 99.73% within ± 3σ in a normal distribution curve.*

- Also refer to tool 119, normal probability distribution, in this handbook.

First, collected scores are sequenced from the lowest to the highest score and placed into a table. See example *Calculating the Standard Deviation—Test Scores*.

Calculate the mean ($\bar{X}$) and subtract from all scores.

Check that the sum of − and + deviation scores (x) = 0.

Square deviation scores and total.

Calculate the variance (S^2). Remember, use n–1 if total scores are less than 30.

Take the square root of the variance to get the standard deviation.

Calculating the Standard Deviation—Test Scores

Training class test scores (10 students)
(100 possible points = 100%)

X	−	$\bar{X}$	=	x	x^2
60	−	82	=	− 22	484
66	−	82	=	− 16	256
67	−	82	=	− 15	225
78	−	82	=	− 4	16
82	−	82	=	0	0
84	−	82	=	+ 2	4
90	−	82	=	+ 8	64
95	−	82	=	+ 13	169
98	−	82	=	+ 16	256
100	−	82	=	+ 18	324
820				0	$\Sigma x^2 = 1798$

$$s = \sqrt{\frac{\Sigma(X - \bar{X})^2}{n - 1^*}}$$

$$s = \sqrt{\frac{1798}{9}} \quad (10 - 1)$$

$$s = \sqrt{199.77}$$

$$\boxed{s = 14.13}$$

The standard deviation = 14.13 for this data set of scores.

$$\bar{x} = \frac{\Sigma X}{n}$$

$$\bar{X} = 82$$

$$s^2 = \frac{\Sigma(X - \bar{X})^2}{n - 1}$$

$$s^2 = 1798$$

Note: For additional information, refer to tool 66, descriptive statistics, in this handbook.

Starbursting generates questions that must be asked by a team in order to clarify issues, probe for potential solutions, or verify resource requirements. Once a topic has been chosen, participants are free to "starburst" any question they feel is relevant to the topic or that needs to be considered and responded to so that nothing is missed in the decision-making process.

- To question how a particular improvement opportunity or problem solution is to be implemented and evaluated.
- To discover, through questioning, what it will take to explore the merits of previously brainstormed ideas.
- To openly voice the questions thought of by team participants during a discussion, presentation, or team meeting.
- To identify early potential problem areas in a change effort.

before

Brainstorming

Observation

Interview technique

Surveying

Questionnaires

after

Critical dialogue

Circles of knowledge

Buzz group

Barriers-and-aids analysis

Cost-benefit analysis

➡ Select and define problem or opportunity	Research/statistics
➡ Identify and analyze causes or potential change	**1** Creativity/innovation
Develop and plan possible solutions or change	Engineering
Implement and evaluate solution or change	Project management
Measure and report solution or change results	Manufacturing
Recognize and reward team efforts	**4** Marketing/sales
	Administration/documentation
	Servicing/support
	2 Customer/quality metrics
	3 Change management

- Just as in brainstorming, no evaluation of questions is allowed during the starbursting process.

The team decides on a topic to be questioned or, as an alternative, displays flip charts of previously brainstormed ideas. See example *Starbursting Questions to Improve Quality*.

The facilitator explains to participants that they may ask as many questions as they wish without having questions evaluated by others.

Questions can be given openly or written on 3×5 cards. All questions are collected and recorded on a whiteboard or flip charts. Checks are made for redundant questions. The purpose for displaying all questions is the possible triggering of other related questions.

When the team runs out of questions, the facilitator asks the team to compare the questions asked with the previously brainstormed ideas, as shown in this example.

Lastly, the team, with the insight gained, discusses the next steps to be taken.

Starbursting Questions to Improve Quality

Date xx/xx/xx

Flip chart 1

Session 8/19/xx

Topic: Improve Quality

- More training
- Short due dates
- Inexperience (more OJT)
- More communications
- Missing information
- What is a defect?
- Constant changes
- No inspections
- Too much work
- Many interruptions
- Group conflict
- Incorrect testing

Flip chart 2

- Lack of proper tools
- Low job satisfaction
- Specifications unclear
- Lack of instructions
- Low morale, motivation
- Lack of metrics
- Involve customers
- Stressful work
- Equipment problems
- Lack of data
- Need problem-solving teams
- No procedures

End of ideas

Previously brainstormed data

Topic: Improve Quality—What Are the Questions?

- How do we involve customers?
- What initiatives are necessary to reduce defect levels?
- What training is appropriate?
- What quality metrics need to be put in place?
- How can we improve intergroup communications?
- What procedures and work instructions need revision?
- How can change be managed more effectively?
- What data needs to be collected and analyzed?
- What can be done to improve morale and job satisfaction?
- Who needs to address work balance and scheduling?
- Why do we have intergroup conflict?
- What does it take to establish problem-solving teams?

The steam-and-leaf display, as developed by John Turkey in 1977, displays the actual numerical values or numbers as collected over a specified period of time. Similar to a histogram, it shows distribution, numerical order, and variation in a process.

- To display original data for further analysis.
- To obtain an idea of overall process variation.

➡ Select and define problem or opportunity
➡ Identify and analyze causes or potential change
  Develop and plan possible solutions or change
  Implement and evaluate solution or change
➡ Measure and report solution or change results
  Recognize and reward team efforts

1 Research/statistics
  Creativity/innovation
  Engineering
  Project management
  Manufacturing
2 Marketing/sales
3 Administration/documentation
  Servicing/support
4 Customer/quality metrics
  Change management

before

Data collection strategy

Frequency distribution (FD)

Checksheet

Normal probability distribution

Questionnaires

after

Histogram

Descriptive statistics

Problem specification

Process analysis

Problem analysis

- Construct a stem-and-leaf display with 5–15 stems. All leaves (scores, numbers, or measurements) are attached to a specific stem.

Collect and summarize the data to be displayed.

Construct a stem-and-leaf display. Stems will reflect the leading digit of numbers: See example *Division "B" Rework Hours for August*.

Insert the leaves on the basis of all numbers collected and recorded, the *raw data*.

Verify that all numbers from the raw data table have been correctly displayed in the stem-and-leaf display. Date the display.

Division "B" Rework Hours for August

Date: xx/xx/xx

Mon	Tue	Wed	Thu	Fri	Sat	Sun
74	67	31	86	95	72	71
40	75	49	48	47	94	56
69	62	22	29	77	61	87
55	86	35	50	36	63	58
71	82	67				

Stem	Leaves
2	2 9
3	1 5 6
4	0 7 8 9
5	0 5 6 8
6	1 2 3 7 7 9
7	1 1 2 4 5 7
8	2 6 6 7
9	4 5

Raw data: 31 days

Organized data

The sticking dots technique introduced by H. Geschka, et al. is a simple, yet effective team rating process. It gives all participants an opportunity to get directly involved and vote for individual preference or priority from a list of ideas or items. Participants indicate their choice(s) by sticking adhesive-backed colored dots next to them on a chart.

- To allow every participant of a team or large group to vote for an idea or item.
- To provide participants direct involvement in a selection process.
- To assign priorities on the basis of collective team input.

before

Double reversal

Brainstorming

Round robin brainstorming

Affinity diagram

Pin cards technique

after

Different point of view

Resource requirements matrix

Team process assessment

Team meeting evaluation

Presentation

Select and define problem or opportunity
Identify and analyze causes or potential change
➡ Develop and plan possible solutions or change
➡ Implement and evaluate solution or change
Measure and report solution or change results
➡ Recognize and reward team efforts

Research/statistics
Creativity/innovation
Engineering
Project management
Manufacturing
3 Marketing/sales
2 Administration/documentation
Servicing/support
Customer/quality metrics
1 Change management

- Participants may be grouped by gender, age, experience, membership, or other characteristics. Assigning different colored dots to particular groups will allow better analysis of preferences, attitudes, or evaluation by participants of each group.
- Colors can also be used to indicate first, second, third priority or preference.
- Recommendation: For 10–40 items give each participant 10–20 colored dots.

The team facilitator displays a list of previously generated ideas or items on a whiteboard or flip charts.

Groups are identified and different colored dots are given to each group. See example *Preference for Tools Training*.

Participants consider their choices and show their preference by sticking dots adjacent to the idea or item listed. Each participant (in this example) has been given 10 dots of the same color.

Facilitator counts the number of dots given to each idea or item and provides a summary to the team for further analysis. Finally, the summary is dated.

Preference for Tools Training

Training Modules Available		Date: xx/xx/xx	
DOE	– Design of experiments	◑◑○◑◑◑◑	7
QFD	– Quality function deployment	◑◑○○○○◑●○◑●	10
SPC	– Statistical process control	○●○●◑○●●	8
BPR	– Business process reengineering	◑◑○◑○●	6
JIT	– Just-in-time	○◑○○○◑◑	7
CSA	– Customer satisfaction analysis	○◑○●◑●●○○●	10
CTM	– Cycle time management	○○○○◑○○○◑○◑	11
MBP	– Management-by-policy	○○◑●	4
TPM	– Total productive maintenance	○○○●●○○	7
IPD	– Integrated product development	◑○●◑○○○◑○○○◑○	⑬
VQA	– Vendor quality assurance	●○○●●●	7

| | | | | Total | 90 |

Note: **Team membership**   **Color dots**   **Quantity**
  Quality (2)   Green – ●   *20*
  Engineering (3)   Red – ◑   *30*
  Manufacturing (4) Blue – ○   *40*

Developed by the Battelle Institute in Frankfurt, Germany, the stimulus analysis tool provides a method of generating problem-solving ideas using unrelated words or objects as potential idea sources. Characteristics of previously brainstormed words or objects are identified and described and then used to stimulate the surfacing of ideas that hold a potential solution to the problem.

- To stimulate the generation of ideas for problem-solving efforts.
- To provide a creativity and innovation method for teams.
- To identify product, process, or service-improvement opportunities.

before

Brainstorming

Circle of opportunity

Circumrelation

Wildest idea technique

Wishful thinking

after

Creativity assessment

Idea advocate

Circles of knowledge

Information needs analysis

Presentation

➡	Select and define problem or opportunity
➡	Identify and analyze causes or potential change
➡	Develop and plan possible solutions or change
	Implement and evaluate solution or change
	Measure and report solution or change results
	Recognize and reward team efforts

	Research/statistics
1	Creativity/innovation
4	Engineering
	Project management
	Manufacturing
3	Marketing/sales
	Administration/documentation
	Servicing/support
	Customer/quality metrics
2	Change management

- Concentrate on one unrelated word or object at a time. If no useful ideas are generated, move on to the next word and repeat the process.

A problem, issue, or concern is displayed to the team. Some discussion or clarification of the technique takes place.

The facilitator prepares three flip charts with headings of *Idea Source*, *Characteristics*, and *Ideas*.

The team brainstorms 8–10 stimulus words or objects that are unrelated to the problem. The facilitator records these on the prepared flip chart *(Idea Source)*. See example *Shared Copier—In Use When Needed*.

Next, the team identifies characteristics such as material, parts, uses, features, etc., for the first stimulus word, as shown in the example *(File Cabinet)*.

Characteristics are recorded and discussed, compared, analyzed, and connected in thought; these are also connected in the search for a problem solution or an improvement idea for the stated problem, issue, or concern.

This process continues until the team has exhausted all possibilities with the particular word or object.

The facilitator records useful ideas and restarts the process with the next word or object *(Fax Machine)*.

Finally, all meaningful, high potential solutions are recorded for further

Shared Copier—In Use When Needed

Idea Source	Characteristics	Ideas
File Cabinet	– Contains files – Four drawers – Is metallic – Has handles – Name plates – Can be locked – Stores info – Stands upright	– Can a copier be called and store repro requests – Call copier to check if not in use; receive "Not In Use" tone

Fax Machine	– Make calls
	– Receive calls
	– Has memory
	– Gives date/time
	– Makes copies
	– Stores calls
	– Stores documents
	– Remote access
	– Signals
		– Have fax send document to copier for
		  reproduction. Copier stores information and
		  rings back when repro job is completed.

Desk	– Wooden	

Storyboarding is a graphically illustrated representation of a complete story, concept, process, or implementation plan. It describes, in logical steps, all of the activities that need to be accomplished to complete a plan and demonstrate the results.

- To provide a flowchart of a process, concept, or planned activity.
- To communicate the sequential activities and requirements of planned change.
- To plan a project or develop a procedure.

Select and define problem or opportunity
➡ Identify and analyze causes or potential change
➡ Develop and plan possible solutions or change
Implement and evaluate solution or change
Measure and report solution or change results
Recognize and reward team efforts

Research/statistics
1 Creativity/innovation
Engineering
2 Project management
Manufacturing
3 Marketing/sales
Administration/documentation
Servicing/support
Customer/quality metrics
Change management

before

Information needs analysis

Brainstorming

Scenario writing

Shewhard PDCA cycle

Deming PDSA cycle

after

Mental imaging

Delphi method

Different point of view

Presentation

Run-it-by

- Storyboarding requires the complete story to be described, and illustrated text and graphics should logically sequence and display what takes place—or what should take place—from the beginning to end of the storyboard.
- Storyboarding is a highly interactive process and requires the application of various tools. A facilitator should be engaged to guide a team through the process.
- All text and graphics *must* be readable.
- A word-processing/graphics software package is needed to finalize team-produced drafts.

The team facilitator reviews the concept and required activities of storyboarding with the participants.

A flip chart is used to record brainstormed ideas or potential problems to serve as a topic for the storyboarding activity.

Once an idea has been selected, the team participants brainstorm the various required activity headings. See example *Continuous Process Improvement (CPI): Training and Development Team Start-up Process*.

Next, each activity is described and graphically illustrated on a whiteboard. All information is sorted, sequenced, and connected to reflect a process flow.

The team continues to create ideas to improve the storyboards. Detail is added until every participant is satisfied with the complete story, as shown in the example.

Finally, the draft is submitted to be finalized.

Continuous Process Improvement (CPI):
Training and Development Team Start-up Process

Note: This is a preliminary draft of a recommended process to become
active within a relatively short period of time. Your suggestions to
improve or enhance this process are important to us!

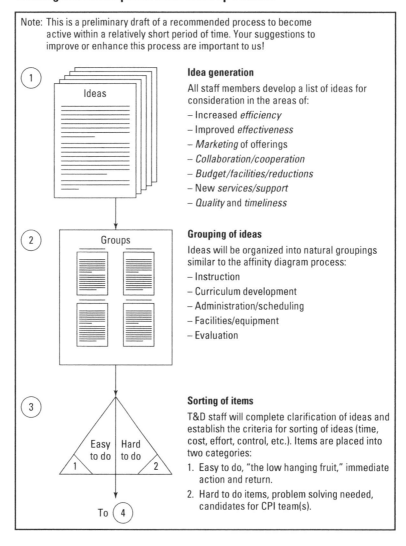

Idea generation

All staff members develop a list of ideas for
consideration in the areas of:

– Increased *efficiency*
– Improved *effectiveness*
– *Marketing* of offerings
– *Collaboration/cooperation*
– *Budget/facilities/reductions*
– New *services/support*
– *Quality* and *timeliness*

Grouping of ideas

Ideas will be organized into natural groupings
similar to the affinity diagram process:

– Instruction
– Curriculum development
– Administration/scheduling
– Facilities/equipment
– Evaluation

Sorting of items

T&D staff will complete clarification of ideas and
establish the criteria for sorting of ideas (time,
cost, effort, control, etc.). Items are placed into
two categories:

1. Easy to do, "the low hanging fruit," immediate
   action and return.
2. Hard to do items, problem solving needed,
   candidates for CPI team(s).

Continuous Process Improvement (CPI):
Training and Development Team Start-up Process *continued*

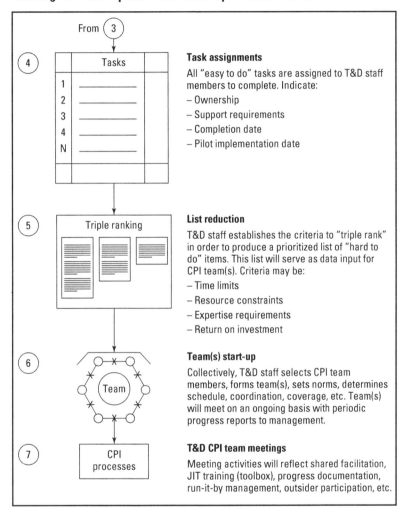

From ③

4 Tasks

1 _____
2 _____
3 _____
4 _____
N _____

Task assignments

All "easy to do" tasks are assigned to T&D staff members to complete. Indicate:
– Ownership
– Support requirements
– Completion date
– Pilot implementation date

5 Triple ranking

List reduction

T&D staff establishes the criteria to "triple rank" in order to produce a prioritized list of "hard to do" items. This list will serve as data input for CPI team(s). Criteria may be:
– Time limits
– Resource constraints
– Expertise requirements
– Return on investment

6 Team

Team(s) start-up

Collectively, T&D staff selects CPI team members, forms team(s), sets norms, determines schedule, coordination, coverage, etc. Team(s) will meet on an ongoing basis with periodic progress reports to management.

7 CPI processes

T&D CPI team meetings

Meeting activities will reflect shared facilitation, JIT training (toolbox), progress documentation, run-it-by management, outsider participation, etc.

The stratification method stratifies (separates) an existing set of data into sub-groups to determine what effect each subgroup of data has on an abnormal pattern or condition. Stratification helps in isolating and unmasking the real cause of a problem.

- To isolate abnormalities among data sets.
- To break down and analyze abnormal distributions.
- To verify the effects of subgroups to identify cause(s).
- To identify root causes of total variation.
- To analyze data to discover improvement opportunities.

➡ Select and define problem or opportunity
➡ Identify and analyze causes or potential change
   Develop and plan possible solutions or change
   Implement and evaluate solution or change
➡ Measure and report solution or change results
   Recognize and reward team efforts

1	Research/statistics
	Creativity/innovation
5	Engineering
2	Project management
3	Manufacturing
6	Marketing/sales
	Administration/documentation
4	Servicing/support
7	Customer/quality metrics
	Change management

- Encode and designate all subgroups plotted. Preferably add the "total group" graph for instant comparisons. Apply the 3:4 ratio graph construction rule.

before

Linechart

Frequency distribution (FD)

Data collection strategy

Checksheet

Observation

after

Variance analysis

Problem specification

Potential problem analysis (PPA)

Trend analysis

Stratum chart

Collect and verify data to be plotted. See example *Shipping Errors Over 8 Weeks*.

	Wk 1	2	3	4	5	6	7	8
Company Total:	40	32	30	34	41	29	39	27
Workshift A	28	20	21	19	33	18	22	18
Workshift B	8	7	4	8	3	6	10	4
Workshift C	4	5	5	7	5	5	7	5

Construct a stratification chart. The height of the vertical axis should be 75 percent of the length (100 percent) of the horizontal axis (3:4 ratio rule).

Plot the data using the error totals for 8 weeks of all 3 workshifts. Also plot the company totals.

Encode plotted data, designate lines, and label axes. Date the stratification chart.

Shipping Errors Over 8 Weeks

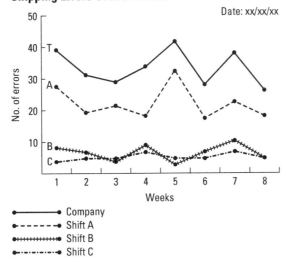

A stratum chart is an effective means to demonstrate cumulative additions of data that range from low to high and that are plotted along a horizontal time scale. Coloring or shading is used to differentiate among variables and to provide a quick interpretation of accumulation and relationships between plotted data.

- To show cumulative changes in data over time.
- To display the effect of plotted variables, each variables' gradual change over time and relationships to each other.

before

Data collection strategy

Checksheet

Frequency distribution (FD)

Trend analysis

Sampling methods

after

Major program status

Process analysis

Monthly assessment schedule

Information needs analysis

Presentation

➡ Select and define problem or opportunity

➡ Identify and analyze causes or potential change

Develop and plan possible solutions or change

➡ Implement and evaluate solution or change

➡ Measure and report solution or change results

Recognize and reward team efforts

1	Research/statistics
	Creativity/innovation
2	Engineering
	Project management
3	Manufacturing
	Marketing/sales
	Administration/documentation
4	Servicing/support
	Customer/quality metrics
	Change management

- Lines or curves cannot overlap.
- Coloring or shading is needed to demonstrate the effect of cumulative changes in data plotted.

Collect historical data for variables to be plotted. See example *TQM-Related Start-up Costs*.

Scale the stratum chart to allow for highest cumulative number.

Plot the data along the horizontal time scale as shown in the example.

Color or provide pattern shading for variable data plotted.

Check the stratum chart for accuracy and provide date of issue.

TQM Related Start-up Costs

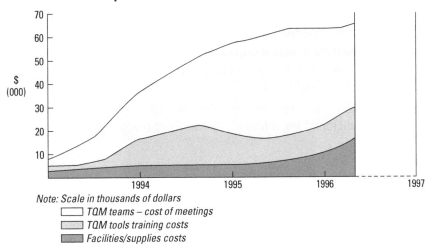

Note: Scale in thousands of dollars
- TQM teams – cost of meetings
- TQM tools training costs
- Facilities/supplies costs

The surveying technique is used to collect large amounts of written or verbal data from customers, employees, or other sources in a very objective, efficient, and organized manner. Applied survey methods such as questionnaires, interviews, observations, and focus groups can provide great flexibility in format and content and usually use data collection instruments that have a high degree of validity and reliability. The type of survey to be used is determined by a team or researcher.

- To collect data for the purpose of solving problems, verifying customer satisfaction, or comparing performance against organizational goals.
- To collect data from a large group of employees to verify job satisfaction, employee morale, or communication problems among organizational units.
- To obtain data, general to specific, on customer perception of quality on products or services.
- To acquire benchmarking information and "best practices" data.

before

Data collection strategy

Random numbers generator

Interview technique

Questionnaires

Observation

after

Frequency distribution (FD)

Response data encoding form

Thematic content analysis

Descriptive statistics

Hypothesis testing (chi-square)

➥ Select and define problem or opportunity	**1** Research/statistics
➥ Identify and analyze causes or potential change	Creativity/innovation
Develop and plan possible solutions or change	Engineering
Implement and evaluate solution or change	Project management
➥ Measure and report solution or change results	Manufacturing
Recognize and reward team efforts	**3** Marketing/sales
	Administration/documentation
	4 Servicing/support
	2 Customer/quality metrics
	5 Change management

Comparison of Survey Methods

Advantages	Mailed Questionnaires	Mass Administered Questionnaires	Face-to-Face Interviews	Self-Administered Questionnaires (Face-to-Face)	Telephone Interviews
• Low cost	High	Med.	Low	Low	Med.
• Speed	Low	High	Low	Low	High
• Anonymity	High	Med.	Low	Med.	Low
• Immediate response— no time pressure	High	Med.	Low	Med.	Low
• Ability to obtain a valid sample from the population*	Low	Low	High	High	Med.
• No interviewer bias	High	Med.	Low	Med.	Low
• Establishing rapport with respondent	Low	Med.	High	Med.	Med.
• Ability to ask complex questions	Low	Med.	High	Med.	Med.
• Ability to get full, detailed responses	Low	Low	High	Low	Med.

* Note: Always refer to a sample size determination table.

A team determines the specific data needed and identifies the data source, and defines the population to be sampled and surveyed.

Team consensus is reached on the type of survey to be used (questionnaires, interviews, observations, focus groups) and the formatting of the data collection instrument.

A survey instrument is developed and field-tested on the basis of valid instrument construction guidelines. See example *Development of Customer Satisfaction Surveys*.

Refer to a more detailed description of the development and administration of the following types of surveys and related tools in this handbook:

- Questionnaires
- Interview technique
- Observation
- Focus group

- Data collection strategy
- Sampling methods
- Random numbers generator
- Response data encoding form

Development of Customer Satisfaction Surveys

Survey Instrument Goal: To obtain written responses on a particular product or service

Survey Instrument Design Considerations:

1. Keep the instrument short. Only ask questions that are absolutely necessary.
2. Restrict the instrument to a single issue, if possible.
3. Provide a cover letter that explains the purpose of the survey, respondent selection process, and the issue of confidentiality. State the return date.
4. Write explicit instructions on how to answer the questions for the respondent.
5. Utilize terms that are clearly understood. Avoid *loaded* words and phrases, avoid jargon.
6. Determine how response data will be analyzed, tested, and displayed.
7. Avoid rank order questions; difficult to analyze.
8. Encode each response when using rating scales.
9. **Development of questions:**
   – Start with nonthreatening, easy to answer.
   – Use general before specific.
   – Use open-ended only if all possible responses are not known.
   – Use multiple-choice for increased data volume.
   – Phrase in positive, rather than in the negative.
   – Avoid researcher bias or prejudice when phrasing.
10. Pretest the instrument for reliability and content validity.

The SWOT analysis is an effective tool to define a situation currently faced by an organization. This analysis identifies internal and external environmental characteristics such as organizational strengths, weaknesses, opportunities, and threats. This tool is instrumental in the strategic planning and goal-setting process.

- To assess the relevant characteristics within an organization in order to verify its strengths and weaknesses.
- To evaluate organizational health.
- To plan for and position an organization in order to capitalize on future opportunities.

before

Affinity diagram
Factor analysis
Circles of knowledge
Critical dialogue
Benchmarking

after

Risk space analysis
Comparison matrix
Gap analysis
Futures wheel
What-if analysis

➥ Select and define problem or opportunity
➥ Identify and analyze causes or potential change
➥ Develop and plan possible solutions or change
　 Implement and evaluate solution or change
　 Measure and report solution or change results
　 Recognize and reward team efforts

1　Research/statistics
　　 Creativity/innovation
　　 Engineering
3　Project management
　　 Manufacturing
　　 Marketing/sales
　　 Administration/documentation
　　 Servicing/support
　　 Customer/quality metrics
2　Change management

- Strengths - Weaknesses - Opportunities - Threats (SWOT) definitions:
  - Strengths: Organizational resources and capabilities available to meet tactical and strategic business goals.
  - Weaknesses: Organizational deficiencies that may inhibit or limit business goal attainment.
  - Opportunities: A product idea, technological change, favorable trend, or market niche that could greatly improve an organization's position in the marketplace.
  - Threats: Performance barriers or obstacles, unfavorable business trends, or operational problems that may have an adverse effect on the organization.

The team engages a facilitator who has considerable experience in organizational analysis.

The facilitator explains the SWOT analysis technique to the participants and draws four headings on a whiteboard or flip charts. These are strengths, weaknesses, opportunities, and threats.

Participants identify items under each heading. The facilitator records them under respective headings. See example *Organizational Positioning Using SWOT Analysis*.

Once the team has slowed generating items, recorded information is reviewed for appropriateness and completeness.

The information is dated and presented to the planning team or committee.

Organizational Positioning Using SWOT Analysis

SWOT Analysis		Date: xx/xx/xx
Team: *Improvers*	**Organization:** *Alpha Research Group*	**Contact:** *W.J.M.*
Internal Analysis		
Strengths	**Weaknesses**	
Good reputation Proprietary materials Technical expertise On-time delivery Strong research capability Process/product innovations	Cannot always meet demand Limited resources Average marketing skills Limited product line Frequent prioritizing	
External Analysis		
Opportunities	**Threats**	
Sell tools for teams on internet Develop custom tools workshops Train-the-trainer Diversify into related services	Consultants reducing fees Loss of interest in TQM work ethic "Stealing shamelessly" by others "Retiree" competitors	

The symbolic flowchart is a useful problem-solving tool for teams in that it visually describes a sequence of specified steps in a work activity. Using a set of standard symbols for certain types of tasks, the flowchart helps to understand the current process and provides the team with insight for the redesign or improvement of the process.

- To analyze basic segments of work, movement of material, and information, and to check if work cells are placed in the most logical place.
- To ensure the understanding of a process by all participants of a problem-solving team.
- To verify work sequence and flow in order to simplify work.
- To reveal no longer needed activities, bottlenecks, redundant tasks, and unnecessarily complex procedures.

before

Systems analysis diagram

Process mapping

Process flowchart

Work flow analysis (WFA)

Process analysis

after

Facility layout diagram

Activity analysis

Cycle time flowchart

Value/non-value-added cycle time

Action plan

➡ Select and define problem or opportunity

➡ Identify and analyze causes or potential change

➡ Develop and plan possible solutions or change

➡ Implement and evaluate solution or change

  Measure and report solution or change results

  Recognize and reward team efforts

  Research/statistics

  Creativity/innovation

3 Engineering

2 Project management

4 Manufacturing

  Marketing/sales

  Administration/documentation

5 Servicing/support

  Customer/quality metrics

1 Change management

- Standard symbols:

  Start or stop   Activity   Meeting

  Document   Decision point   Connector

  ──────▸ Process flow   - - - - -▸ Rework

- A flowchart is drawn from top to bottom and reflects left to right directionality. Avoid crossing flow lines within the chart; use connectors within and from page to page.

The team facilitator assembles a team of participants who have knowledge of the overall process selected to be flowcharted. See example *Facilitate a Process-Mapping Worksho*p.

Participants determine the process start and stop points. Additional discussion should determine the level of detail to be shown.

Next, all major activities and other steps are identified and associated with a standard set of symbols. Symbols and connecting flow lines are used to show process activity and sequence.

The facilitator draws the flowchart on a whiteboard, makes changes, and then continues until the team decides that the complete process has been flowcharted.

Finally, the flowchart is checked by the participants for completeness and to ensure that all symbols are sequenced and interconnected correctly.

The symbolic flowchart is dated and saved for future reference.

Facilitate a Process Mapping Workshop

Date: xx/xx/xx

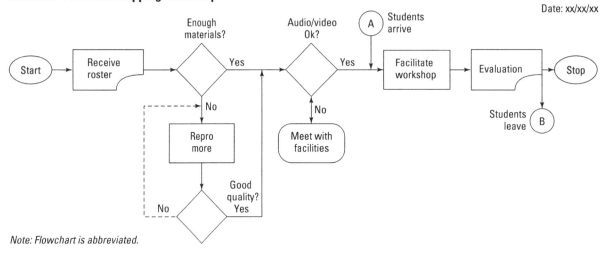

Note: Flowchart is abbreviated.

A system analysis diagram is a tool that systematically illustrates the process flow from the supply side (or input of resources), to the transformation or throughput of product or services, to the output side for final quality verification and release to the customer. This diagram helps to identify interrelationships of major tasks, work phases, and opportunities for improvements through the use of feedback loops at the organization and the customer levels.

- To overview the sequential production or service processes, lines of communication, and quality feedback loops.
- To reach a common understanding using the systems approach.
- To clarify roles, task responsibilities, and system requirements.

before

Block diagram

Organization chart

Organization mapping

House of quality

Process analysis

after

Process mapping

Symbolic flowchart

Cycle time flowchart

Work flow analysis (WFA)

Value/non-value-added cycle time chart

➡ Select and define problem or opportunity

➡ Identify and analyze causes or potential change

➡ Develop and plan possible solutions or change

   Implement and evaluate solution or change

   Measure and report solution or change results

   Recognize and reward team efforts

   Research/statistics

   Creativity/innovation

3 Engineering

2 Project management

6 Manufacturing

   Marketing/sales

5 Administration/documentation

4 Servicing/support

   Customer/quality metrics

1 Change management

- Other headings or designations can be substituted for the generic systems analysis diagram headings:

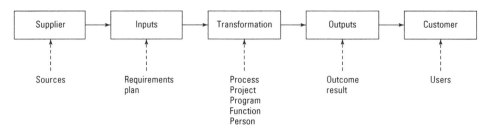

The team develops a Systems Analysis Diagram consisting of five blocks, interconnected, and with internal and external feedback loops added. See example *Application of Major TQM Tools—System Analysis*.

The blocks are designated to contain processing or requirements information as shown in the example.

Using the completed Systems Analysis Diagram as a guide, the team explores potential problem areas and process improvement opportunities.

Application of Major TQM Tools—System Analysis

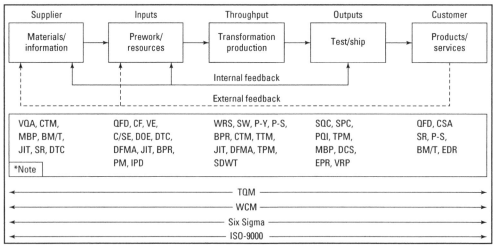

*Note: See tools description chart for definition of the above.

A task analysis is a systematic process used to break down a job into smaller and smaller activities and to identify the skills and knowledge requirements needed to perform the job. This process can also be useful to identify training requirements, tools and equipment, work instructions, and procedure manuals. Task analysis documents provide input data needed to develop training programs and job descriptions.

- To breakdown a job and analyze identified tasks for the purpose of determining skill and knowledge requirements.
- To identify the specific attributes of a complex job.
- To compare the actual performance of a job to the desired performance level.

before

Needs analysis
Activity analysis
Cluster analysis
Symbolic flowchart
Work flow analysis (WFA)

after

Milestones chart
Action plan
Activity cost matrix
Project planning log
Resource requirements matrix

	Select and define problem or opportunity
	Identify and analyze causes or potential change
➥	Develop and plan possible solutions or change
➥	Implement and evaluate solution or change
	Measure and report solution or change results
	Recognize and reward team efforts

1	Research/statistics
	Creativity/innovation
	Engineering
2	Project management
	Manufacturing
	Marketing/sales
3	Administration/documentation
	Servicing/support
4	Customer/quality metrics
	Change management

- A task analysis breaks down any job into duties, tasks, elements of the task, and skill and knowledge requirements to perform the tasks, and it could also indicate task sequence and frequency. On the basis of this data, a training program, work instructions, or a job description can be developed.
- Numbering schema for job-duty-task-element identification:

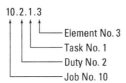

10.2.1.3
- Element No. 3
- Task No. 1
- Duty No. 2
- Job No. 10

First the job analyst reviews the objective and the process of the task analysis. See example *Development of a Training Program*.

Next, all duties of the job are identified and recorded on a whiteboard as shown in the example.

Duties are broken down into tasks. At this level, task frequency and sequence are noted.

This process continues until elements of each task have been identified and recorded on the whiteboard. Again, the sequence of element completion is recorded.

Next, the skills and knowledge required to successfully complete each element are listed. This information is added underneath each element in the task analysis flow diagram.

Lastly, team participants check every duty, task, and task element for special performance conditions or criteria.

The task analysis diagram receives a final check by participants; it is then dated and copied for future reference.

Development of a Training Program

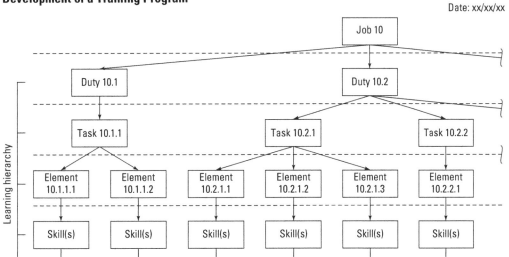

Example: *Job #10*: Final inspector-assembly
Duty 10.1: Circuit Testing
Task 10.1.1: Power-up/down functions
Elements 10.1.1.1: Components A1, C1, toggle switches
Skills and knowledge: Electronic circuit schematics, test equipment, and simulators

The team meeting evaluation surveys provide timely feedback on the effectiveness of the problem-solving process, team dynamics, and the administrative procedures used to ensure that the team stays focused and is moving toward its goals.

- To evaluate a team's process and progress.
- To periodically monitor the effectiveness of team meetings.
- To search for areas of improvements.

	Select and define problem or opportunity
➡	Identify and analyze causes or potential change
	Develop and plan possible solutions or change
	Implement and evaluate solution or change
➡	Measure and report solution or change results
➡	Recognize and reward team efforts

	Research/statistics
	Creativity/innovation
	Engineering
3	Project management
	Manufacturing
	Marketing/sales
	Administration/documentation
	Servicing/support
2	Customer/quality metrics
1	Change management

before

Circle response

Buzz group

Surveying

Relationship map

Interview technique

after

Rotating roles

Team process assessment

Sociogram

Different point of view

Critical dialogue

- Participants' completed meeting evaluation forms should be summarized after each meeting and process/progress results fed back to the team. Use the team process assessment tool for this purpose.
- The use of Likert scale designations (very satisfactory to very unsatisfactory, strongly agree to strongly disagree, etc.) is best determined by the team.

After every team meeting, or periodically if the team decides it, participants fill out the team evaluation survey form.

The team leader or team facilitator summarizes all responses and compares the results with those of the previous meeting. Of particular interest may be the rating averages and any patterns or variations from the expected results.

The rating results and suggestions made are discussed at the beginning of the next scheduled team meeting.

All completed forms should be dated and saved for pattern analysis.

Team Meeting Feedback

Team: *Mfg.–No. 1*	Meeting Evaluation No. 3			Date *xx/xx/xx*	
Please evaluate this meeting by circling your choice 5 = Very satisfactory; 4 = Satisfactory; 3 = Average; 2 = Unsatisfactory; 1 = Very unsatisfactory					
Your observation/perception					
1. The team meeting started/ended on time	(5)	4	3	2	1
2. The agenda was displayed and followed	(5)	4	3	2	1
3. Team members understood meeting's purpose	5	(4)	3	2	1
4. The team's action log was reviewed	5	(4)	3	2	1
5. All team members participated	5	4	(3)	2	1
6. The facilitator kept meeting on topic	5	(4)	3	2	1
7. Team communications were open and supportive	5	(4)	3	2	1
8. The team managed time efficiently	(5)	4	3	2	1
9. Good progress was made during this meeting	(5)	4	3	2	1
10. Team used appropriate decision-making methods	5	(4)	3	2	1
11. Next step action items were assigned	(5)	4	3	2	1
12. The facilitator summarized results	(5)	4	3	2	1
Any suggestions? _____					
Thank You	5s	4s	3s	2s	1s
Total circled	6	5	1	0	0
Total score:	53				
File: Team–Mfg.–No. 1 Average rating:	4.42				

The team mirror technique is used to compare and evaluate team dynamics and performance. It allows teams to view each other and perform a mutual analysis of team effectiveness. All observations are shared for the purpose of furthering team development.

- To allow teams to share perceptions and suggest ways for improved cooperation among teams.
- To train teams.
- To improve team effectiveness.

before

Consensus decision making

Sociogram

Influence diagram

Circle response

Buzz group

after

Team meeting evaluation

Rotating roles

Team process assessment

Different point of view

Fishbowls

Select and define problem or opportunity
Identify and analyze causes or potential change
➡ Develop and plan possible solutions or change
Implement and evaluate solution or change
Measure and report solution or change results
➡ Recognize and reward team efforts

Research/statistics

Creativity/innovation

Engineering

Project management

Manufacturing

Marketing/sales

Administration/documentation

2 Servicing/support

Customer/quality metrics

1 Change management

- This analysis requires one large and one small room for joint and separate team meetings.

Teams agree to mutually analyze their effectiveness and engage an outside facilitator.

The facilitator reviews the team mirror process with both teams and displays a few questions on a flip chart. Both teams are asked to respond to:
- How are we doing?
- How are they doing?
- How do they think we are doing?
- How can we improve?
- How can they improve?
- How can we work together to improve?

One of the teams is asked to move to a separate room (or both teams if two rooms are available) so they can discuss and record their responses. See example *Team Effectiveness Training*.

After approximately 30 minutes both teams rejoin and exchange responses.

Next, the facilitator leads a discussion on improvement opportunities and the teams reach consensus on what changes can be made to increase the effectiveness of both teams.

Team Effectiveness Training

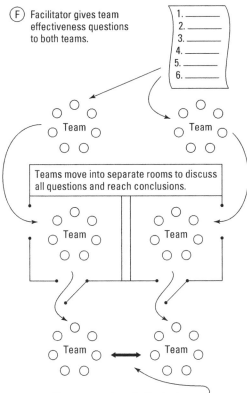

(F) Facilitator gives team effectiveness questions to both teams.

1. _____
2. _____
3. _____
4. _____
5. _____
6. _____

Team

Team

Teams move into separate rooms to discuss all questions and reach conclusions.

Team

Team

Team

Team

Teams present each other's views.

(F) Facilitator leads discussion, teams share ideas and reach consensus on changes to be made to improve team interactions and effectiveness.

The team process assessment technique verifies team performance using a Likert rating scale. Areas of interest such as problem-solving activities, team dynamics, and administrative procedures are rated, and results are fed back to the team for the purpose of continuous improvement.

- To rate a team's process and progress.
- To monitor the effectiveness of team meetings.
- To provide performance feedback.

before

Team meeting evaluation

Surveying

Questionnaires

Interview technique

Gap analysis

after

Rotating roles

Different point of view

Run-it-by

Critical dialogue

What-if-analysis

➥ Select and define problem or opportunity

➥ Identify and analyze causes or potential change

➥ Develop and plan possible solutions or change

    Implement and evaluate solution or change

    Measure and report solution or change results

➥ Recognize and reward team efforts

- Rating averages used:

$\bar{X}$ = item average (sum of item ratings ÷ 8)

$\bar{\bar{X}}$ = overall team average

    (sum of all item ratings ÷ 96)

- Rating scale used: 5 = Very satisfactory

                        4 = Satisfactory

                        3 = Average

                        2 = Unsatisfactory

                        1 = Very unsatisfactory

    Research/statistics

    Creativity/innovation

    Engineering

2   Project management

    Manufacturing

    Marketing/sales

4   Administration/documentation

    Servicing/support

3   Customer/quality metrics

1   Change management

The team leader or facilitator collects all completed team meeting evaluations from the participants. See example *Team Mfg.—No. 1 Assessment*.

Next, all responses are summarized and results are compared to those of the previous analysis. Of particular interest may be the rating averages and any patterns or variations from the expected results.

The rating results and suggestions made by participants are discussed at the beginning of the next scheduled team meeting.

All completed forms are dated and saved for pattern analysis.

Team: Mfg.– No. 1 Assessment

Team: *Mfg.–No. 1* Meeting Evaluation No. 3										Date *xx/xx/xx*
Participants' Observations/Perceptions	**Participant Responses**									**($\bar{X}$)**
1. The team meeting started/ended on time	5	4	5	4	3	4	4	5	—	—	4.25
2. The agenda was displayed and followed	5	3	4	4	5	5	4	5	—	—	4.38
3. Team members understood meeting's purpose	4	4	3	5	3	3	4	5	—	—	3.88
4. The team's action log was reviewed	4	5	4	5	5	5	5	5	—	—	4.75
5. All team members participated	3	2	3	2	3	1	4	3	—	—	2.63
6. The facilitator kept meeting on topic	4	5	4	3	5	5	5	4	—	—	4.38
7. Team communications were open and supportive	4	4	4	5	3	4	5	3	—	—	4.00
8. The team managed time efficiently	5	4	5	4	4	3	3	5	—	—	4.13
9. Good progress was made during this meeting	5	5	4	3	4	3	4	5	—	—	4.13
10. Team used appropriate decision-making methods	4	4	3	1	2	3	5	4	—	—	3.25
11. Next step action items were assigned	5	3	4	3	4	3	5	4	—	—	3.88
12. The facilitator summarized results	5	4	4	4	5	5	5	4	—	—	4.50
File: Team–Mfg.–No. 1									**Overall team average $\bar{\bar{X}}$ = 4.01**	

Notes: 1. See Team Meeting Evaluation Survey
      2. Rating responses: 5 = very satisfactory; 4 = satisfactory; 3 = average; 2 = unsatisfactory; 1 = very unsatisfactory

A thematic content analysis is used to surface clusters or patterns of related data among raw data collected from survey respondents. The purpose for this analysis is to identify major recurring themes that reflect respondents' concerns or perceived problems.

- To uncover concerns, issues, or potential problems in an organizational survey results analysis.
- To count and allocate similar responses into category or major themes.
- To identify related data clusters or patterns among respondents' data.

before

Data collection strategy

Focus group

Surveying

Interview technique

Questionnaires

after

Cluster analysis

Customer satisfaction analysis (CSA)

Consensus decision making

Different point of view

Response data encoding form

Select and define problem or opportunity
➡ Identify and analyze causes or potential change
➡ Develop and plan possible solutions or change
Implement and evaluate solution or change
➡ Measure and report solution or change results
Recognize and reward team efforts

- Typical raw data collection methods are mailed questionnaires, various types of surveys, focus groups, and interviews.

1 Research/statistics

Creativity/innovation

Engineering

Project management

Manufacturing

2 Marketing/sales

Administration/documentation

Servicing/support

3 Customer/quality metrics

Change management

Upon the completion of an organizational survey, employee opinion survey, or other data collection effort, the response data is sorted and identified for a thematic content analysis. See example *Organizational Support for Self-Directed Work Teams*.

A thematic content analysis form is prepared by the data analyst. This form is used to record the responses of interest.

All data are examined and similar responses are combined for each question of interest. Frequency data of how often this response was given is also recorded as shown in the example.

Finally, when all meaningful response data have been recorded and summarized, major themes are identified using linkages, as shown in the example.

The completed document is dated and presented to the quality department's management for further action.

Organizational Support for Self-Directed Work Teams

Raw Data Source: Responses from the SDWT Questionnaires
Example:
Q #8: What is the perception of the current state of team support?
Q #11: What needs to be done to improve interteam communications?
Q #13: What additional resources are needed?

Date: xx/xx/xx

Response Clusters	Frequency	Major Themes
Q #8: – Lack of mgmt. commitment	ⅢⅢ I	
– Not enough support	III	
– Not a high priority	ⅢⅢ III	Lack of time
– Don't have time	ⅢⅢ ⅢⅢ	
Q #11: – Newsletter on team results	II	
– Top mgmt. involvement	ⅢⅢ ⅢⅢ	Management commitment
– Cross-functional sessions	III	for teaming?
– Share lessons learned	ⅢⅢ I	
Q #13: – IPDT training	II	
– Increase meeting time	IIII	
– Require tools training	ⅢⅢ III	More tools
– Need problem-solving tools	ⅢⅢ ⅢⅢ I	training required
– Facilitators	III	

The time study sheet is a recording form that displays the cycle time used to complete a task on the first attempt, second attempt, and so on. It can potentially identify a trend or pattern caused by some process variation or change in the use of tools, layout, or sequence steps. The form is also used to show calculations such as average cycle time, various adjustments, and recommended time to be recorded as a standard.

- To establish criteria of performance.
- To calculate average cycle times for performing tasks.
- To collect cycle time data for constructing a cycle time flow chart.

before

Data collection strategy
Observation
Activity analysis
Checksheet
Task analysis

after

Process analysis
Problem specification
Potential problem analysis (PPA)
Variance analysis
Cycle time flow chart

➥	Select and define problem or opportunity
➥	Identify and analyze causes or potential change
	Develop and plan possible solutions or change
➥	Implement and evaluate solution or change
➥	Measure and report solution or change results
	Recognize and reward team efforts

	Research/statistics
	Creativity/innovation
2	Engineering
3	Project management
1	Manufacturing
	Marketing/sales
	Administration/documentation
	Servicing/support
	Customer/quality metrics
4	Change management

- Record cycle time in seconds, minutes, or hours.
- Make adjustments for performing difficult task elements.
- Make allowances for variations in working conditions.

Identify the tasks and elements to be measured. List them on the time study sheet. See example *Calculating Average Cycle Time for Spring Assembly*.

Determine how often elements of the task are to be measured and take measurements. Record measurements and calculate average cycle time ($\bar{X}$CT).

Note any difficulties; make allowances as deemed appropriate.

Summarize and date the time study sheet as shown in this example.

Calculating Average Cycle Time for Spring Assembly

Time Study Sheet (Recording Cycle Time)											Date xx/xx/xx
Task ID#	**Element Name and ID#**	**Cycles—Repeated Measures**								**$\bar{X}$**	**Observations on Difficulties and Allowances**
		1	**2**	**3**	**4**	**5**	**6**	**7**	**8**		
1	1A. Attach washer, thread nut	8	10	12	9	12	10			10.2	
	1B. Tighten screw to base	10	12	15	16	11	18			13.7	
	1C. Tension spring to spec	25	35	40	28	32	51			35.2	Often difficult to tension
	1D. Measure spring tension	8	12	7	15	9	8			9.8	
2											

Task ID# 1: Total cycle time per task/elements   413

Number of cycle time measures   24

☒ Seconds   ☐ Minutes   ☐ Hours $\bar{X}$CT: 69

Difficulty adjustment: 10

Allowance adjustment: 0

Allowed time: 79

Notes: – $\bar{X}$CT = average cycle time (413 ÷ 6 = 68.8).
– Recheck allowed time periodically.

A timeline chart is used to plot data fluctuations over time. The chart displays trends, patterns, and shifts that may be very useful in problem analysis, measuring change results, or showing trends that may require immediate action.

- To show yields, trendlines, or patterns that may be used to formulate a problem specification.
- To measure results of process changes.
- To track data over time.

before

Data collection strategy

Frequency distribution (FD)

Checksheet

Defect map

Cluster analysis

after

Trend analysis

Monthly assessment schedule

Starbursting

Problem specification

What-if analysis

Select and define problem or opportunity
➥ Identify and analyze causes or potential change
Develop and plan possible solutions or change
Implement and evaluate solution or change
➥ Measure and report solution or change results
Recognize and reward team efforts

4	Research/statistics
	Creativity/innovation
	Engineering
1	Project management
	Manufacturing
	Marketing/sales
3	Administration/documentation
	Servicing/support
2	Customer/quality metrics
	Change management

- Timeline construction: *Time* is always represented on the horizontal axis, frequency and percentage is shown on the vertical axis.

As a preliminary activity, a data collection process records data on a checksheet or some other record.

A timeline chart is drawn. Time intervals are evenly spaced across the horizontal axis, and frequency or percentage is scaled on the vertical axis.

The data (data points) are plotted across the timeline chart, and lines are drawn to connect the data points to show a continuous timeline. See example *Total Monthly TQM Meeting Hours*.

A monthly hours average is computed and drawn on the chart, as shown in this example.

Finally, the timeline chart is checked for data accuracy and dated.

Total Monthly TQM Meeting Hours

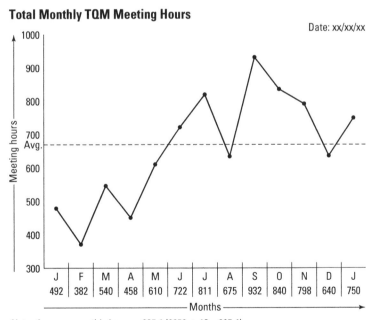

Date: xx/xx/xx

	J	F	M	A	M	J	J	A	S	O	N	D	J
	492	382	540	458	610	722	811	675	932	840	798	640	750

Months

Note: Average monthly hours = 665.4 (8650 ÷ 13 = 665.4)

A top-down flow chart illustrates the major steps in an organizational work process or project. It shows the essential requirements, sequenced from left to right, with a number of substeps listed below each step. This flow chart has an advantage of showing the complete process without too much detail, therefore allowing a team to quickly understand the problem solving or process-improvement opportunities of the process.

- To display all necessary steps in a work process or project.
- To provide an overall picture of a top-level process.

before

Storyboarding

Systems analysis diagram

House of quality

Process selection matrix

Information needs analysis

after

Basili data collection method

Process analysis

Action plan

Resource requirements matrix

Gantt chart

Select and define problem or opportunity
➡ Identify and analyze causes or potential change
➡ Develop and plan possible solutions or change
Implement and evaluate solution or change
Measure and report solution or change results
Recognize and reward team efforts

Research/statistics
Creativity/innovation
1 Engineering
2 Project management
4 Manufacturing
Marketing/sales
Administration/documentation
Servicing/support
Customer/quality metrics
3 Change management

- Designations of Top-Down Flow Chart elements:

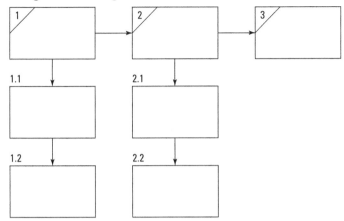

– Recommendation: A top-down flow chart does not exceed seven process steps (across) and no more than five substeps (top-down).

A facilitator explains the purpose of a top-down flow chart to the team participants. The team identifies the process.

The participants identify essential, major process steps.

Team consensus is reached to select a final 5–7 process steps to be drawn on a whiteboard or flip chart. See example *Motorola's Model of "Six Steps to Six Sigma Quality."*

The facilitator draws the top-down flow chart and asks participants to provide 4–5 substeps for each process step drawn.

Identified substeps are discussed, changed, and finally listed under each major step.

Finally, the facilitator provides numerical identification numbers and substep level numbers and dates the flow chart, as shown in the example.

Motorola's Model of "Six Steps to Six Sigma Quality"

Date: xx/xx/xx

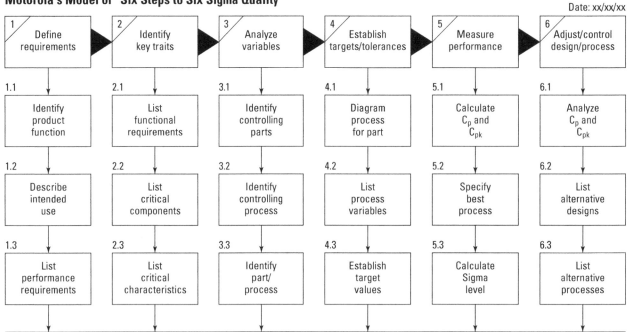

| 1 | Define requirements | 2 | Identify key traits | 3 | Analyze variables | 4 | Establish targets/tolerances | 5 | Measure performance | 6 | Adjust/control design/process |

| 1.1 Identify product function | 2.1 List functional requirements | 3.1 Identify controlling parts | 4.1 Diagram process for part | 5.1 Calculate C_p and C_{pk} | 6.1 Analyze C_p and C_{pk} |

| 1.2 Describe intended use | 2.2 List critical components | 3.2 Identify controlling process | 4.2 List process variables | 5.2 Specify best process | 6.2 List alternative designs |

| 1.3 List performance requirements | 2.3 List critical characteristics | 3.3 Identify part/ process | 4.3 Establish target values | 5.3 Calculate Sigma level | 6.3 List alternative processes |

Note: Only a partial flowdown of requirements is shown.

A tree diagram systematically maps out the detail of smaller activities required to complete a project or reach a primary goal. This tool helps to break down the complexity by logically identifying lower levels of tasks or elements. As a planning tool, it reflects all necessary activities and supporting means to successfully implement a program.

- To logically branch out or flow down levels of detail of projects, problems, or primary goals.
- To break down large activities or goals into smaller and specific tasks.

before

Affinity diagram

Interrelationship digraph (I.D.)

Systems analysis diagram

Symbolic flowchart

Prioritization matrix

after

Activity network diagram

Process decision program chart

Matrix diagram

Five whys

What-if analysis

➡ Select and define problem or opportunity
➡ Identify and analyze causes or potential change
➡ Develop and plan possible solutions or change
    Implement and evaluate solution or change
    Measure and report solution or change results
    Recognize and reward team efforts

    Research/statistics
    Creativity/innovation
    Engineering
2 Project management
    Manufacturing
    Marketing/sales
3 Administration/documentation
    Servicing/support
4 Customer/quality metrics
1 Change management

• Numerical indexing example: Levels of detail.

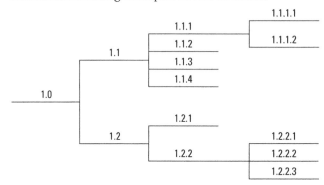

First, determine the project, problem, or primary goal for the tree diagram. This is the first level of detail. See example *Preliminary Planning for Six Sigma Quality.*

Identify the major areas or activities that need to be considered and indicate these as branch headings for the second level of detail.

Continue to break down major areas (branches) into smaller tasks or elements, labeling each branch as shown. This is the third level, etc.

Continue this detailing as required to create lower level branches. At this point, if using the tree diagram as a problem-solving tool, start to identify and circle most likely causes of the problems.

Verify the tree diagram by retracing the branches to the lowest level, checking the logic and flow of activities, and subtasks of supporting elements.

Encode or designate each branch in accordance with the numbering schema shown in *notes and key points*. Date the diagram.

Preliminary Planning for Six Sigma Quality

Date: xx/xx/xx		1.1.1 Company goals	1.1.1.1 Policy
	1.1 Communication	1.1.2 Customers	1.1.1.2 Strategy
		1.1.3 Employees	1.1.1.3 Milestones
		1.1.4 Suppliers	
		1.2.1 Needs analysis	1.2.2.1 Aquisition
		1.2.2 Program development	1.2.2.2 In-house development
1.0 Planning for Six Sigma Quality	1.2 Training plan	1.2.3 Schedule	
		1.2.4 Training	
			1.3.1.1 Identification
		1.3.1 Establish standards	1.3.1.2 Selection
		1.3.2 Definitions	
	1.3 Metrics development	1.3.3 Link to performance	1.3.1.3 Rewards
		1.3.4 Reporting	1.3.1.4 Lessons learned
		1.4.1 Front-end design	1.4.2.1 Documentation
		1.4.2 Manufacturing	1.4.2.2 Rework rate
	1.4 Implementation issues	1.4.3 Admin. cycle time	
	1.5 Customer satisfaction		

Trend analysis tool can project, on the basis of historical data segments, the increase or decrease of what is being measured for the next time segment. Trend analysis is simply comparing performance data and calculating a projection that, if undesirable, may require immediate attention.

- To project future time segment data on the basis of time-series calculations.
- To analyze performance data trends over time.
- To show directionality and variability in measured data.

before

Data collection strategy

Checksheet

Observation

Linechart

Timeline chart

after

Starbursting

Action plan

What-if analysis

Cost-benefit analysis

Countermeasures matrix

➡ Select and define problem or opportunity

➡ Identify and analyze causes or potential change

   Develop and plan possible solutions or change

   Implement and evaluate solution or change

➡ Measure and report solution or change results

   Recognize and reward team efforts

1	Research/statistics
	Creativity/innovation
3	Engineering
2	Project management
4	Manufacturing
	Marketing/sales
	Administration/documentation
	Servicing/support
5	Customer/quality metrics
	Change management

- Recommendation: Use at least nine time intervals of historical data to calculate the "next time interval" projection for costs, defects, time lost, time used, outputs, inventory, activities, events, or other performance measures.
- Equations used to calculate a projection:

$Y^1 = a + bt$ Where: Y^1 = The prediction

a = The average

$a = \dfrac{\Sigma y}{N}$

b = The factor

t = Number of segments of time passed (*including*) the midpoint for which the projection is calculated

$b = \dfrac{\Sigma xy}{\Sigma x^2}$

Σ = The sum of

- As calculated for the example shown:

$a = \dfrac{8650}{13} = 665$ $t = 7$

$b = \dfrac{5613}{182} = 31$ $Y^1 = 665 + (31)(7) = 882$

As a preliminary step, the data collection process determines the specific performance data, the historical time period and number of time segments within, and the next time segment for which the projection is to be calculated.

An odd number of data scores (13 months in this example) is inserted into columns T and Y of the trend analysis worksheet. See example *Projecting Total TQM Meeting Hours for February.*

Column Y is multiplied by column X and the results inserted into column XY. Positive and negative totals are added, and the resultant total reflects the directionality of the trend. The respective values in column X^2 (within the brackets) are also added.

The totals of all columns are used to calculate the average (a), the factor (b), and finally, the projection (Y') as shown in *notes and key points*.

A check is made by adding the factor (b) to the calculated average (a) in column P, as shown in this example. In this case, a repeated addition of 31 for each month (August–February) will result in a February projection of 882 as calculated with $Y' = a + bt$. Note: $t = 7$, the number of segments for this calculation (July–January) as seen in column T. Ensure that the median data score is always placed in the midpoint position of column T in the trend analysis worksheet.

All calculations are verified for accuracy; the trend analysis worksheet is dated and attached to a report.

Projecting Total TQM Meeting Hours for February

	Column T	Column Y	Column X	Column XY	Column X²	Column P (Projected)	
			−10	—	100		
			− 9	—	81		
			− 8	—	64		
			− 7	—	49		
	Jan	492	− 6	− 2952	36		
	Feb	382	− 5	− 1910	25		
	Mar	540	− 4	− 2160	16		
	Apr	458	− 3	− 1374	9		
	May	610	− 2	− 1220	4		
	Jun	722	− 1	− 722	1		
Midpoint →	Jul	811	0	0	0	665 ←	(a) Avg.
	Aug	675	+ 1	+ 675	1	696 Aug	
	Sep	932	+ 2	+ 1864	4	727 Sep	
	Oct	840	+ 3	+ 2520	9	758 Oct	
	Nov	798	+ 4	+ 3192	16	789 Nov	
	Dec	640	+ 5	+ 3200	25	820 Dec	
	Jan	750	+ 6	+ 4500	36	851 Jan	
	Feb	?	+ 7	+	49		
			+ 8	+	64		
			+ 9	+	81		
			+10	+	100		
	$N = 13$	$\Sigma Y = 8650$		$\Sigma + = 15951$	$\Sigma X^2 = 182$	882 Feb ←	(p)
				$\Sigma - = 10338$			
				$\Sigma XY = +5613$			

Note: (a) = Average TQM meeting hours = 665
  (p) = Prediction for February = 882

The triple ranking tool is useful in reducing a long list of items and involves all participants in the discussion, evaluation, and ranking process. The list of items is compared to team-generated criteria, and three rounds of ranking are completed to develop a final list of items that meet the criteria. Open discussions between rounds assist in the clarification and understanding of the listed items.

- To discuss and rank items or issues in order to produce a prioritized list of items or issues necessary as a starting point to build team consensus.
- To reach team agreement on which ideas, problems, or opportunities should receive allocated resources.
- To team select what is perceived to be the most important items from a long list of items.

<table>
<tr><td></td><td>before</td></tr>
</table>

before

Brainstorming

Round robin brainstorming

Interview technique

Thematic content analysis

Affinity diagram

after

Different point of view

Project planning log

Criteria filtering

Responsibility matrix

Action plan

➡ Select and define problem or opportunity	
➡ Identify and analyze causes or potential change	
➡ Develop and plan possible solutions or change	
Implement and evaluate solution or change	
Measure and report solution or change results	
Recognize and reward team efforts	

	Research/statistics
	Creativity/innovation
	Engineering
2	Project management
	Manufacturing
4	Marketing/sales
	Administration/documentation
	Servicing/support
3	Customer/quality metrics
1	Change management

- The team decides on the criteria by which to evaluate each item.
- Three rounds of ranking occur, beginning with selecting many, then three, and finally one item per team participant.

The team decides on the criteria by which each item will be evaluated during the ranking process. The appropriate criteria for the example shown are (a) impact or consequence of effort, (b) support of organizational goals, (c) resource requirements, and (d) employee acceptance and feasibility. See example *Ideas for Quality Improvement*.

Team participants compare the list of items to agreed upon criteria. In round 1 participants choose as many of the items as they think will meet the criteria. All choices are tallied by the team facilitator.

All items that have received at least five tally marks during round 1 will be included in a now-reduced list for round 2. Further discussion and clarification takes place. Team participants explain why certain items were chosen.

Round 2 ranking takes place. This time, each team participant can choose only a maximum of three items. No one can choose a single item more than once per round.

Again the list is rewritten by the team facilitator. The items with three or more tally marks are included in the revised list.

Team participants now complete round 3 by choosing only one of the remaining items. The final list is ranked based on the number of tally marks, highest to lowest number, as shown in the example.

Ideas for Quality Improvement
(Team of Eight Participants)

Date xx/xx/xx

Round 1—Choose Many	Round 2—Choose Three	Round 3—Choose One	
Seminars II			
Surveys IIII IIII	Surveys II		
Tools IIII I	Tools III	Tools I	④
SPC III			
Work Cells IIII			
Teaming IIII I	Teaming IIII I	Teaming III	①
Training IIII II	Training IIII	Training II	③
Books III			
Memberships III			
Interviews IIII III	Interviews II		
SDWT IIII			
Decisions IIII II	Decisions II		
Tapes II			
Visits II			
Practices III			
Meetings IIII			
Customers IIII IIII IIII	Customers IIII	Customers II	②
Rewards IIII			

Note: ① ──▶ ④ Final ranking

A truth table is used to define truth values of statements (sentences) or fundamental operations of symbolic logic. Various types of logical statements or propositions stated in symbolic form can be verified for their truth value or reality. Since symbolic logic is often considered identical with Boolean algebra, truth tables are often used to determine outputs (true or false) of electronic logic gates or circuits.

- To identify relationships among a set of existing conditions.
- To illustrate logical statements using a set of predefined symbols.

before

Venn diagram

Breakdown tree

Influence diagram

Starbursting

Semantic intuition

after

Fault tree analysis

Critical dialogue

Problem specification

Different point of view

Run-it-by

➡ Select and define problem or opportunity

   Identify and analyze causes or potential change

➡ Develop and plan possible solutions or change

   Implement and evaluate solution or change

   Measure and report solution or change results

   Recognize and reward team efforts

   Research/statistics

   Creativity/innovation

1 Engineering

   Project management

   Manufacturing

   Marketing/sales

2 Administration/documentation

   Servicing/support

   Customer/quality metrics

   Change management

- Table of symbols for propositional logic

Symbol	Name	Meaning
$\wedge$	Conjunction	A and B
$\vee$	Disjunction (inclusive)	Either A or B or both
$\underline{\vee}$	Disjunction (exclusive)	Either A or B but not both
$-$	Negation	Not A
$\supset$	Conditional	If A then B
$\rightleftharpoons$	Biconditional	A if, and only if B

- Truth values:
  - A truth value of 1 means a true (T) statement, condition, or logic output of 1 (active).
  - A truth value of 0 means a false (F) statement, condition, or logic gate output of 0 (inactive).
- Truth tables:

A	B	$A \wedge B$	Negation $(-)$
T	T	T	F
T	F	F	T
F	T	F	T
F	F	F	T

A	B	$A \vee B$	$A \underline{\vee} B$
T	T	T	F
T	F	T	T
F	T	T	T
F	F	F	F

A	B	$A \supset B$	$A \rightleftharpoons B$
T	T	T	T
T	F	F	F
F	T	T	F
F	F	T	T

For additional information, refer to a text on critical thinking or reasoning.

- Basic logic gates (building blocks for logic circuits)

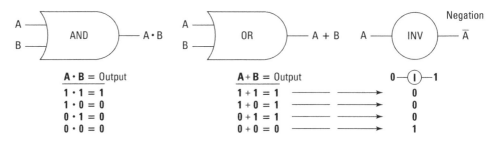

$A \cdot B$ = Output	$A + B$ = Output	
$1 \cdot 1 = 1$	$1 + 1 = 1$	0
$1 \cdot 0 = 0$	$1 + 0 = 1$	0
$0 \cdot 1 = 0$	$0 + 1 = 1$	0
$0 \cdot 0 = 0$	$0 + 0 = 0$	1

0—(I)—1

Symbol Tab	Logic	Gate	Meaning
1	True	Closed	The statement is true, the circuit is closed.
0	False	Open	The statement is false, the circuit is open.
•	Series	A and B	A is in series with B.
+	Parallel	A or B	A is in parallel with B.

A number of logical operations are drawn to produce a certain end result. See example *Telecommunication Equipment Failure*.

Logic gates are connected in an order that produces certain output indications, as shown in this example.

The completed logic circuit sketch is checked by running 1s (active) and 0s (inactive) levels through the circuit.

All input combinations are checked to produce a particular output level as demonstrated by a truth table for the circuit functions under considerations.

Telecommunication Equipment Failure

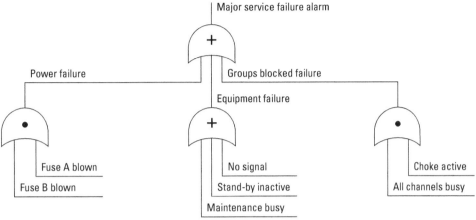

Major service failure alarm

Power failure

Groups blocked failure

Equipment failure

Fuse A blown

Fuse B blown

No signal

Stand-by inactive

Maintenance busy

Choke active

All channels busy

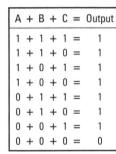

A	·	B	=	Output
1	·	1	=	1
1	·	0	=	0
0	·	1	=	0
0	·	0	=	0

A	+	B	+	C	=	Output
1	+	1	+	1	=	1
1	+	1	+	0	=	1
1	+	0	+	1	=	1
1	+	0	+	0	=	1
0	+	1	+	1	=	1
0	+	1	+	0	=	1
0	+	0	+	1	=	1
0	+	0	+	0	=	0

Notes: – *Any 1 (active signal) into an OR (+) gate will result in a major service failure alarm.*
– *On AND (·) gates, both inputs must be 1 (active signals) to cause a major service failure alarm.*

The two-dimensional survey grid is a powerful data collection tool that is superior to other one-dimensional survey research techniques in that it can be used effectively to establish baselines that would point to needed improvement. It is especially useful in determining existing customer satisfaction levels, identifying performance gaps, or checking perception of quality, morale, or any other people issues.

- To focus problem-solving or process-improvement efforts on concerns or issues most important to the customer.
- To measure and compare performance for internal or external customers.
- To translate and prioritize customer feedback.
- To plot, rank, and interpret survey data for possible corrective action.

before

Audience analysis

Needs analysis

Data collection strategy

Surveying

Questionnaires

after

Consensus decision making

Gap analysis

Interview technique

Focus group

Action plan

➥	Select and define problem or opportunity
➥	Identify and analyze causes or potential change
	Develop and plan possible solutions or change
	Implement and evaluate solution or change
➥	Measure and report solution or change results
	Recognize and reward team efforts

3	Research/statistics
	Creativity/innovation
	Engineering
4	Project management
	Manufacturing
2	Marketing/sales
	Administration/documentation
	Servicing/support
1	Customer/quality metrics
	Change management

• Scaling example: TQM Workshop Participant Survey

Question 1 on performance

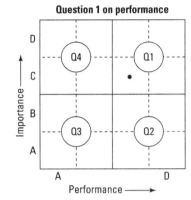

Question 2 on interaction

Importance **to you**
A – To no extent
B – To some extent
(C)– To a great extent
D – To a very great extent

Your satisfaction
A – No satisfaction
(B)– Some satisfaction
C – Great satisfaction
D – Very great satisfaction

Our *performance* in workshop
A – Poor, did not learn anything new
B – Fair, some useful information
(C)– Good, learned a great deal from others
D – Very good, workshop went well

Our group interaction
A – Poor, no interaction
B – Fair, some interaction
(C)– Good, appropriate interaction
D – Very good, excellent interaction

Develop a two-dimensional survey instrument with 10 to 12 questions covering three to four areas of concern. See example *Two Dimensional Grid—Customer Satisfaction Survey.*

Draw and designate grids for each question's related pair of response choice groups seen in the example as *importance to customer* by *quality rated by customer* with respective choices A–D.

Administer the survey, collect the response data and plot corresponding intersects on respective grids.

Assess scatter points (clusters) and determine if improvement action is required. For example, if a cluster of data points falls into quadrant four (Q4), problem-solving or improvement work needs to initiated.

Lastly, summarize the survey results and develop a proposed action plan.

Two Dimensional Grid—Customer Satisfaction Survey

Question #1: Quality of product support documentation　　　　Date: xx/xx/xx

Note: A cluster of points in this grid's quadrant calls for improvement action.

Importance to customer

A – To no extent

B – To some extent

C – To a great extent

D – To a very great extent

Quality rated by customer

A – Poor, major discrepancies

B – Fair, some problem areas

C – Good, updates required

D – Very good, expectations met

A two-directional bar chart is useful to monitor and record percent change from one period of time to another. It can also show positive and negative numbers, above and below normal activity, or any other fluctuations from a zero reference line of the chart.

- To demonstrate percent change of a characteristic over time.
- To measure and show directionality of above-normal and below-normal activity or trends.

	Select and define problem or opportunity
➡	Identify and analyze causes or potential change
	Develop and plan possible solutions or change
➡	Implement and evaluate solution or change
	Measure and report solution or change results
	Recognize and reward team efforts

- The center line, or 0 position on the scale of the two-directional bar chart is the starting point for each bar.
- Changes are plotted in ascending/ descending order.

1	Research/statistics
	Creativity/innovation
	Engineering
	Project management
	Manufacturing
2	Marketing/sales
	Administration/documentation
	Servicing/support
3	Customer/quality metrics
4	Change management

before

Data collection strategy

Checksheet

Linechart

Frequency distribution (FD)

Sampling methods

after

Presentation

Information needs analysis

Problem specification

Problem analysis

What-if-analysis

Construct a table representing the collected data from two or more sources. See example *Percent Change in Teaming Hours*.

Construct a two-directional bar chart, scaling for a highest observed percent change in either direction.

Plot the data as shown in the example.

Check the completed chart for accuracy and provide date of issue.

Percent Change in Teaming Hours

	1995	1996	% Change
Marketing/Sales	200	150	− 25
Engineering	640	800	+ 25
Manufacturing	1400	2100	+ 50
Support/Services	1000	700	− 30
Human Resources	270	300	+11

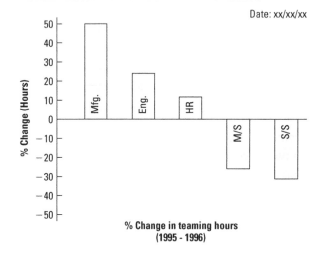

Date: xx/xx/xx

% Change (Hours)

% Change in teaming hours
(1995 - 1996)

The value analysis technique analyzes the functionality of a product, states an estimated cost for each function, and demonstrates a function as compared with that of a competitor's. This technique, therefore, forces an assessment of the manufacturing processes, parts and materials, and design features of a product.

- To identify needed product improvements.
- To lower product costs.
- To prioritize product redesign activities.

before

Linking diagram
Factor analysis
Customer needs table
Truth table
Selection window

after

Influence diagram
Cost-benefit analysis
Activity cost matrix
Different point of view
Idea advocate

➟ Select and define problem or opportunity
➟ Identify and analyze causes or potential change
➟ Develop and plan possible solutions or change
➟ Implement and evaluate solution or change
    Measure and report solution or change results
    Recognize and reward team efforts

    Research/statistics
    Creativity/innovation
    Engineering
    Project management
    Manufacturing
1 Marketing/sales
    Administration/documentation
2 Servicing/support
3 Customer/quality metrics
4 Change management

- The construction of the value analysis table may reflect a different set of factors.
- The primary concern is to determine functions that have a high cost associated with them. These functions often call for a redesign priority.
- Competitors' superior designs must be considered in all redesign efforts.

First, a customer satisfaction survey is completed to collect the customers "wants" or expectations. See example *Designing a Better Mouse Trap*.

As the second step, design engineering and manufacturing examine a number of competitors' products. The team checks for improved functionality, superior designs, and innovation.

A value analysis form is used to list the product's functions and subfunctions. Customer "wants" and competitor data are also filled in.

For every function and subfunction, the estimated cost and percent of total product cost are recorded.

The last step determines the functions that are strong candidates for redesign on the basis of cost and competitors' superior designs.

The completed value analysis form is reviewed, dated, and given to the process owners.

Designing a Better Mousetrap

Product: Mousetrap		Team: Designers			Date xx/xx/xx
Functions – Subfunctions	**Customer Wants**	**Competitor's Design**	**Estimated ($)**	**(%)**	**Redesign Priority**
Quiet operation	Yes	Below	.20	(15)	—
– Instant kill	Yes	Better	.15	(11)	5
– No escape		Not sure*	.05	(4)	
– Does not flip		Below			
Easy to use	Yes	Better	.60	(44)	—
– Finger safe	Yes	Superior	.40	(30)	①
– Easy to bait	Yes	Superior	.10	(7)	
– Easy to set	Yes	Superior	.10	(7)	4
– Easy to remove		Not sure*			
Clean operation	Yes	Same	.05	(4)	
Trigger sensitivity		Superior	.20	(14)	2
Safe for pets	Yes	Same	.10	(7)	
Clear instructions		Same	.05	(4)	
Reliable ops	Yes		.10	(7)	3
Spring force		Better	.05	(4)	

*Notes: – * = Insufficient data*
– Cost per mousetrap = $1.35 = 100%
– Rank 1 is highest priority (.40 ÷ 1.35 = .296 or 30%)

A value/non-value-added cycle time chart displays all activities and the cycle time required from the start point to the stop point of a process. The intent of this tool is to identify non-value-added activities such as lengthy delays, redundant or time-wasting activities, or excessive reviews and approvals. The chart should be constructed by a team that owns the process. Participants have a good understanding of the activities and therefore are best suited to collectively reduce cycle time of the overall process.

- To identify non-value-added activities and excessive delay times in a process.
- To draw a detailed chart for the purpose of completing redesign, problem resolution, and cycle-time reduction activities.
- To capture the "as is" process flow in order to have a common understanding of the process for further problem-solving efforts.

Before

Problem specification

Process mapping

Potential problem analysis (PPA)

Systems analysis diagram

Pareto chart

after

Process analysis

Problem analysis

What-if analysis

Activity analysis

Force field analysis (FFA)

➡	Select and define problem or opportunity
➡	Identify and analyze causes or potential change
	Develop and plan possible solutions or change
	Implement and evaluate solution or change
	Measure and report solution or change results
	Recognize and reward team efforts

	Research/statistics
	Creativity/innovation
	Engineering
2	Project management
3	Manufacturing
	Marketing/sales
	Administration/documentation
4	Servicing/support
	Customer/quality metrics
1	Change management

- Symbols and scale:

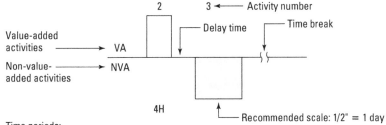

Time periods:
 – (M) minutes, (H) hours, (D) days, (W) weeks

The team facilitator assembles a team that consists of representatives (process owners) of the process to be charted. Flip charts or a white-board is needed to draw the chart.

The team determines the start and stop points of the process. The appropriate scale of time to be used is also determined.

Using the team-provided input, the team facilitator sequentially scales activities, value-added and non-value-added, above and below a drawn line, showing sequence numbers of activities and how much time each activity takes. See example *Department Budgeting Process*.

Next, the team checks the chart for completeness, correct activity sequence, and stated cycle times. Non-value-added activities are shaded in as shown in the example.

Finally, the chart is dated and presented to interested parties for further action.

Department Budgeting Process

Date: xx/xx/xx

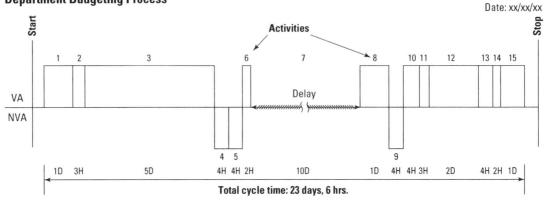

Activities

1	– First notice from finance dept.	9	– Meeting: review dollar rqmts.—all dept. units
2	– Meeting: review rqmts.—all dept. units	10	– Merge budget data—dept. admin.
3	– Assess/forecast staff rqmts.—all dept. units	11	– Budget justification check—dept. mgrs.
4	– Approval by dept. mgrs.	12	– Budget revision—all dept units
5	– Store info.—dept. admin.	13	– Approval by dept. mgrs.
6	– Meeting: review dollar rqmts.—all dept. units	14	– Store finalized budget—dept. admin.
7	– Wait for data—all dept. units	15	– Copy to finance dept.
8	– Collect data—dept. admin.		

A variance analysis tool discovers key process variances or deviations from specifications in a selected process for the purpose of reducing or controlling the serious impact these variances have on service or product quality. In addition, variance analysis allows a closer look at process cycle time, waste, rework, supplier quality, and overall costs.

- To utilize a variance analysis tool after a team has completed process mapping in problem-solving efforts.
- To document key variances that have an overall negative affect on product quality.
- To identify process capability and deviations from customer requirements.
- To perform continuous process improvement and cycle time reduction activities.

before

Brainstorming

Sandard deviation

Process capability ratios

Control chart

Process mapping

after

Pareto diagram

Cause and effect diagram (CED)

Analysis of variance

Activity analysis

Shewhart PDCA cycle

➡ Select and define problem or opportunity
➡ Identify and analyze causes or potential change
   Develop and plan possible solutions or change
   Implement and evaluate solution or change
➡ Measure and report solution or change results
   Recognize and reward team efforts

   Research/statistics
   Creativity/innovation
   Engineering
   Project management
3 Manufacturing
   Marketing/sales
   Administration/documentation
   Servicing/support
2 Customer/quality metrics
1 Change management

- Variance analysis matrix construction:
  - Ensure that all process steps are included and sequenced properly in the matrix. A process map will provide this information.
  - Use a consistent level of detail in listing all variances.
  - Focus on identified key variances that potentially can cause the greatest impact (problems) on the process.
  - Variance impact scale: 5 = *high*, 3 = *medium*, 1 = *low*
  - ⬛12 = variance #12
  - ⓵③ = key variance
  - Key variance control table.

Key Variance Control Table Examples

Key Variance	Root Cause?	Where Observed?	Where Controlled?	How Changed
#3–Old issue parts list	Incorrect documents	Supply/kitting	Engineering repro	Revise documents
#10–Panel wood quality	Defective wood	Parts assembly	Customer complaints	Change supplier
#21–Loose connections	Untightened nuts	Final testing	Assembly operator	Operator training

As a first step, the team process maps a selected process so that all participants acquire a greater understanding of the process.

Next, the team reaches consensus on the input and output requirements based on design criteria and customer expectations.

The team's facilitator explains the concepts of a variance analysis and draws a variance analysis matrix on a whiteboard or on flip charts.

Participants agree on the major process steps and sequentially list all known or potential process variances.

The team establishes variance impact criteria and assigns numerical values to variances that would affect other activities. See example *Assembly of Control Panel Simulators*.

Key variances are identified by adding all impact values underneath each listed variance. The highest totals are considered key variances and their respective variance numbers are circled, as shown in this example.

Next, a variance control table is constructed. This table is used to hold all team-identified key variances.

Systematically, the team completes this table. An example is shown in *notes and key points*. The completion of this table will greatly enhance a team's ability to reduce or at least control the key variances that impact the quality of products or services.

Finally, the variance analysis matrix is dated and presented to the process owners.

Assembly of Control Panel Simulators

Process Steps		Variances	Matrix date: xx/xx/xx

Process Steps	Variance relationship values (left to right)	No.	Variance
Instructions		(1)	Old issue instructions
	5	2	Unclear instructions
Parts Check	5 | 1	(3)	Old issue parts lists (previous model)
	5	4	Wrong toggle switches (2-way vs. 3-way)
	5	(5)	Wrong type of lampcaps
	5	6	Wrong color of lampcaps
	5	7	Missing fuse (AA)
	1	8	Missing washers
	3	9	Wrong size nuts
Parts Assembly		(10)	Panel wood quality (knots)
		11	Panel sizing (holes don't line up)
	5 | 1	12	Panel finish (rough edges)
	3 | 5 | 3	13	Uneven panel cutting
	5 | 3 | 1	14	Uneven stain
	5 | 5	15	Lampholes too large (diameter)
		16	Bent connectors
	3	17	Wires not tagged
Final Inspection	3 | 1	18	Missing final inspection tags
	1 | 3 | 3	19	Scratched panel finish
	3	20	Selector switch hard to rotate
Final Testing	3 | 3	(21)	Loose connections
	5	(22)	Open varistor
	5 | 5	23	Shorted switch terminals
	5 | 5 | 5	24	Open circuit
	5 | 5 | 5 | 5	25	Intermittent operation
Key Variances	16 | 1 | 25 | 5 | 10 | — | — | 5 | 3 | 16 | 7 | 9 | 4 | — | — | — | 8 | — | — | — | 15 | 10 | 5 | 5 | 5		

Note: Impact scale–5 = high, 3 = medium, 1 = low

"Old issue parts list (previous model)" the key variance with the highest count (25), could cause the greatest impact.

A Venn diagram can be used to identify logical relationships, and it is very useful in displaying the union and intersection of events or sets. It can graphically illustrate the mutually exclusive concept and other rules of probability or the outcome of an experiment.

- To illustrate the relationship of events, sets, or behavior.
- To help understand the consequences when two events intersect or are combined.
- To test the validity of a syllogism by applying logical thinking.

before

Influence diagram

Morphological analysis

Organization mapping

Double reversal

Starbursting

after

Mental imaging

Fresh eye

Forced association

Cluster analysis

Truth table

➡ Select and define problem or opportunity

Identify and analyze causes or potential change

➡ Develop and plan possible solutions or change

Implement and evaluate solution or change

Measure and report solution or change results

Recognize and reward team efforts

2	Research/statistics
1	Creativity/innovation
	Engineering
	Project management
	Manufacturing
	Marketing/sales
	Administration/documentation
	Servicing/support
	Customer/quality metrics
	Change management

- Developed by John Venn (1978), a Venn diagram is shown as a rectangle that contains the "sample space" with circles drawn inside to represent all possibilities of interaction and noninteraction of events. To gain more insight into applications within the field of possibility and logic, a textbook on statistics should be referenced.

Identify events or sets and their relationships, interactions or outcomes that may be better understood using a Venn diagram. See example *Venn Diagram Applications*.

Construct a Venn diagram, designate the circles and provide explanations. Run-it-by others for their comments.

Display in training sessions or presentations to facilitate conceptual understanding.

Identify examples to illustrate the concept.

Venn Diagram Applications

Logical Thinking

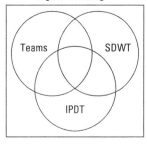

Testing the validity of a syllogism:
– No self-directed work teams (SDWT) are integrated product development teams (IPDT)
– Some teams are SDWTs
– Therefore, some teams are not IPDTs
The shaded area reflects that there are no SDWTs that are also IPDTs!

Relationship/Interaction

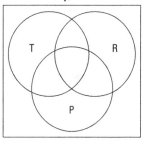

Illustrating the ideal learning approach.
– Theory (T)
– Research (R)
– Practice (P)
The shaded area reflects where all learning is greatly reinforced.

Problem Resolution

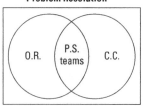

A call for action on the basis of:
– Experiencing customer complaints (C.C.)
– Organization's resources available (O.R.)
– Suggests problem-solving teams
The shaded area reflects an outcome of combining sets.

The weighted voting technique quantifies a preference for a particular choice. Each team participant receives a number of votes for distribution across several choices in accordance with the participant's personal choice. Votes are added for each choice to determine what choice the team is leaning toward.

- To identify participants' preference for a specific choice, product, or service.
- To team vote one option among many.
- To prepare the team for consensus decision making.

before

Brainstorming

Starbursting

Idea advocate

Brainwriting pool

Pin cards technique

after

Consensus decision making

Problem specification

Solution matrix

Nominal prioritization

Importance weighting

➡ Select and define problem or opportunity

➡ Identify and analyze causes or potential change

Develop and plan possible solutions or change

➡ Implement and evaluate solution or change

Measure and report solution or change results

➡ Recognize and reward team efforts

- Assign to team members approximately 50 percent more votes than choices to be voted.

Research/statistics

Creativity/innovation

Engineering

Project management

Manufacturing

2   Marketing/sales

3   Administration/documentation

Servicing/support

Customer/quality metrics

1   Change management

The team facilitator records all choices to be voted on a flip chart. See example *Team Voting to Select a Brainstorming Tool*.

A matrix is constructed listing the participants' names and choices as shown in the example.

Each participant receives eight votes to be distributed across five choices.

The facilitator asks each participant for his or her vote distribution for each choice.

Votes are recorded until all votes have been distributed.

Lastly, the facilitator totals votes for each choice to display the team preferred choice. The flip chart is dated.

Team Voting to Select a Brainstorming Tool　　　　Date xx/xx/xx

Tools / Team Members	Round Robin Brainstorming	Reverse Brainstorming	Crawfort Slip Method	Brainwriting Pool	Brainstorming	
John L.	1	1	1	2	3	
Tony M.	2	0	2	0	4	
Steven K.	2	1	1	2	2	
Gina I.	3	1	1	2	1	**Team Voted for "Brainstorming"**
Jim M.	2	2	0	2	2	
Dana K.	3	0	0	2	3	
Peter A.	1	2	1	2	2	
Vote totals	**14**	**7**	**6**	**12**	**17**	

Note: 7 team members × 8 votes = 56 votes total

The What-if analysis is a very effective idea-generating process that allows a team to question the possible outcomes if a process or procedure is altered. This is also helpful in assessing attempts to do something new or different, or to find a so-far untried solution to a problem.

- To discover and assess alternative ways to use a product or process.
- To question existing practices and applications and to explore potential changes that might yield product or process improvement or a solution to a problem.
- To change one's perspective in the idea-generation process.

before

SCAMPER
Fresh eye
Mental imaging
Problem analysis
Process analysis

after

Creativity assessment
Solution matrix
Opportunity analysis
Activity analysis
Process flowchart

➡ Select and define problem or opportunity
➡ Identify and analyze causes or potential change
   Develop and plan possible solutions or change
➡ Implement and evaluate solution or change
   Measure and report solution or change results
   Recognize and reward team efforts

	Research/statistics
1	Creativity/innovation
3	Engineering
	Project management
	Manufacturing
	Marketing/sales
	Administration/documentation
	Servicing/support
	Customer/quality metrics
2	Change management

Option: On a more detailed level for product improvement or development, the What-if analysis could use the SCAMPER technique to generate new ideas: *What-if we*:

S = Substitute?
C = Combine?
A = Adapt?
M = Modify?, Magnify?
P = Put to other uses?
E = Eliminate?
R = Reverse?, Rearrange?

the material, part, shape, color, purpose, design, sequence, components, procedure, etc.

The team identifies the problem or issue to be analyzed. See example *Defects per Unit (DPU) Reduction Alternatives.*

Team participants discuss and explore the "what-ifs" of the different proposed ways of solving the problem or improving the current situation.

The facilitator records, on a flip chart, all the finalized alternatives suggested by the team that have merit and need further study.

Last, the team prioritizes all potential solutions on the basis of feasibility and resource requirements The flip chart is dated.

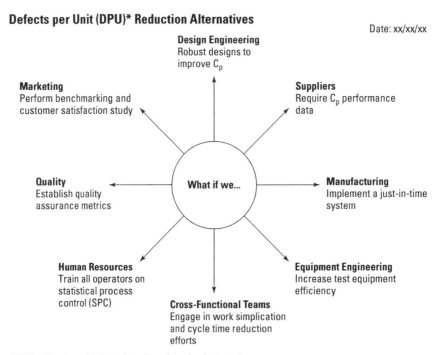

Defects per Unit (DPU)* Reduction Alternatives

Date: xx/xx/xx

Design Engineering
Robust designs to improve C_p

Marketing
Perform benchmarking and customer satisfaction study

Suppliers
Require C_p performance data

Quality
Establish quality assurance metrics

What if we...

Manufacturing
Implement a just-in-time system

Human Resources
Train all operators on statistical process control (SPC)

Cross-Functional Teams
Engage in work simplication and cycle time reduction efforts

Equipment Engineering
Increase test equipment efficiency

*DPU = Number of defects found/number of units tested.

The why/how charting is a sorting tool that clusters ideas regarding *why* particular actions would be supportive of company objectives. Action items necessary to reach objectives were derived by asking *how* they could be accomplished. The information gained is used to determine what next steps need to be taken.

- To reach a common understanding of the objectives and action items necessary in a problem-solving effort.
- To explore different alternatives in an action-planning process.

<table>
<tr><td>

➥ Select and define problem or opportunity
➥ Identify and analyze causes or potential change
➥ Develop and plan possible solutions or change
   Implement and evaluate solution or change
   Measure and report solution or change results
   Recognize and reward team efforts

</td><td>

	Research/statistics
1	Creativity/innovation
	Engineering
	Project management
	Manufacturing
	Marketing/sales
	Administration/documentation
2	Servicing/support
	Customer/quality metrics
3	Change management

</td></tr>
</table>

before

Five whys
Brainstorming
Mind flow
6-3-5 method
Buzz group

after

Actions plan
Consensus decision making
Cost-benefit analysis
Information needs analysis
Presentation

- *Optional*: Draw lines between *objectives* or *action items* to show linkages or interrelationships.
- *Or*, assign numbers to show sequence or priorities of *objectives* or *action items*.

The team facilitator reviews the why/how charting process with the team.

Next, the team agrees on a problem or activity to be charted. See example *Why Not Purchase TQM Video Tapes?*

The facilitator places the problem in the center of a whiteboard and asks the participants to respond to why this problem should be addressed and to discover why certain actions will enable the team to reach the implied objectives.

Next, participants are asked how these actions can be taken. Alternative actions that also have the potential of solving this problem are listed on the whiteboard.

The team visually sorts the information and some linkages; the interrelationships are pointed out to the facilitator, who draws some arrows of directionality.

Finally, the chart is checked and dated. This document is checked to provide input into the action-planning process.

Why Not Purchase TQM Videotapes?

Date: xx/xx/xx

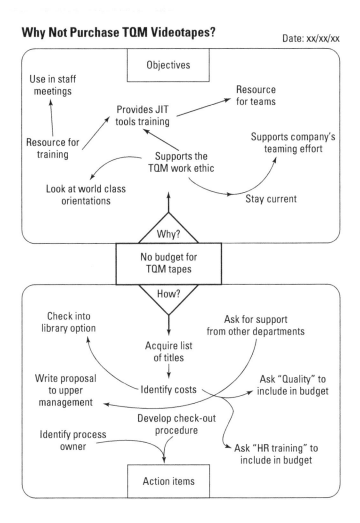

Of all the different variations of brainstorming, the wildest idea technique is perhaps the most challenging and creative activity. This tool encourages participants to perform out-of-the box brainstorming with the goal of generating truly outrageous and wild ideas. The underlying application of this tool is to discover breakthrough ideas for process, product, or service improvements.

- To generate unusual and wild ideas that normal brainstorming methods do not.
- To collect "anything goes" ideas for the purpose of finding practical applications or solutions that normally do not surface during regular sessions.
- To promote creative thinking among brainstorming participants.

before

Brainstorming

Mental imaging

Round robin brainstorming

Interview technique

Buzz group

after

Starbursting

Thematic content analysis

Consensus decision making

Criteria filtering

Multivoting

➡ Select and define problem or opportunity
Identify and analyze causes or potential change
➡ Develop and plan possible solutions or change
Implement and evaluate solution or change
Measure and report solution or change results
Recognize and reward team efforts

Research/statistics
1 Creativity/innovation
Engineering
Project management
Manufacturing
3 Marketing/sales
Administration/documentation
Servicing/support
Customer/quality metrics
2 Change management

- An experienced facilitator can promote more direct participation in this process by applying lessons learned from previous facilitation of round robin, classical, or reversed brainstorming sessions.
- Some wild ideas may need on-the-spot clarification in order to make sense later.

The facilitator introduces this brainstorming variation and provides a rationale for using it.

Brainstorming is started by the facilitator's displaying of several outrageous or impossible ideas to a stated topic, issue, or problem. See example *Employee/Team Recognition and Reward*.

Participants generate other wild, crazy ideas or hitchhike on others already mentioned.

The facilitator records ideas on the flip chart and monitors the process closely to ensure that participants do not revert back to generating more conventional ideas.

The process is continued until all participants run out of wild ideas. The final list of ideas is dated and saved for next steps.

Employee/Team Recognition and Reward	Date xx/xx/xx

- Team gets 10% of profits
- "Honorary Executive" title
- Team success on E-mail distribution
- Teams determine recognition/reward
- Give "markers"
- Open doors for 2 days
- Team goes on cruise
- Job rotation for a week

- President of the company for a day

The window analysis technique is used to determine the potential root causes(s) of a performance problem. Developed by Fyuji Fukuda from Johari's window model, this technique questions any two parties, individuals, or organizational units, if a practice, procedure, or a set of work instructions is known and practiced in order to prevent or minimize performance problems.

- To identify root causes of a performance problem.
- To verify the adherence to company practices, procedures, or work instructions by all organizational units.
- To investigate if performance problems could have been prevented.

before

Five whys

Brainstorming

Cause and effect diagram (CED)

Fault tree analysis

Process analysis

after

Problem specification

Countermeasures matrix

Potential problem analysis (PPA)

What-if analysis

Cost-benefit analysis

➡ Select and define problem or opportunity
➡ Identify and analyze causes or potential change
➡ Develop and plan possible solutions or change
  Implement and evaluate solution or change
  Measure and report solution or change results
  Recognize and reward team efforts

	Research/statistics
	Creativity/innovation
	Engineering
	Project management
2	Manufacturing
	Marketing/sales
	Administration/documentation
3	Servicing/support
	Customer/quality metrics
1	Change management

- Window categories descriptions:
  A: Practices, procedures, or work instructions have been established and both parties (party X and Y) use this information to minimize performance problems. Status: Company directives are followed.
  B: Practices, procedures, or work instructions have been established; however, party X or Y does not use this information correctly. Status: Company directives are not always followed.
  C: Practices, procedures, or work instructions have been established; however, party X or Y does not have this information. Status: Company directives were not communicated to some parties.
  D: Practices, procedures, or work instructions have not been established and, therefore, neither party (party X and Y) has this information. Status: Company directives need to be communicated to make information available to all parties.
- $\overline{\text{Known}}$ = not known (negation of *known*).

For more information: *The Johari Window: A Model for Soliciting and Giving Feedback,* by P. G. Hanson in *1973 Annual Handbook for Group Facilitators,* edited by John. E. Jones and J. William Pfeifer. San Diego, CA: University Associates.

A team is assembled with representation from the organizational units to be analyzed. See example *Lack of Adherence to World Class Practices: Quality Function Deployment (QFD), Design of Experiments (DOE), Cycle Time Management (CTM).*

Participants identify and discuss perceived performance problems. A priority list of no more than five problems is developed.

Using the window diagram, participants systematically explore all squares and discuss each category (A–D) to identify which window square best represents the true situation.

Lastly, participants receive assignments to collect data to prove or disprove a particular category (B–D) previously selected as a potential root cause or the problem.

Lack of Adherance to World Class Practices:
Quality Function Deployments (QFD), Design of
Experiments (DOE), Cycle Time Management (CTM)

Party X — Party Y		Known		$\overline{\text{Known}}$
		Practiced	$\overline{\text{Practiced}}$	
Known	Practiced	A	B	C
	$\overline{\text{Practiced}}$	B	B	C
$\overline{\text{Known}}$		C	C	D

Note: Known: WC practices of QFD, DOE, and CTM are **known** to an organizational unit.
Practiced: WC practices of QFD, DOE, and CTM are **practiced** by an organizational unit.

$\overline{\text{Practiced}}$: WC practices of QFD, DOE, and CTM are **not practiced** by an organizational unit.
$\overline{\text{Known}}$: WC practices of QFD, DOE, and CTM are **unknown** to an organizational unit.

$\overline{\text{Practiced}}$ = The negation of practiced
$\overline{\text{Known}}$ = The negation of known

The wishful thinking tool is based on fantasy and may not be supported by many more pragmatic-minded team participants. Yet a logic-based approach can often overlook new ideas or solutions to a problem, since any deviation from a more structured approach is carefully avoided by many individuals. The wishful thinking tool does provide a way to redefine a problem or situation, which is helpful in gaining new insights.

- To allow fantasy and wishful thinking to produce some novel ideas.
- To use a nonlogical, unstructured method to find potential solutions to a problem.

before

Analogy and metaphor
Wildest idea technique
Fresh eye
Stimulus analysis
Buzz group

after

Creativity assessment
Value analysis
Starbursting
Scenario writing
Run-it-by

Select and define problem or opportunity
Identify and analyze causes or potential change
➡ Develop and plan possible solutions or change
➡ Implement and evaluate solution or change
Measure and report solution or change results
➡ Recognize and reward team efforts

	Research/statistics
1	Creativity/innovation
	Engineering
3	Project management
	Manufacturing
4	Marketing/sales
6	Administration/documentation
5	Servicing/support
	Customer/quality metrics
2	Change management

- A fantasy-based tool for surfacing useful perspectives. A move away from reality to create new thinking modes.

The team defines a problem, issue, or opportunity. See example *Work Redesign Concerns*.

The facilitator provides an overview and some examples of the wishful thinking tool. The team engages in discussion to ensure a shared understanding of the process involved.

Participants engage in fantasizing and make wishful thinking statements such as:

– "We should have the authority to schedule our own work hours (to solve scheduling conflicts).

– "There would be more job satisfaction if we could manage ourselves (communications).

– "They cannot take this job away from me" (job security).

All statements are recorded on flip charts.

Next, participants examine all statements and discuss more practical applications. Back to reality questions are: "How can we really do this?" "What exists today that we could use to respond to the concerns?" "What could happen if we try this idea?"

Steps 3 and 4 can be repeated after restating the problem, issue, or opportunity.

Work Redesign Concerns	Date: xx/xx/xx
Wishful Thinking	**Back to Reality**
• Freedom to schedule working hours	To ——➤ Establish the flextime concept
• Team does not need supervision	To ——➤ Self-directed work teams
• "This job is mine"	To ——➤ Job rights

Note: In some cases wishful thinking has turned into reality!

A work breakdown structure (WBS) is a necessary division of the overall project into major categories of work. Major categories, in turn, are broken down into more defined, specific elements, and then finally down to a work package level. This process provides project management the ability to schedule, assign resources, and report work package completion status.

- To break down a total project's work into definable, manageable, and reportable work packages.
- To reduce the complexity of a project so that interrelated activities and work elements can be clearly understood.
- To identify work packages and resource requirements, and to schedule for completing project activities.

before

Comparison matrix

Project prioritization matrix

Action plan

Objectives matrix

Responsibility matrix

after

Trend analysis

Gantt chart

Activity network diagram

Program evaluation and review technique (PERT)

Major program status

➥ Select and define problem or opportunity

➥ Identify and analyze causes or potential change

➥ Develop and plan possible solutions or change

   Implement and evaluate solution or change

   Measure and report solution or change results

   Recognize and reward team efforts

   Research/statistics

   Creativity/innovation

2 Engineering

1 Project management

   Manufacturing

   Marketing/sales

   Administration/documentation

   Servicing/support

   Customer/quality metrics

3 Change management

• A WBS typically consists of five or more levels of breakdown to reduce a project's scope and complexity:

Level	Description	Designation Example
1	Project	10
2	Category	10.1
3	Subcategory	10.1.1
4	Work element	10.1.1.1
5	Work package	10.1.1.1.1
6	Deliverables	10.1.1.1.1.1

The first step for a project manager's team is to identify the major categories of work to be completed. See example *WBS for Adding an Assembly Line.*

A designation or accounting schema is then established to be able to account for or schedule work. The numbering system used is arbitrary—see example shown.

All work categories are broken down into a lower level of detail. This process continues down to the basic work package level. Typically, five or more levels are diagrammed.

The final WBS diagram should reflect all required work and is used as a resource document for the planning and scheduling of the overall project.

WBS for Adding an Assembly Line

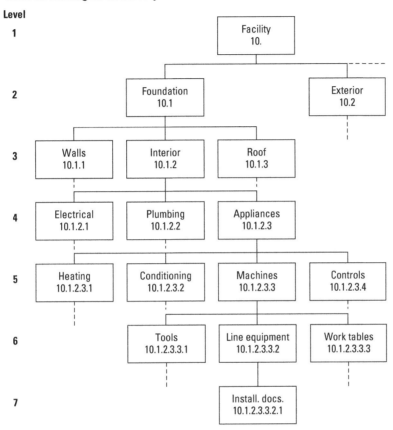

Note: Partial WBS diagram.

The construction of a work flow analysis (WFA) diagram is absolutely necessary to show how work actually (physically) flows from person to person, via groups and departments throughout the organization. Once completed, the work flow diagram will illustrate process flows, methods, information, and material movement.

Work flow analysis is often used as a problem-solving tool to identify process loops, cross-over, redundant moves, bottlenecks, and other inefficient or non-value-adding activities. It is of great assistance in understanding the existing process before improvements can be proposed in process redesign or reengineering efforts.

- To show the sequential steps involved in moving people, material, documentation, or information in a process.
- To diagram or baseline work movement in order for a team to understand the current work-flow sequence.
- To illustrate a system's inefficiency.
- To identify and eliminate illogical process flows.

before

Facility layout diagram

Fault tree analysis (FTA)

Symbolic flowchart

Gozinto chart

Cycle time flowchart

after

Process analysis

Failure mode effect analysis (FMEA)

Action plan

Decision process flowchart

Consensus decision making

Select and define problem or opportunity	
➡ Identify and analyze causes or potential change	
➡ Develop and plan possible solutions or change	
➡ Implement and evaluate solution or change	
Measure and report solution or change results	
Recognize and reward team efforts	

	Research/statistics
3	Creativity/innovation
	Engineering
4	Project management
2	Manufacturing
	Marketing/sales
5	Administration/documentation
	Servicing/support
	Customer/quality metrics
1	Change management

The sequence of flow can be shown as numbering sections of the flow path as shown ──────▶ . Other process paths can be encoded as ┅┅┅┅┅▶ or +++++++++▶ .

The team identifies functions and responsibilities of the work-flow process to be analyzed. See example *Picture Frame Assembly*.

The second step is to obtain a current floor plan and to "walk" the flow of the selected process. Mark up the floor plan displaying the basic "as is" flow. For repeats or different process phases, use different color markers. Timing the process at various stages will provide additional data: the cycle times of tasks, movements, and delays. The resulting diagram is sometimes referred to as a "spaghetti diagram" because of the multiline crossover appearance.

The team then performs an analysis of the current process and recommends a first draft of equipment rearrangements and work flow changes to reduce or eliminate process steps.

Step four requires team consensus to be reached and a presentation given to process owners and other interested parties.

Date the completed work flow analysis diagram.

Picture Frame Assembly

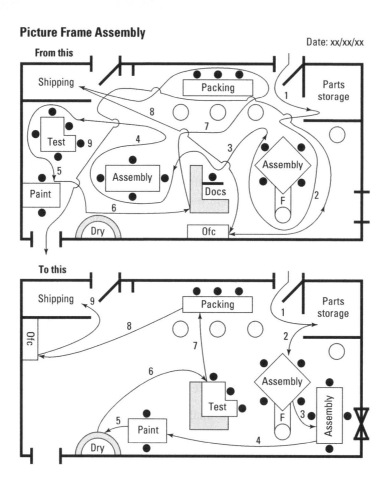

A yield chart shows trends in the quality characteristics of a process; there is also a reflection of process capability. Output data is monitored over time, and the percentage of nondiscrepant (or conforming to specifications) units is identified as the first time yield (FTY). A yield chart can also be used to plot internal or rolled yield, which is the cumulation of individual output yields within a process.

- To measure process variability.
- To identify if problem-solving action needs to be taken at a particular process output stage.
- To track and display the amount of variation in process characteristics.

➡ Select and define problem or opportunity
➡ Identify and analyze causes or potential change
   Develop and plan possible solutions or change
➡ Implement and evaluate solution or change
➡ Measure and report solution or change results
   Recognize and reward team efforts

1	Research/statistics
	Creativity/innovation
3	Engineering
2	Project management
4	Manufacturing
5	Marketing/sales
	Administration/documentation
	Servicing/support
	Customer/quality metrics
	Change management

before

Data collection strategy

Interview technique

Surveying

Information needs analysis

Checksheet

after

Cost-benefit analysis

Monthly assessment schedule

Variance analysis

Process analysis

Problem analysis

- Yield metrics affect many other measurements:
  - Cycle time of processes
  - Schedule linearity or delays
  - Unit costs or total product costs
  - Total costs of operation
  - Indication of defects per unit (DPU) level
  - Indication of process capability (C_p)
  - Indication of stockouts
  - Indication of on-time delivery
- Basic calculations:

$$FTY = \frac{\text{units passed final test/inspection}}{\text{units submitted to final test/inspection}}$$

Rolled yield example: Workstation #2 test 72% units passed $\times$ workstation #3 test 68% units passed = 49% rolled yield (.72 $\times$ .68 = .49).

First, the data collection process is established for the production units to be measured, units to be counted, the time period to be covered, and the frequency with which units are to be measured.

A yield chart is constructed for the production units to be measured. See example *Monthly Production and First Time Yield (FTY)*.

Units produced and units passed are recorded each month. The first time yield (FTY) is calculated and recorded as shown in the example. The start date of the yield chart is shown for historical data trace purposes.

The completed yield chart is submitted to quality or upper management for further analysis and action.

Monthly Production and First Time Yield (FTY)

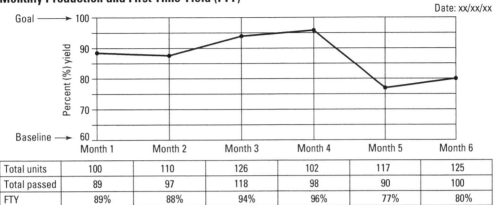

Date: xx/xx/xx

	Month 1	Month 2	Month 3	Month 4	Month 5	Month 6
Total units	100	110	126	102	117	125
Total passed	89	97	118	98	90	100
FTY	89%	88%	94%	96%	77%	80%

Table A: Proportions of Area Under the Normal Curve

How to use this table: Because the normal curve is symmetrical about a mean of zero (the left side being a mirror image of the right side), the areas corresponding to negative z-scores are identical to the areas of positive z-scores. For example, the areas corresponding to a z-score of -1.00 are the same as those areas of a z-score of $+1.00$. Z-scores are given in column A. Areas between (inside) the mean and the z-score are given in column B, and column C contains the area that lies beyond (outside) the z-score. And, since the curve is symmetric, each half of the curve contains .5000 of the total area.

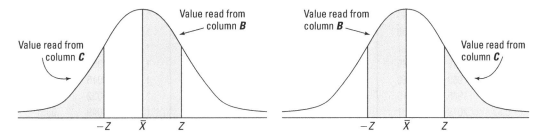

Table A: Proportions of Area Under the Normal Curve

(A)	(B) area inside $\bar{X}$ & Z	(C) area outside Z	(A)	(B) area inside $\bar{X}$ & Z	(C) area outside Z	(A)	(B) area inside $\bar{X}$ & Z	(C) area outside Z
Z			Z			Z		
0.00	.0000	.5000	0.12	.0478	.4522	0.24	.0948	.4052
0.01	.0040	.4960	0.13	.0517	.4483	0.25	.0987	.4013
0.02	.0080	.4920	0.14	.0557	.4443	0.26	.1026	.3974
0.03	.0120	.4880	0.15	.0596	.4404	0.27	.1064	.3936
0.04	.0160	.4840	0.16	.0636	.4364	0.28	.1103	.3897
0.05	.0199	.4801	0.17	.0675	.4325	0.29	.1141	.3859
0.06	.0239	.4761	0.18	.0714	.4286	0.30	.1179	.3821
0.07	.0279	.4721	0.19	.0753	.4247	0.31	.1217	.3783
0.08	.0319	.4681	0.20	.0793	.4207	0.32	.1255	.3745
0.09	.0359	.4641	0.21	.0823	.4168	0.33	.1293	.3707
0.10	.0398	.4602	0.22	.0871	.4129	0.34	.1331	.3669
0.11	.0438	.4562	0.23	.0910	.4090	0.35	.1368	.3632

(continued)

Proportions of Area Under the Normal Curve (continued)

(A) Z	(B) area inside $\bar{X}$ & Z	(C) area outside Z	(A) Z	(B) area inside $\bar{X}$ & Z	(C) area outside Z	(A) Z	(B) area inside $\bar{X}$ & Z	(C) area outside Z
0.36	.1406	.3594	0.75	.2734	.2266	1.14	.3729	.1271
0.37	.1443	.3557	0.76	.2764	.2236	1.15	.3749	.1251
0.38	.1480	.3520	0.77	.2794	.2206	1.16	.3770	.1230
0.39	.1517	.3483	0.78	.2823	.2177	1.17	.3790	.1210
0.40	.1551	.3446	0.79	.2852	.2148	1.18	.3810	.1190
0.41	.1591	.3409	0.80	.2881	.2119	1.19	.3830	.1170
0.42	.1628	.3372	0.81	.2910	.2090	1.20	.3849	.1151
0.43	.1664	.3336	0.82	.2939	.2061	1.21	.3869	.1131
0.44	.1700	.3300	0.83	.2967	.2033	1.22	.3888	.1112
0.45	.1736	.3264	0.84	.2995	.2005	1.23	.3907	.1093
0.46	.1772	.3228	0.85	.3023	.1977	1.24	.3925	.1075
0.47	.1808	.3190	0.86	.3051	.1949	1.25	.3944	.1056
0.48	.1844	.3156	0.87	.3078	.1922	1.26	.3962	.1038
0.49	.1879	.3121	0.88	.3106	.1894	1.27	.3980	.1020
0.50	.1915	.3085	0.89	.3133	.1867	1.28	.3997	.1003
0.51	.1950	.3050	0.90	.3159	.1841	1.29	.4015	.0985
0.52	.1985	.3015	0.91	.3186	.1814	1.30	.4032	.0968
0.53	.2019	.2981	0.92	.3212	.1788	1.31	.4049	.0951
0.54	.2054	.2946	0.93	.3238	.1762	1.32	.4066	.0934
0.55	.2088	.2912	0.94	.3264	.1736	1.33	.4082	.0918
0.56	.2123	.2877	0.95	.3289	.1711	1.34	.4099	.0901
0.57	.2157	.2843	0.96	.3315	.1685	1.35	.4115	.0885
0.58	.2190	.2810	0.97	.3340	.1660	1.36	.4131	.0869
0.59	.2224	.2776	0.98	.3365	.1635	1.37	.4147	.0853
0.60	.2257	.2743	0.99	.3389	.1611	1.38	.4162	.0838
0.61	.2291	.2709	1.00	.3413	.1587	1.39	.4177	.0823
0.62	.2324	.2676	1.01	.3438	.1562	1.40	.4192	.0808
0.63	.2357	.2643	1.02	.3461	.1539	1.41	.4207	.0793
0.64	.2389	.2611	1.03	.3485	.1515	1.42	.4222	.0778
0.65	.2422	.2578	1.04	.3508	.1492	1.43	.4236	.0764
0.66	.2454	.2546	1.05	.3531	.1469	1.44	.4251	.0749
0.67	.2486	.2514	1.06	.3554	.1446	1.45	.4265	.0735
0.68	.2517	.2483	1.07	.3577	.1423	1.46	.4279	.0721
0.69	.2549	.2451	1.08	.3599	.1410	1.47	.4292	.0708
0.70	.2580	.2420	1.09	.3621	.1379	1.48	.4306	.0694
0.71	.2611	.2389	1.10	.3643	.1357	1.49	.4319	.0681
0.72	.2642	.2358	1.11	.3665	.1335	1.50	.4332	.0668
0.73	.2673	.2327	1.12	.3686	.1314	1.51	.4345	.0655
0.74	.2704	.2296	1.13	.3708	.1292	1.52	.4357	.0643

(continued)

Proportions of Area Under the Normal Curve *(continued)*

(A) Z	(B) area inside $\bar{X}$ & Z	(C) area outside Z	(A) Z	(B) area inside $\bar{X}$ & Z	(C) area outside Z	(A) Z	(B) area inside $\bar{X}$ & Z	(C) area outside Z
1.53	.4370	.0630	1.92	.4276	.0274	2.31	.4896	.0104
1.54	.4382	.0618	1.93	.4732	.0268	2.32	.4898	.0102
1.55	.4394	.0606	1.94	.4738	.0262	2.33	.4901	.0099
1.56	.4406	.0594	1.95	.4744	.0256	2.34	.4904	.0096
1.57	.4418	.0582	1.96	.4750	.0250	2.35	.4906	.0094
1.58	.4429	.0571	1.97	.4756	.0244	2.36	.4909	.0091
1.59	.4441	.0559	1.98	.4761	.0239	2.37	.4911	.0089
1.60	.4452	.0548	1.99	.4767	.0233	2.38	.4913	.0087
1.61	.4463	.0537	2.00	.4772	.0228	2.39	.4916	.0084
1.62	.4474	.0526	2.01	.4778	.0222	2.40	.4918	.0082
1.63	.4484	.0516	2.02	.4783	.0217	2.41	.4920	.0080
1.64	.4495	.0505	2.03	.4788	.0212	2.42	.4922	.0078
1.65	.4505	.0495	2.04	.4793	.0207	2.43	.4925	.0075
1.66	.4515	.0485	2.05	.4798	.0202	2.44	.4927	.0073
1.67	.4525	.0475	2.06	.4803	.0197	2.45	.4929	.0071
1.68	.4535	.0465	2.07	.4808	.0192	2.46	.4931	.0069
1.69	.4545	.0455	2.08	.4812	.0188	2.47	.4932	.0068
1.70	.4554	.0446	2.09	.4817	.0183	2.48	.4934	.0066
1.71	.4564	.0436	2.10	.4821	.0179	2.49	.4936	.0064
1.72	.4573	.0427	2.11	.4826	.0174	2.50	.4938	.0062
1.73	.4582	.0418	2.12	.4830	.0170	2.51	.4940	.0060
1.74	.4591	.0409	2.13	.4834	.0166	2.52	.4941	.0059
1.75	.4599	.0401	2.14	.4838	.0162	2.53	.4943	.0057
1.76	.4608	.0392	2.15	.4842	.0158	2.54	.4945	.0055
1.77	.4616	.0384	2.16	.4846	.0154	2.55	.4946	.0054
1.78	.4625	.0375	2.17	.4850	.0150	2.56	.4948	.0052
1.79	.4633	.0367	2.18	.4854	.0146	2.57	.4949	.0051
1.80	.4641	.0359	2.19	.4857	.0143	2.58	.4951	.0049
1.81	.4649	.0351	2.20	.4861	.0139	2.59	.4952	.0048
1.82	.4656	.0344	2.21	.4864	.0136	2.60	.4953	.0047
1.83	.4664	.0336	2.22	.4868	.0132	2.61	.4955	.0045
1.84	.4671	.0329	2.23	.4871	.0129	2.62	.4956	.0044
1.85	.4678	.0322	2.24	.4875	.0125	2.63	.4957	.0043
1.86	.4686	.0314	2.25	.4878	.0122	2.64	.4959	.0041
1.87	.4693	.0307	2.26	.4881	.0119	2.65	.4960	.0040
1.88	.4699	.0301	2.27	.4884	.0116	2.66	.4961	.0039
1.89	.4706	.0294	2.28	.4887	.0113	2.67	.4962	.0038
1.90	.4713	.0287	2.29	.4890	.0110	2.68	.4963	.0037
1.91	.4719	.0281	2.30	.4893	.0107	2.69	.4964	.0036

(continued)

Proportions of Area Under the Normal Curve *(continued)*

(A)	(B) area inside $\bar{X}$ & Z	(C) area outside Z	(A)	(B) area inside $\bar{X}$ & Z	(C) area outside Z	(A)	(B) area inside $\bar{X}$ & Z	(C) area outside Z
Z			Z			Z		
2.70	.4965	.0035	2.94	.4984	.0016	3.17	.4992	.0008
2.71	.4966	.0034	2.95	.4984	.0016	3.18	.4993	.0007
2.72	.4967	.0033	2.96	.4985	.0015	3.19	.4993	.0007
2.73	.4968	.0032	2.97	.4985	.0015	3.20	.4993	.0007
2.74	.4969	.0031	2.98	.4986	.0014	3.21	.4993	.0007
2.75	.4970	.0030	2.99	.4986	.0014	3.22	.4994	.0006
2.76	.4971	.0029	3.00	.4987	.0013	3.23	.4994	.0006
2.77	.4972	.0028	3.01	.4987	.0013	3.24	.4994	.0006
2.78	.4973	.0027	3.02	.4987	.0013	3.25	.4994	.0006
2.79	.4974	.0026	3.03	.4988	.0012	3.30	.4995	.0005
2.80	.4974	.0026	3.04	.4988	.0012	3.35	.4996	.0004
2.81	.4975	.0025	3.05	.4989	.0011	3.40	.4997	.0003
2.82	.4976	.0024	3.06	.4989	.0011	3.45	.4997	.0003
2.83	.4977	.0023	3.07	.4989	.0011	3.50	.4998	.0002
2.84	.4977	.0023	3.08	.4990	.0010	3.55	.4998	.0002
2.85	.4978	.0022	3.09	.4990	.0010	3.60	.4998	.0002
2.86	.4979	.0021	3.10	.4990	.0010	3.65	.4999	.0001
2.87	.4979	.0021	3.11	.4991	.0009	3.70	.4999	.0001
2.88	.4980	.0020	3.12	.4991	.0009	3.75	.4999	.0001
2.89	.4981	.0019	3.13	.4991	.0009	3.80	.4999	.0001
2.90	.4981	.0019	3.14	.4992	.0008	3.85	.4999	.0001
2.91	.4982	.0018	3.15	.4992	.0008	3.90	.49995	.00005
2.92	.4982	.0018	3.16	.4992	.0008	4.00	.49997	.00003
2.93	.4983	.0017						

Critical values computed by John Timko. Used by permission.

Sigma (σ)	Centered		Shifted 1.5 σ	
4.00	63*	99.9937**	6210*	99.379
5.00	0.57	99.999943	233	99.9767
6.00	0.002[†]	99.9999998	3.4[††]	99.99966

Notes:
* Defects per Million Opportunities (DPMO).
** % yield.
[†] At 6 σ, with a centered distribution (no variation shift), this figure is 2 defects per billion opportunities.
[††] At 6 σ, with an off-centered distribution (Motorola's 1.5 σ long-term process variation shift average), is the often quoted statement "No more than 3.4 defects per million opportunities."

Table B: Critical Values for the Distribution of t (Student's t)

How to use this table: The top two rows of the critical values table lists the most common levels of significance for one-tailed and two-tailed tests, respectively. The column of figures on the far left indicates the degrees of freedom for the test.

For the One-Sample t Test: $df = n - 1$
where n represents the sample size.

For the Paired Student's t Test: $df = n_D - 1$
where n_D represents the number of differences between pairs of data.

For the Two-Sample t Test: $df = n_1 + n_2 - 2$
where n_1 represents the number of elements in sample set one and n_2 represents the number of elements in sample set two.

Once the degrees of freedom have been determined and the level of significance has been selected, simply locate the critical value from the table on page 610. If the calculated value of t is equal to or greater than the critical value obtained from the t table, reject the null hypothesis and support the alternative hypothesis. If the calculated value of t is less than the critical value, retain the null hypothesis and reject the alternative hypothesis.

Example: Suppose a researcher has collected data from two independent samples with $n_1 = 13$ and $n_2 = 10$. A student's t of 2.375 is calculated. For a two-tailed test with $\alpha = .05$, $df = 21$, the test statistic exceeds the critical value of 2.080; therefore, the null hypothesis of no significant difference between the means is rejected and the alternative hypothesis is supported.

Note: *When the combined degrees of freedom for a two-sample student's* t *test exceed 30, the distribution of* t *and the distribution of* z *are approximately the same. Therefore, with* df *> 30, the distribution of* z *(Table A) can be used for student's* t *critical values, as well as for finding* **exact** p *values.*

Critical Values for the Distribution of *t* (Student's *t*)

df	Levels of significance for a **one-tailed test**						
	.20	.10	.05	.025	.01	.005	.0005
	Levels of significance for a **two-tailed test**						
	.40	.20	.10	.05	.02	.01	.001
1	1.376	3.078	6.314	12.707	31.821	63.657	636.619
2	1.061	1.886	2.920	4.303	6.965	9.925	31.598
3	0.978	1.638	2.353	3.182	4.541	5.841	12.941
4	0.941	1.533	2.132	2.776	3.747	4.604	8.610
5	0.920	1.476	2.015	2.571	3.365	4.032	6.859
6	0.906	1.440	1.943	2.447	3.143	3.707	5.959
7	0.896	1.415	1.895	2.365	2.998	3.499	5.404
8	0.889	1.397	1.860	2.306	2.896	3.355	5.041
9	0.883	1.383	1.833	2.262	2.821	3.250	4.781
10	0.879	1.372	1.812	2.228	2.764	3.169	4.587
11	0.876	1.363	1.796	2.201	2.718	3.106	4.437
12	0.873	1.356	1.782	2.179	2.681	3.055	4.318
13	0.870	1.350	1.771	2.160	2.650	3.012	4.221
14	0.868	1.345	1.761	2.145	2.624	2.977	4.140
15	0.866	1.341	1.753	2.131	2.602	2.947	4.073
16	0.865	1.337	1.746	2.120	2.583	2.921	4.015
17	0.863	1.333	1.740	2.110	2.567	2.898	3.965
18	0.862	1.330	1.734	2.101	2.552	2.878	3.922
19	0.861	1.328	1.729	2.093	2.539	2.861	3.883
20	0.860	1.325	1.725	2.086	2.528	2.845	3.850
21	0.859	1.323	1.721	2.080	2.518	2.831	3.819
22	0.858	1.321	1.717	2.074	2.508	2.819	3.792
23	0.858	1.319	1.714	20.69	2.500	2.807	3.767
24	0.857	1.318	1.711	20.64	2.492	2.797	3.745
25	0.856	1.316	1.708	20.60	2.485	2.787	3.725
26	0.856	1.315	1.706	20.56	2.479	2.779	3.707
27	0.855	1.314	1.703	2.052	2.473	2.771	3.690
28	0.855	1.313	1.701	2.048	2.467	2.763	3.674
29	0.854	1.311	1.699	2.045	2.462	2.756	3.659
30	0.854	1.310	1.697	2.042	2.457	2.750	3.646
$t \approx z$	**0.842**	**1.282**	**1.645**	**1.960**	**2.326**	**2.576**	**3.291**

Critical values computed by John Timko. Used by permission.

Table C: Critical Values for the Distribution of *F*

When: α = .10 (one-tailed test)   α = .20 (two-tailed test)

v_2 \\ v_1	Numerator Degrees of Freedom									
	1	2	3	4	5	6	7	8	9	10
1	39.86	49.50	53.59	55.83	57.24	58.20	58.91	59.44	59.86	60.19
2	8.53	9.00	9.16	9.24	9.29	9.33	9.35	9.37	9.38	9.39
3	5.54	5.46	5.39	5.34	5.31	5.28	5.27	5.25	5.24	5.23
4	4.54	4.32	4.19	4.11	4.05	4.01	3.98	3.95	3.94	3.92
5	4.06	3.78	3.62	3.52	3.45	3.40	3.37	3.34	3.32	3.30
6	3.78	3.46	3.29	3.18	3.11	3.05	3.01	2.98	2.96	2.94
7	3.59	3.26	3.07	2.96	2.88	2.83	2.78	2.75	2.72	2.70
8	3.46	3.11	2.92	2.81	2.73	2.67	2.62	2.59	2.56	2.54
9	3.36	3.01	2.81	2.69	2.61	2.55	2.51	2.47	2.44	2.42
10	3.29	2.92	2.73	2.61	2.52	2.46	2.41	2.38	2.35	2.32
11	3.23	2.86	2.66	2.54	2.45	2.39	2.34	2.30	2.27	2.25
12	3.18	2.81	2.61	2.48	2.39	2.33	2.28	2.24	2.22	2.19
13	3.14	2.76	2.56	2.43	2.35	2.28	2.23	2.20	2.16	2.14
14	3.10	2.73	2.52	2.39	2.31	2.24	2.19	2.15	2.12	2.10
15	3.07	2.70	2.49	2.36	2.27	2.21	2.16	2.12	2.09	2.06
16	3.05	2.67	2.46	2.33	2.24	2.18	2.13	2.09	2.06	2.03
17	3.03	2.64	2.44	2.31	2.22	2.15	2.10	2.06	2.03	2.00
18	3.01	2.62	2.42	2.29	2.20	2.13	2.08	2.04	2.00	1.98
19	2.99	2.61	2.40	2.27	2.18	2.11	2.06	2.02	1.98	1.96
20	2.97	2.59	2.38	2.25	2.16	2.09	2.04	2.00	1.96	1.94
21	2.96	2.57	2.36	2.23	2.14	2.08	2.02	1.98	1.95	1.92
22	2.95	2.56	2.35	2.22	2.13	2.06	2.01	1.97	1.93	1.90
23	2.94	2.55	2.34	2.21	2.11	2.05	1.99	1.95	1.92	1.89
24	2.93	2.54	2.33	2.19	2.10	2.04	1.98	1.94	1.91	1.88
25	2.92	2.53	2.32	2.18	2.09	2.02	1.97	1.93	1.89	1.87
26	2.91	2.52	2.31	2.17	2.08	2.01	1.96	1.92	1.88	1.86
27	2.90	2.51	2.30	2.17	2.07	2.00	1.95	1.91	1.87	1.85
28	2.89	2.50	2.29	2.16	2.06	2.00	1.94	1.90	1.87	1.84
29	2.89	2.50	2.28	2.15	2.06	1.99	1.93	1.89	1.86	1.83
30	2.88	2.49	2.28	2.14	2.05	1.98	1.93	1.88	1.85	1.82
40	2.84	2.44	2.23	2.09	2.00	1.93	1.87	1.83	1.79	1.76
50	2.81	2.41	2.20	2.06	1.97	1.90	1.84	1.80	1.76	1.73
60	2.79	2.39	2.18	2.04	1.95	1.87	1.82	1.77	1.74	1.71
70	2.78	2.38	2.16	2.03	1.93	1.86	1.80	1.76	1.72	1.69
80	2.77	2.37	2.15	2.02	1.92	1.85	1.79	1.75	1.71	1.68
90	2.76	2.36	2.15	2.01	1.91	1.84	1.79	1.74	1.70	1.67
100	2.76	2.36	2.14	2.00	1.91	1.83	1.78	1.73	1.70	1.66
110	2.75	2.35	2.13	2.00	1.90	1.83	1.77	1.73	1.69	1.66
120	2.75	2.35	2.13	1.99	1.90	1.82	1.77	1.72	1.68	1.65
∞	2.71	2.30	2.08	1.94	1.85	1.77	1.72	1.67	1.63	1.60

Denominator Degrees of Freedom

Critical values computed by John Timko. Used by permission.

Table C: Critical Values for the Distribution of *F*

When: $\alpha = .10$ (one-tailed test) $\alpha = .20$ (two-tailed test)

v_2 \ v_1	Numerator Degrees of Freedom									
	11	12	15	20	24	30	40	60	120	∞
1	60.47	60.71	61.22	61.74	62.00	62.26	62.53	62.79	63.06	63.33
2	9.40	9.41	9.42	9.44	9.45	9.46	9.47	9.47	9.48	9.49
3	5.22	5.22	5.20	5.18	5.18	5.17	5.16	5.15	5.14	5.13
4	3.91	3.90	3.87	3.84	3.83	3.82	3.80	3.79	3.78	3.76
5	3.28	3.27	3.24	3.21	3.19	3.17	3.16	3.14	3.12	3.10
6	2.92	2.90	2.87	2.84	2.82	2.80	2.78	2.76	2.74	2.72
7	2.68	2.67	2.63	2.59	2.58	2.56	2.54	2.51	2.49	2.47
8	2.52	2.50	2.46	2.42	2.40	2.38	2.36	2.34	2.32	2.29
9	2.40	2.38	2.34	2.30	2.28	2.25	2.23	2.21	2.18	2.16
10	2.30	2.28	2.24	2.20	2.18	2.16	2.13	2.11	2.08	2.06
11	2.23	2.21	2.17	2.12	2.10	2.08	2.05	2.03	2.00	1.97
12	2.17	2.15	2.10	2.06	2.04	2.01	1.99	1.96	1.93	1.90
13	2.12	2.10	2.05	2.01	1.98	1.96	1.93	1.90	1.88	1.85
14	2.07	2.05	2.01	1.96	1.94	1.91	1.89	1.86	1.83	1.80
15	2.04	2.02	1.97	1.92	1.90	1.87	1.85	1.82	1.79	1.76
16	2.01	1.99	1.94	1.89	1.87	1.84	1.81	1.78	1.75	1.72
17	1.98	1.96	1.91	1.86	1.84	1.81	1.78	1.75	1.72	1.69
18	1.95	1.93	1.89	1.84	1.81	1.78	1.75	1.72	1.69	1.66
19	1.93	1.91	1.86	1.81	1.79	1.76	1.73	1.70	1.67	1.63
20	1.91	1.89	1.84	1.79	1.77	1.74	1.71	1.68	1.64	1.61
21	1.90	1.87	1.83	1.78	1.75	1.72	1.69	1.66	1.62	1.59
22	1.88	1.86	1.81	1.76	1.73	1.70	1.67	1.64	1.60	1.57
23	1.87	1.84	1.80	1.74	1.72	1.69	1.66	1.62	1.59	1.55
24	1.85	1.83	1.78	1.73	1.70	1.67	1.64	1.61	1.57	1.53
25	1.84	1.82	1.77	1.72	1.69	1.66	1.63	1.59	1.56	1.52
26	1.83	1.81	1.76	1.71	1.68	1.65	1.61	1.58	1.54	1.50
27	1.82	1.80	1.75	1.70	1.67	1.64	1.60	1.57	1.53	1.49
28	1.81	1.79	1.74	1.69	1.66	1.63	1.59	1.56	1.52	1.48
29	1.80	1.78	1.73	1.68	1.65	1.62	1.58	1.55	1.51	1.47
30	1.79	1.77	1.72	1.67	1.64	1.61	1.57	1.54	1.50	1.46
40	1.74	1.71	1.66	1.61	1.57	1.54	1.51	1.47	1.42	1.38
50	1.70	1.68	1.63	1.57	1.54	1.50	1.47	1.42	1.38	1.34
60	1.68	1.66	1.60	1.54	1.51	1.48	1.44	1.40	1.35	1.29
70	1.67	1.64	1.59	1.53	1.49	1.46	1.42	1.37	1.33	1.24
80	1.65	1.63	1.57	1.51	1.48	1.44	1.40	1.36	1.31	1.19
90	1.64	1.62	1.56	1.50	1.47	1.43	1.39	1.35	1.29	1.15
100	1.64	1.61	1.56	1.49	1.46	1.42	1.38	1.34	1.28	1.11
110	1.63	1.61	1.55	1.49	1.45	1.42	1.37	1.33	1.27	1.07
120	1.63	1.60	1.55	1.48	1.45	1.41	1.37	1.72	1.26	1.03
∞	1.58	1.55	1.49	1.42	1.38	1.34	1.30	1.67	1.17	1.00

Critical values computed by John Timko. Used by permission.

Table C: Critical Values for the Distribution of *F*

When: α = .05 (one-tailed test)   α = .10 (two-tailed test)

v_2	Numerator Degrees of Freedom v_1									
	1	2	3	4	5	6	7	8	9	10
1	161.44	199.49	215.71	224.58	230.16	233.99	236.77	238.88	240.54	241.88
2	18.51	19.00	19.16	19.25	19.30	19.33	19.35	19.37	19.38	19.40
3	10.13	9.55	9.28	9.12	9.01	8.94	8.89	8.85	8.81	8.79
4	7.71	6.94	6.59	6.39	6.26	6.16	6.09	6.04	6.00	5.96
5	6.61	5.79	5.41	5.19	5.05	4.95	4.88	4.82	4.77	4.74
6	5.99	5.14	4.76	4.53	4.39	4.28	4.21	4.15	4.10	4.06
7	5.59	4.74	4.35	4.12	3.97	3.87	3.79	3.73	3.68	3.64
8	5.32	4.46	4.07	3.84	3.69	3.58	3.50	3.44	3.39	3.35
9	5.12	4.26	3.86	3.63	3.48	3.37	3.29	3.23	3.18	3.14
10	4.96	4.10	3.71	3.48	3.33	3.22	3.14	3.07	3.02	2.98
11	4.84	3.98	3.59	3.36	3.20	3.09	3.01	2.95	2.90	2.85
12	4.75	3.89	3.49	3.26	3.11	3.00	2.91	2.85	2.80	2.75
13	4.67	3.81	3.41	3.18	3.03	2.92	2.83	2.77	2.71	2.67
14	4.60	3.74	3.34	3.11	2.96	2.85	2.76	2.70	2.65	2.60
15	4.54	3.68	3.29	3.06	2.90	2.79	2.71	2.64	2.59	2.54
16	4.49	3.63	3.24	3.01	2.85	2.74	2.66	2.59	2.54	2.49
17	4.45	3.59	3.20	2.96	2.81	2.70	2.61	2.55	2.49	2.45
18	4.41	3.55	3.16	2.93	2.77	2.66	2.58	2.51	2.46	2.41
19	4.38	3.52	3.13	2.90	2.74	2.63	2.54	2.48	2.48	2.38
20	4.35	3.49	3.10	2.87	2.71	2.60	2.51	2.45	2.39	2.35
21	4.32	3.47	3.07	2.84	2.68	2.57	2.49	2.42	2.37	2.32
22	4.30	3.44	3.05	2.82	2.66	2.55	2.46	2.40	2.34	2.30
23	4.28	3.42	3.03	2.80	2.64	2.53	2.44	2.37	2.32	2.27
24	4.26	3.40	3.01	2.78	2.62	2.51	2.42	2.36	2.30	2.25
25	4.24	3.39	2.99	2.76	2.60	2.49	2.40	2.34	2.28	2.24
26	4.23	3.37	2.98	2.74	2.59	2.47	2.39	2.32	2.27	2.22
27	4.21	3.35	2.96	2.73	2.57	2.46	2.37	2.31	2.25	2.20
28	4.20	3.34	2.95	2.71	2.56	2.45	2.36	2.29	2.24	2.19
29	4.18	3.33	2.93	2.70	2.55	2.43	2.35	2.28	2.22	2.18
30	4.17	3.32	2.92	2.69	2.53	2.42	2.33	2.27	2.21	2.16
40	4.08	3.23	2.84	2.61	2.45	2.34	2.25	2.18	2.12	2.08
50	4.03	3.18	2.79	2.56	2.40	2.29	2.20	2.13	2.07	2.03
60	4.00	3.15	2.76	2.53	2.37	2.25	2.17	2.10	2.04	1.99
70	3.98	3.13	2.74	2.50	2.35	2.23	2.14	2.07	2.02	1.97
80	3.96	3.11	2.72	2.49	2.33	2.21	2.13	2.06	2.00	1.95
90	3.95	3.10	2.71	2.47	2.32	2.20	2.11	2.04	1.99	1.94
100	3.94	3.09	2.70	2.46	2.31	2.19	2.10	2.03	1.98	1.93
110	3.93	3.08	2.69	2.45	2.03	2.18	2.09	2.02	1.97	1.92
120	3.92	3.07	2.68	2.44	2.29	2.17	2.09	2.02	1.96	1.91
∞	3.84	3.00	2.60	2.37	2.21	2.10	2.01	1.94	1.88	1.83

Denominator Degrees of Freedom

Critical values computed by John Timko. Used by permission.

Table C: Critical Values for the Distribution of F

When: α = .05 (one-tailed test) α = .10 (two-tailed test)

V_1 / V_2 (Denominator Degrees of Freedom)	Numerator Degrees of Freedom									
	11	12	15	20	24	30	40	60	120	∞
1	242.98	243.86	245.93	248.01	249.05	250.09	251.14	252.17	253.25	254.33
2	19.41	19.41	19.43	19.45	19.45	19.46	19.47	19.48	19.49	19.50
3	8.76	8.74	8.70	8.66	8.64	8.62	8.59	8.57	8.55	8.53
4	5.94	5.91	5.86	5.80	5.77	5.75	5.72	5.69	5.66	5.63
5	4.70	4.68	4.62	4.56	4.53	4.50	4.46	4.43	4.40	4.36
6	4.03	4.00	3.94	3.87	3.84	3.81	3.77	3.74	3.70	3.67
7	3.60	3.57	3.51	3.44	3.41	3.38	3.34	3.30	3.27	3.23
8	3.31	3.28	3.22	3.15	3.12	3.08	3.04	3.01	2.97	2.93
9	3.10	3.07	3.01	2.94	2.90	2.86	2.83	2.79	2.75	2.71
10	2.94	2.91	2.85	2.77	2.74	2.70	2.66	2.62	2.58	2.54
11	2.82	2.79	2.72	2.65	2.61	2.57	2.53	2.49	2.45	2.40
12	2.72	2.69	2.62	2.54	2.51	2.47	2.43	2.38	2.34	2.30
13	2.64	2.60	2.53	2.46	2.42	2.38	2.34	2.30	2.25	2.21
14	2.57	2.53	2.46	2.39	2.35	2.31	2.27	2.22	2.18	2.13
15	2.51	2.48	2.40	2.33	2.29	2.25	2.20	2.16	2.11	2.07
16	2.46	2.42	2.35	2.28	2.24	2.19	2.15	2.11	2.06	2.01
17	2.41	2.38	2.31	2.23	2.19	2.15	2.10	2.06	2.01	1.96
18	2.37	2.34	2.27	2.19	2.15	2.11	2.06	2.02	1.97	1.92
19	2.34	2.31	2.23	2.16	2.11	2.07	2.03	1.98	1.93	1.88
20	2.31	2.28	2.20	2.12	2.08	2.04	1.99	1.95	1.90	1.84
21	2.28	2.25	2.18	2.10	2.05	2.01	1.96	1.92	1.87	1.81
22	2.26	2.23	2.15	2.07	2.03	1.98	1.94	1.89	1.84	1.78
23	2.24	2.20	2.13	2.05	2.01	1.96	1.91	1.86	1.81	1.76
24	2.22	2.18	2.11	2.03	1.98	1.94	1.89	1.84	1.79	1.73
25	2.20	2.16	2.09	2.01	1.96	1.92	1.87	1.82	1.77	1.71
26	2.18	2.15	2.07	1.99	1.95	1.90	1.85	1.80	1.75	1.69
27	2.17	2.13	2.06	1.97	1.93	1.88	1.84	1.79	1.73	1.67
28	2.15	2.12	2.04	1.96	1.91	1.87	1.82	1.77	1.71	1.65
29	2.14	2.10	2.03	1.94	1.90	1.85	1.81	1.75	1.70	1.64
30	2.13	2.09	2.01	1.93	1.89	1.84	1.79	1.74	1.68	1.62
40	2.04	2.00	1.92	1.84	1.79	1.74	1.69	1.64	1.58	1.52
50	1.99	1.95	1.87	1.78	1.74	1.69	1.63	1.58	1.51	1.46
60	1.95	1.92	1.84	1.75	1.70	1.65	1.59	1.53	1.47	1.42
70	1.93	1.89	1.81	1.72	1.67	1.62	1.57	1.51	1.44	1.39
80	1.91	1.88	1.79	1.70	1.65	1.60	1.55	1.48	1.41	1.36
90	1.90	1.86	1.78	1.69	1.64	1.59	1.53	1.47	1.39	1.33
100	1.89	1.85	1.77	1.68	1.63	1.57	1.52	1.45	1.38	1.30
110	1.88	1.84	1.76	1.67	1.62	1.56	1.50	1.44	1.36	1.27
120	1.87	1.83	1.75	1.66	1.61	1.55	1.50	1.43	1.35	1.25
∞	1.79	1.75	1.67	1.57	1.52	1.46	1.39	1.32	1.22	1.00

Critical values computed by John Timko. Used by permission.

Table C: Critical Values for the Distribution of F

When: $\alpha = .025$ (one-tailed test) $\alpha = .05$ (two-tailed test)

v_2 \ v_1	Numerator Degrees of Freedom									
	1	2	3	4	5	6	7	8	9	10
1	647.56	799.19	864.05	899.47	921.78	937.07	948.19	956.64	963.27	968.62
2	38.51	39.00	39.17	39.25	39.30	39.33	39.36	39.37	39.39	39.40
3	17.44	16.04	15.44	15.10	14.88	14.73	14.62	14.54	14.47	14.42
4	12.22	10.65	9.98	9.60	9.36	9.20	9.07	8.98	8.90	8.84
5	10.01	8.43	7.76	7.39	7.15	6.98	6.85	6.76	6.68	6.62
6	8.81	7.26	6.60	6.23	5.99	5.82	5.70	5.60	5.52	5.46
7	8.07	6.54	5.89	5.52	5.29	5.12	4.99	4.90	4.82	4.76
8	7.57	6.06	5.42	5.05	4.82	4.65	4.53	4.43	4.36	4.30
9	7.21	5.71	5.08	4.72	4.48	4.32	4.20	4.10	4.03	3.96
10	6.94	5.46	4.83	4.47	4.24	4.07	3.95	3.85	3.78	3.72
11	6.72	5.26	4.63	4.28	4.04	3.88	3.76	3.66	3.59	3.53
12	6.55	5.10	4.47	4.12	3.89	3.73	3.61	3.51	3.44	3.37
13	6.41	4.97	4.35	4.00	3.77	3.60	3.48	3.39	3.31	3.25
14	6.30	4.86	4.24	3.89	3.66	3.50	3.38	3.29	3.21	3.15
15	6.20	4.77	4.15	3.80	3.58	3.41	3.29	3.20	3.12	3.06
16	6.12	4.69	4.08	3.73	3.50	3.34	3.22	3.12	3.05	2.99
17	6.04	4.62	4.01	3.66	3.44	3.28	3.16	3.06	2.98	2.92
18	5.98	4.56	3.95	3.61	3.38	3.22	3.10	3.01	2.93	2.87
19	5.92	4.51	3.90	3.56	3.33	3.17	3.05	2.96	2.88	2.82
20	5.87	4.46	3.86	3.51	3.29	3.13	3.01	2.91	2.84	2.77
21	5.83	4.42	3.82	3.48	3.25	3.09	2.97	2.87	2.80	2.73
22	5.79	4.38	3.78	3.44	3.22	3.05	2.93	2.84	2.76	2.70
23	5.75	4.35	3.75	3.41	3.18	3.02	2.90	2.81	2.73	2.67
24	5.72	4.32	3.72	3.38	3.15	2.99	2.87	2.78	2.70	2.64
25	5.69	4.29	3.69	3.35	3.13	2.97	2.85	2.75	2.68	2.61
26	5.66	4.27	3.67	3.33	3.10	2.94	2.82	2.73	2.65	2.59
27	5.63	4.24	3.65	3.31	3.08	2.92	2.80	2.71	2.63	2.57
28	5.61	4.22	3.63	3.29	3.06	2.90	2.78	2.69	2.61	2.55
29	5.59	4.20	3.61	3.27	3.04	2.88	2.76	2.67	2.59	2.53
30	5.57	4.18	3.59	3.25	3.03	2.87	2.75	2.65	2.57	2.51
40	5.54	4.05	3.46	3.13	2.90	2.74	2.62	2.53	2.45	2.39
50	5.34	3.98	3.39	3.05	2.83	2.67	2.55	2.46	2.38	2.32
60	5.29	3.93	3.34	3.01	2.79	2.63	2.51	2.41	2.33	2.27
70	5.25	3.89	3.31	2.98	2.75	2.60	2.47	2.38	2.30	2.24
80	5.22	3.86	3.28	2.95	2.73	2.57	2.45	2.36	2.28	2.21
90	5.20	3.84	3.27	2.92	2.71	2.55	2.43	2.34	2.26	2.19
100	5.18	3.83	3.25	2.91	2.70	2.54	2.42	2.32	2.24	2.18
110	5.16	3.82	3.24	2.90	2.68	2.53	2.41	2.31	2.23	2.17
120	5.15	3.80	3.23	2.89	2.67	2.52	2.39	2.30	2.22	2.16
∞	5.02	3.69	3.12	2.79	2.57	2.41	2.29	2.19	2.11	2.05

Denominator Degrees of Freedom

Critical values computed by John Timko. Used by permission.

Table C: Critical Values for the Distribution of F

When: $\alpha = .025$ (one-tailed test) $\alpha = .05$ (two-tailed test)

v_2 \ v_1	11	12	15	20	24	30	40	60	120	∞
					Numerator Degrees of Freedom					
1	973.02	976.70	984.87	993.10	996.94	1001.2	1005.5	1009.8	1014.0	1018.0
2	39.41	39.41	39.43	39.45	39.46	39.46	39.47	39.48	39.49	39.50
3	14.37	14.34	14.25	14.17	14.12	14.08	14.04	13.99	13.95	13.90
4	8.79	8.75	8.66	8.56	8.51	8.46	8.41	8.36	8.31	8.26
5	6.57	6.52	6.43	6.33	6.28	6.23	6.18	6.12	6.07	6.02
6	5.41	5.37	5.27	5.17	5.12	5.07	5.01	4.96	4.90	4.85
7	4.71	4.67	4.57	4.47	4.42	4.36	4.31	4.25	4.20	4.14
8	4.24	4.20	4.10	4.00	3.95	3.89	3.84	3.78	3.73	3.67
9	3.91	3.87	3.77	3.67	3.61	3.56	3.51	3.45	3.39	3.33
10	3.67	3.62	3.52	3.42	3.37	3.31	3.26	3.20	3.14	3.08
11	3.47	3.43	3.33	3.23	3.17	3.12	3.06	3.00	2.94	2.88
12	3.32	3.28	3.18	3.07	3.02	2.96	2.91	2.85	2.79	2.72
13	3.20	3.15	3.05	2.95	2.89	2.84	2.78	2.72	2.66	2.60
14	3.09	3.05	2.95	2.84	2.79	2.73	2.67	2.61	2.55	2.49
15	3.01	2.96	2.86	2.76	2.70	2.64	2.59	2.52	2.46	2.40
16	2.93	2.89	2.79	2.68	2.63	2.57	2.51	2.45	2.38	2.32
17	2.87	2.82	2.72	2.62	2.56	2.50	2.44	2.38	2.32	2.25
18	2.81	2.77	2.67	2.56	2.50	2.44	2.38	2.32	2.26	2.19
19	2.77	2.72	2.62	2.51	2.45	2.39	2.33	2.27	2.20	2.13
20	2.72	2.68	2.57	2.46	2.41	2.35	2.29	2.22	2.16	2.09
21	2.68	2.64	2.53	2.42	2.37	2.31	2.25	2.18	2.11	2.04
22	2.65	2.60	2.50	2.39	2.33	2.27	2.21	2.14	2.08	2.00
23	2.62	2.57	2.47	2.36	2.30	2.24	2.18	2.11	2.04	1.97
24	2.59	2.54	2.44	2.33	2.27	2.21	2.15	2.08	2.01	1.94
25	2.56	2.51	2.41	2.30	2.24	2.18	2.12	2.05	1.98	1.91
26	2.54	2.49	2.39	2.28	2.22	2.16	2.09	2.03	1.95	1.88
27	2.51	2.47	2.36	2.25	2.19	2.13	2.07	2.00	1.93	1.85
28	2.49	2.45	2.34	2.23	2.17	2.11	2.05	1.98	1.91	1.83
29	2.48	2.43	2.32	2.21	2.15	2.09	2.03	1.96	1.89	1.81
30	2.46	2.41	2.31	2.20	2.14	2.07	2.01	1.94	1.87	1.64
40	2.33	2.29	2.18	2.07	2.01	1.94	1.88	1.80	1.72	1.56
50	2.26	2.22	2.11	1.99	1.93	1.87	1.80	1.72	1.64	1.52
60	2.22	2.17	2.06	1.94	1.88	1.82	1.74	1.67	1.58	1.48
70	2.18	2.14	2.03	1.91	1.85	1.78	1.71	1.63	1.54	1.44
80	2.16	2.11	2.00	1.88	1.82	1.75	1.68	1.60	1.51	1.40
90	2.14	2.09	1.98	1.86	1.80	1.73	1.66	1.58	1.48	1.36
100	2.12	2.08	1.97	1.85	1.78	1.72	1.64	1.56	1.46	1.32
110	2.11	2.07	1.96	1.84	1.77	1.70	1.63	1.54	1.45	1.28
120	2.10	2.06	1.95	1.83	1.76	1.69	1.61	1.53	1.43	1.24
∞	2.02	1.94	1.83	1.71	1.64	1.57	1.48	1.39	1.27	1.00

Denominator Degrees of Freedom (left axis label)

Critical values computed by John Timko. Used by permission.

Table C: Critical Values for the Distribution of F

When: α = .01 (one-tailed test) α = .02 (two-tailed test)

v_2 \ v_1	Numerator Degrees of Freedom									
	1	2	3	4	5	6	7	8	9	10
1	4,052	5,000	5,403	5,625	5,764	5,859	5,928	5,982	6,022	6,056
2	98.50	99.00	99.17	99.25	99.30	99.33	99.36	99.37	99.39	99.40
3	34.12	30.82	29.46	28.71	28.24	27.91	27.67	27.49	27.35	27.23
4	21.20	18.00	16.69	15.98	15.52	15.51	14.98	14.80	14.66	14.55
5	16.26	13.27	12.06	11.39	10.97	10.67	10.46	10.29	10.16	10.05
6	13.75	10.92	9.78	9.15	8.75	8.47	8.26	8.10	7.98	7.87
7	12.25	9.55	8.45	7.85	7.46	7.19	6.99	6.84	6.72	6.62
8	11.26	8.65	7.59	7.01	6.63	6.37	6.18	6.03	5.91	5.81
9	10.56	8.02	6.99	6.42	6.06	5.80	5.61	5.47	5.35	5.26
10	10.04	7.56	6.55	5.99	5.64	5.39	5.20	5.06	4.94	4.85
11	9.65	7.21	6.22	5.67	5.32	5.07	4.89	4.74	4.63	4.54
12	9.33	6.93	5.95	5.41	5.06	4.82	4.64	4.50	4.39	4.30
13	9.07	6.70	5.74	5.21	4.86	4.62	4.44	4.30	4.19	4.10
14	8.86	6.51	5.56	5.04	4.69	4.46	4.28	4.14	4.03	3.94
15	8.68	6.36	5.42	4.89	4.56	4.32	4.14	4.00	3.89	3.80
16	8.53	6.23	5.29	4.77	4.44	4.20	4.03	3.89	3.78	3.69
17	8.40	6.11	5.18	4.67	4.34	4.10	3.93	3.79	3.68	3.59
18	8.29	6.01	5.09	4.58	4.25	4.01	3.84	3.71	3.60	3.51
19	8.18	5.93	5.01	4.50	4.17	3.94	3.77	3.63	3.52	3.43
20	8.10	5.85	4.94	4.43	4.10	3.87	3.70	3.56	3.46	3.37
21	8.02	5.78	4.87	4.37	4.04	3.81	3.64	3.51	3.40	3.31
22	7.95	5.72	4.82	4.31	3.99	3.76	3.59	3.45	3.35	3.26
23	7.88	5.66	4.76	4.26	3.94	3.71	3.54	3.41	3.30	3.21
24	7.82	5.61	4.72	4.22	3.90	3.67	3.50	3.36	3.26	3.17
25	7.77	5.57	4.68	4.18	3.85	3.63	3.46	3.32	3.22	3.13
26	7.72	5.53	4.64	4.14	3.82	3.59	3.42	3.29	3.18	3.09
27	7.68	5.49	4.60	4.11	3.78	3.56	3.39	3.26	3.15	3.06
28	7.64	5.45	4.57	4.07	3.75	3.53	3.36	3.23	3.12	3.03
29	7.60	5.42	4.54	4.04	3.73	3.50	3.33	3.20	3.09	3.00
30	7.56	5.39	4.51	4.02	3.70	3.47	3.30	3.17	3.07	2.98
40	7.31	5.18	4.31	3.83	3.51	3.29	3.12	2.99	2.89	2.80
50	7.17	5.06	4.20	3.72	3.41	3.19	3.02	2.89	2.79	2.70
60	7.08	4.98	4.13	3.65	3.34	3.12	2.95	2.82	2.72	2.63
70	7.01	4.92	4.07	3.60	3.29	3.07	2.91	2.78	2.67	2.59
80	6.96	4.88	4.04	3.56	3.26	3.04	2.87	2.74	2.64	2.55
90	6.92	4.85	4.01	3.54	3.23	3.01	2.84	2.72	2.61	2.52
100	6.90	4.82	3.98	3.51	3.21	2.99	2.82	2.69	2.59	2.50
110	6.87	4.80	3.97	3.50	3.19	2.97	2.81	2.68	2.57	2.49
120	6.85	4.79	3.95	3.48	3.17	2.96	2.79	2.66	2.56	2.47
∞	6.63	4.61	3.78	3.32	3.02	2.80	2.64	2.51	2.41	2.32

Denominator Degrees of Freedom

Critical values computed by John Timko. Used by permission.

Table C: Critical Values for the Distribution of *F*

When: α = .01 (one-tailed test)   α = .02 (two-tailed test)

v_1 / v_2	Numerator Degrees of Freedom									
Denominator Degrees of Freedom	11	12	15	20	24	30	40	60	120	∞
1	6,083	6,106	6,157	6,209	6,235	6,261	6,287	6,313	6,339	6,366
2	99.41	99.42	99.43	99.45	99.46	99.47	99.47	99.48	99.49	99.50
3	27.13	27.05	26.87	26.69	26.60	26.50	26.41	26.32	26.22	26.13
4	14.45	14.37	14.20	14.02	13.93	13.84	13.75	13.65	13.56	13.46
5	9.96	9.89	9.72	9.55	9.47	9.38	9.29	9.20	9.11	9.02
6	7.79	7.72	7.56	7.40	7.31	7.23	7.14	7.06	6.97	6.88
7	6.54	6.47	6.31	6.16	6.07	5.99	5.91	5.82	5.74	5.65
8	5.73	5.67	5.52	5.36	5.28	5.20	5.12	5.03	4.95	4.86
9	5.18	5.11	4.96	4.81	4.73	4.65	4.57	4.48	4.40	4.31
10	4.77	4.71	4.56	4.41	4.33	4.25	4.17	4.08	4.00	3.91
11	4.46	4.40	4.25	4.10	4.02	3.94	3.86	3.78	3.69	3.60
12	4.22	4.16	4.01	3.86	3.78	3.70	3.62	3.54	3.45	3.36
13	4.02	3.96	3.82	3.66	3.59	3.51	3.43	3.34	3.25	3.17
14	3.86	3.80	3.66	3.51	3.43	3.35	3.27	3.18	3.09	3.00
15	3.73	3.67	3.52	3.37	3.29	3.21	3.13	3.05	2.96	2.87
16	3.62	3.55	3.41	3.26	3.18	3.10	3.02	2.93	2.84	2.75
17	3.52	3.46	3.31	3.16	3.08	3.00	2.92	2.83	2.75	2.65
18	3.43	3.37	3.23	3.08	3.00	2.92	2.84	2.75	2.66	2.57
19	3.36	3.30	3.15	3.00	2.92	2.84	2.76	2.67	2.58	2.49
20	3.29	3.23	3.09	2.94	2.86	2.78	2.69	2.61	2.52	2.42
21	3.24	3.17	3.03	2.88	2.80	2.72	2.64	2.55	2.46	2.36
22	3.18	3.12	2.98	2.83	2.75	2.67	2.58	2.50	2.40	2.31
23	3.14	3.07	2.93	2.78	2.70	2.62	2.54	2.45	2.35	2.26
24	3.09	3.03	2.89	2.74	2.66	2.58	2.49	2.40	2.31	2.21
25	3.06	2.99	2.85	2.70	2.62	2.54	2.45	2.36	2.27	2.17
26	3.02	2.96	2.81	2.66	2.58	2.50	2.42	2.33	2.23	2.13
27	2.99	2.93	2.78	2.63	2.55	2.47	2.38	2.29	2.20	2.10
28	2.96	2.90	2.75	2.60	2.52	2.44	2.35	2.26	2.17	2.06
29	2.93	2.87	2.73	2.57	2.49	2.41	2.33	2.23	2.14	2.03
30	2.91	2.84	2.70	2.55	2.47	2.39	2.30	2.21	2.11	2.01
40	2.73	2.66	2.52	2.37	2.29	2.20	2.11	2.02	1.92	1.80
50	2.63	2.56	2.42	2.27	2.18	2.10	2.01	1.91	1.80	1.70
60	2.56	2.50	2.35	2.20	2.12	2.03	1.94	1.84	1.73	1.60
70	2.51	2.45	2.31	2.15	2.07	1.98	1.89	1.79	1.67	1.52
80	2.48	2.42	2.27	2.12	2.03	1.94	1.85	1.75	1.63	1.44
90	2.45	2.39	2.24	2.09	2.00	1.92	1.82	1.72	1.60	1.36
100	2.43	2.37	2.22	2.07	1.98	1.89	1.80	1.69	1.57	1.28
110	2.41	2.35	2.21	2.05	1.97	1.88	1.78	1.67	1.55	1.20
120	2.40	2.34	2.19	2.04	1.95	1.86	1.76	1.66	1.53	1.10
∞	2.39	2.18	2.04	1.88	1.79	1.70	1.59	1.47	1.32	1.00

Critical values computed by John Timko. Used by permission.

Table D: Critical Values for the Distribution of Chi-Square (x^2)

How to use this table: The top row of the chi-square critical values table lists the most common levels of significance. The column of figures on the left indicates the degrees of freedom.

For the chi-square statistic: $\text{df} = (r - 1)(c - 1)$
where r and c represent the number of rows and columns, respectively, in the contingency table.

Example: Suppose a researcher is using a 3×3 contingency table and is testing the null hypothesis of independence at the .01 level of significance. Using the formula above, degrees of freedom for a 3×3 table equal 4. Turn to page 620 and locate 4 in the *df* column. Move 5 columns to the right of 4 df and the critical value is 13.277. Therefore, if the researcher's chi-square statistic were equal to or greater than the critical value of 13.277, the null hypothesis of independence would be rejected at the .01 level of significance, and the alternative hypothesis would be supported.

For the goodness-of-fit statistic: $\text{df} = K - 1$
where K represents the number of attributes (cells) that comprise the variable of interest.

Example: Suppose a researcher is interested in studying the frequency of occurrence of accidents that occur on an hourly basis during an 8-hour shift. Using the formula above, degrees of freedom for a variable comprised of 8 attributes would be equal to 7, that is, ($K - 1 = 8 - 1 = 7$). If the researcher were testing the null hypothesis of no significant difference between observed and expected frequencies at the .10 level of significance, the critical value would be 12.017. Turn to page 620 and locate 7 in the df column. Move 2 columns to the right of 7 df and the critical value is 12.017. Therefore, if the researcher's chi-square statistic for this goodness-of-fit test were equal to or greater than the critical value of 12.017, the null hypothesis of no difference would be rejected at the .10 level of significance, and the alternative hypothesis would be supported.

Note: For chi-square and goodness-of-fit tests, all tests of significance are essentially two-tailed tests. This is because all chi-square and goodness-of-fit tests are nondirectional.

Critical Values for the Distribution of Chi Square (x^2)

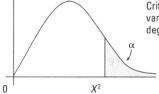

Critical values of X^2 for various values of α and degrees of freedom (df)

df	Levels of significance						
	.20	.10	.05	.025	.01	.005	.001
1	1.644	2.706	3.842	5.024	6.635	7.879	10.828
2	3.219	4.605	5.991	7.378	9.210	10.597	13.816
3	4.642	6.251	7.815	9.348	11.345	12.838	16.265
4	5.989	7.779	9.488	11.143	13.277	14.860	18.459
5	7.289	9.236	11.070	12.832	15.086	16.750	20.515
6	8.558	10.645	12.592	14.449	16.812	18.547	22.458
7	9.803	12.017	14.067	16.013	18.475	20.278	24.321
8	11.030	13.362	15.507	17.534	20.090	21.955	26.124
9	12.242	14.684	16.919	19.023	21.666	23.589	27.876
10	13.442	15.987	18.307	20.483	23.209	25.187	29.586
11	14.631	17.275	19.675	21.920	24.724	26.756	31.261
12	15.812	18.549	21.026	23.336	26.216	28.298	32.906
13	16.985	19.812	22.362	24.735	27.687	29.817	34.524
14	18.151	21.064	23.685	26.118	29.140	31.317	36.117
15	19.311	22.307	24.995	27.488	30.578	32.798	37.690
16	20.465	23.542	26.296	28.845	32.000	34.267	39.244
17	21.615	24.769	27.587	30.191	33.409	35.718	40.780
18	22.760	25.989	28.869	31.526	34.805	37.156	42.301
19	23.900	27.203	30.144	32.852	36.191	38.582	43.807
20	25.037	28.412	31.410	34.170	37.566	39.997	45.300
21	26.171	29.615	32.671	35.479	38.932	41.401	46.797
22	27.301	30.813	33.924	36.781	40.289	42.796	48.268
23	28.429	32.007	35.172	38.076	41.638	44.181	49.728
24	29.553	33.196	36.415	39.364	42.980	45.558	51.178
25	30.675	34.382	37.653	40.646	44.314	46.928	52.620
26	31.795	35.563	38.885	41.923	45.642	48.290	54.052
27	32.912	36.741	40.113	43.195	46.963	49.645	55.476
28	34.027	37.916	41.337	44.461	48.278	50.993	56.892
29	35.139	39.087	42.557	45.722	49.588	52.336	58.301
30	36.250	40.256	43.773	46.979	50.892	53.672	59.703

Critical values computed by John Timko. Used by permission.

Table E: Critical Values for the Pearson's Product-Moment Correlation Coefficient (r)

| | Levels of significance for a **one-tailed test** | | | | | |
	.10	.05	.025	.01	.005	.0005
	Levels of significance for a **two-tailed test**					
n	.20	.10	.05	.02	.01	.001
3	.951	.988	.997	1.000	1.000	1.000
4	.800	.900	.950	.980	.990	.999
5	.687	.805	.878	.934	.959	.991
6	.608	.729	.811	.882	.917	.974
7	.551	.669	.754	.833	.875	.951
8	.507	.621	.707	.789	.834	.925
9	.472	.582	.666	.750	.798	.898
10	.443	.549	.632	.715	.765	.872
11	.419	.521	.602	.685	.735	.847
12	.398	.497	.576	.658	.708	.823
13	.380	.476	.553	.634	.684	.801
14	.365	.457	.532	.612	.661	.780
15	.351	.441	.514	.592	.641	.760
16	.338	.426	.497	.574	.623	.742
17	.327	.412	.482	.558	.606	.725
18	.317	.400	.468	.543	.590	.708
19	.308	.389	.456	.529	.575	.693
20	.299	.378	.444	.516	.561	.679
21	.291	.369	.433	.503	.549	.665
22	.284	.360	.423	.492	.537	.652
23	.277	.352	.413	.482	.526	.640
24	.271	.344	.404	.472	.515	.629
25	.265	.337	.396	.462	.505	.618
26	.260	.330	.388	.453	.496	.607
27	.255	.323	.381	.445	.487	.597
28	.250	.317	.374	.437	.479	.588
29	.245	.311	.367	.430	.471	.579

(continued)

Table E: Critical Values for the Pearson's Product-Moment Correlation Coefficient (r) *(continued)*

	Levels of significance for a **one-tailed test**					
	.10	.05	.025	.01	.005	.0005
	Levels of significance for a **two-tailed test**					
n	.20	.10	.05	.02	.01	.001
30	.241	.306	.361	.423	.463	.570
32	.233	.296	.349	.409	.449	.554
42	.202	.257	.304	.345	.393	.490
52	.181	.231	.274	.322	.355	.444
62	.165	.211	.250	.295	.325	.408
72	.152	.193	.228	.268	.294	.391
82	.142	.181	.214	.252	.277	.345
92	.134	.171	.202	.238	.262	.328
102	.128	.162	.192	.227	.250	.313
122	.116	.149	.178	.208	.229	.288

Critical values computed by John Timko. Used by permission.

Aczel, Amir D. *Complete Business Statistics* (2nd ed.). Homewood, IL: Richard D. Irwin, Inc., 1993.

Aft, Lawrence S. *Productivity, Measurement, and Improvement*. Milwaukee, WI: Quality Press, 1983.

Alreck, Pamela L. and Robert B. Settle. *The Survey Research Handbook*. Homewood, IL: Richard O. Irwin, Inc., 1985.

Alsup, Fred and Ricky M. Watson. *Practical Statistical Process Control*. New York: Van Nostrand Reinhold, 1993.

Amsden, Robert T, Howard E. Butler and Davida M. Amsden. *SPC Simplified*. White Plains, NY: Quality Resource, 1989.

AT&T. *Process Quality Management & Improvement Guidelines*. Indianapolis, IN: AT&T Publication Center, 1988.

AT&T. *Statistical Quality Control Handbook* (Select Code 700-444). Charlotte, NC: Delmar Printing Company, 1985.

Aubrey, Charles A., II and Patricia K. Felkins. *Teamwork: Involving People in Quality and Productivity Improvement*. New York: Quality Resources, 1988.

Backstrom, Charles H. and Gerald Hursh-Cesar. *Survey Research* (2nd ed.). New York: John Wiley & Sons, Inc., 1981.

Berger, Roger W. and Thomas Pyzdek (eds.). *Quality Engineering Handbook*. New York: ASQC Quality Press, 1992.

Bissell, Derek. *Statistical Methods for SPC and TQM*. London: Chapman and Hall, 1994.

Bogan, Christopher E. and Michael J. English. *Benchmarking for Best Practices*. New York: McGraw-Hill, Inc., 1994.

Bolton, Robert. *People Skills*. New York: Simon & Schuster, Inc., 1979.

Born, Gary. *Process Management to Quality Improvement*. New York: John Wiley & Sons, Inc., 1994.

Boshear, Walton C. and Karl G. Albrecht. *Understanding People: Models and Concepts*. San Diego, CA: University Associates Inc., 1977.

Brassard, Michael and Diane Ritter. *The Memory Jogger II*. Methuen, MA: Goal/QPC, 1994.

Braverman, Jerome D. *Fundamentals of Statistical Quality Control*. Reston, VA: Reston Publishing Company, Inc., 1981.

Brown, Mark G. *Baldrige Award Winning Quality* (5th ed.). New York: Quality Resources, 1995.

Burr, Irving W. *Statistical Quality Control Methods*. Milwaukee, WI: ASQC Quality Press, 1979.

Buzan, Tony and Barry Buzan. *The Mind Map Book*. New York: Penguin Group, 1996.

Camp, Robert C. *Benchmarking*. Milwaukee, WI: ASQC Quality Press, 1991.

Carruba, Eugene R. and Ronald D. Gordon. *Product Assurance Principles: Integrating Design Assurance and Quality Assurance*. Milwaukee, WI: Quality Press, 1988.

Christopher, William F. *Productivity Measurement Handbook* (2nd ed.). Cambridge, MA: Productivity Press, 1985.

Cooper, Donald R. and C. William Emory. *Business Research Methods* (5th ed.). Homewood, IL: Richard D. Irwin, Inc., 1995.

Couger, Daniel J. *Creative Problem Solving and Opportunity Finding*. New York: Boyd & Fraser Publishing Company, 1995.

Crosby, Philip B., *Quality Is Free*. Markham, ON: Penguin Books Canada Ltd., 1980.

Daniels, William R. *Group Power: A Manager's Guide to Using Meetings*. San Diego, CA: University Associates, Inc., 1986.

Davenport, Thomas H. *Process Innovation*. Boston, MA: Harvard Business School Press, 1993.

Davis, Duane and Robert M. Cosenza. *Business Research for Decision Making* (3rd ed.). Belmont, CA: Wadsworth Publishing Company, 1993.

De Bono, Edward. Chancen: Das Trainingsmodell fuer erfolgreiche Ideensuche. Duesseldorf, Germany: ECON Taschenbuch Verlag GmbH, 1991.

De Bono, Edward. *Laterales Denken*. Duesseldorf, Germany: ECON Verlag, 1989.

Deeprose, Donna. *The Team Coach*. New York: AMACOM, 1995.

Delbecq, A. L., A. H. Van de Ven and D. H. Gustafson. *Group Techniques for Program Planning*. Glenview, IL: Scott, Foresman, 1975

Deming, W. Edwards. *Out of Crisis*. Cambridge, MA: MIT, Center for Advanced Engineering Study, 1986.

Deming, W. Edwards. *Statistical Adjustment of Data*. New York: John Wiley & Sons, Inc., 1964.

Dockstader, Steven L. *Managing TQM Implementation*, Navy Personnel Research and Development Center. Presented at the DoD Depot Maintenance Seminar, Gettysburg, PA, Nov. 1987.

Dow Chemical Company. "America's Quality Coaches." *CPI Purchasing*, March, 1986.

Dyer, William G. *Team Building* (2nd ed.). Reading, MA: Addison-Wesley Publishing Company, 1987.

Electronic Systems Division. *The ESD Process Improvement Guide*. Hanscom AFB, MA: ESD, MITRE, 1991.

Evans, James R. and William M. Lindsay. *The Management and Control of Quality* (3rd ed.). St.. Paul, MN: West Publishing Company, 1996.

Feigenbaum, Armand V. *Total Quality Control* (3rd ed.). New York: McGraw-Hill, Inc., 1983.

Federal Quality Institute. *Federal Total Quality Management Handbook*. Washington, DC: FQI, 1991.

Felkins, Patricia K., Kenneth N. Chakiris and B. J. Chakiris. *Change Management*. White Plains, NY: Quality Resources, 1993.

Fisher, Kimball. *Leading Self-Directing Work Teams*. New York: McGraw-Hill, Inc., 1993.

Ford Motor Company. *Continuing Process Control and Process Capability Improvement*. Dearborn, MI: Statistical Methods Office, 1984.

Foy, Nancy. *Empowering People at Work*. Brockfield, VT: Gower, 1994.

Francis, Dave and Don Young. *Improving Work Groups*. San Diego, CA: University Associates, Inc., 1979.

Fukuda, Ryuji. *623 623*. Portland, OR: Productivity, Inc., 1997

Gaither, Norman. *Production and Operations Management* (5th ed.). Fort Worth, TX: The Dryden Press, 1992.

Gelb, Michael J. *Thinking for a Change*. New York: Harmony Books, 1995.

Geschka, H. "*Methods and Organization or Idea Generation*." Paper presented at Creativity Week II, Center for Creative Leadership, Greensboro, NC, Sept. 1979.

Goodstein, Leonard, Timothy Nolan and J. William Pfeiffer. *Applied Strategic Planning: A Comprehensive Guide*. New York: McGraw-Hill, Inc., 1993.

Grant, Eugene L. and Richard S. Leavenworth. *Statistical Quality Control* (6th ed.). New York: McGraw-Hill, Inc., 1988.

Greene, Richard. *Global Quality*. Milwaukee, WI: ASQC Quality Press, 1993.

GTE Service Corporation. *Problem Solving Techniques Handbook*. Stamford, CT: GTE, 1986.

Hall, Robert W. *Attaining Manufacturing Excellence*. Homewood, IL: Dow Jones-Irwin, 1987.

Hammer, Michael and James Champy. *Reengineering the Corporation*. New York: Harper Collins Publishers, Inc., 1993.

Harrington, James H. *The Improvement Process*. Milwaukee, WI: Quality Press, 1987.

Harrington-Mackin, Deborah. *The Team Building Toolkit*. New York: AMACOM, 1994.

Harry, Mikel J. *The Nature of Six Sigma Quality*. Government Electronics Group, Motorola, Inc., 1987.

Hayes, Glenn E. *Quality Assurance: Management and Technology* (rev. ed.). Capistrano Beach, CA: Charger Productions, 1983.

Hradesky, John L. *Productivity & Quality Improvement*. New York: McGraw-Hill, Inc., 1988.

Hunt, V. Daniel. *Quality in America*. Burr Ridge, IL: Irwin Professional Publishing, 1992.

Ingle, Sud. *Quality Circles Master Guide*. Englewood Cliffs, NJ: Prentice-Hall, Inc., 1982.

Institute of Industrial Engineers. *Beyond the Basics of Reengineering*. Norcross, GA: Quality Resources, 1994.

Institute of Industrial Engineers. *Business Process Reengineering*. Norcross, GA: IIE, 1993.

Isaac, Stephen and William B. Michael. *Handbook in Research and Evaluation* (2nd ed.). San Diego, CA: Edits Publishers, 1983.

Ishikawa, Kaoru. *Guide to Quality Control*. Tokyo: Asian Productivity Organization, 1986.

Ishikawa, Kaoru. *Introduction to Quality Control*. Tokyo: 3A Corporation, 1989

Jablonski, Joseph R. *Implementing TQM: Competing in the Nineties through Total Quality Management*. Albuquerque, NM: Technical Management Consortium, Inc., 1994.

Jackson, Harry K., Jr. and Normand L. Frigon. *Management 2000: The Practical Guide to World Class Competition*. New York: Van Nostrand Reinhold, 1994.

Jones, Morgan D. *The Thinker's Toolkit*. New York: Random House, Inc., 1995.

Juran Institute. *Quality Improvement Pocket Guide*. Wilton, CT: Juran Institute, Inc., 1993.

Juran Institute. *Quality Planning Ready Reference*. Wilton, CT: Juran Institute, Inc., 1994.

Juran, Joseph M. and Frank M. Gryna. *Juran's Quality Control Handbook* (4th ed.). Milwaukee, WI: Quality Press, 1988.

Juran, Joseph M. *Juran on Planning for Quality*. New York: The Free Press, 1988.

Kan, Stephen H. Metrics and *Models in Software Quality Engineering*. Reading, MA: Addison-Wesley Publishing Company, 1995.

Katzenbach, Jon R. and Douglas K. Smith. *The Wisdom of Teams*. Boston, MA: Harvard Business School Press, 1993.

Kaydos, Will. *Measuring, Managing, and Maximizing Performance*. Cambridge, MA: Productivity Press, Inc., 1991.

Kepner-Tregoe. *Problem Solving and Decision Making*. Skillman, NJ: Kepner-Tregoe, Inc., 1989.

Kerzuer, Harold. *Project Management—A Systems Approach to Planning, Scheduling and Controlling*. New York: Van Nostrand Reinhold, 1992.

King, Bob. *Better Designs in Half the Time* (3rd ed.). Methuen, MA: Goal/QPC, 1989.

Kinlaw, Dennis C. *Continuous Improvement and Measurement for Total Quality*. Homewood, IL: Pfeiffer & Company, 1992.

Kirby, Gary and Jeffery R. Goodpaster. *Thinking*. Englewood Cliffs, NJ: Prentice-Hall, Inc., 1995.

Langley, Gerald J. et al. *The Improvement Guide*. San Francisco: Jossey-Bass Publishing, 1996.

Leedy, Paul D. *Practical Research* (2nd ed.). New York: MacMillian Publishing Company, 1980.

Levin, Richard I. and David S. Rubin. *Statistics for Management* (5th Ed.). Englewood Cliffs, NJ: Prentice-Hall, Inc., 1991.

Levine, Marvin. *Effective Problem Solving* (2nd ed.). Englewoods Cliffs, NJ: Prentice-Hall, Inc., 1994.

Levy, Sidney M., *Project Management in Construction* (2nd ed.). New York: McGraw-Hill, Inc., 1994.

Lewis, James P. *Project Planning, Scheduling & Control*. Boston, MA: Irwin Professional Publishing, 1995.

Manganelli, Raymond L. and Mark M. Klein. *The Reengineering Handbook*. New York: AMOCOM, 1994.

Masaaki, Imai. *Kaizen*. New York: The Kaizen Institute, 1986.

Mason, Robert D. and Douglas A. Lind. *Statistical Techniques in Business and Economics*. Homewood IL: Richard D. Irwin, Inc., 1993.

Mears, Peter. *Quality Improvement Tools & Techniques*, New York: McGraw-Hill, Inc., 1995.

Meredith, Jack R. and Samual J. Mantel, Jr. *Project Management* (3rd ed.). New York: John Wiley & Sons, Inc., 1995.

Messina, William S. *Statistical Quality Control for Manufacturing Managers*. New York: John Wiley & Sons, Inc., 1987.

Michalko, Michael. *Thinkertoys*. Berkeley, CA: Ten Speed Press, 1991.

Michalski, Walter J. *Assessment of an Off-Campus Bachelor of Arts in Management Program*. Unpublished dissertation, Ph.D. Pepperdine University, 1986.

Michalski, Walter J. *Continuous Measurable Improvement Poster (99 Tools)*. Fullerton, CA: Hughes Aircraft Company, 1992.

Michalski, Walter J. *Research and Statistics Primer for College Students*. Huntington Beach, CA: Alpha Research Group, 1989.

Michalski, Walter J. *Statistics for World Class Organizations*. Huntington Beach, CA: Alpha Research Group, 1994.

Michalski, Walter J. *Tools and Notes*. Unpublished collection of approximately 500 tools and techniques for quality and process improvement, collection period 1965–1997.

Michalski, Walter J. *Tools for Teams: Hands-On Problem Solving and Process Improvement Manual*. Huntington Beach, CA: Alpha Research Group, 1994.

Mizuno, Shigeru (ed.). *Management for Quality Improvement*. Cambridge, MA: Productivity Press, 1988.

Moewig, Arthur. *1000 Spiele fuer Gross und Klein*. Rastatt, Germany: Erich Pabel Verlagsunion, 1992.

Moran, John W., Richard P. Talbot and Russell E. Benson. *A Guide to Graphical Problem-Solving Processes*. Milwaukee, WI: ASQC Quality Press, 1990.

Mulvaney, John E. *PERT/CPM as Easy as ABC*. Washington, DC: Management Planning and Control Systems, 1969.

Nadler, Gerald and Shozo Hibino. *Breakthrough Thinking*. Rocklin, CA: Prima Publishing, 1990.

Newstrom, John W. *Still More Games Trainers Play*. New York: McGraw-Hill, Inc., 1991.

Nicholas, John M. *Managing Business & Engineering Projects*. Englewood Cliffs, NJ: Prentice-Hall, Inc., 1990.

Osborn, Jack D. et al. *Self-Directed Work Teams: The New American Challenge*. Homewood, L: Business One Irwin, 1990.

Ott, Ellis R. Process *Quality Control*. New York: McGraw-Hill, Inc., 1975.

Patterson, Marvin L. *Accelerating Innovation*. New York: Van Nostrand Reinhold, 1993.

Pfeiffer, J. William and John E. Jones (eds.). *Handbook of Structured Experiences for Human Relations Training* (Vol. 1–10). San Diego, CA: University Associates, 1974–1990.

Pfeiffer, J. William (ed.). The *1972–1995 Annual Handbooks for Group Facilitators/Developing Human Resources*. San Diego, CA: University Associates, 1972–1991, Pfeiffer & Company, 1992–1995.

Prince, George M. *The Practice of Creativity.* New York: Macmillan Publishing Company, Inc., 1970.

Rabbit, John T. and Peter A. Bergh. *The ISO-9000 Book* (2nd ed.). New York: Quality Resources, 1994.

Re Velle, Jack B. *The New Quality Technology.* Los Angeles, CA: Hughes Aircraft Company, 1992.

Re Velle, Jack B., Norman L. Frigon, Sr. and Harry K. Jackson, Jr. *From Concept to Customer.* New York: Van Nostrand Reinhold, 1995.

Riggs, James L. et al. *Industrial Organization & Management.* New York: McGraw-Hill, Inc., 1979.

Robson, George D. *Continuous Process Improvement.* New York: The Free Press, 1991.

Romig, Dennis A. *Breakthrough Teamwork.* Burr Ridge, IL: Irwin Professional Publishing, 1996.

Rubinstein, Moshe F. *Tools for Thinking and Problem Solving.* Englewood Cliffs, NJ: Prentice-Hall, Inc., 1986.

Rummler-Brache Group. *Introduction to Process Improvement and Management.* Warren, NJ: The Rummler-Brache Group, 1994.

Ryan, Thomas P. *Statistical Methods for Quality Improvement.* New York: John Wiley & Sons, 1989.

Saaty, Thomas L. *Decision Making for Leaders*, University of Pittsburgh, 1988.

Scherkenbach, William W. *Deming's Road to Continual Improvement.* Knoxville, TN: SPC Press, Inc., 1991.

Scholtes, Peter R. *The Team Handbook.* Madison, WI: Joiner Associates, Inc., 1988.

Schonberger, Richard J. *World Class Manufacturing.* New York: The Free Press, 1986.

Senge, Peter M., Charlotte Roberts, Richard Ross, Bryan Smith and Art Kleiner. *The Fifth Discipline Fieldbook.* New York: Currency Doubleday, 1994.

Shores, Richard A. *A TQM Approach to Achieving Manufacturing Excellence.* Milwaukee, WI: ASQC Quality Press, 1990.

Siegal, Andrew F. *Practical Business Statistics* (2nd ed.). Boston, MA: Richard D. Irwin, Inc., 1994.

Silberman, Melvin. *Active Training: A Handbook of Techniques, Designs, Case Examples, and Tips.* Lexington, MA: Lexington Books, 1990.

Sink, Scott D. and Thomas C. Tuttle. *Planning and Measurement in Your Organization of the Future.* Norcross, GA: Industrial Engineering and Management Press, 1989.

Stimson, William A. *The Robust Organization.* Burr Ridge, IL: Irwin Professional Publishing, 1996.

Suzaki, Kiyoshi. *The New Manufacturing Challenge.* New York: The Free Press, 1987.

Suzaki, Kiyoshi. *The New Shop Floor Management.* New York: The Free Press, 1993.

Swanson, Roger C. *The Quality Improvement Handbook.* Delray Beach, FL: St. Lucie Press, 1995.

Swartz, James B. *The Hunters and the Hunted.* Portland, OR: Productivity Press, Inc.,1994.

Tague, Nancy R. *The Quality Toolbox.* Milwaukee, WI: ASQC Quality Press, 1995.

Thompson, Philip C. *Quality Circles.* New York: AMACOM, 1982.

Tichy, Noel M. *Managing Strategic Change.* New York: John Wiley & Sons, Inc., 1983.

Timko, John J. *Statistics By Example* (2nd ed.). Orange, CA: Statistics for Management, 1993.

Utterback, James M. *Mastering the Dynamics of Innovation.* Boston, MA: Harvard Business School Press, 1994.

Van Gundy, Arthur B. *Techniques of Structured Problem-Solving.* New York: Van Nostrand Reinhold Company, 1981.

Vogt, Judith F. and Kenneth L. Murrell, *Empowerment in Organizations*. San Diego, CA: University Associates, Inc., 1990.

Wheeler, Donald J. *Understanding Variation.* Knoxville, TN: SPC Press, Inc., 1993

Xerox Corporation. *Problem-Solving Process User's Manual.* Rochester, NY: Business Products Systems Group, 1987.

Zenger, John E. et al. *Leading Teams.* Burr Ridge, IL: Irwin Professional Publishing, 1994.

Dr. Walter J. Michalski is president of Alpha Research Group, Fountain Valley, California, a consulting firm that assists organizations in their Six Sigma quality and change initiatives. His work experience reflects 30 years in quality assurance, test/process engineering, and process improvement training. He was trained and certified as a Six Sigma instructor by Motorola in 1995. Since then he has conducted approximately 100 various workshop on Six Sigma processes and tools. He has designed many problem-solving workshops and facilitated teams on Six Sigma quality, process reengineering, continuous improvement, measurements, organizational change, and critical-thinking techniques.

Dr. Michalski holds an Ed.D in Institutional Management from Pepperdine University, GSEP, Los Angeles, California. His doctoral dissertation examined the effectiveness of non-traditional college degree programs. As an adjunct professor, he continues to teach at graduate and undergraduate levels in subjects such as research methods, statistics, TQM/TQS, management, and organizational behavior. He also serves as project advisor for students' research projects, practicums, and theses.

Dr. Michalski is available for developing and facilitating "Tools-Strings for Teams" workshops for organizations. He can be reached at:
Dr. Walter J. Michalski, Ed.D.
Alpha Research Group
9882 Osborne Court
Fountain Valley, CA 92708
Tel/Fax: 714-968-0452, e-mail: WMichalski@earthlink.net.

Please check his website, **www.alpharesearchgroup.com**, for the innovative training "Baustein Koncept," "Tools-Strings" for teams, or other customized consulting services. For books on tools and teaming authored by Dr. Michalski, visit the publisher at **www.productivityinc.com** or **www.amazon.com**.

This cross-reference lists 396 tool names in an alphabetical order. Tool cross-references are in parentheses. Numerical designations, for example number **122**, indicate the tool number. Letter designations, for example (IG), indicate tool classification (Idea Generating).

1   (IG)   5W2H method
2   (IG)   6-3-5 method
    Abstraction process (*see* tool 102)
    Accountability grid (*see* tool 166)
    Action and consequences diagram (*see* tool 86)
3   (AT)   Action and effect diagram (AED)
4   (PP)   Action plan
5   (AT)   Activity analysis
6   (DC)   Activity cost matrix
7   (PP)   Activity network diagram
    Affinity analysis (*see* tool 8)
8   (IG)   Affinity diagram
9   (IG)   Analogy and metaphor
10   (AT)   Analysis of variance
    ANOVA, F-test (*see* tool 10)
    Area graph (*see* tool 133)
    Arrow analysis (*see* tool 7)
    Assembly flow (*see* tool 221)
11   (IG)   Attribute listing
12   (PP)   Audience analysis
13   (DM)   Balance sheet
    Bar graph (*see* tool 14)
14   (AT)   Bar chart
15   (CI)   Barriers-and-aids analysis
16   (PP)   Basili data collection method
17   (DC)   Benchmarking
    Benefits and barriers exercise (*see* tool 15)
18   (AT)   Block diagram
    Box and whisker plot (*see* tool 19)
19   (AT)   Box plot
    Brain webs (*see* tool 110)
20   (IG)   Brainstorming
    Brainwriting (*see* tool 21)
21   (IG)   Brainwriting pool
22   (AT)   Breakdown tree
    Bulletin board fishbone (*see* tool 26)
23   (TB)   Buzz group
    Buzzing (*see* tool 23)
    Capability assessment chart (*see* tool 126)
    Capability indices (*see* tool 147)
    Case analysis method (*see* tool 24)
24   (DC)   Case study
    Cause analysis (*see* tool 143)

25   (AT)   Cause and effect diagram (CED)
26   (AT)   Cause and effect diagram adding cards (CEDAC)
    Checkerboard diagram (*see* tool 27)
27   (IG)   Checkerboard method
28   (IG)   Checklist
29   (DC)   Checksheet
    Chi-square analysis (*see* tool 92)
    Circle chart (*see* tool 133)
30   (IG)   Circle of opportunity
31   (DC)   Circle response
32   (TB)   Circles of influence
33   (DC)   Circles of knowledge
34   (IG)   Circumrelation
35   (ES)   Cluster analysis
    Clustering (*see* tool 35)
    Color code audit (*see* tool 103)
    Color dots rating (*see* tool 187)
    Comparative assessment matrix (*see* tool 36)
    Comparative benchmarking (*see* tool 17)
    Comparison grid (*see* tool 128)
36   (ES)   Comparison matrix
37   (AT)   Competency gap assessment
    Concentration diagram (*see* tool 60)
38   (DC)   Conjoint analysis
39   (DM)   Consensus decision making
    Consensus generator (*see* tool 39)
40   (AT)   Control Chart - c (attribute)
41   (AT)   Control Chart - p (attribute)
42   (AT)   Control Chart - $\bar{X}$-R (variable)
43   (DM)   Correlation analysis
44   (AT)   Cost of quality
    Cost of quality analysis (*see* tool 44)
45   (ES)   Cost-benefit analysis
46   (PP)   Countermeasures matrix
47   (IG)   Crawford slip method
    Crawford slip writing (*see* tool 47)
    Creative evaluation (*see* tool 48)
48   (ES)   Creativity assessment
49   (ES)   Criteria filtering
    Criteria ranking (*see* tool 159)
    Criteria rating (*see* tool 160)
    Criteria rating form (*see* tool 135)
50   (IG)   Critical dialogue

51 (DC) Critical incident
Critical path method (CPM) (*see* tool 152)
Cross-functional matrix (*see* tool 85)
Cross-functional process map (*see* tool 150)
52 (AT) Customer acquisition-defection matrix
53 (DC) Customer needs table
54 (AT) Customer satisfaction analysis (CSA)
Customer satisfier matrix (*see* tool 54)
Customer window grid (*see* tool 178)
55 (DC) Customer-first-questions (CFQ)
56 (AT) Cycle time flowchart
Daily operations log (*see* tool 71)
Data collection plan (*see* tool 57)
57 (DC) Data collection strategy
Data entry form (*see* tool 164)
Data matrix (*see* tool 164)
Decision flow analysis (*see* tool 59)
Decision model (*see* tool 58)
58 (DM) Decision process flowchart
59 (DM) Decision tree diagram
Defect location checksheet (*see* tool 60)
60 (DC) Defect map
61 (ES) Delphi method
62 (CI) Deming PDSA cycle
Deming wheel (*see* tool 62)
63 (AT) Demographic analysis
64 (ES) Dendrogram
65 (PP) Deployment chart (down-across)
66 (PP) Descriptive statistics
Dialogue (*see* tool 50)
67 (PP) Different point of view
Dimension map (*see* tool 157)
68 (PP) Dimensions cube
Direct association (*see* tool 81)
Distribution ratio (*see* tool 133)
69 (AT) Dot diagram
Dot plot (*see* tool 69)
70 (IG) Double reversal
71 (CI) Events log
72 (CI) Facility layout diagram
73 (ES) Factor analysis
74 (CI) Failure mode effect analysis (FMEA)
75 (AT) Fault tree analysis (FTA)
Fishbone diagram (*see* tool 25)
76 (TB) Fishbowls
Five w's and two h's (*see* tool 1)
77 (AT) Five whys
Flow methods diagram (*see* tool 194)
78 (DC) Focus group
79 (CI) Fog index
80 (CI) Force field analysis (FFA)
81 (IG) Forced association

82 (DM) Forced choice
Forced comparison (*see* tool 82)
Forced relationship method (*see* tool 34)
Free association (*see* tool 30)
Free-form brainstorming (*see* tool 20)
83 (AT) Frequency distribution (FD)
Frequency table (*see* tool 83)
84 (IG) Fresh eye
Function block diagram (*see* tool 18)
85 (AT) Functional map
86 (AT) Futures wheel
Futuring (*see* tool 86)
Gallery method (*see* tool 21)
87 (PP) Gantt chart
Gantt planning (*see* tool 87)
88 (CI) Gap analysis
Gaussian curve (*see* tool 119)
Goal planning (*see* tool 16)
89 (PP) Gozinto chart
Gunning fog index (*see* tool 79)
90 (AT) Histogram
Histogram analysis (*see* tool 90)
91 (ES) House of quality
Hypothesis testing (ANOVA) (*see* tool 10)
92 (DM) Hypothesis testing (chi-square)
Hypothesis testing (correlation) (*see* tool 43)
93 (ES) Idea advocate
94 (IG) Idea borrowing
Idea box (*see* tool 112)
95 (IG) Idea grid
Imagery (*see* tool 108)
Impact-effort analysis (*see* tool 49)
96 (DM) Importance weighting
Incident analysis (*see* tool 51)
97 (PP) Influence diagram
98 (DC) Information needs analysis
Input-output analysis (*see* tool 195)
Instant priorities (*see* tool 120)
Interaction diagram (*see* tool 182)
Interaction-relations diagram (*see* tool 99)
99 (AT) Interrelationship digraph (I.D.)
100 (DC) Interview technique
Interviewing (*see* tool 100)
Ishikawa diagram (*see* tool 25)
Job analysis (*see* tool 196)
Jury of experts (*see* tool 61)
K-J method (*see* tool 8)
Line graph (*see* tool 101)
101 (AT) Line chart
Link analysis (*see* tool 221)
102 (ES) Linking diagram
List reduction (*see* tool 49)

		Logic diagram (*see* tool 58)
103	(CI)	Major program status
104	(AT)	Markov analysis
		Matrix chart (*see* tool 106)
105	(ES)	Matrix data analysis
106	(PP)	Matrix diagram
107	(ES)	Measurement matrix
		Meeting process check (*see* tool 197)
108	(IG)	Mental imaging
		Metaphorical thinking (*see* tool 9)
109	(PP)	Milestones chart
110	(IG)	Mind flow
111	(IG)	Monthly assessment schedule
112	(IG)	Morphological analysis
		Morphological forced connections (*see* tool 112)
		Multiple line graph (*see* tool 190)
113	(DC)	Multiple rating matrix
		Multiple rating profile (*see* tool 113)
		Multi-var chart (*see* tool 114)
114	(AT)	Multivariable chart
		Multi-vote technique (*see* tool 115)
115	(DM)	Multivoting
116	(AT)	Needs analysis
		Needs assessment (*see* tool 116)
		Network diagram (*see* tool 99)
		Node diagram (*see* tool 7)
		Nominal group process (*see* tool 117)
117	(IG)	Nominal group technique (NGT)
		Nominal grouping (*see* tool 117)
118	(ES)	Nominal prioritization
119	(AT)	Normal probability distribution
120	(ES)	Numerical prioritization
121	(CI)	Objectives matrix (OMAX)
122	(DC)	Observation
123	(ES)	Opportunity analysis
124	(PP)	Organization chart
125	(TB)	Organization mapping
126	(CI)	Organization readiness chart
		Organizational mirror (*see* tool 198)
		Osborne brainstorming (*see* tool 20)
		Outsider's view (*see* tool 67)
127	(TB)	Pair matching overlay
128	(ES)	Paired comparison
		Pairwise ranking (*see* tool 120)
129	(AT)	Panel debate
		Pareto analysis (*see* tool 130)
130	(AT)	Pareto chart
		Pareto principle (*see* tool 130)
		Partner link (*see* tool 127)
		Percent change bar graph (*see* tool 209)
		Performance gap analysis (*see* tool 37)
		Performance index (*see* tool 121)

		Perspective wheel (*see* tool 169)
131	(IG)	Phillips 66
		Phillips 66 buzz session (*see* tool 131)
		Pictogram (*see* tool 132)
132	(PP)	Pictograph
133	(AT)	Pie chart
134	(IG)	Pin cards technique
		Plan-do-check-act strategy (*see* tool 180)
		Planning schedule (*see* tool 109)
135	(DM)	Point-scoring evaluation
136	(AT)	Polygon
		Polygon analysis (*see* tool 136)
137	(AT)	Polygon overlay
		Polygon trend comparison (*see* tool 137)
		Positive-negative chart (*see* tool 209)
138	(CI)	Potential problem analysis (PPA)
139	(PP)	Presentation
		Presentation review (*see* tool 139)
140	(ES)	Prioritization matrix—analytical
141	(ES)	Prioritization matrix—combination
142	(ES)	Prioritization matrix—consensus
143	(AT)	Problem analysis
		Problem definition (*see* tool 145)
144	(ES)	Problem selection matrix
		Problem solution planning (*see* tool 46)
145	(PP)	Problem specification
146	(AT)	Process analysis
147	(AT)	Process capability ratios
		Process cycle time analysis (*see* tool 56)
148	(PP)	Process decision program chart (PDPC)
		Process flow analysis (*see* tool 149)
149	(AT)	Process flowchart
150	(CI)	Process mapping
151	(CI)	Process selection matrix
152	(PP)	Program evaluation and review technique (PERT)
153	(PP)	Project planning log
154	(ES)	Project prioritization matrix
		Pros and cons (*see* tool 13)
155	(CI)	Quality chart
156	(DC)	Questionnaires
157	(AT)	Radar chart
158	(DC)	Random numbers generator
		Random numbers table (*see* tool 158)
159	(ES)	Ranking matrix
160	(ES)	Rating matrix
		Recorded round robin technique (*see* tool 2)
161	(TB)	Relationship map
		Requirements matrix (*see* tool 163)
		Requirements QFD matrix (*see* tool 91)
162	(PP)	Resource histogram
		Resource loading (see tool 162)
163	(PP)	Resource requirements matrix
164	(DC)	Response data encoding form

165	(DC)	Response matrix analysis
166	(CI)	Responsibility matrix
		Results reporting (*see* tool 107)
167	(ES)	Reverse brainstorming
		Reverse fishbone (*see* tool 3)
		Reversed thinking (*see* tool 70)
		Reviewed dendrogram (*see* tool 64)
		Risk management diagram (*see* tool 168)
168	(AT)	Risk space analysis
		Root cause analysis (*see* tool 77)
		Rotating chairs (*see* tool 169)
169	(CI)	Rotating roles
170	(IG)	Round robin brainstorming
171	(AT)	Run chart
172	(AT)	Run-it-by
		Sample analysis (*see* tool 22)
		Sampling (random/systematic/stratified/cluster) (*see* tool 173)
		Sampling chart (*see* tool 158)
173	(DC)	Sampling methods
		Sarape chart (*see* tool 191)
174	(AT)	SCAMPER
		SCAMPER questions (*see* tool 174)
		Scatter analysis (*see* tool 175)
175	(AT)	Scatter diagram
		Scatterplot (*see* tool 175)
		Scenario construction (*see* tool 176)
176	(CI)	Scenario writing
		Second opinion (*see* tool 172)
		Selection grid (*see* tool 177)
177	(ES)	Selection matrix
178	(ES)	Selection window
179	(IG)	Semantic intuition
180	(CI)	Shewhart PDCA cycle
		Situation analysis (*see* tool 193)
181	(AT)	Snake chart
182	(TB)	Sociogram
		Sociometric diagram (*see* tool 182)
		Solution impact diagram (*see* tool 3)
183	(ES)	Solution matrix
		Solutions selection matrix (*see* tool 183)
		Space plot (*see* tool 168)
		Spider chart (*see* tool 157)
184	(AT)	Standard deviation
185	(DC)	Starbursting
		Stem-and-leaf diagram (*see* tool 186)
186	(AT)	Stem-and-leaf display
187	(ES)	Sticking dots
188	(IG)	Stimulus analysis
		Storyboard (*see* tool 189)
189	(PP)	Storyboarding

190	(AT)	Stratification
191	(AT)	Stratum chart
		Surface chart (*see* tool 191)
		Survey analysis (*see* tool 192)
		Survey profiling (*see* tool 165)
192	(DC)	Surveying
193	(PP)	SWOT analysis
194	(AT)	Symbolic flowchart
		Systematic diagram (*see* tool 204)
195	(AT)	Systems analysis diagram
		Tally sheet (*see* tool 29)
196	(AT)	Task analysis
197	(TB)	Team meeting evaluation
198	(TB)	Team mirror
199	(TB)	Team process assessment
		Team rating (*see* tool 187)
		Teardown method (*see* tool 167)
200	(AT)	Thematic content analysis
		Time plot (*see* tool 202)
		Time series analysis (*see* tool 205)
201	CI)	Time study sheet
202	(AT)	Timeline chart
203	(PP)	Top-down flowchart
		Traditional organization chart (*see* tool 124)
		Tree analysis (*see* tool 204)
204	(PP)	Tree diagram
205	(AT)	Trend analysis
206	(ES)	Triple ranking
207	(AT)	Truth table
		Two-dimensional scatter diagram (*see* tool 208)
208	(DC)	Two-dimensional survey grid
209	(AT)	Two-directional bar chart
210	(AT)	Value analysis
211	(AT)	Value/non-value-added cycle time chart
212	(AT)	Variance analysis
		Variance matrix (*see* tool 212)
213	(ES)	Venn diagram
		Visualization (*see* tool 108)
		Voice of the customer (*see* tool 53)
		Weighted averages matrix (*see* tool 96)
214	(DM)	Weighted voting
215	(AT)	What-if analysis
216	(PP)	Why/how charting
217	(IG)	Wildest idea technique
		Wildest idea thinking (*see* tool 217)
218	(AT)	Window analysis
219	(AT)	Wishful thinking
		Work breakdown diagram (*see* tool 220)
220	(PP)	Work breakdown structure (WBS)
221	(CI)	Work flow analysis (WFA)
222	(AT)	Yield chart

The process category index classifies tools into the following eight categories:

TB – Team Building   **ES** – Evaluating/Selecting

IG – Idea Generating   **DM** – Decision Making

DC – Data Collecting   **PP** – Planning/Presenting

AT – Analyzing/Trending   **CI** – Changing/Implementing

Analyzing/Trending

3	Action and effect diagram (AED)
5	Activity analysis
10	Analysis of variance
14	Bar chart
18	Block diagram
19	Box plot
22	Breakdown tree
25	Cause and effect diagram (CED)
26	Cause and effect diagram adding cards (CEDAC)
37	Competency gap assessment
40	Control chart - c (attribute)
41	Control chart - p (attribute)
42	Control chart - $\bar{X}$-R (variable)
44	Cost of quality
52	Customer acquisition-defection matrix
54	Customer satisfaction analysis (CSA)
56	Cycle time flowchart
63	Demographic analysis
69	Dot diagram
75	Fault tree analysis (FTA)
77	Five whys
83	Frequency distribution (FD)
85	Functional map
86	Futures wheel
90	Histogram
99	Interrelationship digraph (I. D.)
101	Line chart
104	Markov analysis
114	Multivariable chart
116	Needs analysis
119	Normal probability distribution
129	Panel debate
130	Pareto chart
133	Pie chart
136	Polygon
137	Polygon overlay
143	Problem analysis
146	Process analysis
147	Process capability ratios
149	Process flowchart
157	Radar chart
168	Risk space analysis
171	Run chart
172	Run-it-by
174	SCAMPER
181	Snake chart
184	Standard deviation
186	Stem-and-leaf display
190	Stratification
191	Stratum chart
192	Surveying
194	Symbolic flowchart
195	Systems analysis diagram
196	Task analysis
200	Thematic content analysis
202	Timeline chart
205	Trend analysis
207	Truth table
209	Two-directional bar chart
210	Value analysis
211	Value/non-value-added cycle time chart
212	Variance analysis
215	What-if analysis
218	Window analysis
219	Wishful thinking
222	Yield chart

Changing/Implementing

15	Barriers-and-aids analysis
62	Deming PDSA cycle
71	Events log
72	Facility layout diagram
74	Failure mode effect analysis (FMEA)
79	Fog index
80	Force field analysis (FFA)
88	Gap analysis
103	Major program status
111	Monthly assessment schedule

121 Objectives matrix (OMAX)
126 Organization readiness chart
138 Potential problem analysis (PPA)
150 Process mapping
151 Process selection matrix
155 Quality chart
166 Responsibility matrix
169 Rotating roles
176 Scenario writing
180 Shewhart PDCA cycle
201 Time study sheet
221 Work flow analysis (WFA)

Data Collecting

6   Activity cost matrix
17   Benchmarking
24   Case study
29   Checksheet
31   Circle response
33   Circles of knowledge
38   Conjoint analysis
51   Critical incident
53   Customer needs table
55   Customer-first-questions (CFQ)
57   Data collection strategy
60   Defect map
78   Focus group
98   Information needs analysis
100 Interview technique
113 Multiple rating matrix
122 Observation
156 Questionnaires
158 Random numbers generator
164 Response data encoding form
165 Response matrix analysis
173 Sampling method
185 Starbursting
208 Two-dimensional survey grid

Decision Making

13   Balance sheet
39   Consensus decision making
43   Correlation analysis
58   Decision process flowchart
59   Decision tree diagram
82   Forced choice
92   Hypothesis testing (chi-square)
96   Importance weighting
115 Multivoting
135 Point-scoring evaluation
214 Weighted voting

Evaluating/Selecting

35   Cluster analysis
36   Comparison matrix
45   Cost-benefit analysis
48   Creativity assessment
49   Criteria filtering
61   Delphi method
64   Dendrogram
73   Factor analysis
91   House of quality
93   Idea advocate
102 Linking diagram
105 Matrix data analysis
107 Measurement matrix
118 Nominal prioritization
120 Numerical prioritization
123 Opportunity analysis
128 Paired comparison
140 Prioritization matrix—analytical
141 Prioritization matrix—combination
142 Prioritization matrix—consensus
144 Problem selection matrix
154 Project prioritization matrix
159 Ranking matrix
160 Rating matrix
167 Reverse brainstorming
177 Selection matrix
178 Selection window
183 Solution matrix
187 Sticking dots
206 Triple ranking
213 Venn diagram

Idea Generating

1   5W2H method
2   6-3-5 method
8   Affinity diagram
9   Analogy and metaphor
11   Attribute listing
20   Brainstorming
21   Brainwriting pool
27   Checkerboard method
28   Checklist
30   Circle of opportunity
34   Circumrelation
47   Crawford slip method
50   Critical dialogue
70   Double reversal
81   Forced association
84   Fresh eye
94   Idea borrowing

95	Idea grid
108	Mental imaging
110	Mind flow
112	Morphological analysis
117	Nominal group technique (NGT)
131	Phillips 66
134	Pin cards technique
170	Round robin brainstorming
175	Scatter diagram
179	Semantic intuition
188	Stimulus analysis
217	Wildest idea technique

Planning/Presenting

4	Action plan
7	Activity network diagram
12	Audience analysis
16	Basili data collection method
46	Countermeasures matrix
65	Deployment chart (down-across)
66	Descriptive statistics
67	Different point of view
68	Dimensions cube
87	Gantt chart
89	Gozinto chart
97	Influence diagram
106	Matrix diagram
109	Milestones chart

124	Organization chart
132	Pictograph
139	Presentation
145	Problem specification
148	Process decision program chart (PDPC)
152	Program evaluation and review technique (PERT)
153	Project planning log
162	Resource histogram
163	Resource requirements matrix
189	Storyboarding
193	SWOT analysis
203	Top-down flowchart
204	Tree diagram
216	Why/how charting
220	Work breakdown structure (WBS)

Team Building

23	Buzz group
32	Circles of influence
76	Fishbowls
125	Organization mapping
127	Pair matching overlay
161	Relationship map
182	Sociogram
197	Team meeting evaluation
198	Team mirror
199	Team process assessment

This cross-reference points to the frequently used tools DFSS (Designing for Six Sigma), PFSS (Processing for Six Sigma), or, if they are used in both:

— The widely adopted General Electric model for DFSS reflects the DMADV phases of activities that stand for <u>D</u>efine, <u>M</u>easure, <u>A</u>nalyze, <u>D</u>esign, <u>V</u>erify.
— The most often applied model for PFSS reflects the DMAIC phases of activities that stand for <u>D</u>efine, <u>M</u>easure, <u>A</u>nalyze, <u>I</u>mprove, <u>C</u>ontrol.

The column before the tool number below represents how these tools are used. For example, "**D**" stands for DFSS, "**P**" stands for PFSS, "**B**" stands for tools are used in both, and "**T**" stands for Team Building or Socio-Metric tools. The letters after the hyphen signify in what phases they are frequently applied.

<u>DFSS example:</u> **D–A, D** tells the reader this tool is often used in the **Analyze** and/or **Design** activities.
<u>PFSS example:</u> **P–A, M, C** tells the reader that this tool could be used in the **Analyze, Measure,** or **Control** activities.

6σ	Tool Number	Class	Title	Page Number
B-M,I	1	(IG)	5W2H Method	1
D-D,A	2	(IG)	6-3-5 Method	3
P-A,I	3	(AT)	Action and Effect Diagram (AED)	6
P-I	4	(PP)	Action Plan	8
P-A,I	5	(AT)	Activity Analysis	11
P-A,I,M	6	(DC)	Activity Cost Matrix	14
P-A,M	7	(PP)	Activity Network Diagram	17
B-D,A	8	(IG)	Affinity Diagram	20
T	9	(IG)	Analogy and Metaphor	23
D-A,D	10	(AT)	Analysis of Variance	26
P-I	11	(IG)	Attribute Listing	31
T	12	(PP)	Audience Analysis	33
P-A,I	13	(DM)	Balance Sheet	35
P-A,M,C	14	(AT)	Bar Chart	37
P-A,I	15	(CI)	Barriers-and-Aids Analysis	39
P-M,C	16	(PP)	Basili Data Collection Method	41
D-D,M,V	17	(DC)	Benchmarking	44
P-A,D	18	(AT)	Block Diagram	47
P-A,M	19	(AT)	Box Plot	50
B-D,D	20	(IG)	Brainstorming	53
D-D,D	21	(IG)	Brainwriting Pool	55
P-A,D	22	(AT)	Breakdown Tree	58

6σ	Tool Number	Class	Title	Page Number
T	**23**	(TB)	Buzz Group	61
P-I, A	**24**	(DC)	Case Study	63
P-A	**25**	(AT)	Cause and Effect Diagram (CED)	66
P-A	**26**	(AT)	Cause and Effect Diagram Adding Cards (CEDAC)	68
D-D,D	**27**	(IG)	Checkerboard Method	71
P-P,A	**28**	(IG)	Checklist	74
P-M,A,C	**29**	(DC)	Checksheet	76
D-D,D	**30**	(IG)	Circle of Opportunity	78
B-D,A	**31**	(DC)	Circle Response	81
T	**32**	(TB)	Circles of Influence	83
B-A,I,V	**33**	(DC)	Circles of Knowledge	86
D-D,D	**34**	(IG)	Circumrelation	89
P-A,I	**35**	(ES)	Cluster Analysis	92
P-A,I	**36**	(ES)	Comparison Matrix	95
P-M,A,I	**37**	(AT)	Competency Gap Assessment	98
D-D,D	**38**	(DC)	Conjoint Analysis	101
B-I,V	**39**	(DM)	Consensus Decision Making	103
P-C	**40**	(AT)	Control Chart — c (Attribute)	105
P-C	**41**	(AT)	Control Chart — p (Attribute)	109
P-C	**42**	(AT)	Control Chart — $\bar{X}$-R (Variable)	113
D-A,V	**43**	(DM)	Correlation Analysis	117
P-M	**44**	(AT)	Cost of Quality	121
B-M,I	**45**	(ES)	Cost-Benefit Analysis	124
P-D,A,I	**46**	(PP)	Countermeasures Matrix	126
D-D,A,D	**47**	(IG)	Crawford Slip Method	128
B-A,M,I,V	**48**	(ES)	Creativity Assessment	131
P-A,M	**49**	(ES)	Criteria Filtering	134
T	**50**	(IG)	Critical Dialogue	136
P-A,I	**51**	(DC)	Critical Incident	139
B-A,V	**52**	(AT)	Customer Acquisition-Defection Matrix	141
D-D,D	**53**	(DC)	Customer Needs Table	144
B-D,I,M	**54**	(AT)	Customer Satisfaction Analysis (CSA)	146
D-D,D	**55**	(DC)	Customer-First-Questions (CFQ)	149
P-A,I	**56**	(AT)	Cycle Time Flowchart	152
P-M	**57**	(DC)	Data Collection Strategy	156
P-D,A	**58**	(DM)	Decision Process Flowchart	158
P-A	**59**	(DM)	Decision Tree Diagram	160
P-I,C	**60**	(DC)	Defect Map	164
B-D,A	**61**	(ES)	Delphi Method	166
P-A,I	**62**	(CI)	Deming PDSA Cycle	169
B-D,A	**63**	(AT)	Demographic Analysis	171
B-D,I	**64**	(ES)	Dendrogram	174

6σ	Tool Number	Class	Title	Page Number
P-M,C	65	(PP)	Deployment Chart (Down-Across)	176
B-AM,C	66	(PP)	Descriptive Statistics	179
B-A	67	(PP)	Different Point of View	183
T	68	(PP)	Dimensions Cube	186
P-A,C	69	(AT)	Dot Diagram	189
B-D,D,V	70	(IG)	Double Reversal	191
P-A,M,C	71	(CI)	Events Log	194
P-A,I	72	(CI)	Facility Layout Diagram	196
B-D,D,I	73	(ES)	Factor Analysis	199
P-C,I	74	(CI)	Failure Mode Effect Analysis (FMEA)	202
P-A,I	75	(AT)	Fault Tree Analysis (FTA)	205
T	76	(TB)	Fishbowls	208
P-A,I	77	(AT)	Five Whys	211
D-D,A,D	78	(DC)	Focus Group	213
T	79	(CI)	Fog Index	216
P-A,I	80	(CI)	Force Field Analysis (FFA)	218
D-D,D	81	(IG)	Forced Association	221
B-A,M,V	82	(DM)	Forced Choice	223
P-A,M,C	83	(AT)	Frequency Distribution (FD)	225
B-D,A,D	84	(IG)	Fresh Eye	228
P-A	85	(AT)	Functional Map	230
P-D,A	86	(AT)	Futures Wheel	233
P-A,M,C	87	(PP)	Gantt Chart	236
P-A,I	88	(CI)	Gap Analysis	239
P-A,I	89	(PP)	Gozinto Chart	241
P-A,M,C	90	(AT)	Histogram	243
D-D,A,D	91	(ES)	House of Quality	246
D-A,D,V	92	(DM)	Hypothesis Testing (Chi-Square)	250
B-A,I,V	93	(ES)	Idea Advocate	254
B-D,A.M	94	(IG)	Idea Borrowing	256
D-A,V	95	(IG)	Idea Grid	259
B-A,M,I	96	(DM)	Importance Weighting	262
P-D,A,I	97	(PP)	Influence Diagram	265
B-D,A,V	98	(DC)	Information Needs Analysis	267
T	99	(AT)	Interrelationship Digraph (I.D.)	270
B-D,A,I,V	100	(DC)	Interview Technique	273
P-A,C	101	(AT)	Line Chart	276
B-A,I,V	102	(ES)	Linking Diagram	278
B-M,C,V	103	(CI)	Major Program Status	280
T	104	(AT)	Markov Analysis	283
P-M,A	105	(ES)	Matrix Data Analysis	286

6σ	Tool Number	Class	Title	Page Number
P-M,A	106	(PP)	Matrix Diagram	288
B-D,M,A	107	(ES)	Measurement Matrix	291
D-D,D	108	(IG)	Mental Imaging	294
P-M,C	109	(PP)	Milestones Chart	296
D-D,D,V	110	(IG)	Mind Flow	298
P-M,C	111	(CI)	Monthly Assessment Schedule	301
D-D,D	112	(IG)	Morphological Analysis	304
P-M	113	(DC)	Multiple Rating Matrix	307
P-M,C	114	(AT)	Multivariable Chart	309
B-D,A	115	(DM)	Multivoting	311
B-A,V	116	(AT)	Needs Analysis	314
B-D,A	117	(IG)	Nominal Group Technique (NGT)	316
P-M,A,I	118	(ES)	Nominal Prioritization	319
D-M,A,D,V	119	(AT)	Normal Probability Distribution	322
B-D,A	120	(ES)	Numerical Prioritization	326
B-D,M,A,C,V	121	(CI)	Objectives Matrix (OMAX)	329
P-A,I	122	(DC)	Observation	332
B-A,M	123	(ES)	Opportunity Analysis	335
T	124	(PP)	Organization Chart	337
B-A,I	125	(TB)	Organization Mapping	339
B-A,I	126	(CI)	Organization Readiness Chart	342
T	127	(TB)	Pair Matching Overlay	344
B-D,A,D	128	(ES)	Paired Comparison	347
T	129	(AT)	Panel Debate	350
B-A	130	(AT)	Pareto Chart	352
D-D,D	131	(IG)	Phillips 66	355
P-M	132	(PP)	Pictograph	357
P-M,C	133	(AT)	Pie Chart	359
P-D,A,I	134	(IG)	Pin Cards Technique	361
P-M,I	135	(DM)	Point-Scoring Evaluation	364
P-M,A,C	136	(AT)	Polygon	366
P-M,A,C	137	(AT)	Polygon Overlay	369
P-A,I	138	(CI)	Potential Problem Analysis (PPA)	372
T	139	(PP)	Presentation	375
P-A,M,I	140	(ES)	Prioritization Matrix—Analytical	377
P-A,M,I	141	(ES)	Prioritization Matrix—Combination	382
P-A,M,I	142	(ES)	Prioritization Matrix—Consensus	385
P-A,I	143	(AT)	Problem Analysis	388
P-A,M,I	144	(ES)	Problem Selection Matrix	391
B-D,A	145	(PP)	Problem Specification	393
P-A,I	146	(AT)	Process Analysis	396
D-M,D,V	147	(AT)	Process Capability Ratios	399

6σ	Tool Number	Class	Title	Page Number
B-A,I	148	(PP)	Process Decision Program Chart (PDPC)	403
P-A,I	149	(AT)	Process Flowchart	406
B-A,I	150	(CI)	Process Mapping	410
P-D,A,I	151	(CI)	Process Selection Matrix	414
P-M,A,C	152	(PP)	Program Evaluation and Review Technique (PERT)	416
P-D,M,C	153	(PP)	Project Planning Log	419
P-D,A,M	154	(ES)	Project Prioritization Matrix	421
P-M,A,I	155	(CI)	Quality Chart	424
P-D,A,V	156	(DC)	Questionnaires	426
P-A,M	157	(AT)	Radar Chart	431
B-D,A	158	(DC)	Random Numbers Generator	433
B-A,M	159	(ES)	Ranking Matrix	436
B-A,M	160	(ES)	Rating Matrix	438
P-A,I	161	(TB)	Relationship Map	440
P-M,A	162	(PP)	Resource Histogram	443
B-M,A	163	(PP)	Resource Requirements Matrix	446
D-D,A,V	164	(DC)	Response Data Encoding Form	448
D-D,A,D	165	(DC)	Response Matrix Analysis	452
B-D,C	166	(CI)	Responsibility Matrix	455
B-A,M	167	(ES)	Reverse Brainstorming	457
P-A	168	(AT)	Risk Space Analysis	459
P-A,I	169	(CI)	Rotating Roles	462
B-D,A,I	170	(IG)	Round Robin Brainstorming	465
P-M,A,C	171	(AT)	Run Chart	468
P-A	172	(AT)	Run-It-By	471
D-D,A,V	173	(DC)	Sampling Method	474
B-A,I	174	(AT)	SCAMPER	477
B-A,M,C	175	(AT)	Scatter Diagram	479
P-A	176	(CI)	Scenario Writing	482
P-A,M,I	177	(ES)	Selection Matrix	484
P-D,A	178	(ES)	Selection Window	486
D-D,A,D	179	(IG)	Semantic Intuition	488
P-A,I	180	(CI)	Shewhart PDCA Cycle	490
P-M,A,C	181	(AT)	Snake Chart	492
T	182	(TB)	Sociogram	494
B-D,A,M	183	(ES)	Solution Matrix	497
B-M,A,D,V,I	184	(AT)	Standard Deviation	499
D-D,A,D	185	(DC)	Starbursting	502
P-A,M,C	186	(AT)	Stem-and-Leaf Display	505
P-M,A	187	(ES)	Sticking Dots	507
D-D,A,D	188	(IG)	Stimulus Analysis	509
B-A,I	189	(PP)	Storyboarding	512

6σ	Tool Number	Class	Title	Page Number
P-M,A,C	190	(AT)	Stratification	516
P-M,A,C	191	(AT)	Stratum Chart	518
D-D,A,D	192	(DC)	Surveying	520
D-D,A,D,V	193	(PP)	SWOT Analysis	523
P-A,I	194	(AT)	Symbolic Flowchart	526
P-D,I	195	(AT)	Systems Analysis Diagram	529
P-A,I	196	(AT)	Task Analysis	531
T	197	(TB)	Team Meeting Evaluation	534
T	198	(TB)	Team Mirror	537
T	199	(TB)	Team Process Assessment	540
T	200	(AT)	Thematic Content Analysis	542
P-M,A,C	201	(CI)	Time Study Sheet	544
P-M,A,C	202	(AT)	Timeline Chart	546
P-A,I	203	(PP)	Top-Down Flowchart	548
P-A	204	(PP)	Tree Diagram	551
P-D,M,A,C	205	(AT)	Trend Analysis	554
B-D,A,M	206	(ES)	Triple Ranking	557
P-D,A	207	(AT)	Truth Table	560
B-A	208	(DC)	Two-Dimensional Survey Grid	564
P-M,A,C	209	(AT)	Two-Directional Bar Chart	567
D-D,A,D,V	210	(AT)	Value Analysis	569
P-A,I	211	(AT)	Value/Non-Value-Added Cycle Time Chart	572
P-A,I	212	(AT)	Variance Analysis	575
T	213	(ES)	Venn Diagram	579
B-D,M,A	214	(DM)	Weighted Voting	581
B-A,I	215	(AT)	What-If Analysis	583
B-A,D,I,V	216	(PP)	Why/How Charting	585
B-A,D,I	217	(IG)	Wildest Idea Technique	588
P-A	218	(AT)	Window Analysis	590
B-D,A,D	219	(AT)	Wishful Thinking	593
P-D,A	220	(PP)	Work Breakdown Structure (WBS)	595
P-A,I	221	(CI)	Work Flow Analysis (WFA)	598
P-M,A,I,C	222	(AT)	Yield Chart	601

#0005 - 250418 - C0 - 229/210/41 - PB - 9781563272950